MW01195058

THE
QUR'AN

A VERSE TRANSLATION

THE
QUR'AN

A VERSE TRANSLATION

M. A. R. Habib and Bruce B. Lawrence

Liveright Publishing Corporation

A Division of W. W. Norton & Company
Independent Publishers Since 1923

For information about permission to reproduce selections from this book, write to
Permissions, Liveright Publishing Corporation, a division of W. W. Norton & Company, Inc.,
500 Fifth Avenue, New York, NY 10110

For information about special discounts for bulk purchases, please contact W. W. Norton Special
Sales at specialsales@wwnorton.com or 800-233-4830

Manufacturing by Lakeside Book Company
Book design by Chris Welch
Production manager: Anna Oler

ISBN 978-0-87140-499-2

Liveright Publishing Corporation, 500 Fifth Avenue, New York, N.Y. 10110
www.wwnorton.com

W. W. Norton & Company Ltd., 15 Carlisle Street, London W1D 3BS

1 2 3 4 5 6 7 8 9 0

CONTENTS

INTRODUCTION

In the cave of Hira on the outskirts of the Arabian city of Mecca, the Prophet Muhammad is said to have received his first revelation. The cave is so small that only one person can enter it; it overlooks a rocky landscape, craggy, rich with bright bronze-colored sand. From this height the Prophet looked down—and meditated on what was right and wrong in the beliefs and practices of his people. He came down from the mountain, ablaze with language that was neither verse nor prose, language that we have ever since been struggling to understand, struggling to render into our own idiom.

Muhammad would meditate in the cave of Hira during the holy month of Ramadan, the time in each year when blood feuds were suspended. It was a time when Meccans who had wealth and leisure retreated to the outskirts of their town, to the hills that enclosed them, and to the caves that offered shelter and repose.

Muhammad had been following this practice for over a decade. Then, one night in Ramadan in the year 610, when he was about forty years old, he felt a strange stirring inside him. He welcomed the nighttime in this special month; it drew him deep into himself and allowed him to resist those impulses that pulled him back to the world, to concerns with family or business or travel. He was alert to repelling those impulses. They clouded his vision, they denied him peace of mind, and above all, they blocked his search for the truth. Yet this was a different stirring. It was deep, arresting. It overpowered him, and then it produced words, words that were not his.[1] He listened:

---

1   The following narrative is based on three literary sources unless otherwise indicated:

(1) The Qur'an itself as it appears in print in what is known as the 'Uthmanic recension, authorized by the third caliph, in the mid-seventh century. Wherever the Qur'an is quoted, it will be noted briefly with English renditions from the current translation.

(2) *Hadith*, which are accounts relating both words and actions of the Prophet Muhammad, gathered in numerous collections of varying authenticity from the eighth century on.

(3) The *sira* or biography of the Prophet, compiled from both *hadith* and Qur'anic passages,

"Read!" And he was shown a piece of silk with words embroidered on it. He did not know how to read. "What shall I read?" he asked.

"Read!" came the command, and again the brocade was thrust before him. He stammered, "But what shall I read?"

Muhammad could not read. All those who accompanied him on caravan trips, whether to Egypt or Syria, to Yemen or Abyssinia, could read commercial symbols but there was not yet a fully developed written Arabic.[2] His companions handled the few documents of exchange that required reading or signing. When Muhammad had to sign, he would ask others to read aloud what was written, then he would sign by pressing the palm of his hand to the paper. Why then did this voice ask him to read?[3]

Even as he was thinking these thoughts, the voice commanded him, for the third time:

"Read!"

"But what, what shall I read?" Then the words appeared:

Read—in the Name of your Lord
Who created—
created humankind from a clot

---

also dating from the eighth century. This biographical account draws largely on two sources: Ibn Ishaq, *Sirat Rasul Allah* (Life of the Prophet of God) written in the mid-eighth century and translated into English by Alfred Guillaume as *The Life of Muhammad* (Karachi: Oxford University Press, 1955), and Martin Lings, *Muhammad: His Life Based on the Earliest Sources* (Rochester, Vt.: Inner Traditions International, 1983).

2   For more on the status of literacy in sixth-century Arabia, see Ahmad al-Jallad, "The Linguistic Landscape of Pre-Islamic Arabia: Context for the Qur'an," in *The Oxford Handbook of Qur'anic Studies*, edited by M. Shah and M. A. S. Haleem (Oxford: Oxford University Press, 2020), 111–27. The author stresses the importance of further analyzing the limited samples of pre-Islamic epigraphy and also conducting "a lexical study of Qur'anic vocabulary in the light of North Arabian inscriptions" (125). Both projects, it is hoped, will provide new insight into the earliest linguistic options for Qur'anic prophecy.

3   There is a persistent ambiguity about what "read" meant as a command to someone who was "illiterate." One could translate the command *iqra'* to mean "recite," but such a rendition weakens the exchange in English. As Muhammad Asad explains, the concept of "reciting" implies no more than the oral delivery—with or without understanding—of something already laid down in writing or committed to memory, whereas "reading" primarily signifies a conscious taking-in, with or without an audible utterance but with a view to understanding them, of words and ideas received from an outside source: see his *The Message of the Qur'an* (Watsonville, Calif.: The Book Foundation, 2003), 1099*n*1.

of blood.
Read—for your Lord
is Most Bountiful,
Who taught by the pen—
taught humankind
what it did not know.

SURA AL-'ALAQ, 96:1–5

According to some traditions, these words appeared on a coverlet of brocade and, urged for the third time, Muhammad somehow read them. But
the Arabic command *iqra'* can mean not only "read!" but "recite!" hence
in other traditions he is said to have recited the words after Gabriel. But in
either scenario, he is said to have related that these words were written on
his heart, through some miracle of comprehension. He wondered, had he
become a man possessed, an ecstatic poet, the kind his clansmen distrusted,
even despised? He had barely absorbed the experience when his whole body
began to tremble. He waited for more counsel. But nothing came. He hurried down the mountain, running toward Mecca. Halfway down the voice
returned. Now it was a booming voice with a face, a man's face. The face
appeared to come from beyond the horizon. The celestial form announced:
"O Muhammad, you are the messenger of God, and I am Gabriel." He tried
to look away but wherever he turned, there was the Archangel Gabriel on the
horizon, meeting his gaze.

Muhammad's encounter on the mountain, in the tiny cave of Hira, was
to change the course of world history. Revelations continued to come for
the next twenty-two years, and they were eventually compiled as the text of
Qur'an (literally, "recitation"), which, along with Muhammad's practice,
became the basis of the religion of Islam. These revelatory experiences raised
him from a humble shepherd and a trader to the rank not only of prophet,
but of statesman, military strategist, ruler, and, above all, a model of conduct
for millions of human beings across the globe. His life can be marked by
five dates: 570 CE,[4] the approximate year of his birth; 595, when he married;

4   Throughout the introduction and the notes, we use CE (common era) to refer to the solar
Julian calendar, distinct from the lunar Islamic calendar, known as AH (*anno hegirae*). The

610, when he was called to prophecy in Mecca; 622, the year of the *hijra* or migration, when he left Mecca for Yathrib (later renamed Medina); and 632, when, after subduing his enemies, he died in Medina. Between the time of his birth and the time of his death, he had transformed and unified the warring tribes of Arabia into a single community of faith, and within fifty years of his death, the vast Islamic empire had overtaken the Persian and Byzantine empires, reaching the very gates of Europe. Today, his followers number almost two billion people.

Early Years

Muhammad was born into the Quraysh, the most powerful tribe of Mecca, and he belonged to the clan of Hashim. He was an orphan, losing his father, Abdullah, in the year of his birth and his mother, Amina, when he was just six. He was adopted first by his grandfather Abd al-Muttalib and then by his uncle Abu Talib; his first cousin 'Ali was a boyhood companion. At this time, Mecca was a thriving center of both religious worship and commerce. Muhammad was employed in its caravan trade. By all accounts, he was a striking young man, handsome, of medium build, with black eyes, a reddish complexion, and hair flowing to his shoulders. He rapidly earned the reputation of being al-Amin (the trustworthy). Hearing of his noble character, a wealthy businesswoman named Khadija sent him on one of her trading caravans to Syria. Khadija was a widow in her forties and she became so enamored of Muhammad's qualities that she proposed marriage to him, which he accepted. They had two sons, who both died young, and four daughters. For twenty-five years he remained devoted to her as his only wife.

   When Muhammad received the first revelation, Khadija was the first person to believe in him and support him. She had sent scouts to the mountain, who found him and brought him home. As soon as they left, he collapsed into her lap, telling her of his experience. "O son of my uncle," she exclaimed, "rejoice . . . and be of good heart. By Him in whose hand is Khadija's soul, I have hope that you will be the prophet of this people."[5] Muhammad received

----

latter commemorates the *hijra* or migration of Muhammad and his followers to the city of Yathrib, later renamed Medina, in 622 CE.

5   Ibn Ishaq, *The Life of Muhammad*, 107.

a similar assurance from Khadija's Christian cousin Waraqa ibn Qusayy. The first man to accept the Prophet's message was ʿAli. Among the early converts to Islam were the respected merchant Abu Bakr, who would later become the first caliph of the Islamic empire, and his uncle Hamza, known for his military prowess. ʿUmar ibn al-Khattab, another prominent noble of Mecca (and later to become the second caliph), was initially shocked on learning that his sister Fatima had converted to Islam; but when he went to her house to upbraid her, he heard the beauty of what she was reciting from the Qur'an and he quickly embraced the new faith.

Opposition to the New Religion

Three years after the first revelation, the Prophet was instructed by the Archangel to disseminate the message of Islam publicly, and this is when resistance grew. Like Christianity, Islam was a revolutionary religion. Just as the values of Christianity were sharply opposed to those of the brutal and materialistic Roman empire, so the early verses of the Qur'an emphatically derided the corruption into which Meccan tribal society had degenerated. The new religion was focused on issues of social and economic justice, insisting on fairness in business transactions, denouncing usury, espousing rights for women and the poor, and prohibiting such savage practices as the burial of newly born unwanted young girls. Since Mecca was an economic and religious center, its Qurayshi leaders saw Muhammad as undermining their entire way of life—not only their idolatrous religion but their commerce and their social practices.

In consequence, the early Muslims were subjected to torture, killing, and confiscation of their property. Muhammad's enemies included some of his own close relatives and tribesmen. Among them was his uncle Abu Lahab, whom God cursed through a revelation, along with his wife. Worst of all was the leader of the Makhzum clan of the Quraysh, Abu Jahl, who would make a mockery of Muhammad and assault his followers. Shortly after the conversion of ʿUmar, the Quraysh publicly ostracized Muhammad and his followers. Notwithstanding the protection afforded to the Prophet by his uncle Abu Talib, the poorer and weaker Muslims were continually subjected to mistreatment. A number of them, with the Prophet's permission, sought refuge in Abyssinia, where they were welcomed by its king, Najashi (the

Negus), despite efforts of the Meccans to dissuade him. This is known as the first *hijra* or migration.

In 619 Muhammad endured his *annus horribilus*. In that year he lost Khadija, his wife, his confidante, and his mainstay in all that he did. Muhammad's monogamous marriage with Khadija for almost twenty-five years was something highly unusual at that time. From the age of fifty until fifty-two he remained unmarried. Thereafter, between the ages of fifty-three and sixty, he married ten women, primarily for political reasons. For example, he married 'A'isha and Hafsa, daughters respectively of the influential leaders Abu Bakr and 'Umar. He also married a Jewish woman, Rehana, to form ties with the tribe of Bani Qurayza, as well as a Christian woman, Maryam, which helped forge a link with Muqawqis, the ruler of Egypt. His marriage to an aging and impoverished woman called Sawda was designed to exemplify kindness to women.

In the same year that Khadija died, Muhammad also lost Abu Talib, his uncle, his father by trust, his protector against hostile clansmen and other Meccan detractors. Abu Talib had been one of the most respected elders of the Quraysh and he had been committed to safeguarding the Prophet even though he himself never converted to Islam. Without his protection, Muhammad and his followers became far more vulnerable to abuse and persecution. Realizing that he could garner no more support in Mecca, the Prophet walked about fifty miles to a neighboring town called Ta'if, hoping to convert people there. But they drove him out, stirring up their slaves to insult him and throw stones at him. Muhammad regarded this as the bitterest day of his life.

After these setbacks, there occurred an extraordinary event in that eventful year of 619. The Prophet was awakened from his sleep at the Ka'ba by the Archangel, who took him on "the night journey" (*isra*) on a white horse from Mecca to the mosque of Al-Aqsa in Jerusalem (originally, the temple built by Solomon). There the Prophet found Abraham, Moses, and Jesus with all the prophets, whom he led in prayer. He was then led through an ascension (*mi'raj*) of the seven heavens, one by one, in which he again met the various prophets, and was finally taken into the Divine Presence, where he received instruction that Muslims were obliged to pray five times daily. On returning, the Prophet met with skepticism when he related his adventure; but Abu Bakr believed instantly, and was thenceforth honored with the title *al-Siddiq*, which means "one who confirms or supports the truth."

The Flight to Medina

Even after the momentous experience of 619, Muhammad continued to face harassment, persecution, and threats of assassination to himself and his followers. He sought help in other oasis towns, with tribes beyond his own. Some 250 miles to the north of Mecca was the town of Yathrib. It was inhabited by tribes that were finding it impossible to live together in peace. They sought in Muhammad—known for his truthfulness and fairness—a just leader who would arbitrate their disputes. Muhammad agreed, on condition that they accept Islam. During the annual pilgrimage in Mecca in 620, a delegation of six men from Yathrib came to meet with Muhammad. Having converted, they agreed to return to Yathrib and deliver the message of Islam to their townspeople. The following year, a delegation of twelve leading men, including five from the previous year, came and pledged allegiance to the Prophet and to Islam at 'Aqaba (known as the First 'Aqaba). In 622 a further delegation of seventy-three men and two women pledged allegiance to the Prophet, again at 'Aqaba, and vowed to protect him if he came to reside in their city (the Second 'Aqaba). These pledges promised hope of an established community with its own sovereign territory—something Muhammad needed if his religion were to survive.

The Prophet now encouraged his followers to migrate to Yathrib; it was not long before most of them had gone, leaving behind in Mecca only Abu Bakr, 'Ali, and the Prophet himself. After a plot by the Quraysh to assassinate Muhammad was foiled, the Prophet also departed, along with Abu Bakr. They stayed initially in a cave in Mount Thaur to the south of Mecca. The Quraysh, who came looking for them with murderous intent, found an acacia tree in front of the cave, with a spiderweb spread between the tree and the mouth of the cave; also, a rock dove had made her nest there. Concluding that no one could be hidden inside, they left.

The Prophet and Abu Bakr, with their Bedouin guide, reached the oasis of Quba', not far from Yathrib, in late September 622. They stayed there for three days during which the Prophet laid the foundations of the first mosque. They departed soon for the city since there was great anticipation in Medina of the Prophet's arrival. A guard of honor from the Yathribi tribes of Aws and Khazraj rode on both sides of the Prophet as he proceeded through the city lined with people gathered to greet him. He ordered that a mosque be built at the courtyard where his camel chose to rest. The Prophet gave the title of *ansar* (helpers) to the Muslims of Medina while the Muslims of the Quraysh and other tribes who had immigrated there were called *muhajirun* (emigrants).

In order to bring peace and unity to the community in his new city, the Prophet made a covenant (later known as the Constitution of Medina) between the eight clans of the *ansar* and the *muhajirun*, as well as between the Jews and the Muslims. The nine Muslim tribes and the Jews of the oasis now constituted a single *umma* or community. Muslims and Jews were to be accorded equal status, with freedom of belief, and they were obliged to fight enemies or to make peace with them as one people. Yathrib was now known as the City of the Prophet or *Madinat al-nabi*, and today simply as Medina. It was from Medina that Muhammad was to begin his journey as a prophet both for fellow Arabs and all humankind. The flight (*hijra*) to Medina in 622 marked the beginning of a new moment and also a new calendar; 622 became the first year for the community who accepted Muhammad, those who prayed with him, those who fought for his cause, those who, like him, waited for guidance from beyond through Gabriel.

Early Wars

The Muslim immigrants to Medina had left their belongings behind in Mecca, which was seized by their opponents. Much of their property had already been confiscated and they were still under threat. Shortly after his arrival in Medina there came to Muhammad the following revelation in the Qur'an:

> Permission to fight is given
> to those who are attacked,
> for they have been wronged.[6]
> And God is All Powerful

---

6 This verse is the earliest pronouncement of what became the principle of self-defense in Islamic law, not invoked until after Muhammad had left Mecca for Medina in 622 CE (1 AH), the *hijra* or migration. Sura 2:190–94, which also permits fighting in self-defense, was revealed about a year later. The reference to "mosques" underscores that the verse was influenced by developments in Medina.

in His support of them—
those driven out of their homes unjustly
—merely for saying, "Our Lord is the One God."
If God did not restrain some people
by means of others, then monasteries,
churches, synagogues, and mosques
—where the name of God
is remembered often—would be torn down.
God will help those who help His cause,
for God is Supremely Strong, Almighty.

SURA AL-HAJJ, 22:39–40

But this was always to be a defensive war, a reluctant recourse to violence when other stratagems had failed. The war Muhammad waged against the Meccans was not a struggle for prestige or wealth; it was a war for the survival of God's Word. The helpers from Medina joined the migrants from Mecca. They provided the migrants with food and shelter from their own resources, but they were all stretched to the limit. They began to raid the caravans of their Meccan foes. They raided only small caravans at first, and never attacked during those times when fighting, especially blood feuds, was prohibited. As someone who had guided many successful caravans, Muhammad knew the routes and the seasons. He also knew the wells where Meccan traders would pass with their camels and their goods.

After the Muslims attacked a Meccan caravan at the oasis of Nakhla in December 623, the provocation to Muhammad's former tribespeople was clear. Muhammad and his followers braced for the next outbreak in what was to become an enduring conflict with their Meccan kinsmen. During the next nine years Muhammad planned thirty-eight battles that were fought by his fellow believers. He himself led twenty-seven military campaigns. The merchant messenger had become not only a recognized prophet but also a successful military strategist.

Muhammad did not have to wait long before leading his first full-scale military campaign. It came at the wells of Badr the following year, in 624. The Muslims chose to attack a caravan coming south from Palestine to Mecca. The Meccans learned of their plan, opposing them with a force of a thousand men and two hundred horses, far outnumbering the Muslim band of three hundred men. Notwithstanding their smaller numbers, the Muslims won a decisive victory. The Qur'an indicated, as yet another divine sign, that they had been helped by a heavenly host:

> God helped you at the Battle of Badr
> when you were but a weak force;
> be mindful, then, of God,
> that you might be thankful.
> Remember when you said
> to the believers, "Is it not enough
> that your Lord reinforced you with
> three thousand descending angels?
> Yes—if you remain patient
> and mindful of God, even if
> the enemy falls upon you suddenly,
> your Lord will reinforce you with
> five thousand assigned angels."
> God made it only a message
> of hope for you, to reassure
> your hearts—there is no help
> except from God,
> the Almighty, the Wise—
>
> SURA AL 'IMRAN, 3:123–26

The Battle of Badr struck fear into the hearts of the Meccans, but it also made some even more firmly resolved to defeat the upstart Muslims. Among the Meccan opponents was Hind ibn 'Utba, the wife of the mighty Meccan warrior Abu Sufyan. Having lost both her uncle and her father at Badr, she incited her husband, even though he was both Muhammad's cousin and his foster brother, to plan for the next encounter. By 625 he had assembled a large army of three thousand men, both foot soldiers and cavalry, which marched toward Medina. The Muslims, a force of only seven hundred men, countered by moving out of the city proper to engage their rivals on the slopes of a nearby mountain, Uhud.

Despite the superior numbers of the Meccans, it went well for the Muslims until some of Muhammad's followers broke ranks too early. Muhammad had placed fifty archers on a hill to protect the rear of his army but forty of them, perhaps anticipating another victory such as Badr and eager for spoils, rushed down the hill. The Meccans counterattacked, and Khalid ibn al-Walid, one of the brilliant Meccan nobles, led his squadron to the unprotected rear of the Muslim formation. Catching them unawares, he began a great slaughter. The Prophet's uncle Hamza was felled by a skilled Meccan javelin thrower paid by Hind, and Muhammad himself, though protected by twenty of his closest followers, was knocked off his horse. One of his teeth was broken, his face gashed, a lip bruised. Daring to hope that Muhammad might die from his wounds, Abu Sufyan began to taunt the defeated Muslim troops. Muhammad sent his trusted lieutenant, 'Umar, to give him the riposte: "God is most high, most glorious," shouted 'Umar. "We are by no means equal: our dead are in paradise, yours are in hell; and by God, you have not killed the Prophet. He hears us even as we speak!"

Not only was Muhammad listening, but he also had resolved to learn the deeper lesson behind this bitter defeat. The defeat of Uhud became as important for Islam as the victory of Badr. It reinforced Muhammad's resolve to secure the loyalty of all his followers—both the Muslims and the non-Muslims bound to him by treaty. There followed some difficult, often bloody purges of tribes near Medina, then a major battle in 627—the Battle of the Trench. A mighty army composed of ten thousand men, four thousand from the Quraysh themselves and the rest from various tribes, was led again by Abu Sufyan, the architect of Uhud. Abu Sufyan had hoped to invade Medina, to defeat and destroy the Muslim upstarts once and for all. The Muslims dug a trench around the city, to which the Meccans laid siege. Three thousand Muslims were encamped outside the city with the trench between them and their foes. Even after several days the Quraysh were unable to cross the trench and hostilities were restricted to a mutual discharge of arrows. The weather was cold and wet and the invading armies were rapidly running out of supplies. Their horses and camels were dying. Then a fierce sandstorm raged over the plain and blew away the tents of the Quraysh. Abu Sufyan told his men to go home, and the allied tribes also deserted their camps. Through this act of God, the Muslims had gained an important victory, which meant their survival.

The Treaty of Hudaybiyya

Inspired by a dream in the year 628, Muhammad instructed his followers to set out for a pilgrimage to the Ka'ba in Mecca, a rectangular shrine regarded as the holiest place on earth by Muslims. They believe the Ka'ba to have been built by Abraham. It was to this place that Abraham sent his concubine Hagar and her son, Ishmael. It was here that, with divine guidance, he had made provision for a branch of his family. The central role of this shrine is voiced by Abraham in the Qur'an:

> Our Lord, I have settled some
> of my offspring in an arid valley,
> near your sacred house, so that
> they might be steadfast in prayer, our Lord.
> So, turn people's hearts toward them,
> and sustain them with fruit, so that
> they might be grateful.
>
> SURA IBRAHIM, 14:37

After the time of Abraham, however, the shrine had become the site of idols that represented local gods and tribal deities. Some believed that these idols possessed a power rivaling the God of Abraham. Others frowned on this polytheism, including local Jews and Christians, as well as some Arabs who traced their views to an ancient Arab prophet, Salih, who had also followed the monotheism of Moses and Jesus. But by the time of Muhammad, idolatry prevailed, and the Quraysh had become guardians of the sanctuary and overseers of the annual pilgrimage that people made from various parts of Arabia and beyond. It was an integral part of Muhammad's mission to rid the Ka'ba of these idols and to reaffirm belief in the one God, Allah.

Muhammad set out with about fourteen hundred followers, each wearing two white cloths, the traditional garb of pilgrims, accompanied by animals garlanded for sacrifice. News of his plans evoked a dilemma among the Quraysh; as guardians of the shrine, they would be violating their own tribal customs if they were to prevent pilgrims from approaching the holy site; yet allowing them entry would represent a moral triumph for Muhammad. They sent the fierce warrior Khalid ibn al-Walid with two hundred horsemen to bar the pilgrims' approach. The Muslims managed to avoid him and made camp at Hudaybiyya en route to Mecca. Eventually, the Quraysh sent Suhayl ibn ʿAmr, an unremittent opponent of the new religion, to negotiate a pact with the Prophet.

The result was the Treaty of Hudaybiyya, which stated that the Muslims would be allowed to perform the pilgrimage only in the following year and, in an important provision, declared a ten-year period of peace, as well as the freedom of people to align themselves with either side. Although some of the Muslims were frustrated at having to postpone their pilgrimage, a revelation from the Qurʾan spoke of the treaty as "a clear victory" (Sura 48:1). It was indeed a victory since it enabled many people to come to the Prophet to declare their faith; over the next two years the Muslim community more than doubled. During this time, the Prophet sent letters inviting a number of rulers to embrace Islam: Heraclius in Byzantium, Khosrow of Persia, Muqawqis in Egypt, and the Negus of Abyssinia. Only the last of these accepted his invitation. Many of the Prophet's former opponents, including Khalid ibn Walid, also embraced Islam and were forgiven for all they had previously wrought against Muhammad.

The Peaceful Entry into Mecca

Their treaty with the Quraysh allowed the Muslims to focus on other dangers. In 629, Muhammad led his forces against the strongholds of Khaybar, a town to the north occupied by a group of Jews who had betrayed their agreement with him. After several days, all the fortresses of the town had been overcome or had surrendered. Muhammad agreed to let the Jews remain on the terms that they themselves had proposed—namely, that they would pay him a yearly rent of half their harvest. In 630 the Treaty of Hudaybiyya was violated by the Meccans, with momentous consequences. The Quraysh helped one of their allied clans in a night raid against a clan allied with the Muslims. Fearing the repercussions of this, the Meccans sent Abu Sufyan to pacify the Prophet, but to no avail. The Prophet prepared a campaign to take Mecca and sent messengers to allied tribes for help. They responded enthusiastically and the Muslim army, composed of Bedouins, immigrants, and helpers, numbered nearly ten thousand men. They encamped on the outskirts of Mecca and the sight of their many thousand campfires that night confirmed the fears of the Quraysh. They once again sent Abu Sufyan, with two other men, to the Prophet, and by the morning all three had declared their faith in the one God and His Prophet. Abu Sufyan returned to tell his fellow Meccans that Muhammad was about to enter the city with an irresistible force. But he also conveyed Muhammad's message that anyone in his house was safe, and that anyone who stayed at home or in the mosque would not be harmed.

It was January in the year 630. The sight of the returning Muslim Meccans and their allies melted the hearts of many who had been their bitter enemies. Tribe after tribe entered the city, each with its banners and pennants, followed by the Prophet's squadron of immigrants and helpers, fully armed so that only their eyes were visible. They entered the city peacefully from four directions, with no bloodshed beyond a small skirmish started by the Quraysh. The Prophet had forbidden any fighting. After his ritual purification with water, Muhammad prayed and then rode to the southeast corner of the Kaʿba to touch the black stone[7] with his staff. Then he performed the traditional seven circumambulations of the shrine. He now turned to the wide circle of 360 idols that surrounded the Kaʿba, pointing at each one with his staff as he rode, and each in turn fell on its face. His cousin ʿAli brought him the key to the Kaʿba, which he entered with two companions. The inside walls were covered with pictures of pagan deities. The Prophet had these effaced; but two icons he preserved, one said to be of Abraham and the other of the Virgin Mary with the child Jesus.

Having ordered that the idols should be broken and burned, Muhammad received the homage of his enemies, who now came to enter Islam, including Hind, the wife of Abu Sufyan. Most of the Meccans pledged their allegiance. He forgave them all.

Final Encounters and the Unification of Arabia

After the conquest of Mecca, the Muslims fought further battles, notably in 630 at the Hunayn valley against tribes to the east and southeast of Mecca who were intent on halting the spread of Islam. The battle at Hunayn proved to be a decisive victory for the Muslims. Later in the same year, a rumor reached Medina that the Byzantine emperor Heraclius, alarmed at the growing power of the Muslims, planned to attack them, and was amass-

---

7   This is a stone set in the southeast corner of the Kaʿba, believed to date back to Adam.

ing his legions along the Syrian frontier. The Prophet decided to meet them at Tabuk, some 350 miles from Medina, with an army of thirty thousand men, the largest he had ever commanded. After spending some twenty days at Tabuk, the Muslims realized that the rumors had been unfounded. They made alliances with local tribes and began the march back to Medina.

Muhammad was now the most powerful leader in Arabia, most of which he had succeeded in uniting under one faith. People were to be bound now not by blood or tribal kinship but by a shared belief in the one God and His final messenger. In the so-called Year of Deputations (632), most tribes had come to him to profess their acceptance of Islam. These included the Bani Thaqif from Ta'if who, some twelve years earlier, had so disdainfully driven Muhammad from their town. The Prophet also stipulated that Jews and Christians should not be compelled to forgo their religion but would pay a poll tax (*jizya*) to protect them and maintain their houses of worship.[8] When the Christians of Najran came to make a pact with the Prophet, he allowed them to pray in the mosque according to their own ritual and guaranteed the safety of their churches and their property.

The expedition to Tabuk and the coming of the numerous delegations convinced some of Muhammad's followers that they would no longer be called upon to fight. They prepared to sell their arms and armor. But the Prophet forbade this, saying that his followers would continue to fight for the truth until the coming of the Antichrist, who would wreak great corruption on the earth. The Prophet foretold the Second Coming of Jesus, who would lead this struggle. Beyond making these predictions about the last days, Muhammad also clarified the essentials of the new religion. His companion 'Umar reported that, one day, while the Prophet was sitting with his followers, a man dressed in pure white came to ask him the meaning of "submission" (*islam*). The Prophet explained that it comprised five obligations: to testify that there is no god other than the one God and that Muhammad is His messenger; to perform the required prayers; to give what is due in charity; to fast during the month of Ramadan; and, if possible, to make the pilgrimage to Mecca during the Hajj season. These were to become known as the five pillars of Islam. The Prophet later explained that the man, who corroborated his answers, was Gabriel, who had come to teach them their religion.

---

8 The poll tax or *jizya* was levied on non-Muslims in return for protection from any invading or attacking force because they were not required to fight in the Muslim army.

The Farewell Pilgrimage

In 632 CE the Prophet undertook his final pilgrimage to Mecca. He was joined by multitudes who gathered from all directions, numbering over thirty thousand men and women. From this time on, no polytheists were allowed into the holy precincts. During the pilgrimage, the Prophet instructed his followers about the rites and customs of the Hajj, and then took up a position on the hill of 'Arafat to address them in his farewell sermon. He told them that their blood and property were sacrosanct; that they would surely meet their Lord and be questioned about their works. He reminded them that usury was abolished and that all blood that had been shed in the pagan period was to be left unavenged. He encouraged them by saying that Satan had despaired of leading them astray in large matters, hence they should beware of his influence in smaller things. He reminded them that husbands and wives had rights over each other. Finally, he told them that he had left two things with them that would prevent their going astray: the Qur'an and his own example.[9]

Soon after his return to Medina, the Prophet had just finished praying for the dead at the local cemetery when he fell ill with an intense headache. He indicated to his companions that he was nearing his end, his meeting with his Lord. He also declared Abu Bakr to be his inseparable friend, and as his illness increased, he instructed that Abu Bakr should lead the prayer in the mosque. The Prophet prayed his final prayer, seated to the right behind his chosen companion. He returned to the apartment of 'A'isha, his youngest wife, and died with his head on her breast. 'Umar did not believe that the Prophet had died and stood in the mosque to tell people that he was still alive. While he was speaking, Abu Bakr arrived and intervened, telling the people that if they worshipped Muhammad, they should know that Muhammad was dead, but if they worshipped God, He was ever living and does not die. He quoted this verse from the Qur'an:

> Muhammad is no more than
> a messenger, and messengers
> passed away before him. If he died

9   Lings, *Muhammad*, 651.

or were killed, would you turn
upon your heels? Whoever so turns
can do no harm to God;
but God will reward those
who are grateful.

SURA AL ʿIMRAN, 3:144

In accordance with his own instructions, the Prophet was buried where he died. It was decided within the community that Abu Bakr should succeed him as its leader and he would become the first caliph of the Islamic empire. People flocked from all over Medina to the Prophet's gravesite to say prayers for him, feeling that a great door—to communications from the beyond—had been closed. Indeed, the revelations had finished, but the miracle of the inimitable Qur'an remained with them.

General Characteristics of the Qur'an

The Qur'an (meaning "recitation") was revealed to the Prophet by the Archangel Gabriel over a period of twenty-three years (610–632). Its Arabic text has survived unchanged for over fourteen centuries, and it is the primary source of authority in Islam, complemented by the *hadith* (traditions or sayings of the Prophet). The Qur'an consists of 114 suras or chapters, which are in turn composed of *ayat* or "verses" (singular: *aya*). The suras are traditionally divided into Meccan and Medinan, named after their place of revelation. The earlier suras revealed at Mecca are shorter, proclaiming God's Oneness, establishing the Prophet's credentials, addressing issues of social justice, and reminding people of impending judgment, with graphic evocations of heaven and hell. The later suras, revealed after Muhammad's migration to Medina, are longer, more prosaic, and concern laws and regulations of various aspects of domestic and social life such as marriage, inheritance, and business transactions; the need to establish a united community; connections with the Jews and Christians (the "people of the Book"); and stories of earlier prophets.

In time, the words Muhammad heard, remembered, and recited became a book. It was confirmed as a canonical written text by his third successor, the Caliph ʿUthman, who arranged all the variants into one standardized version. The order of the suras here is not chronological and generally the longer ones are placed earlier, with the shortest ones at the end. The Qur'an often refers to itself as the book (*kitab*), but a book that is not identical with its physical version (known as *mushaf*). The Qur'an has existed as a written text since the seventh century; excerpts from it are inscribed in stone on the Dome of the Rock, a memorial in Jerusalem, by an early Muslim ruler, the Caliph 'Abd al-Malik.[10] It has been written down by countless generations of Muslims, making calligraphy a major art form in Islamic civilization. The written Qur'an is prized as a sacred object around the world. In many Muslim households, a copy of the Qur'an is set out in a prominent place on a special stand (*kursi*).

The Qur'an speaks of itself as the final stage of four revealed books, the other three being the Torah, the Gospels, and the Psalms.[11] Among the Arabs, those practicing Judaism or Christianity (but not paganism) would have been familiar with its presumption of a single God beyond human knowing. However, in other respects, the new revelation echoed a cosmology that was readily accepted by all—a heaven populated with angels and archangels, a hell strewn with devils, and, in between these, ambiguous creatures called jinn, who are neither angelic nor demonic yet omnipresent and vigilant.

Notwithstanding the rich diversity of its cosmology, the central theme of the Qur'an is the unity of God, who has no partners, a point stressed again and again, as in this verse:

Among His signs are
night and day, sun and moon.
Do not bow before sun and moon,
but bow before God,
Who created them—
if it is Him alone you worship.

SURA FUSSILAT, 41:37

10   See *The Qur'an: A Biography* (2006), chap. 4 for citation, as well as an explanation of the multiple Qur'anic verses from the Dome of the Rock.

11   All four scriptures are related in the Qur'an to their prophetic conduits: the Torah to Moses (Sura 32:33), the Psalms to David (Sura 17:55), the Gospels to Jesus (Sura 5:11), and, of course, the Qur'an to Muhammad.

The sun, moon and stars, men, women, and children, elephants, spiders and ants, trees, plants, and grass—all have been created by a single unitary force, God. God's Oneness is the foundation of the other Qur'anic themes: the attributes of God, as in the ninety-nine Beautiful Names of God, the most prominent among them being the Creator, the Merciful, the Forgiving, and the All Knowing. Acknowledging the unity of God entails complete "submission" to Him.

The one God is the Creator, Ruler, and Protector of all things in the universe. The rhythm of creation reflects His signs (*ayat*), the same word used to denote "verses." Far from being random, creation is designed to reflect the natural—and human—order as He willed it:

> Your Lord is God, Who created
> the heavens and the earth in six days,
> then took up the throne.
> He veils day with night,
> which trails it swiftly.
> He created the sun, moon, and stars—
> all subject to His command.
> Is the creation not His,
> and the command? Blessèd be God,
> Lord of the universe.
>
> SURA AL-A'RAF, 7:54

Other major themes include the obligation of human beings to worship God, not only through prayer but by practicing justice, honesty, and charity, as summarized in this passage:

> Righteousness
> does not reside
> in turning your faces
> toward East or West;
> rather, it resides in those—
> who believe in God
> and the last day,
> in the angels, the Book,

and the prophets;
who give their wealth
—despite their love of it—
for kin, for orphans, the needy,
the traveler, for those who ask,
and for freeing slaves;
who are steadfast in prayer,
who give in charity,
keeping their covenants;
who suffer in patience
hardship, pain, and
times of conflict—
they are the ones
who are truthful, and
they are the ones
mindful of God.

SURA AL-BAQARA, 2:177

The only attribute through which human beings can attain any degree of superiority over others is *taqwa*, or mindfulness of God—which means striving for all the qualities enumerated in this verse. The Qur'an speaks of itself as the final revelation, completing and confirming both the Jewish and Christian scriptures; it accords a very special place to Abraham, Jesus, and the Virgin Mary, while affirming that Muhammad is the last messenger of God, the "seal" of the prophets.

Perhaps the signal characteristic of the Qur'an is its perfection in its original form, its conventionally cited "inimitability," and the inevitable diminishment it suffers when translated into another language. Nonetheless, the majority of the world's Muslims do not read (or comprehend spoken) Arabic and need the Qur'an to be conveyed to them in their own language. No translation can ever substitute for the Qur'an itself, but as we will explain in the next section, we believe that at least some of the power of this majestic book can be conveyed in English.

ABOUT THIS TRANSLATION

Perhaps the greatest obstacle to translating the Qur'an lies in the differences between long-held Western aesthetic assumptions and the compositional features of the Qur'an. Those who read the Qur'an in any of its English renderings bring to it expectations—of unity, coherence, narrative structure—that are inevitably frustrated. Though the Qur'an repeatedly refers to itself as *al-kitab* (the Book), any student of it knows that this term does not signify "book" in a conventional Western sense. It is simply not a book to be read from cover to cover. The Qur'an is meant to be read aloud, and Muslims typically experience it either through listening to the recitation of a religious leader (*imam*) or reciting it themselves.

The oral performance of the Book has been crucial from the earliest years. In religious schools, Muslim children are taught to memorize and recite the Qur'an. Throughout the Muslim world, Arabs and non-Arabs alike participate in annual contests to recite the Qur'an, an exercise known as *qir'at*. The emphasis on performance goes back to Muhammad. When one of his wives, 'A'isha, was asked to describe him, she replied: "He is the walking Qur'an."[12] And so the Qur'an is not just read or recited but embodied. One scholar has even said: "If Christianity's truth is the Word made flesh, Islam's knowledge is the flesh made Word." In other words, the devout Muslim must embody the knowledge of God by hearing, remembering, and performing scriptural directives, by becoming "a walking Qur'an."[13] The Islamic historian Marshall Hodgson famously declared that the Qur'an is not a mere statement

---

12 The actual reference is to the character of Muhammad as "the Qur'an" but it is popularly rendered as "the walking Qur'an." Qatada reported: "I said to 'A'isha, 'O mother of the believers, tell me about the character of the Messenger of Allah, peace and blessings be upon him.' 'A'isha said, 'Have you not read the Qur'an?' I said, 'Of course.' 'A'isha said, 'Verily, the character of the Prophet of Allah was the Qur'an'" (Imam Abul Hussain bin al Hajja et al., eds., Naisiruddin al Khattab, trans., *Sahih Muslim* [Lahore: Darussalam, 2007], *hadith* 746, 2:258).

13 Rudolph T. Ware III, *The Walking Qur'an: Islamic Education, Embodied Knowledge and History in West Africa* (Chapel Hill: University of North Carolina Press, 2014), 254–56.

to be passively received, but "an event, an act."[14] Much more than a conventional book, the Qur'an is the expression of God's spoken message. The goal is nothing short of trying to hear a faint echo of God speaking—a task that is humanly impossible but nonetheless a responsibility.

Collaboration

Translating the Qur'an must therefore be approached with humility. We believe that this task can best be conducted as a collaborative endeavor. The translation of the Qur'an might be seen as a collective enterprise, where each rendering contributes something new or different to the overall endeavor. We undertook this project almost a decade ago, and we continue to be deeply mindful of the long and revered tradition in which we are participating. What distinguishes our translation is that, for the first time, expertise in Arabic/Islamic studies has been brought together with expertise in English. With his broad grounding in Western literature, aesthetics, literary theory, and philosophy, together with his own experience as a poet, Rafey Habib offers a more subtle approach to poetics than has been customary in Qur'an translation. Throughout our joint endeavor, he has considered the challenges of versification, adopting innovative strategies for translating the Qur'an using accentual verse. Having studied Qur'anic Arabic for several years, he has also examined the various modes of recitation of the Qur'an (*tilawa*), as well as insights of scholars into the Qur'an's deployment of *saj'* (rhymed and rhythmic prose).

For his part, Bruce Lawrence brings to this project a deep and intimate knowledge of the Qur'anic text, as well as the history of its translation, in the context of the rich history of Islam. Over the course of his scholarly career, he has often grappled with the idiom of the Qur'an, especially as it pertains to fundamental notions such as the *basmala* (the invocation of God's name) and the ninety-nine Beautiful Names of God as they appear in the Qur'an.

At the foundation of this joint endeavor is our shared recognition that the Qur'an is as much an oral text as a written one. Its style and sound are integral to its meaning—it is a text that is meant to be performed. As the Arabic

---

14   Marshall G. S. Hodgson, *The Venture of Islam*, vol. 1, *The Classical Age of Islam* (Chicago: University of Chicago Press, 1974), 367.

literary scholar Shawkat Toorawa recognizes, its sound effects—including pauses, repetition, rhyme, and assonance—are not somehow supplementary but utterly crucial.[15] Inspired by the insights and the wisdom of many scholars, we have drawn upon the rich history of Qur'an translation and the tradition of *tafsir* (Qur'anic interpretation). We have also sought help from a variety of English-language poets and scholars in our endeavor to produce a translation that not only is accessible and readable but might be considered poetic.

The Qur'an as Verse

Having said this, the Qur'an is not poetry as such. Most of it does not conform to any of the conventional Arabic meters (*al-buhur*), and the text denies its own status as poetry. Early opponents of the new religion claimed that Muhammad was a mere poet and had himself invented the Qur'anic verses. There are no less than six verses in the Qur'an that refer to this accusation. The most emphatic denial of it occurs in Sura Ya Sin (36:69):

> We have not taught poetry
> to the Prophet, nor is it fitting for him.
> This is nothing other than a reminder
> and a clear Qur'an.

Another verse (37:36) links poetry to possession by jinn:[16] in defending their gods, the pagans labeled Muhammad as a "mad poet" (*sha'ir majnun*). Again, at the end of a sura specifically entitled "The Poets" (26:221–26), poets are compared to devils, both of whom are labeled liars:

> Shall I inform you
> on whom the devils descend?

15 Toorawa argues for the vital role of sound in several publications, where he also draws attention to the critical importance of *saj'* (something discussed later in this essay), as in his "'The Inimitable Rose,' Being Qur'anic *Saj'* from Surat al-Duhā to Surat al-Nās (Q. 93–114) in English Rhyming Prose," *Journal of Qur'anic Studies* 8, no. 2 (2006): 143.

16 These are intermediate beings, neither human nor celestial; a more detailed explanation is provided in the glossary (page 531).

They descend on every sinful liar,
they pass on whatever is heard,
and most of them are liars.
And the poets are followed by
those who are astray.
Don't you see them wandering
aimlessly through every valley?
Saying things
that they do not do?

Yet a subsequent verse from the same sura acknowledges that at least some poets can be counted among the righteous:

Except those of them who believe
and do good deeds, and remember God
often, defending themselves
only when wronged.
The wrongdoers shall soon know
their place of return.

SURA AL-SHU'ARA, 26:227

Notwithstanding the ambiguous status accorded to poetry in the Qur'an, it is widely acknowledged that the Qur'anic text itself is deeply poetic. The numerous stylistic virtues of the Qur'an include its use of rhymed and rhythmic prose (saj'), allusions, symbolism, metaphors, similes, and parables; a consciousness of its audience and its place in history; its modulation of its narrative voice; and a range of rhetorical devices, including repetition, stylized and formulaic conversations, and the posing of rhetorical questions. The Qur'an itself states on numerous occasions that it uses the language of allegory, metaphor, or simile (29:43; 13:17; 14:24).

In fact, in a renowned verse the Qur'an distinguishes between its own use of "clear" passages (muhkamat) and "figurative" passages (mutashabihat), affirming that the true meanings of the latter are known only to God (3:7). The voice of the Qur'an extends over many rhetorical and performative situations, with God addressing the Prophet (33:45–46), humankind in general and the believers in particular, speaking in parables, sometimes in the first

person (2:186) and sometimes in the third person (45:12), recounting historical events and moral lessons (36:13–32), as well as dialogues between historical figures (e.g., Moses and Pharaoh, 26:23–28), and offering arguments for
the signs and manifestations of God's existence.

Recently, the Iranian-German literary scholar Navid Kermani has made
a plea to open up study of the Qur'an to the notion of poetic sensibilities.
Acknowledging the Qur'anic declarations that Muhammad is not a poet, he
asserts that Muhammad is not a poet because he was a poet *and something
more*. He quotes two classical scholars—al-Jahiz and al-Jurjani—and also
the modern Lebanese poet Adonis on the surplus nature of God's lyrical elo-
quence, channeled first through Gabriel and then through Muhammad. For
Adonis the Qur'an "is prose, but not like prose; it is poetry, but not like poetry."[17] Not only is the Qur'an aesthetic and musical in nature, but its meaning
is inseparable from its sound. Its sound is more poetic than prosaic, even in
the later legislative Medinan suras. Although the Qur'an may not be poetry,
it is clearly *more* than poetry.

Why, then, have most translators rendered the Qur'an into prose? Their
overriding aim seems to have been clarity. But the text of the Qur'an cannot be called "prose," at least in any conventional Western sense, since it
does not conform to the expectations that a reader of English would bring
to a prose composition. The Qur'anic text does not comprise continuous
narrative, not even Sura Yusuf (Sura 12), which recounts the story of the
prophet Joseph in some detail. Even though the Arabic of the Qur'an *looks*
like continuous prose, many verses are actually independent, and there are
often pauses *within* a verse. Such features create a sound and rhythm when
the Qur'an is recited in Arabic and they are best conveyed by the use of line
breaks within and between verses, enabling greater clarity of meaning and
greater emotive impact.

---

17   Navid Kermani, *God Is Beautiful: The Aesthetic Experience of the Qur'an* (Cambridge: Polity
Press, 2014), 193, 81. Kermani's entire book is teeming with insight into the deeply literary and
lyrical quality of the Qur'an in its own terms, a revelation but one linked to poetry since "poetry
was the only medium besides revelation (and, later mysticism) with an acknowledged claim
to association with a transcendental reality" (288). The age-old prejudice against poetry, and
against any link of the Qur'an to poetry continues in many translations, even by broad-gauged,
well-intentioned scholars, e.g., Ahmad Zaki Hammad, *The Gracious Qur'an: A Modern-Phrased
Interpretation in English* (Lisle, Ill.: Lucent Interpretations, 2007), 1189: "To liken the Qur'an to
poetry is not only fundamentally wrong, but demeaning of its Heavenly Revelation."

Many of the poetic effects of the Qur'an will be entirely lost in a "prose" translation. Consider, for example, the first verse of Sura al-Isra' (17:1), as we have translated it:

> Glory be to the One
> Who took His servant
> on a journey by night
> from the sacred mosque
> to the farthest mosque,
> whose precincts We blessed
> that We might show him
> some of Our signs. He alone
> is the All Hearing,
> All Seeing.

This verse translation aims to create certain effects: there is a slight pause at the end of the first line, allowing the "One" to subsist in momentary independence as the object of glorification, prior to its qualification as a pronoun. There is also a pause after "servant" to reflect a pause in the Arabic. Some of the rhymes in the Arabic are expressed by assonance between "servant" and "journey." The next two lines create a parallel between the two mosques as origin and destination, with the one word visually situated beneath the other. We have consonance between "sacred" and "precincts," as well as an internal rhyme between "night" and "might," and assonance between "might" and "signs." The subject "He alone" enacts its own meaning by being isolated from its predicate (reflecting a pause due to the elongation of the syllables of the Arabic words that mean "truly He"); and there is an emphatic parallelism between "All Hearing" and "All Seeing." Above all, the lines as arranged above force the reader to read slowly, pausing at certain points. These effects are partly visual so that they can register even in a "silent" reading, though they are of course accented when the text is read aloud.

If we render the same lines as "prose," what happens? Nearly all of these effects are lost:

> Glory be to the One Who took His servant on a journey by night from the sacred mosque to the farthest mosque, whose precincts We blessed

that We might show him some of Our signs. He alone is the All Hearing, the All Seeing.

With this version, readerly expectations and assumptions dramatically change. The pace of reading accelerates: the words are read much faster, and all the pauses disappear, as well as one's attention to the aforementioned effects. In a well-known verse, the Qur'an itself instructs the prophet to stand in prayer, "reciting the Qur'an in clear, rhythmic measure" (73:4). A prose translation tends to undermine this meditative mood, impelling the reader to seek forms of coherence and continuity (shaped by centuries of Western aesthetic notions) that are simply not there.

Versification

For all these reasons, we resolved to translate the Qur'an into verse. This itself poses a number of challenges. What does English verse look like in the twenty-first century? Is it free verse, usually said to be marked by absence of regular rhyme, rhythm, or meter? No doubt, most of the poetry produced today appears to be written in free verse. But, as T. S. Eliot remarked, no verse is truly free for the poet who wants to do a good job. According to Eliot, the ghost of some regular meter always lurks behind the arras of metrical irregularity. He affirmed that there "is no escape from metre; there is only mastery." Indeed, he went so far as to deny that free verse exists, as in his renowned assertion that there is only "good verse, bad verse, and chaos."[18] The implication here is that, without a knowledge of regular meters, one cannot know what one is breaking away from. Even free verse must have some discernible pattern and connection to meaning. Free verse at its most effective is a means of enhancing meaning, of enacting meaning, of expressing it more precisely, and adapting to it.

What are the other options for translation beyond free verse? One of the obvious choices is unrhymed iambic pentameter, known as blank verse. Most of the everyday English we speak is iambic, with an unstressed syllable followed by a stressed one, as in the word "defeat" (de-*feat*). So, on the

---

18   The arguments in this section are treated more fully in M. A. R. Habib, "Translating the Qur'an: Towards a New Approach," *Maghreb Review* 46, no. 3 (2021): 314–38.

surface, blank verse would seem to be a natural choice. But we might bear in mind that there is no hard-and-fast rule, no prohibition on using *any* of the traditional verse forms. With an eye to this rich tradition of English letters, we concluded, after much experimenting, that perhaps there is no fixed form or meter into which the Qur'an can be translated. The Qur'an's many styles, many voices, and many rhetorical or performative situations demand an aesthetic versatility, accommodating the use of say, pentameters, tetrameters, trimeters, and free verse—allowing the occasion as it emerges in the Arabic text to dictate our choices in versification.

The Challenge of Qur'anic Rhymed Prose (*Saj'*)

It is widely recognized that the Qur'an often employs the device known as *saj'*, already mentioned.[19] A vivid example occurs at the opening of Sura al-Duha (Sura 93).[20] We can see that the endings of the lines rhyme. Each line below comprises one *saj'* unit, and the *saj'* units can vary in length. Here, each *saj'* unit is progressively longer. Each word in Arabic counts as one beat:

wa-l-duha
by the morning light   } first *saj'* unit: one beat

wa-l-layli | idha | saja
by the night | when | it is still   } second *saj'* unit: three beats

---

19   Since the 1990s, Devin Stewart, drawing on medieval Arab rhetoricians, has produced a great deal of pioneering work on *saj'*. See especially his essay "*Saj'* in the 'Qur'an': Prosody and Structure," *Journal of Arabic Literature* 21, no. 2 (1990): 112–16, to which these sections are indebted. His insights have been valuably developed by Marianna Klar, as documented below. But this work—rather puzzlingly—has not in general informed the process and principles of Qur'an translation.

20   This is how Marianna Klar divides up the *saj'* units of this sura in her essay "A Preliminary Catalogue of Qur'anic *Saj'* Techniques: Beat Patterning, Parallelism, and Rhyme," in *Structural Dividers in the Qur'an* (London: Routledge, 2021), 181–231. See also her situation of *saj'* within a more comprehensive analysis of sura structure in "Text-Critical Approaches to Sura Structure: Combining Synchronicity with Diachronicity in *Sūrat al-Baqara*. Part One," *Journal of Qur'anic Studies* 19, no. 1 (2017): 1–38, and "Text-Critical Approaches to Sura Structure: Combining Synchronicity with Diachronicity in *Sūrat al-Baqara*. Part Two," *Journal of Qur'anic Studies* 19, no. 2 (2017): 64–105.

ma | wadda'aka | rabbuka | wa-ma | qala   third *saj'* unit: five beats
not | abandoned you | your Lord |
and not | abhor

How can we render this structure in English? One way would be to try to match the relative lengths of the three *saj'* units in English:

By the morning light in its brilliance;[21]
by the darkening night in its stillness;
your Lord has not abandoned you, nor is He abhorring [you].

Instead of the end rhymes—which could seem very forced and contrived in English—we have used internal rhymes and assonance ("brilliance," "stillness," "abhorring") as well as the rhymes "light" and "night," "nor" and "abhorring." However, a more effective rendering in English might be to split each *saj'* unit into *two* lines of English verse, like this:

By the morning light
in its brilliance;
by the darkening night
in its stillness;
your Lord has not abandoned you,
nor is He abhorring [you].

There are a number of advantages to this strategy. To begin with, the oath ("By . . . ") as it stands in the first Arabic line is concise, an effect that is lost if we try to express the full meaning of *duha* in five words ("morning light in its brilliance"). Splitting up the lines retains something of the concision, the subject of the oath being the "morning light," with the words "in its stillness" allowed to subsist as a qualification of that light instead of intruding themselves as partial subject of the oath (in other words, the longer line tends to dilute the oath, making it less direct). Second, the rhymes between "light"

21   The word *duha* literally refers to the period of time from after sunrise until before noon. In Sura 91:1 and 79:29, it indicates the full brightness of the sun. Hence, the phrase "morning light" alone would not express the requisite brightness here.

and "night," "brilliant" and "stillness," become more emphatic. Finally, we see in this second version some of the effects of enjambment (continuing a phrase beyond the end of one line into the next), such as the slowing down of the verse into a more deeply meditative mode. When read aloud, there will be slight pauses after "light," "night," and "you." The Arabic text already achieves this effect through the rules of *tajwid* (enunciation) and *waqf* (system of pauses and stops during recitation). So, even a long line in the Arabic is not in danger of being rushed or read aloud in anything but a slow, rhythmic manner.[22] This effect cannot be taken for granted in English. It must be *achieved*—not only by word combination but also by line length and enjambment. In general, enjambed lines bring a slower, attentive pace to verse, prompting an unhurried, contemplative reading.

What options do we have here as translators? To what extent should we try to replicate Arabic verbal structures in translation? The most obvious answer is that there can be no fixed rule and that we should proceed on the basis of each case, which is often unique. If we follow Marianna Klar's division of the entire structure of Sura al-Duha, we'll end up with something like this:

By the morning light in its brilliance;
by the darkening night in its stillness;
your Lord has not abandoned you, nor is He abhorring [you].
What comes hereafter will prove finer for you than what came before;
and your Lord will provide, satisfying you.

---

22   One of the bases of the science of *tajwid* is Sura 73:4, where *tartil* denotes a slow, rhythmic, and distinct recitation. The Prophet is said to have taught his companions how to recite, clearly and precisely, drawing the voice out over the long vowels. There also developed a more specialized and rapid style of recitation known as *hadr* performed by highly trained reciters who needed to cover parts of the Qur'an rapidly. And there is a third style, of medium pace, called *tadwir*. There are also *hadith* that relate the Prophet's manner of pausing during recitation, something that developed into the system of "pauses and resumption" (*waqf wa ibtida'*). And of course there are well-known *hadith* concerning the seven variant dialects of recitation, or 'ahruf (though some subsequent authorities held the number of variant modes to be ten and others fourteen). Some of the most common styles are *tahqiq, hadr, tartil,* and *tadwir.* But the rules of *tajwid* apply to all of them (Frederick Mathewson Denny, "Qur'ān Recitation: A Tradition of Oral Performance and Transmission," *Oral Tradition* 4, no. 1–2 [1989]: 8–10, 19–21; James Robson, *Mishkat al-Masabih: English Translation with Explanatory Notes* [Lahore: Muhammad Ashraf, 1965], 464).

Did He not find you orphaned
and give shelter?
find you seeking and give guidance?
find you needing and suffice you?
Then, as for
the orphan, don't oppress [her]
the one who asks, don't reproach [her]
your Lord's grace, proclaim [it].

The last four lines represent an Arabic construction that is unidiomatic in English. So we would have to change them to something like this:

Do not, then,
oppress the orphan,
nor reproach the one who asks,
but proclaim your Lord's grace.

To our ear, this reads satisfactorily in English. However, it is somewhat imbalanced. In contrast with the Arabic, where each word counts as a beat, in English it is the *syllables* that are counted. Line 3 has fifteen syllables whereas lines 6 and 10 have only three. For the reasons stated above, it would be better, in our view, to divide up the longer lines, so that we have:

By the morning light
in its brilliance;
by the darkening night
in its stillness;
your Lord has not abandoned you,
nor is He abhorring [you].
What comes hereafter
will prove finer for you
than what came before;
and your Lord will provide,
satisfying you.
Did He not find you orphaned
and give shelter?

find you seeking and give guidance?
find you needing and suffice you?
So, do not oppress the orphan,
nor reproach the one who asks,
but proclaim the grace
of your Lord.

The result, we believe, is something that reads like modern English verse while retaining the deep structure of the Arabic text.

English Accentual Verse: A New Strategy in Qur'an Translation

Most English poetry written since the Middle Ages has been *accentual syllabic*, which means that it is based on the accent or stress of syllables, and on the arrangement of stressed and unstressed syllables. So, for example, in the last two lines of Shakespeare's Sonnet 18, the stressed syllables can be represented by a slash and the unstressed ones by an x:

x / x / x / x / x /
So long as men can breathe, or eyes can see,

x / x / x / x / x /
So long lives this, and this gives life to thee.

In this kind of verse, we count *both* the stressed syllables and the unstressed syllables. We can see that each line has ten syllables, following the iambic beat "x /" (unstressed then stressed), the common English form known as iambic pentameter.

However, in *accentual* verse, which was composed orally during the early Middle Ages, we count *only* the stressed syllables, and the total number of syllables in the lines can vary. Usually, there are four beats per line with a pause, or caesura, in the middle of each line. Many nursery rhymes and folk poems adopt this pattern. In the nineteenth century there was some revival of this form, as in the following famed example from Tennyson, which uses three beats per line:

Bréak, bréak, bréak,	(3 syllables)
On thy cóld grey stónes, O Séa!	(7 syllables)
And I wóuld that my tóngue could útter	(8 syllables)
The thóughts that aríse in mé.	(7 syllables)

If we tried to scan this as accentual syllabic meter, it would not make much sense since the number of syllables varies in each line. However, if we look at the lines as accentual verse, we can discern a regular pattern of three strong beats in each line. Given the Qurʾan's oral nature, it is worth experimenting with translations in accentual meter, which might open up new possibilities that have hitherto remained unexplored, allowing for a more effective performance of the English rendition.

Typically, accentual verse was highly alliterative, with regular repetition of consonant sounds (e.g., "The pride and prince"), but we should acknowledge that straining after excessive alliteration in English (as after excessive rhyme) is likely to produce distortions in the meanings of Qurʾanic verses. Rhymes can perhaps be compensated by assonance (in which the English language is rich), and we may find that the structures of Qurʾanic verses lend themselves readily to placing a pause or caesura in the middle of a line. Here is an attempt to "scan" Sura 93 in terms of accentual meter, with "/" representing the pause or caesura in our rendition:

By the mórning líght/
in its brílliance;
by the dárkening níght/
in its stíllness;
your Lórd has not abándoned you,/
nór is He abhórring [you].
What cómes hereáfter/
will prove fíner for you
than what cáme befóre;
and your Lórd will províde,/
sátisfying you.
Did He not find you órphaned/

and give shélter?
find you séeking/ and give guídance?
find you néeding/ and suffíce you?
So, do not oppréss/ the órphan,
nor repróach/ the one who ásks,
but procláim/ the gráce
of your Lórd.

What is stressed in English are the more important or prominent words, and the most we can accomplish is to reflect the major emphases of the Arabic. Hence, we cannot simply replicate the Arabic structure, yet we can keep it in mind as the underlying blueprint, as it were, or substratum.

Saj ' and the Question of Line Length

Two final examples may clarify the possible uses of *saj '*. The first is an example of long *saj '*, namely, Sura 11:9–10. Marianna Klar breaks down the beats of these lines according to the following pattern,[23] which we might initially render into English as:

9 If We grant man a taste of Our mercy, then withhold it from him, he becomes despondent, unthankful.

10 But if We give him a taste of [Our] favor, after hardship has touched him, he'll say, "My troubles have gone," and he becomes exultant, boastful.

In this case, it is relatively easy to come up with an end rhyme in English. However, if we leave our lines like this, with a view to matching the end rhymes of the *saj '*, we will produce a translation that is ineffective. To begin with, the length of these lines is extremely unwieldy in English, and it is difficult to discern any metrical pattern or beat. Moreover, in lines of this length, which tend to invite rapid reading, the grammatical parallelism and other poetic effects are lost. Let's see what happens if we break up the lines:

23 Klar, "A Preliminary Catalogue of Qur'anic *Saj '* Techniques," 211.

₉ If We let humans taste Our mercy,
  then withdraw it from them,
  they become hopeless, thankless.

₁₀ But if We let them taste Our favor,
   after hardship has touched them,
   they say, "Evils are gone from me,"
   and they become joyful, boastful.

Now the actual structure of the verses emerges into sharper relief. The conditional structure of each verse (If...then) stands out clearly, with the condition (if...) on one line, the qualification of the condition on the second (then withhold...; after hardship...), with the consequence (he becomes...) on the third line. Moreover, in this format, "mercy" and "favor" receive an equal and parallel emphasis, by virtue not only of the meter but of their position at the end of the line. Crucially, the parallelism of the Arabic words is somewhat echoed in the parallel between "hopeless, thankless" and "joyful, boastful." Other poetic effects might include assonance between "grant" and "unthankful," as well as between "give/him," "taste/favor," and "touched/troubles/become." Even on a visual level, in silent reading, these parallels strike the eye—and the insertion of an extra clause in the second verse ("they say, 'Evils are gone from me'") is visibly parenthetical in nature and does not obscure the structural symmetry. Finally, with the shorter lines, we can more clearly hear a stress of three beats per line:

₉ If We lét humans táste Our mércy,
  thén withdráw it from thém,
  they becóme hópeless, thánkless.

₁₀ But if We lét them táste Our fávor,
   áfter hárdship has toúched them,
   they sáy, "Évils are góne from me,"
   and they becóme jóyful, boástful.

So, ironically, even though the underlying *saj'* structure is lengthy, it is evinced more clearly by the shorter lines, in which the pattern of beats is heard, and where the various parallelisms are audible and visible.

In our final example, we can see how there might be some flexibility in interpreting and approximating *saj'* structures. Marianna Klar offers two ways in which Sura 19:88–92 might be segmented. The first would divide these verses into three sub-units, which would look like this[24] if we are using our own translation:

88   They say, "The Most Merciful has conceived a child." Assuredly, you
speak of something monstrous—

90   at which the heavens might be cleaved asunder, and the earth burst into
pieces, and the mountains collapse in complete ruin—

91   that they deem the Most Merciful to have a child, for it is not seemly for
the Most Merciful to conceive a child.

The second way of segmenting the verses would look like this:

88   They say, "The Most Merciful has conceived a child."
89   Assuredly, you speak of something monstrous—
90   at which the heavens might be cleaved asunder,
      and the earth burst into pieces, and the mountains collapse in complete
      ruin—
91   that they deem the Most Merciful to have a child,
92   for it is not seemly for the Most Merciful to conceive a child.

In both cases, the rhythm of the lines moves too fast, especially as compared to the slow movement of the Arabic, and the force of the imagery that is stressed in the Arabic is simply lost in this rapid movement.

Here is our version, which expresses the more deliberate cadence of the Arabic and strives to preserve the salience of its imagery:

88   They say, "The All Merciful
      has conceived a child."

---

24   Klar, "A Preliminary Catalogue of Qur'anic *Saj'* Techniques," 190–91.

89 Assuredly, you speak
    of something monstrous—

90 at which the heavens might be
    cleaved asunder, and the earth
    burst into pieces, and the mountains
    collapse in complete ruin—

91 that they deem the All Merciful
    to have a child,

92 for it is not seemly
    for the All Merciful
    to conceive a child.

Instead of the end rhymes of the Arabic—difficult to replicate in English—we have here used assonance, which persists through all the verses, as in "conceived," "speak," "cleaved," "pieces," "complete," "deem," and "seemly." Moreover, the Arabic is marked by a structural contrast, an incongruity between the idea of the Divine and the idea of begetting a child. In our translation, we mark this contrast by allowing "the All Merciful" to stand alone at the end of three lines, with "child" relegated to the next line. Finally, the poetic effect of the prospective disintegration of the heavens, earth, and mountains is expressed by placing "cleaved," "burst," and "collapse" each at the beginning of a new line, where they receive emphasis by departing from the normal iambic rhythm of the English language. In terms of meter, each line contains either two or three stress beats.

Hence, we can't simply replicate in English the structure of the Arabic. This is likely to produce something unnatural and unreadable in English. However, if we adopt the procedures outlined above, we can perhaps more accurately express what we might call the deep structure of the Qur'anic text.

Tilawa (Style of Recitation)

We know that Shakespeare's plays come fully alive only in performance, that their meaning lies relatively dormant until it bursts into life on stage.

The same might be said of the Qur'an. The full potential of its "meaning" is never purely cognitive; it can be brought out only in performance or recitation, when the text (*mushaf*) is transformed into an experience. And usually, that experience is not individual but collective. Hence our rendering of the Qur'an into English must be susceptible of performance, achieving its full effect when read aloud.

There are many different styles of reciting the Qur'an. A given mode of recitation could influence an audience's relation to the text and what the audience might subsequently bring to it. A performance of the text could invest its cognitive meaning with a profound emotional charge.[25] It is not a question of *changing* the meaning but of allowing it to be registered on several levels: cognitive, sensible, psychological, and spiritual. A skillfully performed recitation will enable the text to affect a listener's entire being. It will help render cognitive meaning into an overall aesthetic experience— affecting thought, emotion, senses, and spiritual sensibility.

Here are a few ways in which a given recitation of the Arabic text might affect the process of translation. It could harbor a movement or cadence that is echoed in translation. The pauses effected in recitation might be reflected in line length or spacing. The emphasis on particular words via pitch or tone or timbre or modulation—e.g., rising to a climax—could be embodied in a rhythm that is adopted in translation. And the emotional charge created in recitation could be mirrored or compensated in translation. Above all, the recitation might create an atmosphere or mood that the translator might strive to capture in English. By way of example, we might consider Sura al-Nur (24:35):

God is the Light
of the heavens and of the earth;
His Light is a parable,
of a niche which holds a lamp,
the lamp enclosed in a glass,
the glass which glows like a gleaming star,
lit from an olive tree, blessed,

---

25   Kristina Nelson states that the "melody draws the listener more deeply into the experience, and there is no sense of a separation between the aesthetic and the religious involvement" (*The Art of Reciting the Qur'an* [Austin: University of Texas Press, 1985], 52).

whose soil is neither East nor West;
its very oil would shine forth
though untouched by fire:
Light upon Light.
God guides to His Light whom He will;
He strikes parables for humankind—
for God is Knower of all things.

If we listen to recitations of this verse, we can make a number of obser-
vations. The most striking feature is its slow and steady pace, contrived not
only by the slow cadence but also by significant pauses. At the most basic
level, we might say that the movement of these lines is measured and deliberate, reflecting the cadence of most recitations. Reciters tend to emphasize
through pitch and syllable length the Arabic words for "God," "light," "heavens," and "earth." In our translation, the corresponding words receive stress.
We opted to break the first sentence into two lines so that there is a pause
after "Light" (which is not in the Arabic where, however, the word for "light"
is repeatedly stressed tonally by the reciter). And the entire verse is about the
parable of God's Light, to which we wanted to draw attention. Reciters tend
to place a pause after *ard* (earth), which is optional in the rules of recitation
and which also marks the end of the first phrase of the *saj'* in this verse. So
there is good reason for allowing "earth" to mark the end of the line.

Reciters enact a pause between the two instances of "lamp" and "glass,"
respectively. In the English rendering, we have tried to express this parallel by placing the first instance of "lamp" on one line with an indefinite
article—a line that is made to pause at its end not only by using a comma
but also by mimicking the absence of the verb in Arabic—and the second
occurrence on the next line with the definite article. We've tried to re-create
the metrical balance of the original; the fourth and fifth lines are balanced
by the "holds" and "closed" qualifying "lamp." The same logic applies to our
two citations of "glass"; they are situated on different lines, separated by a
comma, with no verb between them.

Many reciters lengthen the word *nur* ("light") in the clause "Light upon
Light," which, in a way, marks the climax of this entire passage, as its central
clause. We communicate this emphasis in English by giving the expression
an entire line to itself. Reciters end by stretching out the Divine Name *'alim*

("Knower of all things"), and they modulate their pitch at words such as *misbah* ("lamp"), *yudi'* ("glow"), *nur* ("fire"), and *nas* ("humankind").

It's worth bearing in mind that the entire effect of all these pauses and variations in tone and pitch is more than the sum of its parts. Overall, what is created is an atmosphere, a mood, which we can strive to re-create in translation. Our rendering tries to capture something of the slow-moving grandeur of the Arabic as expressed in the pauses and emphases and tonal changes. We are not suggesting that as translators we should be bound by the recitational style of any particular reciter. Rather, we should be aware of the range of styles, of how the Qur'an sounds and is conveyed in performance.

The *Basmala*

The core of Qur'anic rhetoric consists of doublets, the combination of two divine attributes. The first verse of the first sura of the Qur'an includes a doublet: "In the Name of God, the All Merciful, Ever Merciful." This verse has been enshrined in the rhythm of everyday life for most Muslims, an invocation of God that is recited by Muslims before a trip, a meal, or even a simple pause in work. It is a challenge to render in English. The Arabic words are: *bismillah ar-rahman ar-rahim*. The first word elides *bismi* with *Allah*, and hence the whole phrase is known as the *basmala*. The *basmala* effectively defines the entire Qur'an and forms the beginning of all but one of its 114 suras.

In late 1986 Bruce Lawrence and a Jordanian academic, Dr. Ibrahim Abu Nab, spent an entire night talking about just these three words that launch the Qur'an. They agreed to disagree on the initial Name. Abu Nab opted for "Allah," Bruce for "God" if the intended audience was native English speakers. "God" over "Allah" is the same choice made by several translators of the Qur'an, including Yusuf Ali, Asad, and Khalidi (all Muslims), as well as Rodwell, Arberry, and Cleary (all non-Muslims). But it was the echo of the first syllable *rahm* in the second and third words that became the heart of their intense discussion. In approaching each word, verse, or sura of the Qur'an as a translator, argued Abu Nab, one must be wary but also hopeful of finding a counterpart in English that echoes the Arabic original.

But how stubborn was the condensed doublet *ar-rahman/ar-rahim*! How to express in English these two sublime qualifiers for God? Was it possible to use a noun, then an adjective, in English when the two dependent qualifiers of "God" in Arabic were both adjectives? Bruce preferred to render the Arabic phrase as: "In the name of God, Full of Compassion, ever Compassionate," while Ibrahim opted for: "In the name of Allah, the Compassion, the Compassionate." The use of two dependent qualifiers seemed closer to the Qur'anic tone than using a noun and an adjective from the same verbal root or using two adjectives with similar meaning but different verbal roots. The first derived noun qualifying God is the One full of compassion, namely, a reservoir of compassion; God is *full* of compassion." And the second derived noun acknowledges that the One full of compassion is also marked by a consistent, unending reflex of providing compassion to humankind. The One God who is "full of compassion" is at the same time "ever compassionate."

All these reflections circle back to Bruce's work with Rafey Habib. We have now lit on a third option for rendering *ar-rahman ar-rahim* into English: "the All Merciful, Ever Merciful." Sometimes we render it as: "the Most Merciful, Ever Merciful." Either way, it has the required repetition of a single word—"mercy"—but in two different registers: expansive as "the All Merciful" or "the Most Merciful" and continuous as "Ever Merciful." For this insight into the combination of sound and meaning, we are indebted to Ibrahim Abu Nab, who remained in correspondence with Bruce until his death in 1991; although his translation was never completed, its first offerings are available online.[26] His mantra became: "The Qur'anic word cannot be stripped of its light, colors, and music. Otherwise, it will be reduced to a linear meaning in another language. The word of God will lose its many dimensions; it will become linear flat like the word of humans. The word of God cannot be translated yet it must be translated."

The Divine Names

The ninety nine Beautiful Names of God that adorn the Qur'an present us with the same dilemma: they cannot be translated yet must be translated.

26 See https://web.archive.org/web/20211211083354/http:/koraan.info for Ibrahim Abu Nab's original, unprecedented rendition of the final forty-four suras as well as Sura 1, along with an essay outlining his approach to the aural as well as the literary meaning of the Qur'an.

We have elected to highlight the recurrence and importance of these Divine Names by strategic word placement and also by the use of capital letters in a variety of forms. To understand how this protocol works, let us look again at *Ayat al-Kursi* (the Verse of the Throne), arguably the most familiar Qur'anic text after al-Fatiha, the opening sura used in daily ritual prayer. This verse invokes four of the Beautiful Names of God, *al-asma' al-husna*:[27]

> God—there is no god but He,
> the Living, the Self-Subsisting.
> Never can slumber seize Him,
> nor sleep. To Him belongs
> all that is in the heavens, and
> all that is on the earth.
> Who can intercede with Him
> except by His leave? He knows
> what lies ahead, and
> what lies behind.
> None can approach His knowing,
> only as He wills.
> His throne extends
> over the heavens and the earth,
> which He guards and preserves
> with no fatigue,
> for He is Most High,
> Supreme.
>
> SURA AL-BAQARA, 2:255

Our rationale for this rendition is both theological and literary. God is entirely self-sufficient. He is the owner of life. He accepts intercession from

---

27   *Al-asma' al-husna* is the key phrase in Arabic, found in suras 7:180, 17:110, 20:8, and 59:24, that signals the recurrent importance of remembering God and of calling upon him in prayer by multiple names, His "Beautiful Names." Some have said that the Beautiful Names number 99; others reckon that they are beyond calculation; in either instance, they are lodestones of memory and pious mimesis in the Qur'an. For an apt summary of all Qur'anic references to the Beautiful Names, and reflection on their usage, see Shaykh Fadhlalla Haeri, *Calling Allah by His Most Beautiful Names* (Centurion, South Africa: Zahra, 2002).

whom He will. His knowledge is all-encompassing and He grants its light to whom He will; His sovereignty is absolute. However, while God is here described as transcendent in his qualities of uniqueness, universality, and eternity, this verse makes it clear that He is also immanent, that His presence extends throughout creation: ironically, His "throne," the very seat and symbol of His power, is not somehow distant but extends *through* the heavens and the earth. Though not visible, it is palpable. Through His signs God exists everywhere: the One Who is Most High, Supreme, remains the Living, the Self-Subsisting both in His creation above (the heavens) and His creation below (humans).

Translating not only the meanings of divine attributes but also their connotations entails some crucial choices. In the second line, the Arabic *al-hayy-al-qayyum* suggests the attributes of self-subsistence as well as sustaining and protecting all that exists. Because the Arabic expression is extremely concise and has an air of assertive finality, it needs to be reproduced in English by an equivalent brevity. And so we have rendered *al-qayyum* as the "Self-Subsisting," with the connotation that the sustaining capacity, as it marks God Himself, becomes endlessly renewed.

Especially important are the capital letters, a crucial and distinctive feature of our rendition. We use uppercase letters, sometimes together with the intensifying definite article, to underscore a central claim of the entire Qur'an—namely, that it is God alone who bears attributes such as Self-Sufficiency and Eternity. Capitals are used to express the uniqueness of divine qualities, whether they occur as nouns, adjectives, or verbs. It is also important to stress the combinations of Divine Names. While they can and do occur singly, they have a multiplying effect when combined that has to be registered in English as it is in Arabic. One might say that God reveals Himself through the Qur'an as both containing multiple dyads—some complementary such as "All Merciful, Ever Merciful," others contrasting as in "Giver of Death and Giver of Life"—and also excluding contraries within Himself. The Just cannot be "unjust," the One cannot be "many," and the Eternal cannot be "ephemeral." In translation it is as important to be mindful of what is excluded as well as what is included.

The last two lines of the Verse of the Throne turn on how to render the Divine Names. We have avoided saying *the* Most High, and *the* Supreme so as to create an air of absoluteness in these qualities: the word "supreme"

subsists as a line in itself, as if summarizing within itself all of the hitherto enumerated divine qualities. In the end, what we have tried to convey
is something of the sublime nature of the original utterance, which the
Prophet Muhammad called the most exalted verse of the Qur'an.

Another instance where we need to focus on both rhyme and verse in the
Divine Names occurs in Sura al-Hashr (59:22–24). Here we find a large clus-
ter of divine epithets, framed and preceded by a verse that invokes the thunderous process of the Qur'an's disclosure to humankind:

> Had We sent down this Qur'an
> upon a mountain, you would have
> seen it humbled, cleave itself
> into a chasm, in fear of God.
> Such are the parables
> We coin for human beings,
> that they might reflect.
>
> SURA AL-HASHR, 59:21

As a prelude to the disclosure of the Beautiful Names, the revealed Word
of the Qur'an must be declared a supernatural event of unimagined power.
The two actions—the sending down and the cleaving—are linked to the
metaphors or parables calling human beings to reflect. While the first three
lines detail the action, not until the fourth line does one find an accent on "a
chasm, in fear of God." And what is the purpose of that chasm and fear, not
affecting mountains but men and women, all humans (*an-nas*)? That declaration comes as a directive in the last line: "that they might reflect."

Only after the injunction to reflect has been enunciated and remembered
can we contemplate the nature of God as given in His Names. The two most
crucial are those that also frame the *basmala: ar-rahman ar-rahim,* the All
Merciful, Ever Merciful, discussed above.

> God is He, beyond Whom
> there is no god. He knows
> the unseen and the seen;
> He is the All Merciful, Ever Merciful.

What follows in v. 23 is perhaps the most intricate of the many passages in the Qur'an that refer to God's Names, always with a decisive accent on the nature of the Divine source. As in *Ayat al-Kursi*, analyzed above, one has to pay attention to the performed sound, not just the lexical meaning, of each of the words, and one must absorb the words as combined in a growing sequence of solemnity and awe. The sound "s" in English is the crucial link. It occurs in the first three and the final or eighth of the Names here announced, but it also occurs as a form of assonance, or echo of the other Names, in the fourth, "Trustworthy," and the seventh, "Irresistible":

> God is He, beyond Whom
> there is no god, the Sovereign,
> the Sanctified; the Source of Peace,
> the Trustworthy, the Guardian,
> the Almighty, the Irresistible,
> the Supreme; Glorified is He,
> beyond what they affiliate with Him.

Subsequently, in v. 24 we are faced with a different problem: how to reproduce in English the cumulative force of descriptors all of which seem to refer to "creation"?

> He is God, the Creator,
> the Originator, the Shaper of Forms;
> His are the Most Beautiful Names.
> All that is in the heavens and the earth
> glorifies Him, and He is
> Almighty, All Wise.

Does not the first Name, "the Creator," seem to cover the activity and function of the other two? No, since it is precisely the subtle expansiveness of these three words as a chain of related expressions that gives depth to God as Creator. Yes, He is the Creator, but He creates not only as one who originates, *the source*, but also as one who *gives shape* to what He creates, and so the cumulative effect is repetition without redundancy, a recurrent feature of the Qur'an but seldom so important as here. And then the capstone: the identity of all these descriptors as the Beautiful Names of God while also calling on all humankind to glorify, is summarized by two further Names, the Almighty (already introduced in the previous verse) and then All Wise (mentioned here for the first time in this sequence). These words echo, as does the entire sequence of v. 24, the initial verse of Sura al-Hashr. Both can be, and should be, read as simultaneous evocations of the same message, the second confirming and extending the first. The verse amplifies, even as it repeats and reinforces, what is announced in v. 1:

> All that is in the heavens
> and all that is on the earth
> glorifies God,
> for He is Almighty, All Wise.

Again, there is repetition but not redundancy. To stress the sameness as also difference, the last verse condenses the chorus of heaven and earth.

Beyond the nominal or adjectival capitalization for Divine Names, there is also the issue of verbal constructs. Sometimes they replace the Divine Names in translation; in other cases, they reflect the original Arabic text. We have elected to retain capitals for "God Knows," "God Sees," etc. to maintain the heightened sense of divine agency that informs the Arabic. We need to be selective, however; it is only when God is invoked as the Knower/Seer that we capitalize both the agent and the act. Similarly, God "Knowing" is distinguished from God "knowing" when only the former evokes a Beautiful Name. We have pursued this strategy as far as we can without compromising readability and fluency.

We also differ from most translators in according equal weight to *all* Divine Names. No one would dispute that "God" in every instance should be capitalized, but what of the many names of God found in the Qur'an, so many that in Muslim spiritual practice they are reduced to ninety-nine, and readily available in devotional guides or in *tasbih*, rosaries, numbering either thirty-three or ninety-nine to indicate the use of Divine Names? We have opted to capitalize *all* Divine Names, even if they are found only once in the Qur'an. As both agentive nouns ("the Forgiver," "the Guardian") and active participles ("the All-Hearing," "the All-Seeing"), Divine Names are used in many other translations, but few have ventured into the use of verbal constructs ("Swift in Punishment," "Best of Protectors"), which we found necessary to give more clarity and resonance to certain passages. When the qualifier *khayr* "the best" is linked with Divine Names, it seems coherent to make the superlative "best" a capitalized component of the Divine Name, as in Sura Yusuf: "God is the Best of Protectors" (12:64). Another superlative construct in the same sura is: "He is the Most Excellent of Judges" (12:80). In Sura al-Mu'minun, we find two further instances of this superlative form: "You are the Most Merciful of all" (23:109, 118).

Glossary

The Qur'an is polysemous, hence the same word can and should have different renditions in English. There are many instances where we have chosen to provide variants of the same name. In our translation, frequently repeated endnotes refer to the glossary, an appendix where each of the key words mentioned is explained in greater detail. It may be useful to summarize here a few of the most crucial terms.

Among the most elusive terms are *islam* and *muslim*. Both words recur in the Arabic, but not with the current meaning of a discrete religious community (Islam) or its numerous adherents (Muslims). These terms need to be understood in a comprehensive context. We see the Qur'an as an inclusive text, aware of its own position in history, its own theological precedents, and its own status as a confirmation of previous scriptures. The Qur'an projects itself as the culmination of a long process of divine self-disclosure. It affirms a continuity between "Islam" and the earlier religions of Judaism and Christianity, stating on several occasions (e.g., suras 2:136 and 3:84) that there is "no distinction" between any of the prophets in these traditions. The point here is that this continuity rests on a broad definition of "Islam" as "submission" to the will of God, and of "Muslim" as "one who submits." In this sense, Abraham is a "Muslim" (2:128). So, our translation of 2:136 reads:

Say, "We believe in God,
in what has been revealed to us,
and what was revealed to Abraham,
Ishmael, Isaac, Jacob, and the tribes,

and in the Books given to Moses,
Jesus, and the prophets,
from their Lord;
we make no distinction between
any among them,
and to God we submit our will."

But if we translate the last clause *nahnu lahu muslimun* as "We are Muslims" (or, more literally, "We are Muslims to Him"—which makes little sense in English), we are contradicting the spirit of the entire passage by suggesting that "Islam" is an exclusive religion.

A further illustration occurs when Abraham prays (in Sura al-Baqara, 2:128): "Our Lord, make us both, and our descendants, a community that submits to Your will." The Arabic refers to *muslimin* "those who submit" and also to *ummata muslimata*: "a community of those who submit," yet it would be incorrect to refer to either Muslims or Islam—i.e., "the Muslim community"—in this verse. As often explained in footnotes, the accurate way of echoing the original text is to provide its primary meaning "to submit or surrender" in agentive nouns "those who submit or surrender [to God's will]," or as collective entity "a community that submits [to God's will]." Another instance demonstrating the need to pay attention to context and avoid anachronism for *"muslimun"* occurs in Sura al ʿImran (3:52), where Jesus asks his disciples if they will help him in calling people to God. They respond: "We believe in God; so bear witness, that we submit to God's will" (Arabic: *bianna muslimun*). Jesus' disciples were *muslims* but in the broader sense of the term—using the lower, rather than the upper, case.

Another term often repeated in the Arabic is *hanif*, which is linked to Abraham in Sura al-Baqara (2:135) as "the upright," but then clarified in Sura al ʿImran (3:67) as both *hanif* and *muslim*—i.e, one who "believed only in the One God, submitting to God's will." In still other instances, *hanif* is used as a quality that all believers should embrace as upright, as in Sura Yunus: "Set your sight toward the religion of the upright" (10:105) or in Sura al-Rum: "So set your sights, upright, toward the true faith" (30:30).

Several variations in translation of the same term are due to context.

"Those who disbelieve," for instance, is the same as "disbelievers" but often the former seems preferable for sound and rhythm, as is the case for "those who incur loss" instead of "the losers." Beyond its rhetorical limits, the term "losers" also has an unfortunate, popular connotation in contemporary English, as those who lose a public contest or game of chance, not, as suggested by the Qur'an, those destined for eternal punishment. At other times the words themselves can and do have multiple usages in Arabic, and that distinction has to be noted in English. For instance, the word *din* does not mean just "religion," as in Sura al-Kafirun (109:6): "you have your religion and I have mine." It also can mean "debt," "devotion," "duty" or, as in Sura al-Fatiha (1:4), "reckoning": "Ruler of the day of reckoning."

In another instance of Qur'anic polysemy, the word *aya* (plural: *ayat*) would seem to be "verse(s)," but "verse" itself is linked to "sign," and often it is the primary rather than secondary meaning that is intended in the Qur'an. In one instance, in Sura al-Shu'ara (26:128), however, *aya(t)* is neither "verse" nor "sign" but "altar," used with reference to a disobedient people: "You build an altar [*aya*]." The sign here is neither a word nor a phrase but a tangible site of worship. In every instance, sensitivity to English usage, as well as knowledge of Arabic intent, must and does inform our choices.

Lastly, to stress the divine origin of the Qur'an, it seemed that the term "Book" (*kitab*) needed to be capitalized, whether occurring by itself or as the combined phrase "people of the Book" (*ahl al-kitab*). Even while the Qur'an must be performed and not simply read as another book, there is a sense in which it stands for the ultimate Book, *umm al-kitab*: literally, "the Mother of the Book," albeit cited in our rendition as "the basis of the Book" (3:7) and "the origin of the Book" (13:39).

Parenthetical Additions to the Qur'anic Text

During the course of our translation, we have had to recognize some of the difficulties of Qur'anic syntax for an English-speaking listener or reader. There are numerous instances where the Arabic text requires a connecting or explanatory phrase. Such additions are marked by square brackets. Sometimes, at the beginning of a sura there are a few parenthetical insertions needed to clarify the tone and content of what follows. One such instance is the sole sura without a *basmala*: Sura Tawba (Sura 9), which opens with a directive to believers, clarified by the initial insertion:

> [A proclamation] that God
> and His messenger have dissolved
> your treaty with the polytheists.

Similarly, in Sura Quraysh (Sura 106), the context requires an insertion:

> [In gratitude] for the safety
> of the Quraysh[28]—

Still more crucial is the much used Sura 112, widely known as Sura al-Ikhlas. Here, the word "sincerity" is inserted into the title, to indicate that the attributes of the Divine must be uttered with humility, mindfulness, and, above all, sincerity.

There are many more examples of parenthetical inserts that occur in the middle or at the end of verses within a given sura. In the longest sura, Sura al-Baqara (Sura 2), we find nine instances of parenthetical additions, each serving to amplify what is not stated but implied in the Arabic text. The first two occur at the end of a verse:

> 18 deaf, dumb, blind—
> they shall never return [to the path]

> 22 so don't set up rivals with God,
> when you know [the truth].

Another occurs near the beginning of a verse:

> 88 They say, "Our hearts are closed
> [against what you say.]" No—

---

28   This sura should be connected to the previous one, signaling that the Quraysh, the tribe of Muhammad, had survived the mid-sixth century Yemeni assault due to God's grace, not their own military prowess.

God curses them for their disbelief;
and little do they believe.

In each instance the object of the verb is not stated and the parenthetical words complete the thought. Similarly in three other verses from al-Baqara, we find a crucial word—either object or subject or dependent modifier—omitted:

91 but they deny what came after it,
    even though it is the truth
    confirming [the message]
    they already had.

102 From these two, [the disbelievers]
     learned only to sow discord
     between husband and wife,

113 The Jews say, "Christians
     have no basis [for their beliefs],"[29]
     while the Christians say, "Jews
     have no basis [for their beliefs]."

In the first two verses (2:91, 102), the added word completes a thought, while in the third, the assertion itself requires slight adjustment in English to capture the sense of the Arabic.

There are two further instances in al-Baqara where the added word in parenthesis is to explain the addressee of a pronoun, whether the Prophet Muhammad:

144 We see you [Prophet] turning
     your face for guidance toward
     the heavens.

or guardians of the inheritance of widows:

29   Literally, "have nothing to stand upon."

₂₄₀ Those of you who die
and leave widows behind
should bequeath your widows
a year's provision, and not
expel them. But if they leave,
there is no blame on you
[the guardians].

Furthermore, there is an instance of parenthetical addition to note transition within a verse from general declaration to direct quotation, as in:

₂₈₅ They all believe in God, His angels,
His Books, and His messengers.
[They say], "We make no distinction
between any of His messengers."

The protocol throughout is designed to enable the reader/listener to hear, and to feel, the full force of the text without hesitation or puzzlement arising from what remains unsaid yet is clearly implied. There are other moments where subtlety of expression warrants abstention from parenthetical inserts; those are so frequent as to defy even brief summary here.

Changes in Word Order

Sometimes we have found it necessary to change the word order or sequence in a long list of rhymed doublets in Arabic that require a different framing in English. The most evident protocol is to place a Beautiful Name of God in the initial rather than the final part of a sentence. There are numerous instances of such syntactical inversion. For example, the Arabic *Allah 'ala kulli shayin 'alimun* is literally translated as "God, of everything, is the One Knowing." But this is clearly not idiomatic in English, so it is rendered instead as: "He (God) Knows all things." (See, e.g., Sura al-Baqara, 2:29.)

Such changes in word order are designed to make better sense of the Arabic as a performative text in English. Consider, for instance, Sura al-Ahzab (33:35):

For men and women
who submit to the will of God—
believing men and women,
obedient men and women,
truthful men and women,
patient men and women,
men and women with humility,
men and women who give in charity,
who fast, who guard their chastity,
who remember God often—
for all of these God has prepared
forgiveness and a great reward.

Here, it is not a matter of changing the entire list of those favored but combining the names in such a way that the verse remains both accessible and eloquent.

Conclusion

It seems clear that the process of translation is informed by multiple factors, all of which are founded ultimately on the Qur'an's status as oral performance. The notion of *kitab* is itself defined performatively by the Qur'an and does not confirm to Western aesthetic expectations of unity, continuity, and coherence. We have argued that the Qur'an's oral nature favors a verse rendering since verse can more readily accommodate and even highlight features such as repetition, apostrophe, and sound effects, as well as the entire range of rhetorical tropes such as metaphor, simile, assonance, consonance, and alliteration. In our view, diverse kinds of versification should be used to convey the wide range of the Qur'an's rhetorical and performative situations. We have also explored the vast domain of issues raised by *saj'*. We have seen that these include not just rhyme, rhythm, and parallelism but also the possibilities of accentual meter, which might be particularly suited to a text that is to this day conveyed primarily through oral performance.

Of the numerous specific challenges faced by the translator, we have discussed our protocols in translating the *basmala* or invocation of God, and the Beautiful Names of God. In terms of consistency, we have argued that the meaning and connotation of words depends on both their local and broader contexts. Since it is our intention to make our English rendering of the Qur'an as readable and accessible as possible, we have opted to include parenthetical insertions where these clarify the meaning and where the sense of a passage could not be otherwise than as thereby indicated. To the same end—that of making the text readable—we have often had to invert the word order and syntax of the Arabic so that the translation can read idiomatically in English.

In general, we strive to place renewed attention on the somewhat neglected dimension of orality to bear in mind the how the Qur'an is enunciated according to certain rules and the various modes of its recitation. It is in recitation that we witness the Qur'anic text come to life. It is *experienced* on many levels—cognitive, emotional, psychological, spiritual, theological, and legal—as a performance by most of the world's Muslims. We hope that our endeavors will reflect at least to some extent the Qur'an's perennial status as public performance. Translation, after all, is not just interpretation—it is performance.

The strategies described above, whether singly or collectively, do not resolve the lingering tension between a pristine Arabic text and its lyrical English rendition. There can be no final, satisfactory solution to the challenge of translating any classical work, but especially challenging is the tenor and the tone as well as the meaning and understanding of Qur'anic revelation. Because seventh-century Arabic is distant in form as in time from twenty-first-century English, one needs to adopt creative strategies in order to capture an echo of that sublime sound which the renowned Arabist A. J. Arberry characterized as "those rhetorical and rhythmical patterns which are the glory and the sublimity of the Qur'an."[30] We have explored many possibilities in this introduction, but the measure of how well we have succeeded in finding an English version of the Noble Book that not only edifies but elevates will be for the reader to judge in the pages that follow.

---

30   A. J. Arberry, *The Koran Interpreted* (New York: Macmillan, 1955), 25–26.

THE
QUR'AN

The Opening (*Al-Fatiha*)

Some scholars suggest that the opening sura is also known as *umm al-kitab*, the Mother of the Book, and *sab 'an min al-mathani*, the often repeated seven (verses). One of the earliest revelations, it accents the divine attributes of mercy and might, guidance and judgment in succinct, lyrical form.

1 In the Name of God, the All Merciful, Ever Merciful°

2 All praise° be to God,
  Lord of the universe;°

3 The All Merciful,
  Ever Merciful;

4 Ruler of the day
  of reckoning.°

5 You alone we worship;°
  and You alone
  we implore for help.

6 Guide us to the straight path,

7 the path of those
  whom You have favored,
  not of those
  who have incurred Your° wrath,
  nor of those
  who have gone astray.

The Cow (*Al-Baqara*)

The longest sura, it numbers 286 verses and is named "The Cow," designated by God as a sacrificial offering (vv. 67–73). Revealed in Medina, it relates to several prophets, Adam, Moses, and Abraham, with Abraham's home in Mecca depicted as God's house. Detailed instructions cover food, fasting, almsgiving, and prayer but also address fighting, retaliation, writing wills, marriage, divorce, and usury. It has several breaks, allowing the reader to absorb its component parts, especially v. 255, the Verse of the Throne, perhaps the most famous and frequently invoked verse in the entire Qur'an.

In the Name of God, the All Merciful, Ever Merciful

SECTION I

1 *Alif. Lam. Mim.°*

2 This is the Book,
free of doubt—
a guide for those
mindful of the Divine;

3 those who
believe in the unseen
are steadfast in prayer
and give in charity
from what We have given them;

4 those who believe
in what was revealed to you,°
and revealed before you,
those assured
of the hereafter;

5 they are the ones
guided by their Lord
and they are the ones
who will flourish.

6 As for those
who don't believe,
it is the same
whether you warn them or not—
they won't believe.

7 God has set a seal
over their hearts
and their hearing,
and over their sight is a veil—
and they shall face
great torment.

8 Some of the people say,
"We believe in God and
in the last day"—but they do not°—

9 they would deceive God
and those who believe
but they deceive only themselves
though they don't perceive it;

10 their hearts are filled with disease
that God increases, and they
shall face painful torment
for their lying ways.

11 When told, "Don't sow corruption
through the earth," they reply,
"We are just reformers."

12 Wrong—they do spread corruption,
though they don't perceive it.

13 When told, "Believe,
like the others do," they retort,
"What, shall we believe,
like the fools?"
Wrong—they are the fools,
though they don't know it.

14 When they meet believers
they say, "We believe," but
when alone with their demons,°
they say, "Really, we're with you—
we were merely mocking them."

15 It is God Who mocks *them*,
and prolongs their transgression,
leaving them to wander blindly;

16 it is they who have exchanged
guidance for error,

but their trading is profitless,
for they are not guided.

17 They're like people who kindle a
fire—
as it lights up their surroundings,
God banishes their light, leaving
them
in darkness, unseeing—

18 deaf, dumb, blind—
they shall never return [to the path]

19 or, like people hunched beneath
a rainstorm bursting from the sky,
with darkness, thunder, lightning—
at the thunderclaps, they cover
their ears with their hands,
in dread of death—
God besieges the unbelievers
from all sides;

20 the lightning all but blinds their
sight;
whenever it flashes around them,
they walk on,
but when darkness falls upon them,
they stand, transfixed.
Had God willed,
He could have seized
their hearing
and their sight.
He has Power over all things.

SECTION 2

21 Humankind, worship your Lord
   Who created you and those before
      you,
   that you might be mindful of God,

22 Who made the earth
   a couch for you,°
   and the sky a canopy,
   Who sent down rain from the sky,
   and brought out from the earth
   fruits to sustain you—
   so don't set up rivals with God,
   when you know [the truth].

23 And if you doubt
   what We have revealed
   to Our servant, then produce
   a sura like this; and call
   whatever witnesses you have
   besides God,
   if you are being truthful;

24 but if you are unable—and
   you will never be able—to do this,
   then fear the fire, to be fueled
   by humans and stones, prepared
   for the unbelievers.

25 And give joyous news
   to those who believe
   and do good deeds,
   that they shall have gardens
   with flowing rivers beneath;
   whenever they are fed with its fruits,
   they will say, "This

is what we were fed before,"
for they were given the same;
and there they shall have
pure spouses,
and live there forever.

26 God does not recoil
   from coining similes
   using a lowly mosquito
   or higher creatures.
   Those who believe
   know it is the truth from their Lord.
   Those who disbelieve say,
   "What does God mean
   by this simile?"
   We lead many astray by it
   and many We guide by it
   but We lead astray by it
   only the stoutly disobedient.

27 Those who break God's covenant
   after it was ratified,
   and sever the bonds ordained by God
   and spread corruption on the
      earth—
   they will be the ones in loss.

28 How can you deny God,
   when you were dead
   and He gave you life?
   Then He will bring you death,
   and life again, and to Him
   you shall be brought back.

29 It is He who created for you
   all that is on the earth;
   then, turning to the heavens

He fashioned them
as seven heavens°
for He Knows all things.

SECTION 3

30 When your Lord said to the angels,
"I will place a regent on the earth,"°
they said, "Will you place there
one who will sow corruption
and shed blood
while we glorify You with praise
and sanctify you?" He responded,
"I know what you
do not know."

31 And He taught Adam
the names of all things,°
and He brought these things
before the angels, saying,
"Inform Me of their names
if you are right."°

32 They replied, "Glory be to You;
we have no knowledge beyond
what You taught us. You
are the Knowing, the Wise."

33 He said to Adam,
"Inform the angels
of the names of things."
When Adam had done so,
God said, "Did I not tell you
that I know what is unseen
in the heavens and the earth,
that I know what you reveal
and what you conceal?"

34 And when We said to the angels,
"Bow down before Adam,"
they bowed down—all
but Iblis;° he refused, proud—
he became a disbeliever.

35 We said, "Adam,
you and your wife may live
in the garden, and eat from it
wherever you will;
but do not approach this tree
or you will both do wrong."

36 Then Satan caused them
to fall from the garden,
and dislodged them
from their state in it. And We said,
"Go down, all of you,
as enemies of one another;
on earth you shall have a place to
live
and livelihood for a while."°

37 Yet Adam was taught words
[to beg repentance from his Lord],
Who turned to him, relenting—
He is the Ever Relenting,
Ever Merciful.

38 We said, "Go down from here,
all of you. But when My guidance
comes, as it will, those who
follow it shall have no fear,
nor shall they grieve.

39 "But those who disbelieve
and deny Our signs

shall be inmates of the fire,
abiding there forever."

SECTION 4

40 Children of Israel, remember
the blessing I bestowed upon you,
and fulfill your covenant to Me
as I fulfill My covenant to you
and fear Me, alone,

41 and believe in what
I have revealed,
confirming the scripture
already with you;°
don't be the first to deny it,
nor sell My signs for a paltry price
and be mindful of Me, alone;

42 and don't confound truth
with falsehood, nor conceal
the truth, when you know it.

43 Be steadfast in prayer,
practice charity,
and bow down
with those who bow in worship.

44 Do you command people
to righteousness—and
forget it yourselves—
while reciting the Book?
Will you not use reason?

45 Seek God's help, through
patience and prayer—though
this is hard, except for
those who are humble,

46 those assured that they
will meet their Lord, and that
to Him they shall return.

SECTION 5

47 Children of Israel, remember
the blessing I bestowed upon you,
and that I favored you
over all peoples°—

48 so be fearful of a day
when no soul can help another
nor shall any intercession
from it be accepted
nor any compensation—
none shall be helped.

49 And remember when We saved you
from the forces of Pharaoh, who
scourged you with terrible torments,
slaughtering your sons,
sparing only your women.
This was a tremendous trial
from your Lord,

50 and We parted the sea for you,
saving you, and drowning
the forces of Pharaoh
as you looked on.

51 We arranged for Moses to stay
for forty nights [on Mount Sinai];
then, [while he was gone], you took
the calf as an idol°—you did wrong.

52 Even after this, We pardoned you
that you might be thankful,

53 and We gave Moses the Book
and the criterion of right and wrong°
that you might be guided;

54 and Moses said to his people,
"My people,
You have wronged yourselves,
worshipping the calf. So turn,
in repentance, to your Maker,
and kill [the evil in] yourselves.°
That will be better for you
in the sight of your Maker."
Then God relented to you—
He is Relenting, Ever Merciful.

55 And you said, "Moses,
we'll never believe in you
until we see God, appearing."
Then the thunderbolt
struck you, as you looked on.

56 Then We raised you up, after death,
that you might be thankful,

57 and [We brought down]
clouds to shade you,
and We sent down
to you manna and quail, saying,
"Eat of the good things
We have given you,"
for they did not wrong Us
but wronged themselves.

58 And We said, "Enter this town
and eat freely there, wherever
you will, but enter the gate
bowing low, voicing repentance.

We will forgive your mistakes
and increase the reward
of those who do good."

59 But the wrongdoers distorted
the word they had been given,
so We sent down upon them
a plague from the sky
for they were disobedient.

SECTION 6

60 And remember when
Moses prayed for water
for his people. We said,
"Strike the rock with your staff."
Twelve springs gushed out from it,
and each tribe° knew
its drinking place.
"Eat and drink from what God
gives,
and refrain from wicked action,
sowing
corruption in the land."

61 And you° said, "Moses,
we can't abide just one kind
of food, so entreat your Lord,
for us, to bring out what
the earth grows—its herbs,
cucumbers, garlic, lentils,
and onions." He replied,
"Would you exchange
what is better for what is worse?
Go down to any town,
and you shall get what you ask for."

They were struck
with humiliation and misery,
drawing upon themselves
the wrath of God.
They always denied God's signs
and killed the prophets unjustly:
they were always disobedient,
always transgressing.

SECTION 7

62 Those who believe, including
the Jews, Christians, and Sabians°–
all who believe in God
and the last day
and do good works—
they shall have
a reward from their Lord,
and they shall have no fear,
nor shall they grieve.

63 And We took a pledge from you,
and raised the Mount [of Sinai],
towering above you,
[saying], "Hold fast to what
We gave you, and remember
what it contains, that you might
remain mindful of God."

64 But you turned back,
even after that, and
were it not for God's grace
upon you, and His mercy,
you would be in loss.

65 You knew those among you
who broke the Sabbath;

We said to them,
"Become apes, despised."°

66 We made this a deterrent
to those present, as well as those
who came after them—a warning
for those mindful of God.

67 And when Moses told his people,
"God commands you
to sacrifice a cow,"
they retorted,
"Are you making fun of us?"
He responded, "God forbid
that I should be so ignorant."°

68 They said, "Pray to your Lord
to make clear to us what cow it is."
He replied, "He says it should be
neither old nor young
but of middle years;
so do as you're commanded."

69 They said, "Pray to your Lord
to tell us what color it should be."
He replied, "He says it should be
bright yellow, pleasing
to those who see it."

70 They said, "Pray to your Lord°
to tell us exactly which cow—
to us all cows are alike.
We will be guided, if God wills."

71 Moses answered, "He says
it should be a cow not trained
to till the soil, nor

to water the fields;
perfect, without blemish."
They exclaimed, "Now you've
   provided
the facts!"°
Then, still vacillating,
they offered her in sacrifice.

SECTION 8

72 And when you Israelites
killed someone and argued
about who was to blame,
God revealed what
you had concealed.

73 So We said, "Strike
the dead body with a piece
of the cow." This is how
God brings the dead to life
and shows you His signs,
that you might use reason.

74 Yet, even after that, your hearts
were hardened—like rocks,
or harder—for there are rocks
from which rivers gush forth,
and some which split to yield
streams running out,
and others that fall down
in fear of God;
for God is not heedless
of what you do.

75 So, can you believers really hope
that they will believe you,
when a group of them
used to hear the words of God

and distort them willfully,
though they understood them?

76 When they meet the believers,
they say, "We believe." But when
they are with one another in private,
they say, "Why would you tell them
what God has revealed to you—
just so that they could argue it
against you before your Lord?
Do you not understand?"

77 Do they not know that God
knows well what they conceal
and what they reveal?

78 Among them are unlettered people
who don't know the Book;
they take from it notions
to please themselves,
and merely conjecture.

79 And woe to those who write
the Book with their own hands,
claiming, "This is from God"—
selling it for a paltry price.
Woe to them for what
their hands have written,
and what they earn by this.

80 And they say, "The fire will
touch us only for some days."
Say, "Has God promised you this?
—for God never breaks his
   promise—
Or, are you imputing to God
what you do not know?"

81 No, those who reap evil,
    engulfed by their sins,
    shall be inmates of the fire,
    where they shall stay forever.

82 But those who believe
    and do good works
    shall live in the garden,
    where they shall stay forever.

SECTION 9

83 We made a covenant
    with the children of Israel,
    "Worship none but the One God,
    and treat kindly your parents
    and family, as well as orphans
    and the poor. Speak kindly to
        people,
    be steadfast in prayer,
    and give what is due in charity."
    But then, all but a few of you
    turned back—
    and still you turn away.

84 We made a covenant
    with you: do not shed
    one another's blood, nor
    drive one another from your homes;
    you pledged this,
    as you yourselves bore witness.

85 Yet now, you are the ones
    killing one another, driving
    some from their homes,
    helping one another in sin
    and wronging them;

and if they come to you as captives,
you ransom them, though you were
forbidden to expel them.

Do you, then, believe in part
of the Book but deny another part?
What is the reward for those of you
who act like this except
disgrace in this life, and to be
sent back [to your Creator]
for the harshest torment
on the day of resurrection?
God is not heedless of what you do.

86 These are the people who
    trade the hereafter
    for the life of this world;
    their torment shall not be lightened,
    nor shall they be helped.

SECTION 10

87 We gave Moses the Book,
    and We sent after him a series
    of messengers. We gave clear signs
    to Jesus, son of Mary, whom We
    strengthened with the holy spirit.°
    Whenever a messenger
    came to you, bringing what you
    did not desire, did you not grow
        proud,
    denying some and killing others?

88 They say, "Our hearts are closed
    [against what you say.]" No—
    God curses them for their disbelief;
    and little do they believe.

89 When there came to them
    a Book from God, confirming what
    they had before—and though they
    had been praying for victory
    against those who disbelieved—
    even when they knew the truth
    had come to them, they denied it;
    and God curses the disbelievers.

90 They have sold their souls
    for a wicked price, by denying
    what God has revealed, grudging
    that God bestows His grace upon
    whom He chooses of His servants.
    So they have brought upon
    themselves wrath upon wrath;
    and the disbelievers will face
    disgraceful torment.

91 When they are told, "Believe
    in what God has revealed,"
    they say, "We believe
    in what was revealed to us,"
    but they deny what came after it,
    even though it is the truth
    confirming [the message]
    they already had.
    Say, "If you are believers, why
    did you kill God's prophets before?

92 "Moses came to you
    with clear signs; then,
    while he was gone, you took
    the calf as an idol—you did wrong."

93 And We took a pledge from you,
    and raised Mount [Sinai],

towering above you,
[saying], "Hold fast to what
We have given you, and hear Us,"
they said, "We hear and disobey."
And, through their disbelief,
their hearts were made to drink
devotion to the calf.
Say, "If you are believers,
what your faith commands
you to do is wicked."

94 Say, "If the final home with God
    is for you alone, of all peoples,
    you should hope for death—if
    you are being truthful."

95 But they will never hope
    for death—on account of
    the deeds they have accrued;°
    and God Knows all
    that the wrongdoers do.

96 You will find that they
    are the people most attached to life—
    even more than the polytheists.
    Every one of them would love
    to be granted life for a thousand
        years.
    But that life-span would not drag
        them
    away from the punishment,
    for God Sees all that they do.

SECTION 11

97 Say, "As for those who declare
    themselves enemies of Gabriel—

know that it is he
who brought down [this message]
to your heart, by God's leave,
confirming the previous scriptures
you already have, with guidance
and joyous news for the believers—

98 "As for the disbelievers who are
enemies of God, His angels,
and His messengers
—as well as Gabriel and Michael°—
God is *their* enemy."

99 We have revealed to you
clear signs, and only
the disobedient deny them.

100 Whenever they make a covenant,
why does a group of them throw it
aside? Most of them don't believe.

101 And when a messenger came
to them from God, confirming
the scripture they already had,
a group of those among
the people of the Book
ignored the Book of God,°
as if they had not known of it.

102 They followed what
the demons recited about the reign
of Solomon;° it was not Solomon
who disbelieved, but the demons—
they taught people magic and what
was revealed to the two angels
in Babylon, Harut and Marut.°

Yet before they taught anyone,
these two always warned,
"We are only testing you.
So don't disbelieve."
From these two, [the disbelievers]
learned only to sow discord
between husband and wife,
though they could not harm anyone
by it except with God's leave.
And they learned only things
that could harm them, not profit
    them—
knowing that whoever bought
this magic would have no share
in the hereafter.
They sold their souls at
a wicked price—if only they knew.

103 Had they believed and been
mindful of God, they would have had
a better reward from their Lord—
if only they knew.

SECTION 12

104 You who believe, don't say,
"See us," but "Look at us"—and
listen to him.° For the unbelievers
shall face painful torment.

105 The disbelievers among
the people of the Book and
the polytheists don't ever wish
anything good to be sent down
to you from your Lord. But God
chooses for His mercy whom He will;
for God's grace is great.

106 Whenever We abrogate a verse,°
     or let it be forgotten, We bring
     one better than it or similar.
     Do you not know that God
     has Power over all things?

107 Do you not know
     that God holds dominion
     over the heavens and the earth,
     and that beyond Him you will find
     no protector or helper?

108 Would you question
     your messenger, as Moses
     was questioned earlier?
     Whoever exchanges belief
     for disbelief undoubtedly
     strays from the even path.

109 Among the people of the Book
     many wish they could turn you
     back from belief to disbelief—
     out of envy in themselves—even after
     receiving the clear truth.
     But forgive them and forbear
     until God's command comes,
     for God has Power over all things.

110 Be steadfast in prayer,
     and practice due charity,
     for whatever good you do
     for yourselves, you will find it
     laid up with God°—
     God Sees all that you do.

111 And they say, "No one
     shall ever enter paradise unless
     they are Jews or Christians." This
     is nothing but their fancy. Say,
     "Bring your proof, if
     what you say is true."

112 Rather, it is those who
     submit their entire self° to God,
     and do good, who shall have
     their reward with their Lord;
     they shall have no fear,
     nor shall they grieve.

SECTION 13

113 The Jews say, "Christians
     have no basis [for their beliefs],"°
     while the Christians say, "Jews
     have no basis [for their beliefs]."
     Yet they both read the Book,
     and those with no knowledge
     say the same thing.
     But God will judge between them
     on the day of resurrection,
     about the issues they dispute.

114 And who is more unjust
     than someone who prevents
     the remembrance of God's name
     in houses of worship,
     and strives to desolate them?
     Such people should enter
     these houses only with awe;
     they will face disgrace
     in this world, and great torment
     and in the hereafter.

115 To God belong the East
and the West. Wherever you turn—
there is His Face—God,
the All Embracing, All Knowing.

116 They say,
"God has begotten a child."
Wrong—Glory be to Him—
to Him belongs all
that is in the heavens and the earth.
All things devoutly obey Him.

117 He is the Originator
of the heavens and the earth.
When He decrees something,
He says to it, "Be!"—and it is.

118 And those with no knowledge say,
"Why does God not speak to us?"
or "Why does no sign come to us?"
Those before them said the same—
their hearts are alike.
We have indeed made the signs
clear to people of firm faith.

119 Yes, We have sent you,
[Prophet,] with the truth,
to give joyous news and
to give warning. But it's not you
who must answer for
the inmates of the blazing fire.

120 The Jews and Christians will
never be content until you adopt
their creed. Say, "The only guidance
is God's guidance."
If you were to comply with their
desires
after the knowledge that has come
to you,
you would have neither protector
nor helper against God.

121 Those to whom We gave the Book,
those who recite it rightly—
they are the ones who believe in it;
but those who deny it—
they will be the ones who lose.

SECTION 14

122 Children of Israel, remember
the favor I showed you,
choosing you over all peoples—

123 so be fearful of a Day
when no soul can help another,
nor shall any compensation
from it be accepted,
nor shall any intercession
be of benefit to it—
none shall be helped.

124 When Abraham was tried
by his Lord with certain
commands,
which he fulfilled, God said,
"I will make you a leader of nations."
Abraham asked,
"And my descendants also?"
God responded,
"My promise does not extend
to those who do wrong."

125 And We made the House [in Mecca]
a place of assembly for people,
and of sanctuary, saying,
"Take the station of Abraham°
as your place of prayer," and
We made a covenant
with Abraham and Ishmael
that they should purify My House
for those who walk around it,
or stand there in devotion,
or bow and prostrate
themselves in prayer.

126 And when Abraham said,
"My Lord, make this town
a sanctuary, and sustain its people
with fruits—those of them
who believe in God
and the last day," God responded,
"As for those who disbelieve,
I will grant them enjoyment
for a short while, and then
drive them to the torment
of the fire—an evil end."

127 So Abraham and Ishmael
erected the foundations
of the House, saying, "Our Lord,
accept this from us, for You
are the All Hearing, All Knowing."

128 "Our Lord, make us both,
and our descendants,
a community that submits
to Your will.° Show us
the due rites of pilgrimage,
and relent to us.

You are the Ever Relenting,
Ever Merciful."

129 "Our Lord, raise among them
a messenger of their own, reciting
to them Your verses, teaching
them the Book and wisdom,
purifying them. You—
You alone are Almighty, All Wise."°

SECTION 15

130 And who would turn away
from the creed of Abraham
but those who fool themselves?
We chose him in this world,
and in the hereafter he will be
among the righteous.

131 When his Lord said to him,
"Submit to My will," he complied:
"I submit to the Lord
of the universe."

132 And Abraham urged his sons,
as did Jacob, "My sons,
God has chosen this religion for
    you,°
so be sure that you die
submitting [to His will]."

133 Did you witness Jacob's death?°
In fact, when he asked his sons,
"What will you worship after me?"
They said, "We will worship
your God, and the God
of your fathers, of Abraham,

Ishmael, and Isaac—the One God—
and to Him we submit our will."

134 That community° is gone;
what they earned was for them,
and what you earn is for you;
you shall not be questioned
about their deeds.

135 They say, "Become Jews
or Christians—to be rightly guided."
Say, "No—ours is the creed
of Abraham, the upright, who
never ascribed partners to God."

136 Say, "We believe in God,
in what has been revealed to us,
and what was revealed to Abraham,
Ishmael, Isaac, Jacob, and the tribes,
and in the Books given to Moses,
Jesus, and the prophets,
from their Lord;
we make no distinction between
any among them,
and to God we submit our will."

137 If they believe as you believe,
they will be rightly guided; but if
they turn back, they will quarrel.
God is enough to guard you
against them, for He is
All Hearing, All Knowing.

138 [Our religion takes its] color
from God—and who better
to imbue color than God?°
So we worship Him alone.

139 Say [to the Jews and Christians],
"Do you dispute with us about God
when He is our Lord and your Lord?
Your deeds are yours,
and our deeds are ours,
and we are true to Him alone.

140 "Or do you say that Abraham,
Ishmael, Isaac, Jacob, and
the tribes were Jews or Christians?"
Say, "Do you know better
than God? Who is more unjust
than someone who hides
the testimony he has from God?
For God is not unmindful
of what you do."

141 That community is gone—
what they earned was for them,
and what you earn is for you;
you shall not be asked
about their deeds.

SECTION 16

142 The fools among the people
will say, "What has turned them
from the direction of prayer
they used to face?"°
Say, "To God belong the East
and the West; He guides
whom He will to a straight path."

143 And so We made you
a community of moderation°—
to witness the truth
against humankind,

and the messenger a witness
against you.

And We set the direction
you used to face in prayer
that We might set apart°
those who followed the messenger
from those who turned on their heels;
that test was hard except for those
whom God guided;
God would never let your faith
go to waste—
God is Most Kind, Ever Merciful,
toward humankind.

144 We see you [Prophet] turning
      your face for guidance toward
      the heavens. We will turn you toward
      a direction that will please you—
      turn your face
      toward the sacred mosque [in
        Mecca];
      wherever you are,
      turn your faces toward it.
      And those granted the Book
      know it is the truth from their Lord.
      Nor is God heedless of what they do.

145 Even if you brought all the signs
      to those granted the Book,
      they would not follow
      your direction,
      nor shall you follow
      their direction,
      nor will they follow
      one another's direction.
      Were you to follow their desires,

after the knowledge
that has come to you,
you would be among
those who do wrong.

146 Those to whom
      We granted the Book
      know the Prophet
      as well as they know
      their own sons; but a group
      of them conceal the truth
      even though they know it.

147 The truth is from your Lord,
      so don't be one of those who doubt.

SECTION 17

148 Each community° has
      a direction toward which it turns;
      so compete in good works.
      Wherever you are, God shall
      finally bring you all together—
      God has Power over all things.

149 Wherever you start from,
      turn your face toward
      the sacred mosque—
      this is the truth from your Lord,
      nor is God heedless
      of what you do.

150 Wherever you start from,
      turn your face toward
      the sacred mosque; wherever you
        are,
      turn your faces toward it, so that

people have no dispute with you,
except the wrongdoers among them;
and do not fear them, but fear Me,
that I might perfect My favor to you,
and that you might be rightly guided,

151 just as We have sent you
a messenger, from among you,
reciting Our signs, purifying you,
teaching you
the Book and wisdom,
and teaching you
what you did not know.

152 So, remember Me—
and I will remember you.
Show thanks to Me, and
do not be ungrateful.

SECTION 18

153 You who believe, seek help
through patience and prayer;
God is with those who show
    patience.

154 And do not say of those
killed in the cause of God
that they are dead. No—
they are living, though
you don't perceive it.

155 We will try you
with fear and hunger, with loss
of wealth and life and crops;
but give joyous news to
those who show patience,

156 who say, when struck
by calamity, "To God we belong,
and to God we shall return."°

157 They are the ones on whom
their Lord sends blessings and mercy;°
they are the rightly guided ones.

158 The hills of Safa and Marwa
are among the symbols of God,°
so for those performing
the major or minor pilgrimage,°
there is no fault in walking
between them; and if anyone
does good of his own accord,
God is Appreciative, All Knowing.

159 As for those who conceal
the clear signs and guidance
We have revealed
—after We made them clear
in the Book for humankind—
they are the ones whom
God curses and others curse,

160 except those who repent,
reform themselves, and openly
declare [the truth]. To those I relent,
for I am Relenting, Ever Merciful.

161 The curse of God, the angels,
and all humankind shall fall
upon those who disbelieve,
and die as disbelievers.

162 They shall endure this state
forever, without any lightening
of their torment or respite.

163 Your God is One God—
     there is no god but He,
     the Most Merciful, Ever Merciful.

SECTION 19

164 In the creation
     of the heavens and earth,
     in the revolving
     of night and day,
     in the ships that sail upon the sea
     for the gain of humankind,
     in the rain that
     God sends from the sky,
     bringing life to the earth
     after its death,
     in the spreading of every
     kind of beast through it,
     in the directing of the winds
     and clouds, floating
     between heaven and earth—
     in all these are signs for
     people who use reason.

165 Yet some people take others
     as equal to God, loving them
     as they should love God.
     But those who believe
     are stronger in their love for God.
     If only the wrongdoers could see—
     as when they will see
     their punishment—that all power
     belongs to God, and that God
     is Severe in Punishment.

166 When those who were followed
     disown their followers, and they

see the punishment, and all bonds
among them are severed,

167 the followers will say,
     "If only we could go back,
     we would disown them
     as they now disown us."
     So God will make them
     see their deeds with deep regret,
     they will never escape the fire.

SECTION 20

168 "People, eat from what is lawful
     and good upon the earth, and
     don't follow in the footsteps
     of Satan; for he
     is your open enemy.

169 "For he commands you
     to evil and indecency,
     and to say of God
     what you do not know."

170 When told, "Follow what
     God has revealed," they say,
     "No. We follow the ways
     of our fathers." What?
     Even though their fathers
     understood nothing
     nor were rightly guided?

171 Those who disbelieve
     can be compared to one who
     shouts like a shepherd to flocks
     who hear nothing
     but a cry and a call—

deaf, dumb, blind,
they are bereft of reason.

172 You who believe,
eat of the good things
We have given you,
and be thankful to God,
if it is Him you worship.

173 He has forbidden for you
only carrion, blood, the flesh
of swine, and anything on which
some name other than God's
was invoked. But whoever
is constrained—without wanting
to disobey or transgress—
shall remain blameless.
God is Forgiving, Ever Merciful.

174 Those who conceal what
God has revealed in the Book
and trade it for a paltry price—
they shall swallow into their bellies
nothing but fire—
God shall not speak to them
on the day of resurrection, nor
purify them; theirs shall be
a painful punishment.

175 They are the ones who trade
guidance for error, forgiveness
for punishment; how shall they
endure the fire?

176 That is because God revealed
the Book, with truth,
and those who dispute the Book
have gone far astray, in discord.

SECTION 21

177 Righteousness
does not reside
in turning your faces
toward East or West;
rather, it resides in those—

who believe in God
and the last day,
in the angels, the Book,
and the prophets;

who give their wealth
—despite their love of it—
for kin, for orphans, the needy,
the traveler, for those who ask,
and for freeing slaves;

who are steadfast in prayer,
who give in charity,
keeping their covenants;

who suffer in patience
hardship, pain, and
times of conflict—

they are the ones
who are truthful, and
they are the ones
mindful of God.

178 You who believe, you are
commanded to be fair in requital
for murder—free man for free man,
slave for slave, woman for woman.
But if the culprit is pardoned

by his injured brother, he should
seek suitable recompense,
given graciously. This is a mitigation
and a mercy from your Lord.
Whoever transgresses after this
shall face painful torment.

179 The rule of retaliation
preserves life for you—
you people with insight,
so that you might be righteous.

180 When death approaches any of you
who leaves wealth behind—
you are commanded
to make a suitable bequest
to parents and close relatives;
this is a duty imposed on those
who are mindful of God.

181 Anyone who alters the bequest
after hearing it commits a sin—
God is All Hearing, All Knowing.

182 But if anyone suspects that
the testator is mistaken or biased,
it is no sin for him
if he reconciles the two parties.
God is Forgiving, Ever Merciful.

SECTION 22

183 You who believe,
fasting is ordained for you,
as it was ordained for those
before you, so that you might
be mindful of God—

184 fasting for a fixed number
of days. But if any of you is ill,
or traveling, then for a fixed number
of other days.
Those who find it difficult
may compensate by feeding
a needy person. But if anyone
does good of his own accord,
it will be better for him.
And fasting is better for you,
if only you knew.

185 It was in the month of Ramadan
that the Qur'an was sent down,
as a guide for humankind,
with clear signs of guidance and
criteria of right and wrong.
So whoever among you
is present during the month
should fast in it.
And whoever is ill, or on a journey,
should make up a fixed number
of other days. God intends ease,
not hardship, for you—and that
you complete the ordained period,
so that you might magnify Him
for His guidance, and be thankful.°

186 Prophet, when My servants
ask you about Me, I am indeed Near;
I answer the prayer of those
who pray to me. So let them
respond to Me, and believe in Me,
that they might be rightly guided.

187 You are allowed, on the night
of fasting, to approach your wives;

they are your garment and
you are their garment.
God knows that you used to betray
yourselves,° but He turned to you
and pardoned you; so now,
be intimate with them and seek what
God has ordained for you.

Eat and drink until you can
distinguish the white thread of dawn
from the black thread. Then
complete your fast until nightfall,
and don't be intimate with your
    wives
while you are secluded in devotion
in the mosques.

These are the limits set by God,
so do not venture near them.
This is how God makes clear
His signs to humankind,
so that they might be mindful of
    Him.

188 Do not wrongfully consume
one another's property,
and do not use it to bribe judges
in order to consume a portion
of other people's property,
sinfully—and knowingly.

SECTION 23

189 They ask you, Prophet,
about the new moons. Say,
"They signify fixed periods
for people, and for the pilgrimage.

Also, it is not righteous for you
to enter houses by the back door;°
righteousness resides in being
mindful of God.
Enter houses by their main doors.
And be mindful of God
that you might flourish."

190 Fight in the cause of God
against those who fight you,
but do not transgress due limits;
for God dislikes transgressors.

191 And kill them where you
find them, and drive them out
from where they drove you out—
for persecution is worse
than killing.° But do not
fight them at the sacred mosque
unless they fight you there.
But if they do fight you, kill them.
This is the disbelievers' reward.

192 But if they should stop—God
is Forgiving, Ever Merciful.

193 Fight them until there is
no more persecution,
until worship at the sacred mosque
is for God alone. But if they stop,
let there be no more hostility
except against aggressors.

194 Sacred month for sacred month;°
and for all violations, a fair requital.
If anyone assaults you, you may
respond in kind, equally, against them;

but fear God, and know that God
is with those who fear Him.

195 Spend in the cause of God, to
avoid bringing ruin upon yourselves,°
and practice good deeds, for
God loves those who do good.

196 Complete the major or minor
pilgrimage
for the sake of God; if you are
prevented from this, then sacrifice
whatever animal you can,
and do not shave your heads
until the animal reaches
the sacrificial site.

If any of you is ill or has
a malady of the head,
they can compensate by fasting,
or charity or ritual sacrifice.

When you feel secure, those who
have the chance to perform
the minor along with the major
pilgrimage
should offer whatever sacrifice
they can afford; those without
the means should fast for three days
during the major pilgrimage, and
seven days
upon your return, ten days in all.

This is for people whose house
is not near the sacred mosque.
Be mindful of God, and know
that God is Severe in Requital.

SECTION 24

197 The major pilgrimage occurs during
the ordained months; those who
perform the duty of pilgrimage then
should refrain from lewdness,
or wickedness, or quarreling.
And whatever good you do,
God knows it.
Take provision for your journey—
but the best provision
is mindfulness of God.
Be mindful of Me,
you who understand.

198 There's nothing wrong with your
seeking the bounty of your Lord
[while the pilgrimage goes on].°
Then when you leave, going down
from Mount ʿArafat, remember God
at the sacred site of Muzdalifa.°
Remember Him, for He guided you
before, when you were astray.

199 Then leave, going down,
where all the other people go down,
and ask forgiveness of God; for
God is Forgiving, Ever Merciful.

200 When you have finished
your rites of worship, remember
God as you remember
your fathers, or with more fervent
remembrance. For some people
pray, "Our Lord, grant us good
in this world"—they shall have
no share in the hereafter.

201 There are others who pray,
    "Our Lord, grant us good in
    this world and in the hereafter,
    and deliver us from
    the torment of fire."

202 They shall have what they earned;
    for God is Swift in Reckoning.

203 And remember God
    during the appointed days,°
    but if anyone leaves earlier
    —in two days—this is no sin,
    nor if anyone stays longer,
    for those who fear God.
    So fear God, and know that
    you will be gathered to Him.

204 There's a kind of person
    whose talk in this worldly life
    might please you, and they call
    on God to witness
    what is in their heart—
    yet they are the most
    contentious of opponents.

205 When they turn to go away,
    they strive to sow corruption
    in the land, and to destroy
    crops and livestock—
    and God despises corruption.

206 When urged, "Be mindful
    of God," their pride leads them
        to sin.
    Hell shall be ample for them—
    an evil end.

207 But there are also people
    who would sell their own selves
    seeking to please God—and
    God is Most Compassionate
    toward His servants.

208 You who believe,
    submit yourselves entirely,
    and don't follow
    in the footsteps of Satan—
    your open enemy.

209 If you backslide, after
    clear signs have come to you,
    you should know that God
    is Almighty, All Wise.

210 Are they waiting for God
    to come to them in the shadows
    of clouds, with a train of angels?
    No—the entire matter is settled.
    All matters revert to God.

SECTION 25

211 Ask the children of Israel
    how many clear signs
    We sent to them.
    But those who alter
    the blessings of God
    after what has come to them,
    should know that
    God is Severe in Requital.

212 This worldly life is alluring
    to those who disbelieve, and they
    mock those who do believe.

But those who are mindful of God
will be higher than them
on the day of resurrection, and
God provides without measure
for those whom He will.

213 Humankind was one community,
[then they quarreled]
so God sent prophets to bear
joyous news and to warn people.
He sent with them the Book,
with truth, to judge between people
in the things they disputed.
But, in their mutual envy,
those who were given the Book
quarreled, even after receiving
clear signs. So, God guides
the believers to the truth, by His
    will,
in the things they dispute.
And God guides whom He will
to a straight path.

214 Or, do you think you will
enter the garden without facing
the trials imposed
on those before you?
They were struck by misfortune
and hardship, and were so shaken
that their messenger and those
who believed with him
cried, "When will the help
of God come?" Without doubt,
the help of God is near.

215 They ask you what they
should spend in charity.

Say, "Whatever you spend for good
should be for parents, close kin,
orphans, the poor, and travelers.
And whatever good you do,
God Knows it."

216 Fighting is ordained for you
though you find it abhorrent.
But it may be that you abhor
something which is good for you,
and love something
which is bad for you;
for God knows—and you do not.

SECTION 26

217 They ask you about fighting
during the sacred month. Say,
"Fighting in it is a grave offense,
but hindering people from
God's path, disbelieving in Him,
barring access to the sacred mosque,
and driving out its people
are even more grave in God's eyes,
for persecution is worse
than killing." They won't stop
fighting you until they turn you
    back
from your religion, if they can.

And those of you who turn back
from their religion and die
as disbelievers—their deeds
shall be vain in this life
and in the hereafter,
and they shall be inmates
of the fire—forever.

218 Those who have believed,
   migrated, and striven in God's cause
   can hope for God's mercy—
   God is Forgiving, Ever Merciful.

219 They ask you about wine
   and gambling. Say, "In them both
   is great sin, and some gain for people;
   but their sin is greater than their gain."

   They ask you what they should spend
   in charity. Say, "Whatever
   you can spare." In this way,
   God makes clear for you His signs,
   that you might reflect,

220 both in this life
   and the hereafter.
   And they ask you about orphans.
   Say, "Improving their state is best.
   and if you mix with them,
   bear in mind that they
   are your brothers; for God knows
   the difference between those
   who corrupt and those who reform.
   Had He wished, He could have
   made things difficult for you.
   God is Almighty, All Wise."

221 Do not marry women who
   are polytheists, until they believe—
   for a believing female slave
   is better than a polytheist,
   however alluring she is to you;
   nor give your women in marriage
   to men who are polytheists,
   until they believe—

for a believing male slave
is better than a polytheist,
however alluring he is to you.

These beckon you to the fire—
while God beckons to the garden,
and forgives by His leave;
He makes clear
His signs to humankind
that they might take heed.

SECTION 27

222 They ask you about menstruation.°
   Say, "It is an infirmity, so keep away
   from women during menstruation;
   don't approach them
   until they are purified. When pure,
   you may approach them
   as God has ordained."
   God loves those who turn to Him,
   and He loves those
   who keep themselves pure.

223 Your wives are your fields
   so go into your fields
   as you please, advancing
   good deed for yourselves,°
   and be mindful of God;
   know that you will meet Him, and
   give joyous news to the believers.

224 And don't make
   your oaths to God an excuse
   for neglecting good deeds
   or being mindful of God,
   or reconciling between people,

for God is All Hearing, All
    Knowing.

225 God will not call you to account
    for oaths you spoke unintentionally,
    but He will call you to account
    for what your hearts have earned—
    God is Forgiving, Most Forbearing.

226 For those who swear
    to abstain from their wives,
    there will be a waiting period
    of four months—and if
    they go back [to them],
    God is Forgiving, Ever Merciful.°

227 But if they resolve on divorce,
    they should know that God
    is All Hearing, All Knowing.

228 Divorced women shall wait
    for three monthly periods
    [before marrying again],
    and it is not lawful for them
    to hide what God has created
    in their wombs—if they believe
    in God and the last day.

    If their husbands want to reconcile,
    they have more warrant
    to take them back during this time.
    And their rights are similar
    to the rights over them,
    as in what is known to be fair;
    though husbands have
    a degree [of right] over them—
    God is Almighty, All Wise.

SECTION 28

229 Divorce [can be revoked] twice.
    Each time, keep your wife
    on equitable terms, or
    release her in a kindly manner.
    It's not lawful for you to take back
    anything you gave her, unless
    you both fear that you can't adhere
    to the limits set by God;
    if you fear this, there is no blame
    on either of you if the woman
    gives a sum for her release.
    These are the limits set by God,
    so do not transgress them.
    Those who do so are wrongdoers.

230 If a husband then divorces his wife,
    it's not lawful for him
    to remarry her unless she has
      married
    another husband; if *he* divorces her,
    then there is no blame if she and her
    first husband return to each other,
    if they think they can adhere
    to the limits ordained by God.
    These are the limits set by God,
    which He makes clear
    for those who know.

231 When you divorce women,
    and they finish their waiting period,
    either keep them or release them
    on fair terms; but don't keep them
    with intent to harm them, so as to
      transgress.
    Whoever does this

wrongs himself. Do not take
the signs of God in jest—
remember God's favor to you
and the Book and wisdom
He revealed, to instruct you.
Be mindful of God, and know
that God Knows all things.

SECTION 29

232 When you divorce women,
and they finish their waiting period,
don't prevent them from marrying
their former husbands, if they
both agree, on fair terms.
This is counsel for those of you
who believe in God and the last day
to make you more virtuous and
    pure,
for God knows—and you do not.

233 Mothers suckle their offspring
for two whole years, if they wish
to complete the term; the father
should maintain and clothe them
in a suitable manner. No one should
be burdened beyond their limit.
The mother shall not suffer
on account of her child, nor
the father on account of his.
The same duty falls upon
the father's heir. And there's no fault
if the couple, by mutual consulting
and consent, want to wean the child,
nor if you procure a wet nurse
for your child, provided you give
fair payment. Be mindful of God,

and know that God
Sees all that you do.

234 If any of you die and leave
widows behind, they shall wait
for four months and ten days [before
remarrying]; and when they reach
this appointed term, there is no blame
on you [the guardians] if they then
conduct their affairs honorably.°
God is Aware of all that you do.

235 There is no blame on you whether
you hint at a proposal of marriage
to these women or don't disclose it.°
God knows that you want to propose
to them. Don't make a secret contract
with them but speak honorably to them;
and don't bind the knot of marriage
until the appointed period expires.
And know that God knows what is
within you; heed Him, and know
that God is Forgiving, Forbearing.

SECTION 30

236 There is no blame on you
if you divorce women before
you consummate the marriage
and you have not fixed their dowry.
But provide a suitable gift for them,
the rich according to their means,
and the poor according to theirs—
a duty for those who do good.

237 If you divorce women before
you consummate the marriage but

after you have fixed their dowry,
then give them half of the dowry,
unless they—or those holding
the marriage tie°—waive it.
Waiving it comes closer
to being mindful of God. So do not
forget to be generous to one another.
God Sees all that you do.

238 Preserve your practice of prayers,
especially the midafternoon prayer,
and stand before God in devotion.

239 If you are in fear of [an enemy],
then pray on foot, or while riding;
but when you are safe, remember God
in the way He taught you,
which you did not know before.

240 Those of you who die
and leave widows behind
should bequeath your widows
a year's provision, and not
expel them. But if they leave,
there is no blame on you
[the guardians] if they then
conduct their affairs honorably.°
God is Almighty, All Wise.

241 Divorced women should be
fairly provided for—a duty
for those who are mindful of God

242 This is how God makes clear
His signs, so that you might
use your reason.

SECTION 31

243 Won't you reflect on those
who abandoned their homes,
though in their thousands, in fear
of death? God commanded them,
"Die!" But then He brought them
back to life. God is full of favor
toward humankind, yet
most are ungrateful.

244 So fight in the cause of God,
and know that God
is All Hearing, All Knowing.

245 Who will lend to God
a beautiful loan, which He might
multiply for them many times?
It is God who withholds or
grants in abundance—and to Him
you shall be returned.

246 Won't you reflect on the chiefs
of the children of Israel
after the time of Moses?
When they said to the prophet
among them, "Appoint for us a king,
so that we might fight
in the cause of God,"° he answered,
"Perhaps if you were commanded
to fight, you might not fight?"
They said, "How could we not
fight in the cause of God
after we have been turned out
of our homes, with our children?"

Yet when they were commanded
to fight, they turned back
—all but a few—
God Knows those who do wrong.

247 Their prophet said to them,
"God has appointed Saul as your
    King."
They said, "How can he be our king
when we have more right to king-
    ship than him?
And he has not even been granted
much wealth." The prophet replied,
"God has chosen him over you, and
has granted him much knowledge,
and a fair form.
God grants kingship to whom
    He will,
for God is Expansive, All Knowing."

248 And their prophet said to them,
"A sign of his kingship is that
the ark of the covenant° shall come
to you; it shall bear reassurance
from your Lord and relics from
the family of Moses and of Aaron,
which the angels shall bear.
In this is a sign for you
if you are true believers."

SECTION 32

249 Then, when Saul set out with
his armies, he said, "God will
    test you
at the river. Whoever drinks from it
shall not belong with me, and

whoever refrains from tasting it
shall be with me, though those who
take a handful will be excused."

But all except a few drank from it.
When they crossed the river,
he and the believers with him said,
"We lack strength this day against
Goliath and his forces." But those
assured of meeting God responded,
"How often has a small force
vanquished a large one,
by God's leave? For God
is with those who show patience."

250 When they advanced against
Goliath and his armies, they
    prayed,
"Our Lord, fill us with patience,
make firm our feet, and help us
against a disbelieving people."

251 So they defeated them,
by God's leave, and David
killed Goliath; God gave David
sovereignty and wisdom, and
taught him what He wished.

If God did not restrain
some people by others, the earth
would be corrupt—but God is
Full of Grace to humankind.

252 These are the signs of God;
We recite them to you, the truth,
for you are one of the messengers.

253 We favored some
of these messengers over others.
God spoke to some, and raised others
in rank. We gave Jesus, son of Mary
clear proofs, and strengthened him
with the holy spirit. If God had willed,
their descendants would not have
fought one another after clear signs
had come to them. But they disputed,
some believed, others disbelieved;
had God willed, they would not have
fought—but God does as He intends.

SECTION 33

254 You who believe, spend
in charity from what We give you—
before there comes a Day
when there will be
no bargaining,
nor friendship,
nor intercession;
for the disbelievers are wrongdoers.

255 God—there is no god but He,°
the Living, the Self-Subsisting.
Never can slumber seize Him,
nor sleep. To Him belongs
all that is in the heavens, and
all that is on the earth.
Who can intercede with Him
except by His leave? He knows
what lies ahead, and
what lies behind.
None can approach His knowing,
only as He wills.
His throne extends

over the heavens and the earth,
which He guards and preserves
with no fatigue,
for He is Most High,
Supreme.

256 There shall be no compulsion
in religion; true guidance is now
distinct from error.
Whoever denies false gods
and believes in the One God
has grasped the firmest handhold,
which shall never break—for God
is All Hearing, All Knowing.

257 God is the Protector of those
who believe, Who leads them
from darkness into light;
but the protectors of those
who disbelieve are false gods,
who lead them from light
into darkness. They shall be
inmates of the fire—forever.

SECTION 34

258 Have you reflected on the man
who argued with Abraham about
his Lord because He granted him
sovereignty?° When Abraham said,
"My Lord is He Who brings life
and death," he replied, "I bring life
and death." Abraham responded,
"My Lord brings up the sun
from the East—why don't you
try to bring it from the West?"
So the disbeliever was speechless;

God does not guide
a people who do wrong.

259 Or like the man who passed by
a ruined city, its roofs overturned,
and remarked, "How will God
bring it to life after its death?"

Then God made him die
for a hundred years, and
raised him up again.
God asked him,
"How long have you been here?"
He answered,
"I have been here a day or part
of a day." God said,
"No, you have been here
a hundred years;
look at your food and drink—
they have not changed;
and look at your donkey.

"We shall make you a sign
for people.
And look at the bones,
how We raise them and cover
them with flesh."

When it was made clear to him,
he said, "I know that God
has Power over all things."

260 When Abraham said,
"My Lord, show me how
you give life to the dead,"
He said, "Do you not believe?"
He replied, "Yes, but to satisfy
my heart." God said,

"Take four birds, train them
to return to you, then
place pieces of them
on each hill, and call to them.
They will fly back to you in haste—
know that God is Almighty, All
    Wise."

SECTION 35

261 A parable: those who spend
their wealth in God's cause are like
a grain of corn that grows seven ears,
and each ear bears a hundred grains.
God gives in abundance
to whom He will,
for He is Expansive, All Knowing.

262 Those who spend their wealth
in God's cause—without reminders
of their kindness or words that hurt—
their reward is with their Lord;
they shall not fear, nor grieve.

263 Kind words and forgiveness
are better than charity followed
by hurt—and God
is Self-Sufficient, Forbearing.

264 You who believe, don't annul
your acts of charity by reminders
or hurtfulness, like those who
spend their wealth only to be seen
of people—those who don't
believe in God and the last day.

They are like a smooth rock
covered with soil;

heavy rain falls on it
and leaves it bare.
They have no power
over what they reap,
for God does not guide
a people who disbelieve.

265 Another parable: those
who spend their wealth seeking
to please God and assure their souls
are like a garden lodged on a height;
heavy rain falls on it and its yield
is doubled; and if not heavy rain,
even the dew will water it—
God Sees all that you do.

266 Would any of you wish
to have a garden with date palms
and grapevines, and rivers
flowing beneath, in which they have
all kinds of fruit, only to be struck
by old age while their children
are vulnerable, and for it to be
engulfed by a whirlwind of fire
and burned up? This is how
God makes clear for you His signs,
that you might reflect.

SECTION 36

267 You who believe, give
charitably of the good things
you have earned, and of what
We have brought out for you
from the earth; and don't aim
to give shabby things which you
yourselves would only accept
with closed eyes;

and know that God
is Self-Sufficient, Praiseworthy.

268 Satan promises you poverty,
and incites you to indecency;
but God promises you His grace
and forgiveness; for God is
All Embracing, All Knowing.

269 He grants wisdom to whom
He will, and whoever gains wisdom
has been granted great good;
but only those with insight
will take heed.

270 Whatever you spend
or vow to spend in charity,
God knows it; and the wrongdoers
shall have none to help.

271 If you reveal your deeds
of charity, that is fine; but if you
conceal them, and give to the poor,
this is better for you, and will atone
for some of your bad deeds,
for God is Aware of all that you do.

272 It is not for you, Prophet,
to guide them; God guides whom
He will. Whatever you spend
for good, it is for your own souls,
if you spend it solely seeking
the Face of God.

Whatever you spend for good
shall be fully returned to you
and you shall not be wronged.

273 Give in charity to the poor
who are committed to God's cause
and unable to travel in the land.
The ignorant might think them rich
on account of their self-restraint
but you will recognize them
by their trait of refraining from
begging insistently; and whatever
you spend for good, God Knows it.

SECTION 37

274 Those who spend of their wealth
in charity, by night and by day,
in private and in public—
they shall have a reward
with their Lord;
they shall not fear,
nor shall they grieve.

275 Those who devour money
through usury° will stand on the day
of resurrection as people
    confounded
by Satan's touch. That is because
they say, "Usury is merely like trade."
But God has allowed trade
and forbidden usury. Those who
    desist
after receiving admonition
may retain their previous gains,
and their case shall be judged by
    God.
But those who persist in its practice
shall be inmates of the fire; there
they shall stay forever.

276 God will nullify gain from usury
and bless deeds of charity
with increase, for God
dislikes ungrateful sinners.

277 Those who believe,
and do good deeds,
are steadfast in prayer,
and practice charity,
shall have a reward with their Lord;
they shall not fear, nor grieve.

278 You who believe,
be mindful of God
and give up any
gain left from usury
if you are truly believers.

279 If you do not, be warned of
war from God and His messenger.
But if you repent, you can keep
your capital, without wronging
others or being wronged.

280 If the debtor is in hardship,
grant postponement
until their plight is eased.
But if you charitably
forgo the loan,
this is better for you,
if only you knew.

281 And fear the day
when you shall be
brought back to God.
Then every soul shall
be paid what it earned,
and none shall be wronged.

SECTION 38

282 You who believe, when you
contract a debt for a fixed term,
put it in writing;° let a scribe
write it down equitably
between you, and let the scribe
not refuse to write it; let him inscribe
as God has taught him.

So let him write, and
let the debtor dictate and let him
be mindful of God, his Lord,
and not reduce [the debt] at all.
If the debtor is mentally disabled
or weak or unable to dictate, then
let his guardian dictate equitably,
and call two witnesses from
    your men.
If there are not two men, then
    one man
and two women whom you approve
as witnesses; if one forgets,
the other can refresh her memory.

The witnesses should not refuse,
when called. And do not neglect
to write the debt down, whether
small or large, and its term.
This is more equitable in the sight
of God, more upright as testimony,
and more apt to forestall doubts
between you—unless it is
a transaction you conduct
on the spot between you—
then there is no blame on you
if you don't write it down.

And be sure to summon witnesses
    when you
conduct a commercial transaction,
and neither the scribe nor the witness
should be harmed; doing this
is a sin for you. So, be mindful
of God, for it is God
Who will teach you—
God Knows all things.

283 If you are on a journey,
and cannot find a scribe,
then some goods should be
handed over as surety;
but if you trust one another,
let the trustee fulfill his trust and
let him be mindful of God, his Lord.
And do not conceal testimony, for
whoever does so has a sinful heart;
and God Knows all that you do.

SECTION 39

284 To God belongs
all that is in the heavens, and
all that is on the earth;
and whether you reveal
what is within you or conceal it,
God will call you to account for it.
He forgives whom He will, and
He punishes whom He will,
for God has Power over all things.

285 The messenger believes
in what was revealed to him
by His Lord, as do the true believers.
They all believe in God, His angels,

His Books, and His messengers.
[They say], "We make no distinction
between any of His messengers."
And they say, "We hear and we obey.
We seek your forgiveness, our Lord,
and to you is our final journey."

286 God burdens no soul beyond
its means; what it earns
will be for it or against it.

"Our Lord, don't take us to task
if we forget or err.
Don't burden us with the load
you laid upon those before us.
Our Lord, don't lay a burden on us
which we lack strength to bear.
Pardon us, forgive us, and
show mercy to us.
You are our Protector, so help us
against people who disbelieve."

SURA 3

The Family of 'Imran (*Al 'Imran*)

The Family of 'Imran, named after the family of Moses and Jesus (v. 33), numbers 200 verses. It was revealed in Medina following two early battles against Meccan opponents (Badr, 624, and Uhud, 626), though only the first, Badr, is mentioned by name (v. 123). After addressing the divine origin of the Qur'an, it narrates stories of Zachariah, Mary, and Jesus, before critiquing unobservant Jews, then exhorting believers to persist in the face of expulsion, warfare, and also the death of some companions.

In the Name of God, the All Merciful, Ever Merciful

SECTION I

1 *Alif. Lam. Mim.*°

2 God—there is no god but He,
the Living, the Self-Subsisting.

3 He revealed to you the Book
bearing the truth, confirming
what had come before.
He revealed the Torah and the Gospel

4 before, as guidance for humankind.
And He revealed the criterion
[of right and wrong]. Those
who deny the signs of God
shall face severe torment,
for God is Almighty,
Lord of Requital.

5 Nothing on the earth
or in the heavens
is hidden from God.

6 It is He who shapes you
in the womb as He wishes.
There is no god but He,
the Almighty, the Wise.

7 It is He who revealed to you
the Book. Some of its verses
are clear in meaning—these
are the basis of the Book°—
while others are allegorical.
The perverse in heart
follow what is allegorical,
seeking discord, seeking
its deeper meanings.° But none
    knows
its deeper meaning except God.
Those firmly grounded in
    knowledge
say, "We believe in it. All of it
is from our Lord." But only those
who understand will take heed.

8 "Our Lord," they say,
"Let our hearts not deviate
after You have guided us,
but bestow upon us Your mercy;
You are the Ever Giving.

9 "Our Lord, You shall gather
humankind together on a day
of which there is no doubt.
God never breaks His promise."

SECTION 2

10 As for those who deny the truth—
their wealth and their children
cannot help them at all against God;
and they shall be fuel for the fire.

11 Like the people of Pharaoh
and those before them, they denied
Our signs, so God seized them
for their sins; and God
is Severe in Retribution.

12 Tell those who disbelieve,
"Soon you will be overcome, and
gathered into hell—an evil end.°

13 "You had a sign already
in the two armies that met,° the one
fighting in God's cause, the other
disbelieving. The first saw
with their own eyes that the other
was twice its size; but God
reinforces with His help whom
He will. Here is a lesson
for those who perceive."

14 Men's° eyes are allured by love
of what they desire—women,
children, treasures of gold and
    silver,
branded horses, cattle, arable land—
these are provisions of this
worldly life; but the finest home
for our return is with God.

15 Say, "Shall I tell you of things
finer than these, for those mindful
of God? Gardens in God's presence,
with flowing rivers beneath,
abiding there forever, with

pure spouses, and God's good
   pleasure.
For God Sees His servants—

16 "those who say,
   'Our Lord, we do believe, so
   forgive us our sins, and save us
   from the torment of hellfire,'

17 "those who are patient, truthful,
   and devout, who spend in charity,
   and pray for forgiveness
   during the early morning hours."

18 God bears witness that
   there is no god but He—
   as do the angels and those
   with knowledge, who uphold
   justice. There is no god but He,
   the Almighty, the Wise.

19 True religion in the sight of God
   is submission° [to His will].
   Those who were given the Book
   dissented from it through
   mutual envy, only after knowledge
   had been given to them.
   Whoever denies the signs of God
   [should know that] God
   is Swift in Reckoning.

20 So if they dispute with you,
   say, "I have submitted
   my whole self to God,°
   along with those who follow me."
   And ask those given the Book,
   as well as those with no scripture,°

"Do you submit yourselves
to God?" If they do submit,
they are rightly guided,
but if they turn away, your task
is only to convey the message.
For God Sees all things
concerning His servants.

SECTION 3

21 As for those who deny the signs
   of God, killing the prophets
      unjustly,
   and killing those who exhort people
   to be just—announce for them
   a painful punishment.

22 They are the ones whose works
   are vain—in this world and
   the hereafter; and they shall have
   none to help them.

23 Have you not seen those
   who were given part of the Book?
   When asked to use God's Book
   to judge between them, a group
   of them turned away, averse.

24 For they say, "The fire shall
   touch us but for a few days."
   What they have forged
   deludes them in their faith.

25 So how will it be for them
   when We gather them together
   on a day [whose coming]
   is beyond doubt

—when each soul
shall be paid in full
for what it earned—
without being wronged.

26 Say, "O God, Dominion
is Yours. You give dominion
to whom You will, and wrest it
from whom You will.
You exalt whom You will,
and debase whom You will;
all good is in Your Hand; You
have Power over all things.

27 "You fade night into day,
and day into night;
You bring the living from the dead,
and the dead from the living;
and You give provision
to whom You will, without
measure."

28 Believers should not take
unbelievers as allies, rather than
believers; those who do this
will have no kind of bond
with God—unless you do this
out of fear, to protect yourselves.
And it is God Himself
Who warns you°—to God
you will finally return.

29 Say, "Whether you conceal
what is in your hearts or reveal it,
God knows it; and He knows
what is in the heavens and the earth,
for God has Power over all things."

30 "On the day when each soul is
confronted with the good and evil
it has done, it will wish [that evil]
were far, far away. It is God Himself
Who warns you, though He is
Most Kind toward His servants."

SECTION 4

31 Say, "If you love God,
follow me. God will love you
and forgive you your sins, for God
is Forgiving, Ever Merciful."

32 Say, "Obey God
and the messenger."
But if they should turn away,
God does not love the unbelievers.

33 God chose Adam and Noah
and the family of Abraham
and the family of ʿImran
over all peoples,°

34 making them offspring
of one another; and God
is All Hearing, All Knowing.

35 When the wife of ʿImran said,
"My Lord, I vow to you
what is growing in my womb—
to be dedicated to your service,
for You are the All Hearing,
the All Knowing"—

36 then she gave birth, and said,
"My Lord, I have given birth

to a girl." And God knows best
to what she gave birth, for the male
is not like the female.°
"I have named her Mary,
and I seek refuge in You
from the accursed Satan—
for her and her offspring."

37 Her Lord graciously accepted her,
nurtured her immaculately,
entrusting her to the care
of Zachariah. Whenever
he entered her sanctuary, he found her
supplied with provisions. He asked,
"Mary, where did you get these?"
She replied, "They are from God.
God provides without measure
for those whom He will."

38 Then Zachariah
called upon his Lord, "My Lord,
grant me from Your grace°
a pure child. You are the One
Who Hears prayer."

39 The angels called out to him
while he stood praying
in the sanctuary, "God gives you
joyous news of a son, John,
confirming God's Word°—
one noble and chaste, a prophet,
one of the righteous."

40 He asked, "My Lord,
how can I have a son
when old age has withered me
and my wife is barren?"
The angel responded,

"This is how it is:
God does what He will."

41 He said, "My Lord, give me
a sign." The angel said, "Your sign
is that you will not speak to people
for three straight days,
except by gestures.
And remember your Lord often,
glorifying Him evening and
    morning."

SECTION 5

42 The angels proclaimed,
"Mary, God has chosen you
and purified you;
He has chosen you
above all women."

43 "Mary, devote yourself
to your Lord; prostrate yourself
in worship, and bow in prayer
with all those who bow."

44 This is a disclosure from
the unseen, which We reveal to you,
Prophet, for you were not
among them when [the priests]
cast lots to see which of them
should have charge of Mary;
you were not among them
when they argued about this.

45 The angels said, "Mary,
God gives you joyous news
of His Word—He shall be called
the messiah, Jesus, son of Mary,

and he shall be honored in this world
and the hereafter, and he shall be
among those closest to God.

46 "He shall speak to the people
from the cradle and in adulthood,
and he shall be among those
who do good."

47 She said, "My Lord, how
shall I have a son, when no man
has touched me?" He replied,
"So it is—God creates what He will.
When He decrees a thing,
He merely says to it, 'Be' and it is."

48 "And God will teach him
the Book, and wisdom,
the Torah, and the Gospel,

49 "and appoint him as a messenger
for the Children of Israel,
'I have come to you with a sign
from your Lord: I will create for you
the form of a bird from clay, and
breathe into it so that it becomes
a living bird, by God's leave.

" 'I heal the blind and the leper,
and I bring the dead to life,
by God's leave. And I inform you
of what you can eat, and what
you should store in your homes.
In this is a sign for you,
if you are believers.

50 " 'And I have come to confirm
the Torah that came before me,

and to make lawful part of what
was forbidden to you.
And I have come to you with a sign
from your Lord, so be mindful
of God, and obey me.

51 " 'God is my Lord
and your Lord,
so worship Him:
this is a straight path.' "

52 When Jesus sensed some
disbelief among them, he said,
"Who will help me
[in calling people] to God?"
The disciples said,
"We will help in God's cause.
We believe in God: so bear witness
that we submit to God's will."°

53 "Our Lord, we believe
in what You have revealed,
and we follow the messenger.
List us, then, among the witnesses."

54 And the unbelievers schemed;
but God also schemed. And God
is the best of schemers.

SECTION 6

55 God said, "Jesus, I will take you
back and raise you to My presence.
I will purge you of the company
of disbelievers. On the day
of resurrection, I will place those
who follow you above those
who disbelieve. Then you shall all

return to me and I shall judge
between you on the things
you dispute.

56 "As for those who disbelieve,
I shall afflict them with
severe torment in this world
and the hereafter, and they
shall have none to help them.

57 "As for those who believe and
do good deeds, God will give them
their full reward; for God
does not love the wrongdoers.

58 "In this way, We recite to you,
Prophet, some of the signs—
and the wise reminder."

59 In the sight of God,
Jesus is like Adam;
He created him from dust,
saying to him, "Be"—and he was.

60 The truth is from your Lord;
so don't be one of those who doubt.

61 If someone argues with you
after the knowledge given to you,
say to them, "Come, let us call
our sons and your sons,
our women and your women,
ourselves and yourselves,
then let us pray earnestly
and invoke the curse of God
upon those who lie."°

62 —This is the true narrative.
There is no god but the One God,
and God is Almighty, All Wise.

63 If they then turn away,
God Knows all about
those who wreak mischief.

SECTION 7

64 Say, "People of the Book, come,
let there be a common word
between us and you—that we
worship none but the One God,
and associate none with Him,
and not take one another
as lords—only God."
And if they turn away, say,
"Bear witness that we
submit to God's will."

65 People of the Book,
why do you dispute about Abraham,
when the Torah and the Gospel
were not revealed until after him?
Will you not use reason?

66 You are the ones who argued
over things you knew,
so why do you argue now
over things you don't know?
God knows—and you do not.

67 Abraham was not a Jew
nor a Christian; rather,
he believed only in the One God,
submitting to God's will,°

not one of those who
join other gods with God.

68 The nearest among people to
Abraham are those who follow him,
this messenger, and believers.
And God is the Protector
of those who believe.

69 A group of the people of the Book
wish to misguide you, but they
misguide only themselves,
though they don't realize it.

70 People of the Book, why do you
deny the signs of God, when you
yourselves are witness to their truth?°

71 People of the Book, why do you
confound truth with falsehood, and
hide the truth, when you know it?

SECTION 8

72 A group of the people of the Book
say, "Believe in what was revealed
to the believers at the beginning
of the day, then reject it at the end
of the day; perhaps the believers
too will turn back."

73 [And they say,] "Believe only those
who follow your religion."
Tell them, Prophet, "All guidance
is guidance from God." [They say,
"Don't believe] that
anyone can be given
what you have been given,

or dispute with you
before your Lord."
Say, "All grace is in God's hand;
He gives it to whom He will.
For God is Expansive,
All Knowing."

74 He chooses whom He will
for His mercy—
God's grace is great.

75 Among the people of the Book
are some who, if you entrust them
with a great treasure, they'll return it;
and others, if you entrust them
with one dinar,° won't return it
    unless
you stand watching over them,
for they say, "We have no obligation
to the gentiles."
But they lie about God—
and they know it.

76 Yes—God loves those
who fulfill their pledge
and are mindful of Him,

77 but those who sell their pledge
to God and their oaths
for a paltry price shall have
no share in the hereafter;
God shall not speak to them,
nor look at them
on the day of resurrection,
nor shall He purify them.
And they shall face
painful torment.

78 Among them is a group who
distort the Book with their speech,
so you might think it is from
the Book, but it is not;
they say it is from God, but it is not;
for they speak a lie about God,
and they know it.

79 No person to whom God
had given the Book, and wisdom,
and prophethood, would say
to the people,
"Worship me, instead of God."
Rather, he would say,
"Be one of the learned,°
for you have taught the Book,
as you have studied it."

80 Nor would he command you
to take angels and prophets as lords.
Would he command you to disbelief
after you have submitted
to God's will?

SECTION 9

81 God took a pledge
from the prophets, saying,
"If a prophet comes to you,
confirming what I have given you
of the Book and of wisdom,
you must believe in him
and you must support him.
Do you accept and affirm this,
my covenant?"
They responded, "We affirm it."

He declared, "Then bear witness,
and I too shall be a witness."

82 If any turn away after this,
they are transgressors.

83 Do they seek something other
than the religion of God?
For all in the heavens and on earth
submit to Him, willing or
unwilling;
they shall be brought back to Him.

84 Say, "We believe in God,
what has been revealed to us,
and what was revealed to Abraham,
Ishmael, Isaac, Jacob, and the tribes;
and what was given to Moses, Jesus,
and the prophets, from their Lord.
We make no distinction
among any of them, and to Him
we submit our will."

85 If anyone seeks a religion other
than submission to God, it shall
never be accepted of them; and
in the hereafter they shall be
among those in loss.

86 How will God guide a people
who disbelieve after having faith,
who witnessed
that the messenger is true—
and clear proofs had come to them?
God does not guide
a people who do wrong.

87   Their recompense will be
     the curse of God, the angels,
     and all humankind.

88   There they shall stay forever—
     their torment shall not be lightened
     nor shall they find respite,

89   except those who repent,
     after this, and amend themselves;
     for God is Forgiving, Ever Merciful.

90   As for those who disbelieve
     after having faith, and increase
     their disbelief, their repentance
     shall never be accepted, for they
     have gone far astray.

91   As for those who disbelieve
     and die as disbelievers, even though
     they offered as ransom enough gold
     to fill the earth, it would never
     be accepted of any of them.
     They shall face painful torment,
     with none to help them.

SECTION 10

92   You shall never attain
     righteousness unless you give
     freely from what you love; and God
     Knows fully what you give.

93   All food was lawful
     for the Children of Israel except
     for what Israel° forbade himself

before the Torah was revealed.
Say, "Bring the Torah and
recite it, if you speak the truth."

94   Those who invent a falsehood
     about God, after this, do wrong.

95   Say, "God has declared the truth,
     so follow the creed of Abraham,
     who was pure in faith,
     never a polytheist."

96   The first House of worship
     founded for people
     was the one at Mecca°—blessed,
     a guide for humankind.

97   In it are clear signs, as in the
     place where Abraham stood to pray;
     whoever enters it will be safe.
     Pilgrimage to the House is a duty
     to God—for all those
     able to undertake the journey.
     Those who disbelieve should know
     that God is Self-Sufficient,
     beyond need of His creatures.

98   Say, "People of the Book,
     why do you deny the signs of God
     when God Himself is Witness
     to whatever you do?"

99   Say, "People of the Book,
     why do you bar believers
     from the path of God, seeking
     to make it crooked, when you

yourselves are witness to the truth?
And know that God is not
heedless of what you do."

100 You who believe, if you
heed them, a group of those
who were given the Book
would turn you back
into disbelievers—
after you had believed.

101 And how can you disbelieve
when the signs of God have been
recited to you, and His messenger
is among you?
Whoever holds fast to God
shall be guided to a straight path.

SECTION 11

102 You who believe,
be mindful of God, as is His due,
and do not die without
submitting to His will.

103 Hold fast to the rope of God,
all together, and don't be divided.
Remember God's favor to you,
when you were enemies:
He brought your hearts together,
and you became brothers,
by His favor. Even when you were
on the brink of a pit of fire,
He delivered you from it.
In this way, God makes clear to you
His signs, that you might be
    guided.

104 You should be a community
who invite others to what is good,
enjoining what is right,
and forbidding what is wrong—
these are the people who flourish.

105 And don't be like those
who are divided, and dispute
after clear signs have come to them,
for they shall face great torment.

106 On the day when some faces
brighten and others darken, those
with darkened faces shall be asked,
"How could you deny the truth,
after having believed? Taste, then,
the torment for disbelieving."

107 But those with brightened faces
shall live in God's mercy—forever.

108 These are the signs of God;
We recite them to you, Prophet—
the truth—for God desires
no injustice for His creatures.

109 To God belongs
all that is in the heavens
and all that is on the earth—
to God all things shall return.

SECTION 12

110 You are the finest community
raised for humankind; you enjoin
what is right, forbid what is wrong,
and you believe in God.

Had the people of the Book believed,
it would have been better for them.
Among them are true believers
but most of them are transgressors.

111 They can never harm you,
beyond a minor slight. Even if they
fight you, they will soon turn
their backs to you, fleeing;
then they shall find no help.

112 Shame shall fall upon them
wherever they are found—unless
they hold fast to a rope from God
and a rope from humankind.°

They bring down on themselves
the wrath of God, and indigence
shall fall upon them—because
they disbelieved in the signs of God,
killing prophets unjustly—because
they disobeyed, always
    transgressing.°

113 Not all of them are alike:
among the people of the Book
are some who are upright,
who recite the verses°
of God during the hours of night
and prostrate themselves.

114 They believe in God
and the last day;
they enjoin what is right,
and forbid what is wrong;
and they hasten to do good works;
they are among the righteous.

115 None of the good they do
will be rejected, for God well Knows
those who are mindful of Him.

116 As for those who disbelieve,
neither their wealth nor children
will help them in any way
against God; they shall be
inmates of the fire—forever.

117 The parable of what they spend
in this worldly life is that of a wind
which brings a biting frost;
it strikes the harvest of a people
who have wronged themselves
then destroys it. It is not God
who wrongs them, but they
who wrong themselves.

118 You who believe,
don't be close to outsiders
who will spare you no ruin,
and wish only to see you suffer.
Hatred seethes from their mouths,
but what lies hidden in their hearts
is worse. We have made the signs
clear to you, if you use reason.

119 See, you love them—
but they don't love you.
You believe in the Book, all of it.
When they meet you, they say,
"We believe," but when alone,
they gnaw at their fingertips,
raging at you. Say, "Perish
in your fury—God Knows
what is in your hearts."

120 If something good comes
    your way, it grieves them, and
    if any misfortune strikes you,
    they rejoice in it. But if you are
    patient and mindful of God,
    their scheming can't harm you at all.
    God Encompasses all that they do.

SECTION 13

121 Prophet, remember when
    you left your household early
    to assign the believers their
    battle positions?° God
    is All Hearing, All Knowing.

122 Remember when two groups
    of you began to lose heart? But God
    was their ally. So let the believers
    put their trust in God.

123 God helped you at the Battle
       of Badr
    when you were but a weak force;
    be mindful, then, of God,
    that you might be thankful.

124 Remember when you said
    to the believers, "Is it not enough
    that your Lord reinforced you with
    three thousand descending angels?

125 "Yes—if you remain patient
    and mindful of God, even if
    the enemy falls upon you suddenly,
    your Lord will reinforce you with
    five thousand assigned angels."°

126 God made it only a message
    of hope for you, to reassure
    your hearts—there is no help
    except from God,
    the Almighty, the Wise—

127 that He might cut off the flanks
    of the unbelievers' forces, and
    frustrate them, so that they would
    turn back, hopeless.

128 It is not for you [Prophet,
    but for God] to decide
    whether He turns to them,
    relenting, or punishes them—
    they are wrongdoers.

129 To God belongs
    all that is in the heavens
    and all that is on the earth.
    He forgives whom He will
    and punishes whom He will;
    God is Forgiving, Ever Merciful.

SECTION 14

130 You who believe, do not devour
    interest from usury, doubled and
    multiplied; but be mindful of God
    that you might flourish.

131 Be fearful of the fire, prepared
    for those who disbelieve;

132 obey God and His messenger
    that you may obtain mercy.

133 And hasten to forgiveness
from your Lord and a garden
whose expanse spans the heavens
and the earth, prepared
for those mindful of God,

134 those who give freely
in both prosperity and adversity,
who restrain their anger, and
pardon others. For God loves
those who do good,

135 and those who, after committing
indecency or wronging themselves,
remember God and seek forgiveness
for their sins—who forgives sins
except God?—and don't persist
knowingly in doing wrong.

136 Theirs shall be a reward
of forgiveness from their Lord,
and gardens with rivers flowing
beneath, abiding there forever.
How excellent is the reward
of those who labor [to do good].

137 How many ways of life°
have passed before your time.
Travel through the earth, and see
how it ended for those
who denied the truth.

138 Here is a clear lesson for people,
guidance, and admonition for those
who are mindful of God.

139 So don't weaken, or grieve,
for you will prevail—if you believe.

140 If you have suffered a wound,
[remember that] their people
have also borne a wound;°
we give such days to people in turn,
that God may know those
who believe and those
He may take as martyrs°
—God does not love those
who do wrong—

141 and that God may purify
those who believe, and destroy
the disbelievers.

142 Or did you think
you would enter the garden
without God knowing those
who strove so hard among you
and those who remained steadfast?

143 Yes, you used to wish
for death, before you met it;
and now, you've seen it—staring
at it, with your own eyes.

SECTION 15

144 Muhammad is no more than
a messenger, and messengers
passed away before him. If he died
or were killed, would you turn
upon your heels? Whoever so turns
can do no harm to God;
but God will reward those
who are grateful.

145 Nor can a soul die
except by God's leave,
its term decreed.
Whoever desires
the reward of this world,
We shall give it to them;
and whoever desires
the reward of the hereafter,
We shall give it to them;
and We shall reward
those who are grateful.

146 And how many prophets fought,
alongside many pious men,
but they never lost heart when
calamity struck them, in God's path,
nor did they weaken or give up.
God loves those who are steadfast.

147 And the only words they spoke
were "Our Lord, forgive us our sins
and extravagances,°
make firm our feet, and help us
against the disbelievers."

148 And God gave them
the reward of this world
and the more glorious reward
of the hereafter,
for God loves those who do good.

SECTION 16

149 You who believe,
if you heed the disbelievers,
they will drive you back,
on your heels, and you will
turn back, to your own loss.

150 No—God is your Protector,
and He is the Best of Helpers.

151 We shall cast terror
into the hearts of the disbelievers
since they joined partners with God,
for which He revealed no sanction.
Their refuge shall be the fire—
what an evil home for the
wrongdoers!

152 God fulfilled His promise
to you, when, by His leave,
you were routing them—until
you faltered, disputed
the Prophet's command,
and disobeyed it, after
He brought you within sight
of what you coveted.°

Some among you craved this world
while others desired the hereafter.
Then He caused you to retreat
from them, in order to test you. Now
He has forgiven you; for God
is Ever Gracious to the believers.

153 You clambered away from the foe,
without even a glance at anyone,
while the messenger was calling you
from behind. So God gave you grief
upon grief—to teach you not
to lament over what had eluded you
or what had befallen you.
For God is Aware of all that you do.

154 After this grief, He sent down
calm upon you, a sleep that fell over

a group of you, while another group,
caring only about themselves,
entertained false notions of God,
notions from the age of ignorance.°
They said, "Do we have any voice
in the matter?" Prophet, tell them,
"The matter is wholly with God."

They conceal within themselves
what they will not reveal to you.
They say, "If we had had a voice
in the matter, we would not have
been killed here." Say, "Even if
you had stayed at home, those
for whom death was decreed
would still have gone toward
their final place of rest."
This was so that God
could test your hearts,
and purify what was in them°
for God is Aware of whatever
lies within your hearts.

155 As for those of you who
turned back on the day
the two armies clashed,
it was Satan who caused them
to backslide, for something
they had done. But God
has pardoned them. For God
is Forgiving, Forbearing.

SECTION 17

156 You who believe, do not
be like the disbelievers, who say
of their brothers who journeyed
in the land or went on a raid,

"Had they stayed with us, they
would not have died or been killed,"
for God will make [such thoughts]
a source of sorrow in their hearts.
It is God who gives life
and brings death. And God
Sees whatever you do.

157 And if you are killed
in the cause of God, or die,
God's forgiveness and mercy
are better by far than
all the goods they amass.

158 And if you die, or are killed, it is
to God that you will be gathered.

159 It is through the mercy of God
that you dealt gently with them;
had you been rough and
   hard-hearted,
they would have scattered away
from you. So pardon them,
and ask forgiveness for them, and
consult with them in your
   affairs.
Then, when you decide on
   something,
place your trust in God, for God
loves those who trust in Him.

160 If God helps you,
none can overcome you.
If He forsakes you, who
can help you?
So let the believers
trust in God.

161 No prophet would defraud
[anyone of booty from the battle].
If anyone does defraud, he shall bring
his fraud to the day of resurrection—
then, every soul shall receive its due
for whatever it earned; and none
shall be wronged.

162 Can one who seeks to please God
be like one who draws God's wrath
upon himself, whose home
is hell, an evil end?

163 They are ranked differently
in the eyes of God, and God
Sees all that they do.

164 God granted a favor to the
believers when He sent to them
a messenger from their own people,
reciting His verses to them,
purifying them, and teaching them
the Book and wisdom; for
before this, they were clearly astray.

165 Why do you say, when
misfortune strikes you—even though
you have struck your foes with twice
as much—"Where is this from?"
Say, "It is from yourselves—
God has Power over all things."

166 What happened to you
on the day the two armies met
happened with God's leave,
that He might know
who were the true believers,

167 and who were the hypocrites.
They were told, "Come, fight
in the cause of God, or at least
defend yourselves." They replied,
"If we knew how to fight,
we would have followed you."
That day, they were closer
to unbelief than belief.
They say with their mouths
what is not in their hearts; and God
knows best what they conceal.

168 As for those who sat idly behind
and said of their brothers, "If only
they had heeded us, they would not
have been killed," tell them, "Then
avert death from yourselves,
if you speak the truth."

169 Do not think that those
killed in the cause of God
are dead—no, they are living,
with their Lord, enjoying
what He has provided for them,

170 rejoicing in what God
has given them from His grace
and joyful that those left behind
who have not yet joined them
shall neither fear nor grieve.

171 They rejoice in the grace of God
and His favor, knowing that
God will never forfeit the reward
of the believers.

SECTION 18

172 Those who answered the call
    of God and the messenger,
    even after suffering hurt—
    those of them who do good,
    and are mindful of God,
    shall have a great reward;

173 those whose faith was only
    strengthened when people told them,
    "The people have amassed
    a great army against you—
    you should fear them."
    They responded, "God is enough
    for us—He is the best Custodian
    of all affairs."

174 And they returned, through
    God's grace and favor, unharmed,
    for they sought to please God—
    and God is Most Gracious.°

175 It is Satan who fills you
    with fear of his allies. But
    do not fear them—fear Me,
    if you are true believers.

176 And do not be grieved by those
    who hasten to unbelief. They can
    never harm God in any way.
    God intends to give them
    no share in the hereafter, and they
    shall face great torment.

177 Those who exchange faith for
    unbelief

can never do any harm to God, and
they shall face painful torment.

178 Don't let the unbelievers think
    that when We grant them respite,
    it is good for them. We grant respite
    only for them to grow in sin,
    and they shall face disgraceful
        torment.

179 God will not leave you believers
    as you are, without setting apart
    the good from the bad.
    God will not disclose to you
    the unseen, but He chooses
    as His messengers whom He will
    [to give this knowledge]. So believe
    in God and His messenger; and if
    you believe, and are mindful of God,
    yours shall be a great reward.

180 And don't let those who
    greedily withhold what God
    has given them through His grace
    think that this is good for
        them—no,
    it is bad for them. What they withheld
    shall be hung around their necks
    on the day of resurrection; it is God
    Who shall inherit the heavens
    and the earth, and God
    is Aware of all that you do.

SECTION 19

181 God has heard those who taunt,
    "God is poor, while we are rich."

We shall record what they say,
as well as their unjust killing
of the prophets; and We shall say,
"Taste the punishment
of the searing fire."

182 "This is for the bad deeds
you accrued, with your own hands—
God never wrongs His servants."

183 As for those who say,
"God took from us a pledge
that we should not believe
in any messenger until He sent to us
a sacrifice that fire consumes,"
say to them, "Messengers have
come to you before me,
with clear signs, including
what you speak of, so why did you
kill them—if you are speaking the
    truth?"

184 If they deny you, know that
messengers before you were denied,
even though they came with clear
    signs,
scriptures, and an enlightening Book.

185 Every soul shall taste death,
and only on the day of resurrection
shall you receive your recompense.
Whoever is drawn out from
the fire and brought into
the garden shall have triumphed.
For the life of this world gives
but illusory pleasure.

186 You will surely be tested
through your possessions and
your lives, and you shall hear
much that is harmful from
those given the Book before you
and those who are polytheists.
Resoluteness in all things
rests on patience
and mindfulness of God.

187 When God made a covenant
with those given the Book—
"Make it known to the people,
and don't hide it"—they
threw it behind their backs,
and traded it for a paltry price.
How wretched was their bargain!

188 Don't think, Prophet, that
those who rejoice in what
they have brought about
and love to be praised
for what they do not do—
don't think that they will escape
punishment; for they
shall face painful torment.

189 To God belongs dominion
of the heavens and the earth;
and God has Power over all things.

SECTION 20

190 In the creation of the heavens
and the earth, in the revolving
of night and day, are signs
for those with understanding,

191 those who remember God
while standing, sitting, or lying
on their sides, pondering on the
creation of the heavens and the earth,
"Our Lord, You did not create all this
in vain; glory be to You, and
save us from the torment of fire.

192 "Our Lord, You cover with shame
those You cast into the fire—
and the wrongdoers shall find
none to help them.

193 "Our Lord, we have heard the call
of someone calling to the faith,
'Believe in your Lord,'
and we do believe. Our Lord,
forgive us our sins, and absolve
us of our evil deeds, and let us die
in the company of the righteous.

194 "Our Lord, grant us what
You promised us
through Your messengers,
and do not shame us
on the day of resurrection.
You never fail in Your promise."

195 Their Lord answered them,
"I shall not allow the deeds
of any of you—whether you are
male or female to be lost,
you are from one another. As for
those
who migrated, or were driven from,
their homes, or suffered hurt
in My cause, or fought or were killed,

I will absolve you of your
bad deeds, and I will usher you
into gardens, beneath which
rivers flow—a reward from
God Himself, for with God
is the most excellent reward."

196 Do not be deluded by
the unbelievers, strutting about
throughout the land—

197 a brief enjoyment—then
hell will become their home—
a woeful place of repose.

198 But those who are mindful
of their Lord shall have gardens,
beneath which rivers flow,
abiding there forever, a gift from
God Himself—for whatever God has
is better for those who are righteous.

199 And there are those among
the people of the Book
who believe in God, in what
has been revealed to you—and what
was revealed to them; they bow
humbly before God. They do not sell
the signs of God for a paltry price;
they shall have a reward
from their Lord Himself,
for God is Swift in Reckoning.

200 You who believe, be patient—
compete in patience, be constant;
and be mindful of God,
that you might flourish.

Women (*Al-Nisa*)

Late Medinan, this sura numbers 176 verses and concerns women, first those afflicted by war, widowhood, or raising orphans, then those faced with challenges of fornication, divorce, or inheritance. The Prophet's authority as God's emissary and arbiter is extolled, while those deemed hypocrites and people of the Book are reminded of God's transcendence and self-sufficiency: Jesus is the messiah, but also servant of the One with angels stationed near Him (vv. 171–72).

In the Name of God, the All Merciful, Ever Merciful

SECTION I

1 Humankind, be mindful
of your Lord, Who created you
from a single soul, and from this
created its mate, multiplying them
into multitudes of men and women.

Be mindful of God, in whose Name
you ask one another about your rights
and those of your relatives—
God is Ever Watchful over you.

2 Give to orphans whatever wealth
is left to them, and don't substitute
worthless things for things of value;
nor consume their wealth
along with yours—
for that would be a grave sin.

3 If you fear that
you can't be fair to orphan girls,°
then marry other women

who seem suitable to you
—two, or three, or four—
but if you fear that
you can't treat them justly,
then marry only one, or those
you own.° This way, you'll be
less prone to mistreating them.

4 Give women their bridal gift
with goodwill, but if they choose
to forgo a portion, by all means
enjoy it at your pleasure.

5 And don't entrust your property°
to simpletons—for God made it
a means of support for you;
but feed them and clothe them,
and speak to them with kind words.

6 Monitor° orphans until they reach
the age of marriage; then if you find
them to be of sound judgment,
disburse their wealth to them,

and don't consume it wastefully,
or in haste before they come of age.
Let a rich guardian refrain from
using any part of it, while
a poor one can use a fair portion.
When you disburse their wealth,
summon witnesses before them—
for God suffices as Reckoner.

7 There is a portion
   for both men and women
   from what parents
   and near relatives leave
   —whether small or large—
   a specified portion.

8 And if other relatives or orphans
   or the poor are present during
   the distribution, give them a portion
   and speak to them with kind words.

9 And let them show the same
   solicitude [for orphans] as for any
   vulnerable offspring of their own
   that they might leave behind.
   Let them be mindful of God,
   and speak words that are fitting.

10 Those who wrongfully devour
    the wealth of orphans shall devour
    fire into their bellies—burning
    in a blazing fire.

SECTION 2

11 As for your children—in your will,
    God directs you to leave the male
    a portion equal to that of two
        females.
    If there are only daughters—
    two or more—two-thirds
    of the inheritance goes to them;
    if there is only one, she gets half.

Parents get a sixth share each
if [the deceased] leaves children;
but if he leaves no child,
and the parents are his sole heirs,
then his mother gets a third,
unless he has brothers and sisters,
then his mother gets a sixth.

[The distribution of any will
shall be made] after payment of
any bequests or debts.
You do not know which
of your parents or children
will be of more benefit to you—
hence the obligation
laid down by God.
God is All Knowing, All Wise.

12 From what your wives leave,
    your portion is a half, if they leave
    no child. But if they leave a child,
    then yours is a fourth, after payment
    of bequests and debts.
    And from what you leave,
    their share is a fourth, if you leave
    no child. But if you leave a child,
    then theirs is an eighth, after payment
    of bequests and debts.

As for the inheritance
of a man or woman
who has no direct heir
[neither child nor parents]
but has a brother or sister,
each of the two shall get a sixth;
but if more than two,
they will share a third, after payment
of bequests and debts
so that no one suffers loss.
This is the ordinance from God—
God is All Knowing, Most Kind.

13 These are the limits laid down
by God. Those who obey
God and His messenger
shall be brought by Him into gardens
with rivers flowing beneath,
residing there forever—
that is the supreme triumph.

14 But those who disobey
God and His messenger,
and transgress His limits
shall be thrust by Him into fire,
abiding there forever,
in shameful torment.

SECTION 3

15 If any of your women
commits indecency, summon
four witnesses against them
from among you. And if these
attest to their guilt, then
confine them within their home
until death comes to them, or
God finds another way for them.°

16 If two people among you
commit indecency, punish
them both. But if they
repent and amend their ways,
then turn away from them;
for God is Ever Relenting,
Ever Merciful.

17 God accepts the repentance
only of those who do evil
through ignorance and soon
repent. God will turn
to them in forgiveness,
for God is All Knowing, All Wise;

18 but not the repentance
of those who do evil deeds
until death approaches them,
and then say, "Now I repent";
nor the repentance of those
who die as disbelievers.
For these, We have prepared
a painful punishment.

19 You who believe,
it is unlawful for you to inherit
women against their will, or
to treat them harshly,
hoping to take back part of
the bridal gift you gave them, unless
they commit open indecency.
Rather, live with them in kindness,
for if you dislike them, perhaps
you dislike something in which
God imbues much good.

20 But if you intend to take
one wife in place of another,

don't take back any of the
   bridal gift
you gave to the former,
even if it was a substantial sum.
Would you take it by slander
and blatant sinning?

21 For how could you take it
when you have been intimate,
and she has taken from you
a solemn oath?

22 And do not marry
any of the women
your fathers married—
though its past practice
is excused—for it is
an indecency, loathsome,
a wicked custom.

SECTION 4

23 It is forbidden for you
to marry your mothers,
your daughters, your sisters,
your father's sisters,
your mother's sisters,
daughters of brothers,
daughters of sisters,
the foster mothers who nursed you,
the foster sisters nursed with you,
mothers of your wives,
the stepdaughters
in your custody, [born] of the wives
with whom you were intimate
—though if you were not intimate,
there is no blame on you—
the wives of your sons

who are from your loins,
and two sisters at once.

However, the past practice
of all these things is excused—
God is Forgiving, Ever Merciful.

24 Also prohibited are
women already married,
except those you own—this
is what God has decreed for you.

Apart from these, others
are lawful to you, provided
you seek them in marriage,
not in lust, and give them
something of your wealth.

Give the bridal gifts
to those you enjoy thereby,
as an obligation,
but there is no blame on you
if you mutually agree upon
something modifying this
   obligation°—
God is All Knowing, All Wise.

25 And those among you
who can't afford to marry
free chaste believing women,
can marry believers
among your maidservants.°

God best knows your faith;
you belong to one another.

Wed them with permission
of their families, and be fair

in giving them their bridal due.
They should be chaste, not
immoral, taking secret lovers.
Once they are married,
if they commit indecency,
their punishment should be
half of that for free women.
This option is for those of you
who fear falling into sin
by remaining unmarried.
But it is better for you
to be patient—God
is Forgiving, Ever Merciful.

SECTION 5

26 God wants to make
His laws clear to you,
and to guide you in the ways
of those before you. And He
turns toward you, for He
is All Knowing, All Wise.

27 God wants to turn
toward you, but those
who follow their own desires
want you to deviate—
going far astray.

28 God wants to ease
the burdens upon you,
for humans were created weak.

29 You who believe,
do not devour one another's
property wrongfully—
rather, let there be trade
by mutual consent.

Nor kill one another.°
God is Ever Merciful to you.

30 And whoever does this,
spitefully and unjustly,
We shall thrust them
into the fire—
this is easy for God.

31 If you avoid the major sins
that are forbidden to you,
We shall absolve you
of your minor sins,
and let you enter with honor.

32 And do not covet the favors
that God has granted to some
more than others. Men will have
their due share of what they earned,
and women will have
their due share of what they earned.
So entreat God for His favor—
God Knows all things.

33 And for everyone,
We have appointed heirs
to what is left behind by parents
and relatives; so give those
to whom you have pledged
your hand
their due portion—
God is Witness to all things.

SECTION 6

34 Men are maintainers of women,
for God has thereby advantaged one
over the other—and they

support them from their means.°
So righteous women are devout,
guarding [their husband's means
and honor], even in their absence,
what God has guarded.
But if you suspect misconduct
from them, first counsel them,
then withdraw from their beds, then
resort to [harmless] force.° But if
they now obey you, seek no
further course against them—
God is Most High, Most Great.

35 If you fear a rift between husband
and wife, appoint arbiters,
one from his family and one from
    hers.
If they desire to reconcile,
God will bring accord between them
for God is All Knowing, All Aware.

36 Worship God—and do not
associate partners with Him.
Be kind to parents and relatives,
to orphans, and the poor,
to neighbors—both kin and strangers,
to the companions by your side,
to travelers, and to those you own.

God does not love those
who are proud and boastful—

37 nor those who are stingy,
who urge stinginess in others,
and hide what God has given them
by His favor. We have prepared
for the disbelievers
a disgraceful torment—

38 nor those who spend
of their wealth to be seen
of people, but who don't believe
in God and the last day.
Whoever takes Satan
as his companion
has an evil companion indeed.

39 What would they lose
if they were to believe in God
and the last day, and spend
in charity from what God
has provided them?
For God Knows all that they do.

40 God does not wrong anyone
even by the weight of an atom.
If there is any good done,
He doubles it, and He grants
from Himself a great reward.

41 How will it be when We bring
from each people a witness,
and We bring you, Prophet,
as a witness
against these people?

42 On that day, those who
disbelieved and disobeyed
the Prophet will wish
the earth had swallowed them,
but they will never hide
anything from God.

SECTION 7

43 You who believe,
do not come to prayer

intoxicated, but wait until
you know what you are saying.
Nor come in a state
of major ritual impurity,
—unless traveling—until
you have washed yourselves.

If you are ill, or on a journey,
or one of you has answered
a call of nature, or has been
intimate with women, and you can
find no water, then perform
a ritual cleansing with pure soil,
wiping your faces and hands.
God is Ever Pardoning, Forgiving.

44 Have you not seen
those who were given
a portion of the Book
trafficking in error,
wanting you to go astray?

45 God best knows your enemies—
God is sufficient as
both Protector and Helper.

46 Among the Jews are some
who distort the contexts of words,
saying, "We hear and disobey" or
"Hear without hearing" or
"Attend to us," twisting them
with their tongues
and defaming the religion.°

If they had said "We hear and obey"
and "Hear and attend to us,"
it would have been better for them

and more fitting, but God
has cursed them for their disbelief,
for only a few of them believe.

47 You who were given the Book,
believe in what We have now revealed,
confirming what you already have,
before we erase your faces,
turning them backward,
or curse you, as We cursed
those who broke the Sabbath—
God's command is always fulfilled.

48 God does not forgive
the joining of other gods with Him,
but He forgives anything else
for whom He will. And whoever
joins other gods with God
contrives a great sin.

49 Have you not seen those
who claim to purify themselves?
No, it is God who purifies
whom He will; and they
will not be wronged
by even the hair's width
on a date stone.°

50 See how they contrive
a lie about God—
and this itself amounts
to a blatant sin.

SECTION 8

51 Have you not seen those
who were given a portion

of the Book believing
in sorcery and false gods,
and saying that the disbelievers
are better guided on the right path
than the believers?

52 These are the ones
God has cursed.
And you will find
for whoever is cursed by God
none to help them.

53 Or, do they have a share
in His kingdom? Even then,
they would give to people
not even the pith of a date seed.

54 Or do they envy people
for what God has given them
from His grace? But We gave
the people of Abraham
the Book and wisdom,
and We granted them
a great kingdom.

55 Among them, some believed in it,
while others turned away from it.
But hell will suffice as a blazing fire.

56 Soon We shall cast into fire
those who deny Our signs—
whenever their skins
are burned away, We shall
replace these, so they
taste more torment.
God is Almighty, All Wise.

57 But those who believe
and do good deeds,
We shall bring into gardens,
with rivers flowing beneath,
to live there forever,
with pure companions, and
We shall bring them into
shade within shade.

58 God commands you to repay
your trusts to their owners,
and when you judge between
    people,
judge with justice.
Excellent is the advice
God gives you in this—
God is All Hearing, All Seeing.

59 You who believe, obey God
and obey the messenger and those
in authority among you.
If you disagree among yourselves
in anything, refer it
to God and the messenger,
if you believe
in God and the last day—
that is best and most fitting
as the final recourse.

SECTION 9

60 Have you not seen those
who claim to believe in
what was revealed to you and
what was revealed to those
before you, yet wish
to refer judgment to false gods,

though commanded to deny them?
Satan would lead them far astray.

61 And when they are told,
"Come to what God has revealed,
and to the messenger,"
you see the hypocrites turning
away from you, in aversion.

62 When calamity befalls them
—through their own deeds—
how they come to you, swearing
by God, "We wanted merely
to do what was good and
bring about mutual accord."

63 God well knows what is in
the hearts of these people, so turn
away from them, and advise them,
using words that reach
their inmost selves.

64 Any messenger that We sent
was to be obeyed, by God's leave.
If only they came to you, Prophet,
when they had wronged
    themselves,
seeking God's forgiveness,
and the messenger had asked
forgiveness for them—
they would have found God
Ever Relenting, Ever Merciful.

65 No, by your Lord,
they will not believe
until they secure you as judge
in their disputes

and find in themselves
no disquiet about what
you decide, yielding to it,
with full submission.

66 If We had enjoined them
to lay down their lives
or leave their homes,
only a few of them
would have complied.
But had they done
what they were advised to do,
that would have been
better for them, and would have
strengthened them.

67 And then We, from Our grace,
would have given them
a great reward;

68 and We would have
guided them to a straight path.

69 Those who obey God
and the messenger
are in the company of those
whom God has favored
among the prophets,
the truthful, the martyrs,
the doers of good—
noble companions.

70 This is the favor from God,
and God is ample in Knowing.

SECTION 10

71 You who believe,
   take due precautions [in war],
   and advance either in units
   or all together.

72 Yes, there is among you
   the straggler, who says,
   when adversity strikes you,
   "God has favored me
   for I was not there with them."

73 But if good fortune came to you
   from God, he would say
   —as though no affection ever stood
   between you and him—
   "I wish I'd been there with them,
   I would have had great success."

74 Let those fight in the path of God
   who trade the life of this world
   for the hereafter.
   And whoever fights in the path of God
   —whether killed or victorious—
   We shall grant him a great reward.

75 And why should you not fight
   in the path of God
   and of those who are weak
   —men, women, children—
   who cry out, "Our Lord,
   deliver us from this town,
   whose people are tyrants,
   and grant us from Your grace° a
      protector,
   and also from Your grace a helper"?

76 Those who believe fight in the path
      of God,
   and those who disbelieve fight in the
      path of false gods.
   So fight against the allies of Satan.
   Feeble, indeed, are the wiles of Satan.

SECTION 11

77 Have you not seen those who
   were told, "Hold back from fighting,
   to observe prayer and give in
      charity"?
   Then, when commanded to fight,
   a group of them feared people
   as much as—or more than—
   they feared God, and they implored,
   "Our Lord, why did You command
   us to fight? Why did You not grant us
   reprieve for a while?"
   Say, "Enjoyment of the world is brief,
   and the hereafter is better for those
   who fear God—you will not
   be wronged by the hair's width
   on a date seed."

78 "Death will find you,
   wherever you are, even
   if you were in high towers."

   If some good comes to them,
   they say, "This is from God,"
   and if harm comes to them,
   they say, "This is from you, Prophet."
   Tell them, "All is from God."
   Why can these people scarcely
   grasp plain speech?

79 Whatever good comes to you
is from God,
and whatever harm comes to you
is from yourself.
And We sent you, Prophet,
as a messenger to humankind—
God suffices as Witness.

80 Whoever obeys the messenger
is obeying God. As for whoever
turns away—we have not sent you,
Prophet, to be their guardian.

81 They say they obey you,
but when they leave you,
a group of them scheme by night
against what you say. But God
records what they scheme.
So turn away from them
and place your trust in God,
for God suffices as Guardian.

82 Do they not ponder the Qur'an?
Had it been from anyone but God,
they would have found
much incoherence in it.

83 When any news reaches them
concerning security or causing
alarm,
they spread it abroad.
Had they referred it
to the messenger, and those
in authority among them,
these would have known
how to appraise it.
Were it not for God's Favor

to you, and His Mercy,
all but a few of you
would have followed Satan.

84 So fight in the path of God.
You need answer only for yourself,
and urge on the believers; perhaps
God will curb the force
of the disbelievers.
For God is sturdier in force
and sturdier in chastisement.

85 Whoever pleads for a good cause
will gain from it, and
whoever pleads for an evil cause,
will lose from it. For God
is Sustainer of all things.

86 Whenever you are graced
with a greeting, meet it
with one sweeter, or
repeat it. God is Reckoner
of each thing.

87 God—there is no god but He.
He will surely bring you, gathered,
to the day of resurrection,
of which there is no doubt—and who
speaks with greater truth than God?

SECTION 12

88 Believers, why are you
divided about the hypocrites,
when God has curbed them
for what they have done?
Do you wish to guide those

whom God has allowed to stray?
You can never find a way for them.°

89 They would have you disbelieve
as they disbelieve, so that you
will be like them.
So don't take allies from them
until they migrate to the path
of God. But if they renege,
seize them and slay them
wherever you find them,
and do not take from them
any ally or helper—

90 except those who join a group
that has a treaty with you,
or those who approach you
with hearts hesitant to fight you
or to fight their own people.

Had God willed, He could
have empowered them over you
and they would have fought you.
So if they withdraw from you,
don't fight them. And should they
offer you peace, then God
gives you no cause against them.

91 You will find others
who seek to be safe from you
and from their own people.
But when tempted to attack
again, they plunge into it.
If they don't withdraw from you,
offer peace, and restrain themselves,
seize them and slay them
wherever you encounter them.

We have given you
a clear mandate against them.

SECTION 13

92 A believer should never kill
another believer, except in error.
Whoever kills a believer in error
should free a believing slave,
and pay due indemnity
to his family, unless, charitably,
they waive it. If the victim
belonged to a hostile people,
and was a believer, it is enough
to free a believing slave.
But if he belonged to a people
with whom you have a treaty,
then pay due indemnity
to his family, and
free a believing slave.
Let those unable to do this
fast for two straight months,
turning in repentance to God,
for God is All Knowing, All Wise.

93 Anyone who kills a believer
willfully will have hell
as their recompense, to dwell
there forever, with God's wrath
and curse upon them—
God has prepared for them
a great punishment.

94 You who believe, when you
venture out in the cause of God,
be cautious [in telling friend from
    foe],

and don't say to one who greets you
with peace, "You are no believer"
—seeking the fleeting goods
of worldly life—for God
has abundant treasures.

You yourselves were like this
before God showed favor to you.
So, be scrupulous, for God
is Aware of all that you do.

95 The believers who remain behind
—excepting the disabled—
are not equal to those striving
in the cause of God, with their
    wealth
and their lives. God grants
a higher rank to those who so strive
over those who remain.
God has promised good for all,
but He will favor those who strive
over those who remain, with
a great reward,

96 conferring on them exalted rank,
forgiveness and mercy. For God
is Forgiving, Ever Merciful.

SECTION 14

97 When the angels take the lives
of those who wrong themselves,
they will ask,
"What was your plight?"
The wrongdoers will reply,
"We were downtrodden on earth."
The angels will respond,

"Was God's earth not wide enough
for you to find refuge?"
Such people will find their abode
in hell—an evil end—

98 except those who were
indeed downtrodden
—men, women, and children—
with no means and no guidance
to find a way out.

99 Perhaps God will pardon
such people, for He
is Ever Pardoning, Forgiving.

100 Whoever forsakes his home
for God's path will find on earth
many a refuge—and abundance;
and whoever forsakes his home
fleeing toward God and His
    Prophet,
and then is overtaken by death,
shall find his due reward from God,
for God is Forgiving, Ever Merciful.

SECTION 15

101 When you travel in the land
you incur no blame if you
shorten your prayers, fearing
that the disbelievers might
attack you—the disbelievers
are your open enemies.

102 And when you, Prophet,
are among the believers, and
stand to lead them in prayer,

let one group stand with you,
retaining their arms, and
when they finish bowing in prayer,
let them move behind you,
while another group comes forward
to pray with you, using due
   vigilance,
their arms with them.

The disbelievers hope you might
neglect your arms and baggage,
so they might assault you in a
single strike. But there's no blame
if, hampered by rain or illness,
you lay down your arms.
But be vigilant.
God has prepared for the
   disbelievers
a disgraceful punishment.

103 Even after finishing prayer,
keep remembering God,
whether standing, sitting,
or lying on your sides.
And when you feel secure,
resume regular prayer—
prayer is enjoined for believers
at appointed times.

104 And don't falter
in pursuing the enemy.
Though you suffer,
they too suffer like you—
but you have hope in God,
while they have none.
God is All Knowing, All Wise.

SECTION 16

105 We have sent down
to you the Book with the truth
that you might use
what God has shown you
to judge between people—
so do not plead for those
who are treacherous.

106 But seek forgiveness
from God, for God is
Forgiving, Ever Merciful.

107 And do not plead for
those who betray themselves—
for God does not love
the treacherous, the sinful.

108 They try to hide from people,
but they can't hide from God,
for He is with them
when they conspire by night
using words He finds
   displeasing—
God Encompasses all that they do.

109 Here you are, believers,
pleading for them,
in the life of this world—
but who will plead for them to God,
on the day of resurrection?
Who will be their defender?

110 Yet whoever does evil
or wrongs himself, then
seeks forgiveness from God,

shall find God Forgiving,
Ever Merciful.

111   And whoever reaps sin
reaps it for himself—
God is All Knowing, All Wise.

112   But whoever reaps
a wrong or sin, and foists it
on an innocent person
will burden himself
with slander and blatant sin.

SECTION 17

113   Without God's favor to you,
and His mercy, a party of them
would have resolved
to lead you astray. But they
lead only themselves astray,
and cannot harm you in any way,
since God has sent to you the Book
and wisdom, teaching you
what you did not know—
God's favor to you is great.

114   There's no virtue
in most of their furtive talk—unless
one of them enjoins charity,
    kindness,
or harmony between people.
To anyone who does this, seeking
to please God, We shall grant
a great reward.

115   But those who oppose
the messenger, after clear guidance
has come to them, and follow

some other path than that
of the believers, We'll let them follow
what they have chosen—and We shall
burn them in hell—an evil end.

SECTION 18

116   God will not forgive
the joining of other gods with Him,
but He will forgive all else
for whom He pleases.
Whoever joins other gods
with the One God
has wandered far astray.

117   Instead of calling on God,
the polytheists call on goddesses°—
and they call on none
but a rebellious Satan.

118   God cursed him, and Satan said,
"I will take a due quota of your
    servants;

119   "and I *will* lead them astray,
and excite vain desires in them,
and command them to slit the ears
of cattle, and command them
to deface God's creation."

Whoever takes Satan as protector
instead of God
shall suffer glaring loss.

120   Satan makes them promises,
and incites vain desires in them—
but he promises nothing
but delusion.

121 [His followers] shall
have their dwelling in hell,
from which they shall find no
escape.

122 But We shall admit those
who believe and do good deeds
into gardens, with rivers flowing
beneath, dwelling there forever—
the true promise of God. For who
speaks with greater truth than God?

123 Your desires [carry no weight]
nor those of the people of the Book—
whoever does evil shall be
requited for it, and they shall find
no protector or helper besides God.

124 We shall admit into the garden
whoever does good deeds and
believes
—whether male or female—
and they shall not be wronged
by even the breadth of hair
on a date seed.

125 Who is better in religion than
one who submits his entire self
to God, does what is good,
and follows the creed of Abraham,
the pure in faith?°
For God held Abraham as friend.

126 To God belongs
all that is in the heavens and
all that is on the earth—
God Encompasses all things.

SECTION 19

127 They ask you, Prophet,
for your ruling on women. Say,
"God gives the ruling on them—[see]
what is recited to you in the Book
concerning orphan girls whom
you wish to marry, while withholding
their prescribed shares. [God also
gives you the ruling concerning]
children who are helpless: you should
uphold justice for orphans—God
is Aware of whatever good you do.

128 If a wife fears ill conduct
or desertion by her husband,
neither of them will be culpable
if they reach a mutual agreement,
for this is better.°
People are prone to avarice,
but if you do good deeds
and are mindful of Him,
God is Aware of what you do.

129 You will never be able
to deal justly between wives,
however much you may want to.
But don't incline altogether
toward one of them, leaving the other
in abeyance.° If you reconcile,
and are mindful of Him,
God is Forgiving, Ever Merciful.

130 But if they separate,
God will enrich them
from his expanse, for
God is Expansive, All Wise.

131 To God belongs
all that is in the heavens and
all that is on the earth.
We enjoined those
given the Book before you,
as We enjoin you,
to be mindful of God,
but if you disbelieve—still
to Him belongs
all that is in the heavens and
all that is on the earth.
God is Self-Sustaining,
Ever Worthy of Praise.

132 To God belongs
all that is in the heavens and
all that is on the earth. He
suffices as Guardian of all trust.

133 People, if He willed it,
He could remove you,
and replace you with others—
such is His Power.

134 If any desires a worldly reward,
[know that] the reward
of this world and of the hereafter
are both from God—for God
is All Hearing, All Seeing.

SECTION 20

135 You who believe, uphold justice,
as witnesses for God,
even if this proves to be
against yourselves or parents
or kin, whether rich or poor,
for God is closer to both.
Desist from your own desires
that you might behave
justly. If you distort
or turn away from justice,
God is Aware of all that you do.

136 You who believe,
believe in God and His messenger,
and the Book He revealed
to His messenger,
and the Book He revealed before.
Whoever denies God, his angels,
His Books, His messengers,
and the day of reckoning
has gone far astray.

137 God will not forgive
those who believe,
then disbelieve, then
believe again, then
disbelieve again, then
grow in unbelief—
nor will He guide them
to the right path.

138 Tell these hypocrites that they
shall face a painful punishment.

139 As for those who take
disbelievers as allies rather than
believers: is it power they seek
through them? All power
belongs to God alone.

140 He has revealed to you in the Book
that if you hear the verses of God
being denied or mocked [by people],
don't sit with them unless
they turn to some other discourse,
for then you would be like them.
God will gather the hypocrites and
disbelievers all together—in hell.

141 These are the ones who wait on you
[for the outcome of battle],
and if God gives you victory,
they say, "Weren't we with you?"
But if disbelievers make some gain,
they say, "Didn't we have the edge
over you, yet defend you
from the believers?"
But God shall judge between you
on the day of reckoning,
and He shall never grant
    disbelievers
the means of defeating
those who believe.

SECTION 21

142 The hypocrites seek
to deceive God, but it is He
Who will render them deceived.
When they stand in prayer,
they stand shiftlessly, merely
to be seen of people, and little
do they remember God—

143 wavering, between
this and that, for neither

this side nor the other—
You will never find a way
for those whom God leaves astray.

144 You who believe, don't take
disbelievers over believers as allies.
Would you give God
clear proof against yourselves?

145 The hypocrites shall be
in the lowest depths of fire,
and you shall never find
anyone to help them;

146 except for those who repent,
amend themselves, and hold fast
to God, sincere to Him in faith.
They shall be with the believers—
to whom God will grant
a great reward.

147 Why would God punish you
if you are grateful and believe?
For God is Appreciative, All
    Knowing.

148 God dislikes the mentioning
of bad deeds in public, except by
someone who has been wronged;
and God is All Hearing, All Knowing.

149 Whether you reveal
a good deed or conceal it,
or pardon an evil deed—
know that God is Pardoning,
All Powerful.

150 As for those who deny God
     and his messengers, and wish to
     distinguish between God
     and His messengers, saying,
     "We believe in some but deny others,
     and seek a middle way"—

151 they are really disbelievers,
     and We have prepared for them
     a disgraceful punishment.

152 We shall soon grant
     their rewards to those who believe
     in God and His messengers,
     and make no distinction
     among any of them—for God
     is Forgiving, Ever Merciful.

SECTION 22

153 The people of the Book
     ask you to send down to them
     a book from heaven.
     They asked of Moses more
     than this, when they said:
     "Show us God—openly."
     A thunderbolt struck them
     for their offense.° Then,
     they took the calf for worship
     even after clear signs
     had come to them.
     Still, We pardoned them for this,
     and gave Moses clear authority.

154 And We raised Mount Sinai,
     towering over them,
     as they took their pledge,

and We said to them:
"Enter the gate,° prostrating," and
"Do not profane the Sabbath"—
We took from them a solemn pledge.

155 Then We punished them
     for breaking their pledge,
     for denying the signs of God, and
     for killing the prophets wrongfully,
     and for saying, "Our hearts
          are covered"°
     —no, God has sealed them
     in their disbelief;
     so little do they believe—

156 and for their disbelief, and for
     speaking great slander
          against Mary,

157 as well as for saying,
     "We killed Jesus the messiah,
     son of Mary, messenger of God."
     But they did not kill him
     or crucify him, though it appeared
     to them as such.° And those who differ
     on this are full of doubt about it,
     with no knowledge beyond
     the fancies they follow. Assuredly,
     they did not kill him—

158 no—God raised him up to Himself,°
     for God is Almighty, All Wise.

159 And there's not one
     among the people of the Book
     who before death will not
     believe in Jesus°—and on

the day of resurrection
he will be a witness against them.

160 For all these wrongs of the Jews,
We made unlawful certain
    good things
formerly lawful for them,
and for barring people
often from the path of God—

161 and for taking up usury,
which was forbidden to them,
and for wrongfully devouring
the property of people.
We have prepared a painful torment
for the disbelievers among them.

162 However, We shall grant
a great reward to those
firmly rooted in knowledge
among them and the believers,
who believe in what was
revealed to you, and what was
revealed before you;
who are steadfast in prayer,
who give in charity, and
who believe in God
and the last day.

SECTION 23

163 We inspired revelation in you
as We inspired Noah
and the prophets after him.
We also inspired Abraham,
    Ishmael,
Isaac, Jacob, and the tribes,

as well as Jesus, Job, Jonah, Aaron,
and Solomon. And to David
We gave the Psalms.

164 We inspired some messengers
whom We have mentioned
to you before, and others
whom We have not mentioned.
And God spoke directly to Moses.

165 Those messengers were
bearers of joyous news and warning,
so that after them, humankind
should have no alibi before God—
for God is Almighty, All Wise.

166 God Himself bears witness
to the truth He has revealed to you:
He revealed it to you
with His knowledge.°
And the angels too bear witness,
though God suffices as Witness.

167 Those who disbelieve
and bar others from the path of God
have gone far astray.

168 God shall not forgive those
who disbelieve and do wrong,
nor shall He direct them to any path,

169 except the path to hell,
to dwell there forever—
this is easy for God.

170 Humankind, the messenger
has come to you with the truth

from your Lord. It's better
that you believe—for even
if you disbelieve, it is to God
that all in the heavens and earth
belongs; and God
is All Knowing, All Wise.

171 People of the Book,
don't be excessive in your religion,
nor speak anything
but the truth about God.

The messiah, Jesus, son of Mary,
was but a messenger of God—
His Word, conveyed to Mary,
through His spirit.° So believe
in God and His messengers,
and refrain from talk of "trinity"—
restraint will be better for you.

God is the One God, glorified
far above the begetting of any son.
To Him belongs
all that is in the heavens
and all that is on the earth;
and God suffices as Guardian.

SECTION 24

172 The messiah would never spurn
serving God, nor would
the angels close to Him.
He will gather
those who spurn His worship,
those who are proud,
before Him—all of them.

173 He will grant a full reward
to those who believe
and do good deeds, giving them
ever more from His grace.
But He will give painful torment°
to those who are disdainful, proud—
they shall not find any protector
or any helper besides God.

174 Humankind, conclusive proof
has come to you from your Lord,
and We have revealed to you
a Light supremely clear.

175 So, God will admit
into His Mercy and grace
those who believe in Him
and hold fast to Him;
and He will guide them
to Himself on a straight path.°

176 They will ask you, Prophet,
for a ruling. Say, "God gives
the ruling concerning inheritance
[for one with neither parents
nor offspring]:°

If a man dies, leaving a sister
but no child, she shall receive
half of what he leaves.

If she dies leaving no child,
her brother will inherit
everything from her.

If there are two sisters,
they shall have two-thirds
between them of what he leaves.

But if there are brothers and sisters,
the male shall get twice
the share of the female.

God makes this clear for you,
so you do not fall into error—
for God Knows all things.

SURA 5

The Table Spread (Al-Ma'ida)

Middle and late Medinan, this sura numbers 120 verses. "The Table" refers to the table of the Last Supper (v. 114), here sent down from heaven as a sign of Jesus' prophethood. It includes numerous regulations for believers, from injunctions and affirmations to prohibitions and exceptions. It also condemns certain pagan practices, while calling out Jewish rejection of the Prophet's message and Christian error in ascribing partners to God. Near the end, Jesus is lauded for recognizing that he does not know what God knows—"Knower of all that is unseen" (v. 116).

In the Name of God, the All Merciful, Ever Merciful

SECTION I

1 You who believe,
honor your obligations:
it is lawful for you to use
livestock animals for food
except those cited below.
It is not lawful to hunt
while you are on pilgrimage.
God decrees what He will.

2 You who believe,
don't violate the sanctity
of the rites of God,
nor those of the sacred month,
nor of the animals garlanded
for sacrifice,°
nor of those arriving

at the Sacred House,°
striving for the grace
and pleasure of their Lord.

But when you are finished
with the pilgrimage,
you may resume hunting.
And don't let hatred of those who
barred you from the sacred
   mosque
incite you to transgress.

Help one another
to be righteous,
to be mindful of God,
and not to sin and transgress.
Be mindful of God,
for God is Severe in Retribution.°

3 Forbidden to you are carrion,
  blood, and the flesh of swine,
  and anything killed invoking
  some other name than God's,
  as well as anything that has died
  by strangling, beating, falling, or
  being gored, or being eaten
  by a beast of prey—unless
  you can kill it [in the correct way]—
  or what is sacrificed on stone altars,
  or divided by divining arrows,°
  which is grave impiety.

  This day, those who disbelieve
  have despaired of [making you
  abandon] your religion,
  so do not fear them but fear Me.
  This day I have perfected
  your religion for you, and
  I have completed My favor to you,
  and I have chosen as your religion
  submission to My will.°
  But if someone is constrained
  by hunger [to eat what's unlawful],
  without meaning to sin—
  they will find God Forgiving, Ever
    Merciful.

4 They ask you what is lawful
  for them. Say, "It's lawful for you
  to eat things that are good and pure,
  and the things you've taught
  your hunting animals [to catch],
  as God has taught you.
  So eat what they catch for you,
  pronouncing God's Name on it,
  and be mindful of God—
  God is Swift in Reckoning."

5 This day all good things
  have been made lawful for you.
  The food of those given the Book°
  is lawful for you, and
  yours is lawful for them.

  Also lawful are chaste women
  among the believers and among
  those given the Book before you—
  provided you give them their
    dowries,
  as chaste men, with no lewdness,
  not taking them as lovers.

  The work of those who deny faith
  will be in vain—and in the
    hereafter,
  they will be among those in loss.

SECTION 2

6 You who believe,
  before you stand in prayer,
  wash your faces and your arms
  to the elbow, and wipe your heads,
  and wash your feet to the ankles.

  If you're in a condition
  of major ritual impurity,
  purify yourselves by ritual bathing.
  And if you're ill
  or on a journey, or if any of you
  have just relieved yourselves or
  had contact with women
  and do not find water, then
  find for yourself clean sand
  and wipe your faces with it
  and your hands.

God does not want hardship for
    you;
rather, He intends to purify you
and to complete His favor to you,
that you might be grateful.

7 And remember God's favor to you
   and the pledge he took from you
   when you declared, "We hear and
       obey."
   And be mindful of God, for He
       Knows
   what your hearts enclose.

8 You who believe, be steadfast for God,
   as witnesses for justice,
   and don't allow hatred of anyone
   to stop you from acting justly.
   Be just—for that is close to piety.
   And be mindful of God,
   for He is Aware of all that you do.

9 God has promised
   forgiveness and a great reward
   for those who believe
   and do good deeds.

10 Those who disbelieve
   and deny Our signs
   shall be inmates of hellfire.

11 You who believe, remember
   the favor God showed you,
   when a certain people schemed°
   to raise their hands against you,
   and He restrained them.
   So be mindful of God,
   and let the believers trust in God.

SECTION 3

12 God made a covenant
   with the children of Israel,
   and We appointed from them
   twelve captains. And God said,
   "I am with you, if you are steadfast
   in prayer, practice charity, and
   believe in my messengers,
   honoring them, and if you
   lend to God a beautiful loan;°
   then I will expiate your bad deeds,
   and admit you into gardens
   beneath which rivers flow.
   But whoever disbelieves after this
   has strayed from the right path."

13 But because they broke the
       covenant,
   We cursed them and made hard
       their hearts.
   They distort the context of words,
   and forget part of the message
       recalled to them.

   Nor will you cease to find treachery
   among all but a few of them.
   But pardon them,
   and overlook their misdeeds,
   for God loves those who do good.

14 And We made a covenant
   with those who say,
   "We are Christians," but they forgot
   part of the message recalled to them,
   so We aroused among them
   enmity and hatred,
   until the day of resurrection—

then God shall inform them
of all that they have done.

15 People of the Book,
Our messenger has come to you,
making clear many things
that you concealed in the Book,
and overlooking many errors.
A new light has come to you
from God—and a clarifying Book—

16 by which God guides
those who seek to please Him
to the paths of peace.
He leads them
out of darkness into light,
by His leave; and He guides them
to a straight path.

17 Those who proclaim,
"God is the messiah, son of Mary"
are disbelievers. Say,
"Who would have any power
against God if He wished to destroy
the messiah, son of Mary, and
his mother, and all upon the earth?"

To God belongs dominion
over the heavens and the earth
and all that lies between them.
He creates what He will—
God has Power over all things.

18 Jews and Christians both claim,
"We are the children of God,
and loved by Him."

Say, "Why then does He
punish you for your sins?
No—you are merely human beings,
from among those He created.
He forgives whom He will,
and punishes whom He will."

To God belongs dominion
over the heavens and the earth
and all that lies between them.
And to Him is the final return.

19 People of the Book,
Our messenger has come to you,
clarifying things for you
—after a pause in the line
of messengers—so that you
don't claim, "No one came to us
bearing joyous news or warning."
Now, someone *has* come to you
with good news and warning—
for God has Power over all things.

SECTION 4

20 When Moses said to his people,
"My people, remember the favor
God showed you,
when He placed prophets among
   you,
and made you kings, and gave you
what He had not given
to any people in all the world;

21 "my people, enter the holy land,
which God has ordained for you,

and do not turn your backs
for you will then return as losers,"

22 they said, "Moses, a tyrannical
          people
     live in that land, and we will never
          enter it
     until they leave. If they leave it,
     then we will enter."°

23 Then two of the God-fearing men,
     whom God had favored, said,
     "Attack them at the gate—
     once you enter, you will be
          victorious.
     So trust in God, if you are true
          believers."

24 They said, "Moses, we won't enter it
     while they remain there.
     So go, you and your Lord, both—
     and fight, while we stay here."

25 He said, "My Lord,
     I have control only over
     myself and my brother,
     so set us apart in Your sight
     from this disobedient people."

26 God said, "This land
     shall be forbidden to them
     for forty years. They shall wander
     upon the earth, aimless—
     so do not grieve over
     this disobedient people."

SECTION 5

27 Tell them the actual story
     of the two sons of Adam—
     when they both offered a sacrifice.
     It was accepted of one of them
     but not of the other, who said,
     "I'll kill you." The first replied,
     "God accepts sacrifice only
     from those who are mindful
          of Him.

28 "If you raise your hand to kill me,
     I will not raise my hand against you,
          for
     I fear God, Lord of the universe.

29 "I would have you bring upon
          yourself
     my sin as well as yours
     so you'll be among the inmates of
          the fire—
     the reward of wrongdoers."

30 Still, the other sibling's soul
     prompted him to kill his brother—
     now,° he was one of those in loss.

31 Then God sent a raven,
     which scratched the ground
     to show him how to cover
     the dead body of his brother.
     He said, "Alas! Could I not
     have been like this raven
     and covered my brother's body?"
     And he was filled with remorse.

32 On that account, We decreed
for the children of Israel—
if anyone kills a person
—other than for murder or
sowing corruption in the land°—
it will be as if he had killed
all humankind; and if anyone
saves a life, it will be as if he
had saved all humankind.

Our messengers came to them
with clear signs, but even after this,
many among them were
transgressors in the land.

33 The retribution for those
who wage war against God and
his messenger and strive to spread
corruption through the land
is that they be killed or crucified
or their hands and feet cut off
on alternate sides—or that they be
exiled from the land.
Such is their disgrace in this world,
and in the hereafter
they shall face great torment,

34 except for those who repent
before you prevail against them;
know, then, that God
is Forgiving, Ever Merciful.

SECTION 6

35 You who believe,
be mindful of God
and seek the means

to come closer to Him,
and strive in His way,
that you might flourish.

36 As for those who disbelieve,
if they had all that is on the earth,
and twice that, to offer as ransom
for their punishment on the day of
resurrection,
it would not be accepted of them—
they shall face painful torment.

37 They will want to come out of the
fire,
but they shall not escape it,
for they shall face enduring torment.

38 As for the thief—male and female—
cut off their hands:
the recompense they earned—
an example, from God—
for God is Almighty, All Wise.

39 But God will relent, pardoning
those who repent after their crime,
reforming themselves—
for He is Forgiving, Ever Merciful.

40 Do you not know:
to God belongs dominion over
the heavens and the earth?
He punishes whom He will
and He forgives whom He will—
for God has Power over all things.

41 Messenger, don't be grieved
by those who hasten to unbelief—

those who say with their mouths,
"We believe," while their hearts
disbelieve; or those Jews
who listen to falsehood, or to others
who have not come to you [for a
    ruling].

They distort words from
their contexts, and they say,
"If you are given this ruling,
take it, but if not, then beware."°
You have no sway with God
on behalf of those He would test.

They are the ones whose hearts
God has no desire to purify.
They shall be disgraced in this
    world,
and they shall face great torment
in the hereafter—

42 those who listen to lies and
consume what is proscribed.
If they come to you,
judge between them or
turn away from them.
If you turn away,
they can't harm you at all.
And if you do judge, then
judge between them justly—
God loves those who are just.

43 Yet why do they appoint you
as judge when they have their Torah
bearing God's judgment?
And even after this, they turn away,
for they are not true believers.

SECTION 7

44 We revealed the Torah
[to Moses], bearing guidance
and light—by this,
the prophets submissive to God's will
judged for the Jews,
as did the rabbis and the scholars,
by the Book of God
entrusted to their care, and to which
they bore witness.

So do not fear people,° but fear Me,
and do not sell My signs
for a paltry price.

As for those who do not judge
by what God has revealed—
they are the unbelievers.

45 In the Torah We told them,
a life for a life, an eye for an eye,
nose for nose, tooth for tooth,
and fair requital for any wound.
But those who forgo reprisal,
out of charity, will thereby atone
for their bad deeds.

As for those who do not judge
by what God has revealed—
they are wrongdoers.

46 In their footsteps, We sent Jesus,
son of Mary, verifying the Torah
that came before him;
We gave to him the Gospel,
bearing guidance and light,

verifying the Torah
that came before him—
guidance and counsel
for those mindful of God.

47 Let the followers
of the Gospel judge
by what God has revealed in it;
as for those who do not judge
by what God has revealed—
they are the disobedient.

48 And We revealed the Book,
with the truth, to you, Prophet,
verifying the earlier Book,
preserving it. So judge between
   them
by what God has revealed,
and do not follow their desires,
straying from the truth
that has come to you.

For each of you, We made a law
and a path. If God had willed,
He could have made you one people,
but He would test you
in what He has granted you:
so compete in good works.

All of you shall return to God—
He alone shall enlighten you
about the things you dispute.

49 So judge between them
by what God has revealed,
and do not follow their desires—
beware that they don't entice you
away from some of what

God has revealed to you.
And if they turn away, know that
God intends to scourge them
for some of their sins—
for most people are disobedient.

50 Do they seek a judgment
from the days of pagan ignorance?°
Who is better in judging than God
for a people of assured faith?

SECTION 8

51 You who believe, do not take
the Jews and Christians as allies—
they are allies of each other.
Whoever among you turns to them
belongs with them.
God does not guide a wrongful
   people.

52 You see those with sick hearts
hastening to them, saying
"We fear a turn of fortune."
But God may bring you victory,
or a ruling from Himself—
then they will regret what
they hid within themselves.

53 And those who believe
will say, "Are these the ones
who swore the strongest oaths by God
that they were with you?"
All their deeds have been in vain
and they are now the losers.

54 You who believe, if any of you
turn away from their faith, then

God will replace you with a people
whom He loves and who love Him—
humble toward believers, and
robust against disbelievers,
striving in the path of God, not
fearing reproach from anyone.
This is the grace of God, which
He brings to those whom He will,
for God is Expansive, All Knowing.

55 Your allies are God,
His messenger, and the believers
who are steadfast in prayer
and charity, bowing [in worship].

56 The party of God
—those who turn to God,
His messenger, and the believers—
shall be victorious.

SECTION 9

57 You who believe,
do not take as allies those
who take your religion
in jest and sport, among those
who were given the Book
before you and the unbelievers.
Rather, be mindful of God
if you are true believers.

58 When you voice the call to prayer,
they take it in jest and sport—
for they are people void of reason.

59 Say, "People of the Book,
do you resent us just because
we believe in God,

in what was revealed to us
and what was revealed before,
while most of you are disobedient?"

60 Say, "Shall I tell you
who deserved a punishment
worse than this from God?
Those whom God cursed,
His wrath falling on them,
some of whom He turned
into apes and swine,
and who worshipped false gods.
They have an even worse rank
and have strayed farther
from the even path."

61 When they come to you,
they say, "We believe."
But really they enter and leave
in a state of disbelief—and
God knows best what they conceal.

62 And you see many of them
hastening to sin and transgression,
and gorging on unlawful earnings.
How wicked their deeds have been!

63 Why do their rabbis and scholars
not forbid them from speaking sin
and gorging on unlawful earnings?
How wicked their works have been!

64 The Jews say,
"God's hand is chained"—
it is *their* hands that are chained
and they are cursed for what they
assert.

The hands of God are in fact
  outstretched
and He gives as He will.

Your Lord's revelations to you
intensify rebellion and unbelief
in most of them. We have cast
enmity and hatred among them
until the day of resurrection.

Whenever they fuel the fire of war
God extinguishes it. They strive
to sow corruption upon the earth—
and God dislikes those who do this.

65   Had the people of the Book
    believed and had they been mindful
    of God, We would have expiated
    their evil deeds and urged them
    into gardens of bliss.

66   If they had stood firm
    by the Torah and the Gospel
    and what was revealed to them
    from their Lord, then sustenance
    would have showered down on them
    from above, and risen from beneath
    their feet. Among them is a group
    on the right course, yet
    what many of them do is wicked.

SECTION 10

67   Messenger, proclaim all
    that has been revealed to you
    from your Lord—if you don't,
    you won't have conveyed

His message.
And God shall guard you
against people [who oppose you].
God does not guide
people who disbelieve.

68   Say, "People of the Book,
    you stand upon no ground, unless
    you stand firmly by the Torah
    and the Gospel and what was
    revealed to you from your Lord."

But what was revealed to you
from your Lord, Prophet, simply
  deepens
the rebellion and disbelief
of most of them—but do not grieve
over people who disbelieve.

69   Those who believe, including
    Jews, Sabians,° and Christians—
    all who believe in God
    and the last day
    and do good works—
    they shall not fear, nor grieve.

70   We made a covenant
    with the children of Israel,
    and We sent messengers to them.
    Whenever these brought to them
    directives not suiting their desires,
    they rejected some of them
    and killed others.

71   They thought there would be
    no trial—so they became
    blind and deaf.

Yet God turned to them [in mercy],
yet, again, many of them became
blind and deaf—
God Sees all that they do.

72 Those who say,
"God is the messiah, son of Mary"
disbelieve. For the messiah said,
"Children of Israel, worship God—
my Lord and your Lord."
God will bar from the garden those
who associate others with Him;
their home shall be the fire,
and there shall be none
to help the wrongdoers.

73 Those who say,
"God is the third in a trinity"
disbelieve. There is no god
beyond the One God, and if they
don't desist from saying this,
those of them who disbelieve
shall face painful torment.

74 So why don't they turn to God,
seeking His forgiveness?
For God is Forgiving, Ever Merciful.

75 The messiah, son of Mary,
was but a messenger, and before him
other messengers passed away.
His mother was a truthful woman;
they both ate food [like other
     mortals].
See how We make clear
Our signs [to people], and see
how deluded they are!

76 Say, "Do you worship
something other than God
which has the power
neither to do you harm or good?"
God is All Hearing, All Knowing.

77 Say, "People of the Book,
don't trespass, in your religion,
beyond the boundaries of truth.
And don't follow the desires of those
who went astray before
and led many others astray—those
who strayed from the even path."

SECTION II

78 The unbelievers among
the children of Israel were cursed
by the words of David and of Jesus,
son of Mary—for they disobeyed
and were always transgressing.

79 They would not forbid
one another from the iniquities
they committed. The things
they did were wicked.

80 You see many of them
turning to the unbelievers.
The deeds their souls
bring to their own account°
are wicked—God's wrath
falls upon them, and they
will dwell in torment forever.

81 If they had believed
in God and the Prophet

and what has been revealed to him,
they would not have taken
[the unbelievers] as allies.
But most of them are disobedient.

82 You'll find that, of all people,
the Jews and polytheists are
most hostile to the believers;
you'll find those who say,
"We are Christians" nearest
in love to the believers, for
among them are priests and monks
who are not filled with pride.

83 When they hear what
is revealed to the messenger,
you'll see their eyes brim with tears,
for they know the truth. They say,
"Our Lord, we believe, so record us
among the witnesses."

84 "Why would we not believe
in God and the truth that has
come to us? For we yearn
for our Lord to include us
among the righteous people."

85 And God has rewarded them
for what they say, with gardens
with rivers flowing beneath;
there they shall live forever—
that is the reward
of those who do good.

86 But those who disbelieve
and deny Our signs
shall be inmates of hellfire.

SECTION 12

87 You who believe,
do not forbid the good things
which God has made lawful for you,
and do not transgress—for God
does not love transgressors.

88 Eat of the lawful and good things
that God has given, and be mindful
of the One God in Whom you
believe.

89 God will not call you to account
for what you utter unthinkingly
in your oaths,
but He will call you to account
for the oaths you pledge solemnly.

To atone for breaking an oath,
you should feed ten needy people,
as you would feed your families,
or else clothe them, or free a slave.
Whoever finds this beyond their
means
should fast for three days.

This is the atonement for oaths
you have sworn. So keep your oaths.
In this way, God makes clear
His signs for you,
that you might be grateful.

90 You who believe—
wine, games of chance,
sacrifices at stone altars, and
arrows used for divining

are all an abomination—
the work of Satan.
So turn away from them,
that you may flourish.

91 Satan desires merely
to incite enmity and hate
between you, through wine
and games of chance, and
to impede you from
remembrance of God
and from prayer.
Will you not, then, refrain?

92 So, obey God, and obey
the messenger, and be wary;
and if you turn away, know that
Our messenger's task is only
to convey the message clearly.

93 Those who believe and
do good deeds will not be blamed
for what they ate in the past,
if they are mindful of God,
believe, and do good deeds;
then are still mindful of God
and believe;
then are still mindful of God
and do better deeds—
for God loves those who do good.

SECTION 13

94 You who believe, God will
test you through the game you hunt
with your hands and spears
that He may know who fears Him,

even though they cannot see Him;
and whoever transgresses after this
shall face painful torment.

95 You who believe, do not kill prey
while you are dressed as pilgrims.
Those of you who do so willfully
must compensate,
by bringing to the Ka'ba°
a domestic beast as an offering,
equivalent to what they killed,
as judged by two just men among
    you,
or, as atonement, by feeding
needy people or, instead,
by fasting—so that they may taste
the seriousness of their act.
God will pardon a past action,
but if anyone repeats it,
God will requite them,
for God is Almighty,
Lord of Requital.

96 It's lawful for you and travelers
to catch and eat prey from the sea,
but to hunt prey from the land
is unlawful for you while dressed
as pilgrims. And be mindful of God,
to Whom you will be gathered.

97 God made the Ka'ba,
the Sacred House, a secure haven
for humankind, as also
the sacred months, and the animals
for sacrifice, and the garlands—
all, so you might know that
God knows all that is in

the heavens and the earth,
and that God Knows all things.

98 Know also that
God is Severe in Retribution
yet He is Forgiving, Ever Merciful.

99 It is the messenger's task
only to convey the message;
for God knows all that you reveal,
and all that you conceal.

100 Say, "The good and the bad
are not equal, even though
the abundance of bad things
may please you.
So be mindful of God,
You who possess insight,
that you might flourish."

SECTION 14

101 You who believe,
don't ask about things [hidden]
which, if made clear, would grieve
   you.
But if you ask about them
when the Qur'an is revealed,
they will be made clear to you;
and God will pardon your asking,
for God is Forgiving, Forbearing.

102 People before you asked such
   questions
and ended up disbelieving.

103 It was not God who set up
the dedication to idols of

a slit-eared she-camel, nor
a she-camel freed to pasture, nor
a twin-bearing female, nor
a camel stallion freed to stud°—
but rather, those who disbelieve,
inventing a lie against God,
for most of them do not
make use of reason.

104 And when they are told,
"Embrace what God has revealed
to His messenger," they say,
"What our forefathers left us°
is quite sufficient for us."
Really? Even though their
   forefathers
knew nothing and were not guided?

105 You who believe, you are
accountable for your souls.
Those who stray can't harm you
if you are guided. To God
you will all be returned,
and He will inform you
of all that you have done.

106 You who believe, when death
approaches any one of you,
let two just men among you testify
when a will is being made,
or two others from outside
if you are traveling in the land
and happen to meet your death.
If you doubt [the two witnesses],
detain them both after prayer,
and let them both swear by God:
"We shall not sell our testimony,
even for a close relative, and

we shall not hide God's testimony,
for then we would be sinning."

107 But if it is perceived
that these two were guilty
of the sin [of perjury], let
them be replaced by two others
among those who are deemed
more worthy than the first two,
and let them swear by God:
"Our testimony is truer than
that of those two, and
we have not transgressed, for then
we would be doing wrong."

108 This will make them more likely
to give true evidence, or make them
wary that their oaths might be
countered by the oaths of others.
So be mindful of God, and listen—
for God does not guide
a disobedient people.

SECTION 15

109 On the day God gathers
the messengers together,
He will ask,
"How were you answered?"
They will respond,
"We do not know;
You alone Know the unseen."

110 And God will say,
"Jesus, son of Mary, remember
my favor to you and to your mother,
when I strengthened you
with the holy spirit;

you spoke to the people from
the cradle and in maturity, and when
I taught you the Book and wisdom,
the Torah and the Gospel, and when
you created from clay the form of a
    bird
by My leave—you breathed into it
and it became a bird,
by My leave;
and you healed the blind and the
    leper
by My leave;
and when you brought forth the dead
by My leave;
and when I held back from you
the children of Israel, when
you came to them with clear signs,
for the disbelievers among them
    said,
"This is clearly nothing but magic."

111 When I inspired the disciples
of Christ to believe in Me and
in My messenger, they proclaimed,
"We believe—bear witness
that we submit to God's will."

112 When the disciples said,
"Jesus, son of Mary, can your Lord
send down to us from heaven
a table spread with food?
He said, "Be mindful of God
if you are true believers."

113 They said, "We want to eat of it
and ease our hearts, and to know
that you have told us the truth,
so that we may be witnesses to it."

114 Jesus, son of Mary, said,
"O God, our Lord, send to us
from heaven a table spread
with food, as a festival
for the first of us and the last—
as a sign from You.
Provide for us—for You
are the Best of Providers."

115 God responded,
"I am sending it to you,
but I shall punish any of you
who disbelieves after that,
with a punishment such as
I have never imposed on anyone
in all the world."

SECTION 16

116 And when God asked,
"Jesus, son of Mary, did you say
to people, 'Take me and my mother
both as gods instead of God,'"
he will answer, "Glory be to You;
I would never say what I had no right
to say—if I had said it,
You would have known it. You know
what is within me, but I do not know
what is within You—Knower
of all that is unseen.

117 "I said to them only
what you commanded me to,
'Worship God, my Lord and
your Lord,' and I was a witness
to them while I was among them.
When You raised me up, You
were Watching over them, and You
are Witness to all things.

118 "If you punish them,
they are Your servants;
and if You forgive them—
You are the Almighty, All Wise."

119 God will say, "On this day,
the truthful shall benefit from
their truthfulness. They shall have
gardens with rivers flowing beneath;
there they shall live forever. God
shall be pleased with them, and they
with Him—the supreme triumph."

120 To God belongs dominion
over the heavens and the earth,
and all within them. And He
has Power over all things.

Cattle (*Al-An'am*)

Late Meccan with some Medinan additions, this sura numbers 165 verses. It refers to pre-Islamic practices about cattle sacrifice in vv. 138–46 but also offers strong directives about exclusive worship of the one God, ending with exemplary testimony from the Prophet (vv. 161–65).

In the Name of God, the All Merciful, Ever Merciful

SECTION I

1 All praise be to God
Who created the heavens and the
    earth,
Who made the darkness and the
    light—
yet those who disbelieve
ascribe equals to their Lord.

2 It is He Who created you from clay,
then decreed for you a term,
—then a fixed term with Him°—
yet still you are in doubt.

3 And He is God
in the heavens and the earth;
He knows what you conceal
and what you reveal—
He knows what you reap.

4 Yet no sign ever comes
to them from their Lord
but they turn away from it.

5 And so they denied the truth
when it came to them, but soon
the truth of what they ridiculed
shall fall upon them.

6 Don't they see the generations
We destroyed before them?
We had settled them on the earth
more securely than you;
We poured down on them
abounding rain from the sky,
and We made rivers
flow beneath them—but
We destroyed them for their sins,
and We brought forward
other generations after them.

7 Even if We sent you a Book
written on parchment, which
they could touch with their hands,
those who disbelieve would still say,
"This is nothing but plain sorcery."

8 And they ask, "Why isn't
an angel sent down to him?"
Had We sent an angel,

judgment would have been
pronounced on them°—then
they would have no respite.

9 Had We made him an angel,
We would have shaped him
in the form of a human—
furthering their confusion.

10 Messengers before you, Prophet,
were mocked, but those who
        scoffed
were engulfed by what they mocked.

SECTION 2

11 Say, "Wander through the earth
and see how things ended
for those who denied the truth."

12 Ask, "To whom belongs all
that is in the heavens and earth?
Answer, "To God.
He has pledged Himself
to showing mercy;°
He will gather you
on the day of resurrection—
which is beyond doubt;
but those who have lost their souls,
will not believe.

13 To Him belongs all that lives
by night and day—for He is
the All Hearing, All Knowing."

14 Say, "Shall I take as my protector
any but God, Maker of the heavens
and the earth, He Who feeds
and is not fed?" Say,
"I am commanded to be the first
of those who submit to God's will,
so don't *you* be among
those who join others with God."

15 Say, "If I disobeyed my Lord,
I would fear the torment
of a momentous day.

16 "Whoever is spared [torment]
that day—it is through God's
        mercy,
and that will be the clear victory."

17 If God touches you
with affliction, none but He
can remove it;
and if He touches you
with good—it is He
Who has Power over all things.

18 He is the Omnipotent, far above
His worshippers, and
He is the All Wise, All Aware.

19 Ask, "Whose witness carries
the greatest weight?"
Answer, "God is Witness between
        me and you;
and this Qur'an was revealed to me
that I might thereby warn you and
whomever else it reaches.
Can you bear witness that,
besides God, there is another god?"
Say, "I cannot." And say,

"He is the One God, and I disown
whatever you join with Him."

20 Those to whom We gave the Book
recognize it, as they recognize
their own children;
those who have lost themselves
do not believe.

SECTION 3

21 Who does more wrong than
those who invent a lie about God,
and deny His signs?
Those who do wrong shall not
    flourish.

22 One day We shall gather
them all together, then We shall say
to those who ascribed partners to
    Us:
"Where are the partners you
    claimed?"

23 Then, their only plea will be
to swear, "By God, Our Lord,
we did not ascribe partners to You."

24 See how they lie about themselves
and how the gods they invented
have abandoned them.

25 Among them are some who
seem to listen to you.
But We have placed
veils over their hearts—lest they
understand [the Qur'an]—

and deafness in their ears.
And even if they saw every sign,
they would not believe it,
so that, when they come to you,
they dispute with you.
The disbelievers say,
"These are nothing
but tales of the ancients."

26 And they withhold others
from the Qur'an—as they
    themselves
stay away from it; but they merely
bring about their own ruin,
without realizing it.

27 If you could see when they are
made to stand before the fire—
they will say, "If only
we could be sent back—
we would not deny the signs
of our Lord, and we would believe."°

28 No—the truth they used to hide
will become clear to them,
and if they were sent back,
they would just go back
to what was forbidden to them,
for they are liars.

29 They say, "There is nothing
beyond our life in this world,
and we shall not be resurrected."

30 If you could see when they
stand before their Lord—He will say,
"Is this not real?" They will answer,

"Yes, by our Lord." He will say,
"Taste, then, the punishment
for persisting in disbelief."

SECTION 4

31 Those who deny the meeting
with God are lost—until the hour
strikes suddenly, and they say,
"How sorry we are
that we did not heed it!"
For they'll bear their burdens on
their backs—a wicked burden!

32 What is the life of this world
but play and a pastime?
The home of the hereafter is better
for those who are mindful of God.
Will you not, then, use reason?

33 We know that what they say
grieves you, Prophet, but it's
not you they deny—it's the signs
of God the wrongdoers deny.

34 Indeed, messengers were denied
before you, and they bore
denial and injury patiently
until Our help came to them.
For none can alter the words of God—
you have received before now
accounts of the messengers.

35 If it is so hard on you, when they
turn away, what if you could seek
a tunnel in the earth
or a stairway toward the sky,

to bring them a sign?°
If God wished, He could gather
all of them to guidance; so do not
join those who are ignorant.

36 Only those who listen respond;
and God shall bring the dead to life—
then to Him they'll be brought back.

37 And they say, "Why is no sign
sent down to him from his Lord?"
Say, "God has the Power
to send a sign"; but most of them
don't know it.

38 All creatures on the earth,
and all birds that fly on their wings,
are communities,° like you.
We have overlooked nothing
in the Book—then, to their Lord
they shall be gathered.

39 Those who deny Our signs
are deaf and dumb, in darkness—
God allows whom He will to stray,
and He sets whom He will
on a straight path.

40 Say, "Think to yourselves,
if God's punishment or the hour
were to come to you, would you call
on any other besides God,
if what you say is true?"

41 You would call on Him alone;
if He wished, He would remove

the distress that made you call
on Him—and you would forget
the partners you joined with Him.

SECTION 5

42 Yes, We sent messengers
to many nations° before you,
striking them with adversity
and hardship, that they
might learn humility.

43 But when Our adversity
fell upon them, why didn't they
humble themselves? Rather,
their hearts hardened, and Satan
made their actions seem fair to
   them.

44 So, when they forgot
what they had been reminded of,
We opened for them the doors
to all good things,° until
—as they enjoyed their gifts—
We suddenly seized them,
sinking them in despair.

45 So the last vestige
of the wrongdoers was erased°—
praise be to God,
Lord of the universe.

46 Say, "Do you think that,
if God were to take away
your hearing and your sight, and
seal up your hearts, some other god

could restore them to you?"
See how We explain Our signs—
yet still they turn aside.

47 Say, "If God's punishment
fell on you—whether unforeseen
or seen—do you think that anyone
except those who do wrong
would be destroyed?"

48 We send the messengers
only to bring joyous news
and to warn people—
so those who believe
and do good deeds
shall have no fear,
nor shall they grieve.

49 But punishment shall strike
those who denied Our signs,
for they were disobedient.

50 Say, "I do not say to you
that I have the treasures of God,
nor that I know the unseen, nor
that I'm an angel. I merely follow
what is revealed to me." Say,
"Are the blind the same
as those who can see?
Won't you, then, reflect?"

SECTION 6

51 And use this [Qur'an] to warn
those who fear that they will be
gathered before their Lord—so that
they might be mindful of God—

beyond Him they shall have
no protector nor any intercessor.

52 Do not send away
those who call upon their Lord,
morning and evening, seeking
His Face. No part of their reckoning
falls on you, nor yours on them.
Should you send them away,
you would be doing wrong.

53 In this way, We tried
some of them by means of others,
that they might ask,
"Are these the ones God
has favored among us?"
Does God not know best
who are thankful?

54 When those who believe
in Our signs come to you, say,
"Peace be with you."
Your Lord has pledged Himself
to showing mercy.° If any of you
did wrong in ignorance, and then
repented and amended
      themselves—
God is Forgiving, Ever Merciful."

55 In this way, We explain the signs
so that the way for sinners
might be made plain.

SECTION 7

56 Say, "I am forbidden
to worship the gods on whom
you call besides the One God."
Say, "I shall not follow
your desires, for I would stray
and not be rightly guided."

57 Say, "I stand upon clear proof
from my Lord, while you deny it.
What you seek to hasten is
not in my power—the decision is
with God alone. He relates the
      truth,
for He is the Best of Arbiters."

58 Say, "If what you seek to hasten
lay in my power, the matter would
      be
settled between you and me; but
      God
best knows who the wrongdoers
      are."

59 With Him are the keys of the
      unseen,
which none knows but He.
He knows what is on land and sea;
not a leaf falls without
His knowing; nor is there a grain
in the depth of earth's darkness,
nor moisture nor dryness, without
being set down in a clear Book.

60 It is He Who calls back your souls
by night, knowing all you have done

by day; then, He raises you up,
to fulfill the appointed term. To Him
you shall return—then He will
inform you of all you have done.

SECTION 8

61 He is the Forceful, far above
His worshippers, and He sends
guardians over you until,
when death comes to any of you,
Our envoys° take his soul—and they
never fail in their duty.

62 Then they shall be returned
to God, their true Protector.
His alone is the judgment, and He
is the Swiftest of Reckoners.

63 Say, "Who is it that saves you
from the dark depths of land and sea,
when you call on Him
humbly and secretly,
saying, 'If He saves us from this,
We shall truly be thankful'?"

64 Say, "It is God who saves you
from this and every distress—yet still
you ascribe partners to Him."

65 Say, "He is Able to send
punishment to you, from above,
or from beneath your feet,
or split you into factions, to let you
taste one another's aggression."

See how We vary Our signs,
so that they might understand.

66 But your people deny it,
though it is the truth. Tell them,
"I am not your guardian.

67 "There is a given term
for every prophecy—
and soon you will know."

68 When you see people talking idly
about Our signs, turn away from them
until they talk of something else—
if Satan makes you forget,
then, when you remember,
sit apart from those who do wrong.

69 Nothing of their reckoning
falls on those who fear God,
except to remind them that they
should be mindful of God.

70 As for those who take
their religion as play and a pastime,
deluded by the life of this world—
leave them to themselves—but
remind them that a soul
is destroyed by what it reaps;
it shall have no protector besides God,
nor any intercessor; and no matter
what ransom it offered, none
will be accepted from it. Those
are the ones to be destroyed
by what they have reaped; they

shall have scalding water to drink
and painful punishment, for they
always denied the truth.

SECTION 9

71 Say, "Shall we call on others
besides God—who can do us
neither good nor harm?
And shall we turn upon our heels
after God has guided us, like one
seduced by Satan, wandering
bewildered through the land, though
his friends call to him, 'Come to us!'?"
Say, "God's guidance
is the right guidance,
and we have been commanded
to submit our will
to the Lord of the universe,

72 "to be steadfast in prayer, and
to be mindful of Him—
for it is to Him
that you shall be gathered."

73 It is He Who created
the heavens and the earth
with true purpose;° on the day
when He says, "Be," it shall be.
His Word is the truth.
And His shall be dominion
on the day the trumpet is blown—
Knower of the unseen and the seen,
He is All Wise, All Aware.

74 Remember when Abraham
asked his father, Azar,

"Do you take idols as gods?
I see that you and your people
are clearly wrong."

75 And We showed Abraham
the Kingdom of the heavens
and the earth—to assure his faith.

76 When night covered him
with darkness, he saw a star,
and said, "This is my Lord."
But when it set, he said,
"I dislike things that set."

77 When he saw the moon rising,
he said, "This is my Lord."
But when it too set, he said,
"If my Lord does not guide me,
I will be one of those
who've gone astray."

78 When he saw the sun rising,
he said, "This is my Lord.
This is the most great."
But when it too set, he said,
"My people, I renounce
your practice of ascribing
partners to God.

79 "I have set my face toward the One
Who fashioned the heavens
and the earth; upright in faith,
I shall never be a polytheist."

80 His people argued with him.
He said, "Are you arguing with me
about God, when He has guided me?

I have no fear of the gods
you join with Him;
unless He wishes it, [nothing can
     happen].
My Lord embraces all things
in His knowing.
So won't you take heed?

81 "Why should I fear what you
    join with Him, when you
    have no fear of joining partners
    with God, for which no sanction
    has been sent down to you?
    So, which of our two parties
    has more right to feel secure?
    [Tell me], if you know.

82 "Those who believe
    and don't confound their belief
    with doing wrong—they are the
         ones
    who will be secure, for they
    are the rightly guided ones."

SECTION 10

83 This was the argument We gave
    to Abraham against his people.
    We raise in rank whom We will—
    your Lord is All Wise, All Knowing.

84 We gave him Isaac and Jacob,
    and We guided all of them.
    Earlier, We had guided Noah
    and his descendants: David, Solomon,
    Job, Joseph, Moses, and Aaron
    —this is how We reward

those who do good—

85 and Zachariah, John, Jesus, and
       Elijah
    —all were among the righteous—

86 and Ishmael, Elisha, Jonah, and
       Lot—
    We favored them above all peoples,

87 and their fathers, descendants,
    and their brothers—We chose some
    and guided them to a straight path.

88 This is guidance from God;
    He guides by it whichever
    of His worshippers He will.
    If they were to join partners
    with Him, all their deeds
    would be rendered vain.

89 These were the people to whom
    We gave the Book, wisdom,
    and prophethood.
    If now they deny all this,
    We shall entrust it to a people
    who will not deny it.

90 Those were the people God guided,
    so, Prophet, follow the guidance
    that they gained. Say,
    "I ask of you no reward for this—
    this is nothing less than a reminder
    for all the worlds."

SECTION II

91 They fail to appraise
the true measure of God when they
   say,
"God has never revealed anything
to a mere mortal." Say,
"Who revealed the Book
by which Moses brought light
and guidance to his people—
you divide it into parchments,
disclosing some things
but hiding many more?
You were taught
what you did not know—
you nor your forefathers."

Answer, "God revealed it,"
then leave them floundering
in their idle talk.

92 This is a blessèd Book
that We have revealed,
confirming what came before it,
that you might warn
the mother of cities,°
and those around her.

Those who believe in the hereafter
believe in the Book,
and they preserve
their practice of prayer.

93 Who does more wrong than those
who invent a lie about God, or say,
"Revelation came to me"—
when it did not come to them—or,

"I shall reveal something
similar to what God has revealed"?

If you could see the wrongdoers
in the agonies of death, as the angels
stretch out their hands, saying,
"Surrender your souls. Today,
you shall reap the torment
of humiliation for the untruths
you spoke about God, and for your
proud disdaining of His signs."

94 "And [God will say],
Now, you return to Us alone,
as when We first created you:
you have left behind whatever gifts
We granted you. We do not see
any of your intercessors with you—
those you claimed as God's partners
in your affairs. All bonds
between you and them are severed,
and those you claimed as partners
have forsaken you."

SECTION 12

95 It is God who splits open
the seed and the date stone;
He brings the living from the dead
and the dead from the living—
this is God—so how
can you be deluded?

96 It is He Who breaks open the dawn,
Who makes the night for repose,
and the sun and moon for
   reckoning.

This is the providence
of the Almighty, the All Knowing.

97 It is He Who made for you
the stars, to guide you
in the darkness of land and sea.
We have made Our signs clear
for a people who know.

98 It is He who brought you forth
from a single soul, furnishing
a place to dwell and to rest.
We have made Our signs clear
for people who understand.

99 It is He Who sends down rain
from the sky—from this
We bring out every plant, from
    which
We bring greenery, out of which
We bring grain in heaped piles;
and from the spathes of date palm,
low-hanging clusters of dates,
gardens of grapevines, olives, and
pomegranates—all alike yet diverse.

See their fruits as they bear fruit
and ripen—in all this are signs
for people who believe.

100 Yet they ascribe jinn as partners
with God—though He created
    them;
and they falsely ascribe to Him sons
and daughters—without knowledge.
May He be glorified, exalted
far beyond what they ascribe—

SECTION 13

101 the Originator of the heavens
and the earth—how could He
have a son, when He has no consort?
He created all things, and He
Knows all things.

102 This is God, your Lord.
There is no god but He,
Creator of all things—
so worship Him, for He
Oversees all things.

103 No sight can encompass Him,
but He encompasses all sight,
for He is Ever Subtle, All Aware.

104 Now insight has come to you
from your Lord—
those who see, shall do so
for their own good;
and those who are blind, shall be so
to their own cost. Tell them,
    Prophet,
"I am not your guardian."

105 In this way, We explain
and clarify the signs to people
who know, though
[disbelievers] will say to you,
Prophet, "You have been tutored."

106 Follow what your Lord inspired
in you—there is no god but He; and
turn away from those who ascribe
partners to Him.

107 Had God wished it, they would not
have ascribed partners to Him;
but We have not made you
their guardian, nor their overseer.

108 And do not revile
those they call upon besides God
in case they should revile God
through hostility, without knowing.
We made each nation's deeds
seem fair to them, but then
they will return to their Lord,
and He shall inform them
of all that they did.

109 They swear their strongest oaths
by God, that if a sign came to them,
they would believe it. Tell them,
"Signs are in the hands of God
    alone.
What would make you realize,
believers, that even if a sign came
to them, they would not believe?"

110 We would turn away their hearts
and their vision—just as they
did not believe in it at first,
and we would leave them
in their transgression,
wandering blindly.

SECTION 14

111 Even if We sent angels down
to them, and the dead spoke
to them, and We gathered all things
[as evidence] before them,

they would not believe,
unless God wished it—
but most of them are ignorant of
    this.

112 In this way, We made an enemy
for every prophet—demons, among
humans and jinn, urging one
    another
using deceptive rhetoric.°
Had God wished it, they would not
have done this; so leave them,
with their fabrications,

113 so that the hearts of those
who don't believe in the hereafter
might lean toward their deceit,
pleased with it, and so reap
the evil they have sown.°

114 Ask, "Shall I seek some other
judge than God, when it is He
who revealed to you the Book,
explaining all things?

Those to whom We sent the Book
know that it is the truth revealed
by your Lord—so don't be in doubt.°

115 The Word of your Lord
is perfected in truth and justice.
His words cannot be changed,
for He is All Hearing, All Knowing.

116 If you followed most of those
upon the earth, they would make you
stray from the path of God;

they follow nothing but conjecture,
and they do nothing but speculate.

117 Your Lord knows best
who strays from His path;
and He also knows best
who are rightly guided.

118 Eat of animals over which
the name of God has been invoked,
if you truly believe in His signs.

119 Why should you not
eat of animals over which
the name of God has been invoked,
when He has explained to you
what He has forbidden to you,
unless driven by need?
But many lead people astray
by indulging their desires
without knowledge—
God knows best
those who transgress.

120 Avoid sin, open or secret;
those who reap sin shall be
    rewarded
for all that they wrought.

121 Avoid eating animals over which
God's name has not been invoked,
for that is willful disobedience.
Yet the demons are always inciting
their disciples to dispute with you;
but if you should heed them,
you too will be polytheists.

SECTION 15

122 Can a dead person, to whom
We gave life—and a light by which
to walk among people—be
    compared
to someone mired in darkness,
unable to emerge from its depth?
This is how the unbelievers' deeds
seem fair in their own eyes.

123 In this way, We placed in every city
prominent criminals, to contrive
their plots there; yet they merely plot
against themselves—unwittingly.

124 When any sign comes to them
they say, "We'll never believe
until we're given a sign like those
given to the messengers of God."
God knows best where to place
His message. Those who do wrong
shall face humiliation before God,
and severe torment for their
    plotting.

125 God opens the hearts of those
He would guide—to submit to
    Him,°
and He tightens and constricts
the hearts of those He would let
    stray,
as though they were climbing
    toward
the sky. This is how God mires
the disbelievers in their own
    squalor.

126 This is the path of your Lord,
    made straight—We have explained
    the signs to people who take heed.

127 They shall have a home of peace
    with their Lord; in view of their
        deeds,
    He shall be their Protector.

128 On the day He gathers them all,
    saying, "Assembly of jinn, you led
    many humans astray," their allies
    among humankind will say,
    "Our Lord, some of us profited
    from others, and now we reach
    your appointed term for us."
    He will say, "The fire is your home
    forever—unless God wills
        otherwise."
    Your Lord is All Wise, All Knowing.

129 And so We make the wrongdoers
    friends of one another, for the deeds
    they reaped together.

SECTION 16

130 "All you jinn and humankind!
    Did messengers not come to you,
    from among you, reciting My signs,
    and warning you of the meeting
    with God on this day of yours?"
    They will reply,
    "We bear witness against ourselves."

    The life of this world deluded them,
    and they do bear witness

against themselves—
    that they were disbelievers.

131 So [messengers were sent], for
    your Lord would not destroy towns
    unjustly, while their people
    were unaware of the truth.

132 All people are ranked
    by their deeds;
    your Lord is not unaware
    of what they do.

133 Your Lord is Self-Sufficient,
    Full of Mercy; if He wished,
    He could displace you with
    whichever successors He would—
    just as He raised you
    from the offspring of another people.

134 All that has been promised you
    shall come—you shall not escape.

135 Say, "My people, go on
    behaving as you are,° as will I.
    Soon, you shall know whose end
    is best in the home of the hereafter;
    the wrongdoers shall not prosper."

136 They assign to God a share
    of the crops and cattle He created,
    claiming, "This is for God,
    and this is for our idols."
    But their idols' share does not
    reach God, while God's share does
    reach their idols. How iniquitous
    is their judgment!

137 Likewise, their idols
     made the polytheists think that
     killing their children was fine—
     to ruin them, and to confuse them
     in their religion.
     Had God wished, they would not
     have done this. So leave them—
     with their fabrications.

138 And they claim,
     "These cattle and crops are
         forbidden;
     only those we allow may eat them."
     There are some cattle that they
     don't allow to be yoked,
     and others that they slaughter
     without invoking the name of God—
     imputing such invented rules to
         Him.
     Soon He shall requite them
     for their inventions.

139 They say, "The newborn
     from these cattle is only for our men
     and forbidden to our women.
     But if it is stillborn,
     they may share in it."
     Soon shall God requite them
     for their imputations.
     He is All Wise, All Knowing.

140 The losers will be those
     who kill their children in folly,
     without knowledge, and forbid
     the food God has provided,
     inventing lies about God—
     they are astray, without guidance.

SECTION 17

141 It is He Who brings out gardens,
     trellised and untrellised, the date
         palm,
     crops that are various in taste, the
         olive,
     and the pomegranate, alike yet
         diverse.
     Eat of their fruit when they bear fruit,
     and give what is due on harvest day,
     but do not be wasteful, for God
     dislikes those who are wasteful.

142 Some cattle are for burden,
     others for meat. Eat of what
     God has provided for you, and do
         not
     follow in the footsteps of Satan,
     for he is your avowed enemy.

143 God gave you eight animals
     in pairs: two sheep and two goats.
     Say, "Has He forbidden
     the two males or the two females
     or the young in the wombs
     of the two females?
     Inform me—from your
         knowledge—
     if you are speaking the truth."

144 And two camels and two cows.
     Say, "Has He forbidden
     the two males or the two females
     or the young in the wombs
     of the two females?
     Were you witnesses when God

commanded you to do this?
Who does more wrong than
    someone
who invents lies about God,
to lead people astray,
without knowledge?
God does not guide
a people who do wrong."

SECTION 18

145 Say, "In the revelation to me
I do not find any food forbidden
except carrion, flowing blood
or the flesh of swine—for it is foul—
or animals over which a name other
than God's was profanely invoked.
But if someone is compelled
by hunger, without intending to sin
or transgress—God is Forgiving,
Ever Merciful.

146 And for the Jews, We forbade
every animal with claws, the fat
of cows and sheep except what is
on their backs or in their entrails
or attached to bones.
This is how We requited them
for their defiance—
and We speak only the truth.

147 If they deny you, say,
"The mercy of your Lord is wide,
but His wrath cannot be turned
    back
from wicked people."

148 Those who ascribe partners to God
will say, "If God had wished it,
we would not have ascribed
    partners,
nor forbidden anything."
Likewise, those before them denied
until they tasted Our wrath.
Say, "What knowledge can you
produce for us? You follow
nothing but conjecture
and do nothing but speculate."

149 Say, "The conclusive argument
is God's—had He wished,
He would have guided all of you."

150 Say, "Bring out your witnesses
who testify that God forbade this."
And if they testify,
don't testify with them,
and don't follow the desires of those
who deny Our signs, and those
who don't believe in the hereafter,
for they set up equals with their
    Lord.

SECTION 19

151 Say, "Come, I will recite to you
what your Lord has forbidden you:
don't associate anything with him,
be kind to parents, and
don't kill your children out of want;
We shall provide for you and them.
And stay clear of indecency,
either open or concealed;
and do not take life

—that God has made sacred—
except with just cause.
This is what He enjoins you to—
that you might use reason.

152 "Stay clear of an orphan's property
except with the best intentions,
until they reach maturity;
give full measure and weight, justly
—We do not burden any soul
beyond its capacity—
and when you speak, be fair,
even if it is with a relative,
and fulfill God's covenant.
This is what He enjoins you to—
that you might take heed.

153 "And this is My path, straight, so
follow it and don't follow other ways
for they will cleave you from His way.
This is what He enjoins you to—
that you might be mindful of Him."

154 We gave Moses the Book,
perfecting Our favor to those
who do good, explaining all things—
a guide and a mercy—that they
    might
believe in the meeting with their
    Lord.

SECTION 20

155 This also is a blessèd Book
that We have revealed, so follow it,
and be mindful of God,
that you might be shown mercy—

156 in case you say,
"The Book was revealed only
to two communities before us,
and we were unaware
of what they studied."

157 Or in case you say,
"If only the Book had been revealed
to us, we should have been
better guided than them."
But now there has come to you
clear proof, guidance, and mercy
from your Lord.
Who does more wrong than
    someone
who denies the signs of God, and
turns away from them?
We shall requite those who
turn away from Our signs
with a dreadful punishment.°

158 Are they waiting to see
if the angels come to them,
or your Lord Himself,
or some of His signs?

The day such signs° come,
it shall not help any soul
to have faith in them
if it had no faith before,
nor reaped any good
by its faith. Say, "Wait—
we too are waiting."

159 As for those who divide
their religion into sects—
have nothing to do with them;

their case is with God, and He will
inform them of what they've done.

160 Whoever does a good deed
shall reap its reward ten times;
and whoever does a bad deed,
shall reap the reward for it alone;
and they shall not be wronged.

161 Say, "My Lord has guided me
to a straight path, an upright
    religion,
the creed of Abraham, pure in faith,
who was not a polytheist."

162 Say, "My prayer, my sacrifice,
my life and my death, are all for God,
Lord of the universe.

163 "He has no partner—
this is what I am commanded to,

and I am the first
to submit my will to Him."

164 Say, "Shall I seek as Lord
something other than God, when He
is Lord of all things?"
Each soul reaps the reward
only of its own deeds; and no soul
shall bear the burden of another.
Then, you shall return to your Lord
and He shall inform you of the
    things
over which you differed.

165 He Who made you
regents on the earth, and
He raised some of you above others
in rank, that He might test you
through what He has given you.
Your Lord is Swift in Retribution,
yet He is Forgiving, Ever Merciful.

SURA 7

The Heights (*Al-Aʿraf*)

Also late Meccan, this sura of 206 verses was revealed before the preceding
sura but the Heights, mentioned in v. 46, is likely included after the sura called
"Cattle" since it develops similar topics about God's Oneness and the need for
human obedience to divine messengers. The history of earlier prophets, from
Noah to Hud, Salih, Lot, and Shuʿayb, anticipates the long section on Moses (vv.
103–71). There is a central reference to the Beautiful Names (v. 180) that underscores the enduring human need to remember God and seek refuge from Satan,
as also to seek repentance and forgiveness.

In the Name of God, the All Merciful, Ever Merciful

SECTION 1

1 *Alif. Lam. Mim. Sad.°*

2 A Book is revealed to you, Prophet
   —don't let it disquiet your heart—
   that you might use to warn
   and remind the believers.

3 People, follow what is revealed
   to you from your Lord, and
   follow no protector but Him—
   how little you pay heed!

4 See how many towns We destroyed,
   Our wrath falling upon them
   by night or while they slept at
      noon!

5 Their only cry, when Our wrath
   fell upon them, was
   "Yes, we did wrong."

6 We shall question those
   to whom Our message was sent—
   and equally, We shall question
   those who were sent.

7 And We shall recount to them
   [their deeds], with full knowledge—
   We were never away from them.

8 The balance° on that day
   shall be just.
   Those whose balance

is heavy [with good deeds]
shall flourish.

9 And those whose balance is light
   have lost their souls
   for they did injustice to Our verses.

10 We settled you on the earth
    and gave you livelihood there—
    how little you give thanks!

SECTION 2

11 We created you and shaped you;
    then We commanded the angels,
    "Bow down before Adam."
    All bowed down—except Iblis,
    who would not bow.

12 God asked, "What stopped you
    from bowing as I commanded you?"
    He retorted, "I am better than him;
    You created me from fire, but him
    you fashioned from mere clay."

13 God said, "Go down from here;°
    it's not your place to be proud
       here—
    go, for you are truly debased."

14 Iblis said, "Give me reprieve
    until the day that all people
    are raised up from the dead."

15 God answered, "You shall
   be granted a reprieve."

16 Iblis said, "Because
   you've sent me astray,
   I shall lie in wait for them
   on Your straight path.°

17 "I shall come upon them
   from before and behind them,
   from their right and from their left,
   and You will find that most of them
   are not grateful to You."

18 God replied, "Go out from here,
   disgraced and exiled.
   As for those who follow you—
   I shall fill hell with all of you.

19 "Adam, you and your spouse
   may live in the garden, and
   eat wherever you will,
   but do not approach this tree,
   for you would be doing wrong."

20 Then Satan whispered to them both,°
   —so as to expose their shameful
      parts,
   which had been hidden from
      them—saying,
   "Your Lord forbade you to eat
   from this tree only to stop you
   from becoming angels or
      immortals."

21 And he swore to them both,
   "This is sincere advice I offer you."

22 So, through his guile,
   he lured them both [to fall].
   And once they tasted of the tree,
   they realized their nakedness,
   and began to cover themselves
   with leaves from the garden.
   And their Lord called to them both,
   "Did I not forbid you both
   to eat from this tree?
   Did I not tell you both
   that Satan is your open enemy?"

23 They responded, "Our Lord,
   we have wronged ourselves—
   if You do not forgive us
   and have mercy on us,
   we'll be among
   the ones who fall into loss."

24 God said, "Go down from here,
   as enemies of one another;
   you shall have a home
   and livelihood upon the earth—
   for a short while."

25 He said, "There you shall live
   and die, and from there
   you shall be brought out again."

SECTION 3

26 Children of Adam,
   We have given you garments
   to cover your nakedness, and
   to adorn you. But the best garment
   is mindfulness of God.

This is one of the signs of God
that people might take heed.

27   Children of Adam,
      don't let Satan tempt you
      —as he did your parents
      bringing them out of the garden—
      to strip them of their garments,
      and expose their nakedness to them;
      he sees you, he and his tribe,
      from where you can't see them—
      We made the devils allies
      of those who don't believe.

28   When they commit any indecency,
      they say, "This is what we found
      our fathers doing," and
      "God commanded us to do it." Say,
      "God never commands indecency—
      would you say about God
      things you do not know?"

29   Say, "My Lord commands justice,
      so set your faces toward Him
      wherever you pray,°
      and call upon Him, sincere in faith.
      Just as He first made you,
      so you shall return [at last to Him]."

30   He has guided some, while others
      have rightly been left to stray,
      for they have taken devils as allies
      instead of God, thinking that they
      are rightly guided.

31   Children of Adam, wear
      proper clothes wherever you pray;

eat and drink, but not to excess,
for God dislikes the extravagant.

SECTION 4

32   Say, "Who forbids the adornment
      that God furnished for His servants
      and the good things to sustain
         them?"
      Say, "They are for those
      who believed, in the life of this
         world,
      and are only for them
      on the day of resurrection."
      This is how We expound Our signs
      for people who have knowledge.

33   Say, "My Lord has forbidden only
      immoral deeds, open or concealed,
      as well as sin, lawless aggression,
      and your joining partners with
         God—
      for which no sanction has been sent—
      or that you speak about God
      things beyond your knowledge."

34   Each community is assigned
      a fixed time°—when this time arrives,
      they can neither delay nor hasten it—
      not even by an hour.

35   Children of Adam, when
      messengers from your own people
      come to you, reciting My signs,
      those who are mindful of Me
      and amend themselves
      shall neither fear nor grieve.

36 But those who deny Our signs,
    and proudly disdain them
    shall be inmates of the fire—forever.

37 Who does more wrong than those
    who invent lies about God or deny
    His signs? They will get their share
    as decreed in the Book—but when
    Our angels come to take them,
    and ask, "Where are those
    on whom you called besides God?"
    They will answer,
    "They have abandoned us,"
    and they will be witnesses
    against themselves—
    that they were disbelievers.

38 He will say, "Enter the fire,
    with the communities before you—
    jinn and humankind.
    Whenever a people enters,
    it curses its sister community, and
    when they all arrive inside,
    the last of them will say of the first,
    "Our Lord, these are the ones who
    led us astray; so double
    their punishment in the fire!"
    He will say, "It shall be doubled
    for each—though you don't know
        it."

39 The first ones will say to the last,
    "So you were no better than us.
    Taste, then, the punishment
    you have earned!"

SECTION 5

40 The gates of heaven shall never
    open to those who deny Our signs
    and proudly disdain them,
    nor shall they enter the garden,
    until a camel can pass through
    a needle's eye.° This is how
    We reward the sinners.

41 Hell shall be their bed
    and also the covering above them—
    this is how We recompense
    those who do wrong.

42 Those who believe
    and do good deeds—We place
    no burden on a soul beyond its
        limit—
    shall live in the garden, forever.

43 And We shall remove ill feeling
    from their hearts. Rivers will flow
    beneath them, and they will say,
    "Praised be God who guided us
        here;
    we could not have found guidance
    without God—our Lord's
        messengers
    brought the truth."
    And a voice will call to them,
    "This is the garden—yours
    to inherit—for all you have done."

44 The people in the garden
    will call out to the inmates of
        the fire,

"We have found the promise
of our Lord to be true;
have you found it to be true?"
They will answer, "Yes,"
and a herald among them
shall cry out, "The curse of God
is upon those who do wrong,

45 "those who bar others from the path
of God, and seek to make it crooked,
those who deny the hereafter."

46 Between the two groups a barrier
shall stand, with people on its
    heights
—not yet in the garden but hoping—
who recognize all by their marks.
They shall greet the people
in the garden, "Peace be with you!"

47 But when their eyes are turned
toward the inmates of the fire,
they will say, "Our Lord, don't place
us with the wrongdoers."

SECTION 6

48 And the people on the heights
will call out to people they
    recognize
by their marks,
"What did you gain by your
great numbers and proud disdain?

49 "Are these the ones you swore
would not be granted God's mercy?

—who are now told, 'Enter the
    garden—
you shall have no fear, nor grieve'?"

50 The inmates of the fire
will call to the people of the garden,
"Pour water upon us, or whatever
God has given you." They will reply,
"God has forbidden both
to the disbelievers,

51 "those who took their religion
as play and a pastime, those
deluded by the life of this world.
That day We shall forget them,
just as they forgot the meeting
with Us on this day of theirs,
and rejected Our signs."

52 For We brought them a Book,
that We explained—on the basis
of certain knowledge—as guidance
and mercy for people who believe.

53 Are they just waiting
for its warning to be fulfilled?
On the day it is fulfilled, those
who had forgotten it will say,
"Our Lord's messengers
brought the truth. And now,
will anyone intercede for us?
Or can we be sent back
to act differently than we did?"

They have lost their souls,
and their invented idols
shall abandon them.

SECTION 7

54 Your Lord is God, Who created
   the heavens and the earth in six days,
   then took up the throne.
   He veils day with night,
   which trails it swiftly.
   He created the sun, moon, and stars—
   all subject to His command.
   Is the creation not His,
   and the command? Blessèd be God,
   Lord of the universe.

55 Call on your Lord,
   in humility, and secretly—
   He dislikes those who transgress.

56 Don't sow corruption in the land
   now that it has been reformed,
   but call on Him, in fear and hope.
   The mercy of God is near
   for those who do good.

57 It is He who sends the winds,
   bearers of joyous news,
   heralding His mercy;
   when they carry the heavy clouds,
   We drive them to barren land,
   We send rain on it, and
   We raise up from it fruit of all kinds.
   In the same way,
   We shall raise up the dead—
   that you might take heed.

58 Good soil yields rich vegetation,
   by permission of its Lord,
   but bad soil gives a meager yield—

in this way We vary Our signs
to a people who are grateful.

SECTION 8

59 We sent Noah to his people.
   He said, "My people, worship God—
   you have no god but Him.
   I fear for you the torment
   of a momentous day."

60 The leaders of his people retorted,
   "We see that you're clearly wrong."

61 He replied, "My people,
   I am not wrong—I am a messenger
   from the Lord of the universe.

62 "I am conveying to you
   messages from my Lord,
   and I am advising you,
   for I know—from God—
   what you do not.

63 "Do you wonder that a reminder
   has come to you from your Lord
   through a man of your own people,
   to warn you—that you might
   be mindful of God,
   and be shown mercy?"

64 But they denied him,
   so We delivered him,
   and those with him, in the ark,
   and We drowned those
   who denied Our signs—
   a blind people.

SECTION 9

65 And We sent to the people of ʿAd
their brother Hud, who said,
"My people, worship God—
you have no god but Him.
Will you not be mindful of Him?"

66 But the leaders of the unbelievers
among his people retorted,
"We think you're a fool—and a liar."

67 He replied, "My people,
I am no fool—I am a messenger
from the Lord of the universe.

68 "I am conveying to you
messages from my Lord,
and you can trust
the advice I offer you.

69 "Do you wonder that a reminder
has come to you from your Lord
through a man of your own people,
to warn you—remember how
He made you heirs to Noah's people,
and raised you greatly in stature.
Remember the bounties of God,
that you might flourish."

70 They retorted, "Do you come
to tell us to worship God alone, and
forsake what our fathers
worshipped?
Bring us the torment you threatened
if you are speaking the truth."

71 He exclaimed, "Your Lord's torment
and wrath shall fall on you.
Do you argue with me over names°
—that you and your fathers
devised—
for which God has sent no sanction?
Wait, then; and I shall wait with
you."

72 We saved him and those with him,
through Our mercy,
and We erased the last traces
of those who denied Our signs
and remained unbelievers.

SECTION 10

73 We sent to the people of Thamud
their brother Salih, who said,
"My people, worship God—
you have no god but Him.
Clear proof has come to you from
your Lord: this she-camel of God
is a sign for you. So leave her
to graze on God's earth,
and don't harm her,
else a painful punishment
shall overtake you.

74 "Remember how He made you
heirs to ʿAd's people,
and settled you in the land;
you built castles on its plains,
and carved houses in the mountains.
Remember the bounties of God,
and don't act wickedly in the land,
spreading corruption."

75 The leaders of some proud men
among his people said
to the believers they deemed weak,
"Do you know that Salih
is a messenger from his Lord?"
They answered, "We do believe
in the message sent with him."

76 Those proud people declared,
"We deny what you believe."

77 They hamstrung the she-camel,
and disdained their Lord's
    command,
saying, "Salih, bring upon us
the torment you threatened,
if you really are a messenger."

78 So the earthquake shook them,
and by morning they lay fallen
on their faces, dead, in their homes.°

79 Salih turned from them, saying,
"My people, I have conveyed
my Lord's message to you,
and I've advised you—but it seems
you're averse to all advisers."°

80 We also sent Lot,
who said to his people,
"How can you commit indecency—
like none in the world before you?

81 "You lust after men
instead of women; you
exceed all due limits."

82 In response, the only thing
his people could say was
"Drive them out of your town—
these people who are so chaste!"

83 But we saved him and his family,
except his wife, who stayed behind.

84 And we rained down upon them
a rain [of stones]°—observe
the fate of those who sin.

SECTION 11

85 We sent to the people of Midian
their brother Shuʿayb, who said,
"My people, worship God—
you have no god but Him.
Clear proof has come to you from
your Lord—so give
just measure and weight,
and don't give people less
than the value of their goods.
Don't sow corruption in the land
now it has been reformed.
This will be better for you
if you are believers.

86 "Don't lurk on every road,
threatening people, and barring
    those
who believe in God from His path,
seeking to make it crooked.
Remember, when you were few
how we multiplied you.
And observe the fate
of those who sow corruption.

87 "And if some of you believe
   in the message I've been sent with,
   while others don't, be patient
   until God judges between us.
   For He is the Best of Judges."

88 The leaders of some proud men
   among his people said, "Shu'ayb,
   we'll drive you out of our town
   —and those who believe with you—
   unless you return to our creed."
   He retorted, "Even if we abhor it?

89 "We'd be inventing lies about God
   if we returned to your creed after
       God
   had spared us from it; we could not
   return to it unless our Lord God
       wished it.
   Our Lord's knowing embraces
   all things. In God we place our trust,
   'Our Lord, decide justly between us
   and our people—for You
   are the Best of Arbiters.'"

90 The chief unbelievers
   among his people said,
   "If you follow Shu'ayb,
   it will be you who
   fall into loss."

91 So the earthquake shook them,
   and by morning they lay fallen
   on their faces, dead, in their
       homes—

92 as if those who denied Shu'ayb
   had never lived there—
   they were the ones
   who fell into loss.

93 So Shu'ayb turned from them,
   saying, "My people, I have conveyed
   the message of my Lord to you,
   and I gave you sound advice—
   so how can I grieve
   for a people who don't believe?"

SECTION 12

94 Whenever We sent a prophet
   to a town, We inflicted suffering
   and adversity on its disbelievers,
   to instill humility in them.

95 Then We turned their distress
   to prosperity, [but they forgot this],
   and said, "Our fathers too were
   touched by both hardship and
       ease"—
   so We seized them suddenly,
   while they were unaware.

96 If the people of the towns had
   believed and been mindful of God,
   We should have opened the
       blessings
   of heaven and earth to them;
   but they denied Us, so We
   seized them for their misdeeds.

97 Do the people of the towns
   feel certain that Our wrath

will not descend on them
by night, while they sleep?

98   And do the townspeople
feel certain that Our wrath
will not fall upon them
by day, while they idly play?

99   Do they feel secure
against God's plan?
None can feel secure
against the plan of God
except those who
will fall into loss.

SECTION 13

100 Is this not a lesson
for those who inherit the earth
after its former peoples—
that, if We wished, We could
strike them for their sins,
and seal up their hearts,
so that they could not hear.

101 These were the towns
whose stories We have told you—
messengers came to them,
bringing clear proofs,
but still they would not believe
what they had denied earlier—
this is how God
seals the hearts of disbelievers.

102 We found most of them
failing to fulfill their covenant,

and we found most of them
to be disobedient.

103 After them, We sent Moses
to Pharaoh and his chiefs
with Our signs,
but they reviled them—
observe the fate of those
who sow corruption.

104 Moses said, "Pharaoh,
I am a messenger sent
from the Lord of the universe,

105 obliged to speak only the truth
about God. I have brought you
clear proof from your Lord—so
send the children of Israel with me."

106 Pharaoh retorted, "If you
have come with a sign, produce it,
if you are speaking the truth."

107 Then Moses cast down his staff,
and suddenly—it was now
a serpent for all to see.

108 He drew out his hand, and
suddenly—it was gleaming white
for all to see.

SECTION 14

109 Pharaoh's chief people observed,
"This is an expert magician;

110 "he wants to drive you
from your land." Pharaoh asked,
"What do you advise, then?"

111 They replied, "Stall him
and his brother, while you send
scouts to the cities to gather

112 and bring to you
all the expert magicians."

113 When Pharaoh's magicians came,
they asked,
"Shouldn't we be rewarded
if we prevail?"

114 He replied, "Of course,
and you'll be within
my inner circle."

115 They asked, "Moses,
will you throw first, or shall we?"

116 Moses said, "You throw first!"
And when they threw, people were
spellbound, terrified
by what they saw—
such a daunting display of magic.

117 Then We inspired Moses,
"Throw down your staff!"
And suddenly it swallowed
all their concoctions.

118 So the truth was verified
and all their deeds proved vain.

119 Defeated there, humiliated,

120 the sorcerers fell down,
prostrating themselves,

121 proclaiming, "We now believe
in the Lord of the universe,

122 "the Lord of Moses and Aaron."

123 Pharaoh bellowed,
"You believed in Him
before I allowed it?
I'm sure this is a plot
you've planned in the city,
to drive out its people—
but soon you will learn.

124 "I'll cut off your hands and feet
on either side, and crucify you all."

125 They said, "It is certain
that we'll return to our Lord.

126 "You take vengeance on us
only because we believed
in the signs of our Lord
when they came to us.

"Our Lord, fill us with patience,
and let us die submitting to Your
will."

SECTION 15

127 The chiefs of Pharaoh's people
asked him,

"Will you let Moses and his people
wreak mischief in the land,
and forsake you and your gods?"
He answered,
"We'll kill their sons
and spare only their women.
For we have power over them."

128 Moses urged his people,
"Seek God's help, and be patient.
The land belongs to God—
He bequeaths it to whichever
of His servants He will,
and those who are mindful of God
shall triumph in the end."

129 They said, "We were oppressed
both before you came to us, and now,
after you've come." He responded,
"Your Lord may destroy your enemy
and make you successors to the land,
to see how you will behave."

SECTION 16

130 We harried Pharaoh's people
with years of famine
and loss of crops—to warn them.

131 When good things came to them,
they said, "We earned this."
But when misfortune struck them,
they took it as an ill omen from Moses
and his companions, though
their ill omen actually came
   from God,
unbeknown to most of them.

132 They said to Moses,
"No matter what signs
you bring to bewitch us—
we won't believe in you."

133 So We sent the flood upon them,
and a scourge of locusts, lice, frogs,
and blood—all clear signs.
But they remained proud,
a people steeped in sin.

134 Whenever a plague fell on them,
they said, "Moses, call on your Lord,
to fulfill the promise He gave you;
if you free us from the plague,
we'll believe in you—and we'll send
the children of Israel with you."

135 But when We lifted the plague
from them, and gave them a fixed
   time
to fulfill their promise—they
   broke it.

136 So We requited them,
drowning them in the ocean—
for they denied Our signs,
always heedless of them.

137 We made an oppressed people
heirs to the land, both East and
   West,
which We blessed. So your Lord's
wondrous promise to favor
the children of Israel was fulfilled,
for they showed patience; and
We destroyed all that Pharaoh

and his people had wrought,
and all that they had built.

138 We led the children of Israel
across the sea. When they came
upon a people devoted to their idols,
his people said, "Moses, make for us
a god like their gods." He rejoined,
"You are an ignorant people.

139 "The creed of these people
is doomed to die out,
for what they practice is futile."

140 He said, "Would I seek for you
a god other than the One God—
Who favored you over all peoples?"

141 Remember when We saved you
from Pharaoh's people, who
    inflicted
wicked torments on you, killing
your sons, sparing only your women.
This was a great trial from your Lord.

SECTION 17

142 We assigned thirty nights
for Moses, and added ten more,
so he completed in forty nights
the term set by his Lord.° Then,
Moses said to his brother Aaron,
"Take my place among my people,
do good, and don't follow the path
of those who sow corruption."

143 When Moses came
to Our assigned place
and his Lord spoke to him,
he implored, "Show yourself to me,
so I may look upon you."
God said, "Never shall you see me,
but look up at the mountain—
if it stays in place, you will see me.
But when God's glory shone upon
the mountain, it crumbled into dust,
and Moses fell down, unconscious.
Waking, he said, "Glory be to You.
I turn to You, repenting, and
I am the first to believe."

144 God said, "Moses,
I've chosen you above all people,
through My messages, My word.°
So hold fast to what I've given you,
and be grateful."

145 We made laws for him, on tablets,
instructing, and explaining all things.
We told him, "Hold to these firmly,
and enjoin your people to hold fast
to the excellence in them—
I shall show you the final homes
of those who are disobedient."

146 As for those who were proud
—with no right—on the earth,
I will turn My signs away from them.

Even if they saw all the signs,
they would not believe them,
and if they saw the right path,
they would not take it.

Yet if they saw the path of error,
they *would* take it—for they
denied Our signs, always
heedless of them.

147   The deeds of those are vain
who deny Our signs and the meeting
with God in the hereafter.
Will they be rewarded for
anything but their deeds?

SECTION 18

148   While Moses was gone,
his people made the image of a calf
from their ornaments—it seemed
to make a lowing sound.
Did they not see
that it could not speak to them,
or guide them to the right way?
They took to worshipping it—
and became wrongdoers.

149   Realizing that they had strayed,
they said, wringing their hands,
"Unless our Lord shows us mercy
and forgives us, we'll be among
the ones who fall into loss."

150   When Moses came back
to his people, he grew angry
and aggrieved, saying,
"What you've done in my absence
is just wicked. Are you so eager
to bring on your Lord's judgment?"
He flung down the tablets
and seized his brother by the hair,

dragging him close. Aaron said,
"Brother, the people thought me
weak, and almost killed me.
Don't let my enemies rejoice
at my lapse, and don't count me
among the wrongdoers."

151   Moses prayed, "My Lord,
forgive me and my brother, and
admit us into your Mercy, for You
are the Most Merciful of all."°

SECTION 19

152   Those who took to worshipping
the calf shall be visited
by their Lord's wrath, and disgrace
in the life of this world. This is how
We reward those who invent lies.

153   As for those who do bad deeds,
and repent afterward, and believe—
then your Lord is Forgiving,
Ever Merciful.

154   When Moses' anger subsided,
he picked up the tablets—inscribed
on them were guidance and mercy
for those who fear their Lord.

155   And Moses chose seventy men
from his people
for the meeting with Us; when
an earthquake seized them,
he cried out, "My Lord,
had You wished,
You could have destroyed them

and me long ago.
Would you now destroy us
for what the fools among us did?

"This is but a trial from You:
You lead astray by it whom you will,
and You guide whom You will.
You are our Protector, so forgive us
and have mercy on us—
for you are the supreme Forgiver.°

156 "And decree for us what is good,
in this worldly life and the
    hereafter—
for we have turned to You."
God said, "I visit My punishment
on whom I will, but My mercy
encompasses all things;
I shall decree it for those
who are mindful of Me,
who give in charity, and those
who believe in Our signs,

157 "those who follow the messenger,
the 'unlettered prophet,'°
whom they find mentioned
in their own Torah and the Gospel,°
who commands them to do right
and forbids what is wrong;
who makes lawful for them
what is pure, and forbids
what is impure;
who relieves their burdens,
and the shackles weighing on them.

"So those who believe in him,
honor him and help him,

and are guided by the light
sent down with him—
it is they who will flourish."

SECTION 20

158 Prophet, tell them, "People,
I am the messenger of God to you all.
To Him belongs dominion
over the heavens and the earth;
there is no god but He—He gives life
and He brings death. So believe
in God and His messenger,
the unlettered prophet, who
    believes
in God and His words—follow him,
that you might be rightly guided."

159 Among the people of Moses,
there is a group who guide
by the light of truth, by which
they also render justice.

160 We divided them
into twelve tribes or communities.
When his people asked him for water,
We inspired Moses,
"Strike the stone with your staff."
Twelve springs gushed out from it—
each tribe knew its drinking place.

We shaded them with clouds, and
sent down to them manna and quail,
saying, "Eat of the good things
We have provided for you."
They did not wrong Us,
but wronged themselves.

161 Remember when they were told,
"Enter this town, eat where you wish,
but first say, 'Ease our burden,'
and enter the gate bowing low,
[voicing repentance].
We will forgive your mistakes
and increase the reward
of those who do good."

162 But the wrongdoers altered
the words they had been given,
so We sent upon them a plague
from the sky, for the wrong they did.

SECTION 21

163 Ask them, Prophet, about the town
lodged by the sea; its people broke
the Sabbath, because their fish
appeared to abound on the Sabbath
but not on other days.
We tested them in this way
for they were always disobedient.

164 And when a group of them
asked their preachers, "Why preach
to people whom God will destroy
or strike with severe punishment?"
they replied, "To be absolved
[of negligence] before your Lord;
    and
to make them mindful of God."

165 When they forgot
the warnings given to them,
We saved those who forbade evil,
and struck those who did wrong
with a stern° punishment,
for they were always disobedient.

166 When they persisted
in doing what was forbidden,
We told them, "Become apes,
despised."°

167 Then your Lord declared
that He would send people°
to inflict harsh punishment on
    them,
until the day of resurrection.
Your Lord is Swift in Requital,
yet He is Forgiving, Ever Merciful.

168 We divided them
into communities on the earth.
Some of them are righteous
and others are not.
We tested them
with good things and bad,
that they might return
to Our path.

169 After them came a generation
who inherited the Book, but took
instead the goods of this lower life,
saying, "We'll be forgiven."
And if more goods like this came,
they would still take them.

Was a pledge not taken from them,
in the Book, that they would speak
only the truth about God?
They had studied its contents well.°

And the home of the hereafter
is better for those
who are mindful of God.
Will you not, then, use reason?

170 As for those who hold fast
to the Book, and are steadfast
in prayer—We do not overlook
the reward of those who do good.

171 When We raised the mountain
so high above them, like a shadow,
they thought it would fall on them,
We said, "Hold fast
to what We gave you, and
remember what lies within it,
that you might be mindful of God."°

SECTION 22

172 When your Lord drew out
descendants from the loins
of the children of Adam,
and made them testify
about themselves, He asked,
"Am I not your Lord?"
and they answered,
"Yes, we do so testify"—
in case you should say
on the day of resurrection,
"We were unaware of this,"°

173 or plead, "Our fathers before us
were polytheists, and we are merely
their descendants coming after them.
Would you destroy *us*
for the falsehoods they devised?"

174 This is how We explain the signs
that they might return to Our way.

175 Prophet, tell them the story
of the person who cast aside the
    signs
We gave him. So Satan overtook him,
and he went astray.

176 Had We willed, We would have
raised him by Our signs; but he
    cleaved
to the earth, following his own
    desires.
His parable is that of a dog:
if you attack him, he pants,
and if you leave him be, he pants.
This is the parable of a people
who deny Our signs.
So tell them the story, Prophet,
to let them reflect.

177 Those who deny Our signs
set a wicked example—
and they wrong themselves.

178 Those whom God guides
are rightly guided;
but those He leads astray
are the ones who
will fall into loss.

179 We have destined many
jinn and humans for hell—

they have hearts,
yet do not understand;

they have eyes,
yet do not see;
and they have ears,
yet do not hear.

They are like cattle—
no, even more astray—
for they are heedless.

180 The Most Beautiful of Names°
are those of God. So use them
to call on Him; and abandon those
who abuse His names. Soon,
they will be rewarded
for all they have done.

181 There is a community
among all those We created
that guides by the truth
and renders justice [by its light].

SECTION 23

182 We shall gradually draw those
who deny our signs [to
    damnation]—
without their discerning it.

183 I shall grant them respite
for a while—but My scheme
is inexorable.

184 Do they not realize
that their companion is not mad?
That he is merely someone
who gives clear warning?

185 Or, do they not contemplate
the kingdom of the heavens
and the earth,
and all that God has created?
That perhaps the end of their term
is approaching? What message
can they believe after this?

186 Those whom God
allows to stray
shall have no guide;
and He will leave them
transgressing, wandering blind.

187 They ask you about the hour—
When is it due? Say, "My Lord alone
has knowledge of this—only He can
reveal its time—which shall
    resound°
throughout the heavens and the
    earth;
when it comes, it will come
    suddenly."
They ask you as if you knew
about it. Say, "God alone
has knowledge of it, yet most
people don't know this."

188 Say, Prophet, "I have no power
to profit or harm myself—
except as God wishes.
If I had knowledge of the unseen,
I would have amassed good deeds,
and no evil would touch me.
I am merely someone who warns
and bears joyous news
for a people who believe."

SECTION 24

and let them answer you,
if you are speaking the truth.

189 It is He who created you
from a single soul, and
made a mate from him, so that
he might find comfort with her.
Then, when he lies with her,
she carries a light burden,
going about with it.
Then, when she grows heavy,
they both pray to God,
"Our Lord, we'll be thankful
if you grant us a healthy child."

195 "Do they have feet to walk with?
Or hands to grasp with?
Or eyes to see with?
Or ears to hear with?"
Say, "Call upon those
you join with God, and
scheme against me—
without respite,

190 But once He grants them
a healthy child, they claim that
partners of His had a hand in this.
But God is exalted far above
the partners they ascribe to Him.

196 "for my protector is God,
who revealed the Book; it is He
who protects those who do good.

191 Do they ascribe to Him
partners—who can create nothing
and are themselves created?

197 "As for those you call upon
besides God—they can help
neither you nor themselves."

192 And who can neither help them
nor themselves?

198 If you invite them to guidance,
they don't hear. You may see them
looking at you—but they don't see.

193 And if you invite them
to be guided, they won't follow you;
it's the same for you
whether you invite them
or remain silent.

199 Resolve to show forgiveness,
enjoin what is good—and turn away
from those who are ignorant.

194 Say, "Those you call upon
besides God are just His servants,
like you. So, call upon them,

200 Should Satan tempt you
with some wicked prompting,
seek refuge in God—He
is the All Hearing, All Knowing.

201 Those who are mindful of God
remember Him if Satan tempts them
with any wicked prompting—
they will see [what is right].

202 But the disciples° of Satan
plunge them ever deeper
into error—relentlessly.

203 If you don't bring them a sign,
they ask,
"Why have you not devised it?"
Answer,
"I follow only what my Lord reveals
to me. These are insights from
your Lord—guidance and mercy,
for a people who believe."

204 When the Qur'an is being read,
listen to it, attentively,
that you might be shown mercy.

205 And remember your Lord within
yourself, with humility and fear,
without raising your voice,
in the mornings and evenings,
and do not be heedless.

206 Those who are close to your Lord
are never too proud to worship Him;
they hymn His praise,
bowing low before Him.

SURA 8

The Spoils of War (Al-Anfal)

Named after a phrase used in v. 1, this sura of 75 verses was mostly revealed after
the Battle of Badr in 624, though a section (vv. 30–36) was revealed in Mecca and
the final 4 verses came after Badr, anticipating the subject of Sura 9.

In the Name of God, the All Merciful, Ever Merciful

SECTION I

1 They ask you, Prophet,
about the spoils of war. Say,
"The spoils are for God and the
messenger
[to decide], so be mindful of God,
and
make things right among
yourselves.

Obey God and His messenger
if you are true believers."

2 True believers are those
whose hearts tremble in awe
at the mention of God,
and whose faith grows when
His verses are recited to them,
and who trust in their Lord,

3 those who are steadfast in prayer,
  and give in charity from what
  We have given them—

4 these are the believers—
  they shall have a high station
  in the sight of their Lord;
  they shall have forgiveness,
  and a gracious provision.

5 For it was your Lord
  Who made you leave your home,
  for a just cause—despite
  the displeasure of some believers,

6 who disputed with you
  about the truth, even after it
  had been made clear—as if
  they were being driven toward
  a death they could actually see.

7 When God promised you victory
  over one of the two hostile groups,
  you fancied the unarmed group.
  But God wanted to prove
  the truth of His Word—
  and He cut off the unbelievers
  at their source,

8 that He might prove
  the truth to be true,
  and falsehood to be false—
  though the sinners disapproved.

9 When you implored your Lord
  for help, He responded,
  "I will reinforce you

with a thousand angels
row upon row."

10 God made this but a message of
   hope,
   to assure your hearts—
   and there is no help except from
   God;
   God is Almighty, All Wise.

SECTION 2

11 Remember when He shrouded you
   in slumber—to make you feel safe,°
   and sent you rain from the sky
   to cleanse you, and to purge you
   of the stain of Satan, and to
   strengthen
   your hearts and make firm your
   feet.

12 Remember when your Lord
   inspired the angels, "I am with you.
   So strengthen those who believe.
   I shall cast terror into the hearts
   of those who disbelieve—so
   strike above their necks, and
   strike at their fingertips."

13 For they opposed God
   and His messenger; those
   who do oppose them
   should know that God
   is Severe in Retribution.

14 That is your [punishment],
   "So taste it," and know that

the disbelievers shall face
the punishment of fire.

15 You who believe, when you face
the foe advancing in battle,
do not turn your backs to them.

16 If any does turn their back to them
on that day—except as a battle tactic
or to link up with their own forces—
they shall incur the wrath of God,
and their home shall be hell,
a wretched end.

17 It was not you who killed them
but God; it was not you who threw
[sand] at them° but God,
that He might Himself test
the believers through a fine trial.
God is All Hearing, All Knowing.

18 So it is—God will undermine
the unbelievers' designs.

19 Disbelievers—if you were seeking
a judgment, it has come now.
If you stop now,
it is better for you.
But if you return, We shall return.
Your forces shall never help you,
however great in number—
for God is with the believers.

SECTION 3

20 You who believe, obey God
and His messenger, and

do not turn away from him
when you hear him speak.

21 And don't be like those who say,
"We hear," but do not hear.

22 The worst of creatures
in the eyes of God
are the deaf and the dumb—
those who do not reason.

23 If God had seen any good in them,
He would have made them listen;
yet even if He had, they would still
turn away, utterly averse.

24 You who believe, answer God
and His messenger when they
invite you to what will give you life.
And know that God will come
between a person and their heart,
and that you will be gathered to
Him.

25 And beware of any strife
that might harm not just
the wrongdoers among you—know
that God is Severe in Retribution.

26 Remember when you were few—
seen throughout the land as weak,
fearing that people might seize
you—
He sheltered you,
strengthened you with His help,
and provided you with good things,
that you might be grateful.

27 You who believe, do not betray
the trust of God and the messenger,
and do not knowingly betray
what is entrusted to you.

28 And you should know that
your possessions and your children
are merely a trial, and that
there is a great reward with God.

SECTION 4

29 You who believe,
if you fear God,
He will give you a criterion
of right and wrong,
absolve you of your bad deeds
and forgive you—
for God harbors abundant grace.

30 Remember, Prophet, how
the unbelievers schemed against
     you,
to keep you captive, or kill you
or drive you out.
While they were scheming,
God was scheming;
and God is the best of schemers.

31 When Our verses were recited
to them, they exclaimed,
"We've heard this before;
if we wished, we too
could speak like this—
these are merely
tales of the ancients."

32 And they said, "God, if this
really is the truth from you,
rain down upon us a shower
of stones from the sky,
or bring us some painful torment."

33 But God would not punish them
with you among them, Prophet,
nor would He punish them
if they sought forgiveness.

34 And how could they claim
that God should not punish them
when they bar people
from the sacred mosque,°
though they are not its guardians?
Its only rightful guardians
are those who are mindful of God,
though most disbelievers
don't discern this.

35 Their prayers at God's House are
nothing but whistling and
     clapping—
"Taste, then, the punishment,
for your disbelieving."

36 The unbelievers spend their wealth
to bar people from the path of God,
and will keep doing so. In the end,
however, they will regret this—
they will be vanquished.
And the unbelievers
shall be gathered into hell.

37 God will divide
the wicked from the good

and He will heap
the wicked on top of one another,
piling them all together in hell—
they will be the ones who lose.

SECTION 5

38 Prophet, tell the unbelievers—
if they desist, their past deeds
will be forgiven,
but if they persist—[remember]
what happened to their ancestors.°

39 And fight them until
there is no more oppression,
and all religion is for God.
But if they cease—
God Sees all that they do.

40 But if they turn away, know
that God is your Protector—
the best Protector, the best Helper.

41 Know that, of the spoils you take,
one-fifth is for God, the messenger,
relatives, orphans, the needy,
and travelers—if you believe in God
and what was revealed to Our
   servant
on the day when right and wrong
were distinguished,°
the day the two forces met—
God has Power over all things.

42 Remember when you were
on the near side of the valley,
and they on the far side,

with the caravan below you.
Even if you had agreed
to meet in battle,
you would have failed to come.°

But the battle did happen, so that
God might bring to pass
a matter already decreed, so that
those who perished might perish
and those who lived might live
after clear proof had been given.
God is All Hearing, All Knowing.

43 Remember your dream, Prophet,
when God showed them to you as
   few;°
if He had shown them as many,
you would have lost heart, arguing
among yourselves over the issue;
but God preserved you—
He Knows what hearts enclose.

44 And when your forces met,
He made them seem few
in your eyes,
and made you seem few
in their eyes,
so that God might bring to pass
a matter already decreed—
all matters come back to God.

SECTION 6

45 You who believe,
when you meet a hostile force—
stand firm, and keep
remembering God

that you might succeed.

46 Obey God and His messenger,
 and do not quarrel with one another,
 or you may become
 disheartened and dispirited.
 And be patient—
 God is with those who show
  patience.

47 And don't be like those
 who left their homes, boastfully,
 to be seen of people, and
 to bar them from the path of God.
 For God Encompasses
 [in His knowing] all that they do.

48 And remember when Satan
 made their deeds seem fair to them,
 and said, "No force of men
 can vanquish you this day,
 for I am right beside you."°
 But when the two forces
 came within sight of each other,
 he turned on his heels, saying,
 "I disown you—for I see
 what you do not, and
 I fear God—for God
 is Severe in Retribution."

SECTION 7

49 The hypocrites and those
 with sick hearts say about believers,
 "Their religion has deluded them."
 But those who trust in God
 [should know that]

God is Almighty, All Wise.

50 If you could see—when angels
 take the souls of the unbelievers,
 striking their faces and their backs,
 saying, "Taste the torment
 of the blazing fire!"

51 "This is for the deeds
 your own hands have wrought°—
 for God never wrongs His servants."

52 Likewise with Pharaoh's people
 and those before them—
 they denied the signs of God,
 so God seized them for their sins.
 God is Strong, Severe in
  Retribution.

53 For God does not alter the grace
 He grants to people until they change
 what is within themselves—
 God is All Hearing, All Knowing.

54 Likewise with Pharaoh's people
 and those before them—
 they denied the signs of their Lord,
 so We destroyed them for their sins,
 and We drowned Pharaoh's people,
 for they were all wrongdoers.

55 The worst of creatures
 in the eyes of God
 are those who deny the truth,
 and will not believe—

56 those with whom
   you make a covenant, Prophet,
   then break it every time—
   those who don't fear God.

57 If you find them
   on the battlefield, scatter them
   so that those behind them
   will take heed.

58 And if you fear treachery
   from any group, openly
   dissolve your treaty with them,
   for God dislikes the treacherous.

SECTION 8

59 Let the unbelievers
   not imagine that they have won—
   they shall not escape.

60 And prepare against them
   whatever force you can,
   with steeds of war, to strike fear
   into God's enemies and yours,
   and others unknown to you
   but known to God.
   Whatever you spend in God's cause
   you shall get back in full—
   you shall not be wronged.

61 But if the enemy
   inclines toward peace,
   you should also incline to it,
   and put your trust in God—
   He is All Hearing, All Knowing.

62 If they intend to deceive you,
   know that God suffices for you;
   it is He who strengthened you
   with His help, and with the
       believers,

63 and He has brought unity
   between their hearts; had you spent
   all that is on the earth, you could not
   have brought such unity. But God
   has brought it between them—
   He is Almighty, All Wise.

64 Prophet, God suffices
   for you and for the believers
   who follow you.

SECTION 9

65 Prophet, rouse the believers
   to fight: if there are twenty of you
   who are steadfast, they will
       vanquish
   two hundred; and if there are a
       hundred,
   they will vanquish a thousand
   of the unbelievers, for they
   are people void of understanding.

66 God has now lightened
   your burden, for He knows
   the weakness in you—
   if there are a hundred of you
   who are steadfast, they will
       vanquish
   two hundred, and if a thousand,
   they will vanquish two thousand,

by God's leave—for God
is with the steadfast.

67 It is not fitting for the Prophet
to take prisoners of war
before prevailing on the battlefield;
you desire the goods of this life,
but God desires for you the hereafter,
and God is Almighty, All Wise.

68 Had a decree not been
preordained by God,°
you would be punished greatly
for what you have taken.°

69 Enjoy, then, what you have taken,
in a good and lawful manner,
but be mindful of God—
God is Forgiving, Ever Merciful.

SECTION 10

70 Prophet, say to the captives
in your hands, "If God knows
of any good in your hearts,
He will give you something better
than what was taken from you,
and He will forgive you—
God is Forgiving, Ever Merciful."

71 But if they seek to betray you,
they have betrayed God before—
so He has made you
prevail over them—
God is All Knowing, All Wise.

72 Those who believed, emigrated
and strove with their wealth
and their lives in the cause of God,
and those who gave shelter and help,
are allies of one another.°

As for those who believed
but did not migrate,° you are not
obliged to protect them
until they migrate.
But if they seek your help
on religious grounds,°
it's your duty to give them help,
except against any people
with whom you have a treaty—
God Sees all that you do.

73 The unbelievers are mutual allies;
unless you do likewise,
there will be oppression in the land
and much corruption.

74 Those who believe and emigrate,
striving in the cause of God,
and those who give shelter and
   help—
those are the true believers.
They shall find forgiveness
and a gracious provision.

75 Those who believed afterward,
and emigrated and strove with you
in the cause of God—they are of you;
but in the Book of God°
relatives have prior claim
over one another—
God Knows all things.

SURA 9

Repentance (*Al-Tawba*)

The sole sura without the opening *basmala*, or invocation of God's name, its title, "Repentance," comes from v. 104. It consists of 129 verses, closely tied to the themes and issues of Sura 8, especially conduct during and after war. Verses 38–99 refer to the Tabuk campaign in 630, the last battle in which the Prophet Muhammad participated, making this a late Medinan sura revealed shortly before the Prophet's death in 632.

SECTION 1

1 [A proclamation] that God
and His messenger have dissolved
your treaty with the polytheists.

2 Polytheists, you may go about
freely for four months, but know
that
you cannot escape God, and that
God will disgrace the disbelievers.

3 On the day of the greater pilgrimage,
God and His messenger
will proclaim to the people,
"God and His messenger are released
from any treaty with the polytheists.
Polytheists, it will be better for you
if you repent—but if you turn away,
know that you cannot escape God."
Prophet, warn the disbelievers
of severe torment—

4 except for those polytheists who
did not break their treaty with you
or aid anyone against you—fulfill

your treaty with them for its term.°
God loves those who are righteous.

5 But when the forbidden months
are over, kill the polytheists
wherever you encounter them;
seize them and besiege them
and lie in wait for them.
But if they repent, and pray,
and give in charity,
then let them go their way—
God is Forgiving, Ever Merciful.

6 If any of the polytheists should seek
protection from you, grant it to
them
so they might hear the Word of God,
then escort them to a safe place—
they are a people void of
knowledge.

SECTION 2

7 How could polytheists have a treaty
with God and His messenger
except those with whom you made

a treaty at the sacred mosque?
If they remain true to you,
stay true to them—
God loves those who are
    righteous.

8 So how could they° have a treaty—
   if they gain ascendancy over you,
   would they respect your ties of kin
   or pacts of mutual protection?
   They indulge you with their mouths
   but refuse you in their hearts,
   and most of them are rebellious.

9 They sold the verses of God
   for a paltry price,
   and they barred people
   from the path of God.
   How wicked are their deeds!

10 They do not respect
   ties of kin, in believers,
   or pacts of mutual protection—
   they are the transgressors.

11 But if they repent,
   are steadfast in prayer,
   and give due charity, then
   they are your brothers in faith.
   We make clear Our signs
   for a people with knowledge.

12 But if they break their oaths
   after their treaty with you,
   and defame your religion, then
   fight the leaders of disbelief
   —for oaths mean nothing to them—

to make them cease
[their transgression].

13 Won't you fight a people
   who broke their oaths and resolved
   to drive out the Prophet, and
   attacked you first? Do you fear
       them?
   It is God you should rightly fear
   if you are true believers.

14 Fight them—God will punish them
   by your hands, disgrace them,
   and help you vanquish them;
   He will heal the hearts
   of people who believe,

15 and purge the anger
   from their hearts.
   For God ever turns, relenting,
   to whom He will, and God
   is All Knowing, All Wise.

16 Or do you think
   you'll simply be left [untried]
   without God finding out
   those among you
   who strive in His cause,
   who take as allies none but God,
   His Prophet, and the believers?
   God is Aware of all that you do.

SECTION 3

17 It is not for the polytheists
   to maintain God's places of worship
   while attesting to their own unbelief.

The deeds of these people are vain—
they shall stay in the fire forever.°

18　God's places of worship
should be maintained only by those
who believe in God and the last day,
who are steadfast in prayer,
who give due charity,
and fear none but God.
It is they who are rightly guided.

19　Do you think that giving water to
　　pilgrims
and maintaining the sacred mosque
are on the same level as the deeds
of those who believe in God
and the last day, and strive
in the cause of God? These are not
the same in the eyes of God—
for God does not guide
people who do wrong.

20　As for those who believed,
and left their homes,
and strove in the cause of God
with their wealth and their persons—
they shall have the highest rank
in the eyes of God, and it is they
who shall flourish.

21　Their Lord gives them joyous news
of His mercy, His good pleasure,
and gardens for them with lasting
　　bliss,

22　residing there forever—
the greatest reward is with God.

23　You who believe, do not take
your fathers and brothers as allies
if they opt for disbelief over faith;
those who turn to them do wrong.

24　Declare, Prophet, "If your fathers,
sons, brothers, wives, relatives,
the wealth you've acquired,
the trade in which you fear decline,
the homes in which you delight—
if these are dearer to you than God
and His messenger, and striving
in His cause— then wait—until
　　God
brings about His judgment. For God
does not guide disobedient people.

SECTION 4

25　God has helped you
on many plains of battle,
and on the day of Hunayn;°
you were cheered
by your swelling numbers,
but they were of no help to you.
For all its breadth, the earth
seemed to close tight around you,
and you turned in flight.

26　Then God sent down His calm
on the messenger and believers,
and He sent down forces that
you did not see, punishing those
who disbelieved. This is the reward
of the disbelievers.

27 And, after this, God will turn,
   in His mercy, to whom He will—
   God is Forgiving, Ever Merciful.

28 You who believe:
   the polytheists are unclean,
   so don't let them approach
   the sacred mosque after this,
   their final year.
   And if you fear poverty,
   God shall soon enrich you
   from His bounty, if He wishes—
   God is All Knowing, All Wise.

29 Fight those among the people
   of the Book who do not believe
   in God and the last day,
   who do not forbid what God
   and His messenger have forbidden,
   and do not acknowledge
   the religion of truth—until
   they are subdued and
   agree to pay the *jizya* tax.°

SECTION 5

30 The Jews say,
   "Ezra is God's son,"°
   and the Christians say,
   "The messiah is God's son."
   They say this with their own
      mouths,
   but are merely rehearsing what
   disbelievers before them said.
   May God confound them!
   How deluded they are!°

31 They take their rabbis and monks
   as lords, as well as the messiah,
   son of Mary—besides the One God.
   Yet they were commanded to
      worship
   none but the One God. There is no
      god
   but Him. Glorified is He, far above
   the partners they ascribe to Him.

32 With their mouths they would
   extinguish the Light of God;
   but God will only allow
   His Light to be perfected,
   though the disbelievers detest it.

33 It is He who sent His messenger
   with guidance, the religion of truth,
   to make it prevail over all religion,
   though the polytheists detest it.

34 You who believe—
   many of the rabbis and monks
   wrongfully devour people's wealth,
   and bar people from God's path.
   You should warn those
   who hoard gold and silver,
   instead of spending it in God's
      cause,
   of a painful punishment.

35 On the day when
   that gold and silver
   is heated in the fire of hell,
   and their foreheads, sides, and backs
   are branded with it, they will be told,
   "This is what you hoarded

for yourselves—now,
taste what you hoarded."

36 God has decreed twelve months,
ordained in God's Book, on the day
He created the heavens and earth.
Of these, four are sacred;° this
is the upright religion. So do not
wrong yourselves during them;
but fight the polytheists all together
as they fight you all together—
know that God is with the
      righteous.°

37 Deferring the sacred months
is a further act of unbelief.°
Those who disbelieve
are led astray by doing this:
they deem it lawful one year
then forbid it another year
to conform to the number of months
deemed sacred by God,
but in doing this, they deem lawful
what God has forbidden.
Their wicked deeds seem
pleasing to them—
God does not guide
people who disbelieve.

SECTION 6

38 Believers, what's wrong with you—
when told, "Go forward and fight
in God's cause," you seem weighed
down to the ground?° Do you prefer
the life of this world to the hereafter?

Enjoyment of this life is a trifle
compared with the hereafter.

39 Unless you do go forward,
He will punish you severely
and put others in your place,
for you can do no harm to Him—
God has Power over all things.

40 Even if you don't help the Prophet,
God helped him when unbelievers
drove him out [with Abu Bakr].
When the two hid in a cave,
the Prophet told his companion,
"Don't grieve—God is with us."
And God sent His calm upon him,
and strengthened him with forces
that you could not see;
He humbled the disbelievers' words,
and the Word of God was exalted—
for God is Almighty, All Wise.°

41 Advance, lightly or heavily armed,
and strive, with your wealth and
      lives
in God's cause; that is better for you
if only you knew.

42 They would have followed you,
if some gain had been within easy
      reach,
and the journey brief—but
the distance seemed too far for them.
They'll swear by God, "If we could,
we'd come out with you,"
but they condemn themselves,°
for God knows they are lying.

SECTION 7

43 Prophet, may God pardon you;
    why did you exempt them from
        fighting
    before it was made clear to you
    which ones were telling the truth
    and which ones were lying?

44 Those who believe in God
    and the last day do not ask you
    to exempt them from striving
    with their wealth and their lives.
    And God Knows those
    who were mindful of Him.°

45 Only those who don't believe
    in God and the last day
    ask you for exemption—those
    whose hearts are doubtful, wavering
    back and forth, in their doubt.

46 Had they wanted to go and fight
    with you, they would have prepared.
    But God would not countenance
    their going out, so He made them
    lag behind, and they were told,
        "Stay,
    with the others who stay behind."

47 Had they come out with you,
    they would only
    have wrought confusion,
    actively sowing discord
    in your midst—and some among
        you
    would have listened to them—

God has full Knowledge
of those who do wrong.

48 Indeed, they had sought before
    to sow discord, and to overturn
    your plans°—until the truth
        emerged,
    and God's command was revealed,
    though they loathed it.

49 Some of them say,
    "Exempt me from fighting,
    and don't drag me into trial."
    Have they not fallen
    already into trial?
    Hell shall encompass
    the disbelievers.

50 If something good comes to you,
    this grieves them; but if some
        trouble
    comes your way, they say smugly,
    "Well, we already took precautions,"
    and they turn away, exulting.

51 Say, "Nothing shall happen to us
    beyond what God has decreed for
        us;
    He is our Protector—so let believers
    put their trust in God."

52 Say, "What do you expect for us
    beyond one of the two best
        outcomes
    [—martyrdom or victory]?
    What we expect for *you*
    is God's punishment, either

from Himself or at our hands.
So, wait—we are waiting with
    you."°

53 Say, "Whether you give to charity
    willingly or unwillingly,
    it will never be accepted of you,
    for you are disobedient people."

54 Nothing stops their spending
    from being accepted except
    that they disbelieve in God
    and His messenger,
    perform their prayer slothfully,
    and give to charity grudgingly.

55 Don't be dazzled by their wealth
    or their children. God intends
    to punish them by both of these
    in the life of this world,
    and to let their souls take leave
    while they disbelieve.

56 They swear by God
    that they are with you, the believers,
    but they are not—
    for they are cowardly people.

57 If they could find a refuge,
    or some cave or a place to hide,
    they would bolt to it in wild panic.

58 And some of them upbraid you
    about the giving of alms;
    if they receive a share of them,
    they're appeased; if not, they seethe.

59 If only they had been content
    with what God and His messenger
    had given them; if they had said,
    "God suffices for us;
    God and His messenger
    will give us of His bounty—
    we turn in hope to God alone."

SECTION 8

60 Alms° are only for
    the poor, the needy,
    those who administer them,
    those whose hearts
    are to be won,
    the freeing of slaves,
    those in debt,
    those in the cause of God,
    and travelers.
    This is an obligation
    imposed by God—
    God is All Knowing, All Wise.

61 Some of them hurt the Prophet,
    saying "He listens to anything."
    Say, "He listens to what
    is good for you;
    he believes in God,
    has faith in the believers,
    and is a mercy to those of you
    who believe."
    Those who hurt the Prophet,
    shall face painful torment.

62 They swear by God before you
    just to please you;
    but it is God and His messenger

—who have greater claim—
that they should please
if they are true believers.

63 Don't they know that those
who oppose God and His messenger
shall feel the fire of hell—where
they shall stay forever.
That is the supreme disgrace.

64 The hypocrites fear
that a sura will be revealed
exposing what's in their hearts.
Say, "By all means, mock!
For God will bring to pass
exactly what you fear."

65 If you ask them about this,
they'll be sure to say,
"We were just talking lightly,
amusing ourselves."
Say, "Was it God, His signs,
and His messenger
that you were mocking?

66 "Don't offer excuses—
you sank from belief into disbelief.
Even if We pardon some of you,
We shall punish others,
for they were sinners."

SECTION 9

67 The hypocrites, men and women,
are all alike: they urge what is
     wrong,
     forbid what is right,

and are tightfisted.
They have forgotten God,
so He has forgotten them—
the hypocrites are rebellious.

68 God has promised the fire of hell
to the hypocrites, men and women,
as well as the disbelievers—
where they will stay forever.
It is fitting° for them.
God has cursed them, and
they shall face enduring torment.

69 You are just like those before you;
but they were stronger,
with more wealth and children.
They enjoyed their lot
as did you and those before you.
And you indulge in idle talk
just like them. Their deeds
will come to nothing,
in this world and the hereafter,
and they will be the losers.

70 Have they not heard the story
of those before them?
Of the people of Noah, 'Ad,
Thamud, Abraham, Midian,
and the fallen cities?
Their messengers came to them
with clear signs—
it was not God who wronged them,
but they who wronged themselves.

71 The believers, men and women,
are allies of one another.
They enjoin what is right

and forbid what is wrong;
they are steadfast in prayer,
and give duly to charity;
they obey God and His messenger.
They are the ones on whom
God shall have mercy—
God is Almighty, All Wise.

72 God has promised gardens
to the believing men and women,
with rivers flowing beneath,
abiding there forever,
residing in splendid homes
in gardens of lasting bliss.
But greater than this
is the good pleasure of God—
that is the supreme triumph.

SECTION 10

73 Prophet, strive against
the unbelievers and the hypocrites,
and deal firmly with them;
their home shall be hell, an evil end.

74 They swear by God
that they said nothing,
but they did—
they uttered words of disbelief,
and they did disbelieve, having
[pretended to] submit to God's will.

And they vainly plotted [harm
to the Prophet]. This revenge
was their only response after
God and His messenger had
enriched them from God's bounty.°

If they turn to repent,
that will be better for them;
but if they turn away,
God will give them severe torment
in this world and the hereafter,
and they shall have
no protector or helper on the earth.

75 Some of them pledged to God,
"If He gives to us from His bounty,
we'll be sure to give to charity
and we will be righteous."

76 But when He did give them
from His bounty, they were miserly
   with it,
and turned away.

77 He lodged hypocrisy in their hearts,
by way of requital, until the day they
   meet Him—
for they broke their promise to God
and would always lie.

78 Don't they know
that God knows their secrets
and secret counsels,
that He Knows the unseen?

79 Some people reproach believers
who give freely to charity
as well as believers who can give
no more than what they toil for
—they mock them—
but God will mock them,
and they shall face severe torment.

80 Prophet, whether you ask
   forgiveness for them or not,
   [it is all the same]—
   even if you ask seventy times,
   God will not forgive them,
   for they denied God
   and His messenger,
   and God does not forgive
   people who are disobedient.

SECTION II

81 Those who were left behind
   [in the Tabuk mission]
   were happy to stay back,°
   in defiance of God's messenger,
   for they scorned to strive
   with their wealth and lives
   in the cause of God, saying,
   "Don't advance in this heat."
   Say, the fire of hell
   is fiercer in its heat"—if only
   they could understand.

82 So let them laugh a little;
   they will weep a lot—the reward
   they'll reap for all their deeds.

83 Prophet, if God brings you again
   to any group of them, and they ask
   your permission to come out
   and fight alongside you, say,
   "You shall never come out with me,
   and you shall never fight the enemy
   by my side. For you preferred
   to sit idle the first time—so stay now
   with the others who stayed behind."

84 And don't ever pray
   for any of them who died,
   nor stand at their graveside.
   They denied God
   and His messenger,
   and were disobedient
   when they died.

85 Don't be dazzled by their wealth
   or their children. God intends
   to punish them by both of these
   in the life of this world,
   and to let their souls take leave
   while they disbelieve.

86 When a sura is revealed
   exhorting them, "Believe in God,
   and strive alongside His messenger,"
   the wealthy among them ask you
   to exempt them, "Leave us—
   with those who stay back."

87 They prefer to be
   with those who stay back;
   their hearts are sealed
   so they don't understand.

88 As for the messenger
   and those who believe with him,
   striving with their wealth,
      their lives—
   the best things shall be theirs;
   they are the ones who will flourish.

89 God has prepared gardens
   for them, with rivers
      flowing beneath,

to live there forever—
that is the supreme triumph.

SECTION 12

90 Bedouin Arabs° came also,
making excuses, seeking exemption;
those who lied to God and
His messenger also stayed behind.
Severe torment shall strike
the disbelievers among them.

91 There is no blame on those
who can't fight if they are weak,
or sick, or don't have the means
to spend anything—
as long as they are true
to God and His messenger;
nor is there cause to blame
those who do good—
for God is Forgiving, Ever Merciful.

92 Nor is there blame
on those who came to you
asking for mounts to convey them,
and whom you told,
"I can find no mounts for you."
They turned away, their eyes
streaming with tears of grief
because they had no means
to [join the battle].

93 Blame falls only on those
who ask you to exempt them
in spite of their wealth,
and prefer to stay with
the others who stay behind.

God has sealed their hearts,
so they are void of knowledge.

94 When you return [from fighting],
they'll offer their excuses to you.
Say, "Don't offer excuses.
We won't believe you.
God has informed us about you.
God and His messenger
will observe your deeds,
and you will be returned
to the Knower of the unseen
and the seen—
and He will inform you
of all you have done."

95 When you return [from fighting],
they'll swear by God to you—
so you might leave them alone.
So, leave them alone.
They are defiled, and their home
shall be hell—the reward
they reap for all they have done.

96 They swear to you,
in order to please you;
but even if you
were pleased with them,
God is displeased
with disobedient people.

97 The Bedouin Arabs are the worst
of any in disbelief and hypocrisy,
and the least likely to recognize
the limits revealed by God
to His messenger—
God is All Knowing, All Wise.

98 Some of the Bedouin Arabs
         consider
   what they spend in God's cause
   as a loss, and wait for misfortune
   to befall you. It is on them
   that ill fortune shall fall—
   God is All Hearing, All Knowing.

99 But others among the Bedouin
         Arabs
   believe in God and the last day,
   and consider what they spend
   as a means of bringing them
   nearer to God and the prayers
   of the messenger. It is indeed
   such a means for them.
   God will bring them into His
         mercy—
   God is Forgiving, Ever Merciful.

SECTION 13

100 God is well pleased
    with the forerunners°—the first
    emigrants and helpers, and those
    who followed them in good deeds,
    and they are pleased with Him.
    He has prepared gardens for them,
    with rivers flowing beneath,
    to live there for eternity—
    that is the supreme triumph.

101 Some Bedouin Arabs around you
    are hypocrites, as are some people
    of Medina. They persist in
         hypocrisy.
    Prophet, you do not know them—

We do—We shall punish them
      twice,
then they shall be brought again
to face great punishment
[in the hereafter].

102 But others among them
    have acknowledged their wrongs,
    having mingled good deeds with
         bad.
    Perhaps God will turn to them,
    relenting. God is Forgiving,
    Ever Merciful.

103 Accept some gifts for charity
    from their wealth, so that you might
    purge and purify them;
    and pray for them.
    Your prayers will comfort them—
    God is All Hearing, All Knowing.

104 Don't they know that God
    is the One who accepts repentance
    from His servants, and their
         charity—
    that God is the One Who is
    Ever Relenting, Ever Merciful?

105 Say, Prophet, "Do good deeds—
    God, His messenger, and believers
    will see your deeds;
    and you will be brought back
    to the Knower of the unseen
    and the seen,
    and He will inform you
    of all you have done."

106 There are others for whom
     God's decree is pending, whether
     He will punish them
     or turn to them, relenting—
     God is All Knowing, All Wise.

107 Some people set up a mosque
     just to wreak harm, disbelief,
     and division among believers,
     using it as a base for those
     who warred before against God
     and His messenger. They will swear,
     "We only wanted what was best"—
     but God bears witness
     that they are liars.°

108 Prophet, never stand to pray there.
     It's more fitting that you stand
     [in prayer] in a mosque founded
     from the first day
     on mindfulness of God—
     where people like to purify
         themselves;
     God likes those who seek purity.

109 Who, then, is better—
     someone who founds their edifice
     on mindfulness of God
     and His good pleasure,
     or someone who founds it
     at the brink of a precipice
     about to collapse, which crumbles,
     with them, into the fire of hell?
     God does not guide
     a people who do wrong.

110 The edifice they have founded
     will never cease to breed doubt
     in their hearts, until their hearts
     are hewn to pieces—
     God is All Knowing, All Wise.

SECTION 14

111 God has made a trade
     with the believers:
     their lives and their wealth—
     for the gardens of paradise.
     They fight in the cause of God,
     to kill and be killed.
     His promise is true—in the Torah,
     the Gospel, and the Qur'an.
     Who is truer to his promise than
         God?
     So rejoice in the trade you made—
     it is the supreme triumph.

112 Give joyous news
     to the believers—
     those who turn to God, repenting,
     those who worship Him,
     who praise Him,
     who go out [to fight for Him],
     those who bow
     and prostrate themselves,
     those who enjoin what is right,
     and forbid what is wrong,
     and those who observe
     the limits set by God.

113 It is not for the Prophet
     or those who believe to ask

forgiveness for the polytheists
—even if they are near of kin—
once it is clear to them that
they shall be inmates of hellfire.

114 Abraham did ask forgiveness for
      his father,
   only because he had made him a
      promise.
   But when it was clear to him that
      his father
   was an enemy of God, he disowned
      him—
   Abraham was tenderhearted,
      forbearing.

115 God will not let people go astray
   after guiding them,
   without making clear to them
   what they should fear to do.
   God Knows all things.

116 God holds dominion
   over the heavens and the earth;
   He gives life, and He brings death;
   and besides God, you have no
   protector or helper.

117 God turned, in mercy,
   to the Prophet, and the emigrants
   and helpers who followed him
   in the hour of difficulty, though
   some of their hearts almost wavered.
   Then He turned to them, in mercy.
   He is Kind to them, Ever Merciful.

118 [He turned, in mercy, also]
   to the three who were left behind,°
   when the earth, for all its breadth
   closed in around them, and
   their own souls closed in upon them,
   until they were sure there was no
   refuge from God except with Him.
   Then He turned to them, that they
   might turn to Him in repentance.
   God is Ever Relenting,
   Ever Merciful.

SECTION 15

119 You who believe,
   be mindful of God,
   and stand with those
   who are truthful.

120 The people of Medina
   and the neighboring Bedouin Arabs
   should not have stayed behind,
   failing to follow God's messenger;
   nor should they have placed
   their own lives before his—
   for any thirst they suffer,
   any fatigue, any hunger
   in the cause of God,
   any step they take
   to antagonize the disbelievers,
   any harm they inflict on an enemy—
   each of these is recorded
   as a good deed on their behalf.
   God will not overlook
   the reward of those who do good.

121 Whether they spend little or much
in God's cause, or traverse a valley,
it will be recorded on their behalf;
God will reward them
for the best of their deeds.

122 Nor should the believers
all go out to fight together. If a group
from each force should venture out,
to gain understanding of the faith,
they might exhort the others
when they return to them,
so that they might take heed.

SECTION 16

123 You who believe, fight
the unbelievers who lie close to you,
and let them find you standing firm;
know that God is with those
who are mindful of Him.

124 Whenever a sura is revealed,
some of the hypocrites taunt,
"Which of you has it increased in
  faith?"
The faith of those who believe
has indeed increased,
and they rejoice.

125 But for those with diseased hearts,
it adds vileness to their vileness,
and they shall die as disbelievers.

126 Don't they see that they
are tried every year, once or twice?
Yet they don't repent,
nor do they take heed.

127 Whenever a sura is revealed,
they stare at one another, saying,
"Does anyone see you?"
Then they turn away.
God has turned their hearts away,
for they are people
void of understanding.

128 A messenger has come to you
from your own people.
He grieves over your suffering,
cares for you, and is kind,
merciful to the believers.°

129 But if they turn away,
say, "God suffices for me;
there is no god but Him,
and in Him I place my trust;
for He is Lord of the mighty throne."

Jonah (*Yunus*)

A late Meccan sura of 109 verses, this is the first of numerous suras named after one of the many Abrahamic prophets recognized and lauded in Islam. Though Jonah is cited (v. 98), other prophets are also prominent, including Noah, Moses, and Aaron. The final 11 verses (vv. 99–109) are addressed directly to the Prophet Muhammad.

In the Name of God, the All Merciful, Ever Merciful

1 *Alif. Lam. Ra.*°
These are the verses
of the Wise Book.

2 Are people surprised
that We inspired one of them°
to warn humankind,
and to give joyous news
to those who believe,
that they have a firm footing
with their Lord?
The unbelievers say,
"This is a brazen sorcerer."

3 Your Lord is God,
Who created the heavens
and the earth in six days,
then stationed Himself
on the throne, administering
all things. None can intercede
without His leave.
This is God, your Lord,
so worship Him.
Will you not take heed?

4 All of you will return to Him.
The promise of God is true.
It is He who produced creation,
then renewed it, that He might
justly reward those who believe
and do good deeds.
But those who disbelieve
shall taste a boiling potion
and painful punishment,
for their persistent disbelief.

5 It is He who made the sun
radiant and the moon
a softer light,
ordaining phases for it
so you might know
the number of years
and the measure of time.°
God created all this
only with true purpose
He explains His signs
for a people who know.

6 In the revolving cycle
of night and day,
and in all that God created
in the heavens and the earth,
are signs for people
who are mindful of God.

7 As for those who don't
expect to meet with Us,
who are pleased and content
with the life of this world,
and those who are heedless
of Our signs—

8 they shall have the fire
as their home—
for all they have done.

9 But those who believe
and do good deeds,
their Lord will guide them
for their faith;
beneath them will flow rivers
in gardens of bliss.

10 Their refrain there will be
"Glory to You, O God,"
and their greeting there
will be "Peace."
Their refrain will close with
"All praise be to God,
Lord of the universe."

11 If God were to hasten for people
the evil [they reap] just as they
hasten after [worldly] good,
their decreed term
would already have expired.
But We let those who
don't expect to meet Us
wander blindly
in their transgression.

12 When harm befalls someone,
they call to Us—reclining,°
or sitting, or standing.
But when we remove the harm,
they move on as if
they had never called on Us.
This is how the profligates' deeds
are made to seem pleasing to them.

13 We destroyed generations
before you, when they did wrong,
when messengers came to them
with clear signs,
and they would not believe.
This is how We requite sinful people.

14 Then We made you
their successors on the earth,
so We might see what you would do.

15 But when Our clear signs
are recited to them,
those who don't expect to meet Us
say, "Bring us a recitation
other than this, or change it."
Say, "It is not for me to change it
of my own accord; I follow
only what is revealed to me.
If I disobeyed my Lord, I would
fear punishment on the great day."

16 Say, "If God had wished it,
   I would not have recited it to you,
   nor would He make it known to you.
   I was actually among you° a lifetime
   before revelation came.
   Won't you understand?"

17 Who does greater wrong
   than someone who invents lies
   about God or denies His signs?
   Sinners will never flourish.

18 Besides God, they worship things
   that can neither hurt nor profit them,
   yet they say, "These are
   our intercessors with God." Say,
   "Do you presume to tell God
   that there is something
   He does not know
   in the heavens and on the earth?
   Glory be to Him—
   May He be exalted far above
   what they associate with Him."

19 Humankind was one community,
   until they differed among
      themselves.
   Had your Lord not already decreed
   [a deferred punishment for them,]°
   a judgment would have been passed
   concerning their differences.°

20 And they say,
   "Why is no sign sent down to him
   from his Lord?"
   Tell them, "The unseen is known
   to God alone.

So, wait—and I will be waiting
with you."

21 When We let people taste mercy
   after affliction strikes them,
   see how they begin to scheme
   against Our signs. Say,
   "God is swifter in scheming."
   Our messengers are recording
   all that you scheme.

22 It is He who lets you journey
   on land and sea,
   when you are in ships that sail
   with a fair wind, which brings joy.
   Then comes a storming wind,
   waves lashing from every side,
   and they imagine they'll be
      engulfed.
   They cry out to God, sincere
   to Him in faith,
   "If You save us from this,
   we'll be truly grateful."

23 But once he saves them,
   they transgress on the earth
   against all that is right.
   Humankind, you transgress
   against yourselves—
   delighting in the life of the world,
   but you will be returned to Us,
   and We shall show you
   all that you have done.

24 The life of the world
   is merely like the rain
   We send down from the sky,

absorbed by earth's greenery,
from which humans
and animals eat;
once the earth is bedecked
in its gilded beauty,
and its people think they
have power over it,
Our command reaches it,
by night or day,
and We turn it into
a bare harvest,
as if just yesterday
it had never flourished.
This is how We explain Our signs
for a people who reflect.

25 God calls [all people]
to the house of peace
and guides whom He will
to a straight path.

26 Those who do what is good
shall have what is good, and more;
neither darkness nor shame
shall cover their faces.
They shall inhabit
the garden—forever.°

27 But those who did evil
shall reap a reward of equal evil:
they shall be covered with shame,
with no defender against God—
as if their faces were covered
with fragments from the
depth of night's darkness.
They shall be inmates
of the fire—forever.

28 And on the day
we gather them all together,
We shall say to those
who joined other gods with Us,
"Stay in your place,
you and your gods."
And We shall separate
the one from the other.
And those gods will say,
"It was not us whom
you worshipped.

29 "God will suffice as witness
between ourselves and you,
that we were unaware
of your worship of us."

30 There, each of the souls
will be tried for its past deeds;
and they will be returned
to God, their true Master.
And the gods they invented
will abandon them.

31 Say, "Who gives you sustenance
from the sky and earth?" or
"Who controls hearing and sight?
Who brings the living
from the dead, and the dead
from the living?
Who regulates all affairs?"
They will say, "God."
Tell them, "Will you not then
be mindful of God?"

32 This is God, your Lord, the Truth.
What is there beyond truth, but error?
So how can you be turned away?

33 And so the Word of your Lord
has proven true against those who
disobey—they won't believe.

34 Ask, "Can any of the gods
whom you join with God
initiate the creation,
and then renew it?
Say, "It is God alone
who initiates creation,
and renews it. So how
can you be deluded?"

35 Ask, "Can any of the gods
whom you join with God
guide anyone to truth?"
Say, "It is God
Who guides to truth.
Is One Who guides to truth
not worthier to be followed
than one who cannot guide
without being guided?
What is it with you?
How do you judge?"

36 And most of them follow
nothing but opinion.
Opinion cannot prevail
at all against truth.
God is Aware of what they do.

37 This Qur'an could not
be conceived by anyone but God.
It confirms what came before it,
and it explains the scripture
that is free of all doubt,
from the Lord of the universe.

38 Or do they say,
"He [Muhammad] invented it"?
Say to them,
"Then bring a sura like it,
and call on whomever you can
besides God,
if you are speaking the truth."

39 No—they deny it,
whose knowledge
they cannot compass,°
yet its explication
has not come to them.
Those before them
also denied.
Observe, then, the fate
of the wrongdoers.

40 Some of them believe in it,
and others do not—
your Lord knows best
those who wreak mischief.

41 And if they deny you, say,
"My actions belong to me,
and yours to you.
You will not answer for what I do,
nor I for what you do."

42 Some of them seem
to listen to you.
But can you make

the deaf listen,
if they won't use reason?

43 Some of them seem
to observe you.
But can you guide the blind
if they won't see?

44 God does not wrong
human beings at all;
it is humans who
wrong themselves.

45 On the day, He will gather them,
as if they had stayed but an hour
of the day; they'll know one another.
Those who denied the meeting
with God will be lost,
for they were not guided.

46 Prophet, whether We let you see
some of the punishment
We promised them while you live,
or cause you to die before that,
they shall return to Us;
God shall be Witness
to all they have done.

47 A messenger is sent
to every community, and when
a messenger comes to them,
they shall be judged fairly
and shall not be wronged.

48 They ask,
"When shall the promise be
fulfilled,
if what you say is true?"

49 Say, "I have no power over
any harm or good to myself
beyond what God wills.
Every nation has its appointed term.
When their term is due, they can
neither delay it nor advance it—
not even by an hour."

50 Say, "Do you see,
if His punishment came to you
by night or by day—
which part of it would the sinners
seek to hasten?"

51 "Will you believe in it
only when it comes?
Now? Even though [before]
you sought to hasten it?"

52 Then the wrongdoers will be told,
"Taste the eternal punishment.
Are you requited for anything
other than what you reaped?"

53 They ask you, Prophet, "Is it true?"
Say, "Yes, by my Lord, it is true,
and you cannot escape."

54 If every soul that has sinned
possessed all that is on the earth,
it would give it all to ransom itself.
When they saw the punishment

they would repent inwardly—
yet they will be judged with justice,
and they will not be wronged.

55 All that is in the heavens
and earth belongs to God.
The promise of God is true—
yet most people don't know it.

56 It is He Who gives life
and He Who brings death—
to Him you will be returned.

57 People, a warning
has come to you from your Lord,
and healing for what is in your
hearts,
as well as guidance and mercy
for those who believe.

58 Say, "Let them rejoice
in the bounty of God,
and in His mercy—
these are better than the goods
they accumulate."

59 Ask, "Have you seen the provision
that God has sent down for you?
Yet you deem some of it
forbidden, some lawful."
Ask, "Has God given you
permission
for this, or are you inventing
things about God?"

60 As for those who invent lies
about God—what do they think
will happen on the day of
resurrection?
God is Full of Grace to humankind,
but most of them are ungrateful.

61 There is no circumstance
you might be in,
no part of the Qur'an you recite,
no deed that you do,
that We do not witness—whenever
you engage in it.

Nothing escapes your Lord,
not the weight of an atom
in earth or in heaven,
nor anything smaller,
nor larger—all are recorded
in a clear Book.

62 But those who ally themselves
with God shall have no fear,
nor shall they grieve—

63 those who believe
and are mindful of God.

64 There is joyous news for them
in the life of this world,
and in the hereafter.
There is no changing
the words of God—
the supreme triumph.

65 Don't let their words grieve you;
all power belongs to God—
the Hearing, the Knowing.

66   All those in the heavens
      and all those on earth
      undoubtedly belong to God.
      And what do they follow,
      those who call upon others
      besides God?
      They follow nothing
      but opinion,
      and they do nothing
      but guess.

67   It is He Who made for you
      the night, in which you might rest,
      and the day, which gives you sight.
      In this are signs for people who
         hear.

68   They say, "God has a son."
      Praise Him: He is Self-Sufficient—
      to Him belongs
      all that is in the heavens
      and all that is on the earth.
      You have no sanction
      for saying this.
      Would you say about God
      what you do not know?

69   Say, "Those who invent lies
      about God will never prosper."

70   Their span of enjoyment
      in this world is brief—then
      they will return to Us
      and We shall make them taste
      the severest torment
      for their persistent disbelief.

71   Tell them the story of Noah.
      He said to his people,
      "My people, if it vexes you
      that I remain among you,
      and remind you of the signs of God,
      then I place my trust in God.
      So form your plan, openly,
      with your other gods.
      Then inflict it upon me—
      without respite.

72   "But if you turn away, know that
      I have asked no reward of you.
      My reward is with God alone;
      and I have been commanded
      to submit my will to God."

73   Still, they denied him,
      but We delivered him,
      and those with him, in the ark,
      making them heirs to the land,
      and We drowned those
      who denied Our signs—
      observe, then, the outcome
      of those who were warned.

74   After him We sent messengers
      to their respective peoples,
      who brought them clear signs,
      but they refused to believe
      what they had already denied—
      see how We seal up the hearts
      of the transgressors.

75   After them
      We sent Moses and Aaron
      to Pharaoh and his chiefs

with Our signs.
But they were too proud—
a nation of sinners.

76 When the truth came to them
from Us, they said, "Plain sorcery!"

77 Moses asked, "Is this what you say
about the truth, when it comes to you?
Sorcery? Sorcerers have no success."

78 They said, "Have you come
to turn us away from the faith
of our forefathers,
so that you two might gain
stature in the land?
We don't believe you."

79 And Pharaoh said, "Bring
every expert sorcerer to me."

80 When the sorcerers came,
Moses said to them,
"Throw down whatever
you want to throw!"

81 When they had thrown,
Moses told them,
"Everything you come up with
is sorcery—God will nullify it.
God will not rectify the deeds
of those who wreak mischief.

82 "And God proves the truth
by His words, though
the sinners may loathe it."

83 But, apart from some youths,
none of his people believed Moses
for fear that Pharaoh and his nobles
might persecute them—
for Pharaoh was domineering
through the land, given to excess.

84 Moses said, "My people,
if you believe in God,
put your trust in Him,
if you really submit to His will.

85 They said, "We trust in God—
Our Lord, don't let us be oppressed
by an unjust people,

86 "and deliver us
through Your mercy
from this unbelieving people."

87 We inspired Moses and his brother
with these words,
"Settle your people in homes
in Egypt, and make your homes
sanctuaries for worship.°
Be steadfast in prayer,
and give joyous news to
those who believe."

88 Moses entreated,
"Our Lord, you have endowed
Pharaoh and his nobles
with splendor and wealth
in the life of the world—
and they lead people astray
from Your path.
Our Lord, wipe out their wealth

and harden their hearts,
so that they don't believe
until they see
the painful punishment."

89 God said, "Your prayers
are answered, so remain steadfast,
both of you, and don't follow
the path of those who don't know."

90 We took the children of Israel
across the sea.
Pharaoh and his armies, rebellious
and belligerent, pursued them.
Eventually, when he was drowning,
Pharaoh cried out,
"I believe that there is no god
but the One God in Whom
the children of Israel believe,
and I submit to His will."

91 "Now? When before
you were always disobedient,
and wrought mischief?

92 "Yet this day We shall
preserve your body—as a sign
for those who succeed you.
Yet most of humankind
are heedless of Our signs."

93 We settled the children of Israel
in a congenial venue, and gave them
good things to sustain them.
Only when knowledge came
    to them
did they differ among themselves.

Your Lord shall judge between them
on the day of resurrection
concerning the things they disputed.

94 So, Prophet, if you are in doubt
about what We have revealed to you,
ask those who have been
reading the Book before you.
The truth has come to you
from your Lord,
so don't be unsure,

95 nor deny the signs of God—then
you would be among those in loss.

96 Those on whom
your Lord's sentence has passed
will not believe,

97 even if every single sign
comes their way
until they are face-to-face
with the painful torment.

98 Why is it that
not a single town believed,
and benefited from its belief,
except the people of Jonah?
When they believed,
We erased for them the
punishment of disgrace
in the life of this world,
and We granted them
enjoyment for a while.

99 If it had been your Lord's wish,
everyone on earth would believe.

But would you, Prophet,
compel people to believe?

100 No soul can believe, except
by God's leave; He despoils
those who won't use reason.

101 Tell them, "Observe all
that is in the heavens and earth."
But neither signs nor those who
   warn
can help a people who don't believe.

102 Do they wait, then, only
to meet a fate like those
who passed away before them?
Say, "Wait, then—
I will be waiting with you."

103 In the end, We shall save
Our messengers and those
who believe. It is for Us
to save the believers.°

104 Say, "People, if you are still
in doubt about my religion—
know that I do not worship
those you worship besides God,
but I worship the One God,
Who will cause you to die.
And I am commanded
to be a believer.

105 "And [I was commanded],
'Set your sight° toward
the religion of the upright
and do not be a polytheist'

106 "and do not call upon
any besides God, on those
who can neither profit nor harm
   you—
for you would be doing wrong."

107 If God brings adversity to you,
none can remove it but He;
and if He intends good for you,
none can withhold His favor.
He bestows His bounty
on whichever of His servants He
   will,
for He is Forgiving, Ever Merciful.

108 Say, "People, the truth
has come to you from your Lord.
Whoever accepts guidance
does so for their own good,°
and whoever strays,
does so to their own loss°—
and I am not your custodian."

109 So, Prophet, follow
what is revealed to you,
and be patient until God
delivers His judgment for He
is the Most Excellent of Judges.

SURA II

Hud (*Hud*)

Named after an Arabian, non-Abrahamic prophet, linked to the tribe of ʿAd (v. 50), this late Meccan sura of 123 verses begins and ends with addresses to the Prophet Muhammad. It includes accounts of Noah, Salih, Abraham, Lot, Shuʿayb, as well as brief mentions of Moses and Pharaoh (vv. 96–99).

In the Name of God, the All Merciful, Ever Merciful

SECTION I

1 *Alif. Lam. Ra.*°

This is a Book whose verses
are determined and explained°
by the One Who is
All Wise, All Aware,

2 to urge you to worship
none but the One God.
Say, Prophet,
"I have come from Him,
to warn you and to bring
joyous news.

3 "Ask forgiveness of your Lord,
Then turn to him repenting.
He will grant you
gracious enjoyment of life
for a certain time,
and bestow His grace
on those worthy of grace.
But if you turn away,
I fear for you the torment
of a momentous day.°

4 "You will return to God,
Who has Power over all things."

5 See, how they fold up their hearts,
to hide their feelings from Him.
But even when they cover themselves
with their clothes, He knows
what they conceal, and
what they reveal. He Knows
what their hearts enclose.

6 There is no creature on earth
that God does not provide for.
He knows its home and its last
    abode:
all is recorded in a clear Book.

7 It is He who created
the heavens and earth in six days
—with His throne over the waters—
that He might try you, to see
which of you is best in deeds.
But if you were to say to them,
"You shall be raised up after death,"
the disbelievers would say,
"This is nothing but plain sorcery."

8 If We defer their punishment
for a definite term, they will taunt,
"What holds it back?"
But on the day it comes to them,
nothing shall avert it from them,
and it shall besiege them on all
    sides—
the very thing they used to mock.

SECTION 2

9 If We let humans taste Our mercy,
then withdraw it from them,
they become hopeless, thankless.

10 But if We let them taste Our favor,
after hardship has touched them,
they say, "Evils are gone from me,"
and they become joyful, boastful.

11 But those who show patience
and do good deeds
shall be shown forgiveness
and a great reward.

12 You might be inclined to forgo
part of the message revealed to you,
and to let your heart be constrained
by their questioning,
"Why is no treasure sent to him," or
"Why is there no angel with him?"
But you are here merely to warn—
and God is Guardian over all things.

13 Or they exclaim, "He forged it."
Say, "Then bring ten similar verses,
all forged, and call upon what [gods]

you can other than the One God,
if you are speaking the truth."

14 "If [your gods] don't answer you,
you should know that this message
is sent down with God's knowledge,
and that there is no God but Him.
So, will you submit to Him?"

15 As for those who desire
the life of this world and its lure—
We shall recompense in full
their deeds in it,
and they will not be denied
their due in it.

16 The hereafter holds for them
nothing but fire—there, their works
shall be rendered vain, and
all that they did shall be worthless.

17 [Can they really be likened
to] those who have a clear sign
from their Lord, recited by
a witness from Him,
before which the Book of Moses
came as a guide and mercy?
Those people believe in it,
but the sects who deny it
are fated for the fire.°
So have no doubt about it—
it is the truth from your Lord.
Yet most people won't believe.

18 Who does more wrong than those
who forge a lie about God? They
will be brought before their Lord,

and the witnesses will say,
"These are the ones
who lied about their Lord."
See, the curse of God
is upon the wrongdoers,

19 those who bar people
from the path of God,
seeking to make it crooked,
and who deny the hereafter.

20 They will not escape on earth,
with no protectors besides God;
their punishment shall be doubled—
those who could not hear,
and would not see.

21 They are the ones who
have lost themselves
and the gods they invented
have gone from them.°

22 Without doubt, they
will be the ones who lose most
in the hereafter.

23 Those who believe, do good deeds,
and humble themselves before their
  Lord
shall live in the garden—forever.

24 These two groups are like
the blind and deaf alongside
the seeing and hearing—
are the two equal?
Will you not, then, take heed?

SECTION 3

25 We sent Noah to his people, to say,
"I am here to warn you plainly,

26 "not to worship any but God.
I fear for you the punishment
of a painful day."

27 But the leading disbelievers
among his people said,
"We see you as merely human like
  ourselves,
and we see only the lowest of our folk
following you, those rash in their
  opinion;
and we see in you no merit above
  ours.
In fact, we think you're a liar."

28 He replied, "My people, consider:
if I had clear proof from my Lord,
and He granted me His mercy
—though you were blind to this—
could we compel you to accept it
despite your dislike of it?

29 "Also, my people,
I ask of you no wealth,
and I seek no reward
except from God.
I will not drive away
those who believe—
they shall meet their Lord,
but I see that you
are an ignorant people.

30 "Moreover, my people,
who would help me against God,
if I did drive them away?
Will you not, then, take heed?

31 "I don't say to you that
I have the treasures of God,
or that I know what is hidden,
or that I am an angel.
Nor do I say that God will not
grant good to those you despise
—God knows best
what is in their souls—
[if I said such things]
I would be doing wrong."

32 They said, "Noah, you have
argued and argued with us.
Now bring down upon us
[the torment] you threatened us
with,
if you are speaking the truth."

33 He said, "Only God will bring it
upon you,
if He wishes; and you shall not
escape.

34 "Though I wish to advise you,
my advice would not profit you,
if God wished to lead you astray.
He is your Lord—and to Him
you will be returned."

35 Or do they say,
"He has forged the message"?
Say, "Had I forged it, my sin
would be upon me, but
I am free of the sins you incur."°

SECTION 4

36 It was revealed to Noah,
"None of your people will believe
beyond those who already believe,
so don't grieve over what they do."

37 "Build an ark, under Our eyes,
inspired by Us,
and plead with me no further
on behalf of those who do wrong—
for they shall be drowned."

38 He began building the ark
and whenever the chiefs
among his people passed by,
they would mock him.
He said, "Just as you mock us now,
so we shall mock you.

39 "For soon you shall know
who shall face a punishment
that shames them—those on whom
a lasting punishment shall fall."

40 Then, when Our command came,
and earth's fountains overflowed,°
We said, "Load the ark
with a pair of each kind,
and your family
(except those on whom
judgment has been passed)
and those who believe."
Yet few believed with him.

41 So Noah said, "Board the ark.
   Let it sail and let it anchor in the
      name of God—
   my Lord is Forgiving, Ever
      Merciful."

42 So the ark sailed with them
   on the waves towering like
      mountains
   and Noah cried out to his son,
   who was apart, stranded,
   "My son, board with us,
   don't stay with the unbelievers."

43 His son replied,
   "I'll find some mountain
   to save me from the water."
   Noah warned, "This day,
   no one can save anyone
   from the command of God,
   except those to whom
   he shows mercy."
   A wave came between them,
   and his son was among
   those who were drowned.

44 Then a voice said,
   "Earth, swallow up your waters,
   and sky, withhold your rain."
   Then the waters subsided,
   and the command was fulfilled.
   The ark came to rest on Mount Judi.°
   And a voice said, "Gone are the
      people
   who did wrong."

45 And Noah called upon his Lord,
      saying,
   "Lord, my son was one of my family,
   though your promise is true,
   for you are the Most Just of Judges."

46 He replied, "Noah, actually,
   he was not of your family—
   his deeds were unrighteous.
   So do not question me about things
   beyond your knowledge—
   I caution you against such
      ignorance."

47 Noah replied, "My Lord,
   I seek refuge in You
   from asking You about things
   beyond my knowledge,
   and unless You forgive me
   and have mercy on me,
   I too will be among the losers."

48 A voice came, "Noah,
   come down from the ark,
   with Our peace and blessings
   on you and on the nations
   to arise from those with you.
   As for other nations,
   We shall grant them contentment
   for a while, then Our painful
      torment
   will reach them."

49 These are the chronicles
   of the unseen world that
   We revealed to you, Prophet,
   which neither you nor your people

knew before. So, have patience,
for the outcome will favor those°
who are mindful of God.

SECTION 5

50 To the people of ʿAd
We sent their brother° Hud,
who said, "My people, worship God,
for you have no other god but Him—
your gods are merely invented.°

51 "My people, I ask of you
no reward for this.
My only reward is from Him
who fashioned me.
So, won't you use reason?

52 "And, my people,
ask forgiveness of your Lord,
then turn to Him.
He will send abundance of rain
   upon you,
pouring from the sky;
He will add strength to your
   strength,
so do not turn back as sinners."

53 They said,
"Hud, you've brought us no clear
   proof,
and we are not ones to abandon our
   gods
at your word—we don't believe you.

54 "All we can say is that perhaps
some of our gods have harmed you."

He responded, "I call upon God
—and you also—to witness
that I dissociate myself
from the gods you associate°

55 "with Him. So plot against me,
all of you, and give me no quarter.

56 "I trust in God,
my Lord and your Lord.
There is no creature
that He does not hold
by the forelock—
the path of my Lord is straight.

57 "If you turn away, I have,
for my part, conveyed the message
with which I was sent to you;
and my Lord will replace you
with another people; and you
cannot harm Him at all.
My Lord is Watchful
over all things."

58 And when Our command came to
   pass,
We saved Hud and those
who believed with him, through
   Our mercy—
We saved them from a stern
   punishment.

59 These were the people of ʿAd—
they rejected the signs of their Lord,
and disobeyed His prophets,
and followed the commands
of every obdurate tyrant.

60 Shadowed by a curse
in this world and
on the day of resurrection—
See, the people of 'Ad
denied their Lord.
See, the 'Ad are gone,
the people of Hud!

SECTION 6

61 And to the people of Thamud
We sent their brother Salih,
who said, "My people, worship God,
for you have no other god but Him.
It is God Who brought you forth
from the earth and settled you there.
So ask forgiveness of Him and
turn to Him. My Lord is
Ever Near, Responsive."

62 They said, "Salih,
before now, you were our hope.
Do you now forbid us to worship
what our fathers worshipped?
We are in doubt, in distrust,
about what you call us to."

63 He said, "My people, can you see—
if I have a clear sign from my Lord,
and He has shown me His mercy—
who will help me against God
if I disobey Him?
You would increase only my loss.

64 "And, my people,
this is the she-camel of God,
a sign for you.

So let her pasture on God's earth
and do not harm her,
else punishment shall soon
overcome you."

65 But they hamstrung her.
So he said, "Enjoy yourselves
in your homes for three days
    only—
this promise shall not prove false."

66 And when Our command came to
    pass,
We saved Salih and those who
    believed with him,
through Our mercy, from the shame
    of that day.
Your Lord is Powerful, Almighty.

67 The fearsome blast
overcame the wrongdoers,
who lay, fallen, face-down,
in their homes

68 as if they had never
lived and flourished there.
See, the people of Thamud
denied their Lord.
See, the people of Thamud
are gone.

SECTION 7

69 And Our messengers came
to Abraham with joyous news,
and a greeting of "Peace."
"Peace," he responded,

and did not delay
in offering them a roasted calf.

70 But when he saw that
they did not reach for the food,
he found this strange, and began
to fear them. But they said,
"Don't be afraid,
for we have been sent
against the people of Lot."

71 And his wife, standing there, laughed.
But we gave her joyous news,
of a son Isaac, and after him, Jacob.

72 She said, "Alas for me,
how shall I, an old woman,
bear a child, and my husband here
an old man? That would be
an amazing thing."

73 They said,
"Are you amazed at God's
command?
God's mercy and His blessings
be upon you, people of the house.
He is the Praiseworthy, Glorious."

74 When the fear had passed from
Abraham,
and the joyous news reached him,
he began to plead with Us
for the people of Lot.

75 Abraham was forbearing, pitying,
turning always to God in
repentance.

76 "Abraham, turn away from this.
The command of your Lord
has come to pass, and punishment
comes for them—that
cannot be turned back."

77 When Our messengers came to Lot,
he was vexed for them,
and felt powerless to protect them,
saying, "This is a harsh day."

78 And his people came
rushing toward him, those who
before this had performed evil
deeds.
He said, "My people, here
are my daughters for you to marry;
they will be a purer choice for you.°
Be mindful of God, then,
and do not disgrace me
before my guests. Is there not
a right-minded man among you?"

79 They said, "You know well
we have no right to your daughters,
and you know well what we want."

80 He replied, "If only I had power
over you, or could find myself some
forceful support [to resist you]."

81 The strangers said, "Lot,
we are messengers from your Lord.
They shall not reach you.
Go with your family, while
night is still here, and let
none of you look back—

except your wife—what strikes
the rest will strike her.
The appointed hour is
morning. Isn't morning
almost here?"

82 When Our command
came to pass, We turned their town
upside down, and rained upon
it stones of baked clay,
layer upon layer,

83 marked as being from your Lord,°
and never far from the wrongdoers.

SECTION 8

84 And to the people of Midian
We sent their brother Shu'ayb,
who said, "My people, worship God,
for you have no other god but Him.
And do not fall short in measure
and balance. I see you now
in prosperity, but I fear for you
the punishment of a day
that shall encompass all.

85 "And, my people, be just
in measure and balance,
and do not withhold from people
things that are their due,
nor do evil in the land,
sowing corruption.

86 "What rests with God
is better for you, if only you believe.
But I am not your keeper."

87 They said, "Shu'ayb,
do your prayers tell you
that we should abandon what
our forefathers worshipped,
or that we should not do
as we please with our wealth?
You—you who are *so*
forbearing and right-minded!"

88 He replied, "My people,
do you see—if I have a clear sign
from my Lord, who has Himself
given me a good provision—
[should I still not guide you?]
I don't wish to be inconsistent
by doing what I forbid you to do.
I want only your betterment,°
as far as I am able, and my success
can come only from God.
In Him I trust, and to Him I turn.

89 "And, my people,
don't let your opposing me
make you sin, else
there might fall upon you
what fell upon the people of Noah,
or of Hud, or of Salih.
Nor is the fate of Lot's people
far from you.

90 "But ask forgiveness of your Lord,
then turn to Him, for my Lord
is Ever Merciful, Most Loving."

91 They said, "Shu'ayb,
we don't understand much
of what you say, and we see

how weak you are among us.
Were it not for your family,
we would stone you, for you
have no power over us."

92 He said, "My people,
Do you imagine that my family
has more power over you than God?
Have you put Him behind you?
My Lord Encompasses
all that you do.

93 "And, my people,
do whatever you can,
and I shall do what I can.
Soon, you will know who
will meet humiliating punishment
and who is a liar. Be watchful,
for I will be watching with you."

94 And when Our command
came to pass, We saved Shuʿayb
and those who believed with him,
through Our mercy,
but the wrongdoers
were struck by a fearsome blast,
and morning found them
fallen face-down in their homes,

95 as if they had never
lived and flourished there.
See, the people of Madyan
are gone, just as the people
of Thamud are gone.

SECTION 9

96 And we sent Moses,
with Our signs and clear
authority,

97 to Pharaoh and his chiefs,
but they followed the command
of Pharaoh—a command
that was not righteous.

98 He will go before his people
on the day of resurrection,
and lead them into the fire—
wretched is the end
to which they will be led.

99 And they shall be shadowed
by a curse in this life
and on the day of resurrection—
wretched is the gift
they will be given.

100 These are among the chronicles of
cities
that We narrate to you, Prophet.
Some of them still stand, others are
mown down.

101 We did not wrong them,
but they wronged themselves.
The gods on whom they called
besides the One God
did not help them at all.
And when the command
of your Lord came, their gods
brought them nothing but ruin.°

102 This is the punishment
of your Lord when He punishes
communities who do wrong—
His punishment is painful, severe.

103 In this is a sign
for those who fear
punishment of the hereafter.
This is a day on which
humankind shall be gathered,
a day that shall be witnessed.

104 And We shall delay it only
for a limited term.

105 The day it comes,
no soul shall speak
except by His leave.
Among them
some shall be wretched,
others joyous.

106 The wretched shall be
in fire, sighing and wailing,

107 where they will reside
as long as the heavens and earth abide,
except as your Lord wishes.
Your Lord Accomplishes
all that He intends.°

108 And the joyous shall be
in the garden, where they will reside
as long as the heavens and earth
    abide,°
except as your Lord wishes—
an enduring gift.

109 So be in no doubt
about what these people worship:
they worship only what
their forefathers worshipped before.
And We shall repay their portion
in full, undiminished.

SECTION 10

110 We gave the Book to Moses,
but disputes arose over it,
and if a Word from your Lord
had not gone already forth,
[to defer their judgment]
their judgment would have come.
Yet they remain in doubt over it,
mired in mistrust.

111 Your Lord shall requite them
in full for their deeds.
He is Aware of all that they do.

112 Stand firm, then,
as you are commanded,
you and those with you
who turn toward God,
and do not transgress.
He Sees all that you do.

113 And do not lean
toward those who do wrong
for fear the fire might reach you,
for you would have no protectors
besides God, nor
would you be helped.

114 Be steadfast in prayer
at the two ends of the day
and the approach of night.
Good always banishes evil—
this is a reminder
for those who remember.

115 And be patient, for God
will not withhold the reward
of those who do good.

116 In the generations before you,
why were there not people
with a vestige [of good sense]
to prohibit mischief on the earth—
except the few whom We saved?
But the wrongdoers indulged
in the luxuries bestowed on them
and became sinners.

117 And your Lord would not
destroy communities unjustly
if their people were righteous.°

118 Had your Lord wished,
He could have made humankind
one community; but [He wished
otherwise, and] they will not cease
their quarreling,

119 except those to whom
your Lord has shown mercy;
and for this He created them—
that the words of your Lord
might be fulfilled,
"I will fill hell with jinn
and humankind, all together."

120 All We narrate to you, Prophet,
of the chronicles of the messengers
is to strengthen your heart;
these accounts bring truth to you,
as well as lessons, and a reminder
for those who believe.

121 Tell those who don't believe,
"Do whatever you can,
and we shall do what we can.

122 "And wait, for
we too are awaiting
[judgment]."

123 To God belong the unseen realms
of the heavens and the earth,
and to Him all matters are referred.
So worship Him, and trust in Him,
for your Lord is not unmindful
of what you do.

Joseph (*Yusuf*)

The third consecutive sura named after a prophet, this late Meccan sura of 111 verses is devoted in its entirety to the story of the prophet Joseph. This is the only sura consisting almost entirely of narrative. At once poetic and compelling, it has parallels but no direct link to the biblical story of Joseph.

In the Name of God, the All Merciful, Ever Merciful

SECTION 1

1 *Alif. Lam. Ra.°*
These are the verses
of the clear Book.

2 We have sent it
as an Arabic Qur'an,
so you will understand.

3 We narrate to you
the most sublime of narratives
in this Qur'an
that we reveal to you.
Before this, you were unaware
[of those stories].

4 When Joseph said to his father,
"My father, I saw, in a dream,
eleven stars, the sun and moon—
I saw them bowing down
before me,"

5 he replied, "My son, don't tell
your brothers about this dream,
or they might scheme against you—

Satan is an open enemy
to humankind.

6 "This is how your Lord
will choose you, and teach you
the deeper meaning of events,
and perfect His favor to you
and the family of Jacob,
as He perfected it before,
to both your fathers,
Abraham and Isaac—your Lord
is All Knowing, All Wise."

SECTION 2

7 In the story of Joseph
and his brothers are signs
for those who inquire.

8 His brothers said,
"Joseph and his brother
are dearer to father than us,
though we are more in number;°
our father is obviously wrong.

9 "Kill Joseph or cast him out
  to some far land,
  then your father will
  turn his attention° to you alone;
  you can always be righteous
  afterward."°

10 Another one of them said,
  "Don't kill Joseph; if you must
  act on this, throw him down
  to the well's dark depth, so
  some caravan will pick him up."

11 They implored, "Father,
  why won't you trust us with
      Joseph?
  For we only have goodwill for him.

12 "Send him with us tomorrow,
  so he'll enjoy himself and play;
  we'll be sure to guard him well."

13 Jacob said, "It grieves me
  to see you take him, for I fear
  the wolf might eat him
  while you're not minding him."

14 They replied, "If the wolf ate him
  —despite our large number—
  we would indeed be losers."

15 So they took him,
  and they all agreed
  to throw him down
  to the well's dark depth.
  But We inspired him, "In time,
  you will apprise them

of this deed of theirs
when they don't know [you]."°

16 They came to their father
  in the evening, weeping.

17 They said, "Father,
  we went racing, and left
  Joseph with our things; then
  the wolf devoured him.
  You won't believe us,
  even though we speak the truth."

18 They brought out his shirt, soiled
  with false blood. "No!" he cried,
  "Your minds have enticed
  you to some misdeed.°
  Yet patience is a fine thing,°
  and I invoke the help of God
  against what you plead."°

19 A caravan came, travelers, who
  sent their water carrier to the well,
  and he lowered his bucket.
  "What good luck," he cried,
  "Here's a boy!"
  And they stowed him
  in their merchandise—
  God was Aware of what they did.

20 They sold him for a low price,
  a few silver coins,°
  in such low regard did they hold
      him.

SECTION 3

21 The man who bought him
   —an Egyptian—told his wife,
   "Make his lodging comfortable;
   perhaps he'll profit us
   or we'll adopt him as a son."
   And so We settled Joseph in the land,
   that We might teach him
   the deeper meaning of events.
   And so God prevails
   In His affairs; but most
   people don't know.

22 When Joseph reached his prime,
   We endowed him with
   wisdom and knowledge—
   this is how We reward those
   who do good.

23 The woman in whose house
   he stayed tried to seduce him;
   she secured the doors and said,
     "Come here!"
   "God forbid!" he said. "He is my
     master;
   he gave me a comfortable home.
   Those who do wrong cannot
     prosper."

24 She lusted after him,
   and he would have lusted after her,
   had he not seen a token from his Lord;
   so We kept him away from evil and
     indecency,
   for he was one of Our chosen
     servants.

25 They both raced for the door,
   and she tore his shirt from behind;
   they found her husband by the door.
   "What penalty can there be,"
   she cried, "for someone who
   contrived harm against your wife,
   but prison or torture?"

26 He said, "It was she
   who tried to seduce me."
   Someone from her family
   proposed to use as evidence:°
   "If his shirt is torn from the front,
   Then she speaks the truth
   and he is a liar.

27 "But if his shirt is torn from behind,
   then she is lying,
   and he is speaking the truth."

28 So when her husband saw his shirt
   torn from behind, he declared,
   "This is your women's guile,
   what great guile you possess.

29 "Joseph, let this pass,
   and wife, beg forgiveness
   for your sin; you
   are most certainly at fault."

SECTION 4

30 Women gossiped in the city,
   "The governor's wife tried
   to seduce her manservant
   —love for him has stormed her heart—
   we see her clearly straying."

31 When she heard their gossip,
she sent for them and prepared
a banquet for them.
She gave each of them a knife,
and said to Joseph,
"Come before them!"
When they saw him,
they so marveled at him,
they cut their hands, remarking,
"Glory to God! This is no mortal—
this is nothing but a noble angel!"

32 She said, "This is the man
on whose account you reproved me!
Yes, I tried to seduce him
but he refrained.
Yet, if he doesn't do what I
      command,
he'll be thrown into jail, disgraced."

33 He said, "My Lord,
prison is more appealing to me
than the deeds they call me to;
unless you turn their guile
away from me,
I might succumb to them,
in ignorance."

34 Then his Lord answered him
and turned their guile
away from him.
He is All Hearing, All Knowing.

35 Even after they had seen the signs
of his virtue, it seemed to them,
they should imprison him a while
[to quell gossip].

SECTION 5

36 Two young men entered the prison
with him. One of them said,
"I dreamt I was pressing wine."
The other, "I dreamt I was carrying
some bread on my head,
which birds were pecking.
Tell us the deeper meaning—
we can see you're a virtuous
      person."°

37 He said, "Yes, I'll inform you
of the dreams' deeper meaning
even before your food comes
to sustain you. This is part
of what my Lord has taught me.
I reject the creed of a people
who don't believe in God
and who deny the hereafter.

38 "And I follow the creed
of my forefathers, Abraham,
Isaac, and Jacob; it was not for us
to join any other gods
with God. This is due
to God's grace upon us,
and upon humankind,
though most of them
are ungrateful.

39 "My fellow prisoners,
which is better: diverse lords
[differing among themselves],
or the One God, the Unique,
the Omnipotent?

40 "You worship nothing
besides Him but names—invented
by you and your fathers—for which
God has revealed no sanction.
Judgment belongs
to none but God.
He commands you to worship
none but Him.
This is the right religion,
but most of humankind
do not know.

41 "Fellow prisoners, one of you
will serve his lord with wine;
the other will be crucified,
and birds will peck at his head.
This is what is decreed
in the matter on which
you both inquired."°

42 And he said to the one
he thought would go free,
"Mention me to your lord."
But Satan made him forget,
so Joseph remained in prison
for several years more.

SECTION 6

43 The king said, "I saw,
in a dream, seven fat cows,
which seven lean ones devoured;
and seven ears of corn, green,
with seven others, withered.
Counselors, explain my dream to me,
if you can interpret dreams."

44 They said, "[A medley of]
confusing dreams—we are not versed
in the reading of dreams."

45 Of the two prisoners,
the one who was freed
now remembered, after all this time,
and said, "I shall disclose
its deeper meaning to you.
Dispatch me [to visit Joseph]."

46 [On arriving, he asked,]
"Joseph, you who are truthful,
explain [the meaning of] this to us:
seven fat cows,
which seven lean ones devoured;
and seven ears of corn, green,
with seven others, withered—
explain, so I may return
to let the people know."

47 He replied, "You will sow,
as usual, for seven years,
and what you reap, you will store,
leaving it in the ear,
all but a little, from which
you will eat.

48 "After that shall come
seven harsh years
which shall consume
what you have prepared for them,
all but a little, which
you will preserve.

49 "After that shall come
a year in which the people

have abundant rain
and press grapes."

SECTION 7

50 Then the king said,
    "Bring him to me."
    But when the envoy came
    to Joseph, Joseph said:
    "Return to your lord, and ask him
    what was in the minds of the women
    who cut their hands.
    My Lord is Aware of their guile."

51 The king said to the women,
    "What do you have to say about
    your intent to seduce Joseph."
    They said, "Glory to God,
    we know nothing bad about him."
    The governor's wife cried,
    "Now the truth is out:
    It was I who tried to seduce him,
    and he, without doubt,
    is telling the truth."

52 [Joseph said,]°
    "By this, my master may know
    that I never betrayed him
    in his absence, and that God
    does not guide the guile
    of those who are treacherous.

53 "Nor do I absolve my own soul;
    the soul is always prone to evil—
    unless my Lord shows mercy.
    My Lord is Forgiving,
    Ever Merciful."

54 And the king said,
    "Bring him to me, so I may
    keep him in my personal service."°
    When he had spoken with him,
    he said, "Today, we confer on you
    high status and trust."

55 Joseph said, "Let me oversee
    the granaries of the land—
    I will be a prudent custodian."

56 So We settled Joseph
    in the land, to live
    wherever he wished.
    We bestow Our mercy
    on whom We will,
    and We do not withhold the reward
    of those who do good.

57 But the reward of the hereafter
    is better, for those who believe
    and are mindful of God.

SECTION 8

58 Joseph's brothers arrived,
    and came before him;
    he recognized them,
    but they did not know him.

59 When he had provided them
    with supplies, he said, "Bring to me
    your other brother,° who is with
    your father. Do you not see
    that [I trade fairly], giving full
        measure,
    and that I am a most gracious host?

60 "But if you don't bring him to me,
   you'll have no further measure
   of corn from me, nor
   shall you come near me."

61 They replied, "We'll try to get
   his father's consent for him—
   we'll be sure to do it."°

62 Joseph told his servants,
   "Place the goods they bartered
   back in their saddlebags,
   so they'll recognize them
   when they return to their people—
   then they might come back."

63 And when they returned
   to their father, they said,
   "Father, we've been denied
   any further measure of corn;
   send our brother with us,
   so we can procure our measure;
   we'll be sure to protect him."

64 He said, "Shall I trust you
   with him as I trusted you before
   with his brother?
   Yet God is the Best of Protectors,
   and He is the Most Merciful
   of the merciful."

65 When they opened their baggage,
   they found their goods
   returned to them. They said,
   "Father, what more can we want?
   Our goods here are returned to us:
   we'll get food for our household,

   we'll protect our brother;
   and we'll get an extra camel-load
   of grain, an easy load!"

66 Jacob answered, "I'll never
   send him with you, until you pledge
   to me—by God—that you'll bring
       him
   to me, unless you're somehow
       ensnared."
   When they made their pledge,
   he said, "God is Custodian
   over all that we say."

67 He continued, "My sons,
   don't enter by one gate,
   but various gates;
   yet I can't help you at all
   against [the Will of] God.
   Judgment is from God alone:
   I trust in Him—let everyone
   trust in Him."

68 And when they entered
   in the way their father
   had directed, this did not help them
   at all against [the Will of] God,
   for it was just a need in Jacob,
   which he gratified.
   For he possessed knowledge
   that We taught him.
   But most people do not know.

SECTION 9

69 When they came before Joseph,
   he drew his brother to him, saying,

"I am your own brother!
So don't grieve over
what they've been doing."

70 And while he was
preparing their supplies,
he planted a drinking cup
in his brother's saddlebag.
Then a town crier cried aloud,
"You, in the caravan!
You are thieves!"

71 Turning toward them, they said,
"What are you missing?"

72 He said, "We're missing
the chalice of the king;
whoever brings it will get
a camel-load, I pledge."

73 They said, "By God!
You well know, we haven't come
to make mischief in the realm,
nor are we thieves!"

74 He replied,
"Then what penalty
should there be for this,
if you are lying?"

75 They said, "As penalty,
the person who's found with it
in his saddlebag should himself
be detained. That's how
we punish wrongdoers."

76 So Joseph began with their bags,
before searching his brother's bag.

At length, he lifted it out
of his brother's bag.
We contrived this for Joseph,
else he could not detain his brother
within the law of the king,
without God's will.
We raise in station whom We will;
yet above all those who know
is the All Knowing.

77 They said, "If he has stolen,
well, he has a brother who stole
before him." But Joseph said
—to himself, not disclosing
anything to them—
"You are in the worst situation,
and God knows best the truth
of what you claim."

78 They said, "Governor,
he has a father who's very old;
so take one of us in his place;
for we can see that
you're a virtuous person."

79 He responded, "God forbid
that we detain any but the one
caught with our property—
that would be wrong."

SECTION 10

80 Losing hope of persuading him,
they conferred in private.
The eldest spoke, "Don't you know
your father took a pledge from you,

in the name of God—and before
   this,
you failed in your duty with Joseph?
I won't leave this land until my father
gives me leave or God decrees it
   so—
He is the Most Excellent of Judges.

81 "[As for the rest of you],
go back to your father, and say,
'Father of ours, your son
has been stealing—we can tell you
only we what we witnessed;
we could not prevent
something so unforeseen.

82 "'Ask anyone in the town
where we were,
and the caravan we came with—
we're telling the truth.'"

83 [When they said this
to their father,] Jacob replied,
"No, your minds have enticed you
to some misdeed.
But patience is a fine thing;
perhaps God will bring them
all back to me. For He is
the Knowing, the Wise."

84 And he turned away
from them, and sighed:
"How great is my grief
over Joseph!" His eyes
grew white in sorrow,
and he grieved inside.

85 They said, "By God,
will you not cease
to remember Joseph
until you reach
the fatal edge of disease,
or pass away?"

86 He said, "I complain
only to God of my grief,
my sorrow,
and I know from God
what you do not know.

87 "My sons, go to inquire
after Joseph and his brother,
and don't despair of God's grace.
None but disbelievers
despair of God's grace."

88 When they came before Joseph,
they entreated, "Governor,
our family was struck by adversity.
We bring but meager wares,
yet remit a full measure to us,
show charity to us, for God
rewards those who are charitable."

89 He asked, "Do you know
what you did with Joseph
and his brother,
in your ignorance?"

90 They remarked,
"*You* are Joseph, really?"
"I am Joseph, and
this is my brother:
God has been Gracious to us.

He does not overlook
the reward of those
who are pious and patient,
those who do good."

91 They said, "By God!
God has favored you over us,
and we are in the wrong."

92 He said, "Let no reproach
weigh upon you this day.
May God forgive you,
for He is the Most Merciful
of the merciful.

93 "Go, take this shirt of mine,
and throw it over my father's face:
his eyes will light up with sight—
then come back with
your entire family."

SECTION II

94 After the caravan left,
their father said, "I detect
the scent of Joseph—though you
might think me senile."

95 [Those with him] said, "By God,
you still harbor your old delusion."

96 Then the person who came
with good news threw the shirt
over Jacob's face, and he regained
his vision. He proclaimed,
"Did I not say to you
that I know from God
what you do not know?"

97 They implored, "Father,
ask forgiveness for our sins,
for we were at fault."

98 He replied, "Soon I shall ask
my Lord to forgive you,
for He is Forgiving, Ever Merciful."

99 When they came before Joseph,
he embraced his parents, saying,
"Enter into Egypt, in safety,
if this is the will of God."

100 And he raised his parents,
both, on the throne, and
all of them fell down,
bowing before him.
"My dear father, here is
the deeper meaning
of my dream of long ago:
My Lord has brought it to pass.
He was good to me
when He brought me
out of prison
and brought you
out of the desert,
after Satan had sown
discord between me
and my brothers.
My Lord is Subtle
in all that He wills.
He is All Knowing, All Wise.

101 "My Lord, you have given me
authority, and you have taught me
the deeper meaning of events.
Maker of the heavens and earth,

You are my Protector, in this world
and the hereafter. Receive me,
as one who submits to Your will,
and unite me with the righteous."

102 This is from the chronicles
of the unseen, which we reveal
to you.° You, Prophet, were not
with them when they all concocted
their [abominable] plot.

103 Most of humankind
will not believe,
however ardently you strive.

104 And you do not seek reward
from them for this. This is no less
than a reminder to all the worlds.

SECTION 12

105 And how many signs
in the heavens and earth
do they pass by,
turning away.

106 Most of them don't believe in God
without joining other gods with Him.

107 Do they feel safe, then,
from the enveloping calamity
of God's punishment, or
from the sudden descending
of the hour, while they
are unaware?

108 Say, "This is my way;
I call to God, with clear vision,
I, and whoever follows me.
Glory be to God, that I am
not one of those who join
other gods with Him."

109 And We sent before you
only men whom we inspired,
from the people of the cities.
Did they not travel the earth,
and behold the fate
of those before them?
The home of the hereafter
is finer for those who are
mindful of God.
Will you not, then, use reason?

110 When messengers despaired,
thinking they had been denied,
Our help came to them;
We saved whom We will.
But Our wrath will never be
turned from a wicked people.

111 In their stories, there is
a lesson for people of insight.
This is not an invented tale,
but it confirms what came before,
an exposition of all things,
a guide and a mercy
for people who believe.

Thunder (*Al-Ra'd*)

Uncertain in its dating, but probably late Meccan, with some additions from the Medinan period, this sura takes its name from v. 13. "Thunder" focuses on divine guidance, consequential for those who accept but also for those who deny it. Confirmation of prophetic agency recurs through its 43 verses, with Muhammad reassured that the Book common to all prophets was revealed to him in Arabic (v. 37).

In the Name of God, the All Merciful, Ever Merciful

SECTION I

1 *Alif. Lam. Mim. Ra.°*

These are the verses of the Book.
What was revealed to you
from your Lord is truth,
but most people don't believe.

2 It is God who raised up the heavens
with no visible pillars;
then He set Himself upon the throne.
He controlled the sun and moon,
    each
sailing in its orbit for a certain term.
He orders all phenomena,
and explains the signs,
that you might be certain
of meeting your Lord.

3 It is He who spread out the earth,
    set upon it sturdy mountains and
        rivers,

created fruit of every kind, in pairs.
He veils the day with night.
    In all this
are signs for people who think.

4 In the earth are neighboring tracts
and gardens of vineyards, with
sown fields, as well as date palms,
some with clusters, some without,
all watered by the same rain,
yet We make some finer to taste
than others. In all this
are signs for people who reason.

5 Prophet, if you're amazed at all,
you'll be amazed by what they say,
"After we are dust, shall we be
raised again as a new creation?"
These are the people
who deny their Lord;
they shall bear iron collars
around their necks;
they shall be inmates
of the fire—forever.

6 They challenge you
to bring on their punishment,
rather than any reward, even though
many examples of punishment
have passed before them.
Your Lord is Full of Forgiveness
toward people, despite their wrongs.
Yet God is Severe in Requital.

7 And those who disbelieve ask,
"Why hasn't a sign been sent down
to him from his Lord?"
You are only here to warn,
and every people has a guide.

SECTION 2

8 God knows what each female bears,
and how much their womb
contracts or expands; with Him,
all things exist in due proportion.

9 Knowing the unseen and the seen;
He is Great, Most Exalted.

10 It is the same whether any of you
speaks secretly or openly, whether
they hide beneath the cover of night
or walk about freely during the day.

11 Each person has a train of angels
before them and behind them,
guarding them by God's command.
God never changes a people's state
until they change what is in
   themselves.
When God intends ill for a people,

there is no turning it back.
Besides Him, they have no
   protector.

12 It is He who shows you
the lightning, arousing fear and
   hope,
and He raises the clouds,
heavy with rain.

13 The thunder resounds in His praise,
as do the angels, in awe of Him;
and He sends the thunderbolts
to strike whom He will.
Yet still they dispute about God—
He Who is Supreme in Strategy.

14 True prayer is to Him alone.
As for those who pray to others
besides Him, those gods will not
answer them at all, any more than
someone stretching out his hand
toward water to make it reach
his mouth: it will never get there.
The prayer of disbelievers
is nothing but delusion.°

15 All beings in the heavens and earth
bow down to God, willing or
   unwilling,
as do their shadows,
morning and evening.

16 Ask, Prophet, "Who is the Lord
of the heavens and the earth?"
Answer, "God."
Ask, "Do you take other gods

than Him as protectors—who can
neither profit nor harm even
themselves?"
And ask, "Are the blind
and the seeing alike?
Or, is darkness the same as light?"
Do they join other gods with God
who have created, in their eyes,
a creation like His? Then say,
"God is Creator of all things—
He is the One, Omnipotent."

17 He sends down water from the sky,
flowing through valleys,
each to its own depth, and the
    torrents
bear away the rising foam,
just as foam erupts when heating ore
to forge ornaments and utensils.
This is how God exhibits
truth and falsehood:
the froth passes away, worthless,
but what profits humankind
remains in the earth.
This is how God coins parables.

18 Those who respond to their Lord
shall have all that is good; but those
who don't respond—they would
    give
as ransom all that is in the earth,
    and
as much more, if they owned it—
theirs shall be a terrible reckoning,
and their home shall be hell,
a wretched place of rest.

SECTION 3

19 Is someone who knows the truth
of your Lord's revelation to you
the same as someone who is blind?
Only those with insight take heed,

20 those who fulfill their trust
with God, and do not fail
in their pledge,

21 those who join together what
God has commanded to be joined,
those who fear their Lord,
and hold in awe
the terrible reckoning;

22 and those who are patient,
seeking the Face of their Lord,
who are steadfast in prayer,
who spend in charity, both
secretly and openly,
from what We have given them,
who repel evil with good.
Theirs, in the end, shall be
the everlasting home,

23 eternal gardens, which they
shall enter, along with the righteous
among their ancestors, spouses,
and descendants; the angels
shall greet them at every gate:

24 "Peace be with you,
for you showed patience.
How excellent is your
everlasting home!"

25 But those who break God's trust
after giving their pledge,
and who sever what God
commanded to be joined,
and who sow corruption
on the earth—they shall be cursed,
and theirs shall be a wretched home.

26 God enlarges or constricts
His provision for whom He will.
People delight in the life of the world;
yet this life is but a fleeting fancy
when set beside the hereafter.

SECTION 4

27 Unbelievers say, "Why is no sign
sent down to him from his Lord?"
Say, "God lets stray whom He will,
and He guides to Himself those
who turn to Him in repentance,

28 "those who believe,
whose hearts find rest
in remembrance of God—
it is only in remembering God
that hearts find rest;

29 "those who believe
and do good deeds
shall have bliss,
and will return
to a beautiful place."

30 We have sent you to a people
—before whom many peoples
passed away—that you might recite
to them what We inspired in you;
but they denied the All Merciful.
Say, "He is my Lord—
there is no god but Him.
In Him I trust, and to Him I return."

31 If there were a Qur'an by which
mountains could be moved,
or the earth cleaved apart,
or the dead made to speak,
[this would be it].
God's command rules in all things.
Don't the believers realize
that God could have guided
all humankind, had He willed?
As for the unbelievers,
calamity will never cease
to strike them for their deeds,
or lie close to their homes,
God's promise is fulfilled—
God never fails in His promise.

SECTION 5

32 Messengers before you, Prophet,
were mocked, though I gave respite
to the unbelievers. Finally,
I seized them—
how Severe was My Requital!

33 Is He Who stands over
every soul, noting its deeds
[like the other gods they worship]?
Yet they join other gods with God.
Say, "Name them," or "Can you
inform Him of something
He does not know on earth?

Or is this a mere show of words?"
The schemes of the unbelievers
are made to seem pleasing to them,
and they are barred from the path.
And those whom God leaves to stray
shall have no guide.

34 They shall face torment
in the life of this world;
but harsher is the torment
of the hereafter.
And they shall have none
to defend them against God.

35 This is the parable of the garden
—promised to those mindful of
    God—
rivers flow beneath it,
and its food is eternal,
as is its shade. This is the fate
of those mindful of God; the fate
of disbelievers is fire.

36 Those to whom We gave the Book
rejoice in what is revealed to you;
but some factions deny part of it.
Say, "I was commanded only
to worship God, and not to join
other gods with Him. To Him I call,
and to Him is my return."

37 We revealed the Qur'an to render
judgment in the Arabic tongue;
were you to follow their desires, after
the knowledge that has come to you,
there would be none to protect you
against God, or defend you.

SECTION 6

38 We sent messengers before you,
and gave them wives and children.
But it was not for any messenger
to bring a sign without God's leave.
There has been a Book for every age.°

39 God annuls or confirms
what He will; and with Him
is the origin of the Book.

40 Whether We show you part
of the punishment We promised
    them
or cause you to die beforehand,
your part is to convey the message—
Ours is the reckoning.

41 Don't they see how We came
to scale back the borders
of their land? When God judges,
none can undo His judgment;
and He is Swift in Reckoning.

42 Those before them also schemed;
but the ultimate scheme is God's.
He knows what each soul earns;
and the unbelievers shall soon know
who finally has the [best] home.

43 The unbelievers say,
"You are no messenger."
Say, "God suffices as a Witness
between me and you—and those
with knowledge of the Book."

SURA 14

Abraham (*Ibrahim*)

Among the last of the Meccan revelations, this sura is named after its central focus, the "Prayer of Abraham" (vv. 35–41). It totals 52 verses, opening with reference to Moses along with Noah, ʿAd and Thamud, then ending with the threat of torment to wrongdoers (vv. 42–52).

In the Name of God, the All Merciful, Ever Merciful

SECTION I

1 *Alif. Lam. Ra.°*

This is a Book We revealed to you,
that you might bring humankind
from darkness into light,
with their Lord's assent,
to the path of the Almighty,
the Praiseworthy—

2 God, to Whom belongs
all that is in the heavens and earth.
The unbelievers shall know
the sorrow of severe torment°—

3 those who prefer the life
of this world to the hereafter,
and bar people from God's path,
seeking to make it crooked—
they have gone far astray.

4 We never sent a messenger
who did not speak the language
of his people, to make things
clear to them. But God

leaves to stray whom He will
and guides whom He will,
for He is Almighty, All Wise.

5 We sent Moses with Our signs,
saying, "Bring out your people
from darkness into light, and
remind them of the days of God."
In this are signs for all
who are patient and grateful.

6 Then Moses said to his people,
"Remember God's favor to you when
He saved you from Pharaoh's people,
who inflicted dire torments on you,
killing your sons, and sparing
only your women—a terrible trial
from your Lord."

SECTION 2

7 When your Lord declared,
"If you are thankful,
I will grant you increase,
but if you are ungrateful,
My punishment will be severe"—

8 Moses said, "If you are ungrateful,
you and all those on the earth,
know that God is Self-Sufficient,
Praiseworthy."

9 Haven't you heard the story
of those who came before you,
the people of Noah, 'Ad, and
     Thamud,°
and those who came after them?
None but God knows about them all.
Messengers came to them with clear
     proofs,
But, biting their hands [out of spite],°
they cried, "We don't believe in the
     message
sent with you, and we have grave
     doubts
about what you're calling us to do."

10 Their messengers asked,
"Can there be doubt about God,
Creator of the heavens and the earth?
He calls you, that He might
forgive you for your sins, and
give you respite for a decreed time."
They answered, "You're just a
     human,
like us—you want to divert us from
what our fathers worshipped—
bring us some clear sanction for
     this."

11 Their messengers answered,
"Yes, we're just humans, like you;
but God grants His grace
to whom He will of His servants.

And we can't bring you sanction
without His leave—
so let all who believe trust in God.

12 "Why should we not trust in God
Who guided us to this path of ours?
And we will bear with patience
whatever harm you inflict on us—
So let all who trust, trust in God."°

SECTION 3

13 Unbelievers told their messengers,
"Be sure that we'll drive you
from our land, if you don't return
to our creed." But their Lord
revealed to the messengers,
"Be sure that We
will destroy the wrongdoers.

14 "And We'll leave you [believers]
living in the land after them.
This is the reward for those
who fear they will stand before Me,
and those who fear My threat."

15 ° [The messengers]
prayed for victory,° and
every stubborn tyrant came to grief.

16 Ahead of [each of them] lies hell,
and they will drink putrid water.°

17 They will try to gulp it down
but shall scarcely swallow it.
Death will close in on them
from every side, though

they will not die—still ahead of
    them
lies severe torment.

18 Here is a parable
    of those who deny their Lord:
    their deeds are ashes that the wind
    blows wildly on a stormy day;
    they have no power at all
    over anything they've gained—
    this is to go far astray.

19 Do you not see that God
    created the heavens and the earth
    with true purpose?° If He wishes,
    He can remove you and replace
    you with a new creation.

20 This would hardly be
    a huge task for God.

21 They will all be exposed together
    before God; then the weak will say
    to those who were in power,
    "We followed you, but can you now
    help us against God's punishment
    in any way?"
    They'll reply, "Had God guided us,
    we would have guided you."
    It's the same now, whether we rage
    or endure with patience—
    we have no escape."

SECTION 4

22 When all is decided, Satan will say,
    "God made you a promise that was
        true;
    I too made a promise, but I failed
        you.
    I had no authority over you; all I
        could do
    was to call you—yet you responded
        to me.
    So don't blame me—blame
        yourselves.
    I can't help you, nor can you help
        me.
    In fact, I denounce how you part-
        nered me
    with God before. The wrongdoers
    shall face a painful punishment."

23 Those who believed
    and did good deeds
    will be ushered into gardens,
    beneath which rivers flow,
    to live there forever,
    by their Lord's leave.
    There, they'll be greeted
    with "Peace."

24 Do you not see how God
    coins a parable: a good word
    is like a good tree, with roots
    anchored firm, while its branches
    soar into the sky?

25 It yields its fruit in every season
    by its Lord's leave. In this way

God coins parables for humankind,
that they might be reminded.

26 And a bad word
is like a bad tree—
uprooted from the face
of the earth, unstable.

27 God will anchor those who believe
with the Word that stands firm,
in this worldly life and the hereafter.
But He will let the wrongdoers
    stray.
God does all that He will.

SECTION 5

28 Prophet, do you not see those
who bartered God's favor for
    disbelief,
and brought their people to settle
in the house of perdition,

29 hell, where they will burn—
an evil home?

30 And they have set up idols
as equal to God, to mislead people
from His path.
Say, "Enjoy [your time here]
but your path leads to the fire."

31 Tell My believing servants
to be steadfast in prayer,
and to spend in charity
—both secretly and openly—
from what We have given them,

before the coming of a day that
brooks neither trade nor friendship.

32 It is God Who created
the heavens and the earth,
Who sends down rain from the sky,
bringing forth fruits to sustain you.
He subdued to your use
the ships° that sail the ocean
by His command, and subdued
to you the rivers too.

33 And He subdued to your use
the sun and moon, both sailing
steadfast in their orbits;
and He subdued to you
both night and day.

34 And He has given you
all that you asked of Him.
If you tried to count the favors
of God, you could never
number them. Humankind
is truly unjust, ungrateful.

SECTION 6

35 Remember when Abraham said,
"My Lord, make this town secure,
and keep me and my sons
from worshipping idols.

36 "My Lord, those idols
have led many people astray.
Whoever follows me is with me;
as for those who disobey me—
You are Forgiving, Ever Merciful.

37 "Our Lord, I have settled some
of my offspring in an arid valley,
near your sacred house, so that
they might be steadfast in prayer,
        our Lord.
So, turn people's hearts toward them,
and sustain them with fruit, so that
they might be grateful.

38 "Our Lord, you know
what we conceal and what we reveal,
for nothing whatsoever
on earth or in heaven
is hidden from God.

39 "All praise be to God, Who granted
Ishmael and Isaac to me in my old
        age—
My Lord is the One Who Hears
        prayer.°

40 "My Lord, make me steadfast
in prayer, and my offspring too—
our Lord, accept my prayer.

41 "Our Lord, grant forgiveness
to me, my parents, and the believers
on the day the reckoning comes."

SECTION 7

42 Do not think, Prophet, that God
ignores the deeds of those who do
        wrong;
He merely grants them respite
till a day when their eyes
will stare [in horror],

43 racing forward, their heads
craned back, their gaze fixed rigid,°
and their hearts void.

44 So warn the people of a day
when Our torment will fall on them.
Then, the wrongdoers will say,
"Our Lord, grant us respite,
if only for a short while: we'll
answer your call, and we'll follow
the messengers." They will be told,
"But didn't you always swear
that your [power] would never fade?

45 "And you lived in the houses
of those who wronged themselves,
though you were clearly shown
how We dealt with them—
Did We not give examples for you?"

46 Yes, they contrived their plot,
but God has the measure of their
        plot—
even if their plot could move
        mountains.

47 So, Prophet, do not think that God
will fail in His promise to His
        messengers;
God is Almighty, Lord of Requital.

48 One day, when this earth
becomes another earth,
this heaven, another heaven,
with people all exposed before God,
the One, Omnipotent,

49 you, Prophet, will see the sinners
bound together in chains,

50 in garments of tar, their faces
covered by fire—

51 so that God might reward
each soul for what it has reaped—
God is Swift in Reckoning.

52 Here is a message for humankind,
to be warned by it, and to know
that He is the One God, so those
with insight might be reminded.

SURA 15

The Rocky Plain (*Al-Hijr*)

From the middle Meccan period, this sura of 99 short verses takes its name from a place just north of Medina, where the Thamud tribe lived (vv. 80–84). Several passages extol nature and creation but also warn of punishment (vv. 49–84). Among its unusual features is a notable reference to the initial sura, Sura al-Fatiha, as "the seven much-recited verses" (v. 87).

In the Name of God, the All Merciful, Ever Merciful

SECTION I

1 *Alif. Lam. Ra.*°

These are the verses of the Book,
a clear Qur'an.

2 Those who disbelieve may soon wish
they had yielded to God's will.

3 Leave them to eat
and please themselves,
beguiled by hope; soon
they will come to know.

4 We never destroy any town
without decreeing for it a fixed term.°

5 No community can hasten
its term or delay it.

6 They scoff, "You—the one
this message is revealed to—
you are truly mad.°

7 "Why don't you bring the angels
to us, if you're speaking the truth?"

8 We send down the angels
only to bring the truth—and then

there would be no reprieve
[for those who disbelieve].

9 It is We who revealed the message,
and it is We Who watch over it.

10 We sent messengers before you
to former communities,

11 but they mocked every messenger
who came to them.°

12 And so We let it slip
into the hearts of sinners

13 that they would deny the message—
the practice of former peoples.°

14 And even if We opened for them
a gate to heaven, and they rose
through it, higher still and higher,

15 they would only say, "Our eyes
are dazzled—yes, we're bewitched."

SECTION 2

16 We have laid stars out in the sky
in their ordered constellations,
sublime to all who gaze on them,

17 and We guard them against
every accursed devil.°

18 Though any devil who eavesdrops
shall be chased by a luminous flame.°

19 And We have laid out the earth,
set sturdy mountains upon it,
and brought forth on it
all things in due proportion.

20 And We placed in it provision
for you and also for those
outside your care.

21 The treasures of all things
rest with Us, and We send them
down only in due measure.

22 We send the fructifying winds, and
water from the sky for you to drink,
though you cannot store it.

23 It is We who give life,
and We who bring death, and We
shall inherit all things.

24 We know those who go first among
you
and We know those who lag behind.

25 It is your Lord who will
gather them together; He
is the All Wise, All Knowing.

SECTION 3

26 We created humankind
from dried clay,
molded from dark mud.

27 and before that We created jinn
from a scorching fire.

28 Your Lord said to the angels,
    "I shall create a human from dried
        clay,
    molded from dark mud."

29 "Once I have proportioned him,
    and breathed My spirit into him—
    fall down and bow before him."°

30 So the angels all bowed down,

31 except Iblis, who refused to bow
    with the others.

32 God demanded, "Iblis, why
    did you not bow with the others?"

33 Iblis retorted, "I will not bow
    to a human, whom you created from
    dried clay, molded from dark mud."

34 God answered, "Go out, then,
    from here, for you are surely cursed.

35 "And the curse shall stay with you
    until the day of reckoning."

36 Iblis implored, "My Lord,
    grant me respite, till the day when
    all are raised up from the dead."

37 "You shall have respite," said God,

38 "until the appointed day."

39 Iblis said, "My Lord,
    because you have left me to stray,

I will entice them on the earth,
and lead them astray—all,

40 "except those among your servants
    who are chosen."

41 God affirmed,
    "This is a straight path to Me
    [for those who are chosen].

42 "You shall have no authority
    over My servants, except those
    who err, who choose to follow you."

43 And hell is the end
    promised for all of them.

44 It has seven gates,
    each assigned its share of them.

SECTION 4

45 Those who fear God shall be
    amid gardens and fountains;

46 [They shall hear the greeting],
    "Enter in peace and safety."

47 And We will purge their hearts
    of rancor, and they will be kin,°
    arrayed on couches, face-to-face.

48 No fatigue shall reach them there,
    nor will they be made to leave.

49 Let My servants know that I am
    Forgiving, Ever Merciful,

50 and that My punishment
   is a most painful punishment.

51 And let them know about
   the guests of Abraham.

52 When they came to him,
   saying, "Peace," he said,
   "We're afraid of you."

53 They said, "Don't be afraid;
   we bring you good news—of a son,
   to be endowed with knowledge."

54 He answered, "Do you bring
   such good news, when old age
   is already upon me?
   What kind of news is this?"°

55 They said, "We bring you
   good news that is true,
   so don't despair."

56 Abraham replied,
   "Who but those who've gone astray
   despair of their Lord's mercy?"

57 Then he inquired,
   "So, what is your mission,
   you messengers?"

58 They said, "We have been sent
   to a people who are sinful,

59 "except the family of Lot,
   of whom We shall save all

60 "but his wife. We decreed
   that she would be with those
   who stayed behind."

SECTION 5

61 When the messengers came
   to the family of Lot,

62 he said, "You people
   are unknown to us."

63 They responded, "True,
   but We have brought you
   the [very punishment
   the sinners] doubted.

64 "We have brought you the truth,
   and we are being truthful.

65 "So, leave, with your family,
   in the dead of night,
   and stay behind them,
   and let none of you look back,
   but keep going to where
   you are commanded."

66 And We made known to him
   Our decree: the last of those people
   would be wiped out by morning.

67 The people of the town
   came by, exulting.°

68 Lot cautioned them,
   "These people are my guests,
   so don't shame me.

69 "Be mindful of God,
   and don't disgrace me."

70 The townspeople said,
   "Didn't we forbid you from hosting
   or protecting anyone?"°

71 He said, "Here are my daughters,
   if you would behave [acceptably]."°

72 By your very life, Prophet,
   they stumbled blindly in their stupor.

73 But the thunderous blast
   struck them at dawn,

74 and We turned [their town]
   upside down, and rained upon them
   stones of hardened clay.

75 In this are signs
   for the discerning.

76 [And its ruins haunt]
   a road that is still there.

77 In this is a sign
   for those who believe.

78 And the forest dwellers
   were also wrongdoers,°

79 We requited them also.
   Both lie on an open road,
   for all to see.

SECTION 6

80 The natives of al-Hijr°
   also denied the messengers.

81 We sent them Our signs,
   but they always turned
   away from them.

82 They carved their houses
   out of the mountains—
   seeming secure.

83 But the thunderous blast
   shook them in the morning,

84 And the deeds they had done
   were of no help to them.

85 We did not create the heavens
   and the earth, and all between them,
   without true purpose.
   And the hour is surely coming,
   so show them, Prophet,
   gracious forbearance.

86 For your Lord is the Creator,
   the All Knowing.

87 We have given you
   the seven much-recited verses
   and the exalted Qur'an.°

88 Don't strain both your eyes
   gazing at what We have given
   some people to enjoy [while it lasts];
   nor grieve over them;

but lower your wing° [in mercy]
over the believers,

89 and say, "I am someone
who gives clear warning."

90 Just as We sent warning
to those who sought division,

91 dividing the Qur'an
into discrete segments.

92 By your Lord, We shall
question them all

93 for their deeds.

94 So proclaim openly what you
have been commanded to say,

and turn away from those
who join other gods with God.

95 We offer ample defense for you
against those who mock,

96 those who devise, besides God,
some other god—soon
they will come to know.

97 We well know how your heart
is stressed by what they say.

98 So glorify your Lord with praise,
and join those who bow low to Him.

99 And worship your Lord until
[death in its] certainty comes to
you.°

SURA 16

The Bee (*Al-Nahl*)

From the late Meccan period, though the final verses may be Medinan, this sura
of 128 verses lauds creation from heavens and earth to humankind and cattle,
extending to oceans, mountains, and stars (vv. 3–16). Simultaneously it warns of
a painful punishment for disbelievers and promises an eternal reward for believers (vv. 106–28). The title comes from a tribute to the bee, the epitome of divine
disclosure through nature, in vv. 68–69.

In the Name of God, the All Merciful, Ever Merciful

SECTION I

1 What God has decreed is coming,
so do not seek to hasten it.

Glory be to Him, exalted above
the gods they join with Him.

2 He sends down the angels, inspired
  by His command,° to whichever
  of His servants He will, "Warn
      them:
  There is no god but Me, so fear
      Me."

3 He created the heavens and earth
  with true purpose; He is exalted
      above
  the gods they join with Him.

4 He created human beings
  from a tiny globule—yet see
  how openly defiant they are!

5 He created cattle for you,
  giving you warmth and other uses;
  you consume them for food,

6 and you sense a beauty in them
  when you bring them home [at dusk]
  and herd them to pasture [at dawn].

7 And they bear your loads to lands
  you could not reach without
      hardship.
  Your Lord is Most Kind, Ever
      Merciful.

8 And He gave you horses,
  mules, and donkeys, to ride
  as well as for their beauty,°
  and He created other things
  beyond your knowledge.

9 God shows the right path,
  but some paths lead away from this.
  Had He wished,
  He would have guided you all.

SECTION 2

10 It is He who sends down water
   from the sky, which you drink,
   which also brings greenery
   for your livestock to graze.°

11 With it He brings forth for you
   corn, olives, date palms, and vines,
   and all variety of fruit. In this
   is a sign for those who think.

12 And He subdues to your use
   night and day, sun and moon.
   And the constellations are subdued
   by His command. In this
   is a sign for those who reason.

13 And He has multiplied
   all things for you on earth,
   in varying colors. In this
   is a sign for those who take heed.

14 It is He Who subdued the sea
   so you might consume its fish, all
       fresh,
   and bring up from its depth
       ornaments
   to wear. And you gaze upon the ships
   that plow its waves so you might
   seek the bounty of God, and give
       thanks.

15 And He has cast upon the earth
sturdy mountains, to stop it quaking
beneath you; and rivers and paths
so you might be guided,

16 as well as landmarks.
By the stars too, people are guided.

17 Is One who creates the same
as one who cannot create?
Won't you, then, take heed?

18 If you tried to count
the favors of God, you could
never number them. God
is Forgiving, Ever Merciful.

19 And God knows
what you conceal
and what you reveal.

20 Those on whom they call
besides God can create nothing;
they themselves are created—

21 dead, without any life;
nor can they even sense
when they might be resurrected.

SECTION 3

22 Your God is One God. But those
who don't believe in the hereafter
refuse the truth in their hearts,
and they are full of pride.

23 No doubt, God knows
what they conceal
and what they reveal,
and He dislikes those
who are full of pride.

24 When they are asked,
"What has your Lord revealed?"
they scoff in reply,
"Tales of the ancients."

25 So let them bear, on the day
of resurrection, the full weight
of their own burdens, as well as
the burdens of those they led astray
—without any knowledge—
a harrowing burden to bear.°

SECTION 4

26 Those before them also schemed,
but God assailed the very
    foundations
of their building; the roof crashed
down upon them, and His wrath
struck them from places
they could not conceive.

27 Then, on the day of resurrection,
He will shame them, saying,
"Where are My partners—the gods
for whose sake you opposed [Me]?"
Those with knowledge will say,
"Today, shame and misery
shall shroud the disbelievers."

28 Those whose souls the angels
take while wronging themselves
will profess submission:
"We didn't do any evil."

They will be answered,
"But you did—God Knows well
all that you have done.

29 "Enter, then, the gates of hell,
to stay there forever—an evil home
for those who were proud."

30 When those who are
mindful of God are asked,
"What has your Lord revealed?"
they will answer, "All that is good."
Those who do good will reap good
in this world, yet the home
of the hereafter will be better still.
Excellent is the home of those
who are mindful of God.

31 They shall enter eternal gardens,
beneath which rivers flow. There
they shall have all that they desire—
this is how God rewards those
who are mindful of Him.

32 Those whose souls the angels
take while in a state of goodness—
the angels will say to them,
"Peace be with you; enter the
garden,
a reward for all that you did."

33 Are the unbelievers waiting
for the angels to come to them, or
for
your Lord to command [their
doom]?
This is what those before them
did—

it is not God who wrongs them
but they who wrong themselves.

34 They were struck by the evil
of their own deeds, and besieged
by what they used to mock.

SECTION 5

35 The polytheists say,
"If God had wished it,
We would have worshipped nothing
besides Him, we and our ancestors;
and would have forbidden nothing
without his leave." This is what
those before them did.
What is the task of the messengers
but to convey the message clearly?

36 We sent messengers
to every people, saying,
"Worship the One God,
and shun the false gods."
And among them were some
that God guided, and some
deserving to go astray.
Travel, then, across the earth
and observe the fate
of those who denied.

37 Even if you want them
to be guided, God will not guide
those who mislead others,
and there will be none to help them.

38 They swear their strongest oaths
   by God, that God won't raise the
      dead
   —yes, He will; His promise is true,
   but most people don't know it—

39 to make clear to them the things
   they dispute, and to make
      unbelievers
   realize they were lying.

40 When We intend something,
   We merely say, "Be!"—and it is!

SECTION 6

41 To those who were wronged and
   left their homes in God's cause,
   We'll give a good home in this world;
   yet the reward of the hereafter
   is greater—if only they knew.

42 They are the ones who practice
   patience, and trust in their Lord.

43 And We only sent before you
   men whom We inspired
   —ask those who possess the
      message
   if you yourselves don't know—

44 with clear signs and scriptures;
   and We revealed the message to you,
   Prophet, for you to explain to people
   what We sent down to them
   so they might reflect.

45 Can those who devise
   wicked schemes feel sure
   that God won't make the earth
   swallow them up, or that His wrath
   won't strike them from places
   they cannot conceive,

46 or take them suddenly
   as they come and go
   —for they cannot thwart God—

47 or take them by slow attrition?
   Yet your Lord is Most Kind,
   Ever Merciful.

48 Don't they see the things
   that God created—
   how their very shadows incline
   to right and left,
   bowing humbly before God?

49 All in the heavens and all on earth
   bow to God, living creatures
   and the angels—
   for they are not proud.

50 They all fear their Lord, Who
   is high above them, and they do
   as they are commanded.

SECTION 7

51 God has said,
   "Do not worship two gods—
   He is the One, the only God,
   so fear Me alone."

52 To Him belongs all
   that is in the heavens and earth;
   to Him everlasting worship is due.
   Why would you fear any but God?

53 Whatever blessings you have
   are from God alone,
   and when misfortune strikes you,
   you cry to Him alone for help.

54 Yet, when He relieves your
      misfortune,
   some of you join other gods with
      God,

55 ungrateful for what He has given.
   Enjoy your brief time, for soon
   you shall come to know.

56 And they consecrate a portion
   of what We have given them
   to idols, things they don't know.
   By God, you will be asked
   about the things you fabricated.

57 They ascribe daughters to God
   —may He be glorified—
   but for themselves they want sons.°

58 When any of them gets news
   of the birth of a girl, his face darkens
   as he fills with inward gloom.

59 Out of shame, he hides himself
   away from people,
   on account of his bad news.

Should he keep her, to his
   ignominy,
or bury her alive in the sand?°
How wicked is their judgment.

60 Those who don't believe
   in the hereafter are an allegory
   of evil, whereas God is an allegory
   of what is Most High,°
   for He is Almighty, All Wise.

SECTION 8

61 If God took people to task
   for their wrongs, He would leave
   not one living creature on earth, but
   he reprieves them for a given term.
   Once that term ends,
   they cannot delay it, nor hasten it—
   not by one hour.

62 They ascribe to God
   what they themselves dislike,°
   and their tongues mouth the lie
   that the best things° are for them.
   Without doubt, the fire is for
      them—
   in fact, they'll be hurried there.

63 By God, We sent messengers to
      peoples
   before you, but Satan made
   their [wicked] deeds seem fair to
      them;
   he is still their ally today—
   but they shall face a painful torment.

64 We revealed the Book to you
   only for you to clarify for them
   the things they dispute, and as a
      guide
   and mercy to people who believe.

65 And God sends down rain
   from the sky, bringing life
   to the dead earth.° In this
   is a sign for those who hear.

SECTION 9

66 In the uses of cattle, too,
   there is a precept for you:
   We give you drink from their bellies
   —between excrement and blood—
   pure milk, sweet to those who
      drink.

67 And from the fruit of date palm
   and vine, you harvest wine
   as well as wholesome food. In this
   is a sign for those who reason.

68 Your Lord inspired the bee,
   "Build your hives in the hills,
   in trees, and in human dwellings.

69 "So eat of all kinds of fruits,
   and follow the paths made smooth
   by your Lord." From their bellies
   issues a drink of varying hues,
   able to heal people. In this
   is a sign for those who think.

70 It is God Who created you
   and will cause you to die,
   making some of you regress
   to an abject state of old age,
   knowing nothing—after knowing.
   God is All Knowing, All Powerful.

SECTION 10

71 God has favored some of you
   with greater provision than others.
   Those with more would not
      reallocate
   their share to their slaves,
   so as to make them equal. Will they
   deny, then, the blessings of God?

72 God has made spouses for you,
   from yourselves, and from them,
      children
   and grandchildren,
   and He has provided you
   with all that is good.
   Would they still believe in falsehood
   and deny the blessings of God?

73 And would they worship others
   instead of God—who have no power
   to provide them with anything
   from the heavens or the earth,
   and are incapable?

74 Do not coin any likeness of God:
   God has Knowledge—you do not.°

75 God coins a parable: a slave,
   who is owned, with no power

over anything; and a man to whom
We have given ample provision,
who spends in charity both secretly
and openly. How can these be equal?
All praise be to God.
Yet most of them do not know.

76 God coins a parable of two men:
one dumb, with no power to do
anything, is a burden to his keeper—
however he directs him,
he brings no good. Is he
equal to one who enjoins justice
and is set on a straight path?

SECTION II

77 To God belongs all that is unseen
in the heavens and the earth.
The hour of judgment° will come
like the blinking of an eye—
or more swiftly.
God has Power over all things.

78 It is God Who brought you
from the wombs of your mothers,
knowing nothing; and He gave you
hearing, and sight, and hearts,
that you might give thanks.

79 Do they not see the birds,
poised in their skyward flight?
Nothing bears them up except God.
In this are signs
for people who believe.

80 It is God Who made your homes
a place of rest, and made for you,
from the skins of animals, tents
that you find light to bear
when you travel and make camp;
and from their wool, fur, and hair,
you derive furnishings
and supplies to last a while.

81 It is God Who gave you shade,
among the things He created,
and He gave you shelters
in the mountains, and clothes
to shield you from the heat,
as well as armor to shield you
in your warfare. In these ways,
He perfects His favor to you,
that you might submit to His will.

82 But if they turn away,
your task is only to convey
the message clearly.°

83 They recognize God's favors yet
deny them, for most of them
are ungrateful.

SECTION 12

84 One day We shall raise up
a witness among every
people—then
the unbelievers won't be allowed
to make excuses or make amends.

85 When the wrongdoers see
the punishment,

it will not be lightened for them,
nor will they be shown respite.

86 When the polytheists see the gods
they joined with God, they'll say,
"Our Lord, these are the gods
we invoked instead of You."
The gods will throw their words
back at them, "You are liars."

87 On that day, they shall willingly
submit to God, and the false gods
they invented will abandon them.

88 We shall heap torment
on torment upon those who
disbelieved and barred people
from the path of God,
for their breeding of mischief.

89 One day We shall raise up within
every people a witness against them,°
and We shall bring you, Prophet,
as a witness against these people.
We have revealed to you the Book
that clarifies all things—and gives
guidance, mercy, and joyous news
to those who submit to God's will.

SECTION 13

90 God commands justice, goodness,
and generosity to kin. He also forbids
indecency, wrong, and oppression.
He instructs that you might take
heed.

91 So fulfill your pledge to God
once you have made it,
and don't break your oaths
after swearing them, for you
have made God your surety.
God knows all that you do.

92 And don't—like a woman who
untwists the yarn she has spun
firm°—
indulge your oaths to deceive
one another, if one group happens
to outnumber another—
for God will test you by this.
And on the day of resurrection
He will make clear to you
the issues you dispute.

93 Had God wished, He could have
made you one community;
but He leaves to stray whom He will,
and He guides whom He will;
and you shall undoubtedly be asked
about all that you did.

94 Don't indulge your oaths
to deceive one another, else
someone's foot might slip,
though it was firmly fixed,
and you might taste the evil outcome
of your barring people from God's
path,
and face great punishment.

95 And don't barter God's pledge
for a paltry price, for what God has
is better for you, if only you knew.

96 Whatever you have is ephemeral
   but what God has is enduring;
   and We shall reward those
   who practice patience
   for the best of their deeds.

97 Whoever does good
   —whether man or woman—
   and is a true believer,
   We will grant them a good life,
   and We will reward them
   for the best of their deeds.

98 When you read the Qur'an,
   seek refuge in God
   from Satan—the accursed.°

99 He has no sway over those
   who believe and trust in their Lord.

100 His sway is only over those
    who embrace him as an ally,
    and those who, on his account,
    join other gods with God.

SECTION 14

101 When We displace one verse
    with another—and God knows best
    what He reveals—they say,
    "You're nothing but a forger."
    But most of them have no
       knowledge.°

102 Say, "The holy spirit°
    has revealed it [in stages]
    from your Lord, bearing truth,

to strengthen those who believe,
and as guidance and joyous news
for those who submit to God's will."

103 We know well that they say,
    "It's a mere mortal who teaches him."
    But the person they mean
    speaks a foreign tongue°,
    while this is clear Arabic.

104 As for those who don't believe
    in the signs of God—God will not
    guide them, and they shall face
    a painful punishment.

105 Only those who don't believe
    invent lies about the signs of God;
    they are the ones who lie.

106 Those who deny God
    after having faith—unless
       compelled,
    while their hearts kept faith—
    those who open their hearts
    to unbelief, shall incur God's wrath,
    and they shall face great torment.

107 For they preferred the life
    of this world to the hereafter,
    and God does not guide
    a people who disbelieve.

108 They are the ones
    whose hearts, hearing, and sight
    God has sealed,
    for they are heedless.

109 Without doubt, they are the ones
who will lose in the hereafter.

110 But to those who left their homes
after being oppressed, and then
strove
in God's cause with patience,
your Lord will be Forgiving, Ever
Merciful.

SECTION 15

111 One day, each soul
shall come, pleading for itself,
and each soul shall be paid
in full for what it did,
and none shall be wronged.

112 God coins a parable:
there was a town, secure and
content,
with ample supplies from all places;
yet it became ungrateful
for God's favors, so He let it
taste the ravages of hunger and fear
for the things its people did.

113 A messenger, one of their own,
came to them, but they deemed him
a fraud—so punishment struck
them
even as they indulged in
wrongdoing.

114 So eat of the lawful and good
things God has provided for you,

and be grateful for God's favor,
if it is Him that you worship.

115 He has forbidden for you only
carrion, blood, the flesh of swine,
and animals killed by invoking
anything other than God's name.
But if someone is compelled
by hunger, without willful
disobedience or excess, then God
is Forgiving, Ever Merciful.°

116 Don't let your tongues say falsely,
"This is lawful, and this forbidden,"
so as to invent falsehoods about God.
Those who fabricate such lies
shall not prosper—

117 their enjoyment is but brief,
for they shall face painful torment.

118 Prophet, We forbade for the Jews
the things We cited to you earlier,°
for We never wronged them
but they wronged themselves.

119 But to those who do wrong
through ignorance, and then repent
and amend themselves, your Lord
is Forgiving, Ever Merciful.

SECTION 16

120 Abraham was a nation in himself:
devoted to God, upright,
and he was not a polytheist.

121 He was grateful for the favors
of God, Who chose him and
guided him to a straight path.

122 We gave him good in this world,
and he will be among the righteous
in the hereafter.

123 Then We inspired you, Prophet,
"Follow the creed of Abraham,
the upright, who was not a
     polytheist."

124 The [day of the] Sabbath
was decreed only for those
who disputed over it; and
your Lord will judge between them,
on the day of resurrection,
in the things they dispute.

125 Call people to the path
of your Lord with wisdom
and exemplary instruction,
and argue with them
in exemplary fashion.
Your Lord knows best
who has strayed from His path,
and who is rightly guided.

126 If you must respond to aggression,
retaliate only in like measure—
but it will be better for you
if you show patience.°

127 So, Prophet, practice patience—
your patience comes only from
     God;°
don't grieve over them,
and don't distress yourself
over the things they plot.

128 For God is with those
who are mindful of Him,
and those who do good.

SURA 17

The Night Journey (*Al-Isra'*)

From the middle Meccan period, this sura takes its name from the initial verse, depicting Muhammad's journey from Mecca to Jerusalem to heaven and back. Whether as a dream or physical happening, that event (known as the *mi'raj*, or the Prophet's Ascent) has brought acclaim to this sura of 111 verses, though it also contains stories about Israelites as well as the fall of Iblis (vv. 61–65). It further underscores that the Qur'an was revealed in stages (v. 106), inviting believers to call on God with His Beautiful Names (v. 110).

In the Name of God, the All Merciful, Ever Merciful

SECTION I

1 Glory be to the One
Who took His servant
on a journey by night
from the sacred mosque
to the farthest mosque,°
whose precincts We blessed
that We might show him
some of Our signs. He alone
is the All Hearing,
All Seeing.

2 We gave Moses the Book,°
and made it a guide
for the children of Israel, saying,
"Do not entrust your affairs
to anyone but Me,

3 "you descendants of those
We carried in the ark with Noah;
he was a grateful servant."

4 And in the Book We forewarned
the children of Israel:
"Twice you will breed
corruption in the land, and reach
the height of pride."°

5 When the first of the warnings
came to pass, We sent against you
Our servants who had great force;
they entered the inmost precincts
of your homes—the warning
was fulfilled.

6 Then We gave back to you victory
over them, and We reinforced you
with wealth and offspring,
multiplying you.

7 If you do good, you do good
for yourselves; and if you do evil,
it is for yourselves. And when
the second warning came to pass,
[We sent your enemies]
to distress your countenances
and to enter your place of worship
as they did the first time, and
utterly destroy whatever
they had conquered.

8 It may be that your Lord
may yet show you mercy, but
should you turn back,
We shall turn back.
We have made hell
a prison for disbelievers.

9 This Qur'an guides to what
is most right and brings joyous news
to believers who do good deeds—
that they shall have a great reward,

10 and that We have prepared
a harrowing punishment
for those who don't believe,
in the hereafter.

SECTION 2

11 Yet humans pray for evil,
as avidly as they pray for good—
they are always in haste.

12 We made night and day two signs.
We effaced the sign of night,
and gave light to the sign of day,
that you might seek
the bounty of your Lord,
and know the number of years
and the science of calculation.
We have explained all things in detail.°

13 We have fastened
every man's fate
around his own neck;°
on the day of resurrection
We shall bring out
for him a record,
which he shall find
wide open.

14 He will be told,
"Read your record. Your own soul
suffices this day as a reckoning
against you."

15 Whoever receives guidance
is guided for his own good; and
whoever goes astray, strays to his
own harm. And no soul shall bear
another's burden. Nor do We punish
until We have sent a messenger to
warn.

16 When We intend to destroy a town,
We command its wealthy citizens
to obey; but they stubbornly
disobey,
so sentence is passed upon them—
and We destroy them utterly.

17 How many generations
did We destroy after Noah?
For your Lord is fully Aware
and Sees the sins of His servants.

18 Whoever desires this fleeting life,
We hasten whatever We will in it
for them—for whomever We wish;
in the end, We commit them
to hell, in which they will burn,
disgraced, rejected.

19 As for those who desire
the hereafter and duly strive for it
as believers—they are the ones
whose striving will be commended.

20 To each of these,
We extend the gift of your Lord,
a gift unbounded—

21 see, how We have favored
some over others. Yet the hereafter
is higher in rank,
and higher also in favor.

22 Do not set up another god
besides the One God, or you will
be left disgraced, forsaken.

SECTION 3

23 Your Lord has decreed
    that you worship Him Alone,
    and that you be kind to parents.
    Whether one or both of them
    reach old age with you, do not say,
    "For shame!" to them, or spurn them,
    but speak to them with kind words.

24 And lower over them both
    the wing of humility, with mercy,°
    and say, "My Lord, show mercy
    to them, as they nurtured me
    when I was young."

25 Your Lord knows best
    what is in your hearts.
    If you are righteous,
    He is Ever Forgiving of those
    who turn to Him.

26 And render to relatives
    their due, as well as to the needy
    and the traveler; and do not
    spend wastefully.

27 Spendthrifts are brothers
    of Satan;° and Satan
    is ever ungrateful to his Lord.

28 If you must turn from [beggars],
    hoping, by your Lord's mercy,
    [to help them later], at least
    speak to them a gentle word.

29 Don't let your hand be bound
    [tightfisted] to your neck; nor

extend it fully, else you might end up
blameworthy, impoverished.

30 Your Lord extends or restricts
    provision for whom He will.
    He is Ever Aware, Observant
    of His servants.°

SECTION 4

31 And do not kill your children
    through fear of poverty. We provide
    for them as We do for you.
    Killing them is a great sin.

32 Nor venture near adultery
    for it is an indecency,
    an evil way.

33 And do not take life, which
    God has made sacred, except
    for a rightful cause.
    We have authorized the heir
    of anyone killed wrongfully
    [to exact retribution], but they
        should
    not be excessive in taking life,
    for they are already aided.°

34 Nor venture near
    an orphan's property
    except with the best intent,
    until they reach maturity.
    And fulfill every pledge,
    for every pledge
    will be scrutinized.

35 Give full measure when you
   measure; weigh with a true balance:
   that is better and fairer in the end.

36 And do not follow blindly
   things you have no knowledge of—
   your hearing, sight, and heart
   shall all be questioned.

37 Do not walk brazenly on the earth,
   for you cannot pierce [its depth]
   nor reach the height of mountains.

38 All of this is evil,
   odious to your Lord.

39 This is some of the wisdom
   your Lord has revealed to you;
   do not set up any other god with
      God,
   or you will be cast into hell,
   rebuked, rejected.

40 Idolaters, has your Lord
   chosen for you sons, and
   taken for Himself daughters
   among the angels?°
   What you utter is monstrous.

SECTION 5

41 We have offered explanation
   in this Qur'an, that they might heed,
   but it makes them turn further away.

42 Say, "If there were other gods
   with Him, as they claim,
   they would surely have sought

   a way to [overcome]
   the Owner of the throne."

43 May He be glorified and exalted
   far above what they proclaim!

44 He is glorified
   by the seven heavens and the earth,
   and all within them,
   for there is nothing
   that does not glorify Him with praise,
   though you may not grasp
   their mode of glorifying—
   He is Forbearing, Forgiving.

45 When you recite the Qur'an,
   We place an unseen veil
   between you and those who
   don't believe in the hereafter.

46 And We have placed shrouds over
   their hearts, lest they understand it,
   and deafness in their ears.
   And when you talk of your Lord
   as the only God, in the Qur'an,
   they turn their backs, averse.

47 We know best
   what the wrongdoers hear
   when they hear you,
   and the wrongdoers say in private,
   "You follow nothing
   but a man bewitched."

48 See what similes they coin
   about you! But they are astray,
   and cannot find the right way.

49 And they ask,
   "When we are bones and dust,
   will we really be raised up
   as a new creation?"

50 Answer, "Yes—even
   if you were stones or iron,

51 "or anything else in creation
   that your hearts imagine to be even
   harder to bring back to life."°
   They will ask,
   "Who will bring us back?"
   Answer, "He Who created you
   the first time."
   They will shake their heads at you,
   asking, "And when will that be?"
   Answer, "Perhaps soon,

52 "on a day when He calls you—
   you will answer by praising Him,
   and you will imagine
   that you stayed [on the earth]
   for only a short while."

SECTION 6

53 Tell My servants to speak only
   the most exemplary words.°
   Satan brews discord among them—
   always a sworn enemy of
      humankind.

54 Your Lord knows you best—
   if He will, He will show you mercy,
   and if He will, He will punish you.
   We have not sent you, Prophet,
   as their custodian.

55 And your Lord knows best
   all that is in the heavens and earth.
   He favored some prophets
   over others—to David
   We gave the Psalms.

56 Say, "Call upon those you claim
   to be gods besides Him—
   they have no power
   to remove your misfortunes
   or to avert them."

57 Those on whom they call
   themselves seek a way to their
   Lord; which of them is closer?
   They hope for His mercy,
   and fear His punishment—
   your Lord's punishment
   is always to be feared.

58 There is no [evil] town
   that We shall not destroy
   before the day of resurrection
   or punish severely—this
   is inscribed in the Book.

59 Nothing constrains Us
   from sending signs except that
   former peoples denied them.
   We gave the people of Thamud°
   a she-camel as a visible token,
   but they wronged her.
   We send signs only to warn.

60 Prophet, remember when
   We told you that your Lord

Encompasses humankind,
We granted you the vision
We showed you° only as a trial
for people, like the cursed tree
mentioned in the Qur'an.°
We warn them, yet this only
increases their transgression.

SECTION 7

61 And when We said to the angels,
"Bow down before Adam,"
they bowed down except Iblis,
who said, "Shall I bow to one
whom you made of clay?"

62 He added, "Do You see this one
that you have honored above me?
If you grant me reprieve
until the day of resurrection,
I will hold sway over all but a few
of his descendants."

63 God said, "Go out!
If any of them follow you,
hell shall be your reward
[and theirs]—an ample reward.

64 "Rouse those you can
with your voice, assault them
with your cavalry and infantry,
share in their wealth and children,
and make promises to them.
But Satan promises them
only delusion."

65 You have no power over my
servants—

your Lord suffices as their
custodian.

66 It is your Lord Who lets your ships
sail smoothly upon the sea
that you might seek His bounty—
He is Ever Merciful to you.

67 When you meet distress at sea,
the gods you call on besides Him°
abandon you. But when He delivers
you
to land, you turn away.
Humankind is ever ungrateful.

68 Can you feel sure that He
won't make the earth swallow you
when back on land,
or send a hailstorm against you,
so that you find yourselves
with none to protect you?

69 Or can you be sure that He
won't drive you back out to sea
again, and send a hurricane
against you, a gale storm
to drown you for your
ingratitude? Then you would find
none to help you against Us.

70 We have honored the children
of Adam; We have carried them
over land and sea, and provided them
with good things, and favored them
over many others We have created.

SECTION 8

71 On the day We call together
all human beings, with their leaders,
those who are given their book
in their right hand will read it
[with joy], and will not be wronged
by as much as the hair on a date seed.

72 But those who were blind
in this world will be blind
in the hereafter, and even further
astray from the path.

73 Unbelievers almost tempted you
away from Our revelation to you,
hoping that you might
invent something else about Us°—
they would then have
embraced you as a friend.

74 Had We not strengthened
your resolve, you might have
inclined to them a little.

75 We would then have made you
taste a double torment—in this life,
and after death. You would then find
none to help you against Us.

76 Though they were about
to uproot you from the land,
to expel you from it,°
they would not then have been able
to stay there after you
for more than a short while.

77 [This was Our] way°
with the messengers We sent
before you, and you will find
no change in Our way.

SECTION 9

78 You should perform prayer
from the declining of the sun
until the darkening of night,
and recite the Qur'an at dawn—
a recitation ever witnessed
[by the angels].°

79 And in the night, arise to pray,
further, of your own accord,
that your Lord might raise you
to a station of praise.°

80 Say, "My Lord,
let me enter by a gate of truth
and leave by a gate of truth°—
grant me Your own
supportive authority."°

81 Also proclaim, "Truth has come
and falsehood has perished—
falsehood will always perish."

82 We reveal in the Qur'an
what is a healing and a mercy
to believers; yet for wrongdoers,
it merely increases their loss.

83 When We grant favor
to humankind, they turn
proudly away, drawing aside;

yet when evil befalls them,
they slide into despair.

84 Say, "Each person acts
according to their own disposition;
but your Lord knows best
who is rightly guided.°

SECTION 10

85 They ask you about the spirit.
Say, "The spirit comes
by command of my Lord°—
only a small portion
of knowledge is granted you."

86 If we wished, We could take away
what We have revealed to you;
you would then find in this issue
no protector against Us,°

87 without your Lord's mercy—
His favor to you is great.

88 Say, "Even if all humankind
and all jinn gathered together
to produce the like of this Qur'an,
they could not do so, however much
they helped one another."

89 And We have explained
to humankind in this Qur'an
every kind of parable,
yet most of them refuse
to be anything but ungrateful.

90 They say, "We will
never believe you, unless
you make for us a spring
flowing out from the earth,

91 "or you have a garden,
with date palms and grapes,
and cause rivers
to burst forth within it,

92 "or you cause the sky
to fall in fragments upon us,
—as you have claimed°—
or you bring before us
God and the angels,°

93 "or you have a house adorned
with gold, or ascend to the sky—
but we'll never believe you ascended
unless you bring down to us a book
that we might read."
Say, "Glory be to my Lord.
Am I not merely
a mortal, a messenger?"

SECTION 11

94 When guidance came to people,
nothing stopped them from
      believing
except their saying, "Has God sent
a mere mortal as a messenger?"

95 Say, "If the earth were full of
angels walking nonchalantly about,
We would have sent an angel to them
as a messenger from heaven."

96 Say, "God suffices as
    a Witness between me and you;
    He is Ever Aware, Observant
    of His servants."

97 Those whom God guides
    are rightly guided.
    As for those He allows to stray—
    you'll find no protectors for them
    beyond God.
    And We shall gather them
    on the day of resurrection
    fallen on their faces,
    blind, dumb, and deaf.
    Hell shall be their home,
    and whenever the blaze of fire
    subsides, We shall warm it.

98 That is their reward, for they
    rejected Our signs, saying,
    "When we become bones and dust,
    will we really be raised up
    as a new creation?"

99 Don't they see that God,
    Who created the heavens and earth,
    has Power to create their like anew?
    He has assigned a fixed term
    —beyond doubt—for them,
    but the wrongdoers refuse
    to be anything but ungrateful.

100 Say, "If you possessed
    the treasures of my Lord's mercy,
    you would withhold them
    fearful of expending them,
    for humankind is ever miserly."

SECTION 12

101 We gave Moses nine clear signs°
    —ask the Children of Israel.
    When he came to the Egyptians,
    Pharaoh exclaimed to him,
    "Moses, I believe you're bewitched."

102 Moses replied,
    "You well know that only
    the Lord of the heavens and earth
    could reveal these things as proof;
    and I believe that you, Pharaoh,
    shall meet destruction."

103 So he intended to drive them
    from the land; but We drowned him
    and all those with him.

104 Afterward, We told
    the children of Israel:
    "Live in the land," but when
    the promise of the hereafter comes,
    We will bring you together
    in a mingled assembly.°

105 We sent down the Qur'an
    with the truth—and with the truth
    it has come down;
    and We sent you, Prophet,
    only to convey joyous news
    and to warn people.

106 We have divided the Qur'an
    into parts so you might recite it
    to people at intervals, and
    We have revealed it in stages.

107 Say, "Whether *you* believe in it
    or not, those given knowledge
    before it was revealed
    fall down on their faces,°
    bowing, when it is recited to them."

108 They say, "Glory be to our Lord!
    Our Lord's promise is fulfilled."

109 They fall on their faces, in tears,
    and it deepens their humility.

110 Say, "Call upon God
    or call upon the All Merciful—

however you call him,
His are the Most Beautiful Names.°
And do not intone your prayer
loudly nor too softly
but seek a middle way
between these."

111 Say, "Praise be to God
    Who takes no son, and
    Who has no partner in dominion,
    Who needs no protector
    against abasement,
    and magnify Him—magnify
    His Measureless Magnitude."°

SURA 18

The Cave (*Al-Kahf*)

From the middle Meccan period, it derives its name, "The Cave," from vv. 9–26. That segment provides the natural backdrop for the first of three stories woven together in this sura of 110 verses that have inspired commentary and speculation through the ages. All three of these mysterious episodes occur only here in the Qur'an: the cave sleepers (vv. 9–26) is followed by Moses' encounter with a sly stranger at the meeting of waters (vv. 61–83), after which the two-horned figure, perhaps Alexander, builds a (mountain) barrier against Gog and Magog (vv. 84–99).

In the Name of God, the All Merciful, Ever Merciful

SECTION I

1 All praise be to God,
    Who revealed the Book
    to His servant, and made it
    free of deviation,°

2 unerringly straight,° to warn
    of His stern punishment
    and to give joyous news to those
    who believe and do good works
    that theirs will be a rich° reward,

3 [the garden] where
they will stay forever.

4 and to warn those who say,
"God has taken a son."

5 They have no knowledge
of this, nor had their forefathers.
It's a monstrous assertion
that they mouth: they utter
nothing but falsehood.

6 Prophet, you might consume yourself
with grief, because of them,
if they don't believe this message.

7 We have adorned the earth
with all that exists on it
in order to test which of them
are best in their deeds.

8 And We shall turn
all that exists on it
into barren dust.

SECTION 2

9 Prophet, do you think
the companions of the cave°
and the inscription it bears
were a wonder among Our signs?

10 The youths sought shelter
in the cave, and they implored,
"Our Lord, grant us Your mercy
and resolve our dilemma
in a fitting manner."

11 So We sealed their ears
[with sleep] in the cave
for several years.

12 Then We woke them,
so We might know
which of the two parties°
could best calculate
how long they had stayed.

13 We narrate to you their story
as it was:° those youths believed
in their Lord, and We increased
Our guidance for them.

14 We strengthened their hearts
when they stood up and affirmed,
"Our Lord is the Lord
of the heavens and the earth;
never will we call
on other gods than Him,
for we would be voicing
a gross falsehood.

15 "Our people have taken
gods other than Him: why don't they
bring forth a clear sanction for these?
Who does more wrong than those
who invent lies about God?"

16 "Since you have recoiled
from them and what they worship
besides God, seek shelter in the
    cave" [said the chief youth].
"Your Lord will shower you
with His mercy
and ease your plight."

17 You might have seen
the sun, when she rose,
declining away, to the right
of their cave; and when she set,
veering away, to their left
while they lay in the open space
between its walls. This
is among the signs of God:
those whom God guides
are rightly guided; as for
those left astray, you will never
find a protector to guide them
to the right way.

18 You might have thought them
awake though they were sleeping:
we turned them on their right sides
and left sides, their dog stretching
his two paws at the entrance.
If you had seen them,
you would have fled
from them in terror.

19 Then We roused them, so
they might question one another.
One of them asked, "How long
have you been here?" Some said,
"A day or part of a day." Others,
"Your Lord knows best how long.
Now one of you go with money
to the city to find the best food
for your sustenance.
But let him take care
to let no one know about you.

20 "If they recognize you,
they'll stone you or bring you
back to their creed, and then
you will not flourish—ever."

21 We informed people about them,
to let them know that God's promise
is true, that there is no doubt
about the impending hour.
Yet people argued about
the sleepers. Some said,
"Erect a building over them.
Their Lord knows best about them."
Those who prevailed in the matter
said, "We shall build over them
a place of worship."

22 Some say they were three,
and the dog the fourth
of them; others say they were five,
with the dog a sixth—
guessing, without knowing;°
still others say they were seven,
with the dog as eighth.
Say, "My Lord knows best
how many they were;
only a few actually know
about them." So don't argue
over them without tangible proof
nor consult any of these people
about them.

23 Do not say about anything,
"I shall do it tomorrow,"

24 without adding, "if God is willing."°
If you forget, remember your Lord,
and say, "I hope my Lord guides me
closer to righteousness than this."

25 And they stayed in their cave
for three hundred years, some say,
while some figured nine more.°

26 Say, "God knows best
how long they stayed.
His are the secrets of the heavens
and the earth—
how clearly He Sees,
how clearly He Hears.
They have no protector but Him,
He shares His judgment with none."°

27 Recite what was revealed to you
from the Book of your Lord—
there is no changing His words,
and you will find no refuge
beyond Him.

28 Content yourself with
those who call on their Lord
morning and evening,
yearning for His Face;
and do not look beyond them,
yearning for the luster
of worldly life,
nor obey anyone whose heart
We have made heedless
of Our remembrance,
anyone who follows
his own desires, unbridled.

29 And say, "The truth
is from your Lord,"
so let him who will, believe,
and let him who will, deny.
We have prepared a fire

for wrongdoers, whose walls
will enshroud them; and
should they cry for relief,
they will be relieved
with water like molten brass
searing their faces
—a damnable draught—
and an evil abode.°

30 As for those who believe
and do good deeds—We shall not
overlook their reward.°

31 They will have eternal gardens,
with rivers flowing beneath.
There they will be adorned
in bracelets of gold,
and they will wear
robes of green, of fine silk
and rich brocade;
they will recline there
on raised couches—
a blessèd reward,
an excellent home.

SECTION 3

32 Coin for them a parable
of two men—for one of them
We made two vineyards,
bordering them with date palms;
and between them, We placed
fields of crops.

33 Each of the two gardens
yielded its fruit, unfailing

in any respect.
And We made a river flow
between them.°

34 So he had abundant fruit.
While talking with his companion,
he boasted, "I have more wealth
than you, and a greater following."

35 So he entered his garden
and wronged himself, saying,
"I do not think that this
will ever perish,

36 "Nor do I think that the hour
will come; and even if I were
brought back to my Lord,
I would certainly find there
something better than this."

37 Talking with him, his companion
retorted, "Do you deny the One
Who created you from dust,
from a droplet of sperm,
then fashioned you into a man?

38 "As for me,
He is God, my Lord,
and I set up no one as partner
with my Lord.

39 "Why did you not say,
as you entered your garden,
'As God wills'?° There is
no power except God.
Though you see that I have
less in wealth and children,

40 "perhaps my Lord will grant me
something better than your garden,
and will send upon it
a reckoning from the sky,
turning it to sodden dust.

41 "or its water might sink
beneath the ground so you
never find it."

42 And his fruit was beset with ruin,
and he began wringing his hands
over what he had invested in it—
it was collapsed on its trellises.
And he lamented, "If only
I had set up no other god
as partners with my Lord."

43 He had no company
to help him, besides God,
nor could he help himself.

44 [In such crisis], protection
comes from God alone—the True.°
He grants the best in reward,
and the best outcome.

SECTION 4

45 Coin for them a simile
of the life of this world—
it is like rain which We send
down from the sky,
which mixes with earth's greenery,
which then becomes dry stubble,
which the winds disperse.

God alone is Capable
of all things.°

46 The life of this world allures
with wealth and children,
but good works which endure
gain a better reward
from your Lord, and secure
a better hope.

47 One day We shall displace
the mountains
and you will see the earth
as a leveled plain
and We shall gather
all humankind together,
leaving no one behind.

48 They will be marshaled
before your Lord in ranks
and it will be said,
"You have come to Us
just as We created you
at first. Yet you supposed
We would not fulfill
Our promised meeting
with you."

49 The Book of their deeds
will be placed before them,
and you will see the sinners
in terror, on account of
what it holds. They will say,
"Alas for us, what a Book this is—
it leaves nothing, small or great,
out of its account."
They will find presented there

all that they did. And your Lord
will wrong no one.

50 When We said to the angels,
"Bow down before Adam," they all
bowed down except Iblis.
He was one of the jinn,°
and he disobeyed the command
of his Lord. Will you then take him
and his progeny as protectors
instead of Me, though they
are your enemies?
What a wretched bargain
for wrongdoers!

51 I did not make them
witness to the creation
of the heavens and the earth,
or their own creation.
I am not One to
take as aides of Mine
those who misguide.

52 One day He will say,
"Call on the gods you claimed
to be My partners."
And they will call on them,
but those gods will not answer;
and We shall place between them
a deathly chasm.

53 Seeing the fire, the sinners
shall realize they are to fall into it—
they shall find no refuge from it.

54 We have expounded in this Qur'an
parables of every kind for people;

but humankind is most
    contentious.°

55 Once guidance has come to them,
   what prevents people from
   believing and seeking forgiveness
   from their Lord except
   that [they wait for] the fate
   of their ancestors to visit them
   or that their punishment
   visit them face-to-face?

56 We send the messengers
   only to bring joyous news
   and to warn people. But those
   who refuse to believe dispute it,
   using falsehood to impugn
   the truth, even as they mock
   My signs and warnings.

57 And who does greater wrong
   than one who is reminded
   of the signs of his Lord,
   yet turns away from them,
   forgetting what his two hands
   have done?° We have cast
   mantles over their hearts
   —so they will not grasp the
      Qur'an—
   and deafness within their ears.
   If you call them to guidance,
   they will not be guided—ever.

58 But your Lord is Forgiving,
   Full of Mercy. If He took them
   to account for what they earned,
   he would hasten their punishment.

But they have their appointed time,
then they will find no refuge.

59 These cities We destroyed
   when they did wrong;
   and We set an appointed time
   for their desolation.

SECTION 5

60 Moses said to his servant,
   "I won't stop until I reach
   the convergence of the two seas,
   even if I must go on
   for many years."

61 But when they reached
   the convergence of
   the two seas,° they forgot
   about their fish, which bore
   its own course through the sea.

62 When they journeyed farther,
   Moses said to his servant,
   "Bring our meal for us,
   for this journey of ours
   has tired us out."

63 The servant replied, "Did you see?
   When we sheltered under the rock,
   I forgot the fish—it was only Satan
   who made me forget to mention it,
   and it made its way
   wondrously into the sea."

64 Moses said, "That is the place
we were seeking." So they went back,
retracing their footsteps.

65 And they came across
one of Our servants, on whom
We had bestowed Our Mercy,
and whom we had taught
from Our Knowledge.°

66 Moses said to him,
"May I follow you,
so that you might teach me
what you have been taught
of right guidance?"

67 The man said,
"Really, you will never be able
to bear with me patiently.

68 "And how *could* you be patient
about something that's beyond
your knowledge?"

69 Moses said, "You'll find
that I'm patient, if it is God's wish,
and I won't disobey you
in anything."

70 The man said, "If you
would follow me, then
don't ask about anything
until I broach it
in my discourse with you."

71 So they both went on
and° when they embarked in the boat,

the man pierced a hole in it.
Moses demanded, "Did you bore
this hole°
to drown the passengers?
What a strange thing to do!"

72 He replied, "Did I not say that
you could not bear with me
patiently?"

73 Moses implored,
"Don't take me to task for forgetting,
nor be hard on me by making my task
more difficult."

74 So they both went on
and when they met a youth,
the man killed him. Moses asked,
"How could you kill an innocent
person
who had harmed no one?
What a terrible thing you've done!"

75 He replied, "Did I not say that
you could not bear with me
patiently?"

76 Moses said, "If I question you
on any issue after this,
then spurn my company—
you've had [enough] excuse
[to part] from me."

77 So they both went on
and, when they came
to the people of a town,

they asked them for food,
but the people refused them
any welcome. They found there
a wall about to fall down,
but Moses' companion
set it upright. Moses said,
"If you'd wanted, you could have
charged them for doing this."

78 He replied, "Here is where you
and I must part. Now let me tell you
the deeper meaning° of the things
you could not endure with patience.

79 "The boat belonged to
needy people, who worked at sea.
I *meant* to disable it,
for behind them was a king
seizing every [usable] boat by force.

80 "As for the youth, his parents
were both believers, and we feared
he would overwhelm them by
transgressing and disbelieving.

81 "So we wished for their Lord to
bring them another son in his place,
purer and more affectionate.°

82 "And the wall, well, it belonged
to two youths, orphans, in the city.
Beneath it was a buried treasure
which was theirs.
Their father was a righteous
person,
so your Lord intended that

when they reached their maturity,
they should unearth their treasure,
a mercy from Him. So I did not
do this of my own accord. This
is the deeper meaning of the things
you could not endure with patience."

SECTION 6

83 They ask you, Prophet, about Dhu
al-Qarnayn.°
Say, "I'll recite to you a chronicle
about him."

84 We established [his power]
on the earth, and We granted him
a path toward every end.

85 He followed a certain path,

86 and when he reached
the region of the setting sun
to find it setting in a muddy spring,
and found a community near it,
We said, "Dhu al-Qarnayn,
you can either punish them
or treat them well."

87 He said, "We shall punish
whoever does wrong, then
he shall be returned to his Lord,
Who will give him a punishment
even more terrible.

88 "But those who believe
and do good deeds
shall have a fine reward,

and we will command them
to do what is easy for them."

89 Then he continued on the path,

90 and, when he reached
the region of the rising sun,
he found it rising
on a community to whom
We had given no shelter from it.

91 In this way, Our Knowledge
Encompassed everything about
    him.°

92 Then he continued on the path,

93 and, when he reached
a pass between two mountains,
he found, beside them, a community
that could scarcely grasp his speech.

94 They said, "Dhu al-Qarnayn,
Gog and Magog are workers
of mischief in the land.°
If we paid you a tribute,
would you build a barrier
between us and them?"

95 He replied,
"My Lord has empowered me
with something better;
but lend me some strong help,
and I will build a strong rampart
between you and them.

96 "Bring me bars of iron."
Then, when he had filled the chasm
between the two mountainsides,
he said, "Blow with your bellows,"
and when he had made it glow red
    as fire,
he said, "Bring me molten brass
to pour over it."

97 So Gog and Magog
were unable to scale the rampart
or tunnel through it.

98 He said,
"This is a mercy from my Lord.
But when the promise
of my Lord comes to pass,
He will reduce the rampart
to level dust; and His promise
is always true."

99 On that day, We will leave them
surging against one another like
    waves.
The trumpet will sound, and
We shall gather them all together.

100 And on that day We shall lay
hell itself, spread out wide,
before the unbelievers—

101 those whose eyes
were veiled against
remembrance of Me,
those who could not hear.

102 Do those who disbelieve
suppose they can take my servants
as protectors instead of Me?
We have prepared hell
for disbelievers as their home.

SECTION 7

103 Prophet, say to them,
"Shall we inform you
of those whose deeds
will bring them the most loss,

104 "those whose labors have
been wasted in the life of the world,
even as they supposed
they were doing good?

105 "Those who deny
the signs of their Lord
and [their] meeting with Him—
their works shall be in vain,
and We will accord them
no weight on the day
of resurrection."

106 This will be their requital—
hell—for they disbelieved, mocking
My signs and My messengers.

107 Those who believe
and do good deeds shall have
the gardens of paradise
as their home.

108 They will abide there
forever, desiring no change.

109 Say, "If the sea were ink
for the words of my Lord,
the sea would run dry
before the words, even if
We brought another sea just like it."°

110 Say, "I am but a human being
like you; it has been revealed to me
that your God is One God,
so let whoever yearns to meet Him
do good works, and join
none with Him in worship."

SURA 19

Mary (*Maryam*)

A middle Meccan sura, this relates the birth of John and Jesus, highlighting their lives and missions as God's ordained prophets. Its 98 verses provide both comparison and contrast with biblical narratives in the Gospels of Matthew and Luke. Remarkably, it is the sole sura named after a woman, and Mary looms as the major female figure in the Qur'an, her central role in the divine plan extolled in vv. 16–33, and Jesus' role as God's servant, not His son, reinforced toward the end (vv. 88–95).

In the Name of God, the All Merciful, Ever Merciful

SECTION I

1 *Kaf. Ha. Ya. 'Ain Sad.°*

2 This is a reminder
   of your Lord's mercy
   toward His servant Zachariah,

3 when he called to his Lord secretly,

4 "My Lord, my bones are now frail,
   and my hair is ablaze with gray,
   yet never has my prayer to You,
   my Lord, been in vain.

5 "I fear what my kin will do after me,°
   for my wife is barren.
   So grant me an heir—through Your
      grace.

6 "to bear my legacy°
   as well as that of Jacob's family;
   and let him, my Lord, be well
      pleasing."

7 [God replied,]
   "Zachariah, We give you
   joyous news of a son,
   whose name will be John,°
   a name we gave to none before him."

8 "My Lord,° how *can* I have a son,
   when my wife is barren
   and I am withering with extreme
      age?"

9 He replied, "These are the words
   of Your Lord: 'It is easy for Me.
   I created you before°—
   when you were nothing.'"

10 Zachariah said,
   "My Lord, give me a sign."
   "Your sign is this—
   you will not speak to people
   for three straight nights."°

11 So he ventured out to his people
   from his sanctuary, urging them
   by gestures,° to glorify God
   morning and evening.

12 "John," We said,
   "Hold firmly to the Book,"
   and We endowed him
   as a child with sound judgment,

13 and with tenderness, and purity,
   from Our grace.
   He was mindful of God,

14 solicitous of his parents, and
   never imperious° or disobedient.

15 Peace be with him
   the day he was born,
   the day he dies,
   and the day
   he will be raised alive.

SECTION 2

16 And mention in the Book
   the story of Mary,
   when she withdrew from her people
   to a place in the East.

17 She veiled herself from them.
   Then We sent Our spirit,
   appearing to her
   in the perfect form of a man.

18 She said, "I seek refuge from you
   with the All Merciful—withdraw°
   if you fear Him."

19 He said, "I am just a messenger
   from your Lord
   Who grants you a pure son."

20 "How shall I have a son," she said,
   "for no man has touched me,
   and I have not been unchaste?"

21 He replied, "This is how it will be:
   your Lord has said, 'It is easy for Me;
   We will make him a sign
   for humankind, and a mercy from
   Our grace. It is a thing ordained.'"

22 So she conceived him,
   and withdrew with him
   to a place far away.

23 And the pains of labor drove her
   to the trunk of a date palm. She
     cried,

"I wish I had died before this,
   forgotten, and unknown!"

24 But a voice called to her
   from beneath, "Don't grieve—
   your Lord has set a stream
   underneath you.

25 "Shake the trunk of the date palm
   toward you, to make fresh, ripe
     dates
   fall upon you.

26 "So eat and drink; be comforted,
   and if you see anyone, say,
   'I have vowed to the All Merciful
   that I shall fast, and today
   I shall speak with no one.'"

27 Then she came, carrying him,
   to her people. They said, "Mary,
   you've done something scandalous.°

28 "Sister of Aaron, your father
   was not a wicked man,
   nor was your mother unchaste."

29 Then she pointed to the child;°
   they asked, "How can we talk
   with a child in its cradle?"

30 He said, "I am a servant of God;
   He has given me the Book,
   and has made me a prophet.

31 "He blessed me
   wherever I may be,

and enjoined upon me
prayer and charity
as long as I live.

32 "He made me solicitous
toward my mother, and neither
imperious nor wretched.

33 "Peace be with me
the day I was born,
the day I die,
and the day
I will be raised alive."

34 This was Jesus, son of Mary,
this is the true statement°—
about which they dispute.

35 It is not for God to bear a child.
Glory be to Him: when He decrees
something, He merely says to it,
"Be"—and it is.

36 God is my Lord and your Lord,
so worship Him—
this is the straight path.

37 But the sects differed
among themselves; what anguish
will come to those who disbelieve
from the witnessing°
of a momentous day.

38 How keenly they will hear,
how keenly they will see,
on the day they come to Us.

But today the wrongdoers
are clearly astray.

39 Warn them of the day of remorse,
when things will finally be decided
while they are heedless,
and do not believe.

40 It is We who will inherit the earth,
and all those upon it—
to Us they will be returned.

SECTION 3

41 And mention in the Book
the story of Abraham—
he was a man of truth, a prophet.

42 He said to his father,
"Father, why do you worship
what can neither hear nor see,
and cannot profit you at all?

43 "Father, knowledge has come
to me which you do not have.°
So follow me—I will guide you
to an even path.

44 "Father, do not worship Satan,
for Satan is disobedient
to the All Merciful.

45 "Father, I fear that punishment
from the All Merciful will strike you
and you'll become an ally of Satan."

46 His father replied,
"Do you turn away from my gods,
Abraham? If you don't stop,
I shall stone you.
Now keep away from me!"

47 Abraham said,
"Peace be with you; I shall ask
my Lord to forgive you, for He
has been Ever Gracious to me.

48 "But I will turn away from you
and what you call upon besides God,
and I will call upon my Lord.
I trust that my prayer to my Lord
will not be in vain."

49 So when he turned away
from them and those they
worshipped besides God,
We granted him Isaac and Jacob
as sons, and We made
each of them a prophet.

50 We granted Our mercy to them,
and gave them high renown for truth.°

SECTION 4

51 And mention in the Book
the story of Moses—he was chosen,
a messenger, and a prophet.°

52 We called him from the right slope
of Mount Sinai, and We drew him
close for private converse.

53 And through Our Mercy
We granted him
his brother Aaron as a prophet.

54 And mention in the Book
the story of Ishmael—
he was true to his promise,
a messenger, a prophet.

55 He would always enjoin
his people to perform prayer
and charity, and he was always
pleasing to his Lord.

56 And mention in the Book
the story of Idris°—
he was a man of truth, a prophet:

57 And We raised him
to an exalted station.

58 These were among the prophets
God favored, from Adam's progeny,
whom We carried in Noah's ark,
as well as from the descendants
of Abraham and Israel, and from
those
whom We guided and chose.
When verses of the All Merciful
were recited to them, they would
fall, prostrating themselves, in tears.

59 But there came after them
people who neglected prayer
and followed their own desires.
Soon, they will meet perdition.

60 Except those who repent,
   and believe, and do good deeds.
   These will enter the garden
   and will not be wronged
   in any way—

61 eternal gardens, which
   the All Merciful has promised
   to His servants, in the unseen.
   His promise, inexorable,
   shall come to pass.

62 There, they will not hear
   vain discourse—only "Peace."
   And there, they will be provided for,
   morning and evening.

63 This is the garden
   We shall bequeath
   to our servants
   who were mindful of Us.

64 [The angels say,]
   "We descend only
   by command of your Lord.
   To Him belongs
   what lies before us,
   what lies behind us, and
   what lies between.
   Your Lord is never forgetful.

65 "Lord of the heavens and earth,
   and of all that lies between them—
   so worship Him, be steadfast
   in His worship. Do you know
   any who is worthy of His name?"

SECTION 5

66 Humans say, "Once dead,
   shall we be brought to life?"

67 But don't humans recall
   that We created them before,
   when they were nothing?

68 By your Lord, then,
   We shall gather them,
   and the devils, [dragging them]
   around hell, on their knees.

69 Then We shall drag out
   from each sect those who
   most stubbornly opposed
   the All Merciful.

70 For We know best
   those who most deserve
   to burn there.

71 And there is not one of you
   who will not come to it—
   a decree from your Lord
   destined to pass.

72 But We shall deliver those
   who were mindful of God,
   and We shall leave
   the wrongdoers there,
   on their knees.

73 When Our clear signs
   are recited to them,
   the unbelievers taunt those

who believe, "Which of our two
parties is in a better position,
and has superior companions?"

74 Yet how many generations
before them have We destroyed—
who were grander in possessions
as well as in outward pomp?

75 Say, "The Most Merciful prolongs
the straying of those who stray,
until they see the punishment
promised them, either here
or in the coming hour.
Then they will know
who is in the worse position
and is weaker in force."

76 God increases guidance
for those who would be guided.
Enduring good deeds
are the best rewards
in the eyes of your Lord,
and best in their recompense.

77 Have you then seen
the person who denies Our signs,
yet says, "I shall certainly
be given wealth and children?"

78 Has he fathomed the unseen,
or secured an agreement
with the All Merciful?

79 No—We shall record
what he says, and We shall
prolong his punishment.

80 We shall inherit
all that he talks of,
and he shall come
before Us alone.

81 Yet they have taken
gods other than God
to empower them.

82 However, those gods
will reject their worship,
and become their adversaries.

SECTION 6

83 Do you not see—
We have sent devils
against the unbelievers,
inciting them to sin?

84 So make no haste against them,
for We are but counting their
    term.°

85 On the day We gather
the God-fearing to the All Merciful,
as an assembly,

86 and drive the sinners to hell,
like thirsty cows [to water],

87 none shall have power
of intercession, except
those who secure an agreement
with the All Merciful.

88 They say, "The All Merciful
    has conceived a child."

89 Assuredly, you speak
    of something monstrous—

90 at which the heavens might be
    cleaved asunder, and the earth
    burst into pieces, and the mountains
    collapse in complete ruin—

91 that they deem the All Merciful
    to have a child,

92 for it is not seemly
    for the All Merciful
    to conceive a child.

93 There is none in the heavens
    and earth who will not come
    before the All Merciful
    as a servant.

94 He has taken account of each,
    and counted them, every single one.

95 And each one of them
    will come before Him, alone,
    on the day of resurrection.

96 the All Merciful will bestow
    love on those
    who believed and did good works.

97 We have made the Qur'an
    easy, in your own tongue,
    so that you might use it
    to give joyous news
    to those who fear God,
    and warn a stubborn people.

98 And how many generations
    have we destroyed before them—
    can you trace even one of them
    or hear from them
    even a whisper?

SURA 20

Ta Ha (*Ta Ha*)

Dating from the middle Meccan period, this is the first sura to take its name
from the initial and perplexing letters that mark it, as they do twenty-eight other
suras in the Qur'an. Its 135 verses begin with the story of Moses (vv. 9–99), then
the account of Adam and Eve (the latter unnamed—vv. 115–24), and end with
encouragement to Muhammad to endure, pray, be steadfast, watch, and wait
(vv. 130–35).

In the Name of God, the All Merciful, Ever Merciful

SECTION I

1 *Ta Ha.*°

2 We have not revealed
the Qur'an to you
to bring you distress,

3 but rather as a reminder
to those who fear God,

4 a revelation from the One
Who created the earth
and the exalted heavens,

5 the All Merciful, firmly poised
upon the throne.

6 To Him belongs
all that is in the heavens
and all that is on the earth,
all between them,
and all beneath the soil.

7 [Whatever is in your heart]
whether you speak it aloud [or not],
He knows what is secret
and what is most hidden.

8 God—there is no god but He.
To Him belong
the Most Beautiful Names.

9 Have you heard the story of Moses?

10 When he saw a fire,
he said to his family,
"Stay here. I glimpsed a fire—
perhaps I can bring you
a burning brand from it
or find some guidance there."

11 When he drew near,
he was called, "Moses,

12 "I am your Lord,
so remove your sandals,
for you are in
the sacred valley of Tuwa.°

13 "And I have chosen you—
so listen closely
to what is now revealed.

14 "I am the One God—
there is no god but Me,
so worship Me, and
be steadfast in prayer,
remembering Me.

15 "The hour is coming
—though I choose to conceal it—
so that every soul may receive
the reward of its endeavor.

16 "So don't let those
who disbelieve in its coming,
and follow their own desires,
divert you from it,
bringing you to ruin.

17 "And what is this
    in your right hand, Moses?"

18 Moses replied, "This is my staff—
    I lean on it, and with it
    I beat down leaves for my sheep,
    and I have other uses for it."

19 God said,
    "Throw it down, Moses."

20 He threw it down, and see,
    it became a snake, darting quickly.

21 God said, "Take hold of it
    and don't be afraid—
    We shall restore it to its former state.

22 "And place your hand under your arm:
    it will come out gleaming white,
       though
    unharmed—another sign—

23 "so that We might show you
    some of our greatest signs.

24 "Go now to Pharaoh,
    for he has done wrong."

SECTION 2

25 Moses implored, "My Lord,
    enlarge my heart,°

26 "make my task easy for me,

27 "and remove the slur in my speech,°

28 "so that they understand my words,

29 "and give me someone to help,
    from my family,

30 "my brother Aaron—

31 "fortify my strength through him,

32 "and let him share my task,

33 "so that we may glorify You,

34 "and remember you, constantly,

35 "for You always Watch over us."

36 God said, "You are granted
    your request, Moses.

37 "Indeed, We bestowed on you
    a favor once before,

38 "when We inspired
    your mother, saying,

39 "'Place the child in the chest,
    then cast it into the river;
    the river will cast it onto the bank.
    He will be adopted by someone
    who is an enemy to Me and you.'
    But I cast over you My love,
    so you would be reared
    under My eye.

40 "When your sister went out,
    she said, 'Shall I show you
    someone who will nurse him?'

Then we returned you
to your mother, to let her eyes
rejoice and not grieve.
And you killed a man, but
We delivered you from any
    distress,
and We tried you with other tests.
Then you stayed some years
with the people of Midian, and
came at the ordained hour,
    Moses.°

41 "For I have chosen you
    to serve Me.

42 "Go, you and your brother,
    with My signs, and do not relent
    in your remembrance of Me.

43 "Go, both of you, to Pharaoh,
    for he has done wrong.

44 "But speak mildly with him,
    so he might take heed
    or be filled with fear [of God].

45 Moses and Aaron said,
    "Our Lord, we're afraid that
    he'll be harsh with us or
    transgress [still more]."

46 God said, "Don't be afraid.
    I am with you both—
    I see and hear [all things].

47 "So go to him, both of you,
    and say, 'We are messengers
    from your Lord, so send with us

the children of Israel and do not
harass them. We come
with a sign from your Lord.
Peace be upon all who
follow right guidance.

48 "'It has been revealed to us
    that punishment shall fall upon
    those who deny and turn away.'"

49 [Having heard this],
    Pharaoh said, "So, Moses,
    who is the Lord of you both?"

50 He replied, "Our Lord is He
    Who gave each thing its form
    and guided it."

51 Pharaoh said, "What, then,
    [is the status] of former generations?"

52 Moses answered, "The knowledge
    of that is with my Lord, recorded
    in a Book. My Lord does not err,
    nor does He forget."

53 It is He who made for you
    the earth, spread out like a couch,
    and laid out for you paths to travel,
    and sent rain from the sky, with
        which
    We have brought forth plants,
    in pairs, of distinct kinds,

54 so eat, and graze your cattle.
    In this are signs for those
    with understanding.

SECTION 3

55 We created you from the earth,
and to it We shall return you,
and from it We shall bring you again
in another time.

56 We showed all Our signs
to Pharaoh, but he denied
and refused them.

57 He said, "Have you come
to drive us out of our land
with your magic, Moses?

58 "*We* can certainly bring magic
like this to you: arrange a meeting
between us and you, which
neither we nor you shall fail
to honor, in a neutral place."

59 Moses said, "You shall have
your meeting—on the day
of the festival. And let the people
be assembled when the sun is high."

60 So Pharaoh withdrew.
He put together his plan,
and came back.

61 Moses said to him,
"Beware—do not forge
a lie about God, or
He might destroy you with
a severe punishment.
For whoever forges lies
will surely fail."

62 So Pharaoh's ministers
discussed the matter
among themselves, but
kept their discussion secret.

63 They said, "These two
are sorcerers, who intend
to drive you from your land
with their sorcery, and to abolish
your exemplary way of life.

64 "So devise your plan
then draw up in a line.
Whoever wins today
is sure to flourish."

65 They said, "Moses,
shall you throw, or shall we
be the first to throw?"

66 "No, you throw," said Moses,
and suddenly—through their magic,
their ropes and their staffs
seemed to him to be moving.

67 And Moses felt fear
within himself.

68 We told him, "Have no fear,
it is you who will prevail.

69 "Throw what's in your right hand:
it will swallow up what they have
contrived—merely a magician's
    trick,
and no magician can flourish,
no matter where he goes."

70 Then the magicians threw
themselves down, prostrating,°
saying, "We believe in the Lord
of Aaron and Moses."

71 Pharaoh bellowed,
"You believed in Him
before I gave you permission!
He must be your leader,
teaching you magic.
I will have your hands and feet
cut off, on opposite sides,
and have you crucified
on the trunks of palm trees,
so that you will know for sure
which of us gives more severe
and lasting punishment."

72 They said, "We shall never
choose you over the clear proofs
that have come to us or the One
Who created us. So decree
as you will—you decree only
for the life of this world.

73 "We believe in our Lord,
Who may forgive us our faults
and the magic you made us perform;
for God is more worthy and lasting."

74 Those who come to their Lord
as sinners shall attain hell
where they shall find
neither death nor life.

75 But those who come
to Him as believers,

with righteous deeds,
shall attain exalted stations—

76 eternal gardens, beneath which
rivers flow, where they shall
live forever—the reward
of those who attain purity.

SECTION 4

77 We inspired Moses, saying,
"Travel by night with my servants
and break open a dry path for them
through the sea; have no fear
of being overtaken, nor be afraid."

78 Then Pharaoh pursued them
with his forces, but the sea
overwhelmed and covered them.

79 So Pharaoh led his people astray
instead of guiding them.

80 Children of Israel,
We delivered you from your enemy,
and We made a covenant with you
on the right slope of Mount Sinai,
and We sent down to you
manna and quail,

81 saying, "Eat of the good things
We have provided for you,
but do not transgress in this, or
My Wrath may descend upon you.
Anyone on whom My Wrath
descends
is undoubtedly fallen.

82 "Yet I am Forgiving—
    of those who turn in repentance
    and believe and do righteous deeds,
    then stay rightly guided."

83 [When Moses was on the mountain,
    God said,] "What made you
    hasten from your people, Moses?"

84 He replied, "They were close
    upon my heels—and I hastened
    to You, My Lord, to please You."

85 God said, "We tested your people
    after you were gone,
    but the Samiri has led them astray."°

86 So Moses returned to his people
    indignant and aggrieved. He said,
    "My people, did your Lord not
    make you a splendid promise?
    Did the promise seem long
    in coming, or did you want
    your Lord's wrath to descend
    upon you, since you broke
    your promise to me?"

87 They said, "We didn't break
    our promise to you of our own
        accord,
    but we were made to carry
    the people's ornaments,°
    so we threw them [into the fire],
    just as the Samiri did."

88 Then he brought out for them
    the image of a calf, which seemed
    to make a lowing sound,
    so they said, "This is your god,
    and the god of Moses,
    though he has forgotten."

89 Didn't they see that it
    could not answer them a word,
    and had no power either
    to harm or profit them?

SECTION 5

90 In fact, Aaron had said
    to them earlier, "My people,
    you are being tested by this, for
    your true Lord is the All Merciful,
    so follow me, obey my command."

91 And they had retorted,
    "We'll never cease our devotion to it
    unless Moses returns to us."

92 Moses asked,
    "Aaron, when you saw
    they were going astray
    what stopped you

93 "from following me? Did you
    disobey my command?"

94 Aaron replied,
    "Son of my mother, don't seize me
    by my beard or by my hair.
    For I feared that you might say,
    'You have sparked division

among the children of Israel,
and have not respected my word.'"

95 Moses said, "What, then,
do you have to say, Samiri?"

96 He replied, "I saw something in it
that they did not. So I took
a handful of dust from
the messenger's footprint,
and I threw it [onto the calf].
This is what my soul prompted me
to do."

97 Moses said, "Be gone from here.
In all this life you'll be doomed
to say 'Do not touch me,' but
for you there is a promise that
will not fail—look upon your god
to which you're still devoted.
We will burn it and scatter
its ashes into the sea."

98 Your only god is the One God—
there is no god but Him,
Who embraces all things
in His knowing.

99 In this way, We relate to you,
   Prophet,
the narratives of what came
   before—
We send a reminder from Our
   grace.°

100 Whoever turns away from it
shall bear a heavy burden

on the day of resurrection,

101 remaining under it. How wretched
shall be their burden
on the day of resurrection—

102 A day when the trumpet
shall be sounded; a day when
We shall gather the sinners,
blinded, eyes blue with fear,°

103 murmuring among themselves,
"You stayed but ten days on earth."

104 We know best what they say,
for those of them who are exemplary
in conduct will say, "You didn't stay
more than a single day."°

SECTION 6

105 They ask you about the mountains.
Say, "My Lord
shall blast them into fragments.

106 "He will leave them leveled as a
   plain.

107 "You shall see there neither peak nor
   vale."°

108 On that day, they will follow
the caller without deviating.
All voices shall be hushed
before the All Merciful—
you shall hear nothing
but the faintest murmur.

109 On that day, no intercession
can help, except from those
allowed by the All Merciful,
whose words please Him.

110 He knows what lies behind them
and what lies ahead of them, but
their knowing cannot compass
Him.°

111 All faces shall be humbled before
Him,
the Ever Living, Self-Subsisting;°
those who bear the weight of
wrongdoing
shall be in despair.

112 But those who have done
righteous deeds and are true
believers
shall fear no wrong, nor
be deprived of their due.

113 We have revealed a Qur'an
in Arabic, where We gave varied
warnings
to make them mindful of God, or
move them to remembrance of Him.

114 Exalted is God, the true King.
And Prophet, don't be overhasty
reciting the Qur'an before [each]
revelation to you is completed.
Rather, say, "My Lord,
increase my knowledge."

115 We made a covenant with Adam
in an earlier time, but he forgot;
and We found in him no firm resolve.

SECTION 7

116 When We said to the angels,
"Bow down before Adam," they
bowed. But not Iblis—he refused.

117 Then We said, "Adam,
this is an enemy to you
and your wife—so don't let him
drive you from the garden
and bring you to misery.

118 "There is enough in it for you
to be neither hungry, nor naked,

119 "nor suffer from thirst,
nor the sun's heat."

120 But Satan whispered to him,
"Adam, shall I lead you to
the tree of eternal life,
and a kingdom beyond aging?"

121 Then they both ate of it, and
their shame was exposed to them.
They began to fasten leaves
from the garden to cover
themselves.
In this way, Adam disobeyed
his Lord, and fell into error.

122 Later, though, his Lord chose him,
turning to him, and guiding him.

123 [At that time], God said, "Go down,
    both of you, from the garden,
    as enemies to each other. But if
    My guidance comes to you, whoever
    follows it shall not go astray
    nor be brought to misery.

124 "But whoever turns away
    from My remembrance
    shall find a straitened existence,
    and We shall raise him up
    blind on the day of resurrection."

125 He will say, "My Lord,
    why did you raise me up blind,
    when I possessed sight before?"

126 God will say,
    "Just as you forgot Our signs
    when they came to you,
    so this day
    you shall be forgotten."

127 And so We recompense
    whoever transgresses, who does not
    believe in the signs of their Lord—
    and the punishment of the hereafter
    is sterner and more lasting.

128 Is it not a lesson to them
    that We destroyed before them
    generations through whose
        dwellings
    they now walk? In this
    are signs for people of intellect.

SECTION 8

129 Were it not for a decree already
    fixed° by your Lord, and a term
        ordained,
    their end would surely have come.

130 So, Prophet, bear with what
    they say, and glorify your Lord
    with praise, before the sun's rising
    and before its setting. Glorify Him
    during the hours of night,
    and at each end of the day,
    that you may find contentment.

131 And do not strain your eyes
    toward the things We have granted
    some of them to enjoy, the splendor
    of the life of this world—
    that We might test them by these.
    For the provision of your Lord
    is worthier and more lasting.

132 Enjoin your family to pray
    and to be steadfast in this.
    We do not ask you for sustenance—
    It is We Who sustain you.
    And the best outcome shall be
    for those who are mindful of God.

133 But they say, "Why does he not
    bring us a sign from his Lord?"
    Has not a clear sign come to them
    in the earlier scriptures?

134 But if We had destroyed them
    by a punishment before this,

they would have cried, "Our Lord,
why did you not send a messenger
to us? Then we should have
followed your signs before we were
humbled and disgraced."

135 Say, "Each of us is waiting,
therefore, [watch and] wait—
and you shall know
who has adhered to the level path
and who is rightly guided."

SURA 21

The Prophets (*Al-Anbiya'*)

A late Meccan sura, the full roll call of prophets—from Adam to Muhammad—is the focus of its 112 verses. Muhammad becomes the emblematic representative of all prophets with the command "Say" in vv. 4 and 112. After reiterating the Oneness of God, followed by signs of His Power and Providence, the sura cites several prophets, ending with a reference to Mary (vv. 91–94). She is not otherwise heralded as a prophet, although elsewhere (23:50–51) she and Jesus are described as "a sign for all peoples" (v. 91).

In the Name of God, the All Merciful, Ever Merciful

SECTION I

1 The reckoning of humankind
draws near—yet they remain
heedless, turning away.

2 No new message comes to them
from their Lord, without
their listening to it frivolously,

3 their hearts distracted.
The wrongdoers hide
their secret murmurings,
"Isn't this just a human like you?
Would you fall for this sorcery
happening right before your eyes?"

4 Say,° "My Lord knows
whatever is spoken
in the heavens and the earth,
for He is All Hearing, All
Knowing."

5 They say, "Confused dreams!"
or "He's making it up,"
or "He's just a poet!—
Let him bring us a sign
like those sent to peoples of old."

6 The towns We destroyed before
them
did not believe. Will they now
believe?

7 Before you, Prophet, We sent
only men whom We inspired.
You who disbelieve, ask those who
have the message, if you don't know.

8 And We did not give them
bodies that needed no food,
nor were they immortal.

9 In the end We fulfilled
Our promise to them,
and saved them with those
We wished to save,
and We destroyed those
who transgressed.

10 We have revealed to you
a Book to remind you—
will you not, then, use reason?

SECTION 2

11 How many towns We demolished
on account of their wrongdoing,
raising other peoples after them!

12 Then, when they sensed Our wrath
coming upon them, see how they fled!

13 They were told,
"Don't flee, but go back
to the comforts you enjoyed
and to your homes, so that
you might be questioned."

14 They said, "Shame on us!
We were wrongdoers."

15 And their cry did not stop
until We turned them into crops,
lopped and burned to ashes.

16 We did not create
the heavens and earth
—and all that lies between—
for mere amusement.

17 Had We wanted distraction,
We could have found it within Us,
were We so inclined.

18 No—We hurl the truth
against falsehood, shattering
its head. See—it vanishes.
And shame on you for what
you ascribe to God.

19 To Him belong all who are
in the heavens and the earth,
and those in His presence°
are not too proud to worship Him,
nor do they grow weary.

20 They glorify Him
night and day, tirelessly.

21 Have they adopted for worship
gods from the earth?
Can these bring back the dead?

22 If there were other gods beyond
the One God, in both [the heavens
and the earth], both would be in
ruin.

Glory be to God, Lord of the
   Throne,
far above all that they ascribe to
   Him.

23 He cannot be questioned
for anything He does—
it is they who will be questioned.

24 Have they adopted other gods
besides Him? Say, "Bring your
   proof.
This is the message for those
with me and those before me."
But most of them don't know
the truth—they turn away.

25 Before you, Prophet,
We sent no messenger
without revealing to him
the truth that there is no god
but Me—so worship only Me.

26 They say, "The All Merciful
has begotten a child."
Glory be to Him—those
are only His honored servants."°

27 They do not speak before He does,
and act only on His command.

28 He knows what lies before them,
and what lies behind them;
they can intercede only for those
He approves, for they themselves
stand in awe, in fear of Him.°

29 If any of them should claim,
   "I am a god besides Him,"
We shall reward them with hell.
That is how We reward wrongdoers.

SECTION 3

30 Don't the unbelievers know
that the heavens and the earth
were joined together
before We divided them?
And We made from water
every living thing.
Will they still not believe?

31 We have set upon the earth
firm mountains, to stop it quaking
beneath them, and We have
placed on it wide highways,
so they might find their way.

32 And We raised the sky,
a secure canopy, yet still
they turn away from Our signs.

33 It is He who created
night and day, sun and moon,
each sailing in its own orbit.°

34 We have not granted immortality
to any human before you, Prophet.
If even you are destined to die,
can the disbelievers be immortal?

35 Every soul shall taste death;
We test you by evil and good—a trial;
to Us you shall be returned.

36 When the unbelievers see you,
they just sneer at you, "Is this the
one
who talks about your gods?"
They shun any remembrance
of the All Merciful.

37 Humankind was created hasty by
nature.
Soon I shall show you My signs,
so don't ask Me to hasten their
coming.

38 They demand of you,
"When will this promise be
realized,
if you are speaking the truth?"

39 If only the unbelievers knew
about the time to come, when,
unable to fend off the fire
from their faces or their backs,
they shall find no help.

40 No—the hour will fall upon them
suddenly, confounding them;
unable to hold it back,
they shall find no respite.

41 Messengers before you were
mocked,
but those who scoffed were besieged
by [the very wrath] they used to mock.

SECTION 4

42 Say, "Who can protect you
during the night and the day
from the All Merciful?"
But no—they turn away
from all remembrance of their Lord.

43 Do they have gods who can
defend them against Us?
Those gods cannot help themselves,
nor can they be protected from Us.

44 We let these men and their fathers
enjoy comforts through a long life.
But don't they see
how We came upon their land,
to scale back its borders?
Can they then prevail?

45 Say, "I am merely warning you
according to the revelation."
But the deaf will not hear the call
even when they are warned.

46 Yet if the mere scent of punishment
reached them from your Lord,
they would cry out, "Shame on us—
we really were wrongdoers."

47 We shall set up a just balance
on the day of resurrection, so that
no soul shall be wronged at all;
and We shall bring into account
even the weight of a mustard seed,
for We are proficient in
Reckoning.°

48 We gave Moses and Aaron
   the criterion of judgment,
   a light and a reminder
   for those who are mindful of God—

49 those who fear their Lord
   in the unseen, and hold in awe
   the impending hour.

50 This Qur'an that We revealed
   is a blessèd reminder—
   will you, then, reject it?

51 In earlier days, We made Abraham
   righteous, knowing him well.

52 When he asked his father
   and people, "What are these images
   to which you're devoted?"

53 They answered, "We found
   our ancestors worshipping them."

54 He exclaimed,
   "You and your forefathers
   have clearly gone astray."

55 They retorted,
   "Have you brought us the truth,
   or are you joking?"

56 He said, "No. Your Lord
   is the Lord of the heavens and earth;
   it is He Who made them,
   and I bear witness to this.

57 "And by God, I'm planning
   something for your idols,
   once you've turned your backs!"

58 Then he smashed them to pieces,
   all except the biggest one—
   so that they might come back to it.

59 They fumed, "Who has done this
   to our gods? Some wrongdoer!"

60 People said, "We heard a youth
   called Abraham, ranting about
      them."

61 They urged, "Bring him here, then,
   before the eyes of the people,
   so they can see for themselves."

62 And they asked, "Was it you
   who did this to our gods, Abraham?"

63 He answered, "No. It was done
   by this one, the biggest of your idols.
   Ask the idols—if they can speak."

64 They turned upon
   one another,° saying,
   "It's you who are in the wrong!"

65 Then they turned about:°
   "You know full well
   these idols can't speak."

66 Abraham said, "So, you worship
   —instead of God—things that can
   neither profit nor harm you?

67 "Shame on you and those
you worship instead of God!
Won't you use reason?"

68 They said, "Burn him,
and uphold your gods,
if you want to do something."°

69 We said, "Fire, be cold,
and keep Abraham safe!"

70 Then they aimed
to plot against him,
but We made them
the ultimate losers.

71 We delivered him and Lot
to the land We blessed
for all peoples.

72 We also gave him Isaac and Jacob,
and We made all of them
righteous.

73 We made them leaders,
to guide people by Our command,
and inspired them to do good deeds,
be steadfast in prayer,
and give in due charity—
they were Our true servants.

74 We endowed Lot
with wisdom and knowledge,
and We saved him from the town
that practiced abominations—
they were a wicked,
disobedient people.

75 We received him into Our mercy,
for he was one of the righteous.

SECTION 5

76 When Noah cried out to Us,
in earlier days, We answered him,
saving him and his family
from the great calamity.

77 We helped him against a people
who denied Our signs.
They were a wicked people,
so We drowned them all.

78 When David and Solomon
passed judgment concerning a field
into which the sheep of certain
       people
had strayed by night, We witnessed
their judgment in the matter,

79 and gave Solomon
a sound grasp of it,
though We gave to both of them
shrewd judgment and knowledge.
We made the mountains and birds
echo Our glory, along with David.
It was We Who brought about
all these things.

80 It was We Who taught him
how to make coats of mail,
to protect you in warfare:
will you, then, give thanks?

81 And [We subdued] the wind
   to Solomon, so that it flew
   by his command to the land
   which We had blessed—
   for We know all things.

82 And We made some of the demons
   dive into the sea for him,
   and do other work,
   while We watched over them.

83 When Job cried out to his Lord,
   "Misfortune is upon me,
   yet You are the Most Merciful
   of the merciful,"

84 We answered him,
   removing his misfortune,
   restoring his family to him,
   and its like along with them,
   as a mercy from Our grace
   and a reminder to Our servants.

85 And then there were Ishmael, Idris,
   and Ezekiel, all steadfast in patience,

86 whom We received into Our mercy,
   for they were undoubtedly righteous.

87 And Jonah strode off in anger,
   imagining We had no sway over him.
   But then he called out
   through the dark depths,
   "There is no god but You.
   Glory be to You.
   It was I who was wrong."

88 So We answered him,
   and saved him from distress—
   as We save believers.

89 When Zachariah called to his Lord,
   "My Lord, don't leave me childless
   and alone—though You are
      doubtless
   the best of heirs,"

90 We answered him,
   and gave him a son, John,
   curing his barren wife.
   They would always hasten
   to do good deeds,
   and would call upon Us
   in hope and fear,
   humbling themselves before Us.

91 We breathed Our spirit into Mary°
   who preserved her chastity;
   We made her and her son
   a sign for all peoples.

92 This community of yours is one,
   and I am your Lord, so worship Me.

93 But [subsequent generations]
   became divided into sects—
   to Us they shall all return.

SECTION 6

94 The labor of those
   who do good deeds and are believers
   shall never be rejected,
   and We shall record it on their behalf.

95   But no town
     that We have wiped out
     shall rise again°

96   till the people of Gog and Magog°
     are unleashed, swarming down
     from every slope,

97   and the true promise draws near.
     Then, the eyes of the disbelievers
     will stare in horror, and they will say,
     "Shame on us, we were heedless
     of this—we did wrong."

98   You polytheists and those
     you worship instead of God
     shall be fuel for hell—to which
     you shall assuredly come.

99   If these idols had been gods,
     they would not have ended up there;
     but there they shall all stay forever.

100 There, the disbelievers
     shall groan in anguish,
     and they shall hear nothing.

101 But those to whom
     We have promised good things
     shall be far removed [from hell];

102 they will not hear a whisper
     from it, and will live forever
     with all that they desire.

103 The great horror
     shall not grieve them;

angels shall greet them,
"This is your promised day."

104 On that day We shall
     roll up the heaven, like a scroll
     folding away its writing.
     Just as We induced the first creation,
     so We shall reproduce it anew—
     This is Our promise,
     which We shall fulfill.

105 In the Psalms, as in earlier
        scriptures,
     We declared, "My righteous servants
     shall inherit the earth."°

106 This Qur'an bears a message
     for those who worship God.

107 We sent you, Prophet, only
     as a mercy to humankind.

108 Say, "What has been revealed
     to me is that your god is One God—
     so will you not submit to His will?

109 But if they turn away from you,
     say, "I have proclaimed the message
     to all of you alike.
     But it's not for me to know
     if the judgment promised you
     is near or far.

110 "It is He Who knows
     what is openly spoken,
     and what you hide.

111 "I do not know if this
is a trial for you—
a brief time of enjoyment."

112 Say,° "My Lord, judge justly—
our Lord, the All Merciful,
Whose help we seek against
the falsehoods you ascribe to Him."

The Pilgrimage (*Al-Hajj*)

Both Meccan and Medinan, this sura totals 78 verses. They underscore the antiquity of the Hajj rite going back to Abraham (vv. 25–29) but also herald the ubiquity of hope for all those who believe (v. 17). While reinforcing the need to struggle and strive on behalf of truth (vv. 39ff.), this sura acknowledges that God has "assigned rites of worship for every people to perform" (v. 67). The Prophet's duty is to remind them (of their rites), but defer until the day of resurrection all matters on which they dispute with him (vv. 68–69).

In the Name of God, the All Merciful, Ever Merciful

SECTION I

1 Humankind, be mindful of your
Lord,
for the trepidation° of the hour
shall be a tremendous thing.

2 The day you see that dreadful hour,
every nursing mother shall forget
her child, and every pregnant female
miscarry her fetus, and you'll see
people seeming to move
in drunken stupor, though not
drunk—
so severe will be the wrath of God.

3 Yet some people still argue about
God,
without knowledge; they follow
every
obstinate, rebellious devil.

4 As decreed, the devil will lead astray
those who turn to him, guiding
them
to the punishment of blazing fire.

5 Humankind, if you are in doubt
about the resurrection, know that
We created you from dust, then
from sperm, then a clot of fluid,
and then an embryonic mass,
both formed and unformed—

to make clear to you [Our Power].
We allow what We will
to stay in the womb for a fixed term,
then We bring you out as infants,
to grow and reach maturity.
Some of you die young,
while others reach senility,
bereft of the knowledge they had.
You see the earth barren;
then We send rain to make it stir
and swell, sprouting exquisite
[plants of] all kinds in their pairs.

6 For God is the True Reality,°
He Who brings life to the dead,
He Who has Power over all things.

7 And the hour is on its way—
let there be no doubt about this,
or that God will raise up
all people from their graves.

8 But among the people are some
who argue about God,
without knowledge, or guidance,
or any illuminating Book,

9 twisting their necks away
in disdain that they may
lead some people astray
from God's path.
Disgraced in this world,
We will yet make them taste
the torment of the blaze
on the day of reckoning,

10 telling them, "This is for the deeds
you amassed with your own hands,
for God never wrongs His servants."

SECTION 2

11 Some of the people serve God
as if on the verge [of doubt]—
if good fortune falls to them,
they feel content.
But if they are tested,
their faces turn about, reverting—
they have lost both this world and
the hereafter—a distinct loss.

12 They call on gods other than God
—who can neither harm nor help
them—
and thereby stray far away.

13 They call on one more disposed
to harm than help°—a wicked
patron,
a wicked companion.

14 God will usher those who believe
and do good deeds into gardens,
beneath which rivers flow—
for God does all that He intends.

15 Whoever thinks that God
will not help him in either this world
or the hereafter, let him stretch
a rope to the ceiling, [hang himself
from it,] and cut off his life,
to see if his recourse
removes the source of his rage.°

16 We reveal the Qur'an
in clear verses;
God guides whom He will.

17 Those who believe,
and the Jews, Sabians, Christians,
Magians,° and polytheists—
God will judge between them
on the day of resurrection,
for God is Witness to all things.

18 Do you not see that all things
in the heavens and on the earth
bow down before God—
the sun, moon, stars, mountains,
trees, animals, and many people,
though many deserve to be
    punished?
No one can raise to honor
those whom God disgraces,
for God does all that He will.

19 Both believers and unbelievers
dispute over their Lord.
A robe of fire shall be tailored
for those who deny, and scorching
water poured over their heads,

20 melting their insides and skins,

21 iron maces restraining them.

22 Whenever they venture, in anguish,
to break out, they shall be forced
    back
and told, "Taste the suffering of fire."

SECTION 3

23 But God will usher those who
    believe
and do good deeds into gardens
beneath which rivers flow. Bracelets
of gold and pearl shall adorn them,
and their clothes shall be of silk.

24 For they were guided
toward virtuous words,
and toward the path
of the Praiseworthy.

25 As for the disbelievers, who
bar people from the path of God
and the sacred mosque
(which We made for humankind,
residents and visitors alike),°
the disbelievers who
aim to deviate and do wrong—
We shall make them taste
a painful torment.

SECTION 4

26 We entrusted to Abraham the site
of the sacred house, saying,
"Do not join other gods with Me
in worship, and purify My house
for those who circle round it,
those who stand to pray, and those
who bow and prostrate themselves.

27 "And proclaim to all people
the duty of pilgrimage.
They will come to you on foot,

and on every kind of swift camel;
they will come out from every
far and deep mountain pass,

28 "so they might see some gain
and remember the name of God
on the designated days,
pronounced over the cattle
He has provided for them.
Eat from them, and also
feed those who are destitute, poor.

29 "Then let them complete their rites
of cleansing, fulfill their vows,
and circle the ancient house."°

30 This [is how to perform
the pilgrimage]: those who honor
the sacred rites of God
will find this better for them
in the sight of their Lord.
And livestock are lawful to you,
except what is already banned.°
Refrain from the abomination
of worshipping idols, and refrain
from uttering what is false.

31 Be upright in faith to God,
never joining other gods with Him;
whoever does this is like a person
who has fallen from the sky
and is plucked away by birds, or
blown by the wind to a far-off place.

32 This is how it is—those
who honor the rituals of God°
do so from the piety of their hearts.

33 Livestock will yield benefits
for you, for a limited time;
then, their place of sacrifice
shall be near the ancient house.

SECTION 5

34 We designated rites of sacrifice
for every community, so they might
remember the name of God over
the livestock he gave to sustain them.
For your God is One God,
so submit to Him alone,
and give joyous news to those
who humble themselves,

35 those whose hearts fill with awe
when the name of God is spoken,
who show patience
when adversity strikes them,
those who are steadfast in prayer,
and spend in charity from what
We have given them.

36 We have made for you
among the rituals of God
the sacrificial camels and cows;
in them is much good for you.
So, invoke the name of God
over them as they are lined up
for sacrifice. Then, when they
are fallen, lifeless, on their sides,
eat from them, and feed the needy,
those who ask and those who don't.
Hence We subdued to your use
these sacrificial beasts,
that you might give thanks.

37 It is not their meat that reaches God,
nor their blood; what reaches Him
is your piety. Hence He subdued
them
to your use, that you might glorify
God
for guiding you. So give joyous news
to those who do good deeds.

38 God will defend the believers;
He has no love for the traitors
or those who are ungrateful.

SECTION 6

39 Permission to fight is given
to those who are attacked,
for they have been wronged.°
And God is All Powerful
in His support of them—

40 those driven out of their homes
unjustly
—merely for saying, "Our Lord is
the One God."
If God did not restrain some people
by means of others, then
monasteries,
churches, synagogues, and mosques
—where the name of God
is remembered often—would be
torn down.
God will help those who help His
cause,
for God is Supremely Strong,
Almighty;

41 those who, once We settle them in
the land,
are steadfast in prayer, give in
charity,
enjoin what is right and forbid the
wrong.
With God rests the outcome of all
things.

42 Prophet, if they deny you,
know that before them
the people of Noah, 'Ad,
and Thamud denied them,

43 as did the people
of Abraham and Lot,

44 and those of Midian.
Even Moses was denied.
I granted respite
to the unbelievers for a while,
and then I seized them—
how dire was My punishment!

45 How many towns did We destroy,
as they fell into wrongdoing?
Their walls fell down with their
roofs.
How many wells lie deserted,
how many proud palaces?°

46 Have they not journeyed
through the land
with hearts to reason,
and ears to hear?
It is not their eyes that are blind,
but the hearts within their breasts.

47 Taunting, they ask you to hasten
the punishment. But God will not
    fail
in His promise. A day for God is like
a thousand years in your
    counting.°

48 How many were the towns
to which I granted respite,
which fell into wrongdoing?
Afterward, I seized them;
their final destination is to Me.

SECTION 7

49 Say to them, "People, I am here
only to give you clear warning:

50 "Those who believe
and do good deeds
shall find forgiveness
and rich provision.

51 "But those who strive
against Our signs,
vainly opposing [Our might]—
they shall be inmates
of hellfire."

52 We never sent a messenger
or prophet, who aspired [high]
without Satan infusing [doubt]
into his aspiration. But God
    removes
what Satan infuses, and He
reinforces His signs, for God
is All Knowing, All Wise.

53 [God does this] to make
what Satan infuses a trial
for those whose hearts are sick,
and those whose hearts are
    hardened
—the wrongdoers are mired
in deep resistance to truth—

54 and so that those given knowledge
might know that the Qur'an
is the truth from your Lord,
and believe in it, humbly submitting
their hearts to Him.
For God Guides those who believe
to the straight path.

55 But those who disbelieve
won't cease to doubt it, until
the hour falls upon them suddenly,
or the torment of a day of
    desolation.

56 Dominion on that day
shall belong to God, and
He shall judge between them.
Those who believed
and did good deeds
shall find themselves
in gardens of bliss,

57 while those who disbelieved
and denied Our signs
shall face disgracing torment.

SECTION 8

58 God shall give a fine provision
   to those who leave their homes
   in the cause of God,
   and are then killed or die—
   He is the Best Provider.°

59 He will bring them into a place
   most pleasing to them,
   for God is All Knowing,
      Forbearing.

60 So it will be. If someone requites
   a wrong in like measure, and is
   wronged again, God will help
      them—
   He is Pardoning, Forgiving.

61 So it will be. For God
   fades night into day
   and day into night. God
   is All Hearing, All Seeing.

62 So it will be. For God is Reality,
   and those they call on besides Him
   are illusion. And God is Most High,
   the Most Great.

63 Do you not see how God
   sends down rain from the sky,
   and the earth turns green.
   God is Most Subtle, All Aware.

64 To Him belongs
   all that is the heavens
   and all that is on the earth.
   He is Self-Sufficient, Praiseworthy.

SECTION 9

65 Do you not see that God
   has subdued to your use
   all that is on the earth
   and the ships that sail the sea
   by His command? That He
   prevents the sky from falling
   onto the earth, without His leave?
   God is Most Kind, Ever Merciful
   toward humankind.

66 It is He Who gave you life,
   will make you die, and give you life
   again. Yet humankind is ungrateful.

67 We have assigned rites of worship
   for every people to perform, so
   don't let them dispute this with you,
   Prophet, but call them to your Lord,
   for you are guided on a straight
      path.

68 If they should dispute with you,
   say, "God knows best what you do.

69 "God will judge between you
   on the day of resurrection
   concerning the things
   over which you dispute."

70 Do you not know that God knows
   all that is in the heavens and earth?
   All this is inscribed in a record—
   and this is easy for God.

71 Yet they worship, instead of God,
   things for which no sanction

has been revealed to them,
things they have no knowledge of;
and there will be none to help
those who do wrong.

72 When Our clear verses are recited
to them, you'll observe recalcitrance
on the faces of those who
    disbelieve—
they would almost do violence
to those who recite our verses to
    them.
Say, "Shall I tell you of something
worse than [your anger]?
The fire of hell—which God has
promised for those who
    disbelieve—
an evil destination."

SECTION 10

73 People, here is a parable, so hear it
with due care: those you invoke
besides God could not create a fly—
though they all combined in trying.
And if the fly snatched something
from them, they couldn't take it back.
How feeble are those who seek
and those who are sought.

74 They fail to assess God
in His true measure—for God
is Supremely Strong, Almighty.

75 God chooses messengers
from angels and humans,
for God is All Hearing, All Seeing.

76 He knows what lies before them
and what lies behind them;
and all issues return to Him
for resolution.

77 You who believe, bow down,
prostrate yourselves,
worship your Lord, and do good,
that you might flourish.

78 And strive for God
with due effort. He has chosen you,
and imposed upon you
no hardship in religion.
It is the creed of Abraham.
God named you as those
who submit [to His will],° both
before and in this [Book], so that
the messenger might be a witness
for you, and you for humankind.
Be steadfast, then, in prayer,
give in charity, and hold fast to God,
for He is your Protector—
the Supreme Protector,
the Supreme Helper.

The Believers (*Al-Mu'minun*)

Late Meccan, this sura of 118 verses underscores the benefit of faith for true believers, invoked in v. 1 and addressed throughout. Instances of God's power and protection abound (vv. 12–22) and the role of messengers is extolled, including Jesus (vv. 50–51) while the certainty of resurrection is marked by a barrier (*barzakh*, v. 100), evident for all to see on the Last Day (vv. 101–15).

In the Name of God, the All Merciful, Ever Merciful

SECTION I

1 The true believers shall succeed,

2 those who pray humbly,

3 who turn away from idle speech,

4 who perform deeds of charity,

5 and preserve their chastity,

6 except with their spouses or
    servants,
  for then they are not blameworthy.

7 But those who seek to exceed
  these limits are transgressors.

8 Those who observe
  their covenants and trusts,

9 who preserve their practice of
    prayer—

10 shall be the heirs

11 who inherit the highest paradise,
  living there through eternity.

12 We created humankind
  from a substance of clay,

13 which We lodged as a drop
    [of sperm]
  within a secure, stable home.

14 We turned the sperm drop
  into a clot, and the clot
  into an embryonic mass;
  We turned the mass into bones,
  clothing the bones with flesh,
  to produce from this
  a new being.° Blessed be God,
  the Most Excellent of Creators.

15 After this, you will die,

16 and be raised up again
  on the day of resurrection.

17 We created seven spheres above
    you,°
   never heedless of Our creation.

18 We sent down water from the sky
   in due measure, and caused it
   to soak the earth. Yet We always
   have the Power to withdraw it.

19 We use it to grow gardens for you
   of date palms and grapevines,
   yielding abundant fruit for you
        to eat,

20 and a tree springing from Mount
    Sinai,°
   yielding oil and relish for your food.

21 There is a lesson for you
   in the example of livestock—
   from their bellies We give you milk
   to drink, and they have many uses
   for you; you also feed on them,°

22 and you are carried
   on them, as you are in ships.

SECTION 2

23 We sent Noah to his people.
   He said, "My people, worship God.
   you have no god other than Him,
   so will you not be mindful of Him?"

24 The chiefs of the unbelievers
   among his people retorted,
   "This is but a human, like you,

wanting to show that he is
   superior to you. If God had willed it,
   He could have sent angels.
   We never heard such talk as this
   among our ancestors of old.

25 "He's merely a madman,
   so let's wait for a while
   [to see what might happen]."

26 Noah pleaded, "My Lord, help me,
   for they accuse me of lying."

27 So We inspired him,
   "Build the ark, under Our gaze
   and Our inspiration. Then,
   when Our command comes,
   and the springs of the earth gush
        out,
   take on board a pair of every species
   and your family, except those
   already sentenced.
   Do not plead with Me
   for the wrongdoers—
   they will be drowned.

28 "And when you and your crew
   have embarked on the ark, say,
   'All praise be to God, Who saved us
   from a people who do wrong.'

29 "And say, 'My Lord, let me
   disembark in a blessèd harbor,
   for You bestow the best of
        harbors.'"

30 In this are signs—for We have
      always
   put human beings through trials.

31 After them We raised
   another generation.

32 And We sent a messenger to them,
   one of their own, who urged,
   "Worship God, you have no god
   but Him—so will you not
   be mindful of Him?"

SECTION 3

33 But the chiefs of those
   who disbelieved among his people
   —who denied the meeting with God
   in the hereafter, and to whom
   We had granted the luxuries
   of the life of this world—
   said to them, "This prophet
   is but a human like you.
   He eats what you eat,
   and drinks what you drink.

34 "And if you obey a mere human
   like yourselves, you will lose out.

35 "Does he promise that when you die,
   and are nothing but dust and bones,
   you'll be raised up once more?

36 "What you're promised
   is far, far-fetched.

37 "There's nothing beyond
   our life in this world.
   We die and we live—
   but we shall never
   be raised up again.

38 "He's just a man who invents
   a lie about God,
   and we don't believe him."

39 The prophet said,
   "My Lord, help me,
   for they accuse me of lying."

40 God replied, "Soon, they will
   begin to feel remorse."

41 Then the blast struck them,
   and We reduced them to debris
   of dead leaves. Away, then,
   with a people who do wrong!

42 After them, We raised
   other generations.

43 No community can hasten
   its term, nor delay it.

44 We sent Our messengers, in turn.
   Every time a people's messenger
   came to them, they denied him.
   So We made them follow one
      another,
   and We made them an example—
   a tale of warning. Away, then,
   with a people who will not believe!

45 Then We sent Moses
and his brother Aaron,
with Our signs,
with clear authority

46 to Pharaoh and his chiefs,
but they were proud, arrogant
people.

47 They said, "Shall we believe
in two men like ourselves,
whose people merely serve us?"

48 So they accused them of lying
but they were themselves
destroyed.

49 And We gave Moses the Book
so that his people might be guided.

50 We made the son of Mary
and his mother a sign for
humankind,
and We gave them shelter
on a serene hill, with a flowing
spring.

SECTION 4

51 "Messengers, eat food
that is wholesome and good,
and do good works,
for I Know all that you do.

52 "This community of yours
is one community,

and I am your Lord,
so be mindful of Me."

53 But they split up their religion,
among themselves, into sects,
each faction happy with its own
beliefs.°

54 So leave them,
in their confusion,
for a while.

55 Do they think that, because
We gave them wealth and sons,

56 We will hasten to grant them
all good things?
No—but they don't know it.

57 Those who live in awe,
fearing their Lord,

58 those who believe
in the signs of their Lord,

59 those who don't join
other gods with their Lord,

60 and those who give in charity
with hearts trembling, knowing
they will return to their Lord°—

61 they are the ones who hasten
to do good deeds, foremost in this.

62 We never burden any soul

beyond its capacity.
And We have before Us a Book
that speaks the truth,
so they shall never be wronged.

63 But the hearts of disbelievers
are confused over this,
they perform other [evil] deeds—

64 until We seize and punish
those among them mired in
    wealth;
then they will cry out for help.

65 But they will be told,
"Don't cry for help—
you shall never get help from Us.

66 "Whenever My signs
were recited to you, you would
turn back, on your heels,

67 "conversing by night, in your pride,
indulging in idle jokes about the
    Book."

68 Do they not ponder over the
    Word?
Has something new come to them
that never came to their ancestors?

69 Or is it that they don't recognize
their messenger, and so deny him?

70 Or do they say, "He's possessed"?
No. He has brought them the truth,
but most of them hate the truth.

71 If the truth had complied
with their desire,
then the heavens, the earth,
and all within them
would be in ruins.
We gave them their reminder,
yet they turn away from it.

72 Prophet, do you ask of them
any recompense? The recompense
of your Lord is better—
He is the Best of Providers.

73 Though you call them
to a straight path,

74 those who don't believe
in the hereafter
veer from that path.

75 Even if We showed mercy to them
and removed their distress,
they would keep transgressing
wandering blindly around.

76 We seized and punished them,
yet still they would not submit
to their Lord, nor will they
humble themselves

77 until We open for them
a door to severe torment—
then they'll be in despair.

SECTION 5

78 It is He Who engendered in you
hearing, and sight, and feeling—
but seldom are you grateful.

79 It is He Who multiplied you
through the earth, and to Him
you shall be gathered.

80 It is He Who gives life and death,
and rules the cycle of night and
    day—
Will you not, then, use reason?

81 No—like ancient peoples, they say,

82 "What? Once we're dead,
and turned to dust and bones,
will we be raised up again?

83 "Such promises were made before
to us and our ancestors—they are
nothing but tales of the ancients."

84 Say, "To whom
does the earth belong,
and all those upon it—
if you truly know?"

85 They will answer, "To God."
Say, "Then will you not take heed?"

86 Say, "Who is Lord
of the seven heavens,
and Lord of the mighty throne?"

87 They will say, "God."
Say, "Will you not, then,
be filled with awe?"

88 Say, "In whose hand
lies the dominion of all things,
Who protects all,
Who is the One against Whom
there is no protection—
say, if you know?"

89 They will reply, "God."
Say, "Why, then, are you deluded?"

90 We did bring them the truth,
but they are lying.

91 Nor did God beget a child,
for there is no god besides Him—
else each god would take
what he had created
and some would overpower others.
May God be glorified above
what they ascribe to Him!

92 Knower of the unseen
and the seen, may He be exalted
above the gods they join with Him.

SECTION 6

93 Say, "My Lord, if you
must show me° what [torment]
they are promised,

94 then do not, my Lord, place me
among the wrongdoers."

95 We are quite Able to show you
the torment We have promised them.

96 Repel whatever is wicked
with whatever is most excellent;
We know best
what they ascribe to Us.

97 And say, "My Lord,
I seek refuge with you
against the devils' promptings,

98 "and I seek refuge with you,
my Lord, should they be near me."

99 And when death comes
to any of them, they plead,
"My Lord, send me back

100 "so I can do the good deeds
I left undone." Never.
These are mere words they speak.
Behind such people shall remain
a barrier—until the day they are raised.

101 On the day the trumpet sounds
all bonds between them will be gone,
and none will ask about another.

102 Those whose balance is heavy
—they shall flourish.

103 But those whose balance is light—
they shall have lost their souls,
and they shall stay in hell forever.

104 The fire will burn their faces,
grimacing with twisted lips.

105 "Were my verses not recited
to you—which you kept denying?"

106 They will say, "Our Lord,
our perversity overcame us, and
we were a people gone astray.

107 "Our Lord, take us out of here,
and if we relapse,
we'll indeed be wrongdoers."

108 He will say, "Stay there,
and do not address Me.

109 "When a group of My servants
would pray, 'Our Lord, we believe,
so forgive us, and show us mercy,
for You are the Most Merciful of all,'°

110 "you mocked them—
so much so, that you forgot
to remember Me
as you laughed at them.

111 "This day I have rewarded them
for their patience—and they
are the ones who will triumph."

112 He will say, "How many years
did you stay on the earth?"

113 They will answer, "We stayed
a mere day or part of a day—but ask
those who are tasked with reckoning."

114 He will say, "You stayed only
a short while—if only you knew.

115 "Did you think
We created you in vain,
and that you would not
be brought back to Us?"

116 Exalted be God, the true King—
there is no god but Him,
Lord of the glorious throne.

117 Whoever calls on any god
beyond the One God
—for which they have no proof—
shall face their reckoning
with their Lord.
The disbelievers shall never
flourish.

118 Say, then, "My Lord,
show forgiveness and mercy,
for You are the Most Merciful
of all."

SURA 24

Light (*Al-Nur*)

Medinan, this sura numbers 64 verses, highlighted by the mystical verses (vv. 35–40), but also includes ethical mandates for slander and fornication, deriving from the rumor concerning the prophet's wife 'A'isha (vv. 11–20). The obligation to be mindful of slaves, children, women, the blind, and the sick concludes this litany of divine signs (vv. 58–61), with the reminder of God's surveillance and omniscience (vv. 63–64).

In the Name of God, the All Merciful, Ever Merciful

SECTION I

1 We have revealed this sura,
whose decrees are binding.
We have revealed in it clear signs,
so that you might take heed.

2 Give the adulteress and
adulterer a hundred lashes each.
Don't let pity for them keep you

from the judgment of God
if you believe in God
and the last day;
and let a group of believers
witness their punishment.

3 The adulterer shall marry
only an adulteress, or a polytheist;
and the adulteress only an
adulterer or a polytheist—

this is forbidden for believers.°

4 As for those who accuse
   chaste women without then
   bringing four witnesses—
   give them eighty lashes,
   and reject their testimony
   ever after; they are transgressors—

5 except those who then repent,
   and amend themselves,
   for God is Forgiving, Ever Merciful.

6 Let those who accuse their wives
   of adultery, with no witnesses
   but themselves, each bear witness
   four times before God
   that he is being truthful,

7 and the fifth time,
   that the curse of God
   be upon him if he is lying.

8 But the wife shall suffer
   no punishment if she bears witness
   four times before God
   that he is lying,

9 and the fifth time,
   that the wrath of God
   be upon her if he is being truthful.°

10 If not for God's grace
   upon you and His mercy, and
   that God is Relenting, All Wise.°

SECTION 2

11 It was a group among you
   who propagated the lie°—don't
   think of it as a bad thing for you.
   No, it was for your good:
   every one of them
   will answer for his sin, and the one
   who played the major part
   will incur great torment.

12 When you heard the lie,
   why didn't believing men and
      women
   think better of their own people
   and declare, "This is an obvious lie"?

13 Why didn't the accusers
   bring four witnesses to vouch for it?
   Since they didn't, it is they
   who are liars in the eyes of God.

14 If not for the grace
   of God upon you, and His mercy
   in this world and the hereafter,
   immense punishment would have
   struck you for indulging [such
      calumny],

15 when you took it on your tongues°
   and spewed from your mouths
   what you did not know—
   you took lightly
   what was weighty with God.

16 And when you heard it,
   why didn't you say,
   "It's not for us to speak of this.

Glory be to You—
this is a great slander"?

17 God warns you
not to repeat the like of this
—ever—if you are believers.

18 And God makes the signs
clear for you,
for God is Knowing, Wise.

19 Those who enjoy spreading
lewdness among the believers
shall face a painful punishment
in this life and the hereafter;
for God knows—and you do not.

20 If not for the grace
of God upon you, and His mercy,
and that God is Most Kind,
Ever Merciful.

SECTION 3

21 You who believe, do not follow
in the footsteps of Satan,
for he incites those who do so
to indecency and evil.
Were it not for the grace
of God upon you and His mercy,
not one of you would be pure, ever;
but God purifies whom He will,
for God is All Hearing, All
Knowing.

22 Let those among you blessed
with bounty and largesse not refuse

to help their kin, the needy, and
those
who left their homes in God's cause.
Let them forgive and pardon—
would you not like God to forgive
you?
God is Forgiving, Ever Merciful.

23 Those who accuse chaste women,
who are believing but careless,
are cursed in this life
and in the hereafter, and
shall face great punishment

24 on the day when their tongues,
their hands, and their feet
shall bear witness against them
for all their deeds.

25 On that day God will give them
their due recompense in full,
and they will know that
God is the clarifying Truth.

26 Lewd women are for lewd men
and lewd men for lewd women;
good women are for good men
and good men for good women—
they are innocent of what
people say about them;
they shall be shown forgiveness
and a noble provision.

SECTION 4

27 You who believe, do not
enter houses other than your own
without asking permission

and greeting those within—
this is better for you,
so that you might be heedful.

28 If you find no one
in the house, don't enter it
without permission,
and if you are told, "Go away," go—
this is more decent° for you,
and God Knows all that you do.

29 There is no blame on you
if you enter uninhabited houses
that you can use—
for God knows what you reveal
and what you conceal.

30 Tell believing men
to lower their gaze
and preserve their chastity;
that is more decent for them,
and God is Aware
of all that they do.

31 And tell believing women
to lower their gaze,
to preserve their chastity,
and not to expose their adornment
beyond what normally shows;
to draw their scarves over
their bosoms, and not to show
their adornment, except
to their husbands, their fathers,
their husbands' fathers,
their sons, their stepsons,
brothers, brothers' or sisters' sons,
their women and their servants,

their male attendants freed of desire,°
and children who are oblivious
of women's nakedness.
Tell them not to stamp their feet
to flaunt their hidden adornments.°
And believers, all: turn toward God,
repenting, that you might prosper.

32 Marry those who are single
among you, and the righteous
among your male and female slaves;
if they are poor, God will enrich them
from His grace, for God
is Expansive, All Knowing.

33 Let those without the means to
    marry
keep chaste until God
enriches them from His grace.

Give a written contract of freedom
to those of your slaves who seek this
if you see some good in them,
and give them some of the wealth
God has given you.

Don't force your maids
into prostitution° if they want
to be chaste, just for the gain
of this worldly life.
If anyone does compel them,
God is Forgiving, Ever Merciful.

34 We revealed to you clear signs,
and a parable of those who passed
before you—an admonition
for those who are mindful of God.

SECTION 5

35 God is the Light°
of the heavens and of the earth;
His Light is a parable,
of a niche which holds a lamp,
the lamp enclosed in a glass,
the glass which glows like a gleaming star,
lit from an olive tree, blessed;
whose soil is neither East nor West;°
its very oil would shine forth
though untouched by fire:
Light upon Light.
God guides to His Light whom He
   will;
He strikes parables for humankind—
for God is Knower of all things.

36 His Light abides in houses,
sanctified by God to be raised high,
where His Name is remembered.
There is He glorified, morning and
   evening,

37 by men whom neither trade
nor profit can divert
from remembrance of God
or steadfastness in prayer,
and giving of charity;
whose sole fear is for the day
when hearts and vision
are upturned,°

38 when God rewards their best deeds
giving ever more from His grace,
for God furnishes without measure

those whom He will.

39 But behold the unbelievers—
their deeds are like a mirage
in the burning desert:
the parched man's eyes see
water in the distance; approaching,
he finds nothing; beside him,
he finds God, before Whom
he must answer—and God
is Swift in Reckoning.

40 Or, like darkness
on a fathomless sea,
wave upon wave, overcast by cloud:
darkness upon darkness;
if a man stretch out his hand,
he can scarce see it.
For one deprived of God's Light
there is no light.

SECTION 6

41 Do you not see that all praise God—
all in the heavens and earth,
like the birds with wings spread wide?
Each creature knows its prayer,
its mode of praise;
and God Knows all that they do.

42 To God belongs dominion
of the heavens and the earth, and
to God is the final destination.

43 Do you not see that God
drives the clouds, then gathers them
together, then amasses them

into heaps until you see
rain burst forth from their midst?
From these mountains
in the sky He sends down
hail, striking with it
whom He will, and averting it
from whom He will; the flash
of His lightning almost
blinds the eyes.

44 God alternates night and day—
in all this is a lesson
for those with sight.

45 God created every animal from water.
Some crawl on their bellies,
some walk on two legs, some on four.
God creates what He will—
God has Power over all things.

46 We have revealed clear signs;
and God guides whom He will
to a straight path.

47 They say, "We believe
in God and in the Prophet,
and we obey." But afterward,
some of them turn away—
they are not believers.

48 And when they are summoned
to God and His messenger
so He might judge between them,
some of them turn aside.

49 But if they presume they are right,
they hurry to him, abject.

50 Is there a disease in their hearts?
Or are they in doubt?
Or do they fear that God and
His messenger will be unjust to
    them?
No—they are the wrongdoers.

SECTION 7

51 When believers are summoned
to God and His messenger
so he might judge between them,
their only response is,
"We hear and we obey"—
those are the ones who will flourish.

52 Those who obey God
and His messenger, fear God
and are mindful of Him—
those are the ones who will triumph.

53 They swear their solemn oaths
by God, promising that
if you commanded them,
they would march out.
Say, "Do not swear;
but offer due obedience.
God is Aware of all that you do."

54 Say, "Obey God, and obey
the messenger. But if you turn away,
know that he is liable
only for the duty placed on him,
and you for the duty placed on you.
If you obey him, you will be guided;
the messenger's only task is
to convey the message clearly."

55 God has promised those of you
who believe and do good deeds
that He will make you inherit
the land, as He did with those
before you. And He will establish
the religion He has favored for them,
and replace their fear with security:
They shall worship me, and not
associate anything with me.
Those who deny after this
are the disobedient ones.

56 Be steadfast, then, in prayer,
and give in charity,
and obey the messenger,
so you might be shown mercy.

57 Do not think that
the unbelievers shall escape
God on earth; their home
is the fire—a wretched end.

SECTION 8

58 You who believe, let your slaves
and those yet to reach puberty
ask your permission before they enter
at these three times:
before the dawn prayer,
when you undress at midday,
and after the evening prayer—
these are your three times of
    privacy.
At other times, there is no blame
upon you or upon them
if you move around one another
    freely.

In this way, God makes clear for you
His signs—God is Knowing, Wise.

59 But when the children among you
reach puberty, let them also seek
permission, like others before them.
In this way, God makes clear for you
His signs—God is Knowing, Wise.

60 There is no blame on elder women
beyond the age of childbearing,°
if they take off their outer robes,
without flaunting their adornments;
but if they refrain, that is better
for them—God is Hearing,
    Knowing.

61 No blame will fall upon
the blind, the lame, the sick, nor
upon yourselves, if you eat
in your own houses, or the houses
of your fathers or the houses
of your mothers, or the houses of
your brothers or sisters, or of
your paternal uncles and aunts,
your maternal uncles and aunts,
or houses in your possession,°
or those of any friend.

No blame will fall upon you
whether you eat together
or separately. And when
you enter a house, greet one another
with a greeting as from God,
one that is blessed and gracious.
In this way, God makes clear to you
His signs, so you might understand.

SECTION 9

62 Only those are believers who
believe in God and His messenger,
who, when they are gathered
with him for some common
    concern,
do not leave until they have asked
his permission. Those who do so
are the ones who believe in God
and His messenger.
And when they ask your permission
for some affair of theirs, grant it
to those whom you will among
    them,
and seek God's forgiveness for them;
for God is Forgiving, Ever Merciful.

63 Do not treat the messenger's
calling of you as you do your
calling of one another;
God knows those among you
who slip away in stealth.
So let those who oppose
his command beware, else
some trial or painful torment
might befall them.

64 To God indeed belongs all
that is in the heavens and on earth;
He knows your state, and
on the day they are brought back
to Him, He shall inform them
of all they have done—
for God is Knower of all things.

SURA 25

The Criterion (*Al-Furqan*)

Middle Meccan and numbering 77 verses, this sura takes its name from the initial verse. Relying on the second-person singular in several verses, it can be referring either to the Prophet Muhammad or more generally to all believers. The depiction of *barzakh* as two seas (v. 53) is among its prominent literary tropes.

In the Name of God, the All Merciful, Ever Merciful

SECTION I

1 Blessèd is He Who revealed
the criterion° of right and wrong
to His servant, to warn all peoples;

2 He Who has dominion over
the heavens and the earth.
He has no child, nor any partner
who shares in His dominion.
He created all things, and
determined them in due proportion.

3 Yet they have adopted other gods
besides Him—who create nothing
and are themselves created,
who can bring neither harm
nor profit to themselves,
and have no power over
death or life—or resurrection.

4 The disbelievers say,
"This is just a lie he's forged
with the help of others." But it's they
who promote injustice and
falsehood.

5 And they say,
"Mere tales of the ancients
which he has had put into writing;
they're dictated to him
morning and evening."

6 Say, "He Who knows the mystery
of the heavens and earth revealed
it—
He is Forgiving, Ever Merciful."

7 They say, "What kind of messenger
is this, who eats food and walks
around the markets?
Why hasn't an angel been sent
to give warning with him?"

8 Or "Why isn't he given treasure
or a garden° from which to eat?"
The wrongdoers say,
"You merely follow a man
who's bewitched."

9 See what similes they coin for you!
But they are astray
and cannot find the way.

SECTION 2

10 Blessèd is He Who could give you
better things than these, if He
willed—
gardens, beneath which rivers flow,
with palaces He could build for you.

11 But they deny the hour,
and We have prepared
for those who deny it
a blazing fire—

12 when it sees them, from far away,
they will hear its raging and roaring.

13 And when they are cast into it,
constricted, and chained together,
they shall plead for death.

14 They will be told,
"Don't plead, this day, for one death—
plead, rather, for many deaths!"

15 Say, "Is this better,
or the eternal garden,
promised to the righteous,
as both their reward and end?°

16 "They shall have there
all that they desire,
abiding there forever—a promise
assured by your Lord."

17 When He gathers them
together, on the day,
with the other gods
they worshipped besides God,
He will ask,
"Was it you who led astray
these servants of Mine, or was it they
who strayed by themselves
from the true way?"

18 They will say, "Glory be to You.
We should not have taken
protectors other than You.
But you granted them comforts,
and their fathers too, so they forgot
to remember You—and became
a lost people."

19 [God will reply,] "Your false gods
prove that what you say is lies—
so you cannot avert [your
   punishment]
nor find help. We shall make
those of you who do wrong
taste great torment."

20 We sent no messengers before you
who did not eat food
and walk through the markets.
We made some of you a test for
   others.
Can you show patience?°
For your Lord is All Seeing."

SECTION 3

21 As for those who don't expect
to meet with Us—

they taunt, "Why aren't angels
sent down to us?" or
"Why can't we see our Lord?"
They are proud within their hearts
and show the utmost insolence.

22 On the day they see the angels—
that day, there will be no
welcome news for the sinners.
The [inmates of hell] will cry,
"A barrier, forbidden!"°

23 Then We shall proceed to consider
their deeds, and scatter them like
   dust.

24 On that day,
the people of paradise
will be in a better home,
reposing in a fairer place.

25 On the day the sky with its clouds
is burst asunder,
and hosts of angels are sent down—

26 on that day, the Most Merciful
shall have true dominion—
a bitter day for unbelievers.

27 On that day the wrongdoer
will bite his own hands, and cry,
"If only I had taken
the path with the messenger!

28 "A pity for me°—if only I hadn't
taken so and so for a friend.

29 "They diverted me from
remembrance [of the Book]
after it had come to me—
Satan always betrays humankind."

30 The messenger said, "My Lord,
my people have forsaken this
Qur'an."°

31 In this way We gave every prophet
enemies among the sinners;
but your Lord suffices
as a guide and a helper.

32 The disbelievers ask,
"Why wasn't the Qur'an revealed
all at once?" We revealed it
like this so it might fortify your heart,
reciting it in due measure, over time,°

33 and so they can't bring
any example to you
that We don't explain best,
bringing you its truth.

34 Those gathered into hell,
lying on their faces,
shall be in an evil place,
farthest astray from a straight path.

SECTION 4

35 We gave Moses the Book,
and his brother Aaron to help him.

36 And We commanded,
"Go, both of you, to the people
who have denied Our signs"—

Then, We destroyed the people.

37 And when the people of Noah
denied the messengers,
We drowned them—
making them a sign for humankind.
We have prepared a painful torment
for those who do wrong.

38 So too with the people of 'Ad,
Thamud, and Rass,°
and many generations in between.

39 We produced parables
warning each of them,
and each We destroyed.°

40 Disbelievers must have come upon
the town showered with
brimstone°—
did they not see it? No—they don't
expect to be resurrected.

41 When they see you,
they merely mock you,
"Is this the one whom God sent
as a messenger?

42 "He might have led us astray
from our gods, had we not stayed
steadfast by them."
But soon they shall know
—when they see the punishment—
who is more astray from the true way.

43 Have you seen those who take
their own desire as their god?
Are you their guardian?

44 Do you think most of them listen
or understand? They're like cattle—
even more astray from the true way.

SECTION 5

45 Don't you see how your Lord
lengthens a shadow? If He wished,
He could make it stand still—
We made the sun its sign,

46 then We draw it in toward Us,
phase by phase.

47 It is He Who makes the night
a robe for you, and sleep a repose,
and the day for you to rise again.

48 And it is He Who sends the winds
as omens, heralding His mercy;
and We send pure water from the sky

49 to give life thereby to a dead land,
and drink to those We created—
so many livestock and people:

50 We have distributed
[the water] among them,
that they might remember.
But most of them refuse
to be anything but thankless.

51 Had We wished, We could have
sent someone to warn every town.

52 So don't heed the unbelievers
but strive hard against them,
using the Qur'an.

53 It is He Who merged the two seas
—one fresh and sweet, the other
salty and brine—and placed
between
them a barrier, forbidden.°

54 And it is He Who created
the human being from water,
and ties of blood and marriage;
for your Lord is All Powerful.

55 Yet they worship, besides God,
things that can neither profit
nor harm them; and the disbeliever
always helps those opposed to God.

56 We sent you, Prophet, only as a
bearer of joyous news and warning.°

57 Say, "I ask no reward for what I do,
only that those who desire it
take the path to their Lord."

58 And trust in the Living God
who never dies, and hymn His
praise;
for He is Well Aware
of the sins of His servants.

59 It is He Who created the heavens
and earth and what lies between
them
in six days, then took up

the throne—the Most Merciful—
ask a learnèd person about Him.

60 When they are told, "Bow down
before the Most Merciful," they ask,
"What is the Most Merciful?
Shall we bow down
to anything you command us to?"
So their aversion grows.

SECTION 6

61 Blessed is He Who graced the skies
with starry constellations, placing
    there
a beaming lamp and gleaming
    moon.

62 It is He Who made night and day
in seamless sequence so that
those inclined might be mindful
or show that they are grateful.

63 The worshippers of the Most
    Merciful
are those who walk humbly upon
    the earth,
and, when the ignorant address them,
respond with "Peace";

64 those who spend the night bowing
and standing [in prayer] before their
    Lord;

65 those who plead, "Our Lord,
avert from us the torment of hell,
for its torment always cleaves—

66 "it is an evil home
an evil place to repose—"

67 those who are neither prodigal
in spending, nor miserly,
but achieve a mean between these;

68 those who don't invoke
any other god than the One God,
nor take a life—that God
has made sacred—without just
    cause,
nor engage in fornication.
Those who do these things
shall face a penalty,

69 their torment doubled on the day
of resurrection, and there
they shall stay forever, disgraced—

70 except those who repent,
and do good deeds.
God will displace their bad deeds
with good ones;
for God is Forgiving, Ever Merciful.

71 And those who repent
and do good deeds
have truly turned again to God;

72 those who refrain
from bearing false witness; who,
when they hear vain talk, pass it by,
retaining their dignity;

73 those who, when reminded
of the signs of their Lord,

do not stumble over them
as if they were deaf or blind;

74 and those who pray, "Our Lord,
grant us spouses and offspring
who will bring comfort to our eyes,
and make us leaders of the
    righteous."

75 Those are the ones to be rewarded
with the highest mansion in
    paradise,
—for they were patient—where they

will be met with greetings and
    peace,

76 to live there forever—a beautiful
home, a beautiful place of repose.

77 Say to the disbelievers,
"My Lord will not care for you
if you do not call on Him.
You have denied Him, and soon
the inexorable torment
will fall upon you."

SURA 26

The Poets (*Al-Shuʿara*)

Middle Meccan, this sura contains terse narratives in short verses of several prophets, beginning with Moses and Abraham, but also including Noah,
Hud, Salih, Lot, and Shuʿayb. The final verses (192–227) extol belief, and caution against poets (hence the title) who go astray and lead others to follow them
(223–26).

In the Name of God, the All Merciful, Ever Merciful.

SECTION I

1 *Ta. Sin. Mim.*°

2 These are verses of the clear Book.

3 Prophet, you would perhaps
distract yourself to death
[grieving] that they won't believe.

4 If We wished, We could send
down to them a sign from heaven,
before which their necks
would humbly bow.

5 But as soon as a reminder comes
to them from the All Merciful,
they turn away from it.

6 Yes, they deny it, but soon
the truth of what they scorn
will come to them.

7 Don't they see the earth—
how many noble species
We have caused to grow in it?

8 In this is a sign,
yet most of them won't believe.

9 And your Lord Alone
is the Almighty, Ever Merciful.°

SECTION 2

10 When your Lord called to Moses,
"Go to the people who do wrong,

11 "the people of Pharaoh—
will they not be mindful of God?"

12 He said, "My Lord, I fear
that they'll say I am lying.

13 "My chest will tighten,
and my tongue will falter,
so send Aaron also.

14 "Besides, they have charged me
with a crime,°
and I fear they'll kill me."

15 God answered, "Never.
Go, both of you, with Our signs.
We will be with you, listening.

16 "So present yourselves
before Pharaoh, both of you,
and say, 'We bring a message
from the Lord of the universe—

17 "'that you send with us
the children of Israel.'"

18 Pharaoh retorted, "Did we not
nurture you as a child among us,
and did you not stay among us
for many years of your life?

19 "Yet you committed that deed,
ungrateful as you are."

20 Moses replied, "I did it
at a time when I was astray,°

21 "Then I fled from you
when I was afraid of you;
but my Lord granted me wisdom,
and made me one of the messengers.

22 "And is this the favor
you have done me—that you
enslaved the children of Israel
[but spared me]?"

23 Pharaoh inquired, "And what is
this Lord of the universe?"

24 Moses responded, "The Lord
of the heavens and the earth,
and all that lies between them—
if only you could be convinced."

25 Pharaoh said to those around him,
   "Do you not hear what he says?"

26 Moses continued, "Your Lord,
   and the Lord of your forefathers."

27 Pharaoh retorted, "Your messenger,
   the one sent to you, is surely a
      madman."

28 Moses went on,
   "Lord of the East and the West and
   all that lies between them—
   if only you could use reason."

29 Pharaoh said,
   "If you take anyone but me as god,
   I shall have you imprisoned."

30 Moses asked, "Even if I bring
   before you convincing proof?"°

31 Pharaoh said, "Bring it, then,
   if you speak the truth."

32 So Moses threw his staff,
   and behold, it became,
   quite plainly, a snake.

33 And he drew out his hand,
   and behold, it gleamed white
   for all to see.

SECTION 3

34 Pharaoh said to the courtiers
   around him, "This is indeed
   an expert magician!

35 "He wants to drive you
   from your land by magic.
   What do you advise?"

36 They said,
   "Detain him and his brother,
   while you send
   scouts to the cities to gather

37 "and bring before you all
   the expert magicians."

38 So the magicians were gathered
   at an appointed time
   on an announced day,

39 and the people were asked,
   "Will you too gather?"

40 They replied, "We might follow
   the magicians if they prevail."

41 So when the magicians arrived,
   they asked Pharaoh,
   "There'll be a reward for us,
   of course, if we win?"

42 He replied, "Of course,
   and you shall be among
   my inner circle."

43 Moses said to them,
    "Throw down whatever
    you want to throw!"

44 So they threw their ropes
    and their staffs, saying,
    "By the might of Pharaoh,
    it is we who will win!"

45 Then Moses threw down his staff,
    and it soon devoured their
        concoctions.

46 Then the magicians fell down,
        prostrate,

47 exclaiming, "We believe
    in the Lord of the universe,

48 "the Lord of Moses and Aaron."

49 Pharaoh said,
    "You believed in Him
    before I gave you permission?
    He must be your elder, who has
    taught you magic. But soon
    you shall know! I shall cut off
    your hands and feet on either side,
    and crucify you all."

50 They said,
    "No harm shall befall us;
    we shall turn back
    to our Lord.

51 "We hope our Lord
    will forgive us our sins,
    since we were the first to believe."°

52 And We inspired Moses—
    "Travel by night, with my servants,
    for you will be pursued."

SECTION 4

53 Then Pharaoh sent scouts
    to all the cities,

54 saying, "These Israelites
    are a feeble band of men,

55 "yet they have enraged us,

56 "and we are a large force,
    on full alert."

57 So We expelled [the Egyptians]
    from their gardens and springs,

58 their treasures and noble homes.°

59 So it was. And later We made
    the children of Israel their heirs.

60 But as the sun rose
    Pharaoh's forces pursued them.

61 And when the two hosts
    saw each other, Moses' companions
    exclaimed, "We're about
    to be overtaken."

62 Moses responded, "No!
My Lord is with me,
He will guide me."

63 We then inspired Moses—
"Strike the sea with your staff."
So it parted, each side like
a mighty mountain.

64 And We brought the others near,

65 so We delivered Moses
and all who were with him,

66 then We drowned the others.

67 In this is a sign—
yet most of them won't believe.

68 And your Lord Alone
is Almighty, Ever Merciful.

69 And recite to them
the story of Abraham.

SECTION 5

70 When he said to his father
and his people,
"What do you worship?"

71 They replied, "We worship idols,
and will remain devoted to them."

72 He asked, "Do they listen to you,
when you call on them?

73 "Or do you any good or harm?"

74 They responded, "No, but
this is what our forefathers did."°

75 He asked, "Have you reflected on
what you have been worshipping,

76 "you, and those before you?

77 "They are an enemy to me—
unlike the Lord of the universe

78 "Who created me;
it is He Who guides me,

79 "Who gives me food and drink,

80 "and Who cures me when I am ill,

81 "Who will cause me to die,
and then give me life,

82 "and Who, I hope,
will forgive me my faults
on the day of reckoning.

83 "My Lord, grant me wisdom
and unite me with the righteous,

84 "and let later generations
speak honorably of me,

85 "and let me be among those
who inherit the garden of bliss;

86 "Forgive my father—he is
among those who are astray,

87   "and let me not be disgraced
on the day when all are raised up,

88   "the day when neither wealth
nor children° will avail,

89   "but only those who bring
to God a pure heart."

90   And the garden will be
brought near, to those
who were mindful of God,

91   while hellfire shall
appear plainly before those
who were misguided.

92   And they shall be asked,
"Where are the gods
you used to worship,

93   "besides God? Can they help you
—or themselves?"

94   Then they will be thrown,
face-down, into hell, with those
who misguided them,

95   and all the hosts of Iblis.

96   There, they will say,
as they quarrel,

97   "By God, we were
in clear error

98   "when we held you as equals
with the Lord of the universe,

99   "it was the sinners
who led us astray.

100   "And now there is no
intercessor for us,

101   "nor any loyal friend.

102   "If only we could return,
we would be believers."

103   Surely, in this is a sign,
yet most of them won't believe.

104   And your Lord Alone
is Almighty, Ever Merciful.

SECTION 6

105   The people of Noah
denied the messengers

106   when their brother Noah
said to them, "Will you not
be mindful of God?

107   "I am a trustworthy messenger
sent to you.

108   "So be mindful of God,
and obey me.

109   "I ask of you no reward.
My only reward is with
the Lord of the universe.

110   "So be mindful of God,
and obey me."

111 They said,
"Should we believe in you
when it's only the lowest
who follow you?"

112 He said, "What do I know
of what they do?

113 "Their reckoning is only
with my Lord—if only
you could perceive.

114 "I am not one to drive away
the believers.

115 "I am merely one
who gives clear warning."

116 They said, "Noah,
if you don't desist,
you will be stoned."

117 He said, "My Lord,
my people have denied me.

118 "So judge decisively
between me and them,
and deliver me and those
with me who believe."

119 So we delivered him
and those with him,
in the laden ark.

120 Then We drowned the rest.

121 Surely in this is a sign,

yet most of them won't believe.

122 And your Lord Alone
is the Almighty, Ever Merciful.

SECTION 7

123 The people of 'Ad denied
the messengers

124 when their brother Hud
said to them, "Will you not
be mindful of God?

125 "I am a trustworthy messenger
sent to you.

126 "So be mindful of God,
and obey me.

127 "I ask of you no reward.
My only reward is with
the Lord of the universe.

128 "You build an altar°
on every high hill, out of vanity?

129 "And establish
fortresses, thinking you
will live in them forever?

130 "And when you seize [someone]
by force, you seize them like tyrants?

131 "Be mindful of God,
and obey me.

132 "Be mindful of Him,
Who has provided you
with all that you know.

133 "He has provided you
with livestock and children,

134 "gardens and springs.

135 "I fear for you the punishment
of a momentous day."

136 They said, "It's the same to us
whether you warn us or not.

137 "It's only the custom
of our forefathers
[that we follow].

138 "And we are not
going to be punished."°

139 They denied him,
and so We destroyed them.
Surely, in this is a sign,
but most of them won't believe.

140 And your Lord Alone
is the Almighty, Ever Merciful.

SECTION 8

141 The people of Thamud denied
the messengers

142 when their brother Salih
said to them, "Will you not

be mindful of God?

143 "I am a trusted messenger
sent to you.

144 "So be mindful of God,
and obey me.

145 "I ask of you no reward.
My only reward is with
the Lord of the universe.

146 "Do you imagine that you
will be left secure
with all that you have here—

147 "gardens and springs

148 "cornfields and date palms,
soft in their clusters,

149 "and carving houses out of
mountains, with such skill?

150 "So be mindful of God,
and obey me.

151 "And do not follow the bidding
of transgressors

152 "who spread corruption in the land
and will not pursue the common
good."°

153 They said, "You're just bewitched.

154 "You are a mere mortal

like us. Bring a sign
if you are being truthful."

155 He said, "Here is a she-camel—
she has a right to drink,
and you have a right to drink,
each on an appointed day.

156 "Do not harm her, or
the punishment of a momentous day
shall overtake you."

157 But they hamstrung her;
and were then regretful.

158 So the punishment overtook them.°
Surely, in this is a sign;
but most of them won't believe.

159 And your Lord Alone
is the Almighty, Ever Merciful.

SECTION 9

160 The people of Lot denied
the messengers

161 when their brother Lot
said to them, "Will you not
be mindful of God?

162 "I am a trustworthy messenger
sent to you.

163 "So be mindful of God,
and obey me.

164 "I ask of you no reward.
My only reward is with
the Lord of the universe.

165 "Must you, alone among creatures,
lust after males

166 "forsaking the mates
that your Lord created for you?
You transgress all bounds."

167 They said,
"Lot, if you don't stop,
you'll be among those
who are thrown out."

168 He rejoined, "I am among those
who abhor what you do.

169 "My Lord, save me and
my family from what they do."

170 So We saved him
and all his family,

171 except an old woman
who lingered behind,

172 then We destroyed the rest.

173 We rained down
a hail of brimstone° on them,
a wicked rain on those forewarned.

174 In this is a sign,
yet most of them won't believe.

175 And your Lord Alone
    is the Almighty, Ever Merciful.

SECTION 10

176 The forest dwellers also denied
    the messengers

177 when Shu'ayb said to them,
    "Will you not be mindful of God?

178 "I am a trustworthy messenger
    sent to you.

179 "So be mindful of God,
    and obey me.

180 "I ask of you no reward.
    My only reward is with
    the Lord of the universe.

181 "Give just measure,
    and do not sell short,

182 "but weigh with an
    even balance,

183 "and don't withhold from people
    the things that are due to them,
    nor work evil in the land,
    spreading corruption,

184 "and be mindful of the One
    Who created you and
    the generations before you."

185 They said, "You're just bewitched.

186 "You are a mere mortal like us.
    In fact, we think you are a liar.

187 "Cause fragments of the sky
    to fall on us,
    if you are telling the truth."

188 He said, "My Lord knows best
    what you do."

189 But they denied him,
    so the punishment of the day
    of shadow overcame them,
    the punishment of a momentous day.

190 In this is a sign,
    yet most of them won't believe.

191 And your Lord Alone
    is the Almighty, Ever Merciful.

SECTION 11

192 This is a revelation
    from the Lord of the universe—

193 The trustworthy spirit°
    brought it down

194 to your heart, Prophet,
    that you might warn people

195 in a clear Arabic tongue.

196 And this was in the scriptures
    of ancient peoples.

197 Is it not a sign to them
that the learnèd people
of the children of Israel
know it?

198 Had We revealed it
to any of the non-Arabs,

199 and had he recited it to them,
they would not have believed in it.

200 In this way, We have
made it pass into the hearts
of the sinners—

201 they will not believe in it
until they see
the painful punishment,

202 which shall fall upon them
suddenly, while they are unaware.

203 Then they will say,
"Can't we be granted respite?"

204 Or, would they
hasten Our punishment?

205 See, if We let them
enjoy a few years,

206 and then they were struck
with the punishment promised
them,

207 what they enjoyed
would not help them.

208 We never destroyed a town
without sending people to warn it,

209 as a reminder—
for We are never unjust.

210 It was not any devils
who brought down this revelation.

211 It is not allowed them,
nor would they be able.

212 In fact, they are prevented
from hearing it.

213 So do not call on any
other god with God,
else you may be among
those who are punished;

214 and warn your closest kin,

215 and lower your wing°
over the believers who
follow you.

216 If they disobey you, say,
"I am free [of the guilt]
of your actions."

217 And trust in the Almighty,
the Ever Merciful,

218 Who sees you when you
stand [in prayer],

₂₁₉ and when you bow among
those who prostrate themselves.

₂₂₀ For He is the All Hearing,
All Knowing.

₂₂₁ Shall I inform you
on whom the devils descend?

₂₂₂ They descend on every sinful liar,

₂₂₃ they pass on whatever is heard,
and most of them are liars.

₂₂₄ And the poets are followed by
those who are astray.°

₂₂₅ Don't you see them wandering
aimlessly through every valley?°

₂₂₆ Saying things
that they do not do?

₂₂₇ Except those of them who believe
and do good deeds, and remember
God
often, defending themselves
only when wronged.
The wrongdoers shall soon know
their place of return.

SURA 27

The Ants (*Al-Naml*)

Like "The Bee" (Sura 16) and "The Spider" (Sura 29), this middle Meccan sura
of 93 verses is named after lowly creatures of great industry and subtlety, also
emblematic of God's creative expanse. They were singled out as insects that even
Solomon respected when he entered "the valley of the ants" (v. 18). The hoopoe,
other birds, and also Sheba (described but not mentioned by name) figure prom-
inently in the initial verses (vv. 16–44), while the stories of Thamud and Lot precede a long invocation—and warning—about God's signs (vv. 59–93).

In the Name of God, the All Merciful, Ever Merciful

SECTION I

₁ *Ta Sin.*°
These are verses

of the Qur'an,
a clear Book,

₂ a guide, and joyous news
for believers,

3 those who are steadfast in prayer
give in charity, and are certain
of the hereafter.

4 As for those who don't believe
in the hereafter, We have made
their deeds seem fair to them—
so they wander blindly.

5 They shall face severe torment,°
and in the hereafter
they shall bear the greatest loss.

6 Prophet, you receive the Qur'an
from One Who is All Wise, All
   Knowing.

7 Moses said to his family,
"I see a fire; I will bring you
word from it, or a lighted torch
to warm yourselves."

8 But when he came to the fire,
a voice called out, "Blessed is the One
who is at the fire and whoever is
   around it.°
And glory be to God,
Lord of the universe.

9 "Moses, I am the One God,
the Almighty, the All Wise.

10 "Now, cast down your staff."
But when he saw it stirring
like a snake,° he turned away,

fleeing, without returning.
"Moses," said the voice, "Don't fear:
messengers have no fear
in My presence.

11 "As for those who do wrong,
then turn to good after evil—
I am Forgiving,
Ever Merciful.

12 "Now, place your hand
by your breast,° and it will
come out gleaming white,
though unharmed.
This is among nine signs
you will take to Pharaoh
and his people—
a disobedient people."

13 But when Our signs were
shown to them, they said:
"This is obviously magic."

14 And they rejected the signs
through their iniquity and pride
though in themselves
they were convinced.
See, then, the fate
of those who wreak corruption.

SECTION 2

15 We gave knowledge
to David and Solomon,
who both said,

"Praise be to God Who
has favored us over many
of His believing servants."

16 And Solomon was David's heir.
He said, "People, we have been
     taught
the speech of birds,° and we have
been endowed with all things—
an evident favor from God."

17 And gathered before Solomon
were his hosts of jinn and men
and birds, all arrayed in rows.

18 When at length they came
to a valley of ants, an ant said,
"Ants, disperse to your homes
or Solomon and his armies
might unwittingly crush you."°

19 Solomon smiled, laughing
at its speech, and said,
"My Lord, grant that I have strength
to give thanks for Your favor
which You have bestowed
on me and on my parents,
and grant that I may perform
righteous deeds that please you,
and bring me, through Your Mercy,
to be among your righteous
     servants."

20 He inspected the birds, and said,
"Why do I not see the hoopoe?°

Is he absent?

21 "I'll punish him severely,
or execute him, unless
he brings me a clear reason
[for his absence]."

22 But the hoopoe, who was
not long gone
[drew near] and explained,
"I have learned something
that you don't know,°
and I come from Saba'°
with decisive news.

23 "I found there a woman
ruling over them,
possessed of everything.
And she has a mighty throne.

24 "I found her and her people
bowing before the sun instead of
     God,
for Satan has made their deeds
seem fair to them, barring them
from the path, leaving them
without guidance,

25 so they don't bow before God
Who brings forth what is hidden
in the heavens and the earth, and
Who knows what you conceal
and what you reveal.

26 God—there is no god but He,
Lord of the mighty throne."

27 Solomon responded,
"Soon we shall see whether
you have told the truth or lied.

28 "Go, with this letter of mine,
and deliver it to them. Then,
withdraw from them, and await
the answer they bring back."

29 The Queen said, "Counselors,
here is a royal letter, delivered to me.

30 "It's from Solomon, and it reads,
'In the Name of God,
the All Merciful, Ever Merciful;°

31 "'do not exalt yourselves
above me, but come to me
in submission.'"°

SECTION 3

32 She said, "Counselors,
advise me in this matter—
I don't decide on any matter
without your presence."

33 They said, "Though we have
strength and great power in war,
yours is the command.
So consider what you
would like to command."

34 She said, "When kings enter a town,
they ravage it, and humiliate
its noblest inhabitants—
this is what they typically do.

35 "But I will send them a gift
and see what response
my envoys bring back."

36 When the envoys came to him,
Solomon said, "What, are you
offering me wealth?
What God has granted me is better
than what He grants you.
In fact, it's you who
rejoice in your own gift.

37 "Go back to your people—
and be sure we'll come upon them
with irresistible forces, and
expel them from there,
humiliated, and abased."

38 He said to his own men,
"Counselors, which of you can
bring me her throne before
they come to me in submission?"

39 An 'ifrit among the jinn said,°
"I will bring it to you
before you rise from your place;°
I assuredly have the strength
and can be trusted to do this."

40 Another, who had knowledge
of the Book, said, "I will bring it
to you before you even blink."°
Then, when Solomon saw it
placed before him, he exclaimed,
"This is by the grace
of my Lord to test whether
I would be grateful or ungrateful.

Whoever shows gratitude does so
only to his own gain, but whoever
is ungrateful—my Lord
is Self-Sufficient, Munificent."

41 He said, "Disguise her throne
so she won't recognize it.
Let's see whether she is guided
or one of those without guidance."

42 When she arrived, she was asked,
"Is your throne like this?" She
    answered,
"It looks like it." [Solomon said],
"Knowledge was granted to us
    before her,
and we submitted to God's will,

43 "while she was prevented
by her worship of others
besides God; for she was from
a disbelieving people."

44 "Enter the palace," she was told.
But when she saw it, she thought
its [floor] was a [shining] lake, so
    she
uncovered her shins. He explained,
"It is in fact a palace paved smooth
with glass." She said, "My Lord,
I have wronged myself, and
I submit, with Solomon, to God,
Lord of the universe."

SECTION 4

45 We sent to the people of Thamud
their brother Salih,° who urged
    them,
"Worship God." But they split
into two factions, quarreling.

46 He said, "My people,
why do you seek to bring on evil
before good? Why not seek
forgiveness of God,
so you might be shown mercy?"

47 They said, "We see you
and those with you as an ill omen."
He replied, "Your ill omen
is a matter for God; and you are
a people undergoing trial."

48 There were in the city
nine [heads of families],
spreading corruption in the land,
and they would not reform.

49 They said, "Swear to one another
an oath by God that we'll launch
a night attack on him and his
    family,
and that we'll say to his heir [when
he seeks vengeance], 'We never saw
the destruction of his family,
and we're speaking the truth.'"

50 So they plotted and planned,
but We also planned,
though they were not aware.

51 See, then, the outcome
of their plot—We destroyed
them and all their people.

52 These were their houses—
now in utter ruin, for they were
wrongdoers. In this is a sign
for people with knowledge.

53 And We saved those
who believed and were
mindful of God.

54 We also sent Lot, who said
to his people, "How can you
commit such indecency,
which you can clearly see [is wrong].

55 "Would you really lust after
men rather than women?
What an ignorant people you are!"°

56 But the only response
of his people was "Drive out
the family of Lot from your town!
They are truly people
who fancy themselves pure!"

57 But We saved him
and his family, except his wife
whom We destined to be
among those left behind.

58 And We rained down on them
a rain of brimstone°—
on those who had been warned.

SECTION 5

59 Say, "Praise be to God,
and peace be upon His servants,
whom He has chosen."
Who is better—God, or the gods
they join with Him?

60 Who created the heavens and earth,
and sends down upon you water
from the sky? With it, We grow
gardens of beauty and delight.
It is not in your power
to grow their trees.
Is there any god besides God? No.
Yet they are a people
who ascribe equals to Him;

61 Who made the earth a secure home,
and wrought rivers in its midst,
and made firm mountains for it,
placing
between the two seas a barrier?°
Is there any god besides God?
Yet most of them do not know;

62 Who answers the distressed person
calling on Him, relieves their
anguish,
and makes you regents on the earth?
Is there any god besides God?
How little you remember!

63 Who guides you through
the darkness of land and sea?
Who sends the winds as joyous
news,

heralding His mercy?
Is there any god besides God?
Exalted is God, above
the gods they join with Him.

64 Who brings about Creation,
then renews it, Who sustains you
from the heavens and the earth?
Is there any god besides God?
Say, "Bring your proof
if what you say is true."

65 Say, "None in the heavens
or on the earth knows the unseen
except God, nor can they fathom
when their resurrection will come."

66 Even less can their knowledge
reach into the hereafter: they remain
in doubt over it, blind to it.

SECTION 6

67 The unbelievers ask,
"What, when we are dust, with our
fathers,
will be really be brought back?

68 "Yes, we've been promised this
before—we and our fathers. But
these
are merely tales of the ancients."

69 Say, "Wander through the earth
to see what was the fate of the
sinful."

70 But don't grieve on their account,
nor let their plotting distress you.

71 And if they ask,
"When will this promise come to
pass,
if what you say is true?"

72 Say, "It may be that
some of the things
you seek to hasten
are close behind you."

73 And your Lord is Full of Favor
toward humankind,
though most of them are ungrateful.

74 And your Lord knows
what their hearts conceal
and what they reveal.

75 Nor is there anything hidden
in the heavens and the earth
that is not [recorded] in a clear
Book.

76 This Qur'an explains
to the children of Israel
most of the things
about which they differ.

77 It is a guide and a mercy
for the believers.

78 Your Lord will decide
between them, with His judgment,
for He is Almighty, All Knowing.

79 So, trust in God—you stand
   upon the clear truth.

80 You cannot make the dead hear
   or the deaf hear the call,
   when they turn away, recoiling.

81 Nor can you guide the blind
   from their straying;
   you can only make those hear
   who believe in Our signs,
   those who submit to Our will.

82 And when the sentence
   is passed on them,
   We shall bring forth for them
   a beast° from the earth
   to tell them that
   humankind was uncertain
   about Our signs.

SECTION 7

83 On that day, We shall gather
   from every people a troop of those
   who denied Our signs, in ranks.

84 Then, when they come
   to judgment, God will say,
   "Did you deny My signs,
   without knowledge of them—
   what were you doing?"

85 And the sentence will be passed
   on them, for they did wrong,
   and they will be unable to speak.

86 Do they not see that
   We made the night,
   in which they might rest,
   and the day, bringing light
   to the eyes? In this are signs
   for a people who believe.

87 On the day the trumpet
   is sounded, all in the heavens
   and all upon the earth
   shall be filled with terror,
   except some by the will of God.
   And all shall come
   before Him, humbled.

88 You see the mountains
   and think them firmly fixed;
   but they shall pass,
   like the passing clouds—
   this is the artistry of God,
   Who brings all things
   to their perfection.
   He is Aware of all that you do.

89 Those who come bringing good
   shall receive even better,°
   and they will be safe from
   the terror of that day.

90 Those who come bringing evil—
   their faces shall be cast into the fire,
   "Are you not rewarded precisely
   for what you have done?"

91 I have been commanded only
   to worship the Lord of this city,
   the One Who has sanctified it,

to Whom all things belong.
I have been commanded to be
   among
those who submit to God's will,°

92 and to recite the Qur'an.
Whoever takes guidance
takes it only for his own good;

and say to whoever strays,
   "I am only one of those who warn."

93 And say, "Praise be to God
Who will soon show you His signs,
so you shall know them."
Your Lord is not unmindful
of what you do.

SURA 28

The Story (*Al-Qasas*)

The "story" is about Moses and Pharaoh, who occupy the first part of this late Meccan sura, numbering 88 verses. It also includes a cautionary tale about Qarun, a wealthy Israelite whose fortune did not save him, or his house, from being swallowed by the earth (v. 82). Anticipating Sura 55:26–27, the last verse declares, "All things shall pass away except His Face" (v. 88).

In the Name of God, the All Merciful, Ever Merciful

SECTION I

1 *Ta Sin Mim.*°

2 These are verses of the clear Book.

3 We recite to you the story
of Moses and Pharaoh—the truth
for people who believe.°

4 Exalting himself in the land,
Pharaoh split its people into factions.
Oppressing a group of them,
he killed their sons

but spared their women.
He always sowed corruption.°

5 But We intended to favor those
who were oppressed in the land,
to make them leaders, and heirs,

6 to empower them in the land,
to bring before° Pharaoh, Haman,°
and all their forces
what they had always feared.

7 We inspired Moses' mother,
saying, "Suckle your child,
but if you fear for him,

place him in the river—
and do not fear or grieve.
We shall restore him to you,
and We shall make him
one of Our messengers."

8 Then the family of Pharaoh
picked him up—who would
become an enemy to them
and a source of grief—
Pharaoh, Haman, and their forces
were always sinners.

9 Pharaoh's wife cried,
"Here's a joyful sight
for me and you! Don't kill him.
Perhaps he'll be of use to us, or
we might adopt him as a son"—
they were unaware [of God's plan].

10 But a void opened up
in the heart of Moses' mother,
who might have disclosed his plight,
had We not strengthened her heart,
to make her a believer.

11 She said to his sister,
"Follow Moses."°
So she watched him from a distance,
though [the people of Pharaoh]
were unaware.

12 We had ordained earlier
that he should not suckle
from wet nurses, so
his sister asked [Pharaoh's house],
"Shall I show you
the people of a house

who will rear him for you
and take good care of him?"

13 So We returned him to his mother,
that she might be comforted
and not grieve, and know
that God's promise is true.
Yet most of them don't know.°

SECTION 2

14 When Moses reached
his maturity and manhood,
We endowed him with wisdom
and knowledge; this is how
We reward those who do good.

15 He entered the city at a time
when its people would not notice.
He found two men fighting there,
one from his own people
and the other an enemy.
The former sought his help
against his enemy.
Moses struck him with his fist,
killing him.° He said,
"This must be Satan's work,
for he is clearly an enemy
who leads astray."

16 He prayed, "My Lord,
I have wronged myself: forgive me."
And God did forgive him—
He is Forgiving, Ever Merciful.

17 He said, "My Lord,
because You have favored me,
I shall never support those who sin."

18 As the morning came,
   he was in the city, fearful, wary,
   when the man who had sought
   his help the day before
   called out to him for help again.
   Moses said, "Clearly, it's you
   who are in the wrong!"

19 Then, when Moses showed
   his intent to strike the man who was
   their common enemy, the man said,
   "Moses, do you want to kill me
   as you killed a person yesterday?
   You want to be a tyrant in the land,
   not someone who fosters the good."°

20 Then a man came, running,
   from the farthest end of the city,
   crying, "Moses, the chiefs
   are conferring about you,
   proposing to kill you. So leave!
   This is my sincere advice to you."°

21 So he left from there,
   fearful, wary, praying, "My Lord,
   save me from people who do
      wrong."

SECTION 3

22 And when he turned his face
   toward the land of Midian,° he said,
   "May my Lord guide me
   to the right way."

23 And when he came to
   the wells of Midian,
   he found a group of men there
watering their flocks,
and beside them two women
holding back their flocks. He asked,
"What's the matter with you?"
They explained,
"We can't water our flocks
until the shepherds drive theirs
   back—
our father is a very old man."

24 So he watered their flocks for them.
   Then, turning back toward the shade,
   he sighed, "My Lord, I am truly
   in need of whatever good
   You might send down to me."

25 Later, one of the two women
   came to him, walking shyly,
   "My father invites you,
   so he might reward you
   for watering our flocks."
   When Moses came to him and
   narrated his story, the father said,
   "Don't be afraid—you have escaped
   from people who do wrong."

26 One of the women said,
   "My father, hire him—
   the best person to hire is someone
   strong and trustworthy."

27 The father said to Moses,
   "I want to wed you to one
   of my two daughters here,
   if you'll serve me for eight years.
   But if you were to complete ten,
   that would be up to you.°
   I don't want to burden you;

you'll find me, God willing,
to be a righteous person."

28 Moses replied, "Let that be
the agreement between me and you.
Whichever of the two terms I fulfill,
don't harbor animosity toward me,
for God is Witness to what we say."

SECTION 4

29 When Moses had fulfilled the term,
and was traveling with his family,
he glimpsed a fire
on the side of Mount Tur.
He said to his family, "Stay here,
I glimpsed a fire;
perhaps I can bring you
some word from it°
or firewood to warm yourselves."

30 But when he came to the fire,
he was called by a voice
from the right slope of the valley,
from a tree on hallowed ground,
"Moses, I am the One God,
Lord of the universe.

31 "Now, throw down your staff."
But when Moses saw it stirring,
like a snake, he turned in flight,
and did not return.
"Moses, draw near, and
don't fear, for you are safe.

32 "Slip your hand into your cloak—
it will come out gleaming white,
unharmed.
Drop your hand by your side,
free from fear.° These shall be
two proofs from your Lord
to Pharaoh and his chiefs—
they are a wicked people."

33 Moses said, "My Lord,
I have killed one of them,
and I fear they will kill me.

34 "Also, my brother Aaron
is more eloquent in speech than me,
so send him with me, as an aide,
to confirm what I say, for I'm afraid
they will call me a liar."

35 God said, "We shall strengthen
your arm through your brother,
and invest you both with authority,
beyond their reach. With Our signs
you and those who follow you
will be victorious."°

36 But when Moses came to them
with Our clear signs, they said,
"This is nothing but contrived
magic.
We never heard the like of it
from our ancestors."

37 Moses replied, "My Lord knows
best
who has come with guidance

from Him, and whose outcome
will prevail in the hereafter.
The wrongdoers will never thrive."

38 Pharaoh said, "Counselors,
I know of no god for you but me.
So, Haman, kindle for me
a fire to bake clay bricks,
and make me a towering edifice
so I may look upon
the God of Moses,
for I consider him a liar."

39 Hence Pharaoh and his forces
behaved arrogantly in the land
beyond their right, thinking
they would never be returned to Us.

40 So We seized him and his forces,
and cast them into the sea—
observe the end of those
who do wrong!

41 We made them leaders
who summon people to the fire;
on the day of resurrection
they shall find no help.

42 In this world,
We laid a curse upon them,
and on the day of resurrection,
they shall be among the despised.

SECTION 5

43 We gave the Book to Moses
—after We destroyed earlier
    generations—
to give insight to humankind,
as well as guidance and mercy,
that they might be reminded.

44 You, Prophet, were not there
on the western side of the
    mountain°
when We decreed the
    commandment
to Moses—you were not a witness.

45 We raised up generations over
long eras—you, Prophet, did not live
among the people of Midian,
reciting to them Our signs—
it is We who send [messengers].

46 Nor were you at the side
of Mount Sinai when We called
to Moses;° yet you are sent
as a mercy from your Lord
to warn a people to whom
no one before you came to warn,
that they might be reminded,

47 and may not say, if calamity
—brought by their own hands—
befalls them, "Our Lord,
if only You had sent us a messenger,
we would have followed Your signs
and would have been believers."°

48 But now, when the truth
has come to them from Us, they say,
"Why is he not given signs
like those given to Moses?"
And did they not also deny
what was given to Moses before?
"Two brands of sorcery,
hand in hand," they say
and "We deny it all," they say.

49 Say, "Then bring a Book from God,
a better guide than either of these,
so I may follow it,
if you are speaking the truth."°

50 But if they don't answer you,
know that they only follow
their own desires—who
goes further astray than someone
who follows their own desire
without guidance from God?
God does not guide
a people who do wrong.

SECTION 6

51 And now indeed We have
conveyed to them the Word,
that they might be reminded.

52 Those to whom
We gave the Book before
believe in it;

53 and when it is recited to them,
they say, "We believe in it—it is
indeed the truth from our Lord.

In fact, even before it came,
we submitted to His will."°

54 They will be twice rewarded
for they have been patient,
they avert evil with good,
and spend in charity from
what we have given them;

55 and when they hear idle talk,
they turn away from it, saying,
"Our deeds belong to us,
yours to you. Peace be with you.
We do not seek out the ignorant."

56 You, Prophet, cannot guide
all those you love.
But God guides whom He will,
and He knows best those
who will be guided.

57 They say, "If we followed
the guidance with you, we would be
swept away from our land."
Have We not set up for them
a safe sanctuary,° where fruits
of all kinds are brought,
as sustenance from Us?
Yet most of them do not know.

58 And how many towns have
We destroyed, which exulted
in their easy living. And after them,
their homes were scarcely lived in—
We are the sole Heirs.°

59 Your Lord never destroyed
the towns until he had sent
to their center° a messenger,
reciting to them Our signs;
nor would He have destroyed
these towns unless their people
had been wrongdoers.

60 Whatever things you are given
are fleeting joys, adornment
of the life of this world;
but whatever is with God
is better and enduring.
Will you not, then, use reason?

SECTION 7

61 Is a person to whom We made
a good promise and sees it fulfilled
like the person to whom We gave
the joys of the life of this world,
then, on the day of resurrection,
will be brought out [for
    punishment]?

62 On the day that God
calls to them, He will ask,
"Where are the other gods
you claimed to be My partners?"

63 Those with proof against them
will say, "Our Lord, these are the ones
we led astray. We led them astray
as we ourselves were led astray. Now
we disavow them before you;
it was not us that they worshipped."

64 They will be told,
"Call upon your other gods."
They will call them, but they
will not answer. Then they
will see the punishment—if only
they had let themselves be guided.

65 On the day that God calls them,
He will ask, "How did you answer
the messengers?"

66 All news will seem
dubious to them on that day,
when they cannot query one
    another.

67 But those who repent,
believe, and do good deeds
may be among
those who succeed.

68 For your Lord creates what He will,
and it is He Who chooses—
there is no choice for them.
Glory be to God—
may He be exalted above
the gods they join with Him.

69 And your Lord knows
what their hearts conceal
and what they reveal.

70 For He is God: there is
no god but Him. His is the praise
in this world and the next.°
His is the judgment; and to Him
you shall be returned.

71 Say, "Do you see? If God
  enshrouded you in unending night
  until the day of resurrection,
  what other god could bring you light?
  Will you not, then, listen?"

72 Say, "Do you see? If God
  exposed you to unending day
  until the day of resurrection,
  what other god could bring you night
  in which you might repose?
  Will you not, then, perceive?

73 "But through His mercy,
  He made for you the night,
  where you might repose,
  and the day, where you might
  seek His bounty,
  that you might give thanks."

74 On the day that God
  calls them, He will ask,
  "Where are the gods
  you claimed to be My partners?"

75 And from each people
  We shall draw a witness,
  saying, "Bring your proof."
  Then they shall know
  that the truth is with God—
  and the gods they invented
  will abandon them.

SECTION 8

76 Korah belonged to the people
  of Moses,° but he oppressed them.

We gave him treasures whose
very keys would weigh down
a company of strong men.
His people told him, "Don't
flaunt [your wealth], for God
does not love those who boast.

77 "But rather, seek through what
  God has given you the house
  of the hereafter.
  Don't neglect what you have
  in this world,° but do good
  as God has been good to you,
  and do not seek corruption
  in the land, for God does not love
  those who sow corruption."

78 He said, "This was granted me
  on account of my knowledge."
  Did he not know that God
  had destroyed generations
  before him, greater than him
  in strength and possessions amassed?
  The sinners shall not be asked
  about their sins.

79 So he went out among
  his people in his finery,
  and those hankering after
  the life of this world remarked,
  "Ah, if only we had the like
  of what Korah has been given!
  What a great fortune he has!"

80 But those endowed with knowledge
  retorted, "Shame on you!
  God's reward is better, for those

who believe and do good deeds,
and none will attain it except
those who practice patience."°

81 Then We roused the earth
to swallow him and his house.
There was none° to help him,
beyond God, nor could he
defend himself.

82 By morning, those who yesterday
had coveted his position
began to say, "Indeed—
God enlarges provision
or restricts it for whom He will
of his servants. If God did not
favor us, He could have
roused the earth to swallow us.
Indeed—those who deny God
shall not prosper."

SECTION 9

83 We shall grant the house
of the hereafter to those
who don't seek to be exalted
in the land or to sow corruption,
and the best outcome will be
for those mindful of God.

84 Those who bring good
will receive what is better;
as for those who bring evil—
their recompense will equal
their evil deeds.

85 He who assigned you
[to convey] the Qur'an
will bring you back,
to the place of return.°
Say, "My Lord knows best
who comes with guidance and
who is clearly in error."

86 Nor had you, Prophet,
expected the Book
to be sent to you; it was
but a mercy from your Lord.
So, never support the disbelievers.

87 And never let them turn you
away from the verses of God
once they are revealed to you.
Call people to your Lord,
and never be among those
who ascribe partners to God.

88 Nor call on any other god
besides the One God.
There is no god but Him.
All things shall pass away
except His Face. His is
the judgment; and to Him
you shall be returned.

The Spider (*Al-'Ankabut*)

Taking its name from v. 41, this late Meccan sura of 69 verses warns all those who take anyone but the One God as their support. Not only Qarun but Pharaoh and Haman (v. 39) are marked as proud profligates who disregarded God's signs. No less unmindful are seafarers who call on God at sea but forget him when they land safely (v. 65).

In the Name of God, the All Merciful, Ever Merciful

SECTION I

1 *Alif Lam Mim.*°

2 Do people imagine
that they'll be left alone
after saying, "We believe,"
and that they won't be tested?

3 Yes, We tested those before them—
and God knows those who are
    truthful
and those who lie.

4 Do those who do bad deeds
think they can elude Us?
How bad their judgment is!

5 For those who hope to meet God,
the hour appointed by God°
will surely come—
for He is All Hearing, All Knowing.

6 And whoever strives
strives only for himself,
for God is Self-Sufficing,
free of all need
of created beings.°

7 As for those who believe
and do good deeds,
We shall wipe out their misdeeds,
and reward them
for the best of their deeds.

8 We have enjoined people
to be kind to parents;
but if they strive to make you
associate things with Me
of which you have no knowledge,
then don't obey them. To Me
is your return, and I will inform you
of all you have done.

9 As for those who believe
and do righteous deeds,
We shall admit them
among the righteous.

10 Some of the people say,
   "We believe in God."
   But when they are harmed
   in the cause of God,
   they equate people's duress
   with God's punishment;
   and if help comes to you
   from your Lord, they say,
   "We were always with you."
   Does God not know best
   what lies within the hearts
   of His creatures?°

11 And God knows those who believe,
   just as He knows the hypocrites.

12 Those who disbelieve
   say to those who believe,
   "Follow our way, and
   we will bear your sins."
   But they cannot bear
   any of their own sins—
   they are nothing but liars.

13 They *will* bear their own burdens
   and other burdens besides—
   they shall be questioned,
   on the day of resurrection,
   about their fabrications.

SECTION 2

14 We sent Noah to his people,
   and he stayed with them
   for a thousand years less fifty,
   but the flood overcame them
   for they were wrongdoers.

15 But We saved him
   and the people of the ark,
   and We made it a sign
   for all nations.°

16 And We sent Abraham,
   who said to his people,
   "Worship God, and
   be mindful of Him.
   That is better for you,
   if only you knew.

17 "You worship instead of God
   only idols, and you invent falsehood.
   Those you worship instead of God
   can give you no provision,
   so seek provision from God,
   worship Him, and be grateful to
      Him—
   to Him you will be returned.

18 "And if you deny the message,
   as nations before you denied it,
   know that the messenger's task
   is only to convey it clearly."

19 Do they not see how God
   originates creation and
   then renews it?
   This is easy for God.

20 Say, "Travel through the earth
   and see how He originated creation;
   then God will bring about
   a new creation,
   for God has Power over all things.

21 "He will punish whom He will,
and show mercy to whom He will,
and to Him you will be turned back."

22 "You cannot evade Him
on the earth nor in the heavens,
Nor shall you find beyond God
any protector or helper."

SECTION 3

23 As for those who deny the signs
of God and the meeting with Him,
they have despaired of My mercy,
and theirs shall be a painful
    torment.

24 His people's only reply was
"Kill him or burn him,"
but God saved him from the fire.
In this are signs
for people who believe.

25 Abraham responded,
"You have adopted idols
instead of God,
out of love for one another
in the life of this world. But on
the day of resurrection, you will
deny and curse one another,°
and your home shall be the fire—
with none to help you."

26 But Lot believed in Him.
He said, "I will flee to my Lord,
for He is Almighty, All Wise."

27 And We granted to Abraham
Isaac and Jacob, and We placed
within his progeny prophethood
and the Book, and We gave him
his reward in this world;
and in the hereafter
he will be among the righteous.

28 Recall when Lot said to his people,
"You commit an indecency
without precedent by anyone
in the world before you.

29 "Do you approach men,
cut off their path,
and commit wickedness
when you gather together?"
His people's only reply was
"Bring on God's punishment,
if you are speaking the truth."

30 He said, "My Lord,
help me against a people
who breed corruption."

SECTION 4

31 When Our messengers came
to Abraham with joyous news
[of his son's birth], they said,
"We are going to destroy
the people of this town—
they are given to wrongdoing."

32 He said, "But Lot is there!"
They rejoined,
"We well know who is there;

we shall save him and his family—
except for his wife,
who will be among those
who stay behind."

33 When Our messengers came to Lot,
he felt vexed and constrained
on their behalf, powerless
to protect them, but they said,
"Don't fear and don't grieve.
We shall save you and your family—
except for your wife,
who will be among those
who stay behind.

34 "We are going to bring down
retribution on the people of this town,
for they are given to transgression."

35 And We have left its ruins°
as a clear sign
for people who use reason.

36 And We sent to the people
of Midian their brother Shu'ayb,
who said, "My people, worship God,
be wary of the last day,
and don't do evil on the earth,
sowing corruption."

37 But they denied him—
then the earthquake shook them,
and they lay fallen,
face-down, in their homes.

38 The fate of the people of 'Ad
and Thamud is clear

from [the ruins] of their homes.
Satan made their deeds
seem fair to them,
hindering them from the path,
though they possessed insight.

39 Moses came to Korah and Pharaoh
and Haman with clear signs,
but they were proud upon the earth—
still they could not elude Us.

40 We seized each of them for his sin.
Against one We sent a hailstorm;
another was gripped by a great blast,
and the other We caused to be
swallowed up by the earth,
and yet another We drowned.
It was not God who wronged them
but they who wronged themselves.

41 The parable of those who
take protectors other than God
is the house the spider builds.
It is the frailest of houses—
if only they knew.°

42 God knows all
that they call upon besides Him—
for He is Almighty, All Wise.

43 Such are the parables
We coin for humankind;
but only those with knowledge
can fathom them.

44 God created the heavens and earth
with true purpose—in this is a sign
for those who believe.

SECTION 5

45 Recite what was revealed to you
of the Book, and be steadfast in
        prayer;
prayer forestalls indecency and evil.
Paramount is remembrance of God,
for God knows all that you do.

46 And do not argue
with the people of the Book,
except using the best
        means—unless
it is with the wrongful among
        them.
And say, "We believe
in what was revealed to us
and what was revealed to you;
our God and your God is One;
and to Him we submit."

47 This is how We sent
to you the Book; those given
the Book before believe in it,
and some of these [pagan Arabs]
believe in it. None but
unbelievers deny Our signs.

48 You did not recite from any book
before this, nor did you write it
with your right hand, else
the falsifiers would have doubted.

49 No, these are clear signs
in the hearts of those endowed
with knowledge; and none but
the wrongdoers deny Our signs.

50 Yet they say,
"Why are signs not sent down
to him from his Lord?"
Say, "The signs are only
with God; and I am only
here to give plain warning."

51 Is it not enough for them
that We have sent down to you
the Book, as recited to them?
In this is a mercy and a reminder
for people who believe.

SECTION 6

52 Say, "God suffices as Witness
between me and you;
He knows what is in the heavens
and the earth. And those who
believe in falsehood and deny God
shall be the ones in loss."

53 They taunt you—to hasten
the punishment; had it not been
appointed for a fixed time,
punishment would surely
have come upon them,
and it will come suddenly to them,
while they are unaware.

54 They taunt you—to hasten
the punishment;
but hell shall encompass
the disbelievers,

55 on the day the punishment
enshrouds them from above,

and from below their very feet—
and He will say, "Taste the deeds
that you have done!"

56 My servants, who believe—
My earth is wide indeed,
so worship only Me.

57 Every soul shall taste death;
then to Us
you shall be brought back.

58 As for those who believe
and do good works,
We shall give them a home
in the garden, in raised halls,
beneath which rivers flow,
to dwell there always—
how superlative the reward
of those who labor,

59 those who practice patience,
and trust in their Lord.

60 How many are the creatures who
do not shoulder their own provision.
It is God Who provides for them
and for you—
for He is All Hearing, All Knowing.

61 If you ask them,
who created the heavens and the
earth,
and who controls the sun and moon,
they will surely say, "God."
So how are they deluded?

62 God enlarges or restricts
provision
for whom He will of His servants—
God is Knower of all things.

63 And if you ask them
who sends down rain from the sky
to give life to the earth after its
death,
they will surely say, "God."
Say, then, "Praise be to God."
Still, most of them do not discern.

SECTION 7

64 What is the life of this world
but amusement and play?
The home of the hereafter
is true life—if only they knew.

65 Whenever they set sail by ship,
they call on God, on Him alone,
yet when He delivers them to dry
land,
see how they join other gods
with Him in worship.

66 Let them be ungrateful
for what We have given them
Let them enjoy themselves—
soon, they shall know.

67 Don't they see that We've made
a secure sanctuary, while people are
plucked away all around them?
Do they still believe in falsehood,
ungrateful for the favor of God?

68 Who does more wrong
than those who invent
a lie about God,
or deny the truth
when it reaches them?
Is there not in hell a home
for the disbelievers?

69 As for those who strive
in Our cause,°
We shall guide them in Our ways,
for God is with the righteous.

SURA 30

The Byzantines (*Al-Rum*)

A rare reference to actual historical events, the title of this middle Meccan sura numbering 60 verses refers to Byzantines or Greeks, cited in v. 2. who were enemies of the pre-Islamic Arabs and conquered by the new Muslim polity. God's promises etched as His signs are repeatedly extolled, providing hope for believers, at the same time that God "sets a seal on the heart of those who don't know" (v. 59).

In the Name of God, the All Merciful, Ever Merciful

SECTION I

1 *Alif Lam Mim.*°

2 The Empire of the Byzantines
lies defeated

3 in a neighboring domain,
yet soon after this defeat
they shall triumph

4 within a few years—
God is ever in command,
both before and after—
and on that day
the believers shall rejoice°

5 in the help of God.
He helps whom He will,
for He is Almighty,
Ever Merciful.

6 God's promise—He never breaks it.
but most people do not know.

7 They know only the surface
of the life of this world, and they
remain heedless of the hereafter.

8 Do they not reflect
upon themselves?
God did not create the heavens

and the earth and all
that lies between them
without true purpose
and for an appointed time.
Yet most people deny
that they will meet their Lord.

9 Do they not travel
through the earth and observe
how those before them
met their end?
They were stronger than these,
they plowed the earth
and built upon it more than these.
Their messengers came to them
    [in vain]
with clear proofs—
God did not wrong them
but they wronged themselves.

10 Those who did evil
met an evil end, for they
denied the signs of God,
and mocked them.

SECTION 2

11 God originates creation
then renews it, then to Him
you shall be returned.°

12 On the day when the hour comes,
the guilty shall be in despair.

13 None of the gods
they joined with God

shall intercede for them
and they will deny belief
in these gods.°

14 On the day when the hour comes,
people will be sorted [into two
    groups]:

15 those who believed
and did good deeds,
will be filled with delight
in a lush meadow,

16 while those who disbelieved,
denying Our signs and
the meeting in the hereafter
shall be brought forward
for punishment.

17 So hymn the glory of God
when you reach evening and rise at
    dawn

18 —praise be to Him throughout
the heavens and earth—
and in your late afternoons
as well as your midday hour.°

19 He brings the living from
the dead, and the dead from
the living, and brings the earth
to life after its death. Likewise,
you shall be brought back
[to life after death].

SECTION 3

20 Among His signs is that
    He created you from dust, then,
    see, you became humans,
    scattered wide.

21 And among His signs is that
    He created partners for you
    from among yourselves,
    to live serenely with them;
    and He placed between you
    love and mercy.
    In this are signs
    for a discerning people.

22 And among His signs is
    the creation of the heavens
    and the earth, the diversity
    in your languages and colors.
    In this are signs
    for people who know.°

23 And among His signs
    is that you sleep by night and
    seek His bounty by day.
    In this are signs
    for people who hear.

24 Among His signs—
    He shows you the lightning,
    that engenders fear and hope, and
    he sends down rain from the sky
    bringing life to the earth
    after its death.
    In this are signs
    for people who reason.

25 Among His signs is that
    the heaven and the earth
    stand by His command, then
    once He calls you—see,
    you shall come forward.

26 To Him belong
    all in the heavens
    and on the earth—
    and all obey Him.

27 He originates creation,
    then renews it;
    this is most easy for Him,
    He is beyond analogy
    in the heavens and the earth,
    for he is Almighty, All Wise.

SECTION 4

28 He coins for you this analogy
    from your own lives: Do you make
    your slaves your partners, with
    equal part in what we gave you?
    Do you fear them as you fear
    one another? This is how
    We clarify Our signs°
    for a people who reason.

29 Yet the wrongdoers follow
    their own desires, without
        knowledge.
    And who will guide those
    whom God allows to stray?
    They shall have none to help them.

30 So set your sights, upright,
toward the true faith,° the nature°
from which God created
    humankind.
No change can there be
in God's creation.
This is the upright faith,
but most of humankind don't know.

31 Turn to Him, and
be mindful of Him;
be steadfast in prayer,
and don't be one of those
who join other gods with God,

32 nor those who sunder
their religion, becoming sects,
each party exulting
in what it has.

33 When calamity strikes people,
they call upon their Lord, turning
to Him. Then, when he lets them
savor His mercy, some of them
join other gods with Him,

34 ungrateful for what
We have given them.
Enjoy yourselves, then—
for soon you shall know.

35 Did We reveal to them any
    authority,
sanctioning the partners
they join with God?

36 When We let people savor Our
    mercy,
they rejoice in it.
But if some evil befalls them
—wrought by their own hands—
see how they despair.

37 Don't they see that God
enlarges or restricts provision
for whom He will? In this
are signs for people who believe.

38 So give what is due
to relatives, the poor,
and the traveler.
This is better for those
who seek the Face of God—
it is they who shall flourish.

39 What you lend with usury
to reap interest through
the wealth of others
shall reap no interest with God.
But what you give in charity,
seeking the Face of God,
shall be multiplied.

40 It is God Who created you,
then gave you sustenance;
He will bring you to death, then
    to life.
Can any of the gods you join
    with Him
do any of these things? Glory be
    to Him,
and exalted is He over
the gods they join with Him.

SECTION 5

41 Corruption has surfaced
on land and sea, through
the hands of humankind,
and He will let them taste the [fruits]
of some of their deeds,
that they might return [to Him].

42 Say, "Travel through the earth
and observe what was the end
of those before you.
Most of them joined
other gods with God."

43 So direct your face
toward the steadfast faith,
before there comes from God
a day that cannot be averted.
On that day, humankind
will be divided—

44 as for those who disbelieved—
their disbelief will stand against them;
while those who did good deeds
make provision for themselves,

45 so that out of His bounty
He may reward those
who believed and did good deeds
for He does not love
those who disbelieve.

46 Among His signs is that
He sends the winds, bearing joyous
      news,
so you might savor His mercy.

Your ships sail by His leave,
so you may seek His bounty,
and be grateful.

47 And We sent, before you,
messengers to their own peoples,
coming to them with clear proofs.
We requited those who sinned—
It is always Our province
to help those who believe.

48 It is God Who sends
the winds that raise up the clouds,
which He spreads across the sky
as He will, bursting them
into fragments; you see the rain
pouring from within their midst,
and when he makes it fall
upon His servants, as He will—
see how they rejoice,

49 though before—before
it was sent down upon them—
they were in despair.

50 Consider then the traces
of God's mercy, how He gives life
to the earth after its death.
He is Restorer of life to the dead,
and He has Power over all things.

51 Yet, if We sent a [scorching] wind
so they saw their crops all yellowed,
they would still disbelieve.°

52 Prophet, you cannot
make the dead hear, nor can you

make the deaf hear your call
when they turn their backs to you,

53 nor can you guide the blind
from their straying. The only ones
you can make hear are those
who believe in Our signs,
those who submit to Our will.°

SECTION 6

54 It is God Who
created you weak,
then gave you strength,
then made you weak again
with gray hair.
He creates what He will,
for He is All Knowing,
All Powerful.

55 On the day when the hour comes,
the sinners will swear that they
lingered but an hour [on earth]—
they were always deluded like this.

56 Those given knowledge and faith
will say, "Actually, you lingered,
by God's decree until
the day of resurrection.

The day of resurrection is *now*,
but you—you did not know."

57 On that day
the wrongdoers' excuses
won't help them,
nor can they beg
to make amends.

58 We have contrived in this Qur'an,
every kind of parable for
    humankind—
yet if you bring them a sign,
the unbelievers declare,
"You are merely falsifiers."

59 In this way God sets a seal
on the hearts of those who don't
    know.

60 So, be patient. God's promise
is true. And do not let those
who lack all conviction
lighten your resolve.

Luqman (*Luqman*)

A pre-Islamic wise man or sage, Luqman appears only here in the Qur'an. The heart of this middle or late Meccan sura of 34 verses is the section of advice given by Luqman to his son, featured in vv. 12–19.

In the Name of God, the All Merciful, Ever Merciful

SECTION I

1 *Alif Lam Mim.*°

2 These are verses
of the wise Book,

3 a guide and mercy
for those who do good,

4 who are steadfast in prayer,
give in charity, and
are certain of the hereafter.

5 It is they who are rightly
guided by their Lord—
they who will succeed.

6 But among the people, there's a person
who invests in idle tales°—without
knowledge—
to mislead people, away from God's
path,
seeking to mock it. Shameful torment awaits him.

7 When Our signs are recited to him,
he turns away in pride, as if he hadn't
heard them, as if his ears
were weighed down in deafness.°
Warn him, then, of painful torment.

8 Those who believe and do good deeds,
shall enter gardens of bliss,

9 to live there forever.
God's promise is true—
He is Almighty, All Wise.

10 He created the heavens [raised up]
with no visible supports;
He set upon the earth firm
mountains
so it would not quake beneath you;
He spread throughout it animals
of all kinds; and We sent down
rain from the sky, so that fine plants
of all kinds might bloom in pairs.

11 All of this is God's creation;
now show Me what those other gods
have created—the wrongdoers
are clearly mistaken.

SECTION 2

12 We gave Luqman wisdom:
"Be thankful to God—
whoever gives thanks,
does so for his own sake,
and as for the thankless—
[they should know that] God
is Self-Sufficient, Praiseworthy."

13 Luqman cautioned his son,
"My son, don't worship any
but God, for joining gods
with the One God
is a great wrong."

14 And We commanded people
to honor their parents;
their mothers bore them,
strain upon strain, weaning them
after two years—Be thankful, then,
to Me and to your parents,
for your destination ends with Me.

15 But if your parents urge you
to join other gods with Me
—about whom you know nothing—
don't obey them. However,
be kind companions to them
in this world while following
the path of those who turn to Me—
to Me you shall return,
and I shall inform you
of all you have done.

16 "My son," said Luqman,
"if even the slightest thing

—like a mustard seed°—
were hidden in a rock, or
anywhere in the heavens or earth,
God would bring it into sight,
for He is Subtle, All Aware.

17 "My son, be steadfast in prayer,
commend what is right,
and forbid what is wrong;
endure with patience
whatever befalls you—
this is the true resolve
in all affairs.

18 "And don't shun people,
turning your face away from them;
nor walk haughtily upon the earth,
for God does not like
the proud and boastful.

19 "Walk in a modest way,°
and lower your voice,
for the harshest of voices
is the braying of an ass."°

SECTION 3

20 Don't you see that God
has subdued [to your use]
all that is in the heavens,
and all that is on the earth,
that He has multiplied
His blessings upon you,
both seen and unseen?
Yet some people dispute over God,
without knowledge, or guidance,
or recourse to an illuminating book.°

21 And when they are told,
"Follow what God has revealed,"
they say, "No. We'll follow
the ways of our fathers."°
Really? Even if Satan
were beckoning them to the
torment of blazing fire?

22 Whoever submits wholly to God,
and does good, has surely grasped
the securest handhold—
for all affairs are concluded in God.

23 And don't be grieved
by the disbelief of those
who deny: to Us they shall return,
and We shall inform them
of all that they did.
God is Aware of all
that their hearts contain.

24 We grant them enjoyment
for a while, but then
We shall force them
into harsh torment.

25 If you ask them who created
the heavens and the earth,
they will say, "God."
Say, "Praise be to God."
Yet most of them don't know.

26 To God belongs all
that is in the heavens and earth.
God is Self-Sufficient, Praiseworthy.

27 If all the trees on earth
were pens, and the seas were ink,
with seven more seas beyond,
still the Word° of God
would not be exhausted.
God is Almighty, All Wise.

28 Nor was the creation
and resurrection of you all
any more for Him
than that of a single soul.
God is All Hearing, All Seeing.

29 Do you not see how
God fades night into day,
and day into night,
and holds sway over sun
and moon, each sailing in
its own domain for its
ordained term?
And that God is Aware
of all that you do?

30 All of this is because
God is the Truth, and those
they invoke besides Him
are false; and because God
is Most High, Most Great.

SECTION 4

31 Do you not see that
ships sail upon the sea
by God's grace, that He might
show you His signs?
In this are signs for all

who are patient, and all
who are grateful.

32 When a towering wave hangs
over them, like a darkened vault,
they call upon God, with sincere
faith in Him; but once We deliver
them safely on land, some begin
to waver. Only the treacherous
and thankless dispute Our signs.

33 Humankind, be mindful
of your Lord, and fearful
of a day when no father
can help his son in anything,
nor any son his father.

The promise of God is true,
so don't let the life of this world
deceive you, nor let the deceiver
deceive you about God.

34 God alone has knowledge
of the hour. It is He
Who sends down rain, and He
Who knows what is closed within
the womb. No soul knows what
it will reap tomorrow,
nor does any soul know
in which land it will die.
God is All Knowing,
All Aware.

SURA 32

Prostration (*Al-Sajda*)

A late Meccan sura of 30 verses, it extols the act of prostration (v. 15), which characterizes the believers, those who fall down, prostrate, in praise of God when they "are reminded of" His verses.

In the Name of God, the All Merciful, Ever Merciful

SECTION I

1 *Alif Lam Mim.*°

2 This is the revelation
of the Book—free of doubt—
from the Lord of the universe.

3 Yet they ask, "Has he forged it?"
No—it is the truth from your Lord,
so you might warn a people
warned by none before you,°
so they might be guided.

4 It is God Who created
the heavens and the earth,
and all between them, in six days,

then set Himself upon the throne.
You have no protector or intercessor
beside Him—so will you not heed?

5   He oversees all things
from heaven to earth.
All things shall rise to Him,
on a day which spans
a thousand years in your counting.

6   This is the Knower
of the unseen and seen—
the Almighty, Ever Merciful,

7   He Who perfected in its excellence
each thing that He created. He
    began
the creation of humankind from
    clay,

8   then made its offspring
from the essence of a lowly fluid.

9   He then proportioned it,
and breathed into it His Spirit;
and He gave you
hearing, seeing, and feeling°—
though little do you give thanks.

10 And they say, "When we
are buried beneath the earth,
will we be created anew?"
Yes, the disbelievers
deny the meeting with their Lord.

11 Say, "The angel of death
in charge of you shall take you;

then, you shall be returned
to your Lord."

SECTION 2

12 If only you could see how
the sinners will hang their heads
before their Lord, saying, "Our Lord,
we have seen and we have heard.
So send us back, and we will do
good deeds—for now we are certain."

13 Had We wished, We could have
given guidance to each soul.
But My words will come true,
"I will fill up hell with jinn
and humans—all together.

14 "Taste, then—for you forgot
the meeting on this day of yours,
and We too will forget you—
taste the eternal punishment
for what you have done."

15 Only those people believe
in Our verses who, when
they are reminded of them,
fall down, prostrate, and
glorify their Lord with praise—
for they are not too proud.

16 They° forsake their beds
to call upon their Lord, in fear and
in hope; and they spend in charity
from what we have given them.

17 Nobody knows
what joy and comfort
lie hidden for them in reward
for what they have done.

18 Is a person who believes
like a person who is defiant?
They are not the same.

19 Those who believe and do good
deeds,
shall have gardens as their home,
a reward for what they have done.

20 As for those who still disobey,
their home shall be the fire.
Whenever they wish to escape it,
they shall be brought back to it,
and told, "Taste the torment of fire—
which you always denied."

21 And We shall make them taste
the nearer torment [of this life]
before the ultimate torment, so they
might return [to the straight path].

22 Who does more wrong
than those who turn away
when the verses of their Lord
are recited to them?
We shall requite the sinners.

SECTION 3

23 We gave the Book to Moses,
so be in no doubt, Prophet,
about receiving it—

We made it a guide
for the children of Israel.

24 We made leaders among them,
giving guidance by Our command,
for they were patient,
and assured of Our signs.

25 Your Lord will judge between them
on the day of resurrection
in the things they dispute.

26 Will they not learn from
the number of generations
We destroyed before them,
in whose homes they now tread?
In this are signs—
so will they not listen?

27 And do they not see that
We drive the rain to parched soil,
and bring from it crops from which
they and their livestock eat?
So will they not see?

28 And they say,
"When will this verdict come,
if you are speaking the truth?"

29 Say, "On the day of the verdict,
it will not profit the disbelievers
to then believe—for then
they will be granted no respite."

30 So turn away from them, and wait—
they too are waiting.

SURA 33

The Allied Forces (*Al-Ahzab*)

A Medinan sura, this takes its name from the forces who opposed Muhammad and his followers at the Battle of the Trench, which took place in 627, five years after the *hijra*, the exodus from Mecca to Medina. Elements of that encounter occupy vv. 9–27 while the remainder of its 73 verses deal with kinship and covenant (vv. 4–8) and guidelines for regulating behavior in general but also among Muhammad's wives (vv. 28–60). Perhaps the most memorable verse occurs toward the end, in v. 72, when the burden of moral trust is refused by all except humankind who "bore it, being unjust and ignorant."

In the Name of God, the All Merciful, Ever Merciful

SECTION I

1 Prophet, be mindful
of God, and do not heed
the unbelievers and hypocrites.
God is All Knowing, All Wise.

2 Rather, follow what is
revealed to you from your Lord—
God is Aware of all that you do.

3 And trust in God,
for God suffices as Guardian.

4 God has not made two hearts
within any man;
nor has He made your wives
—whom you liken
to your mothers°—
your actual mothers;
nor has He made
your adopted sons your actual sons.°

Such is the talk that comes
out of your mouths.
But God speaks the truth,
and He guides to the path.

5 Name [your adopted sons]
after their fathers; this is more just
in the sight of God. But if
you do not know their fathers,
[treat them as] your brothers
in religion, as relatives.°
There is no blame on you
if you err in this—only for
what your hearts intend.
For God is Forgiving,
Ever Merciful.

6 The Prophet is closer to believers
than they are to themselves,
and his wives are their mothers.
And blood relatives are closer,
in God's decree, than other believers

and emigrants, though you should
still treat your friends with kindness.°
This is written in the Book.

7 And We took a pledge
from the prophets, as from you,
from Noah, Abraham, Moses,
and Jesus, son of Mary—
We took from them a solemn pledge:

8 God will question the truthful
about their truthfulness,
and has prepared for disbelievers
a painful punishment.

SECTION 2

9 You who believe, remember
God's favor to you when legions
descended upon you°—We sent
against them a mighty wind
and legions beyond your seeing.
For God Sees all that you do.

10 When they came upon you
from above you and below,
your eyes were frantic [with fear],
your hearts swelled into
your throats, and you started
to harbor doubts about God.

11 There the believers were tested
and shaken—severely.

12 The hypocrites and the sick in heart
said, "God and His messenger
promised us nothing but delusion."

13 A party of them urged,
"People of Yathrib,° you cannot
withstand the onslaught, so retreat!"
And a group of them asked
the Prophet's permission to retreat,
saying, "Our homes lie exposed"
—though they were not—
they merely wanted to flee.

14 Had the city been
breached from all sides,
had they been urged to rebel,
they would have done so
with barely a qualm.

15 Yet they had already pledged
to God not to turn their backs—
one is always answerable
for a pledge to God.

16 Prophet, tell them,
"Fleeing won't help you.
Even if you flee from death
or killing, you'll be granted
but a brief respite."

17 Say, "Who can shield you
from God whether He intends
ill for you or mercy?"
Nor will they find, besides God,
any protector or helper.

18 God knows those among you
who hold others back,
and those who say to their brothers
"Come and join us," those who
barely come out to fight,

19 begrudging you [their help].
Yet, when fear overcomes them,
you'll see them looking to you,
their eyes rolling, as if shadowed
by death. And once fear leaves them
they abuse you sharply with their
tongues,
begrudging in doing good.
These are the ones who never
believe,
hence God makes vain their deeds—
that is always easy for God.

20 They think the allied forces°
have not gone; and if those allies
should come, they would wish
they were nomads
among the Bedouin Arabs,
asking for news of you° [from afar].
Even if they were with you,
they would hardly fight.

SECTION 3

21 You have an excellent example
in the messenger of God—
for those who repose their hope
in God and the last day,
and remember Him often.

22 When they saw the allied forces,
the believers said, "This is what God
and His messenger promised;
what God and His messenger
said was true," and it only increased
their faith and submission to God.

23 Among the believers
are men who remained true
to their covenant with God;
and among them are those
who fulfilled their vow;° also
among them are those who still
wait—
who have not reformed at all.

24 Accordingly, God will reward
the truthful for remaining truthful,
and punish the hypocrites, if He
will,
or turn to them, relenting.
God is Forgiving, Ever Merciful.

25 God repulsed the disbelievers
in their rage,° and they made no
gain.
God suffices for the believers in war,
for God is Powerful, Almighty.

26 He cast down from their strongholds
the people of the Book who helped
them
and He cast terror into their hearts.
A group of them you slew,
and another you took captive;

27 and He made you heirs
to their land, their homes,
and their possessions—
a land where you
had not set foot before—
for God has Power over all things.

SECTION 4

28 Prophet, say to your wives,
    "If you yearn for the life
    of this world, and its ornament,
    then come, I will provide
    for you and release you
    with a handsome allowance.

29 "But if you yearn for God
    and His messenger,
    and the home of the hereafter,
    God has prepared a great reward
    for those of you who do good."

30 Wives of the Prophet,
    whoever among you
    commits obvious indecency
    shall be doubly punished—
    that is always easy for God.

31 Whoever among you
    obeys God and His messenger
    and does good works,
    We shall grant her a double
        reward—
    We have prepared
    a noble provision for her.

32 Wives of the Prophet, you
    are not like any other women.
    If you are mindful of God,
    do not be too soft in speech
    —or those sick in their hearts
    might be moved with desire—
    so speak with propriety.

33 Remain in your homes,
    and refrain from adorning
        yourselves
    in display, as in the former time
    of [pagan] ignorance.
    Be steadfast in prayer, give in
        charity,
    and obey God and His messenger.
    God wishes only to remove
    all abomination from you, people
    of the [Prophet's] household,
    and to perfect you in purity.

34 And remember what is
    recited in your homes
    from the verses of God
    and His Wisdom.
    God is Ever Subtle, All Aware.

SECTION 5

35 For men and women
    who submit to the will of God—
    believing men and women,
    obedient men and women,
    truthful men and women,
    patient men and women,
    men and women with humility,
    men and women who give in charity,
    who fast, who guard their chastity,
    who remember God often—
    for all of these God has prepared
    forgiveness and a great reward.

36 It is not fitting for
    any believing man or woman
    to claim choice in any matter

where God and His messenger
have ruled. For whoever disobeys
God and His messenger
has clearly gone astray.

37 When you said to the one
whom God and you had favored,
"Keep your wife, and be mindful
of God," you kept in your heart
what God would reveal.
You feared the people, but God
has a greater right to your fear.
So when Zayd ended his marriage
to her, with due procedure,
We gave his wife to you
so there would be no blame
on believers for marrying the wives
of their adopted sons once they have
ended their marriage with them,
with due procedure.
God's command will be fulfilled.°

38 There can be no blame
upon the Prophet in what
God has ruled for him.
This was God's way
with those who passed before
—for God's command is ordained—

39 and with those who convey
the message of God, who fear Him,
fearing none but God—
God suffices as Reckoner.

40 Muhammad is not father
to any among your men,
but is the messenger of God,

the seal of the prophets°—
God is Knower of all things.

SECTION 6

41 You who believe,
remember God often,

42 and glorify Him
morning and evening.

43 It is He Who bestows
blessings upon you, as do
His angels, to bring you
from darkness to the light,
for He is Ever Merciful
to the believers.

44 Their greeting on the day
they meet him will be "Peace."
And He has prepared for them
a noble reward.

45 Prophet, We have sent you
as a witness, a bearer of joyous
  news,
and one who gives warning;

46 as one who calls to God,
by His leave, as a lamp,
whose light shines.

47 So give the believers
joyous news that they
shall have from God
a great favor.

48 And don't heed the disbelievers
    and hypocrites. Ignore the harm
    they wrought, and trust in God,
    for God suffices as Guardian.

49 You who believe,
    when you marry believing women,
    then divorce them before touching
       them,
    you should impose no "waiting
       period"°
    but give them due provision
    and release them
    with a handsome allowance.

50 Prophet, We made lawful to you
    the wives whose bridal gift you paid,
    and those God gave you
    to own as captives;
    the daughters of your paternal
    uncles and aunts;
    the daughters of your maternal
    uncles and aunts, who emigrated
    with you; any believing woman
    who dedicates herself to the Prophet
    and whom he wishes to wed—this is
    for you only, not for other believers.
    We know precisely what we have
    made obligatory for them
    concerning their wives and those
    whom they own as captives—so that
    no blame will fall upon you.
    God is Forgiving, Ever Merciful.

51 You may defer [a wife's turn]
    and receive any of [your wives]
    as you wish. Nor will you be

at fault if you take one that you
had set aside. This is more likely
to comfort them, so they
will not be vexed, and will all be
content with what you give them.
For God knows what is in your
   hearts.
And God is All Knowing,
   Forbearing.

52 It is not lawful for you, Prophet,
    to marry more women after this,
    nor to exchange them for [other] wives,
    even though their beauty may allure
       you—
    except those you own as servants.
    God is Ever Watchful over all things.

SECTION 7

53 You who believe, do not enter
    the Prophet's apartments for a meal,
    awaiting its due time, without his
       leave.
    But when you are invited, enter,
    and when you have eaten, disperse,
    and don't stay to indulge in talk,
    for that would offend the Prophet,
    and he would refrain from asking
       you
    to leave. But God does not refrain
    from speaking the truth. And when
    you ask [his wives] for something,
    ask from behind a screen—
    that is purer for your hearts and
       theirs.
    It is not fitting for you

to offend the messenger of God,
or ever to marry his wives after him—
something gross in the sight of God.

54 Whether you reveal something
or conceal it—God Knows all things.

55 There is no blame
on the Prophet's wives [if
they appear before] their fathers,°
their sons, their brothers,
their brother's sons,
their sister's sons,
their women, or those they own.
[Wives of the Prophet]:
Be mindful of God,
for God is Witness to all things.

56 God and His angels
invoke blessings on the Prophet;
So, you who believe, you also
invoke blessings on him,
and meet him
with greetings of peace.

57 As for those who offend God
and His messenger—
God has renounced them
in this world and the hereafter,
and has prepared for them
a humiliating punishment.

58 As for those who unduly offend
believing men and women—
they bring upon themselves
calumny and flagrant sin.

SECTION 8

59 Prophet, tell your wives,
daughters, and believing women
to wrap their robes
about them in public;
this is most appropriate
so they will be known
and not open to offense.
God is Forgiving, Ever Merciful.

60 If the hypocrites,
the sick in heart,
and rumormongers in the city
don't desist,
We will rouse you against them
and they won't stay long in it
as your neighbors,

61 and will be cursed.
Wherever they are found,
they will be taken
and executed.

62 This was God's way
with those who passed before;
and you will find no change
in God's way.

63 People ask you about the hour.
Say, "Knowledge of that
lies with God alone."
And how could you know this?
Perhaps the hour draws near.

64 God has cursed the disbelievers,
and has prepared for them a blazing
fire,

65 where they shall stay forever;
    they shall find no protector,
    nor any helper.

66 That day, their faces
    will be turned around in the fire;
    they will say, "If only
    we had obeyed God
    and obeyed the messenger."

67 And they will say,
    "Our Lord, we in fact obeyed
    our chiefs and our great ones,
    and they led us astray
    from the path.

68 "Our Lord, double
    their punishment, and curse
    them with a great curse."

SECTION 9

69 You who believe,
    don't be like those
    who offended Moses,
    whom God absolved
    of their charges,
    and was honored
    in the sight of God.

70 You who believe,
    be mindful of God, and speak
    in a forthright manner,

71 that He might reform
    your deeds and forgive your sins.
    Whoever obeys God
    and His messenger
    has surely gained a great victory.

72 We offered the [burden
    of moral] trust
    to the heavens and the earth
    and the mountains, but
    they refused to bear it,
    fearing it.°
    Yet humankind bore it,
    being unjust and ignorant,

73 so God will punish
    hypocritical men and women,
    and idolatrous men and women,
    but God will turn in mercy to
    the believing men and women—
    for God is Forgiving, Ever Merciful.

Sheba (*Saba'*)

This late Meccan sura of 54 verses warns of judgment, death, and disaster, citing David and Solomon as forewarners, with the people of Sheba in Yemen their primary audience (vv. 15–21).

In the Name of God, the All Merciful, Ever Merciful

SECTION I

1 All praise be to God,
   to Whom belongs
   all that is the heavens and
   all that is on the earth;
   to Whom belongs
   all praise in the hereafter—
   He is All Wise, All Aware.

2 He knows all that goes into the
      earth
   and all that comes out of it,
   all that comes down from the sky
   and all that goes up to it—
   He is Ever Merciful, Forgiving.

3 The unbelievers say,
   "The hour shall never fall upon us."
   Tell them, "No! It will
   befall you—by my Lord,
   Knower of the unseen,
   Whom even an atom's weight
   cannot escape, in the heavens or
      earth,
   nor anything smaller or greater,
   for all is recorded in a clear Book

4 "so He might reward those who
      believe
   and do good deeds: they shall know
   forgiveness and a rich provision."

5 Those who strive against Our signs,
   trying to undermine them
   shall face painful torment.

6 Those who were granted knowledge
   of what your Lord revealed to you
   see that it is the truth,
   which guides to the path
   of the Almighty, the Praiseworthy.

7 The unbelievers say,
   "Shall we show you a man
   who tells you that when
   you are wholly decomposed,
   you'll be re-created anew?

8 "Has he invented a falsehood
   about God, or is he mad?"
   No—those who disbelieve
   in the hereafter
   shall face punishment,
   for they are far astray.

9 Don't they see what lies before them
and behind them, in heaven and earth?
If We willed, We could make the earth
swallow them, or fragments of sky
fall on them. In this is a sign
for every servant who turns to God.

SECTION 2

10 We graced David with Our favor,
"You mountains, hymn with David
Our praise, and you birds too!"
And we made iron pliable for him,

11 saying, "Make armor of chain mail,
measuring the links correctly,
and do righteous deeds,
for I See all that you do."

12 We subdued the wind to Solomon;
its morning journey took a month,
its evening course a month.
And We made to flow for him
a fountain of molten brass,
and some jinn worked for him
with their Lord's leave,
but if any turned from Our command,
We made them taste
the torment of blazing fire.

13 They worked to make him all
that he wanted: places of worship,
statues, basins large as cisterns,
and anchored cauldrons.
"Work, people of David, with
gratitude,
for few of my servants are grateful."

14 When We decreed Solomon's death,
nothing showed the jinn that he was
dead
except an earthworm gnawing at his
staff.
So, when he fell down, it was clear
to them—
had they known what is in the
unseen,
they would not have remained
in degrading torment [of this labor].

15 There was a sign for Sheba's people
in their own home—two gardens,
right and left: "Eat of what your Lord
has provided, and be thankful to
Him—
a good land and a Forgiving Lord."

16 But they turned away, so We sent
upon them a flood from the dam,°
replacing their two gardens
with two others bearing bitter fruit,
tamarisks, and a few lote-trees.

17 This is how We rewarded them,
for they were ungrateful—
and who but the ungrateful
would We reward like this?

18 Also, We placed between them
and the towns We had blessed,
other towns, clearly visible,
between which We placed easy
stages:
"Travel through them safely,
by night and by day."

19 But they said, "Our Lord,
lengthen the stages of our journeys,"°
and they wronged themselves.
So We made an exemplary tale
of them, scattering them into
        fragments.
In this are signs for all
who are patient and thankful.

20 Iblis proved his view of them
to be true,° for they followed him
—all but a group of believers—

21 though he would have had
no authority over them—
only so that We might show
who believes in the hereafter,
and who is in doubt over it,
for your Lord is Guardian
over all things.

SECTION 3

22 Say, "Call on those you claim
besides God—they don't control
even an atom's weight in either
the heavens or the earth; they hold
no share in either,
nor can any of them help Him.

23 "No intercession can help with Him
except by those He allows."
Once fear is driven from their hearts
they'll ask the intercessors,
"What did your Lord say?"
They'll answer, "The truth,
for He is Most High, Most Great."

24 Say, "Who gives you provision
from the heavens and the earth?"
Say, "It is God. And either we or you
are rightly guided, while [the other]
has clearly gone astray."

25 Say, "You won't be questioned
about the sins we committed,
nor will we be questioned
about what you did."

26 Say, "Our Lord shall gather us
together and shall decide justly
between us, for He is the Judge,°
the All Knowing."

27 Say, "Show me the gods
you have joined with Him—
no—He alone is God,
the Almighty, the Wise."

28 We sent you as a messenger
to all peoples, only to bring
joyous news as well as warning;
but most people won't understand.

29 They say, "When will this promise
come to pass,
if you are speaking the truth?"

30 Say, "Your meeting [with God]
is on a day
that you can't put back or forward—
even by one hour."

SECTION 4

31 The disbelievers say,
"We shall never believe this Qur'an
or what came before it."
If you could see the wrongdoers,
arrayed before their Lord,
flinging back rebukes on
    one another.
The oppressed will accuse
their oppressors, "If not for you,
we would have been believers."

32 The oppressors will reply
to the oppressed, "Was it we
who kept you from true guidance
after it had come to you?
No, *you* were sinners."

33 The oppressed will rejoin, "No,
it was your scheming, night and day,
urging° us not to believe in God
and to set up equals beside Him."
When they see the punishment,
they will feel inward remorse,
and We shall shackle the necks
of the disbelievers.
How should they be rewarded
except for what they did?

34 Whenever We sent someone
to warn a town, its wealthy people
would say, "We don't believe
in the message you're sent with."

35 And they would say,
"We have more wealth and children,
and we won't be punished."

36 Say, "My Lord enlarges provision
or restricts it for whom He will,
yet most people don't know."

SECTION 5

37 It is not your wealth or children
that will bring you close to Us,
only those who believe
and do good deeds—they shall reap
a double reward for their deeds
and high mansions, safe
    [in paradise].

38 Those who strive against Our signs,
trying to undermine them
shall be brought for punishment.

39 Say, "My Lord grants more or less
to whom He will of his servants;
and whatever you spend
[in His cause], He will restore,
for He is the Best of Providers."

40 One day He shall gather them
all together, and ask the angels,
"Were these the ones
who used to worship you?"

41 They will say, "Glory be to You—
You are our Protector, not they.
In fact, they worshipped the jinn,
and most believed in them."

42 And on this day,
none of you will have power
to help or harm the others,
and We shall say to the wrongdoers,
"Taste the torment of fire—
which you denied."

43 When Our clear signs
are recited to them, they sneer,
"This is just a man who wants
to bar you from what your fathers
worshipped," and they jeer,
"This is just a lie, concocted."
Even when the truth comes
    their way,
unbelievers say, "This is plain magic"

44 —though We had not given them
any books to study,
nor sent anyone to warn them.

45 Those before them also denied,
and these people have achieved
not a tenth of what We gave *them*.
When they denied My messengers,
[see] how I rejected them!

SECTION 6

46 Say, "I counsel you
on one thing only: stand
    before God,
in pairs or individually, and reflect:
your companion is not possessed;
he simply warns you
of impending, severe torment."

47 Say, "I ask of no reward
from you—it is all for you.
My only reward is from God,
for He is Witness to all things."

48 Say, "My Lord casts down
the truth before you—
Knower of the unseen."

49 Say, "The truth has come,
and falsehood can neither
originate nor resurrect a thing."

50 Say, "If I am astray, it is to my loss,
but if I am rightly guided,
it is by what my Lord reveals to me.
He is All Hearing, Ever Near."

51 If you could see how terrified
they will be—there shall be no escape,
when they are seized from a
    nearby place.°

52 And they will say,
"We believe in it now,"
but how can they attain it
from such a distant place,°

53 since they denied it before
and conjectured about the unseen
from that distant place?

54 A barrier shall be imposed
between them and their desires,
as was done with their kind before,
for they have always been
deep in grave doubt.°

The Originator (*Fatir*)

Another late Meccan sura, this stresses human moral responsibility in response to recognition of, and gratitude for, creation (hence the title). The Book of God is extolled as the resource and reminder for both rewards and punishments, with the latter underscored as the outcome for evil schemers in the final verses (vv. 42–45).

In the Name of God, the All Merciful, Ever Merciful

SECTION I

1 All praise be to God, Originator
of the heavens and the earth, Maker
of the angels, messengers with wings,
two, three, or four pairs.
He adds to His creation
   what He will;
He has Power over all things.

2 Whatever mercy God bestows
on humankind, none can withhold;
and what He withholds,
none can disburse,
for He is Almighty, All Wise.

3 Humankind, call to mind
God's favor to you—
is there a creator besides God
who provides for you
from the heavens or the earth?
There is no god but Him—
so how can you be deluded?

4 And if they deny you,
messengers before you
were likewise denied.
All matters fall back to God
for resolution.

5 People, God's promise is true,
so never let the life of this world
deceive you, nor let the deceiver
deceive you about God.

6 Satan is your enemy,
so treat him as one.
He calls his supporters—
though only to be inmates
of the blazing fire.

7 Those who disbelieve
shall face severe torment;
but those who believe
and do good deeds shall see
forgiveness and a rich reward.

SECTION 2

8 What of the person whose bad deed
   seems alluring, good to them?
   God leaves to stray whom He will
   and He guides whom He will.
   Prophet, don't weigh down your soul
   with remorse for them,
   for God Knows all that they do.

9 It is God Who sends the winds
   to stir up the clouds, and
   We drive them to dead land
   to bring life to the earth after
      its death.
   The resurrection will be just like this.

10 Whoever seeks honor—[know that]
   all honor belongs to God. To Him
   rises up all the good that is spoken°
   and He raises up each good deed.
   But those who scheme evil things
   shall face severe torment
   and their schemes shall perish.

11 God created you from dust,
   then a drop of sperm, then made you
   into pairs. No female conceives
   or gives birth without His knowing.
   No life is lengthened or shortened
   that is not recorded in the Book.
   All this is easy for God.

12 The two seas are not alike,
   one fresh, sweet, pleasing to drink,
   the other brinish and bitter.
   Yet from each you eat fresh meat,

and retrieve gems to wear;
and you see ships streaming
through the seas, that you
   might seek
His bounty—and be grateful.

13 He fades night into day
   and day into night, and subdues
   sun and moon, each sailing
   in its own orbit for a fixed term.
   This is God, your Lord, to Whom
   belongs all dominion. And the gods
   on whom you call besides Him
   control nothing—not even
   the membrane of a date seed.

14 If you call them,
   they don't hear your call,
   and if they heard it,
   they would not answer you.
   On the day of resurrection,
   they'll deny your association
   of them with God;
   and none can better inform you
   than the One who is All Aware.

SECTION 3

15 Humankind, it is you
      who need God,
   but God is He Who needs no one,
   He alone is Praiseworthy.

16 If He wishes, He can efface you,
      and bring in a new creation—

17 and that would not be hard for God.

18 No soul can bear another's burden°
and if a soul with a heavy burden
should call on another to
     bear its load,
none of its burden can be taken,
even by one who is close in blood.
You can only warn those
who fear their Lord,
     though unseen,°
and are steadfast in prayer.
Those who purify themselves
do so for their own soul—
the final journey is to God.

19 The blind and the seeing
are not alike;

20 nor are the depths
of darkness and the light;

21 nor are the cool shade
and the heat of the sun;

22 nor alike are the living and the dead.
God can make whom He will hear,
but you cannot make
those in their graves hear.

23 You are here merely to warn.

24 We have sent you with the truth,
to give joyous news and to warn
no nation was without warning.°

25 If they deny you,
     earlier peoples did the same—
messengers came to them

with clear signs, scriptures,
and an illuminating Book.

26 In the end, I seized the disbelievers—
how dreadful was my reprimand!

SECTION 4

27 Don't you see how God
sends down rain from the sky,
with which We raise fruit
in varying colors?
And the mountains bear tracts
of red and white,
in varied hues, and deep black.

28 Likewise, people, wild beasts,
and livestock are in varying colors.
Only those of His servants
with knowledge truly fear God—
God is Almighty, Forgiving.

29 Those who recite the Book of God,
are steadfast in prayer, and spend
     in charity
from what we give them, secretly
     and openly—
can hope for a commerce that will
     never fail.

30 For He will reward them in full
and give even more from His grace;
He is Forgiving, Appreciating.

31 What was revealed to you
from the Book was truth,
confirming what came before it;

God is All Aware,
Seeing everything about
    His servants.

32 We gave the Book as a legacy
to Our servants whom We favored.
Some of them wrong their
    own souls,
some are moderate, and others
by God's leave are foremost
in good deeds—the greatest grace.

33 They shall enter eternal gardens,
adorned there with bracelets of gold,
and pearls, in robes of silk.

34 And they will say, "Praise be to God,
Who removed our sorrow.
Our Lord is Forgiving,
    Appreciating,"

35 "Who, in His grace, settled us
in a lasting home, where no fatigue
or weariness shall fall upon us."

36 But those who disbelieve
shall know the fire of hell,
where no death is decreed for them,
nor relief from its torment.
This is how We reward
every disbeliever.

37 There, they will cry out,
"Our Lord, let us out.
We'll do good deeds—
not those we did before."
"Did We not give you life

long enough, for those willing
to be heedful, to be warned?°
And someone did come to warn you.
So taste [the reward]—there is none
to help the wrongdoers."

SECTION 5

38 God Knows all that is unseen
in the heavens and the earth;
He Knows all that lies
in human hearts.

39 It is He who made you
regents on the earth.°
The ungrateful will pay
for their ingratitude;°
it adds only to their odium
in the sight of their Lord,
and to their loss.

40 Say, "Have you seen the gods
you invoke besides God?
Show me what they've created
on the earth.
Or, do they have a share
in the heavens?
Or, have We given them a Book,
on which they can ground
clear proofs?
No—the wrongdoers promise
one another
nothing but delusion."

41 It is God Who keeps
the heavens and earth
in their ceaseless being;

and if they should cease,
none beyond Him could stop this.
He is Forbearing, Most Forgiving.

42 Swearing by God the strongest
of their oaths, they claimed that
if someone came to warn them,
they would be more rightly guided
than other nations.
Yet when someone did come,
it only increased their aversion

43 because of their pride on earth
and their evil scheming.
But their scheming shall
    confound *them*.
Do they expect anything
But the fate of earlier peoples?
You will never find any change
or variation in God's way.

44 Have they not traveled
through the land and seen
the fate of those before them—
though they were more powerful?
God is not to be frustrated
by anything in the heavens
or on the earth—
He is All Knowing, All Powerful.

45 If God took people to task
for the deeds they earned,
he would not leave any creature
on the face of the earth.
But He gives them respite
for a fixed term,
and when that term expires
[they will know that]
He Sees everything
about His servants.

Ya Sin (*Ya Sin*)

A middle Meccan sura, this takes its name from the initial and perplexing letters that mark it, as they do twenty-eight other suras. After the initial sura, "The Opening," it is perhaps the most liturgically important sura in the entire Qur'an. With its accent on the afterlife in the last part (vv. 51–83), it provides the fitting recitation for someone who has died, and its verses are often spontaneously recited by a devout Muslim on hearing of another's demise.

In the Name of God, the All Merciful, Ever Merciful

SECTION 1

1 *Ya Sin.*°

2 By the wise Qur'an,

3 you, Prophet, are truly
   one of the messengers

4 on a straight path.

5 It is a revelation sent down from
   the Almighty, the Ever Merciful,

6 that you might warn a people
   whose forefathers had no warning,
   who therefore are heedless.

7 Sentence has been passed
   on most of them,
   for they won't believe—

8 We placed yokes
   around their necks,
   drawn up to their chins,
   forcing up their heads,

9 and We placed a barrier
   before them and behind them,
   and shrouded them so
   they cannot see.

10 It's the same to them
   whether you warn them or not—
   they won't believe.

11 You can warn only those
   who follow the message and fear
   the All Merciful, though unseen.°
   So give joyous news to them,
   of forgiveness and a noble reward.

12 We bring the dead back to life,
   and We transcribe all the deeds
   they send before them
   and all they leave behind,
   and We have accounted all things
   in a clear record.

13 Coin for them a parable,
   of a people to whose town
   messengers came.

SECTION 2

14 When We sent two messengers°
   to them, they denied them both.
   So We reinforced them with a third,
   and they declared,
   "We have been sent
   as messengers to you."

15 The people said,
   "You're merely humans like us,
   and the All Merciful
   has not sent anything.
   You are just lying."

16 They said, "Our Lord knows
   that we have been sent
   as messengers to you."

17 "And our task is only
   to convey [the message] clearly."

18 The people retorted,
   "We think you're an evil omen.
   If you don't desist, we'll stone you
   and subject you to painful torment."°

19 They replied, "Your evil omen
   is within yourselves. [Do
        you say this]
   because you have been reminded?
   No—you people are given to excess."

20 A man came running from
   the outskirts of the city, saying,
   "My people, follow the messengers.

21 "Follow those
   who ask of you no reward,
   and who are rightly guided.

22 "Why should I not worship Him
   Who created me? To Him
   you will be returned.

23 "Should I take other gods
   besides Him? If the All Merciful
   intended harm for me,
   their intercession could not
   help in any way, nor
   could they save me.

24 "I would clearly be wrong.

25 "I believe in your Lord;
   so hear me."

26 He was told, "Enter the garden."°
   He said, "If only my people knew

27 "how my Lord has forgiven me
   and has set me among those
   held in honor."

28 We did not send down,
   after him, any hosts from heaven
   against his people,
   nor would We deign to—

29 there was but a single blast,
   and they were gone.

30 Alas, for My servants—
   no messenger came to them
   whom they did not mock.

31 Don't they see how many
   generations before them
        We destroyed,
   so none would come back to them?

32 And every one, all together,
   will be brought before Us.

SECTION 3

33 A sign for them
   is the dead earth:
   We bring it to life,
   and bring from it
   grain which they eat.

34 And We placed upon it gardens,
with palm groves and grapevines,
We made springs burst forth there,

35 so they might eat of its fruit,
which their hands did not make;
will they not, then, be grateful?

36 Glory be to Him Who
created in pairs
all that the earth yields,
and their own selves,
and also things of which
they are unaware.

37 And a sign for them is the night—
we strip away from it the light of day
so they are left in darkness,

38 and the sun, coursing
through her appointed path
by decree of the Almighty,
the All Knowing,

39 and the moon, for whom
We ordained phases, so it returns,
curved like a dried, date stalk of old.

40 The sun may not outrun the moon,
nor the night outstrip the day—
each glides in its own orbit.

41 And a sign for them
is that We bore their offspring
in the loaded ark,

42 and We have created for them
such vessels in which they sail.°

43 If We wished, We could
drown them, and they would
have no helper,
nor would they be saved,

44 except by Our mercy,
for a fleeting reprieve.

45 When they are told,
"Have fear of what lies before you
and what lies behind you,
that you might be shown mercy,"

46 they turn away from every sign
that comes to them from their Lord;°

47 and when they are told,
"Spend in charity from what God
has given you," those
    who disbelieve
say to those who believe,
"Should we feed those whom
God could have fed, had
    He willed?
You are clearly wrong."

48 They say, "When will this promise
[of resurrection] come to pass,
if you are speaking the truth?"

49 But they wait [unaware]
only for a single blast,
which will seize them
while they dispute.

50 They won't be able
    to disburse any bequest,
    or return to their own people.

SECTION 4

51 The trumpet shall be sounded,
    and behold, how they will hasten
    from their graves to their Lord.

52 They will say, "Alas for us!
    Who has raised us from our place
    of sleep?" A voice will answer,°
    "This is what the All Merciful
        promised:
    the messengers spoke the truth."

53 It will be but a single blast,
    then they shall all
    be brought before Us.

54 On that day, no soul
    shall be wronged in any way,
    and you shall be requited
    only for what you have done.

55 On that day,
    the people of the garden
    shall be gladly occupied,

56 they and their spouses,
    in the shade,
    reclining on couches.

57 There, they shall have fruit,
    and all that they ask for.

58 "Peace"—the word [of welcome]
    from a Lord Ever Merciful.

59 It will be said, "This day,
    stand apart, you sinners."

60 "Children of Adam,
    did I not enjoin you
    not to worship Satan,
    —for he is your open enemy—

61 "and to worship Me?
    —this is a straight path.

62 "But he led astray
    a great many of you—
    did you not use reason?

63 "This is hell,°
    which you were promised.

64 "Burn in it, this day,
    for you went on disbelieving."

65 This day, We shall seal
    their mouths; but their hands
    shall speak to Us, and their feet
    shall bear witness to what they reaped.

66 Had We wished, We could
    have extinguished their sight,
    then they would grope to find
    the path, but how should they see it?

67 Had We wished, We could
    have transfixed them in their place,
    unable to move forward or go back.

SECTION 5

68 To whomever We grant long life,
    We reverse their faculties—
    will they not, then, use reason?

69 We have not taught poetry°
    to the Prophet, nor is it fitting for him.
    This is nothing other than a reminder
    and a clear Qur'an,

70 so that those who are living
    might be warned, and the Word
    can be vindicated
    against those who disbelieve.

71 Don't they see that We created for them
    —among the things that Our hands
        have made—
    livestock, which they own,

72 and which We made tame for them,
    some to ride and others to eat?

73 And they yield further uses,
    and give drink.
    So won't they be thankful?

74 Yet they still take
    other gods beside God,
    hoping they might be helped.

75 Those gods have no power
    to save them, even if they were
    an army assembled.°

76 So do not be grieved, Prophet,
    by what they say—

We know all that they conceal
and all that they reveal.

77 Do human beings not see
    that it is We who created them
    from a drop of semen? Yet, see,
    they are openly adversarial°

78 and coin allegories about Us,
    forgetting their own creation,
    asking, "Who can bring life
    to bones that have decomposed?"

79 Say, "He will bring life to them
    Who first composed them,
    for He Knows every creation.

80 "It is He who made fire
    for you from the green tree,
    and see, you light from it
    your own fires."

81 Is He Who created the heavens and
        earth
    not able to create the like of human
        beings?
    Of course—for He is the Creator,
    the All Knowing.

82 When He intends something,
    His only command is to say to it:
    "Be," and it is.

83 So glory be to Him
    in Whose hand is dominion
    over all things; and to Him
    you will be returned.

Arrayed in Ranks (*Al-Saffat*)

An early Meccan sura, its title appears to come from the initial verse, then confirmed by later verses (vv. 164–66), presupposed to be ranks of angels. It begins by extolling the awesome creative power of God, then warns of the disparate fates awaiting believers and disbelievers. Prophets from Noah to Jonah are lauded, while any link of God with daughters or with jinn is rejected (vv. 149–59). The final verses extol God, Lord of the universe (vv. 180–82).

In the Name of God, the All Merciful, Ever Merciful

SECTION I

1 By those arrayed in ranks,°

2 those who cry out a warning,

3 reciting a reminder—

4 your God is One,

5 Lord of the heavens, of the earth,
and all that lies between,
Lord of every place
where the sun rises.°

6 We have graced
the lower heaven
with stars

7 to guard against
every rebellious devil,

8 to bar them from hearing
the highest assembly [of angels];
they are pelted from every side,

9 repelled; and they shall face
lasting torment.

10 Any who eavesdrops, snatching
an overheard fragment,
shall be pursued by a piercing flame.

11 So, Prophet, ask the disbelievers,
are they more difficult to create
than the other things We have created?
We created them from clinging clay.

12 How you marvel [at God's creation],
while they mock,

13 and when reminded,
they do not take heed;

14 and when they see a sign,
they mock it,

15 saying, "This is nothing
   but obvious magic.

16 "When we die, when
   we are dust and bones,
   shall we then
   be raised up again,

17 "with our forefathers of old?"

18 Say, "Yes, indeed,
   and you shall be brought low."

19 There will be a single cry,°
   and behold, they will see,

20 and they will say, "Alas for us!
   This is the day of reckoning."

21 A voice will say,°
   "This is the day of decision,
   which you denied.

SECTION 2

22 "Gather all the wrongdoers
   and their spouses, together
   with what they worshipped

23 besides God, and guide them
   to the path of the blazing fire,°

24 and stop them, to be questioned,

25 'What is wrong with you,
   why do you not help one another?'"

26 On that day, they shall indeed
   submit to the will of God.°

27 And they will turn to
   one another, questioning,

28 "It was you who came to us,
   with authority, [urging us to evil]."°

29 The others will rejoin, "No,
   it was you who were not believers;

30 "we had no authority over you.
   You were rebellious people.

31 "Now the Word of our Lord
   is proven against us,
   and we must taste [the torment].

32 "We led you astray—
   we ourselves were astray."

33 On that day, they will share
   the same punishment.

34 This is how We deal
   with the sinners.

35 When it was said to them,
   "There is no god but [the One]
      God,"
   they remained proud,

36 saying, "Shall we forsake our gods
   for the sake of a mad poet?"

37 No—he brings the truth, and
confirms the [earlier] messengers.

38 You shall surely taste
the painful punishment—

39 you will be requited
only for what you have done—

40 as for the chosen servants of God,

41 they shall enjoy
an endowed provision

42 of fruits; and they shall be honored

43 in gardens of bliss,

44 facing one another,
arrayed on couches.

45 Around them will be passed
a goblet from a spring,

46 white, delicious
to those who taste it,

47 neither impairing
nor intoxicating them.

48 Beside them will be
females of modest glance,
and lustrous eyes,

49 like sheltered eggs.°

50 They will turn to one another,
inquiring.

51 One will say, "[On earth]
I had a close companion

52 "who used to ask,
'Are you really one of those
who believe?

53 "'When we die and become
dust and bones, shall we
really be brought [for
reckoning]?'"

54 The other will say,
"Will you look down?"

55 So he'll look down
and see his companion
in the midst of hellfire.

56 He said, "By God,
You almost brought me to ruin."

57 "If not for the grace of my Lord,
I should have been brought to it."

58 [To those with him he shall say,]
"Shall we really not die

59 "beyond our first death,
and not be punished?

60 "This is surely
the supreme triumph."

61 Let all who strive
   strive for the like of this—

62 is this the better welcome
   or the tree of Zaqqum?°

63 We made Zaqqum
   a trial for wrongdoers,

64 for it is a tree that comes
   from the pit of hellfire;

65 its fronds like the heads
   of devils.

66 They will eat from it,
   filling their bellies with it;

67 then they shall have a brew
   of scalding water,

68 and then shall return
   to the blaze of hellfire.

69 Yes, they found
   their forefathers astray

70 yet they hastened
   in their footsteps.

71 Before them, indeed,
   most of the ancients were astray,

72 though We had sent
   messengers to warn them.

73 Observe, then, the outcome
   of those who were warned—

74 all but the chosen
   servants of God.

SECTION 3

75 Noah cried out to Us—
   and how excellent was Our
      response,°

76 We saved him and his people
   from great distress,

77 enabling his offspring to survive,

78 and We left him [a good name]
   with posterity,

79 "Peace be to Noah
   among all beings"°—

80 this is how We reward
   those who do good.

81 For he was among
   Our believing servants.

82 Then We drowned the rest.

83 Abraham was of his creed°

84 when he approached his Lord
   with a pure heart.

85 He said to his father
   and his people,
   "What are you worshipping?

86 "Do you desire false gods
   instead of the One God?

87 "What are your thoughts
   on the Lord of the universe?"

88 Then he turned his gaze
   toward the stars,

89 and said, "Actually, I am unwell."

90 So they turned their backs to him,
   and left.

91 Then he turned to their gods,
   "Why do you not eat?

92 "Why is it that you do not speak?"

93 He turned toward them, and
   struck them with his right hand.

94 At this, his people
   rushed toward him,

95 so he asked, "Do you worship
   what you yourselves have sculpted,

96 "when it is God who created you
   and what you make?"

97 They cried, "Build a pyre° for him
   and throw him into the blazing
      fire!"

98 So they plotted against him,
   but We brought them low.

99 He said, "I will go to my Lord—
   He will guide [me].

100 "My Lord, grant me
    a righteous child."

101 So We gave him joyous news
    of a son who would be forbearing.

102 When the boy was old enough
    to help his father, Abraham said,
    "My son, I saw in a dream
    that I was offering you as a
       sacrifice.
    See, now—what do you think?"
    The son replied, "My father,
    do as you are commanded. God
       willing,
    you shall find me patient."°

103 And when they had both
    submitted to the will of God,
    and Abraham had laid him
    face-down on his forehead,

104 We called to him, "Abraham,

105 "you have fulfilled the vision."
    This is how We reward
    those who do good;

106 this indeed was a clear trial.

107 We ransomed his son
    with a crucial sacrifice,°

108 and We left Abraham
    a good name with posterity,

109 "Peace be with Abraham."

110 This is how We reward
those who do good—

111 for he was among
Our believing servants.

112 And We gave him joyous news
of a son Isaac—a prophet,
one of the righteous.

113 We blessed him and Isaac.
and among their progeny
were some who were good,
and some who clearly
wrong themselves.

SECTION 4

114 We also bestowed Our favor
on Moses and Aaron;

115 We delivered them both
and their people from great
distress;

116 We helped them,
so they were victorious;

117 and We gave them
the illuminating Book;

118 We guided them to the straight path,

119 and We left them a good name
with posterity—

120 "Peace be with Moses and Aaron"—

121 this is how We reward
those who do good;

122 they were both among
Our believing servants.

123 Elijah, too, was one of the
messengers.

124 He said to his people,
"Will you not be mindful of God?

125 "Do you call upon Ba'al
and forsake the Best of Creators—

126 "the One God, your Lord,
and Lord of your forefathers?"

127 But they denied him,
for which they will surely
be brought [for punishment]—

128 all but the chosen servants of God.

129 and We left him a good name
with posterity—

130 "Peace be with Elijah"—

131 this is how We reward
those who do good,

132 for he was among
Our believing Servants.

133 Lot also was one of the messengers.

134 We delivered him and all his people,

135 save an old woman with those
who lingered behind;

136 then we destroyed the rest.

137 You pass by their ruins, morning

138 and night—will you not,
then, use reason?

SECTION 5

139 Jonah, too, was one of the
messengers.

140 When he fled to the loaded ship,

141 they cast lots, and he lost;°

142 then the whale swallowed him,
for he had incurred blame.

143 Had he not then glorified God,

144 he should surely
have stayed in its belly
until the day of resurrection.

145 But We cast him, sick,
onto a barren shore,

146 and let a tree of gourd fruit
grow above him.

147 We sent him [as a messenger]
to a hundred thousand or more,

148 and they believed—
so We let them enjoy life
for a while.

149 Prophet, ask the disbelievers,
"Does your Lord have daughters
while they have sons?"

150 Did We create the angels
as females, while they looked on?

151 No—and it's one of their lies
when they say,

152 "God has begotten."
They are liars indeed.

153 Did He really choose
daughters over sons?

154 What is wrong with you?
How do you form your judgment?

155 Will you not reflect?

156 Or do you have clear authority
[for your claims]?

157 Then bring your scripture,
if you are speaking the truth.

158 And they assert kinship
between Him and the jinn,

yet the jinn surely know that
they will be brought [for reckoning].

159 —May God be glorified, above
what they ascribe to Him—

160 all but the chosen servants of God.

161 And neither you
nor those you worship

162 can beguile any away from [God]

163 but those who will burn
in the blazing fire.

164 [The angels say], "Every one of us
has an appointed place;

165 "we are arrayed in ranks

166 "and we are the ones
who glorify God."

167 Yet [the disbelievers] say,

168 "If only we had a reminder
like former peoples,

169 "we would have been
chosen servants of God."

170 Now they deny [the Qur'an];
but soon they shall know.

171 Our Word has already
been given to Our servants,
the messengers,

172 that they shall be helped,

173 and that Our forces
shall be victorious.

174 So, Prophet, turn away
from the disbelievers for a while,

175 and see what becomes of them;
for soon they shall see.

176 Do they wish to hasten
Our punishment?

177 When it descends
upon their courtyards,
it will be an evil morning
for those forewarned.

178 So turn away from them
for a while,

179 and see what becomes of them;
for they shall soon see.

180 Glory be to your Lord,
the Lord of Majesty, far above
what they ascribe to Him;

181 peace be to the messengers;

182 and praise be to God,
Lord of the universe.

SURA 38

Sad (*Sad*)

Middle Meccan, this sura is named after its first letter, not otherwise explained. Numbering 88 verses, it condemns those who had vilified Muhammad and other messengers before him. Some of the messengers (like Elisha and Dhul Kifl, v. 48) are seldom or never mentioned except here. The penultimate section concerns the story of Iblis—his creation, disobedience, and dismissal (vv. 71–85). The final directive underscores Muhammad as an authentic and selfless messenger (vv. 86–88).

In the Name of God, the All Merciful, Ever Merciful

SECTION I

1 *Sad.*°
By the Qur'an with its reminder—

2 the unbelievers are steeped
in self-glory and dissent.

3 How many generations
We destroyed before them.
Then they cried out for escape
when it was too late.°

4 They're bemused that
one of their own
has come to warn them;
and the unbelievers cry,
"This is a lying sorcerer.

5 "Has He made all the gods
into One God? How bizarre!"

6 Their leaders stride away, saying,
"Walk on, and stay steadfast to your
gods,
for there's some motive°
within this [against us].

7 "We never heard the like of this
in previous religious creed.°
It's nothing more than a fiction.

8 "Out of all of us, the message
was sent to *him*?" Yes
—they doubt My message—
they have yet
to taste My punishment.

9 Or do they possess the treasures
of the mercy of your Lord,
the Almighty, the Bestower?

10 Or do they have dominion
over the heavens and the earth
and all that lies between?

Then let them ascend
by whatever means° they can
[to bring down revelation].

11 The armies there,
of their allies,
shall be vanquished.

12 Before them, the people of Noah,
'Ad, and Pharaoh of the stakes°
denied [the messengers],

13 as did Thamud, the people of Lot,
and the forest dwellers°—
these were the allies.

14 Every one of them
denied the messengers,
so My punishment
came justly upon them.

SECTION 2

15 These disbelievers but await
a single blast, which cannot be
delayed.

16 They taunt, "Our Lord,
hasten for us our share
of punishment—even before
the day of reckoning!"

17 Bear with patience what they say,
and bear in mind Our servant David,
who was strong, ever turning to God.

18 We made the hills
hymn Our glory, along with him,
at evening and at sunrise,

19 as well as the birds in flocks—
all turning to Him.

20 We fortified his kingdom,
gave him wisdom, and made him
decisive in discourse.

21 Have you heard the story
of the two litigants, who climbed
the wall to reach his private
quarters?°

22 When they came upon David,
he was terrified of them.
They said, "Don't be frightened.
We are two litigants, and one of us
has wronged the other. So, judge
between us fairly, and don't be unjust,
but guide us to the right path.

23 "This is my brother.
He has ninety-nine ewes
and I have just one. Yet he says,
'Let me have charge of her,'
and his words overwhelmed me."°

24 David said,
"He has wronged you
in demanding that your ewe
be added to his ewes.
Many business partners
wrong each other
except those who believe

and do good deeds—
but they are few."

Then David knew—
We were testing him.°
He begged forgiveness of his Lord;
he fell down, bowing,
and turned [to God again].

25 We forgave him this [lapse],
   and he will be brought close to Us,
   with the best home for his return.°

26 "David, We made you
   a regent on the earth,
   so judge between people justly,
   and don't follow your desires,
   for they will lead you astray
   from God's path. Those who stray
   from the path of God shall face
   severe torment, for they
   have forgotten the day
   of reckoning."

SECTION 3

27 We did not create in vain
   heaven and earth and all between
   —that is what the unbelievers
      think—
   what torment awaits them in the
      fire!

28 Should We treat those who believe
   and do good deeds as We would
      those
   who work mischief on earth?

Or, should We treat the righteous
as We would the wicked?

29 This is a blessèd Book
   We have revealed to you,
   that they might ponder its signs,
   and people of insight
   might remember.

30 We gave David a son, Solomon
   —an excellent servant—
   he always turned to Us.

31 When swift steeds, well bred,
   were brought before him
   near the day's end,

32 he said, "I loved fine things
   rather than remembering my Lord."

When the horses vanished,
veiled from sight,°

33 [he commanded],
   "Bring them back to me,"
   then he began to stroke
   their legs and necks.°

34 And We tested Solomon:
   We reduced him to a lifeless body
   on his throne. Then he turned
   to Us in repentance,

35 saying, "My Lord, forgive me,
   and bestow upon me a kingdom
   such as none after me can acquire,
   for You alone are the Bestower."

36 Then We subdued the wind to him,
   coursing gently by his command,
   wherever he directed;

37 and the devils, every kind
   of builder and diver,

38 as well as others, bound in chains.°

39 "This is Our gift,
   so grant or withhold [it]
   without measure."

40 and he will be brought close to Us,
   an excellent home for his return.

SECTION 4

41 Remember Our servant Job
   who called out to his Lord,
   "Satan has brought me distress
   and torment."

42 [He was told,]
   "Stamp the ground with your foot.
   Here is cool water to bathe in,
   and to drink."

43 We restored his family to him,
   and more like them—a mercy
      from Us,
   and a reminder to those with insight.

44 [We told him,]
   "Take a bundle of reeds in your hand
   and strike [her] with it°
   so as not to break your oath."

We found him to be patient,
   an excellent servant, who turned
      to Us.

45 And remember Our servants
   Abraham, Isaac, and Jacob,
   who possessed strength and vision.

46 We chose them, for their fervent
   remembrance of the final home.

47 In Our sight, they were among
   the elect, the best.

48 And remember Ishmael, Elisha,
   and Ezekiel°—all among the best.

49 This is a reminder:
   those who are mindful of God
   shall have the best abode
   for their final return.

50 Eternal gardens, whose gates
   shall always stay open to them.

51 There they shall recline
   and call [at their pleasure]
   for fruit in abundance
   and refreshing drink.

52 With them will be companions
   of modest glance, well matched.

53 This is what you are promised
   for the day of reckoning.

54 This is Our provision—
   that never ends.

55 So it will be.
   But those who transgress
   shall have an evil home
   for their final return—

56 Hell—where they will burn—
   a wretched dwelling place.

57 So it will be for them:
   let them taste boiling liquid
   and purulent fluid

58 and [face] other such torments
   of various kinds.

59 [The leaders of the unbelievers
   shall say to one another,]
   "Here is a group
   bursting in to join you.
   They are not welcome—
   they shall burn in the fire."

60 [The followers shall reply
   to their leaders,] "No, *you*!
   You are not welcome!
   You brought us to this—
   a wretched home."

61 The followers will say, "Our Lord,
   let those who brought this upon us
   bear a doubled punishment in
        the fire."

62 And they will say,
   "Why don't we see those
   we used to consider wicked,

63 "those we ridiculed?
   Or have our eyes missed them?"

64 This is how things will transpire—
   squabbling among people in the fire.

SECTION 5

65 Say, "I am here only to warn:
   there is no god
   but the One God, Supreme.

66 "The Lord of the heavens and earth
   and all that lies between,
   Almighty, Forgiving."

67 Say, "This is momentous news,

68 "yet you turn away from it.

69 "I know nothing of what
   the highest [angels] discuss.

70 "It is only revealed to me,
   that I am to give clear warning."

71 Your Lord declared to the angels,
   "I shall create a human from clay.

72 "When I have proportioned him
   and breathed My spirit into him,
   bow down before him."

73 So the angels bowed down, all,

74 except Iblis, who was too proud,
and became a disbeliever.

75 God demanded, "Iblis,
what stops you from bowing
to what I created with My own
hands?
Are you too proud, or too exalted?"

76 Iblis retorted,
"I am better than him.
You created me from fire,
but him from mere clay."

77 God answered, "Well, go from here,
for you are cursed.

78 "And the curse shall stay with you
until the day of reckoning."

79 Iblis implored, "My Lord,
grant me respite, till the day
when they are raised [from the
dead]."

80 "You shall have respite," said God,

81 "until the appointed day."°

82 Iblis said, "I swear, by your might,
I will lead them astray—all.

83 "except those among them
who are Your chosen servants."

84 God said, "This is the truth
—for I speak the truth—

85 "that I will fill hell
with you and those of them
who follow you—all."

86 Say, Prophet,
"I ask no reward of you,
nor am I an impostor.

87 "This is no less than a reminder
to all the worlds,

88 "and, in time, you shall know
the truth it holds."

SURA 39

The Crowds (*Al-Zumar*)

A late Meccan sura of 75 verses, this declares God's unity and creative intent. Repeatedly the fate of believers and disbelievers is contrasted, before concluding with a vivid depiction of the day of resurrection (vv. 67–75).

In the Name of God, the All Merciful, Ever Merciful

SECTION I

1 A revelation of the Book
from God—
the Almighty, the Wise.

2 We revealed the Book to you
with truth—
so serve God with true devotion.°

3 True devotion is for God alone.
Those who take gods other than
    Him
as protectors claim, "We serve them
only to bring us closer to God."
God will judge between them
in the things they dispute.
God does not guide those
who lie and disbelieve.

4 Had God wanted a child,
He could have chosen whom
He wished from His creation.
Glory be to Him—
He is the One God, Omnipotent.

5 He created the heavens and earth
with true purpose. He enfolds day
within night and night within day,
and he subdues the sun and moon,
each sailing for an appointed
    term—
He is truly the Almighty, Forgiving.

6 He created you from a single soul
then from it made its mate;

and He gave you four kinds°
of livestock, in pairs.
He creates you in the wombs
of your mothers, in stages, one upon
another, in threefold darkness.°
This is God, your Lord,
Who has dominion over all.
There is no god but Him—
so, how can you turn away?

7 If you disbelieve, know that
God is Free of all need of you;
but His servants' ingratitude
does not please Him.
If you are grateful,
He will be pleased with you.
None can bear another's burden.
In the end, you will return to
your Lord and He will inform you
of all you have done—
He Knows what is in your hearts.

8 When harm strikes people,
they call on their Lord
and turn to Him.
But then, when He grants them
His favor, they forget the One
they called on before,
and they set up against God
rivals, who will lead them
from His path. Say,
"Enjoy your disbelief for a while.
You shall be inmates of the fire."

9 [Are such people better] than
those who devote themselves

during the night, prostrating
and standing, fearful
of the hereafter, and hopeful
of their Lord's mercy?
Say, "Are those who know
the same as those who don't?"
Only the discerning take heed.

SECTION 2

10 Say, "My servants who believe,
be mindful of your Lord.
Those who do good in this world
shall be rewarded with good.
God's earth is wide.
Those who are patient shall know
a reward beyond measure."

11 Say, "I am commanded
to serve God with true devotion.

12 "And I am commanded
to be the first of those
who submit their will to God."

13 Say, "If I disobeyed my Lord,
I would fear the torment
of a momentous day."

14 Say, "It is God whom I serve,
with true devotion.

15 "So serve what you will
besides Him." Say,
"The true losers are those who
lose themselves and their families

on the day of resurrection.
That is the clear loss."

16 Layers of fire shall engulf them,
above and below. This is how God
puts fear into His servants:
"So, be mindful of Me, My
     servants."

17 But there is joyous news for those
who spurn the worship of false gods
and turn to God. So give
this joyous news to My servants—

18 those who hear the Word
and follow the best in it.
Those are the ones God guides—
they are the discerning ones.

19 What of those
who are justly sentenced?
Can you rescue those
already in the fire?

20 But those mindful of their Lord
shall have high mansions
raised for them, one upon another,
with rivers flowing beneath.
This is God's pledge—
He never fails in His promise.

21 Don't you see how God
sends down rain from the sky,
guiding it through earth's springs,
to bring out crops of varying colors?
Then, as they wither, you see them
yellowing, crumbling.

In all this is a reminder
for people of insight.

SECTION 3

22 What of those whose hearts
    God has opened to bow to His will,
    who live by their Lord's light?
    Woe to those whose hearts are
        hardened
    against remembrance of God—
    they have clearly gone astray.

23 God has revealed
    the most sublime of narratives
    as a Book, its parts consistent,
        paired°—at which
    those who fear their Lord
    tremble in their skins,
    then their skins and hearts
    are soothed by His remembrance.
    This is God's guidance, by which
    He guides whom He will.
    But those whom God leaves astray
    have none to guide them.

24 What of those who have only
    their faces to shield them
    from extreme torment
    on the day of resurrection?
    The wrongdoers will be told,
    "Taste what you have earned."

25 Those before them disbelieved,
    and punishment came to them
    from places they could not imagine.

26 So God made them taste
    disgrace in the life of this world;
    but punishment in the hereafter
    is greater—if only they knew.

27 We have coined for people
    all kinds of parables in this Qur'an,
    that they might take heed—

28 an Arabic Qur'an,
    with no deviation,
    that they might be mindful.

29 God offers a parable:
    is a man owned by shared masters
    —all squabbling—equal to a man
    owned by one master?
    Praise be to God—
    most of them don't know.

30 It is certain that you will die,
    and they too will die.

31 Then, on the day of resurrection,
    you will bring your disputes
    before your Lord.

SECTION 4

32 Who does more wrong
    than those who lie about God
    and deny the truth when it comes
    to them? Is there not a home in hell
    for those who disbelieve?

33 But the one who brought the truth
    and those who affirmed it—

they are the ones mindful of God.

34 They shall have all that they desire
from their Lord—the reward
of those who do good;

35 God shall erase their worst deeds
and reward their best ones.

36 Does God not suffice
for His servant?
Yet they threaten you
with other gods.°
Those whom God leaves astray
have no guide.

37 And none can lead astray
those whom God guides. Is God not
Almighty, Lord of Requital?

38 If you ask them, who created
the heavens and the earth,
they will surely say, "God."
Say, "Consider those
you call on besides God—
if God wanted harm for me,
could they remove it?
And if he wanted mercy for me,
could they withhold it?
Say, "God suffices for me—
let those who trust,
trust in Him."

39 Say, "My people,
do whatever you can;°

and I will do what I can—
for soon you will know

40 "who shall face degrading torment
and on whom
lasting punishment will descend."

41 Prophet, We revealed the Book
to you, with truth, for humankind.
Those who receive guidance
do so to their own gain;
but those who go astray
do so to their own loss—
and you are not their custodian.

SECTION 5

42 God takes the souls of people
at the hour of their death,
and of those asleep who are not
dead.
He keeps the souls of those
for whom He has decreed death,
and the others He sends back
until an appointed time—in all this
are signs for those who think.°

43 Do they take intercessors
other than God? Say, "Even though
they have no power [to intercede]
and no understanding?"

44 Say, "All power to intercede
belongs to God alone—His
is dominion of the heavens and
earth;
in the end, you will return to Him."

45 When the One God is mentioned,°
the hearts of those who don't believe
in the hereafter recoil in aversion,
but when other gods are spoken of,
they exult and rejoice.

46 Say, "O God, Originator
of the heavens and the earth,
Knower of the unseen
and the seen—it is You Who
will judge between Your servants
on the things they dispute."

47 If the wrongdoers possessed
all that is on the earth—twice
over—
they would offer it as ransom
for the dreadful torment
of the day of resurrection—
but God will bring before them
something they had not conceived.

48 The evil deeds they reaped
will come before them,
and they shall be engulfed
by what they mocked.

49 When adversity strikes someone,
they cry out to Us. But when
We grant them Our favor, they say,
"I'm given this for my knowledge."
Wrong—such favor is a trial,
but most of them don't know.

50 Those who came before them

said the same thing. But the deeds
they reaped were of no use to them.

51 The evil they reaped
overtook them; and the evil reaped
by the wrongdoers among *these*
shall overtake them—
they shall not escape.

52 Don't they know that God
enlarges provision and restricts it
for whom He will? In this
are signs for people who believe.

SECTION 6

53 Say, "My servants, who have
transgressed against yourselves—
do not despair of God's mercy.
God forgives all sins.
He is Forgiving, Ever Merciful.

54 "Turn to your Lord and bow
to His will, before punishment
overcomes you—then
you will not be helped.

55 "And follow the best
of what is revealed to you
from your Lord, before punishment
overcomes you—suddenly,
while you are unaware,

56 "and your soul says,
'Alas for me, for my neglect
of what was due to God—
I was among those who mocked.'

57 "Or, 'If only God had guided me—
I would have been among the
     righteous.'

58 "Or [when it sees the punishment],
'If only I could have another chance—
I'd be among those who do good.'

59 "[A voice will then reply,]
'No—My signs came to you
and you denied them, through pride—
you were among the disbelievers.'"

60 On the day of resurrection
you'll see those who lied about God
with faces blackened—is there not
a home in hell for the proud?

61 But God will deliver the righteous
to their salvation. No evil shall
touch them, nor shall they grieve.

62 God is the Creator of all things;
it is He Who Oversees all things.

63 His are the keys of the heavens
and the earth, and those who deny
the signs of God shall suffer loss.

SECTION 7

64 Say, "Do you command me
to worship something other than God,
you who are so ignorant?"

65 It has been revealed to you
and those before you, that if you join

other gods as partners with God,
your works will be vain,
and you will be among
those who suffer loss.

66 No—worship God, and be
among those who are grateful.

67 They have not reckoned God
in His true measure; on the day
of resurrection, the whole earth
will be folded in His grasp,
and the heavens rolled up
in His right hand. Glory be to Him,
exalted beyond the other gods
they partner with Him.

68 The trumpet shall be sounded
and all in the heavens and earth
shall fall dead, except those
God wishes. Then, it will be
     sounded
again, and they shall stand, staring.

69 And the earth will shine
with the Light of its Lord;
the Book will be laid open
and the prophets and witnesses
brought forward. Fitting judgment
shall be passed on them
and they shall not be wronged.

70 Every soul shall be paid
in full for its deeds;
and God knows best
all that they do.

SECTION 8

71 The unbelievers will be driven
toward hell in throngs. When they
reach it, its gates shall open,
and its keepers shall ask,
"Did messengers not come to you
from among yourselves, reciting
to you the verses of your Lord,
and warning you of the meeting
with God on this day of yours?"
They will answer, "Yes, indeed."
The threat of torment for
    unbelievers
has proven to be true.

72 They will be told,
"Enter the gates of hell
to dwell there forever—
a wretched home for the proud."

73 But those who were mindful
of their Lord will be urged toward

the garden, in throngs. When they
reach it, its gates shall open,
and its keepers proclaim,
"Peace be with you.
You have done well. Enter here,
where you shall live forever."

74 They will say, "All praise be to God,
who has fulfilled His promise to us,
and has made us heirs to this realm.°
We can live where we will
in the garden,
how excellent is the reward
of those who labor [for God]."

75 And you shall see the angels
surrounding the high throne, as
they hymn the praise of their Lord.
Fitting judgment shall be passed
among them, and these words
shall resound, "All praise be to God,
Lord of the universe."

SURA 40

The Forgiving (Al-Ghafir)

A late Meccan sura, 85 verses in length, this is the first of seven consecutive suras that begin with the same two Arabic letters—*ha mim*. It begins with an encomium to God marked by six Divine Names, accenting the importance of belief and prayer. After a detailed story of Moses (vv. 23–53), the sura circles back to God, extolling the majesty and inviolability of the Creator who is also the Judge (vv. 54–85).

In the Name of God, the All Merciful, Ever Merciful

SECTION 1

1 *Ha Mim.*°

2 This Book is a revelation from God,
   the Almighty, the All Knowing,

3 Forgiving of sin,
   Accepting of repentance,
   Severe in Requital,
   Encompassing in Abundance°—
   there is no god but Him.
   To Him is the final return.

4 None dispute the signs of God
   but the disbelievers—
   don't let their [proud] ventures
   in the land deceive you.

5 Before them, the people of Noah
   denied [the truth], as did factions
   after them. Every nation schemed to
   seize its messenger, and they
      disputed,
   using falsehood to impugn the truth.
   So I seized them—
   how severe was My requital!

6 Hence your Lord's promise
   [to punish] the disbelievers
   was proven true—
   they shall be inmates of the fire.

7 Those who bear the throne,
   and those around it, hymn the praise
of their Lord; they believe in Him
and ask forgiveness for those
who believe, "Our Lord,
You encompass all things
with mercy and knowledge—
so forgive those who repent
and follow Your path, and
save them from the torment of hell.

8 "Our Lord, usher them
   into everlasting gardens
   which You have promised them
   and the righteous among their
      fathers,
   their wives, and their children—
   for You are Almighty, All Wise.

9 "And save them from all evils
   —those whom you save on that day
   are surely granted Your mercy—
   that is the supreme triumph."

SECTION 2

10 The disbelievers will be told,
    "God's loathing of you
    is greater than your self-loathing
    for you were called to the faith
    but you refused."

11 They will say, "Our Lord,
    twice you placed us in a state
    of non-being,° and twice
    you brought us to life, and
    now we acknowledge our sins—

is there no way out of this?"

12 [They will be answered,]
"This is because, when the One God
was invoked, you disbelieved.
But when other gods were joined
with Him, you believed—
judgment belongs to God,
the Most High, Most Great."

13 It is He Who shows you His signs,
and sends down sustenance from
    the sky.
But only those who turn to God,
repenting, will take heed.

14 So call upon God, with sincere faith
though disbelievers may hate this.

15 Exalter of rank, Lord of the throne,
He sends the Spirit by His command
to whom He will of His servants,
to warn of the day of meeting—

16 the day they will all
come forward. Nothing of them
is hidden from God—
Who holds dominion on this day?
God—the One, the Invincible.

17 On that day every soul
shall be requited for what it earned.
No injustice shall occur that day—
God is Swift in Reckoning.

18 Warn them of the approaching day
when their hearts will rise
to their throats, choked.
The wrongdoers will have no friend,
no intercessor who will be heeded.

19 God knows their furtive glances
and what their hearts conceal.

20 God will judge with justice—those
other gods they invoke besides Him
shall judge with nothing. It is God
Who is All Hearing, All Seeing.

SECTION 3

21 Don't they travel through the earth
and see the fate of those before
    them—
superior to them in strength
and influence on the earth?
Yet God seized them for their sins—
against God they have no protector.

22 For messengers came to them
with signs, but they denied them,
so God seized them.
He is Strong, Severe in Requital.

23 Earlier, We sent Moses
with Our signs, and clear authority,

24 to Pharaoh, Haman, and Korah,°
but they retorted, "Lying sorcerer!"

25 When he brought them the truth
from Us, they said, "Kill the sons

of those who believe with him,
and spare only their women."
The disbelievers' scheming is
    misconceived.

26 Pharaoh said, "Let me kill Moses
even as he calls upon his Lord.
I fear that he'll change your faith
or spread disorder through the
    land."

27 Moses said, "I have sought refuge
in my Lord and your Lord
from every proud person
who does not believe
in the day of reckoning."

SECTION 4

28 A believing man from Pharaoh's
    people
who had concealed his faith said,
"Would you kill a man just for
    saying,
'My Lord is the One God,'
and who has brought you clear
    proofs
from your Lord? If he is a liar,
the lie shall fall upon his own head.
But if he is truthful, some of the
    things
he threatens could fall upon you.
God does not guide
the liar and transgressor.

29 "My people, today, as masters,
you hold sway in this land—but
who will help us against God's wrath

if it falls upon us?" Pharaoh
    retorted,
"I merely tell you my view
and guide you to the right path."

30 The believer responded,
"My people, I fear for you
a day like that which fell
upon factions before you—

31 "like the plight of the people
of Noah, 'Ad, Thamud, and those
who came after them—
though God never intends injustice
toward His servants.

32 "And, my people,
I fear for you a day when
you will cry out to one another,

33 "a day when you shall
turn and flee—you shall have
no protector against God—
and those whom God leaves to stray
shall have no guide.

34 "And when Joseph came to you
in earlier times with clear proofs,
you never ceased to doubt his
    message,
and when he died, you proclaimed,
'God shall never send a messenger
after him.' So, God leaves to stray
those who doubt and transgress,

35 "who dispute the signs of God
without being granted any
    sanction—

this is abhorrent in the sight of God
and the believers. Thus God seals up
the heart of every proud tyrant."

36 Pharaoh said, "Haman, build me
a high tower so I can climb the
paths°—

37 "the paths to the heavens
to gaze upon the god of Moses,
for I deem him a liar."
And so, Pharaoh's evil deeds
were made to seem fair to him,
he was barred from the right path;
and Pharaoh's scheming led
to nothing but ruin.

SECTION 5

38 The man who believed said,
"My people, follow me—
I'll guide you to the right path.

39 "My people, the life of this world
is merely a passing pleasure
but the hereafter is a lasting home.

40 "Whoever does a wicked deed
shall be requited only with its like;
but whoever does good deeds,
—whether male or female—
and is a true believer,
shall enter the garden,
with provision beyond measure.

41 "And, my people, how is it that I
call you to salvation, while you
call me to the fire?

42 "You call me to disbelieve in God
and to join with Him partners
—of which I have no knowledge—
while I call you to the One
Who is Almighty, Forgiving.

43 "Without doubt, what you call me to
has no claim to be invoked either
in this world or the hereafter.
We shall return to God,
and the transgressors shall be
inmates of the fire.

44 "Soon you will remember
what I am saying to you:
I commit my affairs
to God—God Sees all
concerning His servants."

45 So God saved him
from their wicked scheming;
and dire punishment
engulfed Pharaoh's people.

46 They will be brought before the fire
morning and evening; and on the day
when the hour falls, a voice shall say,
"Strike the people of Pharaoh
with the most severe torment."

47 See, they will quarrel with one
another
in the fire. The weak will say to the
proud,
"We were but your followers. So can
you
avert from us some portion of the
fire?"

48 The proud will answer,
"We are all in this together—
God has judged
between His servants."

49 The people in the fire will plead
with the keepers of hell,
"Call on your Lord to lighten
our punishment for a day."

50 But they will answer,
"Did messengers not come to you
with clear proofs?" "Yes, indeed,"
the inmates will say. And the keepers
will retort, "Plead, then"—
but the pleas of disbelievers
will be misconceived.

SECTION 6

51 We shall help Our messengers
and those who believe,
both in the life of this world
and on the day when
witnesses will rise,

52 the day when the excuses
of the wrongdoers
shall be of no use to them—
they shall be cursed
and have a wretched home.

53 We gave guidance to Moses,
and We made the children of Israel
heirs to the Book—

54 a guide and a reminder
for people of insight.

55 Be patient, then—God's promise
is true; ask forgiveness for your sin,°
and hymn the praise of your Lord
evening and morning.

56 Those who dispute the signs
of God
without being granted any sanction
have in their hearts only pride
that they will never satisfy.
Seek refuge, then, in God,
for He is All Hearing, All Seeing.

57 Creation of the heavens and earth
was a greater thing
than the creation of humans,
yet most of humankind
do not know.

58 The blind are not equal
to those who see;
nor are those who believe,
doing good deeds, equal
to those who commit evil deeds.
How little you take heed.

59 The hour will undoubtedly come,
yet most people don't believe.

60 Your Lord says, "Call upon Me
and I shall answer you.
But those too proud to worship Me
shall enter hell—in disgrace."

SECTION 7

61 It is God Who has made the night
in which you might rest, and the day

giving light to your eyes. God is
Full of Grace toward humankind,
yet most of them are ungrateful.

62 This is God, your Lord,
Creator of all things.
There is no god but Him—
so how can you be deluded?

63 This is how deluded they are—
those who deny the signs of God.

64 It is God Who made the earth
a place for you to live, and the sky
a canopy. He gave you form,
perfected your forms, then provided
good things for your sustenance.
This is God, your Lord—blessed
is He, Lord of the universe.

65 He is the Living—there is no god
    but He
so call upon Him, with sincere faith.
All praise be to God, Lord of the
    universe.

66 Say, "I am forbidden to worship
those you call upon besides God
since clear proofs have come to me
from my Lord. I am commanded
to submit to the Lord of the
    universe."

67 It is He Who created you
from dust, then from sperm,
then from a clot of blood;
He then brings you out as infants,
till you reach maturity, and old age

—though some of you die young—
to reach your appointed term,
to make you understand.

68 It is He Who gives life
and brings death; and
when He decrees something,
He merely says, "Be!" and it is.

SECTION 8

69 Don't you see those
who dispute the signs of God,
how perverted they are?°

70 Those who deny the Book and
what We sent with Our
    messengers—
but soon they shall know,

71 when they are dragged,
with yokes and chains
around their necks,

72 into the boiling fluid,
then burned in the fire.

73 Then they'll be asked, "Where
are the other gods you worshipped

74 "besides God?" They will say,
"They have abandoned us—in fact,
we were calling upon nothing."
In this way, God leaves
the disbelievers to stray.

75 [They will be told,] "That is because
   you exulted on earth without right°
   and because you were insolent.

76 "Enter the gates of hell,
   to stay there forever—wretched
   is the home of the proud."

77 So be patient, Prophet, for God's
      promise
   is true; and whether we show you
   something of [the punishment] We
      promised them
   or make you die before that,
   to Us they shall be returned.

78 We sent messengers before you;
   We told you the stories of some
   and not others. No messenger
   brings signs without God's leave.
   And when God's command comes,
   fair judgment will be passed—
   and there, those who
   incite falsehood shall lose.

SECTION 9

79 It is God who made livestock for
      you,
   some for you to ride, others for you
      to eat,

80 and they have other uses for you;
   through them you can fulfill

your hearts' desire, and you are
   carried
upon them, as you are upon ships.

81 He shows you His signs—
   which, then, of the signs of God
   would you deny?

82 Don't they travel through the earth
   and see the fate of those before
      them?
   They were greater in number,
      strength,
   and in their impact on the
      earth—yet
   their achievements proved no use to
      them.

83 When their messengers came
   to them with clear proofs,
   they merely exulted
   in what they already knew—
   but they were engulfed
   by what they mocked.

84 Only when they saw Our torment
   did they say, "We believe
   in God alone, and we deny
   the other gods we joined with Him."

85 But their "faith" after seeing
   Our torment did not avail them.
   This has always been God's way
   with His servants—
   there, the disbelievers lost.

Explained in Full (*Fussilat*)

Still another late Meccan sura, but only 54 verses long, this accents the Qur'an as something explained in full and in Arabic (v. 3), at once a guide and a cure for those who believe but conveying only deafness and blindness for those who disbelieve (v. 44).

In the Name of God, the All Merciful, Ever Merciful

SECTION I

1 *Ha Mim.*°

2 A revelation from
the Most Merciful, Ever Merciful—

3 a Book whose verses are explained
in clear detail, an Arabic Qur'an
for people who know,

4 bringing joyous news
and warning—but most of them
turn away so they don't hear.

5 They say, "Our hearts are shielded°
from what you call us to,
and our ears sunk in deafness;
between us and you is a veil,
so do as you will—and so shall we."

6 Say, "I'm just a human, like you.
It's revealed to me that your God
is One God—so seek a straight path
to Him, and ask forgiveness of Him."

Wretched are those who join
other gods with Him,

7 those who don't give in charity,
and who deny the hereafter.

8 Those who believe
and do good deeds
shall know an unceasing reward.

SECTION 2

9 Say, "Do you deny the One
Who created the earth in two days?°
Do you set up others as His equals?
This is the Lord of all Creation."

10 He set firm mountains on [the
earth],
high above, and blessed it, and
measured
its sustenance according to the
needs
of those who seek it—in four days.

11 Then He set Himself toward the sky,
a mere mass of smoke, and
commanded
both it and the earth, "Come into
being,
willing or unwilling." They answered,
"We are coming into being,
willingly."

12 He perfected them as seven heavens
in two days, and He revealed
to each heaven its role.
We adorned the lower heaven
with lamps and rendered it secure.
This is the order ordained
by the Almighty, the All Knowing.

13 But if they should turn away,
then say, "I have warned you
of a thunderbolt—like the one
that struck 'Ad and Thamud."°

14 When messengers came to them
from all perspectives,° urging,
"Do not worship anything other
than the One God," they responded,
"If our Lord had wished,
He would have sent down angels—
we deny the message sent with you."

15 The people of 'Ad strutted proudly
through the land, without just cause.°
They would say,
"Who is our superior in strength?"
Don't they see that God
—Who created them—
is far superior to them in strength?

Yet they continued to deny Our
signs.

16 So We sent against them
a roaring wind, through days
of misfortune, to let them taste
the torment of disgrace
in the life of this world—
though torment in the hereafter
shall be more disgraceful,
and they shall not be helped.

17 As for the people of Thamud—
We gave them guidance but
they preferred blindness to guidance,
so they were struck by a thunderbolt
as punishment, disgracing them
for their misdeeds.

18 But We delivered those
who believed and feared God.

SECTION 3

19 On the day the enemies of God
are gathered toward the fire
and are driven in ranks—

20 when they come to [the fire],
their hearing, and sight
—their very skins—
shall testify against them
on account of their deeds.

21 They will ask their skins,
"Why do you testify against us?"
and their answer will be,

"God gave us speech—He
Who gives speech to all things.
It is He Who created you
in the beginning, and to Him
you will be returned.

22 "Yet you did not try to hide, to
stop your hearing, sight, and skins
from testifying against you—
but you thought God unaware
of much of what you did.

23 "This is what you thought
of your Lord, and it is this thought
that has brought you to ruin—
you are now among those
who will suffer loss."

24 Even if they can endure it,
the fire shall be their home;
if they ask to redeem themselves,
they shall not be allowed.

25 And We have decreed
[evil] companions for them
who made their present and past°
seem fair to them; but the decree°
of their punishment proved true
as with the generations
of jinn and humans who came
before them—they were the losers.

SECTION 4

26 The unbelievers say, "Don't listen
to this Qur'an: drown it in idle noise—
that way, you'll have the last word."°

27 But We will make the unbelievers
taste severe torment,
and We will requite them
for the worst of their deeds.

28 This is the requital
for the enemies of God
—the fire, their eternal home—
their requital for denying Our signs.

29 And the unbelievers will say,
"Our Lord, show us the jinn and
    humans
who misled us—we'll trample them
beneath our feet, forcing them
to be among the lowest [in hell]."

30 The angels will descend to those
who say, "Our Lord is the One God,"
and are upright, [saying to them],
"Have no fear, do not grieve,
and receive joyous news
of the garden you were promised.

31 "We are your protectors
in the life of this world
and the hereafter.
There you shall have
all that your souls desire,
all that you ask—

32 "a welcoming gift from
the Forgiving, the Ever Merciful."

SECTION 5

33 Who speaks better than one
who calls people to God,
does good deeds, and speaks
the words, "I am one of those
who bow to God's will."°

34 Good and evil are not equal.
Counter [evil] with something better,
then the person who was your foe°
will become like a close friend.

35 But none is granted this [goodness]
except people who show patience,
those with great righteousness.°

36 If any evil prompting from Satan
should whisper within you,
seek refuge in God—
He is All Hearing, All Knowing.

37 Among His signs are
night and day, sun and moon.
Do not bow before sun and moon,
but bow before God,
Who created them—
if it is Him alone you worship.

38 But if [the unbelievers]
strut proudly, [it is of no account],
for those with your Lord
hymn His glory night and day,
without fatigue.

39 And among His signs is this:
you see the earth barren, and when
He sends down rain upon it,

it stirs into life, and swells.
He Who gives it life can surely
bring life to the dead—
He has Power over all things.

40 Those who distort
what is in Our signs
are not hidden from Us.
Who is better—a person
who is hurled into the fire,
or someone who comes through
secure on the day of resurrection?
Do what you will—
He is Aware of all that you do.

41 Those who reject the message
when it comes to them—
it is a Book of great power,

42 that no falsehood might reach
from any side,° revealed by
the All Wise, the Praiseworthy—

43 [should know that] nothing is said
to you that was not said
to the messengers before you.
Your Lord is Full of Forgiveness
and Severe in Requital.

44 Had We produced this Qur'an
in a foreign tongue, they would say,
"Why are its verses not explained
in full? A foreign [Book
brought by] an Arab!° Say,
"It is guidance and healing
for those who believe,
but for those who disbelieve,
it brings deafness to their ears,

and blindness—as if they
were being called from afar."

SECTION 6

45 We gave the Book to Moses
but disputes arose over it.
Had your Lord not issued a decree,°
judgment would have been passed
between them. But they remain
in anxious doubt over it.

46 Whoever does good deeds,
does so for himself;
and whoever does bad deeds,
does so against himself.
Your Lord is never unjust
to His servants.

47 Knowledge of the hour
lies with Him alone.
No fruit emerges from its sheath,
no female conceives or gives birth
without His knowing.
And on the day He calls to them,
"Where are My partners?"
they will say, "We confess to you
that none of us can attest [to them]."

48 The gods they called on before
will forsake them, and they will see,
for sure, that they have no escape.

49 People never cease to pray for good,
but when evil touches them,
they lose hope and despair.

50 When We let them taste Our
mercy
after adversity touches them,
they will say, "This my due—
I don't believe that the hour
will ever transpire, yet even if
I am brought back to my Lord,
He will surely have the best
reward
for me." But We shall inform
the disbelievers of what they did
and We shall make them taste
severe punishment.

51 When We bestow Our favor
on people, they turn away,
staying far [from Us].
But when misfortune touches
them,
they turn [to Us], full of prayer.

52 Say, "Did you ever reflect:
what if this [revelation] is truly
from God—yet you still deny it?
Who can be more astray than one
so far opposed to it?"

53 Soon We will show them
Our signs—on the far horizons
and within themselves
until it becomes clear to them
that this is the truth.
Is it not enough that your Lord
is Witness to all things?

54 Indeed, they remain in doubt about
the meeting with their Lord—yet
He surely Encompasses all things.

Consultation (*Al-Shura*)

A Meccan sura with some Medinan verses, this also is comparatively short (53 verses). Unlike other suras that begin with multiple mysterious letters, it frames them in two verses (vv. 1–2) not a single verse (as in Maryam, Sura 19). It extols settling affairs by consultation (v. 38), accented in the title. At the same time, it highlights the value of the Qur'an in Arabic (v. 7), a guiding light for Muhammad, unversed yet commanded through a divine spirit (v. 52).

In the Name of God, the All Merciful, Ever Merciful

SECTION I

1 *Ha Mim.*

2 *'Ayn Sin Qaf.°*

3 This is how He reveals to you,
   as to those before you—
   God, the Almighty, All Wise.

4 To Him belongs
   all that is in the heavens
   and all that is on the earth—
   for He is the Most High, Most
      Great.

5 The heavens are almost
   rent from on high,
   while the angels glorify
   their Lord with praise,
   and pray for forgiveness
   for all those on earth.
   God is the One Who
   is Forgiving, Ever Merciful.

6 As for those who take others
   as protectors,° God Watches them,
   and you are not their keeper.

7 We have hereby revealed
   to you an Arabic Qur'an
   that you might warn
   the mother of cities°
   and those around her,
   warn them of the day of gathering
   —of which there is no doubt—
   with one group in the garden,
   the other in the fire.

8 Had He wished, God would
   have made them one people,
   but He admits into His mercy
   whom He will;
   and the wrongdoers
   shall have no protector
   and no helper.

9 Or, have they taken as protectors
   others besides Him?

For God is the Protector,
the Restorer of life to the dead,
and He has Power over all things.

SECTION 2

10 Whatever issue you dispute,
it is for God to judge—
this is God, my Lord:
in Him I trust
and to Him I turn.

11 Creator of the heavens and earth,
He has made for you mates
from among yourselves, and mates
between the animals, multiplying
    you.
There is nothing like Him—
He is the All Hearing, All Seeing.

12 His are the keys
of the heavens and the earth:
He extends and restricts provision
for whom He will—
He Knows all things.

13 He has ordained for you
the religion that He enjoined
upon Noah, that We revealed
to you, Prophet,
and that We enjoined upon
Abraham, Moses, and Jesus.
"Establish the religion, and do not
divide yourselves within it."
What you call the polytheists to do
is hard for them;
God chooses for Himself

whom He will,
and He guides to Himself
whoever turns toward Him.

14 They divided, out of mutual envy,
only after knowledge came to them.
If judgment on them had not been
deferred until an appointed time
by a previous word from your Lord,
sentence would have been passed
between them. And those
who inherited the Book after them
are vexed with doubt over it.

15 So, call people to the [Book],
stand firm as commanded,
and do not follow their fancies;
say, rather: "I believe in the Book
which God has revealed,°
and I have been commanded
to dispense justice among you.
God is our Lord and your Lord;
our deeds belong to us,
and yours to you—so let there be
no dispute between us and you.
God will gather us together,
and to Him is our final return.

16 As for those who dispute over God
after accepting the message,°
their dispute is vain
in the eyes of their Lord—
His wrath falls on them,
and severe torment awaits them.

17 It is God Who sent down
the Book, with truth,

as well as the balance
[to weigh truth and falsehood].
And what would make you know
that the hour may be near?

18 Those who don't believe in it
seek to hasten it,
while those who believe in it
are fearful of it,
knowing it to be true.
Those who argue about the hour
have gone far astray.

19 God is Most Gentle
toward His servants;
He provides for whom He will.
He is All Powerful, Almighty.

SECTION 3

20 For those who desire
the harvest of the hereafter,
We shall increase their harvest;
and for those who desire
the harvest of this world,
We shall grant them some of it,
but they shall have no portion
in the hereafter.

21 Or, do they have gods
ordaining for them in religion
what God has not permitted?
Had it not been for a decisive word
[from God], sentence would already
have been passed between them.
The wrongdoers shall face
a painful punishment.

22 You will see the wrongdoers
fearful on account of what they
earned,
and what will surely befall them.
But those who believe
and do good deeds shall be
in the gardens' flowering meadows.
They will have all they wish for
from their Lord—
that is the abundant grace.

23 This is the joyous news
which God gives to His servants
who believe and do good deeds.
Say, "I ask of you no reward for this
beyond the love due
to those who are close to you."
As for those who do good,
We shall increase its good for them°—
God is Forgiving, Appreciative.

24 Or, do they say,
"He has coined a lie about God"—
even though, if God wished,
He could seal up your heart?
For by His words
God abolishes falsehood
and verifies truth—
He Knows what hearts contain.

25 It is He Who accepts
the repentance of His servants
and pardons wrongful deeds;
He knows all that you do.

26 He answers those
who believe and do good deeds,

and grants them ever more
from His grace. But those
who disbelieve shall face
severe punishment.

27 Had God extended [boundless]
provision° to His servants,
they would have tyrannized the
earth.°
But He sends down in due measure
what He will, for He is All Aware,
All Seeing, of His servants.

28 It is He Who sends down
rain—after people have despaired—
and spreads His mercy far,
for He is the Protector,
the Praiseworthy.

29 Among His signs is creation
of the heavens and the earth,
and the creatures He dispersed
throughout both—
He is All Powerful, Able
to gather them when He will.

SECTION 4

30 Whatever misfortune befalls you
is wrought by your own hands,
yet He pardons much.

31 Nowhere can you escape
throughout the earth;
nor, do you have besides God
any protector or helper.

32 Among His signs are the ships,
sailing [high] on the seas,
like mountains.

33 If it were His wish,
He could lull the wind,
then the ships would be motionless
on the back of the ocean.
In this are signs
for all who are patient
and full of thanks.

34 Or He could wreck [the ships]
on account of what [their crew]
has earned, yet He pardons much.

35 So let them know, those
who dispute over Our signs—
there is no escape for them.

36 Whatever you are given
is but a passing pleasure
of the life of this world.
But what God will give to those
who believe and trust in their Lord
is far better and will endure—

37 those who avoid the major sins
and indecencies, and forgive,
even when angry;

38 those who answer their Lord,
are steadfast in prayer,
and settle their affairs
by mutual consultation,
and who give [in charity]
from what We have given them;

39 and those who defend themselves
   when oppression falls upon them.

40 The requital for a wrong
   is an equal wrong; but whoever
   pardons and reconciles
   will find his reward with God,
   for He does not love
   those who do wrong.

41 But there is no reproach on those
   who defend themselves when
      wronged.

42 Reproach falls only on
   those who oppress people and
   tyrannize the earth lawlessly.
   Theirs shall be a painful torment.

43 But whoever forbears
   and forgives, displays in this
   an ideal resolve.°

SECTION 5

44 And whoever God allows to stray
   shall no longer have a protector.
   And you shall see the wrongdoers say,
   when they see the punishment,
   "Is there any way [for us] to return?"

45 You will see them exposed
   to [the punishment], humbled,
   humiliated, glancing, with furtive
      eyes,
   and the believers will say,
   "The losers are those who have

lost themselves and their kin
on the day of resurrection.
The wrongdoers will abide
in enduring torment."

46 And they have no protectors
   to help them beyond God;
   and whoever God allows to stray
   shall find no way forward.

47 Answer your Lord before
   the coming of a day, from God,
   which cannot be turned away.
   On that day there will be no asylum
   for you, no denial.

48 If still they turn away, [remember,]
   We have not sent you, Prophet,
   to be their guardian. Your task
   is only to convey [the message].
   When We grant humankind
   a taste of Our mercy, they rejoice
      in it;
   but when some harm befalls them
   —by their own hands—
   then humankind becomes
      ungrateful.

49 To God belongs dominion
   of the heavens and the earth.
   He creates what He will;
   He grants to whom He will
   female or male offspring;

50 or grants both males and females,
   and makes barren whom He will—
   He is All Knowing, All Powerful.

51 It is beyond any mortal
   that God would speak to him
   except by revelation
   or from behind a veil
   or by sending a messenger
   to reveal, by His leave,
   what He will.
   He is the Most High, All Wise.

52 Hereby, We have revealed
   Our command to you, Prophet,
   through a spirit. You were unversed

in the Book, and in faith;
but We made it a Light,
by which We might guide
whom We will of Our servants—
you truly guide to a straight path,

53 the path of God,
   to Whom belongs
   all that is in the heavens
   and all that is on the earth.
   All affairs are destined
   ultimately to God.

SURA 43

Gold Adornments (*Al-Zukhruf*)

A Meccan sura of 89 verses. Its short, pithy verses extol the virtues of Abraham, Moses, and Jesus while also condemning those who rejected them and persisted in idolatry or disbelief. The final command to Muhammad is to "turn away from them, and say 'Peace,' for soon they shall come to know" (v. 89).

In the Name of God, the All Merciful, Ever Merciful

SECTION I

1 *Ha Mim.*°

2 By the clarifying Book,

3 which We have made
   an Arabic Qur'an
   to make you understand.

4 It is in an archetypal Book,°
   kept by Us, Exalted, Most Wise.

5 Should We take this message
   away from you, disregarding you,
   since you are a people who
      transgress?

6 How many messengers
   did We send to earlier peoples,

7 yet no prophet came to them
   whom they did not mock.

8 And We destroyed people
mightier than these—examples
of earlier peoples have passed.

9 If you asked them, "Who created
the heavens and the earth?"
they would surely say,
"They were created by
the Almighty, the All Knowing,"

10 Who made the earth a place
of repose for you, and traced roads
throughout it to guide you.

11 And it is He Who sends down
rain from the sky, in due measure,
and We revive thereby a dead
    earth—
likewise, you will be raised up again.

12 It is He Who created all things
in pairs, and made for you the ships
and livestock on which you ride,

13 so that, securely mounted
on their backs, you might recall
your Lord's favor to you, and say,
"Glory be to Him, Who subdued
all this [to our use],
for we were unable to do this.

14 "And We shall turn
back to Our Lord."

15 Yet they attribute
to some of His servants
a share with Him [as His
    daughters]°—
humankind is blatantly ungrateful.

SECTION 2

16 Or, has He taken daughters
from what He himself created
and chosen sons for *you*?

17 When one of them hears
of [the birth of a daughter]
—a creature he has likened to
    God—
his visage darkens, and he is
choked with grief.°

18 "[Am I to have a daughter]—
who is nurtured among trinkets
and cannot form a clear argument?"°

19 They also deem the angels
—who are themselves servants
of the Most Merciful—to be female.
Did they witness their creation?
Their testimony will be recorded
and they shall be questioned.

20 They say, "If the All Merciful
had willed it, we would not
have worshipped them."
But they have no knowledge of this,
and do nothing but speculate.

21 Or, did We give them
a Book before this,
to which they hold fast?

22   No—they say,
     "We found our fathers
     practicing [this] religion,
     and we are guided
     by their footsteps."

23   Likewise, whenever We sent
     someone before you, to warn a
        town,
     their affluent people affirmed,
     "We found our fathers
     practicing [this] religion,
     and we are guided
     by their footsteps."

24   The Prophet retorted,
     "Even if I brought you better
        guidance
     than what you found
     your ancestors practicing?"
     They answered, "We deny
     the message you have brought."

25   So We requited them—
     observe, then, the fate of those
     who denied the truth.

SECTION 3

26   Abraham said to his father
     and his people, "I repudiate
     what you worship.

27   "[I worship] none but the One
     Who made me,
     and He will guide me."

28   He made this a lasting declaration°
     to his descendants,
     so they might return to God.

29   Still, I let these people and their
        fathers
     enjoy this life for a while,
     until the truth came to them, and
     a messenger who made things clear.

30   But when the truth came to them,
     they declared, "This is sorcery—
     we don't believe it."

31   And they ask,
     "Why wasn't this Qur'an
     revealed to some prominent man
     from one of the two cities?"°

32   Is it they who apportion
     the mercy of your Lord?
     It is We Who apportion among them
     their livelihood in the life of this
        world.
     We raise some of them above others
     in rank, so they take them into
        service.
     And the mercy of your Lord
     is better than
     all the worldly goods they hoard.

33   We could have lavished on those
     who deny the All Merciful
     roofs of silver for their houses,
     and stairways to ascend
     —if this did not risk uniting them
     into one disbelieving community—

34 as well as doors
    for their homes, and
    beds on which to rest,

35 as well as ornaments of gold.
    But all these are merely amusements
    of the life of this world. The hereafter,
    with your Lord, is for the righteous.°

SECTION 4

36 If anyone turns away from
    the message of the All Merciful,
    We appoint for him a devil,
    to be his companion.

37 Such [devils] hinder them from
    the right path, though they think
    they are being rightly guided.

38 Until, when they come to Us,
    they say [to their devil companion],
    "If only there were a distance
    between us, as between East and
        West.
    What a wretched companion!"

39 [They will be told],
    "Since you did wrong,
    having partners in punishment
    won't help you now."

40 Can you make the deaf hear,
    or guide the blind,
    or those who are clearly astray?

41 Either We shall take you
    [from this life],
    and requite them

42 or We shall show you
    the fate We promised them—
    for We have power over them.

43 So hold fast to what
    was revealed to you,
    for you are on a straight path.

44 And [the Qur'an] is a reminder
    for you and your people—soon
    you shall all be questioned.

45 And ask the messengers
    We sent before you,
    did We appoint any gods
    to be worshipped
    other than the All Merciful?

SECTION 5

46 We sent Moses with Our signs
    to Pharaoh and his chiefs.
    He announced, "I am a messenger
    from the Lord of the universe."

47 But when he came to them
    with Our signs, they laughed at them.

48 We showed them sign after sign,
    each greater than its predecessor,°
    then We seized them with torment
    so they might turn back [to Us],

49 and they replied, "Sorcerer,
pray for us to your Lord
by virtue of His covenant with
　　you—
then we will be guided."

50 But once We removed their torment,
they broke their word.

51 Pharaoh called out to his people,
"My people, do I not hold dominion
over Egypt, over these rivers flowing
beneath me? Do you not see?

52 "Am I not better than
this vile wretch, who can scarce
express himself in plain speech?

53 "Why is he not adorned
with bracelets of gold, and escorted
by a host of angels?"

54 And so he fooled his people,
who obeyed him, for they were
a disobedient people.

55 So, when they angered Us,
We requited them,
and drowned them all.

56 And We made them
a precedent—an example
for generations to come.

SECTION 6

57 When [Jesus], son of Mary,
is offered as an example,
your people laugh about him,

58 saying, "Are our gods better,
or him?" They mention him
to you merely to argue,
for they are a contentious people.

59 He was only a servant—
to whom We granted favor, and
whom We offered as an example
to the children of Israel.

60 Had it been Our wish,
We could have made
some of you angels,
succeeding one another
on the earth.

61 And [Jesus] is a portent
of the impending hour,°
so do not harbor doubt about it,
and follow Me.
This is a straight path.

62 And don't let Satan bar you
[from the path]—
he is your open enemy.

63 When Jesus came
with clear testimony, he said,
"I come to bring you wisdom,
and to clarify some of the things

over which you dispute—
so, fear God, and obey me."

64 "For God is my Lord
and your Lord.
So worship Him alone—
this is a straight path."

65 Yet the various sects still
disputed among themselves.
Let those who did wrong
beware the torment
of a painful day.

66 Are they just waiting
for the hour to fall upon them
suddenly, while they are heedless?

67 On that day, friends
will become foes of one another—
except those who are righteous.

SECTION 7

68 My servants—on that day,
you shall have no fear
nor shall you grieve—

69 those who believed in Our signs
and bowed to Our will—

70 enter the garden, you
and your spouses, rejoicing.

71 Plates and goblets of gold
shall be passed among them.
And there, they shall have

all that their souls desire
and all that delights the eyes.
And you shall abide there forever.

72 This shall be the garden
bequeathed to you as its heirs
in virtue of your deeds.

73 There you shall have
fruit in abundance to eat.

74 But the sinful shall see
the torment of hell,
abiding there forever.

75 Their torment shall not be
lightened—
they shall be mired in despair.

76 We have not wronged them—
it is they themselves who did wrong.

77 They will cry, "Malik,°
let your Lord put an end to us!"
He will reply, "You must abide."

78 We have brought you the truth
but most of you abhor the truth.

79 Have they contrived a scheme?
We too shall conceive a scheme.

80 Or do they think We can't hear
their covert talk and whispered
counsels?
Our envoys are with them,
recording.

81 Say, "If the All Merciful
did have a child, I would be
the first to worship [him]."

82 Glory be to the Lord
of the heavens and the earth,
Lord of the throne—far above
what they ascribe to Him.

83 So leave them to gossip
and frolic—until they encounter
their promised day.

84 He is God in heaven
and God on earth,
He is Wise, All Knowing.

85 Blessed is He who has dominion
over the heavens and the earth
and all that lies between them;
He alone has knowledge of the hour,
and to Him you shall be returned.

86 And those they call on besides God
have no power to intercede—
only those who bore witness
to the truth and know [it].

87 If you, Prophet, asked them
"Who created the heavens and
earth?"
they would surely say, "God."
How, then, can they be deluded?

88 [God hears the] lament
[of the messenger],°
"My Lord, these are a people
who do not believe."

89 So, turn away from them,
and say, "Peace,"
for soon they shall come to know.

SURA 44

Smoke (*Al-Dukhan*)

For this Meccan sura of 59 verses, the distinctive image is "a pall of smoke" marking the day of resurrection (v. 10). It suggests that the Qur'an was revealed "on a [single] blessèd night" (v. 3), anticipating al-Qdar, Sura 97. It also recounts the story of Pharaoh, his punishment, and the rescue of the people of Israel (vv. 17–33). It ends with a direct command to Muhammad: "Wait," as the unbelievers also are waiting (v. 59).

In the Name of God, the All Merciful, Ever Merciful

SECTION I

1 *Ha Mim.*°

2 By the clarifying Book,

3 which We revealed on a blessèd
   night
   —We constantly give warning—

4 a night where every matter
   was wisely determined

5 by Our command—
   We constantly send [revelation]

6 as a mercy from your Lord—
   He is All Hearing, All Knowing,

7 Lord of the heavens and earth,
   and of all that lies between—if only
   you were assured in faith.°

8 There is no god but He—
   He Who gives life and brings death,
   your Lord, and Lord of your
      forefathers.

9 Yet they idle around, in doubt.

10 Watch out, then, for a day
   when the sky pours out
   a pall of smoke, for all to see,

11 enveloping humankind—
   a painful torment.

12 [They will cry,] "Our Lord,
   remove this torment from us—
   we are true believers."

13 How can they be reminded
   —a messenger already came to them
   with a clear message,°

14 they turned away from him,
   exclaiming, "A tutored madman."

15 If We remove the torment
   for a while, you will revert
   [to your former ways].

16 The day We seize them
   with overwhelming force,
   We shall exact retribution.

17 Before them, We tested
   the people of Pharaoh—
   a noble messenger came to them,

18 saying, "Deliver God's servants to
      me—
   I am a trustworthy messenger sent
      to you,

19 "and do not exalt yourselves
   over God—I come to you
   with clear authority.

20 "Should you seek to revile me°
   I seek refuge with my Lord
   and your Lord.

21 "If you don't believe me,
then keep away from me."

22 So Moses cried to his Lord,
"These people are a nation of
sinners."

23 [The reply came:]
"Set out by night with My servants,
for you are sure to be pursued.

24 "And leave the sea as it is—
divided°—behind you,
for their army shall be drowned."

25 How many gardens and springs
they left behind,

26 with fields of corn
and splendid structures,

27 and pleasant things° in which
they had known delight.

28 This [was their end],
and We made other peoples
heirs to those things.

29 Neither heaven nor earth
wept for them,
nor were they granted any respite.

SECTION 2

30 We delivered the children of Israel
from disgraceful torment

31 by Pharaoh, foremost
among the transgressors.

32 And We chose them,
with full knowledge,
over all peoples,°

33 and granted them signs
that would clearly try them.°

34 As for these people
[the Meccan disbelievers], they say,

35 "There is nothing beyond
our first death—we shall not
be raised again.

36 "Bring back our ancestors
if what you say is true."

37 Are they better than the people
of Tubba'° and those before them?
We destroyed them
for they were always sinners.

38 We did not create the heavens
and earth and all between them
for mere amusement.

39 We created them only
with true purpose; yet
most of them fail to understand.

40 The day of decision
is appointed for them all.

41 A day when no friend
can help another friend

and none shall be helped,

42 except those to whom
God shows mercy—
for He is Almighty, Ever Merciful.

SECTION 3

43 The tree of Zaqqum°

44 shall be the sinners' food;

45 it will boil, like molten lead,
in their bellies,

46 like scalding water.

47 [A voice will command,]
"Seize him, and drag him
to the depths of blazing fire.

48 "Then pour scalding water
over his head as punishment."

49 "Taste [this], you
who were mighty and noble.

50 "This is what you always doubted."

51 But those who fear God
shall be in a secure place,

52 amid gardens and springs,

53 in fine silk and rich brocade,
arrayed facing one another.

54 So it will be. We shall join them
as spouses to fair maidens, large
eyed.

55 They shall call for all kinds of fruit
in tranquility;

56 nor shall they taste death there,
beyond the first death,
and He will save them
from the torment of blazing fire,

57 a favor from your Lord—
the supreme triumph.

58 We have made this Qur'an easy,
in your tongue, so they might take
heed.

59 So, wait—they° too
are waiting.

Kneeling (*Al-Jathiya*)

A short Meccan sura of 37 verses, this extols the several signs of God in creation and the natural world (vv. 3–13), culminating with a scene where each community will be kneeling on judgment day, attesting to its record, literally, its book (v. 28).

In the Name of God, the All Merciful, Ever Merciful

SECTION I

1 *Ha Mim.*°

2 The revelation of the Book
 is from God, the Almighty, All
  Wise.

3 In the heavens and on earth
 are signs for those who believe.

4 In your own creation,
 and in the creatures God dispersed
 throughout the earth, are signs
 for those with firm faith.

5 In the cycle of night and day,
 and in the sustenance God sends
 from the sky, giving life
 to the earth after its death,
 and in His steering of the winds
 are signs for people who reason.

6 These are the verses of God
 which We recite to you with truth.

So, in what message can they believe
 after rejecting God and His signs?

7 Woe to every lying sinner

8 who hears the verses of God
 recited to him, yet persists in pride,
 as though he had not heard them.
 Warn him, then, of painful torment.

9 Even when he learns something
 of Our signs, he mocks them.
 Disgraceful torment awaits him.

10 Before such people lies hell,
 and what they earned will be
 of no use to them, nor those they
  took
 as protectors instead of God;
 they shall face great torment.

11 This is true guidance—
 and those who deny
 the signs of their Lord
 shall face painful torment.

SECTION 2

12 It is God Who has subdued to you
the sea, on which ships might sail
by His command, so you might seek
His bounty, and show thanks.

13 And He has subdued to you
all that is in the heavens
and all that is on earth—a favor
from Him. In all this are signs
for a people who reflect.

14 Tell those who believe to forgive
those who do not truly expect [to see]
the days of God°—
so that He might requite people
for what they have earned.

15 If anyone does good,
it is for himself; if he does evil,
it is against himself.
In the end, you shall all
be brought back to your Lord.

16 We gave the children of Israel
the Book, wisdom, and
        prophethood;
We sustained them with good things
and favored them above all nations.

17 We gave them clear proof
on questions [of religion].
Yet they quarreled, through mutual
        envy,
even after knowledge came to them.
On the day of resurrection
your Lord will judge between them

concerning the things they dispute.

18 Now We have set you, Prophet,
on a proper path [of religion]°—
so follow it, and don't follow
the desires of those who don't know.

19 They will be of no help to you
against God, for the wrongdoers
are protectors of one another,
while God is Protector of those
who are mindful of Him.

20 These are insights° for humankind,
as well as guidance and mercy
for those of firm faith.

21 Do those who commit evil deeds
imagine that We will treat them like
those who believe and do good
        deeds,
making their lives and deaths alike?
How perverse is their judgment!

SECTION 3

22 God created the heavens and earth
with true purpose, so that each soul
might be recompensed for what it
        earned—
and none of them shall be wronged.

23 Have you observed
the [kind of] person who takes
his own desire as his god?
Knowing this, God has let him stray,
placing a seal upon his hearing and
his heart, and a veil over his sight—

who can guide him after God
[has let him stray]?
Will you not, then, take heed?

24 And they say, "There is nothing
but our life in this world.
We die and we live—only time
destroys us." Yet they know nothing
of this, and merely conjecture.

25 When Our clear verses are
recited to them, they merely retort,
"Bring back our forefathers
if what you say is true."

26 Say, "It is God Who gives life
to you, then brings you death;
He will gather you all together
on the day of resurrection—
of which there is no doubt,
though most people don't know."

SECTION 4

27 To God belongs dominion
of the heavens and the earth,
and on the day when the hour falls,
it is the falsifiers who will lose.

28 You will see all peoples kneeling.
Each will be called to its record:°
"This day, you shall be requited
for all that you did.

29 "Our record here speaks the truth
about you—We have transcribed
in it
all that you did."

30 He will admit into His mercy those
who believed and did good deeds—
that is the distinct triumph.

31 Those who denied will be asked,
"Were My verses not recited to you?
Yet you remained proud,
a sinful people."

32 When it was said,
"The promise of God is true,
there is no doubt about the hour,"
you retorted,
"We don't know what the hour is—
we think it is mere speculation
and we're not convinced."

33 The evil of their deeds
will appear before them,
and they will be engulfed
by what they used to mock.

34 They will then be told,
"Today, We will forget you
just as you forgot the meeting
[with Us] on this day of yours.
Your home shall be the fire
and you shall have no helper.

35 "This is because you mocked
the signs of God, deluded by the life
of this world." So on this day,
they shall not be brought out
of the fire, nor shall they
be able to atone.

36 Praise be to God,
Lord of the heavens
and Lord of the earth—
Lord of the universe.

37 His is the Grandeur
throughout the heavens and earth—
He is Almighty, All Wise.

SURA 46

Sand Dunes (*Al-Ahqaf*)

This is the final of seven Meccan suras that begin with the same disconnected letters, *ha mim*. Like others in the series, its 35 verses extol the sending down of the Qur'an while condemning idolaters' recalcitrance in the face of God's signs. It also brings into the chorus of believers a group of spirits (jinn), who are moved by the Qur'anic message, "a Book, revealed after Moses, confirming what came before it" (v. 30).

In the Name of God, the All Merciful, Ever Merciful

SECTION I

1 *Ha Mim.*°

2 The revelation of the Book
is from God,
the Almighty, All Wise.

3 We created the heavens and earth
and all that lies between them
only with true purpose°
and for an appointed term.
Those who disbelieve turn away
from the warnings given to them.°

4 Say, Prophet, "Do you see
what it is you call upon besides God?
Show me what they have created
of the earth, or what share
     they have
of the heavens. Bring me a Book
[revealed] before this one,
or a trace of [earlier] knowledge
if you are speaking the truth.

5 And who could be more astray than
those who call on other gods besides
     God
—others who will not answer them

until the day of resurrection,
who will not heed their prayers?

6 And when humankind
are gathered together,
[those other gods]
will be their enemies, and
will deny their worship.

7 When Our clear verses are recited
to them, the disbelievers say
—of the truth that has reached them—
"This is clearly just sorcery."

8 Or they say, "He has invented it."
Say, "Had I invented it,
you would have no power
[to intercede] for me with God.
He knows best what you say about it.
He will suffice as Witness
between you and me—
He is Forgiving, Ever Merciful."

9 Say, "I am not new
among the messengers,
nor do I know what will be done
with me or with you.
I merely follow what
is revealed to me,
and I am merely someone
who gives clear warning."

10 Say, "Have you thought—
what if this [Book] *is* from God
and you deny it, while a witness
from the children of Israel attests
that it is like [previous scripture]

and believes, while you [turn away]
in your pride? God does not guide
a wrongdoing people."

SECTION 2

11 The unbelievers say about the
believers,
"If [this message] had merit,
they would not have embraced it
before we did." And since [the
unbelievers]
will not be guided by it,
they say, "This is an ancient lie."

12 Yet, before this, the Book of Moses
was a guide and a mercy—
this Book confirms it
in the Arabic tongue
to warn those who do wrong
and bring joyous news
to those who do good.

13 As for those who say,
"Our Lord is God,"
and remain steadfast—
they shall have no fear,
nor shall they grieve.

14 They shall reside in
the garden, abiding there forever—
a reward for all they did.

15 We have enjoined man
to be kind to his parents;
in pain his mother bore him
and in pain she gave birth to him.

Bearing him and weaning him
took a full thirty months.
When, eventually, he reaches
maturity—forty years—
he [should] say, "My Lord,
give me strength to be grateful
for Your favor to me
and to my parents.
Let me do good deeds
that are pleasing to You,
and make my offspring righteous—
for I turn to You [repenting]
and I am among those
who bow to Your will."°

16 From them We shall accept
the best of their deeds, and overlook
their bad deeds. They shall be
among those who live in the garden—
fulfilling the promise given to
them.°

17 But some person might chide
his parents, "Confound you both—
do you really promise me that
I'll be raised up again—even though
generations before me have passed
on?"
But both parents seek God's help,
saying, "Shame on you! You should
believe—for the promise of God is
true."
Yet still he retorts, "These are merely
fables of the ancients."

18 Sentence shall be passed on
such people, along with generations
of jinn and men that have passed
before them—they shall suffer loss.

19 All shall be ranked by degrees
in virtue of what they did,
so that God might
requite them for their deeds—
and none of them shall be wronged.

20 The day unbelievers are exposed
to the fire [they will be told],
"You exhausted your share of the
good things in the life of this world
and you enjoyed them. But this day
you shall be requited
with humiliating torment,
for you were proud
upon the earth, without due right,
and were always disobedient."

SECTION 3

21 Recount [the story of Hud]
of the tribe of ʿAd, when he warned
his people amid the sand dunes
—others had come to warn them
before and after him—
"Worship none but God,
for I fear for you the torment
of a momentous day."

22 They retorted, "Have you come
to turn us away from our gods?
Then bring down upon us

the torment you threaten us with,
if you are speaking the truth."

23   He said, "Knowledge of that
rests with God alone. I merely convey
the message with which I am sent.
Yet I see you are an ignorant people."

24   Then, when they saw a cloud
looming over their valleys,
they exclaimed, "Here is a cloud
bearing rain for us"—"No.
It is [the threat] you asked
to be hastened—a stormy wind
bearing painful torment,

25   "destroying all before it
by its Lord's command."
By morning, nothing could be seen
except their homes [in ruins]—
this is how We requite
a sinful people.

26   We established them
with [such power and authority]
as we have not endowed you.
We gave them
hearing, sight, and hearts—but
    none
of these—hearing or sight or
    hearts—
availed them at all, for they denied
the signs of God, so they were
    engulfed
by the very thing they would mock.

SECTION 4

27   We destroyed towns around you,
after giving them diverse signs
that they might return [to Our path].

28   Why then did their gods
not help them—those they had taken
as gods instead of the One God
to bring them closer to Him?
Instead, they abandoned them—
that was the lie they invented.

29   We sent to you, Prophet, a group
of jinn, to listen to the Qur'an,
and, while they attended it,
    they said,
"Listen in silence."
When it was concluded, they turned
back to their people to warn them.

30   They said, "Our people,
we have heard a Book, revealed
after Moses, confirming what came
before it. It guides to the truth
and to a straight way.

31   "Our people, answer the one who
calls [us] to God, and believe in Him.
God will forgive you your sins
and deliver you from painful
    torment.

32   "Those who fail to answer the one
who calls [us] to God shall find
no escape throughout the earth,

nor any protectors besides God—
they are clearly wrong."

33 Do they not see that God is the One
Who created the heavens and the
    earth,
unfatigued by their creation?
He is Able to give life to the dead—
He has Power over all things.

34 On the day the unbelievers
are exposed to the fire,
[they will be asked,] "Is this not real?"
They will reply, "By our Lord, it is."

[They will be told,]
"Taste the punishment
for your disbelief."

35 Be patient, then, as the messengers
of firm resolve° were patient,
and do not seek to hasten [torment
for the unbelievers]. On the day
they see the torment promised them,
it will seem as if they had stayed
[in this life] a mere hour of one day.
[This Qur'an] is a message.
Shall any be destroyed
but those who were disobedient?

SURA 47

Muhammad

A Medinan sura of 38 verses, this deals with historical events around the Battle of Badr (624 CE), which occurred two years after Muhammad's move to
Medina. The rare mention of Muhammad by name in the Qur'an (v. 2) is the
reason this becomes the title of the sura.

In the Name of God, the All Merciful, Ever Merciful

SECTION I

1 God will nullify the deeds
of those who disbelieve
and bar [people] from His path.

2 But for those who believe
and do good deeds, who believe
in what was revealed to Muhammad
—the truth from their Lord—

He will nullify their misdeeds
and rectify their condition.

3 For those who disbelieve
pursue falsehood,
while those who believe
pursue the truth
from their Lord. This is how God
mirrors for people their true
    likeness.°

4 When you meet the unbelievers
  [in battle], strike at their necks,
  and when you have subdued them,
  bind them firmly, then you can
  either be gracious [and free them]
  or hold them for ransom, once
  the weight of war has lifted.
  That [is Our command].
  Had God wished, He Himself
  could have requited them,
  but He would test you
  against one another.
  And the deeds of those killed
  in God's cause shall never be lost.

5 He will guide them and
  and rectify their condition,

6 and bring them into the garden—
  as He has made known to them.

7 You who believe—if you help
  in the cause of God, He will help
     you
  and plant your feet firmly.

8 As for the disbelievers—
  destruction awaits them
  and their deeds shall be lost.

9 For they hate what God has
     revealed,
  so He has nullified their deeds.

10 Don't they travel through the earth°
   and see the fate of those before
      them?

God brought destruction to them;
the unbelievers shall see the same
   end.

11 For God is Protector
   of those who believe,
   but the unbelievers
   have no protector.

SECTION 2

12 God will bring those who believe
   and do good deeds into gardens,
   with rivers flowing beneath.
   The unbelievers enjoy [this world]
   and eat as cattle eat; but the fire
   shall be their [eternal] home.

13 How many cities We destroyed
   that had more power than your city
   which drove you out—
   and there was none to help them.

14 Is a person who acts
   on clear proof from his Lord
   the same as someone whose
   wicked deeds seem fair to him,
   or the same as those
   who follow their own desires?

15 [Here is] a parable of the garden
   promised to those who fear God:
   It has rivers of pure water,
   and rivers of milk whose taste
   never changes, and rivers of wine,
   delicious to those who drink,
   and rivers of purified honey.

It has every kind of fruit for them,
and forgiveness from their Lord.
Are such people like
those who abide in eternal fire,
those given scalding water to drink,
that tears apart their bowels?

16 Among them are some
who listen to you,
but when they leave you,
they say to those
who have received knowledge,
"What was it he said just now?"
They are the ones
whose hearts God has sealed,
for they follow only
their own desires.

17 But God increases guidance
for those who will be guided,
and He makes them mindful of Him.°

18 Do they but wait, then, for the hour
to fall upon them suddenly?
Some tokens of it have already
    come—
and once it has fallen upon them
what good is it then for them
to remember God's warning?

19 Know, then, that there is
no god but the One God,
so ask forgiveness for your sin,
and for believing men and women.
For God knows where you move
and where you rest.°

SECTION 3

20 Those who believe say,
"Why is a sura not revealed
[commanding us to fight]?"
But when a sura is revealed that
clearly mentions fighting, you'll see
the sick-hearted staring at you
with the look of one about to faint
at the prospect of death.
More appropriate for them

21 would be obedience
and upright words.°
And once the stratagem [of war]
is resolved upon,°
it would be better for them
to stand true to God.

22 If you turn away, would you
sow corruption in the land,
and cut your bonds of kinship?

23 These are the ones God has cursed,
making them deaf
and taking away their sight.°

24 Do they not reflect on the Qur'an—
or are there locks on their hearts?

25 As for those who turned their backs
after clear guidance was given them—
it was Satan who enticed them,
and prolonged them in [false] hope.

26 For they declared to those
who hate what God has revealed,

"We'll obey you in some things"—
but God knows what they keep
    secret.

27 How will it be when the angels
take their souls at death,
striking their faces and their backs?

28 For they pursued what angered God
and were loath to please Him,
so He shall nullify all their deeds.

SECTION 4

29 Or do those with sick hearts think
that God will not expose their hatred?

30 Had We wished, We could have
shown them to you and you would
    have
known them by their marks––
but you'll know them indeed
by their tone of speech.
And God knows all that you do.

31 And We shall test you, to see°
which of you strive [in God's cause]
and are steadfast—We shall test
the truth of what is said by you.°

32 As for those who disbelieve,
who bar people from God's path,
and oppose the messenger
after clear guidance was given
    them—
they cannot harm Him at all—
but He shall render their deeds void.

33 You who believe: obey God,
obey the messenger, and
do not render vain your own deeds.

34 As for those who disbelieve
and bar people from God's path,
then die as disbelievers—
God shall never forgive them.

35 So do not weaken and cry for peace
while you have ascendancy,
for God is with you;
He will never deprive you
of the reward for your deeds.

36 The life of this world
is but a pastime and a sport;
but if you believe, and fear God,
He will give you your reward;
nor is He not asking you
to give up your possessions.

37 If He were to ask you this,
and press you, you would hold back,
and He would expose your ill will.

38 See—you are the ones called upon
to spend in the cause of God,
but some of you still hold back.
Those who hold back do so
at the cost of their own souls—
for God is Self-Sufficient,
while you are in need [of His mercy].
If you turn back, He will replace you
with another people—
who will not be like you.

Victory (*Al-Fath*)

Another Medinan sura with historical resonance, its opening verse, "We have given you a clear victory," could refer to the Battle of Badr, noted in the previous sura, or it could be an anticipation of the victory that would come later (after the Peace of Hudaybiyya in 628 CE) when the Muslims delayed their reentry to Mecca in exchange for permission to go later (630). Its notable verses refer to God's serenity being sent down on Muhammad and believers after Hudaybiyya (v. 26), and the marks left on foreheads of the devout at prayer (v. 29).

In the Name of God, the All Merciful, Ever Merciful

SECTION I

1 We have given you a clear victory,

2 such that God might forgive you
your past and future sins,
fulfill His favor to you,
and guide you to a straight path,

3 granting you His mighty help.

4 It is He Who sent down serenity
into believers' hearts to increase
their faith—the forces of the
heavens
and earth belong to God;
God alone is All Knowing, All
Wise—

5 so that He might usher
the believing men and women
into gardens, beneath which
rivers flow, abiding there forever,

and so that He might absolve them
of their bad deeds—in God's eyes
that is the supreme triumph—

6 and that He might punish
the hypocrites, both men and
women,
and the polytheists, men and
women,
who harbor a wrongful conception
of God. Around them is
a circle of evil, and the wrath of God
is upon them. He has cursed them
and prepared for them hell—
an evil destination.

7 For the forces of the heavens
and earth belong to God;
God alone is Almighty, All Wise.

8 We have sent you, Prophet,
as a witness, a bearer of joyous news,
and as one who warns

9 so that [all of] you might believe
   in God and His messenger,
   honoring God, revering Him,°
   glorifying Him morning and evening.

10 Those who pledge allegiance
   to you, Prophet, pledge allegiance
   to God—the Hand of God
   is over their hands.°
   And those who break their oath
   thereby harm their own soul.
   But He will grant a great reward
   to those who fulfill
   their covenant with God.

SECTION 2

11 The Bedouin Arabs who stayed back
   will say to you, "Our properties
   and our families kept us busy,
   so seek forgiveness for us"—
   their tongues speak what
   is not in their hearts. Say,
   "Who has power to intervene for
        you
   with God, should He intend
   either harm or gain for you?
   Indeed, God is Aware
   of all that you do.

12 "Indeed—you thought the
        messenger
   and the believers would never
   come back to their families,
   and this pleased your hearts—
   but your thought was wicked—
   you are a ruined people."

13 As for those who do not believe
   in God and His messenger—
   We have prepared a blazing fire
   for such disbelievers.

14 To God belongs dominion
   of the heavens and the earth;
   He forgives whom He will,
   and punishes whom He will—
   He is Forgiving, Ever Merciful.

15 When you set out for [the site] where
   you might grasp the spoils of war,
   Those who stayed back will say,
   "Allow us to follow you"—they want
   to change the words of God. Say,
   "Never shall you follow us—
   God said this before." They will say,
   "The truth is that you envy us."
   No—the truth is that they
   have little understanding.

16 Say to the Bedouin Arabs who
        stayed back,
   "You will be called [to fight] against
   a people of great military might.
   You shall fight until they submit,
   and if you obey, God will grant you
   a fine reward, but if you turn back,
   as you did before, He will punish you
   with a painful torment."

17 The blind, the lame, and the sick
   won't be blamed [if they don't fight].
   God will usher those who obey Him
   and His messenger into gardens,
   beneath which rivers flow, but

He will punish those who turn away,
with a painful torment.

SECTION 3

18 God was pleased with the believers
when they pledged allegiance to you
beneath the tree.° He knew
what was in their hearts, so He sent
down serenity upon them, and
rewarded them with a swift victory,

19 and many spoils of war yet to take,
for God is Almighty, All Wise.

20 God promised that you will take
many spoils of war, and He hastened
this for you, restraining the hands
of those against you—as a sign
for the believers, and so He might
guide you to a straight path.

21 And there are more gains,
over which you have no power,
which God oversees,
for God has Power over all things.

22 If the unbelievers had fought you,
they would have turned their backs—
finding then no protector or helper.

23 This has been God's way,
as before—you will never find
any change in God's way.

24 It was He Who restrained the hands
of those fighting against you, and

yours from them, in the valley of
   Mecca,
after He gave you victory over them—
for God Sees all that you do.

25 They are the ones who disbelieved,
barred you from the sacred mosque
to stop the offering from reaching
its sacrificial site. Had there not
   been
believing men and women whom
you did not know among them,
whom you might have trampled,
unaware, thereby incurring blame,
[God would have let you advance
but instead held you back] so that
He might admit whom He will
into His mercy—if they had been
separated, We would have punished
the unbelievers among them
with a painful torment.

26 While the unbelievers' hearts
seethed with rage—ignorant rage—
God sent His serenity upon
His messenger and the believers,
making them cleave to their word
to be true to Him,° for they were
more deserving and worthy of this—
God is Knower of all things.

SECTION 4

27 God has fulfilled the truth
of His messenger's vision—
you shall enter the sacred mosque
   safely,

if God is willing, with shaved heads
or shortened hair, without fear—
for He knew what you did not know,
and decreed for you, besides this,
an imminent victory.

28 It is He Who has sent
His messenger with guidance
and the religion of truth
to display its preeminence
over all [other] religion—
for God suffices as Witness.

29 Muhammad is the messenger of God;
those with him are firm with
   unbelievers
and compassionate with one
   another—

you will see them bowing [in prayer]
and prostrating, seeking God's favor
and His good pleasure. Their
   foreheads
bear the marks° of their
   prostrations.
This is how the Torah and the Gospel
present a parable of them: [they are]
like a seed which sends out its shoot
and makes it strong; then it thickens
and stands upon its own stem,
delighting those who sowed it°—
so that God might exasperate
the unbelievers by their means.
God has promised those among
   them
who believe and do good deeds
both forgiveness and a great reward.

SURA 49

The Private Apartments (*Al-Hujurat*)

A short (18 verses) late Medinan sura, this cites the protocol for behavior of believers with the Prophet (vv. 2–5), especially when they contact him from outside his private apartments (v. 4), and concludes with a critique of the Bedouin Arabs (vv. 14–18).

In the Name of God, the All Merciful, Ever Merciful

SECTION I

1 You who believe, do not
put your own decisions
before those of God
and His messenger°—
rather, be mindful of God,

for God is All Hearing,
All Knowing.

2 You who believe, do not
raise your voices above the voice
of the Prophet—and do not
speak loudly to him, as you might do

among one another, else
your deeds might be rendered vain
without your knowing it.

3 Those who lower their voices
in the presence of God's messenger
are the ones whose hearts
God has tested for righteousness.
They shall find forgiveness
and a great reward.

4 As for those who call you, Prophet,
from behind your private
    apartments—
most of them fail to understand.

5 If they had patience—[to wait]
until you came out to them—
that would be better for them.
But God is Forgiving, Ever
    Merciful.

6 You who believe—
if a wicked person comes to you
with news, see if it is true—
so you don't harm people
through ignorance, and then
feel regret for what you did.

7 And know that God's messenger
is among you. If he were to heed
your wishes in many things,
you would surely suffer.
But God has endeared the faith to
    you
and beautified it in your hearts,
making disbelief, transgression,

and disobedience hateful to you—
such are those who are rightly
    guided—

8 a grace and favor from God,
for God is All Knowing, All Wise.

9 If two parties among the believers
fight, make peace between them.
If one seeks to oppress the other,
then oppose that party until they
    abide
by God's command; when they do so,
make peace between them justly, and
be fair—God loves those who are fair.

10 The believers are kin, so
make peace between your kin,
and be mindful of God
that you might be shown mercy.

SECTION 2

11 You who believe—
Let no people [among you]
ridicule any other people,
for perhaps they are better than
    them;
nor should any group of women
ridicule another group,
for perhaps they are better than
    them;
nor revile, nor call one another
by [hurtful] nicknames. How
    terrible
to be called out in mockery
after embracing faith.

And those who don't repent
are wrongdoers.

12 You who believe,
   avoid excessive suspicion, for
   some kinds of suspicion are a sin.
   And do not spy on one another,
   nor backbite—would you like
   to eat the flesh of your dead brother?
   Of course not—you would hate it.
   So, be mindful of God—
   God is Ever Relenting, Merciful.

13 Humankind, We created you
   from a male and a female, then
   We made you into nations and
      tribes,
   that you might know one another.
   The most noble of you in God's sight
   is the most mindful of Him—
   God is All Knowing, All Aware.

14 The Bedouin Arabs say, "We
      believe."
   Say to them, "You do not believe.
   Rather, you should [first] say,
   'We have submitted to God's will,'°
   for belief has not yet entered
   your hearts. But, if you obey God
   and His messenger, He will not
   withhold from you at all

the reward for your deeds—
God is Forgiving, Ever Merciful."

15 True believers are those
   who believe in God and His
      messenger
   and do not then fall into doubt;
   who strive with their wealth and
   give their lives in the cause of
      God—
   they are the ones who are truly
      sincere.

16 Say, "Would you presume
   to instruct God in religion?
   God knows all that is in the heavens
   and all that is on the earth—
   God is Knower of all things."

17 They consider it a favor to you
   that they've submitted to God's will.
   Say, "Don't think your submission
   a favor to me; rather, God has
      favored you
   in guiding you to the faith,
   if you are truly sincere."°

18 God knows all that is unseen
   in the heavens and the earth—
   He Sees all that you do.°

Qaf (*Qaf*)

This Meccan sura begins with a single Arabic letter (*qaf*) elided into the opening verse. Its 45 verses appeal to God's might and mercy in affirming resurrection from the dead (vv. 2–11). It contains a graphic account of two recording angels on the day (vv. 17–29) and ends with an injunction to the Prophet that he should "remind them, with the Qur'an—those who fear My warning" (v. 45).

In the Name of God, the All Merciful, Ever Merciful

SECTION I

1 *Qaf.*°
By the glorious Qur'an—

2 they wonder why one of their own
has come to warn them;
the unbelievers say, "How strange,

3 "when we die and turn to dust
[shall we rise again]?
Such a return is a remote prospect."

4 We know well how the earth
decomposes them;° We have a Book
that preserves everything.°

5 But they denied the truth
when it came to them,
and now they are confused
[as to right and wrong].

6 Don't they see the sky above them—
how We fashioned and furbished it,
with no fracture in it?

7 And We spread out the earth, setting
firm mountains upon it, and made
to flower
every kind of exuberant plant—

8 to provide insight and a reminder
for every repenting servant.

9 And We send down from the sky
rain that is blessed, and We raise
with it gardens and harvest grain,

10 and tall palm trees, laden
with clusters of dates, layer on layer,

11 as sustenance for Our servants,
and with rain We bring life to dead
soil—
this is how [the dead] will come out.

12 Before them,
the people of Noah disbelieved,
as did the people of Rass, Thamud,

13 'Ad, Pharaoh, the brothers of Lot,

14 the people of Midian,
and the nation of Tubba'°
—all denied the messengers,
so My warning was fulfilled.

15 Did the first creation fatigue Us?
No—yet they doubt
the promise of a new creation.

SECTION 2

16 We created man, and We know
what his soul whispers to him;
We are closer to him
than his jugular vein.

17 Two angels,° seated on the right
and left, record everything.

18 No word does [a person] utter
but an observer is with him,
ready [to record it].

19 And the stupor of death
will bring out the truth—
"This is what you tried to elude."

20 And the trumpet will be blown—
"This is the promised day."

21 And each soul shall come,
with one angel to urge it on,
another to serve as witness:

22 "You were heedless of this.
Now, We have removed your veil—
on this day your sight is keen."

23 And his attendant will say,
"I have his record here, ready."

24 "Hurl into hell every
stubborn disbeliever

25 "who always forbade
what was good, transgressed,
and remained in doubt,

26 "who set up another god
besides the One God.
Hurl him into severe torment."

27 His companion will say, "Our Lord,
I didn't make him transgress—
he was already far astray."

28 God will say, "Don't dispute
with each other in My presence.
I sent you a warning—

29 "My Word shall not be changed,
nor am I unjust to My servants."

SECTION 3

30 On the day We ask hell,
"Are you full?" it will answer,
"Are there more?"

31 But the garden shall be drawn
near for those who feared God,
distant no more.

32 "This is what you were promised—

for all who turned [to God,
   repenting]
keeping [Him in mind],

33 "who feared the Most Merciful,
though unseen, and turned to Him
with a penitent heart.

34 "Enter it, in peace; this day
begins eternity."

35 They shall have there
all that they desire,
and more besides, from Us.

36 How many generations
did We destroy before them,
though they were stronger,
and had explored many lands—
could they find no refuge?

37 In this is a reminder for whoever
has a heart, and listens, as a witness.

38 We created the heavens and earth,
and all between them in six days,
yet no fatigue could reach Us.

39 So bear with patience
whatever they say,
and hymn your Lord's praise
before sunrise and sunset,

40 hymn His glory during the night,
and after bowing in prayer.

41 And listen for a day
when the caller calls
from a nearby place,

42 the day they hear the actual blast—
that will be the day they come out
[from their graves].

43 It is We Who give life
and bring death:
to Us is the final return—

44 the day the earth is
cleaved asunder beneath them,
with people rushing away—
such a gathering of them all
will be easy for Us.

45 We know best what they say,
and it is not for you, Prophet,
to compel them.
So remind them, with the Qur'an—
those who fear My warning.

Scattering Winds (*Al-Dhariyat*)

Also Meccan and also evoking judgment by an appeal to nature (the widely scattering winds, v. 1), this sura recounts Abraham's hospitality to his honored guests (vv. 24–37), as well as the punishment meted out to Pharaoh and other disbelievers (vv. 38–54). It culminates with a reminder to Muhammad to remind believers: "I have created jinn and humankind only so that they might worship Me" (v. 56).

In the Name of God, the All Merciful, Ever Merciful

SECTION I

1 By the widely scattering [winds];

2 and those bearing [clouds of rain];

3 and those flowing with ease;

4 and those spreading
   [rain and other blessings]
   as ordained;°

5 what you are promised is true:

6 the reckoning will surely come.

7 By the sky, copious with paths—

8 you differ in what you say;

9 those who turn away
   are thereby turned away;

10 may those who lie perish,

11 those who flounder in
    heedlessness—

12 they ask, "When will be
    the day of reckoning?"

13 It will be a day when
    they are tried by fire.

14 "Taste your ordeal—this
    is what you sought to hasten."

15 Those who were mindful of God
    shall be in gardens and springs,

16 gaining what their Lord gives them,
    for their good deeds in the past.

17 They would sleep just
    a small part of the night,

18 and in the hours before dawn
    they would ask for forgiveness;

19 and give their due share of wealth
to beggars and those in need.°

20 There are signs on the earth
for those assured in their faith,

21 and also within your own selves—
will you not, then, see?

22 The heavens hold your sustenance
and all that you are promised.

23 By the Lord of the heavens
and earth, this is the truth,
as true as the fact that you speak.

SECTION 2

24 Has the story of Abraham's
honored guests reached you?

25 When they came to him,
they said, "Peace." He replied,
"Peace to you, strangers."

26 Then he went back to his family
and brought out a fattened calf,

27 which he placed before them.
"Won't you eat?" he asked,

28 feeling some fear of them.
They said, "Don't be afraid,"
and they gave him joyous news
of the birth of a learnèd son.

29 Then his wife came forward,
hollering—cuffing her face,
she scoffed, "A barren old woman?!"

30 They said, "It will be so,
says your Lord,
and He is Almighty, All Knowing."

31 Abraham asked, "Messengers,
what is your mission?"

32 They said, "We have been sent
to a nation of sinners,

33 "to send down brimstone
upon them,

34 "marked by your Lord
for those who transgress."

35 Then We brought out
the believers who were there,

36 but We found in one house only
those who submit their will to God,°

37 and We left there a sign for those
who fear a painful torment.

38 In Moses [was a further sign],
when We sent him to Pharaoh
with clear sanction.

39 But [Pharaoh] turned away
with his retinue, saying, "He's either
a sorcerer or simply possessed."

40 So We seized him with his forces
and cast them into the sea
for he was blameworthy.

41 [There is also a sign]
in the people of ʿAd—against whom
We sent a barren wind

42 that left nothing in its trail
but utter destruction.

43 And [another sign]
in the people of Thamud
who were told, "Enjoy this life
for a short while."

44 But they defied
their Lord's command,
so a thunderbolt struck them
as they looked on.

45 Unable even to stand,
they were utterly helpless.

46 Like Noah's people before them,
they were a disobedient people.

SECTION 3

47 We forged the sky with Our might,
and We spread it throughout space.

48 Then We spread out the earth—
how excellently expansive!

49 And We created pairs of each thing
that you might be reminded.

50 [Prophet, urge them,]
"Hasten toward God—
I am sent to you from Him
to give clear warning.

51 "Set up no other god
besides the One God;
I am sent to you from Him
to give clear warning."

52 Likewise, no messenger came
to the peoples before them
without their saying, "He's either
a sorcerer or simply possessed."

53 Is this what they have
told one another? No!
They are a transgressive people.

54 So turn away from them—
for you have incurred no blame.

55 But remind them [of the message]
for a reminder profits believers.

56 I have created jinn and humankind
only so that they might worship Me.

57 I desire no sustenance from them
nor do I wish them to feed Me.

58 For God is the Sustainer,
Possessor of Power,
Supreme in Strength.

59 The wrongdoers will be punished
    like their predecessors—so let them
    not urge Me to hasten this.

60 Woe to the unbelievers,
    on the day promised to them.

SURA 52

Mount Sinai (*Al-Tur*)

Opening with a reference to Mount Sinai, this Meccan sura of 49 verses highlights the certainty and the accountability of judgment day (vv. 9–28), with a
stern reminder to Muhammad that he is neither a poet nor a soothsayer nor a
madman (vv. 29–30), and that he should show patience while praising God day
and night (vv. 48–49).

In the Name of God, the All Merciful, Ever Merciful

SECTION I

1 By Mount [Sinai],

2 by a Book that is inscribed°

3 in a scroll unfolded;

4 by the house° that is visited
   time after time,

5 by the canopy° raised high;

6 and by the brimming sea,
   [unconfined]

7 the torment of your Lord
   shall come to pass—

8 none can prevent it.

9 On the day when the sky
   rocks back and forth,

10 and the mountains roll
    violently around—

11 woe on that day
    to those who deny,

12 who idle away their time
    in trifling talk—

13 on that day they shall be
    thrust into the fire of hell.

14 "This," [they will be told,]
    "is the fire you denied.

15 "Is this sorcery, then,
    or do still you not see?

16 "Burn in it—it is the same for you
  whether you endure it or not—
  You are merely requited for what
    you did."

17 Those who were mindful of God
  shall be in gardens, in bliss,

18 relishing their Lord's gifts to them,
  and their Lord shall deliver them
  from the torment of blazing fire.

19 [They will be told,]
  "Eat and drink, to your content—
  for all that you have done."

20 Reclining on couches,
  arrayed in rows—
  We shall wed them
  to houris, large eyed.

21 We shall unite those who believe
  with those of their offspring
  who followed them in faith.
  We shall not withhold at all
  the reward for their deeds—
  every person is bound
  by° what they have earned.

22 And We shall extend to them
  all the fruit and meat they desire.

23 There, they shall pass around
  a cup among themselves, inducing
  neither idle talk nor sin.

24 Youths as fair as hidden pearls
  shall circle among them,

25 and they will turn to
  one another, asking questions,

26 saying, "When we were
  with our families before
  [on earth], we were fearful.

27 "But now God has favored us,
  and saved us from
  the torment of scorching wind.

28 "Even then, we would call on Him—
  for He is Most Kind, Ever Merciful.

SECTION 2

29 So remind them, Prophet—
  for, by the grace of your Lord,
  you are neither a soothsayer
  nor a madman.

30 Or, do they say, "A mere poet—
  for whom we anticipate
  some misfortune in time!"

31 Say, "Wait, then—
  and I shall be waiting with you."

32 Do their minds urge them
  to [say] this, or are they
  a rebellious people?

33 Or, do they say,
"He has invented it"?
They just don't believe.

34 Let them produce a discourse like it
if they are speaking the truth.

35 Were they created from nothing—
or are they themselves creators?

36 Or, did they create the heavens
and the earth? No, they have no
assurance [of the truth].

37 Or, do they possess the treasures
of your Lord, or control them?

38 Or, do they have a stairway
to climb and hear [the secrets
of heaven]? If so, let those
who heard bring clear proof.

39 Or, does He have daughters
while you yourselves have sons?

40 Or, do you ask them for payment
that would weigh them down in
debt?

41 Or, do they have knowledge
of the unseen,
which they can transcribe?

42 Or, do they intend to scheme
against you?—those who disbelieve
are already being outschemed.

43 Or, do they have a god
other than the One God?
Glory be to God, far above
what they join with Him.

44 Even if they saw a fragment
of the sky falling down on them,
they would say,
"It's merely a mass of clouds."

45 So leave them, Prophet, until
they come face-to-face with their
day
when they shall faint,
thunderstruck.

46 The day when their scheming
shall help them in no way,
and they receive no other help.

47 As for those who do wrong
there is yet more torment beyond
this
though most of them do not know it.

48 So await with patience
the judgment of your Lord
—for you are in Our sight—
and hymn your Lord's praise
when you rise,

49 hymn His praise by night,
and by the evanescing stars.

SURA 53

The Star (*Al-Najm*)

Like many suras, including the preceding three, its name comes from the opening verse. An early Meccan sura of 62 verses, it also interpolates later verses (vv.
13–18) that refer to the Prophet's Ascent (the initial topic of "The Night Journey,"
Sura 17). The exchange with the three goddesses (vv. 20–21) has occupied many
commentators, but central to the Prophet's vision, and his mission throughout,
is his connection to prior prophets, and their messages, here highlighted as the
scrolls of Abraham and Moses (vv. 36–37).

In the Name of God, the All Merciful, Ever Merciful

SECTION I

1 By the star when it descends—

2 your companion is neither
astray nor misguided,

3 nor does he voice his own desire.

4 It is nothing less than revelation
that is sent down to him,

5 one mighty in power°
has taught him,

6 one imbued with great strength,
who stood

7 at the horizon's peak

8 then approached, coming down

9 to within two bow-lengths away
or closer—

10 until he revealed to God's servant
what He revealed.

11 His heart did not mistake
what it saw.

12 Will you then dispute with him
what he saw?

13 He saw [Gabriel]
descending again

14 Near the lote-tree
on the farthest horizon,

15 near the garden of repose,

16 when the tree was cloaked
[in sublime splendor].°

17 His sight never wavered,
   nor did it venture beyond,

18 for he saw the most sublime
   signs of his Lord.

19 Have you seen the "goddesses"
   Al-Lat and Al-Uzza,

20 and a third, Al-Manat?°

21 For you the male
   and for Him the female?°

22 This apportioning would be unjust.

23 These are merely names
   you and your forefathers
   have devised, for which
   God has revealed no sanction.
   They merely pursue conjecture
   and what they themselves desire—
   even though guidance has come
   to them from their Lord.

24 Or shall humankind have
   whatever it wishes for?

25 No—both beginning and end
   belong to God.°

SECTION 2

26 How many angels there are in the
      heavens
   whose intercession will be of no help—

except after God grants leave for
   those
whom He will and approves?

27 Those who don't believe
   in the hereafter
   assign female names to the angels.

28 But they have no knowledge of this.
   They pursue mere conjecture—
   which is of no use against truth.

29 So turn aside from those
   who turn away from Our message,
   desiring only the life of this world.

30 Such is the extent
   of their knowledge.
   It is your Lord Who best knows
   who strays from His path
   and who is guided.

31 To God belongs
   all that is in the heavens,
   and all that is on the earth.
   He will requite those who do evil
   for what they did, and reward those
   who do good with what is best,°

32 those who avoid major sins
   and indecencies, though falling into
   minor sins. Your Lord is Expansive
   in forgiveness. He knows you well
   since He brought you out of the
      earth,
   and since you were mere fetuses

in the wombs of your mothers.
So do not claim to be pure—
He knows best who is mindful of Him.

SECTION 3

33 Have you see the one
who turns away,

34 who gives a little
then holds back?

35 Does he have knowledge
of the unseen, so that he can see?

36 Has he not been told of what
the scrolls of Moses hold?°

37 And of Abraham,
who fulfilled his trust?°—

38 that none shall bear
the burdens of another;

39 and that humans can have
only what they strive for;

40 and that their striving
will soon be seen,

41 then they will be rewarded for it
with a full reward

42 that the final goal is
to your Lord;

43 that it is He Who makes people
laugh and cry;

44 that it is He Who
brings death and gives life;

45 that it is He Who created
male and female in pairs

46 from a drop of sperm, discharged;

47 that He will bring forth
a second creation;°

48 that it is He Who
enriches and suffices;

49 that it is He Who is Lord
of Sirius;°

50 that it is He Who destroyed
the ancient people of ʿAd

51 and the people of Thamud,
without sparing them,

52 and the people of Noah
before them—they were most unjust
and most rebellious.

53 and He brought low
the overturned cities
[of Sodom and Gomorrah],

54 covering them?°

55 Which of the favors of your Lord
would you, then, doubt?

56 This is one who warns,
like those who warned
in former times.

57 The impending hour
draws near.

58 None but God
can unveil it.

59 Do you yet wonder
at this message?

60 And laugh, rather than cry?

61 Immersed, as you are, in vanities?

62 Bow down before God
and worship Him alone.

SURA 54

The Moon (*Al-Qamar*)

A middle Meccan sura, its 55 verses begin with a cosmic sign—some would say, miracle—that portends the day of reckoning. "The moon torn asunder" evokes not just the final judgment but also the roll call of prophets honored, like Noah and Lot but also people condemned, like 'Ad and Thamud as well as the family of Pharaoh. None escapes "the book of deeds" in which "each matter, small and great, is recorded." (vv. 52–53).

In the Name of God, the All Merciful, Ever Merciful

SECTION I

1 The hour draws near,
and the moon is torn asunder.°

2 If they see a sign, they turn away,
saying, "The sorcery continues."°

3 They deny the signs
and follow their own desires—
yet every affair will be resolved.

4 Stories of former peoples
have already come to them,
to deter them,

5 stories consummate in wisdom—
but the warnings are of no use.

6 So turn away from them, Prophet.
On the day the caller summons
them
to something terrible,

7 they will emerge from their graves,
   eyes downcast, swarming like
      locusts,

8 scrambling toward the caller.
   The unbelievers will cry,
   "This is a harsh day."

9 Before them, Noah's people
   denied [the truth],
   denying Our servant,
   saying "He is possessed"—
   and he was reproved.

10 Then he called on his Lord,
    "I am overcome—so help me!"

11 So We opened the gates
    of heaven, with water
    cascading down.

12 And We made the earth
    burst open with gushing springs—
    the waters came together as decreed.

13 But We carried Noah
    on [an ark] made of planks and nails

14 sailing secure beneath Our gaze—
    a reward for the one
    who had been spurned.

15 And We have left this [ark]
    as a sign—so will any take heed?

16 How [dire] were My torment
    and My warnings.

17 We have made the Qur'an
    easy, on mind and memory—
    so will any take heed?

18 The people of 'Ad also denied
    [the truth]—how [dire]
    were My torment and My warnings.

19 For We sent against them
    a furious wind, on a day
    of unrelenting calamity,

20 plucking people out like stumps
    of uprooted palm trees.

21 How dire were My torment
    and My warnings.

22 We have made the Qur'an
    easy, on mind and memory—
    so will any take heed?

SECTION 2

23 The people of Thamud [also]
    denied the warnings.

24 For they said, "Shall we follow
    a mere mortal from among
       ourselves?
    We would fall into error and folly!

25 "Was the reminder sent to him
    alone of all those among us?
    It can't be—he's an insolent liar."

26 They shall know tomorrow
who the insolent liar is.

27 We will send the she-camel
as a trial for them. So, watch them,
Salih, and be patient.

28 Inform them that the water
is to be shared among them,
each drinking in turn.

29 But they called their comrade
who took a sword°
and hamstrung the camel.°

30 How dire were My torment
and My warnings.

31 For We hurled against them
a single fearsome blast
that turned them into
the like of dry twigs
used by a builder of fences.

32 We have made the Qur'an
easy, on mind and memory—
so will any take heed?

33 The people of Lot [also]
denied the warnings.

34 We hurled against them
a shower of brimstone—except
the family of Lot, whom we saved
at the hour of dawn,

35 by Our grace. In this way
We reward those who are grateful.

36 Lot warned them
that We would seize them,
but they disputed the warnings,

37 and even solicited his guests
[to seduce them]—
but We blinded them—
"Taste My torment
and the truth of My warnings."

38 Early in the morning
a relentless torment seized them—

39 "Taste My torment
and the truth of My warnings."

40 We have made the Qur'an
easy, on mind and memory—
so will any take heed?

SECTION 3

41 Warnings came
to the people of Pharaoh.

42 They denied all Our signs,
so We seized them with the power
of the Almighty, the All Powerful.

43 Are the unbelievers among you
better than them?
Or, were you granted
exemption in the scriptures?

44 Or, do they say,
   "We are a strong force,
   and we shall win"?

45 But their force shall be vanquished
   and they will turn their backs,
        fleeing.

46 But the hour—as promised to
        them—
   the hour shall be
   most grievous, most bitter.

47 It is the sinners who have fallen
   into error—and madness;

48 on the day they are dragged
   into the fire, their faces down,
   [they will be told,]
   "Taste the embrace of hellfire."

49 We created all things
   in due measure,

50 Our command works in one flash
   like the blinking of an eye.

51 We have destroyed your kind
   before—so will any take heed?

52 Each thing they do
   is recorded in the book of deeds

53 each matter, small and great,
   is recorded.

54 The righteous shall be among
   gardens and rivers,

55 in a seat of honor,
   near the All Powerful King.

SURA 55

The All Merciful (*Al-Rahman*)

Early Meccan in origin, according to modern scholars, this sura of 78 verses echoes one of God's Beautiful Names, the one most revered after Allah: Rahman, "the All Merciful." In a refrain that recurs thirty-one times from v. 13 to v. 77, it addresses both humankind and jinn, valuing each as an audience for divine commands and as recipients of divine blessings. The rhetorical use of the Arabic dual marks it as an extraordinary oral performance, one requiring parallel effort in its English rendering.

In the Name of God, the All Merciful, Ever Merciful

SECTION I

1 The All Merciful:

2 He taught the Qur'an,

3 He created man,

4 He taught him speech.

5 Both sun and moon,
  exact in their span,

6 and stars and trees, both bow down;

7 and the sky He raised high,
  setting up the balance,

8 that you might not infract
  what is due in balance;

9 set up [your] weights justly, then,
  and do not fall short in balance.

10 And He laid out the earth
   for His creatures,

11 with her fruit and date palms
   with clustered sheaths;

12 and corn, with husks,
   and scented plants.

13 Which, then, of your Lord's favors
   would you both deny?

14 Humankind He created from
   dry clay, like earthen pots,

15 and jinn He created from
   smokeless fire.

16 Which of your Lord's favors
   would you both then deny?°

17 Lord of the two Easts°
   and Lord of the two Wests.°

18 And which of your Lord's favors
   would you both deny?

19 He let the two seas flow,
   so they might converge:

20 between them a barrier,
   where they shall not merge—

21 so which of your Lord's favors
   will you both deny?

22 Out of them both come
   pearls and coral.

23 Which, then, of your Lord's favors
   will you both deny?

24 And His are the ships sailing high
   on the seas, like mountains.

25 So which of the favors of your Lord
will you both deny?

SECTION 2

26 All things upon [the earth] shall
  perish,

27 while the Face of your Lord
Abides Forever,
in Majesty and Munificence.

28 Which, then, of your Lord's favors
will you both deny?

29 All that is in the heavens and earth
implores Him,
each day His decree exists.°

30 Which of your Lord's favors
will you then both deny?

31 Soon We shall attend to you,
you hosts [of jinn and humankind].

32 Then which of your Lord's favors
will you both deny?

33 Assembly of jinn and humankind—
if you can pass beyond the realms
of heaven and earth, then pass—
yet you shall not pass
without [Our] warrant.

34 And which of your Lord's favor
will you both deny?

35 Against you both will be hurled
a fiery flame, and smoke—
you shall find no quarter.

36 Which, then, of your Lord's favors
will you both deny?

37 When the sky is torn asunder,
turning crimson like red leather.°

38 Which of your Lord's favors
will you then both deny?

39 On that day, none will be
questioned about his sin,
neither humans nor jinn.

40 And which of your Lord's favors
will you both deny?

41 The sinners shall be known
by their marks, and seized
by their forelocks and their feet.

42 Which, then, of your Lord's favors
will you both deny?

43 This is hell, which sinners deny—

44 they will wander in circles
between it and boiling water.

45 Which, then, of your Lord's favors
will you both deny?

SECTION 3

46 But whoever fears [the day]
   when he stands before his Lord—
   shall have two gardens—

47 so which of your Lord's favors
   will you both deny?

48 With spreading branches.

49 So which of your Lord's favors
   will you both deny?

50 In them both will be
   two fountains, flowing.

51 So which of your Lord's favors
   will you both deny?

52 In them both will be fruits
   of every kind, in pairs.

53 So which of your Lord's favors
   will you both deny?

54 Reclining on couches,
   lined in rich brocade,
   with fruit of both gardens
   within close reach.°

55 So which of your Lord's favors
   will you both deny?

56 In the gardens will be females
   of modest glance, untouched
   before by human or jinn—

57 so which of your Lord's favors
   will you both deny?

58 [In beauty] like rubies and coral.

59 So which of your Lord's favors
   will you both deny?

60 What is the reward for goodness,
   beyond goodness?°

61 Which, then, of your Lord's favors
   will you both deny?

62 And besides these two,
   shall be two more gardens—

63 which, then, of your Lord's favors
   will you both deny?

64 Both hued in deepest green.

65 And which of your Lord's favors
   will you both deny?

66 In them both will be
   two fountains, overflowing.

67 Which, then, of your Lord's favors
   will you both deny?

68 In them both will be fruit,
   date palm, and pomegranate.

69 Which, then, of your Lord's favors
   will you both deny?

70 In them will be maidens,
   virtuous and beautiful—

71 which of your Lord's favors
   would you then both deny?

72 Houris,° large eyed,
   secluded in pavilions—

73 and which of your Lord's favors
   will you both deny?

74 Untouched before by human or jinn.

75 Which, then, of your Lord's favors
   will you both deny?

76 Reclining on cushions of green
   and luscious carpets.

77 Which, then, of your Lord's favors
   will you both deny?

78 Blessed is the Name
   of your Lord, forever,
   in Majesty and Munificence.

SURA 56

The Inexorable Event (*Al-Waqi'a*)

As with many suras, the opening verse of its 96 verses provides the title for this early Meccan invocation of "a noble Qur'an, in a Book well guarded" (v. 77–78). It begins with a vivid description of judgment day, then divides those arrayed into the ones nearest to God, followed by those on the right, and those on the left (vv. 10–56). Signs of God's power and providence (vv. 57–74) underscore the universal need to acknowledge "the truth, certain," glorifying "the Name of your Lord, Most Great" (vv. 95–96).

In the Name of God, the All Merciful, Ever Merciful

SECTION I

1 When the inexorable event arrives,

2 none shall deny its arrival.

3 Many will it abase
  and many will it exalt—

4 when the earth is convulsed
  to its core,

5 and the mountains crumbled

6 to dust, scattered wide—

7 then you shall be ranked

into three groups:

8 some on the right—who?°

9 and some on the left—who?

10 While the foremost [in faith]
   shall be foremost [in place];

11 these will be nearest to God°

12 in gardens of bliss:

13 many from the first generations,

14 few from later generations,

15 on couches adorned with gold,

16 reclining, facing one another.

17 Immortal youths shall pass
   among them, [serving them]

18 with goblets, jugs, and a cup
   [filled] from a flowing stream,

19 inducing neither headache
   nor stupor;

20 and whatever fruits they choose;

21 and the flesh of whatever
   fowl they desire;

22 and houris, large-eyed,

23 like pearls preserved
   in their shells—

24 a reward for all their deeds.

25 There, they will hear neither
     gossip
   nor sinful talk—

26 only the words "Peace . . . peace."

27 Those on the right—
   how will they be?

28 [They will be] among lote-trees
   shorn of their thorns,°

29 among acacias laden with fruit,

30 under spreading shade,

31 with flowing water,

32 and fruit in abundance

33 without limit or constraint,

34 seated on couches raised high.

35 We created companions,

36 whom We have made chaste,

37 loving, and well suited°—

38 for those on the right—

SECTION 2

39 many from former times,

40 and many from later generations.

41 Those on the left—
     how will they be?

42 They will be in scorching wind
     and scalding water,

43 in the shade of black smoke

44 neither cool nor soothing.

45 Before this, they had indulged
     in luxury,

46 persisting in great sin,

47 and they used to say,
     "So when we die, and turn to
     dust and bones, will we
     really be resurrected—

48 "along with our ancestors?"

49 Say, "Yes, both former
     and later generations

50 "shall be gathered together
     at an appointed time
     on a stipulated day.

51 "Then you who are astray,
     and deny the truth,

52 "shall eat from the bitter
     tree of Zaqqum,°

53 "filling your bellies with it,

54 "while drinking scalding water,

55 "slurping it like thirsty camels."

56 This will be their welcome
     on the day of reckoning.

57 It is We Who created you—
     so why will you not accept the truth?

58 Do you see the [semen]
     that you emit?

59 Did you create it,
     or are We the Creator?

60 We decreed death
     to be your common lot°—
     nor could We be thwarted°

61 [if We wished] to transform
     your form and re-create you
     in forms unknown to you.

62 And of course you know well
     your original form of creation—
     so why will you not take heed?°

63 Do you see the seed
     that you sow?

64 Is it you who cause it to grow
     or We?

65 Had We wished, We could have
   crushed it to rubble,
   and left you musing,

66 "We are deep in debt,

67 "in fact, we're dispossessed."

68 Do you not see the water
   that you drink?

69 Is it you who send it down
   from the rain clouds—or We?

70 If We willed, We could make it
   bitter [and undrinkable]—
   so why will you not give thanks?

71 Do you see the fire
   that you light?

72 Is it you who produce
   the tree that fuels it, or We?

73 We made it a reminder,
   and a provision for desert travelers.

74 So glorify the Name
   of your Lord, Most Great.

SECTION 3

75 Indeed—I swear
   by the setting of the stars°

76 —this is a momentous oath,
   if only you knew—

77 that this is a noble Qur'an,

78 in a Book well guarded,

79 which only the pure shall touch—

80 a revelation from
   the Lord of the worlds.

81 Would you, then,
   take this message lightly?

82 And do you make your living
   by denying it?

83 Why do you not [intercede]
   when the [soul of a dying man]
   wells up to his throat,

84 while you merely gaze on?

85 We are nearer to him
   than you are—but you do not see.

86 And why, if you are exempt
   from judgment,

87 do you not bring back [his soul],
   if you are speaking the truth?

88 If [that dying person] is among
   those brought near to God,

89 they shall have repose,
    fragrant delight,
    and a garden of bliss.

90 And if he is one of those
    on the right,

91 [he shall hear the greeting]
    "Peace be to you" from those
    on the right.

92 But if he is one of those
    who denied [Our message]
    and went astray,

93 his welcome will be
    scalding water,

94 and burning in hellfire.

95 This is the truth, certain.

96 So, glorify the name
    of your Lord, Most Great.

SURA 57

Iron (*Al-Hadid*)

Only 29 verses, this early Medinan sura takes its title from the mention of iron, sent down to provide "great strength and benefits for people" (v. 25). Extolling the glory of God and His messenger (vv. 1–11), it then separates the believers and hypocrites, with disparate fates awaiting each (vv. 12–20) and an appeal to believers: "Race to gain forgiveness from your Lord" (v. 21). It concludes with praise for the earlier followers of Noah, Abraham, and Jesus and emphasis on the light as a mark of God's guidance and forgiveness (v. 28).

In the Name of God, the All Merciful, Ever Merciful

SECTION I

1 All that is in the heavens and on
   earth

hymns the glory of God,
for He is Almighty, All Wise.

2 His is the dominion

over the heavens and the earth;
He gives life and brings death,
and He has Power over all things.

3   He is the First and the Last,
the Manifest and the Hidden,
Knower of all things.

4   It is He Who created
the heavens and the earth
in six days, then took up the throne.
He knows what enters the earth
and what leaves it,
what descends from the sky
and what ascends to it.
He is with you wherever
you are—for God Sees
all that you do.

5   His is the dominion
over the heavens and the earth,
and all affairs are returned to God.

6   He fades night into day,
and day into night; and He Knows
what your hearts contain.

7   Believe in God and His messenger,
and give freely° from what
He has entrusted to you. For those
of you who believe and give freely,
there is a great reward.

8   Why do you not believe in God
when the messenger calls you
to believe in your Lord
—and has taken a pledge from you—
if you are truly believers?

9   It is He Who sends clear signs
to His servant, so he might lead you
out of the darkness into light—
for God is Most Kind,
Ever Merciful.

10 And why do you not spend
in God's cause? For the legacy of
the heavens and the earth is God's.
Not all among you are equal:
those who gave and fought
before the victory°
are higher in rank than those
who gave and fought afterward.
But God has promised all
a fine reward—
for God is Aware of all that you do.

SECTION 2

11 Who will lend to God
a beautiful loan, that God
will multiply for them?
Theirs will be a noble reward.

12 On a day when you see
the believers, men and women,
with their light moving before them,
on their right, [they will hear,]
"What joyous news for you this
      day—
gardens, beneath which rivers flow,
to live there forever—
that is the supreme triumph."

13 On that day, the hypocrites, both men
and women, will say to the believers,
"Wait for us! Let us share

some of your light." They will
  be told,
"Go back behind and seek a light."
Then a wall shall be raised
between them, with a door—
mercy inside it and torment outside.

14 [Those outside] will call out,
"Were we not with you?
[The others] will reply,
"Yes, but you fell into temptation.
You were hesitant, in doubt,
and false desires deceived you—
until God's command came.
The deceiver deceived you about God.

15 "This day no ransom
shall be accepted of you, nor
of the disbelievers. Your home
is the fire, your true patron—
a wretched destination."

16 Has not the time come
for the believers to humble
their hearts in remembrance of God
and of the truth revealed [to them],
and not to be like those who were
given the Book earlier,
whose hearts grew hard over time,
many of whom were disobedient.

17 Know that God gives life
to the earth after its death;
We have made the signs clear to you
that you might comprehend.

18 For the men and women
who give in charity, and lend to God

a beautiful loan—it will be
  multiplied
and theirs will be a noble reward.

19 Those who believe in God
and His messengers are truthful—
they will bear witness
before their Lord.
They shall have their reward
and their light.
But those who disbelieve
and deny Our signs
shall be inmates of hellfire.

SECTION 3

20 Know that the life of this world
is but play and idle pastime, with
adornment and mutual boasting,
and rivalry for gain in wealth
and children. It is like the rain
bringing up [a crop],
which delights the tillers.
But then it dries, and
you see it turn yellow, then
to stubble. In the hereafter
there is severe torment, but also
God's forgiveness and approval—
for the life of this world is nothing
but diversion, delusion.

21 Race to gain forgiveness
from your Lord, and a garden
as wide as the heaven and earth,
prepared for those who believed
in God and His messengers.
This is the grace that God
grants to whom He will,

for God's grace is great.

22 No misfortune can occur
on the earth or in yourselves
without being recorded before
We brought it into being—
that is easy for God—

23 so that you don't grieve
over what eludes you, nor exult
in what He has given you,
for God does not like
the proud and boastful,

24 those who are miserly and
encourage others to be so.
As for those who turn away—
God is Self-Sufficient, Praiseworthy.

25 We sent down Our messengers
with clear proofs, and We sent
with them
the Book and the balance°
that people might uphold justice.
And We sent down iron, which has
great strength and benefits for
people—
so that God might know who will
help [His cause] and His messengers
[though He is] unseen.
For God is All Powerful, Almighty.

SECTION 4

26 We sent Noah and Abraham,
and bestowed prophethood
and the Book upon their descendants.

Some among them were rightly
guided,
but many were disobedient.

27 Then We brought [more of]
Our messengers to follow
in their footsteps. After them
We sent Jesus, son of Mary,
to whom We gave the Gospel.
We placed compassion and mercy
in the hearts of his followers.
But they invented monasticism
—which We did not ordain for
them—
to seek God's good pleasure—
though they failed to observe
it duly.°
Then we rewarded the believers
among them—but many were
disobedient.

28 You who believe, be mindful
of God, and believe in His messenger.
He will grant you a twofold portion
of His mercy; He will make a Light
for you, in which you shall walk,°
and He will forgive you—for God
is Most Forgiving, Ever Merciful—

29 so that the people of the Book
might know that they have no power
whatsoever over the grace of God,
that this grace lies in His hands,
and He gives it to whom He will—
for God's grace abounds.

The Woman Who Pleads (*Al-Mujadila*)

This Medinan sura of 22 verses takes its name from its subject: a woman who challenges her husband's right to divorce her with a pre-Islamic formula (vv. 1–4). Stressing God's omniscience and omnipotence (vv. 6–13), it also warns those who deceive or oppose Muhammad (vv. 14–21) and concludes with a promise that God will strengthen believers with His own spirit (v. 22).

In the Name of God, the All Merciful, Ever Merciful

SECTION I

1 God has heard the words
of the woman who pleads with you
concerning her husband, and
refers her complaint to God.
And God hears both sides
of your exchange, for God
is All Hearing, All Seeing.

2 As for those of you
who divorce their wives° by
pronouncing *zihar* against them
[misnaming them "mothers"]—
they are not their mothers.
Their mothers are only those
who gave them birth.
So what they say
is both wicked and false.
But God is Pardoning, Forgiving.

3 But those who divorce their wives
in this way, then wish to go back
on what they have said,
should free a slave
before any mutual touching.
This is what you are enjoined to do,
for God is Aware of all that you do.

4 And those without the means
[to do this] should fast for
two consecutive months
before any mutual touching.
And those unable to do this
should feed sixty poor people.
This is so you will believe in God
and His messenger, for these are
the limits set by God.
And a painful torment
awaits the disbelievers.

5 Those who oppose God and His
messenger
will be disgraced—like those before
them.
For We have sent down clear signs.
And degrading torment awaits the
disbelievers

6 on the day that God raises them up
   together,
and informs them of all they have
   done.
God has recorded it though they
   have forgotten it.
For God is Witness to all things.

7 Do you not see that God knows
all that is in the heavens and
all that is on the earth—there is no
whispered converse between three
   people
but He is the fourth, nor between
   four
but He is the fifth, nor between five
but He is the sixth—nor fewer
nor more but He is with them
wherever they are. Then, on the day
of resurrection, He shall inform
   them
of all they have done.
For God is Knower of all things.

8 Have you not seen those
who were forbidden from furtive talk
revert to doing what was forbidden,
conspiring in what is sinful, hostile,
and disobedient to the Prophet.
When they come to you,
they address you as God would never
address you,° and they say
to themselves, "Why does God
not punish us for what we say?"

Hell is enough for them, and
they shall burn in it—an evil end.

9 You who believe—when you hold
secret counsel, do not conspire
   in sin,
hostility, and disobedience to the
   Prophet;
converse, rather, with a view
to righteousness and mindfulness
of God. Be mindful of God—
   the One
to Whom you will be gathered.

10 Furtive talk is prompted by
Satan, to breed grief among
   believers.
But He cannot harm them at all
without leave from God.
So let the believers trust in God.

11 You who believe, when told
to make room for one another
in the assemblies, do so—
God will make room for you.
And when you are told to rise, do
   so—
God will raise up in rank
those among you who believe
and who have been given
   knowledge.°
For God is Aware of all that you do.

12 You who believe, when you
consult in private with the Prophet,
first offer alms. This will be better

for you, and more purifying.
But if you do not find
[the means to do this],
God is Forgiving, Ever Merciful.

13 Were you afraid of not being able
to give alms before consulting
with the Prophet? If you did not,
and God relents toward you,
be steadfast in prayer,
give in charity, and obey God
and His messenger.
For God is Aware of all that you do.

SECTION 3

14 Do you not see those who befriend
people who have incurred God's
    wrath?
They are not of you, nor you of
    them.
And they swear knowingly to what
    is false.

15 God has prepared severe torment
for them; what they have done is evil.

16 They have made their oaths
a screen [for their misdeeds], and
they bar [others] from the path of
    God—
theirs shall be a disgracing torment.

17 Their wealth and their children
shall prove no use to them against
    God.

They are inmates of hellfire
where they shall dwell forever.

18 On the day that God
raises them up together,
they will swear to Him,
as they swear to you—they think
they have something to stand on—
wrong—they are liars.

19 Satan has overcome them.
making them forget remembrance
of God. They are the party of
    Satan—
a party that will lose out.

20 Those who oppose God
and His messenger
shall be the most humiliated.

21 God has decreed: "It is I
and My messengers who will
    prevail."
God is All Powerful, Almighty.

22 You will not find any people
who believe in God and the last day
befriending those who oppose
God and His messenger—even if
they are their fathers, sons,
    brothers,
or relatives. He has inscribed faith
within their hearts, strengthening
    them
with His own spirit.° He shall usher
    them
into gardens beneath which rivers flow,

to live there forever. God will be
    pleased
with them, and they with Him. They

are the party of God, and it
    is God's party
who will surely succeed.

The Gathering (*Al-Hashr*)

A middle Medinan sura, its 24 verses stress the gathering (hence the title) of a
Jewish tribe that first supported, then opposed the Prophet. The central verses
concern this episode (vv. 2–17), followed by verses exhorting believers to remember God (vv. 18–21), above all to glorify Him by reciting His "Most Beautiful
Names" (vv. 22–24).

In the Name of God, the All Merciful, Ever Merciful

SECTION I

1 All that is in the heavens
and all that is on the earth
glorifies God,
for He is Almighty, All Wise.

2 It is He Who expelled the
    disbelievers
among the people of the Book
from their homes,
at the first gathering of forces.°
You did not think they would go
and they themselves thought
their fortresses would defend them
from God. But God
came upon them from where
they least expected, and cast
terror into their hearts.
Their homes were destroyed by
their own hands, and the hands

of the believers. So take heed,
you who are able to see.

3 Had God not decreed
banishment for them,
He would have surely
punished them in this world.
In the hereafter, they shall face
the torment of hellfire.

4 That is because they
opposed God and His messenger.
Whoever opposes God—[know that]
God is Stern in Requital.

5 Whether you cut down
[their] palm trees or left them
standing on their roots, it was
by God's leave, that He might
shame the disobedient.

6 You had to make no expedition
  of horse or camels for the spoils God
  gave to His messenger from them,
  for God empowers His messengers
  over whom He will, and God
  has Power over all things.

7 Any spoils God gave to His
    messenger
  from the people of the towns
  belongs to God, the messenger,
  kinsfolk, orphans, the needy,
  and the traveler—so they should not
  circulate between the rich among you.
  So take whatever the messenger
  gives you, and refrain from
  whatever he disallows you,
  and be mindful of God,
  for God is Stern in Requital.

8 [A share is due] to the poor
  among the emigrants, who were
  expelled from their homes
  and their possessions
  while seeking the grace of God
  and His good pleasure
  in helping [the cause of] God
  and His messenger.
  These are the truthful people.

9 [A share is also due]
  to those, already settled
  before them in their homes
  [in Medina], and firm in faith,
  who show love for those
  who came to them for refuge,
  and find in their hearts no need

for what has been given to the
    refugees,
preferring them over themselves,
even though they too are poor:
those who are saved from the greed
of their own souls,
are the ones who will succeed.

10 Those who have come after them
  say, "Our Lord, forgive us and our
  brothers who came before us in faith
  and don't leave a grudge in our hearts
  against those who believe. Our Lord,
  You are Compassionate, Ever
    Merciful."

SECTION 2

11 Have you not seen the hypocrites
  say to their disbelieving brothers
  from the people of the Book,°
  "If you are expelled, we will surely
  go with you; we will never listen
  to anyone who speaks against you;
  if you're attacked, we shall surely
  help you." But God bears witness
  that they are lying.

12 If they are expelled,
  they will never go with them,
  and if they are attacked,
  they will not help them,
  and if they did help them,
  they would turn their backs:
  so they would not be helped.

13 You are more fearsome
  in their hearts than God.

That is because they are people
who will not understand.

14 They will not fight you, even when
united, except in fortified towns,
or from behind walls; their violence
among themselves is great:
you think them united,
but their hearts are divided.
That is because they are people
who are averse to reason.

15 Like those who came
just before them, they have tasted
the grievous fruit of their actions,
and they shall face painful torment.

16 Like Satan, when he says
to humankind, "Do not believe!"
But when humankind disbelieves,
he says, "I disown you: I do fear God,
Lord of the universe."

17 Both will end in the fire,°
to remain there forever.
Such is the reward of wrongdoers.

SECTION 3

18 You who believe, be mindful
of God; and let every soul
look to [the deeds] it sends forth
for tomorrow; be mindful
of God, for God is Aware
of all that you do.

19 And do not be like those
who forget God, whom He causes

to forget themselves—
they are the disobedient.

20 Those in the fire
and those in the garden
are not equal—
those in the garden
are the triumphant.

21 Had We sent down this Qur'an
upon a mountain, you would have
seen it humbled, cleave itself
into a chasm, in fear of God.
Such are the parables
We coin for human beings,
that they might reflect.

22 God is He, beyond Whom
there is no god. He Knows
the unseen and the seen;
He is the All Merciful, Ever
    Merciful.

23 God is He, beyond Whom
there is no god, the Sovereign,
the Sanctified; the Source of Peace,
the Trustworthy, the Guardian,
the Almighty, the Irresistible,
the Supreme; Glorified is He,
beyond what they affiliate with Him.

24 He is God, the Creator,
the Originator, the Shaper of Forms;
His are the Most Beautiful Names.°
All that is the heavens and the earth
glorifies Him, and He is
Almighty, All Wise.

The Woman Tested (*Al-Mumtahana*)

This late Medinan sura is very brief, with the title and purpose referring to v. 10. Its 13 verses focus on categories of women caught between two groups, Muslims and their opponents, in skirmishes just before the Prophet's reentry to Mecca in 630 CE. The purpose of testing these women is to determine the sincerity of their belief once they confirm their intent to remain with the ascendant Muslim community.

In the Name of God, the All Merciful, Ever Merciful

SECTION I

1 You who believe, do not take
as allies My enemies and yours,
offering them friendship, when they
disbelieve in the truth that came
to you, driving out the messenger
and yourselves, because you
    believed
in God, your Lord—if indeed
you emigrated to strive in My cause
and to seek My good pleasure.
You show them secret affection,
    but I know
what you conceal and reveal.
Those of you who do this
stray from the level path.

2 If they gain ascendancy over you,
they will become your enemies
and reach out against you
with their hands and tongues,
with wicked resolve,
for they want you to disbelieve.

3 Your relatives and children
will be of no use to you
on the day of resurrection.
He will judge between you,
for God Sees all that you do.

4 You have an excellent example
in Abraham and those with him,
when they said to their people,
"We dissociate ourselves from you
and what you worship besides
the One God. We reject you,
and the enmity and hatred risen
between us shall endure until you
believe in God—and Him alone."
Except when Abraham said to
    his father,
"I will ask forgiveness for you, but
I have no power at all on your
    behalf
with God." [He and his people
    prayed,]
"Our Lord, we trust in You, we turn
    to You,
and our final return is to You.

5 "Our Lord, do not make us
   [a means] of trial for the
      unbelievers,
   and forgive us, Our Lord.
   You are Almighty, All Wise."

6 They were an excellent example
   for you—for those whose hope
   lies in God and the last day.
   As for those who turn away—
   God is Self-Sufficient, Praiseworthy.

SECTION 2

7 It may be that God will induce
   love between you and those
   you held as enemies,
   for God is All Powerful,
   and God is Forgiving,
   Ever Merciful.

8 God does not forbid you
   from being kind and just to those
   who don't fight you over religion
   or try to drive you from your homes,
   for God loves those who are just.

9 God only forbids you from taking
   as allies those who fight you,
   drive you from your homes,
   and help [others] to drive you out.
   Those who take them as allies
   are wrongdoers.

10 You who believe—
   when the believing women come
      to you

as emigrants, test them.
God best knows their faith.
Once you know them to be believers,
don't send them back
to the disbelievers—for whom
they are no longer lawful, nor
are the disbelievers lawful for them.
Rather, give [their unbelieving
   husbands]
whatever they paid [as bridal dues]—
nor do you incur blame if you
   marry them
once you pay them their bridal dues.
Do not hold to your marriages
with unbelieving women.
Ask for return of the bridal dues
you paid, and let the unbelievers
ask for return of what they paid.
This is God's judgment—
it is He Who judges between you,
for God is All Knowing, All Wise.

11 And if any of your wives deserts you
   for the unbelievers, then in your turn,
   give to those whose wives have gone
   what they spent [as bridal dues]—
   and fear God, in whom you believe.

12 Prophet, when the believing women
   come to you—pledging not to
   associate anything with the One God,
   not to steal, commit adultery,
   nor kill their children, nor forge
      any lie

about who has fathered their
　　children,
nor disobey you in what is
　　righteous—
then, accept their pledge, and ask
forgiveness for them from God,
for God is Forgiving, Ever Merciful.

13 You who believe,
　　do not seek as allies those
　　who have incurred God's wrath,
　　and who despair of the hereafter
　　just as the disbelievers despair
　　that those in their graves
　　[will be brought back to life].

SURA 61

In Ranks (*Al-Saff*)

An early Medinan sura, it is short (14 verses). Extolling those who "fight in His cause, in battle lines (v. 4)," it invokes the examples of Moses and Jesus as stalwart messengers who helped God's Light to shine (vv. 4–8), auguring a messenger named Ahmad with the religion of truth (vv. 6, 9), whose followers will be victorious (v. 14).

In the Name of God, the All Merciful, Ever Merciful

SECTION I

1 All that is in the heavens and earth
　　hymns the glory of God—
　　He is Almighty, All Wise.

2 You who believe,
　　why do you profess
　　what you do not practice?

3 It is loathsome in the sight of God
　　that you profess
　　what you do not practice.

4 God loves those who fight
　　in His cause, in ranks,
　　like a firmly wrought structure.

5 Moses said to his people,
　　"My people, why do you vex me
　　when you know that
　　I am God's messenger to you?"
　　When they deviated, it was God
　　Who caused their hearts to deviate—
　　for God does not guide
　　people who transgress.

6 Jesus, son of Mary, said,
　　"Children of Israel, I am God's
　　messenger to you, confirming

the Torah that came before me,
and bringing joyous news
of a messenger to come after me,
whose name will be Ahmad."
Yet when he came to them
with clear signs, they declared,
"This is clearly sorcery."

7 Who does greater wrong than those
who invent a lie about God,
even when invited to submit to Him—
God does not guide
a people who do wrong.

8 With their words,° they wish
to extinguish the Light of God.
But God will perfect His Light
though disbelievers may detest it.

9 It is He Who sent His messenger
with guidance and the religion of truth
to exalt it over all religion,
though the polytheists may detest it.

SECTION 2

10 You who believe, shall I lead you
to a transaction that will save you
from painful torment?

11 Believe in God and His messenger
and strive in the cause of God
with your possessions and your lives—
that is better for you, if only you knew.

12 He will forgive you your sins
and usher you into gardens
beneath which rivers flow, into
splendid dwellings in eternal
gardens—
that is the supreme triumph.

13 And another [favor] you will love—
help from God and imminent victory.
So, give the joyous news
to those who believe.

14 You who believe, be helpers
[in the cause] of God. As when Jesus,
son of Mary, said to the disciples,
"Who will help me in God's cause?"
They responded, "We shall."
Of the children of Israel,
one group believed
while another disbelieved.
So We supported those
who believed against their enemy—
and they were victorious.°

The Friday Prayer (*Al-Jumu'a*)

A short Medinan sura, its 11 verses address God's power (vv. 1–4), then Jewish opponents (vv. 5–8), with an appeal to believers to pray and remember God (vv. 9–11) "for God is the Best of Providers" (v. 11).

In the Name of God, the All Merciful, Ever Merciful

SECTION I

1 All that is in the heavens and earth
  hymns the glory of God—
  the Sovereign, the Holy,
  the Almighty, All Wise.

2 It is He Who has sent a Prophet
  to the unlettered people,° one of
      their own,
  who recites for them His signs,
  who sanctifies them, teaching them
  the Book and wisdom—
  though before this
  they were clearly astray—

3 [the Prophet was sent to them and
  to] others who have yet to join them.
  For God is Almighty, All Wise.

4 This is the grace of God
  which He grants to whom He will
  for God is Full of Grace.

5 Those entrusted with
  bearing the Torah
  and who failed in this
  are like a donkey bearing books.
  Wicked are the likes
  of people who deny
  the signs of God—
  and God does not guide
  a people who do wrong.

6 Say, "Those of you who are Jews,
  if you claim you have a bond
      with God°
  —excluding all [other] people—
  then hope for death
  if you are speaking the truth."°

7 But they will never hope for death
  given the deeds they have accrued°—
  God Knows those who do wrong.

8 Say, "The death you flee from
  will overtake you. Then you will
  be sent back to the Knower
  of the unseen and the seen
  and He will inform you
  of all that you have done.

SECTION 2

9 You who believe, when the call
to Friday prayer is made,
hasten to remember God
and leave your trading.
That is better for you,
if only you knew.

10 And when the prayer is concluded,
disperse through the land, seeking
the bounty of God—

and remember God often,
that you might prosper.

11 Yet when they see some trading
or play, they disperse, running
toward it, and leave you standing
  alone.
Say, "What is with God is
  far better
than trade or play. For God
is the Best of Providers."

SURA 63

The Hypocrites (*Al-Munafiqun*)

Another short Medinan sura of 11 verses, this addresses first hypocrites (vv.
1–8), then believers (vv. 9–11), reminding the latter that "God is Aware of all that
you do" (v. 11).

In the Name of God, the All Merciful, Ever Merciful

SECTION I

1 When the hypocrites come to you,
they say, "We bear witness that you
are truly the messenger of God."
God knows well that you
are His messenger—
and He bears witness
that the hypocrites are liars.

2 They have made their oaths
a screen [for their misdeeds], and

they bar [people] from God's path—
what they have done is wicked.

3 That is because they believed,
then disbelieved. So a seal
has been set upon their hearts—
hence they don't understand.

4 When you see them, their looks
please you, and when they speak,
you listen to what they say.
Yet [in truth], they are like

beams of timber, propped up.
They think that every cry
is against them. But they
are the enemy, so be wary of them.
May God curse them—
how deluded they are.

5 And when it is said to them,
"Come, the messenger of God
will ask forgiveness for you,"
they turn their heads aside
and turn away in their pride.

6 It's the same for them whether
you ask forgiveness for them
    or not—
God will not forgive them.
God does not guide
people who are disobedient.

7 They are the ones who say,
"Don't give anything to those
who are with God's messenger—
then they will disband."
But the treasures of the heavens
and earth belong to God, though
the hypocrites don't understand.

8 They say, "If we return to Medina
The more powerful° will expel
the weaker ones from it." But power
belongs to God, His messenger,
and the believers,
though the hypocrites
have no knowledge [of this].

SECTION 2

9 You who believe, don't let
your wealth and your children
distract you from remembrance
of God—those who do this
will be the ones who suffer loss.

10 Spend [in charity] from what
We have given you, before death
comes to any one of you,
and they should say,
"My Lord, why don't you
grant me respite for a short term,
so that I can give in charity,
and be among the righteous?"

11 But God will not grant respite
to any soul once its term
    becomes due.
For God is Aware of all that you do.

Mutual Fraud (*Al-Taghabun*)

Either Meccan or Medinan, its 18 verses begin with extolling God (vv. 1–4), then recall the punishment of earlier generations (vv. 5–6), before announcing the different fates of believers and disbelievers (vv. 7–10). While believers face trials and temptations (vv. 11–16), they should remain confident of God's forgiveness—"for God is Appreciative, Forbearing—Knower of the unseen and the seen, the Almighty, the All Wise" (vv. 17–18).

In the Name of God, the All Merciful, Ever Merciful

SECTION I

1 All that is in the heavens
and all that is on the earth
hymns the glory of God.
His is all dominion, and
His is all praise—
He has Power over all things.

2 It is He Who created you.
Some of you are disbelievers
while others believe—
and God Sees all that you do.

3 He created the heavens and earth
with true purpose, and formed you
in beautiful forms—and to Him
you shall finally return.

4 He knows all that is in the heavens
and on the earth. He knows
what you conceal and reveal.
He Knows what lies hidden in hearts.

5 Has word not reached you of those
who disbelieved in the past?
They tasted the evil fruit of
their deeds
and theirs was a painful torment.

6 For° their messengers came to them
with clear proofs, but they said,
"Shall we be guided by a mere
mortal?"
and, disbelieving, they turned away.
But God does not need them,
for God
is Self-Sufficient, Worthy of Praise.

7 The unbelievers claim that they
will not be raised from the dead.
Say,
"By my Lord, you *will* be raised up,
and then informed of all that
you did—
this is easy for God."

8 So, believe in the One God
and His messenger, and in the Light
We have sent down.° For God
is Aware of all that you do.

9 When He gathers you together
on the day of gathering—that
will be the day when you suffer
mutual fraud.
As for those who
believe in God and do good deeds,
He will absolve them
of their misdeeds,
and usher them into gardens
beneath which rivers flow,
dwelling there for eternity.
That will be the supreme triumph.

10 But those who disbelieve
and deny Our Signs, shall be
cast into the fire, dwelling there
forever—a wretched destination.

SECTION 2

11 No kind of calamity can strike
without God's leave. God guides
the heart of any who believe
in Him—
and God is Knower of all things.

12 So obey God, and
obey His messenger;
but if you turn back,

Our messenger's task
is only to convey
the message clearly.

13 God—there is no god but He—
so let the believers trust in God.

14 You who believe—some among
your wives and children may be
your enemies, so beware of them.
But if you pardon, forbear, and
forgive,
God is Forgiving, Ever Merciful.

15 Your wealth and your children
are merely a test for you.
But the greatest reward is with God.

16 So be mindful of God—
as much as you are able.
Hear, and obey, and spend
in charity—for your own sake.
Those who are saved from
their own greed are the ones
who will prosper.

17 If you lend to God a beautiful loan°
He will multiply it for you,
and forgive you, for God is
Appreciative, Forbearing—

18 Knower of the unseen
and the seen,
the Almighty, the All Wise.

Divorce (*Al-Talaq*)

A Medinan sura of 12 verses, this begins with a commentary on divorce laws (vv. 1–7) and then warns of punishment for disbelievers as well as blessing for believers (vv. 8–12), concluding as do many suras, with invoking Divine Names: "God has Power over all things, and that His Knowledge encompasses all things (v. 12).

In the Name of God, the All Merciful, Ever Merciful

SECTION I

1 Prophet, when any of you
divorces women, do so when
their waiting period starts,°
and keep count of the period,
remaining mindful of God,
your Lord. Don't expel them
from their homes, and they
themselves should not leave
unless they are guilty
of some clear indecency.
These are the limits set by God,
and those who transgress
those limits wrong themselves.
You do not know if God, after this,
will bring something else to pass.

2 Then when their term of waiting
expires—either keep them or
part with them—in a kindly manner,
and call two just men among you
as witnesses, to give upright
testimony for the sake of God.
This is counsel for those who
believe in God and the last day.

God will find a way out for those
who are mindful of Him.

3 And He provides for them
from sources they could not
    imagine.
God is sufficient for those
who place their trust in Him.
He brings about what He decrees
and sets a measure for all things.

4 If you are in doubt, the waiting
period will be three months for
those women past menstruation
and those not yet menstruating.
For those who are pregnant,
the waiting period shall expire
when they deliver.
God will make things easy
for those who are mindful of Him.

5 This is the command of God,
which He has revealed to you.
He will absolve of their bad deeds
those who are mindful of Him
and make great their reward.

6 Let the women you are to divorce
  live in your homes, as you can afford;
  don't harm them, to cause distress.
  And if they are pregnant,
  maintain them until they deliver.
  If they suckle your offspring,
  compensate them. Consult together
  in a kindly manner,
  but if you find this too arduous,
  let another woman suckle the child.

7 Let affluent people spend
  according to their means,
  and let those of spare means
  spend from what God has given
      them.
  God puts no burden on any soul
  beyond the means He has given it—
  and after hardship He brings relief.°

SECTION 2

8 How many towns did We bring
  to stern account, which rebelled
      against
  the commandment of their Lord
  and His messengers—subjecting
      them
  to Our severe torment?

9 So they tasted the evil fruit
  of their deeds—and the result
  of their deeds was utter ruin.

10 God has prepared for them
   a severe torment—so be mindful
   of God, you people who understand,
   who believe—God has sent down
   a message to you,

11 a messenger, who recites to you
   clear verses from God, to lead those
   who believe and do good deeds
   from darkness into light.
   Those who believe in God
   and do good deeds shall be
   urged into gardens, beneath which
   rivers flow, to dwell there forever—
   what an excellent provision
   God has in store for them.

12 It is God Who created seven
   heavens and their like in earths.°
   His command descends through
       them
   to let you know that God
   has Power over all things,
   and that His knowing
   encompasses all things.

Prohibition (*Al-Tahrim*)

This Medinan sura of 12 verses opens with directives about Muhammad's wives (vv. 1–5). It then addresses general guidelines for believers, disbelievers, and the Prophet (vv. 6–9), closing with examples from prior times (Noah's wife, Lot's wife, Pharaoh's wife, and Mary, the daughter of 'Imran; vv. 10–12).

In the Name of God, the All Merciful, Ever Merciful

SECTION I

1 Prophet, why do you prohibit
what God has made lawful for you,
seeking to please your wives!
Yet God is Forgiving, Ever Merciful.°

2 God has ordained that you
might be freed from such oaths,
for God is your Protector,
and He is All Knowing, All Wise.

3 When the Prophet confided
something to one of his wives,
and she divulged it [to another wife],
God made this known to him,
and he confirmed part of it,
without disclosing the rest.
When he told her about it,
she asked, "Who informed you
about this?" He replied,
"I was informed by the One
Who is All Knowing, All Aware."

4 If your wives both turn
to God in repentance [it will

be better]—for your hearts
have deviated; so if you support
each other against the Prophet,°
[know that] God is his Protector—
along with Gabriel
and the righteous believers;
the angels too will support him.

5 It may be that if he divorced you,
God would give him in exchange
wives better than you—who submit
to God, who believe, are devout,
repentant, worshipping, and who
    fast°—
both previously wed and virgins.

6 You who believe, save yourselves
and your families from a fire
whose fuel is humans and stones,
over which angels stand guard
who are stern and severe, never
disobeying the commands of God,
who do as they are commanded.

7 [They will say,] "Unbelievers,
don't make excuses this day—

you are merely being requited
for all that you did."

SECTION 2

8 You who believe, turn to God
with sincere repentance. Perhaps
God will erase your bad deeds,
and usher you into gardens,
with flowing rivers beneath.
On that day, God will not
disgrace the Prophet and those
who believed with him.
Their light will precede them,
on their right, and they shall say,
"Our Lord, perfect our light,
and forgive us, for You
have Power over all things."

9 Prophet, strive hard against
the disbelievers and hypocrites,
and be firm with them. Their home
will be hell, an evil end.

10 God sets outs a parable
for the unbelievers—

the wife of Noah and the wife of Lot.
They were married to two
of Our righteous servants
but they betrayed them,
and their husbands could not
help them against God.
They were told, "Enter the fire
along with the others."

11 And God sets out a parable
for the believers—
the wife of Pharaoh, who said,
"My Lord, build me a home near You,
in the garden, and save me
from Pharaoh and his deeds,
and from a wrongdoing people."

12 And Mary—the daughter of
'Imran—
who preserved her chastity.
We breathed Our spirit into her,
and she affirmed the truth of the
words
of her Lord, and of His Books,
for she was among the devout.

SURA 67

Dominion (Al-Mulk)

A middle Meccan sura, its 30 verses divided into four segments: extolling God's glory (vv. 1–4); enumerating punishment for the devil and his minions (vv. 5–11); an invocation of God's might (vv. 13–22); and directives to the Prophet (vv. 23–30). The conclusion is capped by a reminder of divine control of even daily drinking water: "Say, 'Have you considered—if one morning all your water were to sink into the earth, who would bring you water that is flowing and clear?'" (v. 30).

In the Name of God, the All Merciful, Ever Merciful

SECTION I

1 Blessed is He Whose hands
hold dominion—
He Who has Power over all things—

2 He Who created death
and life, that He might test
which of you is best in deeds.
He is Almighty, Forgiving—

3 He Who created the seven
   heavens,
one above another. You will see
no flaw in the creation of
the Most Merciful. Look again—
do you see any flaws?

4 Look again, a second time—
your sight will return to you
humbled and fatigued.

5 And We have adorned
the lowest heaven with lamps,
making them missiles
against the devils,
for whom We have prepared
a torment of blazing fire.

6 Those who denied their Lord
shall face the torment of hell,
an evil end.

7 When they are thrown into it,
they will hear it bubbling,
as it boils up,

8 almost bursting with fury.
Whenever some group is thrown
into it, its keepers will ask,
"Did no one come to warn you?"

9 They will reply, "Indeed,
someone did come to warn us
but we denied him, saying,
'God never sent down any message.
You are gravely mistaken.'"°

10 And they will say,
"Had we listened,
or used our reason,
we would not now be
inmates of the blazing fire."

11 So they will confess
their sins—so much for the inmates
of the blazing fire!

12 As for those who fear
their Lord, unseen—
they shall have forgiveness
and a great reward.

13 And whether you conceal
your speech or proclaim it openly,
He Knows what lies
in the hearts [of humankind].

14 Would He not know—
He Who created them? He is
Most Subtle, All Aware.

SECTION 2

15 It is He Who has made
the earth subservient to you,
so walk in its pathways,
and eat of His provision—
[returning] to Him
you shall be resurrected.

16 Do you feel assured° that
He Who is in heaven will not
make the earth swallow you up
when it shakes violently?

17 Or do you feel assured
that He Who is in heaven
will not send against you
a hailstorm, that you might
know what My warning is?

18 And those who came
before them also denied—
[see] how I rejected them!

19 Don't they see the birds
above them, spreading and folding
their wings? None upholds them
but the All Merciful—
He Sees all things.

20 Who can help you—even
an army—besides the All Merciful?
The disbelievers are merely
sunk in delusion.

21 Or who can provide for you
if He withholds His provision?

Yet they persist in insolence
and aversion to truth.

22 Is someone who walks
with his face down better guided
than someone who walks upright
on a straight path?

23 Say, "It is He Who
brought you into being,
and gave you hearing, sight,
and hearts—
how little you give thanks."

24 Say, "It is He Who
multiplied you throughout
the earth, and to Him
you shall all be gathered."

25 They ask, "When will
this promise be fulfilled—
if you are speaking the truth?"

26 Say, "God alone has
[that] knowledge. I am merely
one who gives clear warning."

27 But when they see it near them,
the disbelievers' faces shall
be distressed, and they will be told,
"This is what you called for."

28 Say, "Have you considered—
if God were to destroy me
and those with me, or if He
were to have mercy on us—
who could save the disbelievers
from painful punishment?"

29 Say, "He is the All Merciful.
We believe in Him,
and trust in Him.
Soon, you shall know
who is clearly wrong."

30 Say, "Have you considered—
if one morning all your water
were to sink into the earth,
who would bring you water
that is flowing and clear?"

SURA 68

The Pen (Al-Qalam)

A Meccan sura, probably very early, of 52 verses, this extols the pen (v. 1) before offering a retort to the challenge that Muhammad is "possessed," posed by some wealthy but vitriolic Meccan opponents (vv. 2–18). There follows a parable of proud owners of a garden (vv. 13–34), and the sura closes with a vigorous polemic (vv. 35–46) and invocation of Jonah's good fortune (vv. 48–50), a reminder to those who think Muhammad possessed (vv. 51–52).

In the Name of God, the All Merciful, Ever Merciful

SECTION I

1 Nun.° By the pen,
and by what they write—

2 by the grace of your Lord,
you are not possessed;

3 and for you there will be
unending reward.

4 for you are most exalted
in moral character.

5 Soon you shall see
—and they shall see—

6 which of you is afflicted
[with madness].

7 It is your Lord who best knows
who has strayed from His path,
and it is He Who knows best
who is rightly guided.

8 So, don't heed those
who deny the truth.

9 They want you to compromise
so they can compromise.

10 And don't heed some wretched
swearer of oaths,

11 some slanderer, spreading
malicious gossip,

12 a sinful transgressor,
thwarting what is good,

13 cruel, and above all, ignoble°—

14 all on account of his wealth and sons.

15 When Our signs are recited
to him, he cries,
"Fables of the ancients!"

16 Soon We shall brand him
on the snout.

17 We tested them, just as
We tested the owners of the garden
when they swore to pluck its fruit
in the morning,°

18 without making allowance
[for God's will].

19 So a calamity from your Lord
struck the garden
while they were sleeping,

20 [and the orchard was desolated,]
as though it had been harvested.

21 As morning broke, they called
out to one another,

22 "Go to your crop early
if you want to harvest its fruits."

23 So they went, whispering,

24 "Let no poor person
enter the garden today
[without your consent]."

25 And they went early,
strong in this resolve.

26 But when they saw the garden, they
said,
"We must have lost our way.

27 "Oh no—we are ruined."

28 One of them, more moderate than
the rest,
said, "Did I not tell you to glorify
God?"

29 They said, "Glory be to our Lord.
We have done wrong."

30 Then they turned to blame one
another,

31 saying, "Alas, we have transgressed.

32 "But perhaps our Lord
will replace this garden
with something better, for
we turn to Him, in hope."

33 Such is the punishment
in this life. But in the hereafter
it will be greater still—
if only they knew.

SECTION 2

34 Those mindful of God
shall have gardens of bliss
with their Lord.

35 Would We treat alike
those who submit [to God's will]
and those who sin?

36 What is wrong with you?
On what grounds do you judge?

37 Or, do you have a Book
from which you learn

38 that you can have there
whatever you choose?

39 Or do you have a covenant
with Us, enduring until the day
of resurrection, that you will have
what you deem [to be yours]?

40 Ask them, which of them
will guarantee this?

41 Or do they have some divine partners?
Then let them bring forward these
partners,
if they are speaking the truth.

42 On the day of apocalypse,
they shall be called
to bow down—but will be unable.

43 Their eyes downcast,
shame will fall over them—

they were called to bow down
when they were sound [in body].

44 So, Prophet, leave to Me
those who deny this message:
We shall lead them on, step by step,
in ways they can't imagine.

45 I will grant them some respite—
My intent is resolute.

46 Or, is it that you ask of them
some payment, that would
burden them with debt?

47 Or is the unseen within their grasp,
so they can transcribe it?

48 Await patiently, then,
your Lord's judgment, and
don't be like Jonah in the whale°
who called out in distress—

49 had his Lord's grace
not reached him, he would have
been
cast on the naked shore, disgraced.

50 But his Lord chose him,
and made him one of the righteous.

51 When the unbelievers hear
this message, they would almost
strike you down° with their glances,
and they say, "He is possessed."

52 But this is nothing less
than a reminder for all the worlds.

Reality (*Al-Haqqa*)

A Meccan sura, in 52 verses, this references several previous peoples who disbelieved and were destroyed (vv. 1–12). The sura describes the joy of judgment day for believers (vv. 13–24), with the opposite fate for sinners (vv. 25–37), culminating in a paean to the Qur'an (vv. 38–52), announced as "certain truth" (v. 51).

In the Name of God, the All Merciful, Ever Merciful

SECTION I

1 The reality [of resurrection].

2 What is the reality of resurrection?

3 What would make you grasp
the reality of resurrection?

4 The people of Thamud and 'Ad
denied the thundering calamity.°

5 So the Thamud were destroyed
by an overwhelming blast,

6 and the 'Ad were destroyed
by a screaming, violent wind.

7 He made it rage against them
for seven nights and eight days
together—so you see its people
fallen down dead, like trunks
of hollow palm trees.

8 Do you see any trace of them now?

9 Pharaoh and those before him,
and the overturned cities
all committed grave sins,

10 and disobeyed each
messenger of their Lord,
so He seized them
with a deathly grasp.

11 When the water flooded,
We carried you in the floating ark,

12 to make it a reminder for you—
so listening ears might take heed.

13 Then, when a single blast
blares from the trumpet,

14 and the earth and mountains
are raised and crushed
with a single stroke—

15 on that day the event will come,

16 and the sky will be torn asunder,
for it will be frail that day.

17 and on its verges, the angels
will stand, and eight of them,
that day, shall bear above them
the throne of your Lord.

18 On that day, you shall be
exposed, and no secret of yours
shall stay concealed.

19 Then those given their record
in their right hand will each say,
"Here, read my record;

20 "I was certain that I would
come to my reckoning."

21 And he will be
in a pleasing life,

22 in a high garden,

23 with its clusters of fruits
hanging near.

24 "Eat and drink to your content—
for the deeds you accrued
in days gone by."

25 And those given their record
in their left hand will each say,
"I wish I were not given my record,

26 "and that I did not know
what my reckoning was.

27 "I wish that death had made
an end of me!

28 "My wealth is of no use to me.

29 "My power has gone from me."

30 [A voice will say,] "Seize him
and shackle him,

31 "then burn him
in the blazing fire,

32 "and bind him in a chain
of seventy cubits—

33 "he would not believe
in God, the Supreme,

34 "and never urged the feeding
of the poor,

35 "so he has no friend here today,

36 "nor any food except the pus

37 "that only sinners eat."

SECTION 2

38 Yes—I swear by what you see

39 and what you do not see,

40 that this is the word
of a noble messenger;

41 it is not the word of a poet—
how little you believe!

42 Nor the word of a soothsayer—
how little you pay heed!

43 This is a message revealed
from the Lord of the worlds,

44 if the messenger had contrived
any statements in Our Name,

45 We would seize him
by his right hand,

46 and cut off his heart's aorta—

47 nor could any of you
prevent him from this.

48 But this is a message for those
who are mindful of God,

49 and We know that some
among you deny it—

50 it is a cause of dismay
to those who disbelieve,

51 but it is the certain truth,

52 so glorify the Name of your Lord,
the Supreme.

SURA 70

The Paths of Ascent (*Al-Maʿarij*)

A Meccan sura, with some later interpolations, its 44 verses include an opening query about paths of ascent (v. 3) with a command for patience (vv. 5–7), followed by a recapitulation of judgment day (vv. 8–35). It extols those on the right (vv. 22–35), but closes with a warning to those on the left (vv. 36–44).

In the Name of God, the All Merciful, Ever Merciful

SECTION I

1 Someone inquired about
the punishment to come—

2 it will fall upon the disbelievers—
none can avert it—

3 from God, Who controls
the paths of ascent.

4 The angels and the spirit
ascend to Him on a day whose span
is fifty thousand years.°

5 So practice patience—
beautiful patience.

6 They see the day
as far away,

7 while We see it
as near—

8 a day when the sky will be
like molten brass,

9 and the mountains
like carded wool,

10 no friend will ask
after any friend,

11 even though they are placed
within sight of each other.
The sinner would ransom himself
from the torment of that day
by offering his children,

12 his spouse and his brother,

13 his near kin who sheltered him,

14 and everyone on the earth—
if this could save him.

15 No—it will be
a flame of hell

16 that strips his scalp,

17 calling to all those
who turned their backs
and turned away,

18 amassing wealth, only
to hoard it.

19 Humans are created anxious,

20 fretful when misfortune
touches them,

21 and miserly when good fortune
reaches them—

22 except those who pray,

23 who remain constant
in their prayers,

24 and those whose wealth
bears an acknowledged share

25 for the beggar
and the deprived,

26 those who accept the truth
of the day of reckoning,

27 and are fearful
of their Lord's punishment

28 —from which none
can feel secure—

29 and those who preserve
their chastity,°

30 except with their wives
or their slaves—for which
they incur no blame

31 —but those who venture
beyond this are transgressors—

32 while those who fulfill
their trusts and covenants,

33 those who are upright
in their testimonies,

34 and those who preserve
the practice of their prayers

35 shall all be
in gardens, honored.

SECTION 2

36 What is it with the disbelievers—
who rush toward you, Prophet,

37 from the right, from the left,
in crowds?

38 Does every one of them
long to enter the garden of bliss?

39 No—they know
from what We created them!

40 No—I swear by the Lord
of every sunrise and sunset°
that We have the Power

41 to replace them with others,
who are better—and
nothing can thwart Us.°

42 So leave them to gossip
and frolic, until they encounter
their day—as promised°—

43 a day when they will rush out
from their graves, as if racing
toward a goal,

44 eyes downcast, and covered
in disgrace—this is the day
they were promised.

SURA 71

Noah (*Nuh*)

Likely a Meccan sura, this recalls and lauds the encounter of God with Noah, ending with a plea from Noah that crowns its 28 verses: "My Lord, forgive me, my parents, those who enter my house as believers and all believing men and women" (v. 28).

In the Name of God, the All Merciful, Ever Merciful

SECTION I

1 We sent Noah to his people:
  "Warn your people before
  painful punishment falls on them."

2 He said, "My people,
  I give you clear warning

3 "that you should worship God,
  be mindful of Him, and obey me.

4 "He will forgive you your sins
  and grant you respite for
  an appointed term.
  When that term from God expires,
  it cannot be prolonged—
  if only you knew."

5 He said, "My Lord, I have called
  to my people night and day,

6 "but my call merely makes them
  fly further away,

7 "And every time I call them
  —so that you might forgive them—
  they block their ears with their
      fingers
  and hide their heads in their robes,
  obstinate, inflated with pride.

8 "So I called to them openly,

9 "declaiming to them in public
  and addressing them in private,

10 "urging them,
   'Seek forgiveness from your Lord,
   for He is Ever Forgiving.

11 "'He will send you
   abundant rain from the sky,

12 "'bestow wealth and children
   upon you, and grant you
   gardens and rivers.

13 "'What is wrong with you—
   Why don't you look toward
   the majesty of God?

14 "'Who created you in stages?

15 "'Do you not see how
   God created the seven heavens,
   one above the other?

16 "'And made the moon
   a light within them,
   and the sun a lamp?

17 "'And made you grow, surging
   out of the earth?°

18 "'And will return you into it
   and bring you out again, anew?

19 "'God made the earth
   an expanse for you,

20 "'That you might wander
   along its wide paths.'"

SECTION 2

21 Noah said, "My Lord,
   they have disobeyed me
   and they follow those
   whose wealth and children
   merely increase their loss.

22 "And they have devised
   a great plot,

23 "saying, 'Don't abandon
   your gods—*Wadd, Suwaʻ,*
   Yaghuth, Yaʻuq, and Nasr.'°

24 "They have misled many—
   let the wrongdoers
   sink only deeper into error."°

25 On account of their sins
   they were drowned, and made
   to enter the fire. They found
   none to help them besides God.

26 And Noah said, "My Lord,
   don't leave a single one
   of the disbelievers on earth!

27 "For if you leave them,
   They'll mislead your servants,
   and they'll breed nothing
   but wicked disbelievers.

28 "My Lord, forgive me,
   my parents, those who enter
   my house as believers,
   and all believing men and women—
   but let the wrongdoers
   sink only deeper into ruin."

SURA 72

The Jinn (*Al-Jinn*)

Middle or late Meccan, this sura of 28 verses is unusual in that it addresses the
jinn as curious listeners, then converted believers. Its style is also unusual, with
the first fifteen verses directed to the Prophet, and then the remainder (vv. 16–
28) a string of dicta he addresses to the jinn.

In the Name of God, the All Merciful, Ever Merciful

SECTION I

1 Say, Prophet, "It has been
   revealed to me that a group of
      jinn°

listened to [to a recitation] and said,
'We've heard a wondrous Qur'an,

2 "'that guides to the right path,
   so we believe in it, and shall never

associate any other with our Lord;

3   "'and that He—exalted be
the Majesty of our Lord—
has neither spouse nor son.

4   "'but that some foolish one
among us would say
outrageous things about God,

5   "'and that we had thought
no human or jinn
would ever lie about God.

6   "'and that some humans
sought shelter with the jinn,
merely increasing their
misguidance,

7   "'and that they thought,
as you did, that God would
never raise anyone back to life.

8   "'and that we tried to reach heaven,
but we found it full of stern guards
and flaming stars.

9   "'and that we would sit there
at various stations, trying to hear.
But any who tries to listen now
will find a flaming star
waiting for him.°

10   "'And that we don't know whether
evil is meant for those on earth
or whether their Lord means
them to be rightly guided.

11   "'And that some among us
do good deeds while others do not—
we follow divergent paths.

12   "'And that we recognized
we could not escape God on earth
nor escape Him by flight.

13   "'And that when we heard
the message of guidance,
we believed it. And that whoever
believes in their Lord shall fear
neither loss nor injustice.

14   "'And that among us are some
who submit their will to God
while others are unjust.
Those who submit have
sought the right path.

15   "'But those who are unjust
shall be fuel for hellfire.'"

16   Had they stayed steadfast
on the right path, We would have
given them abundant rain,

17   a test for them. As for those who
turn away from their Lord's
     message—
He will give them severe torment.°

18   Know that the places of worship
are for God alone, so do not call
on any but the One God.

19 Yet when God's servant°
stood to pray, they almost
crowded in upon him.

SECTION 2

20 Say, "I call only upon my Lord,
and I associate none with Him."

21 Say, "It is not in my power
either to harm you
or to make you upright."

22 Say, "None can protect me
from God, nor can I find
any refuge except in Him.

23 "I only convey what is from God
and His messages. Those who
disobey God and His messenger
shall face the fire of hell,
to dwell there forever.

24 "When they see for themselves

what was promised them,
they will know whose helpers
are weaker and who are fewer."

25 Say, "I do not know whether
what you are promised is near
or whether my Lord has fixed
a distant term for it.

26 "He alone is Knower
of the unseen, and He reveals
to none what lies in the unseen,

27 "except a messenger He chooses,
placing a guard
before him and behind him°—

28 "so he might know that
each messenger has conveyed
the messages of his Lord.
He Encompasses everything
about them,
and He reckons all things."

SURA 73

The One Enwrapped (*Al-Muzzammil*)

One of the earliest Meccan revelations, its last verse (v. 20) is clearly Medinan, expanding the conditions but also exemptions for Qur'an recitation. Initially addressed to the Prophet alone (vv. 1–8), these exemptions are extended to all believers, including those "fighting in God's cause" (v. 20), a reference to jihad that took place only after the *hijra* (622 CE).

In the Name of God, the All Merciful, Ever Merciful

SECTION I

1 You, who lie enwrapped
   in your mantle—

2 stand in prayer°
   for the night,
   all but a small part—

3 half of it, or a little less,

4 or more, reciting the Qur'an
   in clear, rhythmic measure.

5 Soon We shall send down
   to you a Word
   of momentous weight.°

6 Rising in the night is austerer,
   [achieves deeper self-harmony,]
   more suited to
   reciting of the Word.

7 During the day you are
   occupied at length,

8 but remember the Name
   of your Lord, and devote
   yourself wholly to Him—

9 Lord of the East and the West;°
   there is no god but He,
   so take Him as your Guardian.

10 Bear patiently what they say,
   and depart from them, graciously,

11 and leave to Me
   those who disbelieve,
   the ones who live in ease—
   and endure them for a while.

12 We have shackles for them
   and a blazing fire,

13 as well as food that chokes,
   and a painful torment

14 on a day when the earth
   and the mountains shake,
   and the mountains crumble to
   heaps of sand.

15 People, We have sent
   a messenger, as a witness to you,
   as We sent a messenger to Pharaoh.

16 But Pharaoh disobeyed
   the messenger, so We brought
   ruinous torment upon him.

17 If you disbelieve, then,
   how can you be mindful
   of a day that will turn
   the hair of children gray,

18 when the sky is torn asunder,
   and the promise of God fulfilled?

19 This is a reminder—
so, let those who desire it
take a path to their Lord.

SECTION 2

20 Your Lord knows that you
stand in prayer almost two-thirds
of the night, and sometimes a half
or a third of it, along with a group
of those with you. God determines
night and day in due measure.
He knows that you cannot
keep count, so He turns to you,
relenting. Recite, then, as much
of the Qur'an as you can with ease.

He knows that some of you are ill,
or traveling the earth seeking
the bounty of God, or fighting
in God's cause.° So read as much as
you can with ease, be steadfast
in prayer, and give what is due
in charity—lend to God a beautiful
loan.° For whatever good you accrue
in your deeds, you shall find it
there with God—better, and
   greater,
in reward. And seek God's
   forgiveness,
for He is Forgiving, Ever Merciful.

SURA 74

The One Enfolded (*Al-Muddaththir*)

The opening verse from this very early Meccan sura of 56 verses refers to the Prophet as wearing a *dithar* or mantle. It enjoins him to patience (v. 7) but also excoriates one who opposes him (vv. 11–31), detailing the punishment of hell-fire with reference to its nineteen custodians (v. 30). The remainder of the sura expands the warning to humankind, with a decisive reminder that God alone is "the Source of Mindfulness, the Source of Forgiveness" (v. 56).

In the Name of God, the All Merciful, Ever Merciful

SECTION 1

1 You who are enfolded
in your mantle,°

2 arise and warn!

3 And magnify your Lord,

4 keeping your garments
pure,

5 shunning uncleanliness.

6 Do not give
   in order to seek gain,

7 but be patient in the cause
   of your Lord.

8 When the trumpet is sounded,

9 that day will be a harsh day

10 with no ease
   for those who disbelieve.

11 Leave me to deal with
   the person I created,° alone,

12 to whom I granted
   extensive wealth,

13 and children by his side,

14 he for whom I laid out
   a path of ease,

15 still, he wishes that I give more!

16 No—for he has stubbornly
   defied Our signs.

17 Soon I will place him
   in steep hardship,

18 for he pondered
   and plotted—

19 may he perish
   for the way he plotted,

20 yes, may he perish
   for how he plotted.

21 First, he looked,

22 then he frowned and scowled,

23 then turned away
   in his pride,

24 saying, "This [Qur'an]
   is but old-style sorcery,

25 "it is nothing but
   the speech of a mortal."

26 Soon I shall burn him
   in the fire of hell.

27 And what would make you grasp
   what the fire of hell is?

28 It spares none,
   and it leaves none,

29 scorching the flesh of humans.

30 Nineteen guardians stand over it.°

31 And We have placed none
   but angels as guardians of the fire;
   We have fixed their number
   only as a trial for disbelievers,
   so that those given the Book
   will be certain, and that believers
   might be stronger in faith.
   Neither those given the Book

nor the believers will harbor
   doubt,
but those whose hearts are
   diseased
and the disbelievers will say,
"What does God mean by this
   parable?"
In this way, God lets stray whom
He will, and guides whom He will—
and none knows your Lord's forces
but He; and this is nothing less
than a message for all humankind.

SECTION 2

32 No—by the moon,

33 and by the night
   as it recedes,

34 by the dawn
   as it rises into light,

35 This is one of the greatest signs,

36 a warning to humankind,

37 to any among you who
   advances or retreats,

38 Every soul will be bound
   by its deeds,

39 except for those on the right,

40 who will be in gardens—
   asking one another

41 concerning the sinners,

42 "What led you into
   the fire of hell?"

43 They will answer, "We were
   not among those who prayed,

44 "nor did we feed the poor,

45 "rather, we indulged
   with others in idle talk,

46 "and denied the day
   of reckoning,

47 "until there came upon us
   the certainty [of death]."°

48 Then no intercession
   by any intercessors
   shall help them.

49 What is wrong with them—
   what makes them turn away
   from the message?

50 As if they were
   frightened wild asses

51 in flight from a lion?

52 Yes, each one of them
   wants to be furnished with
   scrolls, unfurled.°

53 No—they have no fear
   of the hereafter.

54 Yes—this is a reminder—

55 Let those who will
   keep it in mind.

56 Yet none will keep it
   in mind, except as God wills—
   He is the Source of Mindfulness,
   the Source of Forgiveness.°

SURA 75

Resurrection (*Al-Qiyama*)

A series of short passages, this early Meccan sura of 40 verses deals with familiar themes of resurrection (vv. 1–15) and judgment (vv. 20–30). It also contains
instruction on Qur'an recitation (vv. 16–19) and the rebuke of a denier (vv. 31–
35), with reminders for all humankind (vv. 36–40).

In the Name of God, the All Merciful, Ever Merciful

SECTION I

1 Indeed, I swear by the day
  of resurrection,

2 and indeed I swear by the
  self-reproaching soul—

3 do humans think We won't
  reunite their bones?

4 In fact, We're able to remold
  their very fingertips.

5 Yet humans want to deny
  what lies before them,

6 asking, "When is the day
  of resurrection?"

7 When their sight is dazzled,

8 and the moon eclipsed,

9 and the sun and moon
  are joined together—

10 that day, people will say,
   "Where is any escape?"

11 But no—there will be no refuge.

12 That day, the only repose
   will be with your Lord.

13 That day humans will be told
what they did and did not do.°

14 Yes, humans will
witness against themselves,

15 though they offer
their excuses.

16 Prophet, do not scramble
your tongue, hurrying
[to recite the Qur'an];

17 it is We who will ensure its
collection and recitation.

18 When We recite it,° follow
the recital precisely;

19 then it is for Us
to make it clear.°

20 Yet you still love the now,
all of you,

21 and neglect the hereafter.

22 Some faces, that day,
will be gleaming,

23 as they look toward their Lord,

24 and other faces, that day,
will be filled with gloom,

25 imagining the calamity
about to crush them.

26 When the soul rises up
to the throat
[on its way out of the body],

27 and it is asked,
"Who can convey him?"°

28 and when he grasps that
this is the parting
[of soul from body]

29 his legs locked together—

30 on that day, he will be driven
toward your Lord.

SECTION 2

31 He neither believed
the truth nor prayed.

32 Rather, he denied the truth
and turned away,

33 going back to his people,
swaggering,

34 Closer and closer
to you is woe,

35 closer still and closer.°

36 Do humans think
they will be left unquestioned?

37 Were they not at first
a drop of ejected sperm

38 that became a clot?
    God created and shaped it,

39 making from it two sexes,
    male and female.

40 Is He, then, not Able
    to bring the dead back to life?

SURA 76

Humankind (*Al-Insan*)

A middle Meccan sura of 31 verses, this extols creation and reprimands the disbeliever (vv. 1–5) before detailing how the righteous will be rewarded (vv. 5–22). It
closes with a firm reminder of the Prophet "to wait patiently for your Lord's judgment" (v. 24) and to trust the will of God, Who is "All Knowing, All Wise" (v. 30).

In the Name of God, the All Merciful, Ever Merciful

SECTION I

1 Was there not a time when
   when humankind was nothing
   to speak of?

2 We created humankind
   from a drop of mingled sperm,
   to try them. We gave them
   hearing and sight.

3 We have shown them the way—
   whether they are grateful or not.

4 For the disbelievers
   We have prepared chains,
   shackles, and a blazing fire.

5 The righteous shall drink
   from a cup tinged with camphor,

6 a fountain where God's
   servants drink, flowing
   freely at their will.

7 They fulfill their vows, and fear
   a day whose misery shall be
   spread far and wide;

8 and, despite their love of it,
   they donate [their] food
   to the poor, the orphan,
   and the prisoner of war,

9 saying, "We feed you,
   seeking only the Face of God;
   we desire from you
   neither reward nor thanks.

10 "We only fear, from our Lord,
   a day of wrath and distress."

11 But God will save them
    from the misery of that day,
    and will cast over them
    radiance and joy.

12 He will reward them
    for their patience—with a garden
    and robes of silk.

13 Reclining there on couches,
    they shall know neither burning sun
    nor biting cold.

14 The shades of the gardens
    shall spread over them, its fruits
    lowered before them.

15 And there shall be passed
    among them vessels of silver
    and goblets of crystal—

16 crystal clear, silver,
    in what measure they will—

17 they will be given drink
    from a cup flavored with ginger

18 from a fountain there
    called Salsabil.°

19 And there shall pass among them,
    immortal youths to serve—
    to see them, you would think
    they were pearls, scattered.

20 And when you look,
    you will see there only bliss
    and a glorious kingdom.

21 They shall be robed
    in garments of green silk
    and rich brocade, adorned
    with bracelets of silver;
    and their Lord will give them
    a pure drink,

22 [saying,] "This is your reward,
    your endeavor is commended."

SECTION 2

23 It is We Who have revealed
    to you the Qur'an in stages.°

24 So, wait patiently
    for your Lord's judgment;
    take no heed of the sinners
    and disbelievers among them.

25 And remember the Name
    of your Lord, morning and evening;

26 bow down to Him
    in the night, glorifying Him
    during the long hours of night.

27 These people love
    the life here, leaving aside
    all thought of a coming day
    that shall weigh heavily.

28 It is We Who created them
and strengthened their forms;
but whenever We will,
We can replace them.

29 This is but a reminder—
let those who will, take a path
toward their Lord.

30 Yet you do not will
except as God wills—for God
is All Knowing, All Wise.

31 He will admit into His mercy
whom He will; but for wrongdoers
He has prepared a painful torment.

SURA 77

Those Sent Out (*Al-Mursalat*)

An early Meccan sura, its 50 verses set forth the signs and certainty of the day of decision (v. 13), before elaborating on the calamities that will befall schemers, deniers, and liars on that day (vv. 14–50).

In the Name of God, the All Merciful, Ever Merciful

SECTION I

1 By the [winds] sent out,
one after another,

2 which storm violently,

3 scattering widely,

4 and those who distinguish
by a criterion,°

5 bringing down a reminder

6 forestalling all excuse or
issuing warning—

7 what you are promised
shall come to pass.

8 When the stars are
extinguished,

9 when the sky is
torn asunder,

10 when the mountains are
blown away in dust,

11 when the messengers are
gathered at a chosen time—

12 for which day
are these events held back?

13 For the day of decision.

14 And what would make you grasp
what the day of decision is?

15 Woe, that day, to those
who deny the truth.

16 Did We not destroy
earlier peoples?

17 And shall We not make
later peoples follow them?

18 This is how We deal
with sinners.

19 Woe, that day, to those
who deny the truth.

20 Did We not create you
from a lowly fluid

21 which We lodged in a
secure home

22 for a decreed time?

23 It is We Who decree—and
how superlatively!

24 Woe, that day, to those
who deny the truth.

25 Did We not make
the earth a vessel

26 for the living and the dead,

27 and place there sturdy,
high mountains, and give you
sweet water to drink?

28 Woe, that day, to those
who deny the truth.

29 They will be told, "Go—
to what you always denied.

30 "Go—to the shadow of smoke
rising in three pillars,°

31 "that yields no shade,
and will be of no help
against the flame.

32 "It throws out sparks
as large as castles,

33 "as if they were
yellow camels."

34 Woe, that day, to those
who deny the truth.

35 That will be a day
they are unable to speak,

36 nor will they have leave
to make pleas.

37 Woe, that day, to those
who deny the truth.

38 That will be the day
of decision. We shall gather
you and those before you.

39 So if you have a scheme,
scheme against Me [now]!

40 Woe, that day, to those
who deny the truth.

SECTION 2

41 The righteous shall be
among shades and springs,

42 with whatever fruits they desire.

43 "Eat and drink, to your content,
[a reward] for all your deeds."

44 In this way, We reward
those who do good deeds.

45 Woe, that day, to those
who deny the truth.

46 They will be told,
"Eat and enjoy for a while—
you who are sinners."

47 Woe, that day, to those
who deny the truth.

48 And when they are told,
"Bow down,"
they do not bow.

49 Woe, that day, to those
who deny the truth.

50 In what message, ever,
will they believe after this?

SURA 78

The Announcement (*Al-Naba'*)

Middle Meccan, this sura of 40 verses opens with a pronouncement of imminent judgment (vv. 1–5) before citing God's might and majesty (vv. 6–16) and
then concluding with a vivid scenario of the day of decision (vv. 17–40).

In the Name of God, the All Merciful, Ever Merciful

SECTION 1

1 About what
do they ask one another?

2 About the momentous
announcement

3 over which they dispute.

4 Indeed, they shall find out—

5 yes, they shall soon find out.

6 Did We not spread out
   the earth like a couch?

7 And anchor the mountains like
   posts?

8 Did We not create you in pairs,

9 and make your sleep for rest,

10 the night a cover,

11 the day for livelihood?

12 Have We not built above you
    seven secure heavens,

13 placing there a flaming lamp?

14 And do We not send down
    water from the rainclouds,
    pouring profusely,

15 to bring forth grain and greenery,

16 and gardens with luscious growth?

17 The day of decision
    has an appointed time—

18 a day when the trumpet shall be
    sounded
    and you will come forward in
    crowds;

19 the sky will be opened like doors,°

20 and the mountains moved,
    vanishing into a mirage.°

21 Hell, for sure, lies waiting—

22 the final end for transgressors

23 where they will stay for eons.

24 They will taste nothing cool there,
    nor any drink,

25 just scalding water and
    purulence—

26 a fitting recompense.

27 For they never expected
    any reckoning

28 and utterly denied Our signs.

29 We have recorded all things
    in a Book.

30 "So taste this—We will grant you
    only more torment."°

SECTION 2

31 Those who were mindful of God
    shall flourish

32 in gardens with grapevines

33 with companions, well suited,

34 and a cup overflowing.

35 There they shall hear
no idle talk nor falsehood—

36 a reward from your Lord,
a fitting gift

37 from the Lord of the heavens and
the earth,
and all that lies between them—the
All Merciful—
none shall have power to address
Him—

38 on the day that the Spirit°

and the angels stand in ranks,
none shall speak but those
permitted by the All Merciful—
and they will say only what is right.

39 That will be the day of truth—
so let those who wish, take a path
back to their Lord.

40 We have warned you
of impending torment, on a day
when every person will see
[the deeds] his hands have wrought,
when the disbelievers cry, "Alas,
I wish I were nothing but dust!"°

SURA 79

Those Who Force Out (*Al-Nazi'at*)

This early, possibly middle Meccan sura, 46 verses long, begins with a series of invocations, likely angels commanding souls, on the day of resurrection (vv. 1–14). It then shifts to the story of Moses (vv. 15–26) before an appeal to nature as God's masterpiece (vv. 27–33) and ending with a reminder of the imminent hour (vv. 34–46).

In the Name of God, the All Merciful, Ever Merciful

SECTION I

1 By the angels who force out
[the souls of the wicked];

2 by those who ease out
[the souls of the blessèd];

3 by those who glide, swimming,

4 and those who strive, racing

5 to arrange the world's affairs
[as commanded]—

6 the day when all shall shake
in violent convulsion
[with the first trumpet sound],

7 and more convulsion
[with the second sound]—°

8 Hearts shall quake that day,

9 their eyes downcast, [in dread].

10 Now they say, "Shall we
really be brought back
to our former state

11 "when we are rotting bones?"

12 They say, "This would be
a ruinous return."

13 There will be but a single
deafening blast

14 and they shall rise, on a wide
expanse.

15 Has the story of Moses
reached you,

16 when his Lord called to him
in the sacred valley of Tuwa?°

17 "Go to Pharaoh,
for he has transgressed,

18 "and ask, 'Are you willing
to purge yourself

19 "'and have me guide you
to your Lord,
whom you might then fear?'"

20 Then Moses showed him
a most stupendous sign°

21 but Pharaoh denied it
and disobeyed;

22 then he turned his back,
striving [against God].

23 He gathered his people,
declaring to them,

24 "I am your Lord,
the Most High."

25 So God punished him
as an example, in this life
and the next.°

26 In this is a lesson
for those who fear God.

SECTION 2

27 Are you harder to create
than the sky that God made?

28 He raised its canopy
and proportioned it,

29 immersing its night in darkness
and revealing its morning light.

30 And after this,
he spread out the earth,

31 bringing out its water
and its pasture;

32 —anchoring the mountains—

33 to provide for you
and for your herds.

34 When the great calamity strikes

35 on the day that humankind
recalls all that it strove for,

36 and the fire of hell appears
for all to see.

37 Then, those who transgressed,

38 and preferred the life
of this world,

39 shall have the fire of hell
as their home.

40 But those who feared [the day]

when they would stand before their
Lord,
and restrained the desires of self,

41 shall have the garden
as their home.

42 They ask you about the hour—
"When will it come?"

43 But how would you speak of this?

44 Its time is known only
to your Lord.

45 You merely warn those
who fear it.

46 The day they see it,
it will seem as though
they had stayed [on earth]
for but an evening
or a morning.

He Frowned ('*Abasa*)

An early Meccan sura of 42 verses, this offers a divine rebuke to Muhammad for ignoring a blind man (vv. 1–10). It then proceeds to extol scripture as "honored scrolls" (v. 13b) and to chastise humankind as ungrateful (vv. 17–23), even for the food they consume (vv. 24–31), before evoking a scene of the last day (vv. 33–42).

In the Name of God, the All Merciful, Ever Merciful

1 [The Prophet] frowned,
and turned away°

2 because the blind man
came to him.

3 Prophet, how would you know—
perhaps he might purge himself of sin,

4 or heed the teaching°
that might profit him?

5 Yet some uncaring person°

6 claims your attention

7 —though you are not to blame
if he fails to purge himself of sin—

8 while the one who came to you
[eagerly] in haste,

9 and in awe,

10 you dismiss.°

11 Why, no! This is a reminder

12 for *any* who would heed it,

13 [inscribed] in honored scrolls,

14 exalted, and kept pure,

15 borne by the hands of scribes

16 who are noble and righteous.

17 Woe to humankind—
how ungrateful they are!

18 From what did He create them?

19 He created them from
a sperm drop
and proportioned them,

20 then made their path easy.

21 Then He caused them to die,
brought them into their grave;

22 then, when He wishes,
He will raise them up again.

23 Yet they have not fulfilled
what God commanded them.

24 Let humankind consider
the food they consume:

25 We pour down water
plentifully,

26 then We cleave the ground,

27 bringing out of it grain,

28 vines and vegetation,

29 olives and date palms,

30 with lush gardens,

31 fruits and pasture,

32 to provide for you

and your livestock.

33 But when the deafening blast comes,

34 that day, a man will flee
from his own brother,

35 from his mother and father,

36 his spouse and his children.

37 Each of them, that day,
will be immersed
in their own concerns—

38 a day on which some faces
shall beam,

39 laughing, rejoicing,

40 while other faces that day
shall be covered with dust,

41 shrouded in darkness—

42 these will be the disbelievers,
the iniquitous.

SURA 81

The Folding Up (Al-Takwir)

A Meccan sura, its 29 verses open with a vivid scene of the last day (vv. 1–14) conveyed to underpin Muhammad's authority against his critics (vv. 15–29), vouchsafed by the will of God, Lord of the universe (v. 29).

In the Name of God, the All Merciful, Ever Merciful

SECTION I

1 When the sun is folded up,

2 when the stars fall down, scattered,

3 when the mountains
   move, [vanishing,]°

4 when camels, pregnant to term
   are left untended,

5 when the wild beasts
   are herded together,

6 when the oceans boil over,

7 when souls are paired;°

8 when the infant girl,
   buried alive, is asked

9 for what crime she was killed,

10 when the scrolls of deeds
   are opened wide,

11 when the sky is
   torn away,

12 when the fire of hell
   is set ablaze,

13 and when the garden
   is brought near—

14 then each soul shall know
   what it has wrought.

15 So, I swear by
   the receding [stars]

16 that sail and disappear

17 and by the night
   as it fades away,

18 and by the dawn
   as it breathes,

19 this is the word
   of a noble messenger,°

20 imbued with strength,
   honored by the Lord of the throne,

21 obeyed and deemed
   worthy of trust.

22 Your companion
   is not possessed,

23 for he saw the Archangel
   on the clear horizon,°

24 and he does not withhold
   what he knows of the unseen.

25 Nor is this the word
of some accursed demon.

26 So, where are you all heading?

27 This is nothing less
than a message
for the whole universe,°

28 for those among you who wish
to follow a straight path,

29 But you shall not will
except as God wills—
Lord of the universe.

The Cleaving Asunder (*Al-Infitar*)

An early Meccan sura of 19 verses, this registers the day of reckoning as a celestial cataclysm (vv. 1–4). Its reckoning certain for each soul (vv. 5–16), it will be "the day when God's command is absolute" (v. 19).

In the Name of God, the All Merciful, Ever Merciful

1 When the sky
is cleaved asunder,

2 when the stars
are scattered,

3 when the oceans burst
over their shores,

4 when graves are turned
upside down—

5 then each soul shall know
[the good deeds] it has accrued,
and those it has left undone.

6 Humankind, what has misled you,
away from your Noble Lord,

7 Who created you, shaped you,
and proportioned you,

8 molding you into
whatever form He wished?

9 Yet still you deny
the reckoning.

10 But watching over you
are angels,

11 noble recorders,

12 who know all that you do.

13 Those who were righteous
shall be in bliss,

14 while the wicked
   shall be in hellfire,

15 where they will burn
   on the day of reckoning,

16 nor will they be
   removed from it.

17 What would make you grasp
   what the day of reckoning is?

18 Yes, what could make you grasp
   what the day of reckoning is?

19 The day when no soul
   can help another soul at all,
   the day when God's command
   is absolute.

SURA 83

Those Who Defraud (*Al-Mutaffifin*)

It's uncertain whether this is an early or late Meccan sura. It begins by denouncing those who cheat others (vv. 1–17), reminding them of how they will be evaluated "on a momentous day" (v. 5). The second segment of its 36 verses lauds the pious (vv. 18–28) before declaring that they, not the disbelievers, will have the last laugh (vv. 29–36).

In the Name of God, the All Merciful, Ever Merciful

1 Woe to those who defraud,

2 who, when receiving from people,
  exact full measure,

3 but when giving or weighing
  for them, fall short in measure.

4 Do they not reckon
  that they will be resurrected

5 on a momentous day,

6 a day when humankind shall stand

before the Lord of the universe?

7 Indeed, the record of the wicked
  is housed in Sijjin.°

8 And what would make you grasp
  what Sijjin is?

9 —a record, inscribed.

10 Woe on that day to those
   who deny—

11 those who deny

the day of reckoning.

12 And none will deny it
but sinful transgressors.

13 When Our signs are recited
to them, they exclaim,
"Tales of the ancients!"

14 Their hearts are covered with rust
by all that they have done.

15 On that day, they shall be
veiled from their Lord,

16 then they shall burn
in the fire of hell.

17 They will be told,
"This is what you denied."

18 Indeed, the record of the righteous
shall be housed in Illiyyun.°

19 And what would make you grasp
what Illiyyun is?

20 —a record, inscribed,

21 to be witnessed by those
close to God.

22 The righteous shall
be in bliss,

23 on couches, observing all—

24 you will know in their faces
the radiance of bliss.

25 They shall be served
with pure wine, sealed,

26 with the seal of musk.
Let all who strive, strive for this.

27 It will be mixed
with the water of Tasnim,°

28 a spring, from which those drink
who are close to God.

29 Those given to sin would laugh
at those who believed,

30 winking at one another
whenever they passed by them;

31 and would return jesting
to their own people;

32 and whenever they saw believers,
they would say,
"These are the ones who are astray."

33 But they were not sent
as custodians
over the believers

34 And on this day, the believers
will laugh at the disbelievers

35 on couches, observing all,

36 [they will say to one another,]
"Are not the disbelievers
requited for what they did?"

The Splitting Asunder (*Al-Inshiqaq*)

An early Meccan sura of 25 verses, it opens with sky splitting asunder on the day when humans meet their Lord (vv. 1–15). There follows another invocation of the twilight, night and moon (vv. 16–18) before disbelievers face a painful punishment (vv. 19–24) while believers are rewarded (v. 25).

In the Name of God, the All Merciful, Ever Merciful

1 When the sky is split
asunder,

2 hearing its Lord,
as it must;

3 when the earth
is spread out,

4 casting out its contents,
empty,

5 hearing its Lord,
as it must;

6 you humans—laboring toward
your Lord—will meet Him.

7 Then those given their record°
in their right hand

8 will have an easy reckoning

9 and will turn to their people
rejoicing.

10 But those given their record
behind their backs

11 will cry for their end

12 and burn in blazing fire.

13 They went among their people
rejoicing.

14 They thought they would
never return [to Us].

15 But no—their Lord was always
watching them.

16 I swear by the gleaming twilight,

17 by the night and what it enfolds,

18 by the moon in its fullness—

19 you will journey
from stage to stage.

20 So why will they not believe?

21 And when the Qur'an
is read to them,
why do they not bow down?

22 But no . . . the disbelievers deny it.

23 But God knows best
what they keep within themselves.

24 So announce to them
a painful torment,

25 except for those who believe
and do good deeds—theirs shall be
a reward without end.

SURA 85

The Constellations (*Al-Buruj*)

Early Meccan, this sura consists of 22 verses that begin with the constellations
as witness (vv. 1–3). It evokes the story of a pit made in pre-Islamic times for
the murder of Christians. The account of Pharaoh and Thamud (vv. 17–18) is
a reminder that God encompasses disbelievers from all sides (vv. 19–20), and
that He is custodian of "a glorious Qur'an, inscribed on a preserved tablet" (vv.
21–22).

In the Name of God, the All Merciful, Ever Merciful

1 By the heaven, that holds
the constellations;

2 by the promised day;

3 by the Witness
and what is witnessed—

4 may they perish who made the pit°

5 with fire full of fuel

6 while they sat around it,

7 bearing witness to all they did
against the believers—

8 whom they begrudged
only because they believed in God,
the Almighty, the Praiseworthy,

9 to Whom belongs dominion
of the heavens and the earth;
God is Witness to all things.

10 Those who persecute
the believing men and women
and do not then repent—
theirs shall be the torment of hell;
theirs the torment of blazing fire.

11 As for those who believe
and do good deeds—

theirs shall be the gardens
with rivers flowing beneath—
that is the great triumph.

12 Your Lord's onslaught
   is severe.

13 It is He Who brings life
   and restores life;

14 for He is Forgiving, Loving,

15 Lord of the glorious throne,

16 Who does all that He intends.

17 Have you heard the story
   of the forces

18 of Pharaoh and Thamud?°

19 Yet the disbelievers
   persist in denying.

20 But God Encompasses them
   from all sides.°

21 For this is a glorious Qur'an,

22 inscribed on a preserved tablet.°

SURA 86

The Night Traveler (*Al-Tariq*)

A Meccan sura of 17 verses, this opens with a celestial oath (vv. 1–4) before graphically depicting human creation (vv. 5–7) as a reminder that return to God is as inevitable as "the sky and its cycle of rain" (v. 11). Just as the Qur'an is "a decisive Word, not to be taken lightly" (vv. 13–14), so God is the ultimate schemer whom disbelievers cannot escape (vv. 15–17).

In the Name of God, the All Merciful, Ever Merciful

1 By the sky and the traveler
  by night—

2 what would make you grasp
  what the night traveler is?

3 It is the star of piercing light.

4 Every soul has its guardian.

5 Let humans consider
  from what they were created—

6 from a drop of fluid, ejected,

7 arising between
  the backbone and the ribs.

8 God indeed has the Power
  to bring it back to life.

9 On the day when the secrets
  of humankind are exposed,

10 they shall have no power,
   and no helper.

11 By the sky
   and its cycle of rain,°

12 and by the earth
   bursting with greenery,

13 this is a decisive Word,

14 not to be taken lightly.

15 The disbelievers are scheming,

16 but I am outscheming [them].

17 So give respite
   to the disbelievers;
   give them respite
   for a short while.

SURA 87

The Most High (Al-Aʿla)

A paean to the Most High (one of God's Beautiful Names), this Meccan sura of
19 verses recalls creation and destruction (vv. 1–5) before commanding recitation
(vv. 6–9), mindful that some will heed and others will not (vv. 10–13). Not only
the Qur'an but "the scriptures of Abraham and Moses" are commended (v. 19).

In the Name of God, the All Merciful, Ever Merciful

1 Glorify the name of your Lord,
  the Most High,

2 Who created and proportioned
  [all things],

3 Who determined [their destinies]
  and guided them,

4 Who brings forth pasture,

5 then turns it to dark stubble.

6 We shall teach you to recite
  so you do not forget,

7 except as God wills.
  He knows what is open
  and what is hidden.

8 And We shall make
  your path easy.

9 So remind people,
  if this should profit them.

10 Those who fear God
will heed it.

11 But the wretched will
avoid it—

12 those who will burn
in the great fire,

13 where they will
neither die nor live.

14 But those who purify themselves
shall flourish,

15 those who remember
the name of their Lord,
and pray.

16 But no—you prefer the life
of this world,

17 though the hereafter
is better and enduring.

18 This is indeed
in previous scriptures,

19 the scriptures of
Abraham and Moses.°

SURA 88

The Overshadowing Event (*Al-Ghashiya*)

This early Meccan sura of 26 verses is divided into two sections. The first (vv. 1–16) contrasts the fates of disbelievers and believers on "that day" (vv. 2, 8). The second part (vv. 17–26) invokes nature's signs before underscoring Muhammad's sole duty to remind disbelievers; it will be for God "to call them to account" (v. 26).

In the Name of God, the All Merciful, Ever Merciful

1 Have you heard about
the overshadowing event?

2 Some faces, that day,
will be downcast,

3 laboring, weary,

4 they shall burn in a blazing fire,

5 given drink from a boiling spring,

6 with no food but bitter thorns

7 which will neither nourish
nor quell hunger.

8 Other faces, that day,
  will be joyful,

9 pleased with their striving,

10 in a lofty garden,

11 where they shall hear
   no idle talk;

12 where there shall be
   a flowing spring,

13 and raised couches,

14 and goblets laid out,

15 with cushions arrayed
   in rows,

16 and carpets spread out.

17 Do they not look at camels,
   and how they are created?

18 And at the sky, and
   how it is raised high?

19 At the mountains, and
   how firmly fixed they are?

20 At the earth, and
   how it is spread wide?

21 So, remind people—
   you are only one who reminds.

22 You don't control
   their affairs.

23 But those who turn away
   and deny God—

24 God will punish them
   with great torment.

25 To Us they will return,

26 then it will be for Us
   to call them to account.

SURA 89

The Breaking Dawn (*Al-Fajr*)

Early Meccan, this sura of 30 verses begins with a nocturnal oath (vv. 1–4) that segues into a recap of how two Arab tribes, 'Ad and Thamud, along with Pharaoh, meet with torment for their transgressions (vv. 5–14). Honor and humility are lauded (vv. 15–16), and these virtues entail respecting orphans and feeding the poor (vv. 17–18). Those who neglect such directives will be punished (vv. 19–26) while others, their soul content (v. 27), will be told: "enter among My servants, enter My garden" (vv. 29–30).

In the Name of God, the All Merciful, Ever Merciful

1 By the breaking dawn,

2 by ten nights,°

3 by the even and the odd,°

4 and by the night
  when it fades—

5 is this oath not enough
  for those who understand?

6 Have you not considered
  how your Lord dealt
  with the people of ʿAd,

7 of the city of Iram
  with its towering columns,

8 the likes of which
  were not wrought in any city,

9 and with the people of Thamud°
  who hewed rocks within the valley,

10 and with Pharaoh,
  with his great forces?°

11 All of these transgressed
  in their lands

12 where they spread great corruption.

13 So your Lord poured upon them
  a scourging torment,

14 for your Lord is Ever Watchful.

15 As for humankind—
  whenever their Lord tries them,
  honoring and favoring them,
  they each say,
  "My Lord honors me."

16 But when he tries them
  by reducing their provisions,
  they each say,
  "My Lord humiliates me."

17 But no—you do not
  respect orphans,

18 nor do you urge one another
  to feed the poor;

19 rather, you greedily devour
  entire inheritances,

20 and you love wealth
  with excessive love.

21 No—when the earth
  is pounded into powder,

22 and your Lord comes
  with His angels, row upon row,

23 and hell, that day, is brought
  before them—that day, humankind
  will take heed, but of what use
  will it be for them?

24 They will each say, "If only
   I had accrued good deeds
   for the life to come."°

25 For on that day, He will punish
   as no other could punish,

26 and He will bind
   as no other could bind.

27 "You, serene of soul,

28 "return to your Lord
   well pleased, and pleasing Him,

29 "enter among My servants,

30 "enter My garden."

SURA 90

The City (*Al-Balad*)

An Early Meccan sura, its 20 verses invoke the city to warn against the ease of abundant wealth (vv. 1–10) and to enjoin instead "the steep path'" (vv. 11–12), requiring right action as well as true belief, assisting others who are "on the right" (vv. 13–18), remembering that fire closes in those on the left (vv. 19–20).

In the Name of God, the All Merciful, Ever Merciful

1 I swear by this city,

2 this city, in which you live freely,

3 I swear by parent and child,

4 We have created humankind
   for toil and labor.

5 Do they think that none
   has power over them?

6 They might each say,
   "I have thrown away wealth
   in abundance."

7 Do they think that none
   sees them?

8 Have We not made for them
   a pair of eyes,

9 a tongue, and a pair of lips,

10 and shown them the two paths?

11 But they have not ventured
   on the steep path.

12 And what would make you grasp
   what the steep path is?

13 It is freeing a slave,

14 or giving food at a time
   of severe hunger,

15 to an orphan, near of kin,

16 or to the poor,
   mired in misery,

17 and to be one of those
   who believe, and urge one another
   to patience and compassion.

18 These shall be on the right,

19 but those who deny Our signs
   —they shall be on the left

20 with fire closing in
   around them.

SURA 91

The Sun (*Al-Shams*)

This brief early Meccan sura (15 verses) begins with an oath invoking celestial elements (vv. 1–7) to stress the vigilance required for purifying the soul (vv. 8–10). The example of those who fail to take heed are the people of Thamud, who hamstrung a she-camel, bringing divine retribution (vv. 11–15).

In the Name of God, the All Merciful, Ever Merciful

1 By the sun
  and her splendor;

2 by the moon
  as it trails her;

3 by the day as it
  displays her;

4 by the night as she
  veils her;

5 by the heaven and He
  Who framed her;

6 by the earth and He
  Who extended her;

7 by the soul and He
  Who proportioned her;

8 for He inspired her
  to know the evil
  and the piety within her;

9 He surely succeeds
who purifies her,

10 and he fails
who defiles her;

11 the nation of Thamud
denied [their prophet Salih],°
for they were transgressors,

12 when they deputed
their most wicked offender
[to denounce him].

13 God's messenger
advised them:
"This is a she-camel of God,
so let her drink."

14 But they denied him
and hamstrung her.
So for their sin, their Lord
destroyed [their nation],
and leveled it.

15 Nor does He fear
what will become of it.

SURA 92

Night (*Al-Layl*)

An early Meccan sura, its invocation (vv. 1–4) precedes a listing of right and wrong behavior, with good and bad outcomes detailed in the remaining verses (vv. 5–21).

In the Name of God, the All Merciful, Ever Merciful

1 By the night when it cloaks
the light,

2 by the day when it breaks
into splendor,

3 by Him Who created
male and female—

4 you strive for widely
diverging ends:

5 those who give in charity
and are mindful of God,

6 and affirm what is best—

7 We will make smooth for them
the path to ease.°

8 But those who are miserly,
self-satisfied,

9 and reject what is best—

10 We will make smooth for them
the path to hardship;

11 nor will their wealth help them
when they fall [into the fire].

12 It is for Us to guide,

13 and to Us belong both
end and beginning.

14 So I warn you
of a blazing fire,

15 in which none shall burn
but the most wretched,

16 those who deny the truth and
turn away.

17 But the most righteous shall be
turned aside from it—

18 those who give away their wealth
to purify themselves,°

19 not as recompense for favors
received from someone,

20 but only to seek
the Face of their Lord,
the Most High;

21 And they shall be
well pleased.

SURA 93

Morning Light (*Al-Duha*)

One of the earliest Meccan suras, its 11 verses crystallize the patient persistence required of the Prophet. Morning and night are invoked (vv. 1–2) to ensure God's providence (vv. 4–5) before the specific promises of shelter, guidance, and sufficiency (vv. 6–8), echoing a command for all believers to care for the orphan, heed the beggar, and proclaim God's grace (vv. 9–11).

In the Name of God, the All Merciful, Ever Merciful

1 By the morning light
in its brilliance;°

2 by the darkening night
in its stillness;

3 your Lord has not abandoned you,
nor is He abhorring [you].°

4 What comes hereafter
will prove finer for you
than what came before;

5 and your Lord will provide,
satisfying you.

6 Did He not find you orphaned
and give shelter?

7 find you seeking and give guidance?

8 find you needing and suffice you?

9 So, do not oppress the orphan,

10 nor reproach the one who asks,

11 but proclaim the grace
of your Lord.

SURA 94

The Broadening (*Al-Sharh*)

A very short Meccan sura, its 8 verses console the Prophet for the burden of his
task (vv. 1–4) and promise a relief from hardship for all who seek God in earnest
(vv. 5–8).

In the Name of God, the All Merciful, Ever Merciful

1 Have We not made your heart
broader than before,

2 and taken from you
the burden° you bore,

3 that weighed sore
upon your back,

4 making your name soar
in esteem?°

5 With every hardship comes ease—

6 yes, with every hardship
comes ease.

7 So, when you cease
your task, increase
your striving,

8 and seek your Lord
eagerly.°

The Fig (*Al-Tin*)

This very early Meccan sura of 8 verses invokes Mount Sinai to underscore human potential and weakness (vv. 1–5), heralding the certainty of reckoning by "the Most Just of Judges" (vv. 6–8).

In the Name of God, the All Merciful, Ever Merciful

1 By the fig
and the olive,

2 by Mount Sinai,

3 and this secure city,°

4 We created humankind
in the best of forms;

5 then We reduced them to
the lowest of the low

6 except those who believe
and do good deeds—
theirs shall be a ceaseless reward.

7 What, after this, could make you
deny the reckoning?°

8 Is not God the Most Just
of Judges?

Clot of Blood (*Al-ʿAlaq*)

The first five verses of this sura are heralded as the initial revelation to Muhammad in the cave of Hira, with the remaining fourteen verses (vv. 6–19) focused on the disbelief and opposition of one of Muhammad's early enemies.

In the Name of God, the All Merciful, Ever Merciful

1 Read—in the Name of your Lord
Who created—

2 created humankind from a clot
of blood.

3 Read—for your Lord
is Most Bountiful,

4 Who taught by the pen—

5 taught humankind
what it did not know.

6 But humans transgress
all bounds,

7 thinking themselves
self-sufficient—

8 all shall return to your Lord.

9 Do you observe the person
who prevents°

10 Our servant from prayer?

11 Do you see whether he is guided

12 or enjoins mindfulness of God?

13 Do you see whether
he denies the truth
and turns away?

14 Does he not know
that God observes?

15 Let him beware—
if he does not stop, We shall
drag him by the forelock—

16 a lying, sinful forelock.

17 Let him call his companions—

18 We will call the angels of hell.

19 No—do not heed him,
but bow down, and come
closer to God.

SURA 97

The Night of Decree (Al-Qadr)

Likely Meccan, this sura condenses into 5 verses the disclosure of the Qur'an as celestial decree, honored as a special night of vigil during Ramadan, when angels with the spirit descend and linger until dawn (vv. 4–5).

In the Name of God, the All Merciful, Ever Merciful

1 We revealed this Word°
on the night of decree.

2 And what would make you grasp
what the night of decree is?

3 The night of decree is better
than a thousand months.

4 In this night the angels
with the spirit descend

by their Lord's leave
for every task.

5 Peace reigns until
the rise of dawn.

SURA 98

Clear Proof (*Al-Bayyina*)

A sura that is Medinan in origin, its 8 verses trace the divisions caused by disbelievers and polytheists (vv. 1, 5–6) despite the clear proof brought by the Prophet
(vv. 2–4), with a reminder that those who believe and do good deeds will have
their reward (vv. 7–8).

In the Name of God, the All Merciful, Ever Merciful

1 The disbelievers among
the people of the Book
and the polytheists
were not going to leave their ways
until clear proof came to them—

2 a messenger from God
reciting from untainted scrolls,

3 containing unerring scriptures.

4 Those given the Book
did not fall into factions until
clear proof had come to them.

5 They were merely commanded
to worship God, the One God,
sincere in faith to Him alone,°
to be steadfast in prayer

and to give in charity—
for this is the upright religion.

6 The disbelievers among
the People of the Book
and among the polytheists
shall be in the fire of hell
to dwell there forever.
They are the worst of creatures.

7 But those who believe
and do good deeds
are the best of creatures.°

8 Their reward rests with God—
eternal gardens, beneath which
rivers flow, to dwell there
eternally. God shall be pleased
with them, and they with Him—
all this for those who fear their Lord.

The Earthquake (*Al-Zalzala*)

This sura is early Meccan, and in 8 verses it heralds the end of time (vv. 1–5), capping the news of that day with anticipation of serial, individual judgment, focused on the smallest of deeds (vv. 6–8).

In the Name of God, the All Merciful, Ever Merciful

1 When the earth is shaken
with a great earthquake,

2 and she lays bare
all her burdens,

3 and humankind cries,
"What is happening to her?"

4 On that day she will
proclaim her story,°

5 for your Lord inspired her.

6 On that day humankind
will emerge in scattered groups
to be shown what they have done.

7 Then whoever has done
an atom's weight of good
shall see it.

8 And whoever has done
an atom's weight of evil
shall see it.

Racing Steeds (*Al-'Adiyat*)

This sura is probably Meccan; its 11 verses begin with a stunning image of galloping horses (vv. 1–5), likely referring to uncontrolled human desires (vv. 6–8). Talking of the human lust for wealth, the sura issues a warning that on the day of judgment all will be revealed because God is "fully Aware" (vv. 9–11).

In the Name of God, the All Merciful, Ever Merciful

1 By those racing
  like steeds, panting,°

2 striking sparks with their hooves,

3 raiding at dawn,

4 raising clouds of dust,

5 thrusting through the center
  of enemy lines—

6 humans are ungrateful
  to their Lord,

7 as they themselves
  bear witness,

8 and their love of [the world's] good
  is intense.

9 Do they not know—
  when what is buried in graves
  bursts out,

10 and what lies in human hearts
   is exposed—

11 that on that day, their Lord
   shall be fully Aware of them?

SURA IOI

The Thundering Calamity (*Al-Qari'a*)

Early Meccan with 11 verses, this sura evokes the day of judgment in stark terms, with opposite outcomes for those with heavy scales (i.e., good deeds) and those with light scales (i.e., few deeds counted as "good"), vv. 6–9.

In the Name of God, the All Merciful, Ever Merciful

1 The thundering calamity°—

2 What is the thundering calamity?

3 What would make you grasp
  what such calamity is?

4 —the day when humankind

  shall be like moths, scattered,

5 and the mountains
  like carded wool—

6 then those whose balance
  is heavy,

7 will find themselves
  in a pleasing life.

8 But those whose balance
   is light

9 shall find their home
   in the abyss.

10 And what would make you grasp
    what that is?

11 It's a fire—blazing.

SURA 102

Competing for Worldly Gain (*Al-Takathur*)

The 8 verses of this early Meccan sura dismiss and condemn the unbridled pursuit of wealth and status, counterposed to certain knowledge (v. 5) and assured vision (v. 7).

In the Name of God, the All Merciful, Ever Merciful

1 Competing for worldly gain
   distracts you—

2 until you reach your graves.

3 But soon you shall know.

4 Yes, soon you shall know.

5 Indeed, if you had
   sure knowledge,°

6 you would see the fire of hell.

7 Yes, you would see it
   with sure vision.°

8 Then, on that day,
   you shall be asked
   about your worldly bliss.

SURA 103

Time (*Al-'Asr*)

Early Meccan, this sura has only 3 verses. Two short verses are followed by a longer final verse highlighting the collective effort to believe and do good—to wit, urging others to truth and to patience.

In the Name of God, the All Merciful, Ever Merciful

1 By time, passing,

2 humankind is in a state
  of loss,

3 except those who believe,
  and do good deeds, urging
  one another toward truth,
  and urging one another
  toward patience.

SURA 104

The Backbiter (*Al-Humaza*)

Early Meccan, its 9 verses focus on the person of a wealthy slanderer, likely referring to numerous Meccan opponents, reminding them of not just hellfire but the fire of God that will close upon them (vv. 6–8).

In the Name of God, the All Merciful, Ever Merciful

1 Woe to every backbiting slanderer

2 who amasses wealth,
  always counting it—

3 thinking that his wealth
  will make him live forever.

4 No—he will be thrown
  into the pulverizing fire.

5 And what would make you grasp
  what such a fire is?

6 —A fire that God has kindled,

7 which pierces people's hearts.

8 It will close upon them,

9 in soaring pillars.°

SURA 105

The Elephant (*Al-Fil*)

Early Meccan with 5 verses, this sura refers to a historical event, the unsuccessful attack of a Yemeni ruler on the Quraysh, possibly just before Muhammad's birth (ca. 570 CE). The Quraysh response is given in the next sura.

In the Name of God, the All Merciful, Ever Merciful

1 Have you not considered
how your Lord dealt
with the people of the elephant?°

2 Did He not confound
their plot?

3 He sent against them
birds in flocks,

4 pelting them with stones
of baked clay.

5 Then He left them
like stubble—chewed up.

SURA 106

Quraysh (*Quraysh*)

Early Meccan, its 4 verses depict the twofold gratitude expected of the Quraysh after their rescue from Yemeni attack (Sura 105): for food when hungry, and for safety when afraid (v. 4).

In the Name of God, the All Merciful, Ever Merciful

1 [In gratitude] for the safety
of the Quraysh°—

2 safe for both their journeys,
winter and summer—

3 Let them worship the Lord
of this House,

4 Who has given them food
to forestall hunger,
and safety, to forestall fear.

SURA 107

Small Kindnesses (*Al-Ma'un*)

An early Meccan sura of 7 verses, this underscores the double ethical mandate—to heed the orphan and feed the poor—as requisite for "the reckoning to come" (v. 1).

In the Name of God, the All Merciful, Ever Merciful

1 Have you seen the person who
denies the reckoning to come?

2 This is the one who
pushes aside the orphan,

3 and does not urge others
to feed the poor.

4 Woe, then, to those who pray,

5 but don't heed their prayer,

6 those who do it
just to be seen,

7 yet refuse even small deeds
of kindness.

SURA 108

Abundance (*Al-Kawthar*)

Early Meccan, this sura of 3 verses is the shortest sura yet it uplifts the Prophet's
spirit, reassuring him that progeny is more than siring a son.

In the Name of God, the All Merciful, Ever Merciful

1 We have given to you
in abundance°—

2 So pray to your Lord
and make sacrifice,

3 for it is your enemy
who will be cut off.°

SURA 109

Those Who Disbelieve (*Al-Kafirun*)

Early Meccan, its 6 verses set the marker for confirming, and upholding, the gap
between believers and disbelievers.

In the Name of God, the All Merciful, Ever Merciful

1 Say, "You who disbelieve,

2 "I do not worship
what you worship,

3 "nor are you worshippers
of what I worship,

4 "and I am not a worshipper
of what you worship,

5 "nor are you worshippers
of what I worship—

6 "you have your religion
and I have mine."

Help (*Al-Nasr*)

A Medinan sura, this is perhaps the last sura to be revealed. In 3 verses it assures the Prophet of victory, for himself and his community, and the proper response should be not gloating over success but praising God and asking for forgiveness.

In the Name of God, the All Merciful, Ever Merciful

1 When God's help comes
and His victory,

2 and you see people flocking
in multitudes
to the religion of God,

3 hymn the praise of your Lord
and seek His forgiveness;
He is the Ever Relenting.

The Palm Fiber (*Al-Masad*)

Early Meccan, its 5 verses are the only direct diatribe against one of the Prophet's opponents, and his wife, also a fierce detractor of the Prophet in word and deed.

In the Name of God, the All Merciful, Ever Merciful

1 Perish the hands
of Abu Lahab, Father of Flame!°
And may *he* perish!

2 He'll profit nothing
from all his wealth,
and all his gains.

3 Soon he shall burn in a fire
blazing with flame.

4 His wife shall bear the wood,

5 a rope of palm fiber
twisted about her neck.

SURA 112

Unity/Sincerity (*Al-Ikhlas*)

Early Meccan, its 4 verses are heralded as the epitome of the Qur'anic message.
It stresses God's oneness, immutability, and uniqueness. Also apotropaic, its
power is in direct proportion to the sincerity (*ikhlas*) of its reciter.

In the Name of God, the All Merciful, Ever Merciful

1 Say, He is God, the One,

2 God, the Absolute.°

3 Neither did He beget,
nor was He begotten.

4 His like or equal there is none.

SURA 113

The Dawn (*Al-Falaq*)

Early Meccan, like the next sura with which it is linked, this sura of 5 verses is
apotropaic, seeking God's protection from evil.

In the Name of God, the All Merciful, Ever Merciful

1 Say, "I seek refuge with the Lord of the breaking dawn,°

2 "from the evil in those° He created;

3 "from the evil in darkness when it descends;

4 "from the evil of those° who blow on knots;

5 "and from the evil of the envier, when he envies."

SURA 114

Humankind (*Al-Nas*)

The final sura, also early Meccan and apotropaic, its 6 verses stress that jinn as well as humankind must seek refuge in God from sinister forces.

In the Name of God, the All Merciful, Ever Merciful

1 Say, "I seek refuge with the Lord of humankind,

2 "the Ruler of humankind,

3 "the God of humankind,

4 "from the evil of the one who whispers°, and recoils [from the Name of God]—

5 "the one who whispers into the hearts of humankind—

6 "from among jinn, and humankind."

ACKNOWLEDGMENTS

This translation represents a journey spanning some ten years. Traveling on that path together, we have incurred profound debts to those who aided us in navigating its sometimes arduous and steep terrain. We would both like to thank:

—those who shared their Qur'anic expertise with us: the scholars of the University of al-Azhar in Cairo, Ahmad Elezabi, Amr Saleh, and the late Ahmed Shafik al-Khatib; the Qur'anic scholars Carl W. Ernst, Shawkat Toorawa, Azdeddine Chergui, Omid Safi, Michael Sells, Brett Wilson, Ulrika Martensen, Khalid Saqi, Marianna Klar, Assya Elhannaoui, and Musharraf Hussain;

—those who gave us inspired feedback on our rendering: Jerry and Betty Eidener, Carl and Janet Edwards, Harry and Peregrine Kavros, Scott Kugle, Sohaib Khan, Safaa Al-Saeedi, Michael Beard, J. T. Barbarese, Ernest Hilbert, Kimberly V. Adams, Aaron Hostetter, Piers Smith, Daniel Simmons, Nader El-Bizri, Irfaan Nooruddin, Reza Aslan, Magda Hasabelnaby, Leonard Neidorf, Ali Ansari, Areej Al-Harbi, Rahaf Al-Mubarak, Norah Roudhan, Wadha Alessa, Waed Al-Azemi, Muntassir Ibrahim Altamy, Adrian Day, and Siddiqua Shabnam;

—those who facilitated presentations and conferences for us: Sahar Muradi and the high school teachers of City Lore and Poets House in New York City; M. A. S. Abdel Haleem of the School of Oriental and African Studies in London; Mohamed Ben-Madani, for allowing us to use material from the *Maghreb Review*; Omar Ali de Unzaga of the Institute of Ismaili Studies in London; Rob Gleave, Mustafa Baig, and William Gallois, who organized a Qur'an conference at the University of Exeter in England; Recep Senturk, Heba Raouf, and Ercument Asil, who invited us to present at the Alliance of Civilizations Institute (MEDIT) at Ibn Haldun University in Istanbul; Mohammed Ben Romdhane and Shahd Al-Shammari who helped us obtain a generous grant from KFAS to present at the Gulf University of Science and Technology in Kuwait; and Salwa El-Awa, who invited our participation in a conference at the University of Swansea;

—those who merit a very special note of gratitude for their countless hours of dedication and expertise in helping us negotiate the Arabic text of the Qur'an: Ismail Lala and Ahmed Zafar;

—the wonderfully insightful editorial team at Liveright, including our editor Peter Simon, whose feedback at every stage was crucial; our meticulous copyeditor, Trent Duffy; our project editor, Robert Byrne; and the project's various editorial assistants over the years, including Katie Pak, Olivia Atmore, and Zeba Arora—as well as the talented professionals who made this book so beautiful: our production director, Anna Oler, and our art director, Ingsu Liu. Although our journey with them has barely begun, we also wish to thank the extraordinary publicity and marketing team at Liveright who will help get this book into readers' hands: Peter Miller, director of publicity; Fanta Diallo, publicist; Clio Hamilton, publicity assistant; and Nick Curley, marketing director;

—our respective life partners: miriam cooke, whose deep expertise in Arabic and warm and friendly help over the years were an endless source of inspiration; and Yasmeen Habib, who was lovingly supportive, sharing her insights into the rules of recitation and the system of pauses in the Qur'anic script.

The journey is far from over. No translation of the Qur'an can ever hope to do more than gesture toward the inimitable splendor of the original. The voyage that began as a voice on a mountain in the lonely cave of Hira is one which will continue through many voices, into many futures, forever echoing down from the sublimity of that height.

M. A. R. Habib and Bruce B. Lawrence

GLOSSARY

The following are often-cited, important Arabic terms in the Qur'an. These notes explain why some are rendered consistently throughout this translation while others vary according to context. A selective list is provided of the occurrence of each term in Qur'anic verses.

ahl al-kitab — "people of the Book." This term refers to the Jews and Christians (and also Muslims). See 2:41ff., as well as 3:3, 4:47, 5:46, 6:92, and 89:91. The first reference (2:41ff.) is dedicated to retelling the story of the Children of Israel. *Ahl* is also the first of five technical terms referring to "people." Each has its own nuance, with *ahl* closest to familial, *qawm* to tribal, while *umma* accents collective coherence apart from family or tribe. Both *nas* and *insan* refer to humankind at large.

ajal — "a period" / *ajal musamma*: "a fixed period." These terms are used specifically in some suras and by implication in others. Either one can refer to the destined period of existence for individuals (6:2), communities (23:43), and the entire universe (46:3). This period lies within the purview of God's omniscience; it can be lengthened or shortened only by His direction (35:4). It can also be elided with the Mother of the Book (*umm al-kitab*; see below), a relationship depicted in 13:38–39.

'alamin — "universe" (1:2 – genitive plural of *'alam*, world), denoting the fact that all the "worlds" created by God ultimately comprise a unity; also rendered as "all peoples" (3:33), "all the worlds" (5:20, 115), "all worlds" (5:28; 10:10, 37; and 12:104), "[created] beings" (29:6), "creatures" (29:10, 28), and "peoples" (37:79). In each case, the sense of the surrounding passage dictates the choice of translation. At 1:2, the original Arabic refers to *'alamun* (nominative pl. of *'alam*), literally, "the worlds, or all worlds"; it connotes "universe" because it covers the spectrum of creations in the heavens and earth, land and sea, while at the same time including other creatures who are nonhuman, both *jinn* (see below) and angels.

amr — literally, "command" (16:2), but also "clear signs" as in 2:87, 253; 5:110; 16:2; 40:15; 42:52; 65:12; and 97:4.

al-asma' al-husna — "the Beautiful Names" / *asma' Allahi al-husna*: "the Beautiful Names of God." The Beautiful Names, sometimes known as the Most Beautiful Names or the Beautiful Divine Names, are invoked in prayer by multiple names. Some have said that the Beautiful Names number ninety-nine, while others reckon that they are beyond calculation; in either instance, they are lodestones of memory and pious mimesis, both in the Qur'an and in Muslim ritual devotion. In this rendition, the Beautiful Names have been capitalized in every instance where they occur or can be inferred. For further details, see pages li–lvii as well as The Beautiful Names (page 534).

ayat — literally, "signs" (of God and God's power), but also "verses" or "words" (of God), as in 3:112–13. In one case (26:128), the singular *aya* means "altar" or "monument."

barzakh — a Persian word. At 23:100 and 25:53, it's rendered as "barrier," but at 55:20, it's rendered as a "limit," since it is both a barrier and a bridge, not mixing yet connecting two distinct elements or states or levels of existence.

dhikr — "remembrance" (of God or the Qur'an), "reminder," or "message." It is used almost three hundred times in reference to either God or the Qur'an.

din — "reckoning" or "religion." As discussed in the note for 1:4, in the phrase *malik yawm al-din* it is clearly the final day or the day of reckoning, with the promise of reward or punishment. Elsewhere, the word is best rendered as "faith" (e.g., 9:11, 122). Another example of *din* as "reckoning" occurs in 37:20, "day of reckoning," similar to *yawm al-qiyama*, "day of resurrection."

furqan — 2:53; 3:2 and 25 (passim), with multiple meanings. Often translated as "measure" or "criterion," *furqan* is a technical term indicating an absolute dividing line or demarcation between two opposites or binaries, especially the good and the bad.

al-ghaib — what lies beyond human knowing, i.e.,"the unseen," as in 2:33; 6:50, 59; 7:188; and 13:9.

hanif — "one pure in faith" (3:67, 95) or "monotheistic in faith" (10.105 and also 16:120–23). It is the antonym of *kafir* (see under *kufr*, below).

haqq/haqqa — "truth" or "reality," but also "right" or "duty." *Haqq* can refer not just to truth but the possession of right, as in 9:13, 146, and 33:37, where God is cited as having "more right" to be feared than others. In terms of duty, see 2:180, where making provision for one's survivors is "a duty upon those who are mindful of [the One] God."

Iblis — see *Shaytan* below.

al-insan — "person" (36:77), "man" (55:3), or "humankind" (12:5 and 55:14, 33). To be gender inclusive, *insan* has often been rendered as "humans" (instead of the singular) or "humankind." Also see *ahl* under *ahl al-kitab*, above.

islam — "submission" / *muslim*: "one who submits" (to God). See, however, 5:3, where the name "Islam" is used; see also 2:128 and 3:85. The root verb, *s-l-m*, refers both to peace (*salam*) and submission (*islam*). In the period when the Muslim movement had not yet coalesced into a community aware of itself as such, the emphasis was on submitting to God and to God's will, both as individuals and as a group. Multiple references to *muslimun* (i.e., "muslims") are to those who submit from every tradition honoring the One God, not solely to those who follow Muhammad and later become part of Islam.

jinn — "spirits." Neither angelic nor human, yet both at once. They abound in literary circles of the premodern world, with their equivalent in English being "genie." They can be either evil or good, depending on circumstance. See especially suras 55 and 72.

kufr — "disbelief" or "lie," but also "ingratitude." Hence a *kafir* is a disbeliever and *kafirin* are liars, but all are, firstly, ungrateful. The contrast is between *kufr* and *shukr* ("gratitude"), as in 2:152: "Show thanks to me, and do not be ungrateful."

al-mathal — "parable" (36:13), "simile," or "comparison" (36:78).

muqatta'at — "disconnected" / *al-huruf al-muqatta'at*: "disconnected letters." These Arabic letters that appear at the beginning of several suras have become the subject of extensive commentary, with occasional efforts to translate them (as in Sura 36, Ya Sin). They are often termed mystical or mysterious letters whose meanings are known only to the Lord of all that is seen and unseen. There is a suggestive tone of authority in several suras; it comes in the phrase right after the opening letters. In 2:2 we are told that the Book "provides guidance for those mindful of the Divine"; elsewhere it can refer to the Book as clear and decisive (e.g., suras 15, 36, 38, and 50) or to the process of revelation (e.g., suras 3, 7, and 40–46). Because this last group (40–46) all start with the same letters (*ha* and *mim*), they are often called the *Hawamim*.

muslim — "one who submits" (to the will of God). See *islam* above on the variability of *islam*/*muslim* as both terms evolved during the early decades of the Qur'anic revelation.

muttaqi — "one mindful of God." Also see *taqwa* below.

nas — "people," "man," "humankind" (10:2, 11, 19, 21, and 23; 24:3; and 114 passim), but also "human beings" (10:44), or "humans" (10:44). See *ahl* under *ahl al-kitab*, above.

naskh — "abrogation" (2:106 and 3:7). The replacement of one verse by other verses, it has become the basis for juridical efforts to see shifts within the Qur'an at several points. However, other commentators have disputed whether the Qur'an itself changes or if it instead challenges each reader/believer/submitter to explore depths of meaning not readily apparent in God's Word. See also 3:7 for the Qur'an's own distinction between verses clear in meaning and those deemed allegorical or metaphorical. One needs to be constantly aware of how images, such as the Hand of God (e.g., 48:10) or the Face of your Lord (e.g., 55:27), are metaphorical rather than literal.

qawm — "peoples" (10:74) or "nation" (10:75). The Qur'an speaks of humankind as one people (in 2:213), but as many elsewhere: 5:48, 11:118, 16:93, 42:8, 43:33, and especially 10:19. Also see *ahl* under *ahl al-kitab*, above.

ruh — "spirit." Suras 4:171, 16:2, 17:85, 19:17, 40:15, 42:52, 58:22, and 78:38 all include reference to *ruh al-quds* ("holy spirit"), not be confused with "the Holy Spirit," a central component of the Christian doctrine of the Trinity (eschewed by Muslims). Wherever the text refers to the Arabic *ruh al-quds* (literally, "spirit of the holy" or "holy spirit"), Gabriel is the agent.

Shaytan — *Iblis* is another name for Shaytan (Satan), the enemy of humankind. Iblis's refusal to bow down to Adam is cited in several passages: 2:34, 7:11, 17:61, 18:50, 20:116, and 38:74–75.

sihr — "magic" (5:110 and 20:71, 73), "magician" (20:69 and 38:4), "magicians" (20:70), "sorcery" (6:7, 11:7, 20:63, 37:15, 43:30, and 54:2), "sorcerer" (43:49 and 51:39, 52), "manifest sorcerer" (10:2), or "sorcerers" (20:63). See also 5:110, 27:13, 34:43, 46:5, 61:6, and especially 10:75–81.

sura — sura, referring to the sections into which the Qur'an is divided (24:1). See also 10:38 and 11:13.

taqwa — "mindfulness of God" / *muttaqi*: "mindful of God or in 2:2 "mindful of the Divine." Also rendered as "fear of God" (9:108–9, 115) and "God-fearing" (19:97 and 41:18).

umm al-kitab — literally, "the Mother of the Book." In 3:7 and 13:39 it is rendered as "the origin of the Book," while in 43:4 it is described as "the archetypal Book" that records all deeds of humankind, and is also the source of all scripture.

umma — "community" (7:34, 10:19, and 43:21), "nation" (10:47, 49, and 16:120), or "people" (5:48 and 42:8). The plural is *umam*. Note two further uses—11:8: *illa ummatin ma'dudatin*, "for a definite term"; and 12:45: *ba'd ummatin*, "after all this time." See also *ahl* under *ahl al-kitab*, above.

zabur — the Psalms (4:163, 17:55, and 21:105), but also "scriptures" in general (3:184; 16:44; 23:53; 26:196; 35:25; and 54:43, 52).

THE BEAUTIFUL NAMES OF GOD

The Beautiful Names (*al-asma' al-husna*) or the Beautiful Names of God (*asma' Allahi al-husna*) recur throughout the Qur'an. They have been extracted and counted as ninety-nine in devotional practice and in numerous commentaries though their actual usage exceeds ninety-nine. We have capitalized their various forms in all but a few cases where doing so might compromise our general aim of producing a readable and fluent translation.

Abiding Forever—*al-Baqi*: **55**:27

The Absolute—*al-Samad*: **112**:2

Accepting of repentance – *Qabil al-tawb*: **40**:3

The Accomplisher/Doer—*al-Fa''al*: **11**:107; **85**:16

The [All] Aware/Ever Aware—*Khabir/al-Khabir*: **2**:234, 271; **3**:153, 180; **4**:94, 128, 135; **5**:8; **6**:18, 73, 103; **9**:16; **10**:19, 50, 111; **17**:30, 96; **22**:63; **24**:30, 53; **25**:58; **27**:88; **31**:16, 29, 34; **33**:3, 34; **34**:1; **35**:14, 31; 42: 27, **48**:11; **49**:13; **57**:10; **58**:3, 11, 13; **59**:18; **63**:11; **64**:8; **66**:3; **67**:14; **100**:11

The All Encompassing—*al-Muhit*: **2**:19; **3**:120; **4**:108, 126; **8**:47; **48**:21; **65**:12; **85**:20

The [All] Forgiving, Ever Merciful—*Ghafur Rahim*: **2**:173, 182, 192, 199, 218, 226; **3**:31, 89, 129; **4**:23, 25, 96, 100, 106, 110, 129, 152; **5**:3, 34, 39, 74, 98; **6**:54, 145, 165; **7**:153, 167; **8**:69, 70; **9**:27, 91, 99, 102; **10**:107; **11**:41; **12**:53, 98; **14**:36; **15**:49; **16**:18, 110, 115, 119; **24**:5, 22, 33, 62; **25**:6, 70; **27**:11; **28**:16; **31**:2; **33**:5, 24, 50, 59, 73; **39**:53; **41**:32; **42**:5; **46**:8; **48**:14; **49**:5, 14; **57**:28; **58**:12; **60**:7, 12; **64**:14; **66**:1; **73**:20

The All Hearing—*Sami'/al-Sami'*: **2**:127, 137,181, 224, 227, 244, 256, **3**:34, 35, 38, 121; **4**:58, 134, 148; **5**:76; **6**:13, 115, 200; **8**:17, 42, 53, 61; **9**:98, 103; **10**: 65; **12**:34; **14**:39; **17**:11; **21**:4; **22**:61, 75; **24**:21, 60; **26**:220; **29**:5, 60; **31**:28; **34**:50; **40**:20, 56; **41**:36; **42**:11; **44**: 6; **49**:1; **58**:1

The All Kind/Ever Forbearing/Most Forbearing—*al-Halim*: **2**:225, 235, 263; **3**:155; **4**:12; **5**:101; **11**:87; **17**:44; **22**:59; **33**:51; **35**:41; **64**:17

The [All] Knowing/Knower/Aware—*'Alim/al-'Alim*: **2**:29, 32, 95, 115, 137, 158, 181, 215, 224, 231, 246, 247, 256, 261, 268, 273, 282, 283; **3**:34, 35, 63, 73, 92, 115, 119, 121, 147, 148, 154; **4**:11, 12, 17, 24, 26, 32, 35, 39, 70, 92, 104, 111, 127, 147, 148, 170, 176; **5**:7, 54, 76, 97, 116; **6**:13, 59, 73, 83, 96, 101, 115, 128, 139; **7**:200; **8**:17, 42, 43, 53, 61, 71, 75; **9**:15, 28, 44, 47, 60, 78, 94, 97, 98, 103, 105, 106, 110, 115; **10**:36, 65, 79; **11**:5; **12**:6, 19, 34, 50, 76, 83, 100; **15**:25, 86; **16**:28, 70; **21**:4; **22**:52, 59; **23**:51; **24**:18, 21, 28, 32, 35, 41, 58, 59, 60, 64; **26**:220; **27**:6, 78; **29**:5, 60, 62; **30**:54; **31**:23; **33**:1, 40, 51, 54; **34**:3, 26, 48; **35**:8, 38, 44; **36**:38, 79, 81; **39**:7, 46; **40**:2; **41**:12, 36; **42**:12, 24, 50; **43**:9, 84; **44**:6; **48**:4, 26; **49**:1, 8, 13, 16, 18, **51**:, 30; **57**:3, 6; **58**:7; **59**:22; **60**:10; **62**:7, 8; **64**:4, 11, 18; **65**:12; **66**:2, 3; **67**:13; **73**:26; **76**:30 ; **84**:23

The All Merciful/Most Merciful—al-Rahman

    a. **17**:110; **19**:18, 26, 44, 45, 58, 61, 69, 75, 78, 85, 87, 88, 91, 92, 93, 96; **20**:5, 90, 108, 109;
       21:26, 36, 112; **25**:26, 59, 60, 63; **26**:5; **36**:11; **15**:23, 52; **41**:2; **43**:17, 19, 20, 33, 36, 45, 81;
       50:33; **55**:1; **59**:22; **67**:3, 19, 20, 29; **78**:37, 38

    b. The All Merciful, Ever Merciful—al-Rahman al-Rahim: **1**:1, 3; **2**:163; **27**:30; **41**:2;
       59:22. Also, as doublets, they precede **2**:1–**114**:1, introducing all suras except 9.

The [All] Powerful/Able—Qadir/al-Qadir: **2**:20, 106, 109, 148, 259, **2**:284; **3**:26, 29,165;
    189; **4**:133, 149; **5**:17, 19, 40, 120; **6**:17, 37, 65; **8**:41; **9**:39; **11**:4; **16**:70, 77; **17**:99; **22**:6,
    39; **23**:18; **24**:45; **25**:54; **29**:20; **30**:50, 54; **33**:27; **35**:1, 44; **41**:39; **42**:9, 29, 50; **46**:33,
    48:21; **57**:2; **59**:6; **60**:7; **64**:1; **65**:12; **66**:8; **67**:1; **75**:40; **86**:8. (See also The One Hold-
    ing Sway/All Powerful—al-Muqtadir.)

The All Seeing/All Watchful/Observant—Basir/al-Basir: **2**:96, 110, 233, 237, 265; **3**:15, 20,
    156, 163; **4**:58, 134; **5**:71; **8**:39, 72; **11**:112; **17**:1, 17, 30, 96; **20**:35, 125; **22**:61, 75; **25**:20;
    31:28; **33**:9; **34**:11; **35**:31, 45; **40**:20, 44, 56; **41**:40; **42**:11, 27; **48**:24; **49**:18; **57**:4; **58**:1;
    60:3; **64**:2; **67**:19; **84**:15

The [All] Wise—Hakim/al-Hakim: **2**:32, 129, 209, 220, 228, 240, 260; **3**:6, 18, 62, 126; **4**:11,
    17, 24, 26, 56, 92, 104, 111, 130, 158, 165, 170; **5**:38, 118; **6**:18, 73, 83, 128, 139; **8**:10, 49, 63,
    67, 71; **9**:15, 28, 40, 60, 71, 97, 106, 110; **12**:6, 83, 100; **13**:4; **14**:4; **15**:25; **16**:60; **22**:52;
    24:10, 18, 58, 59; **27**:6, 9; **29**:26, 42; **30**:27; **31**:2, 9, 27; **33**:1; **34**:1, 27; **35**:2; **36**:2; **39**:1;
    40:8; **41**:42; **42**:3, 51; **43**:9, 84; **45**:2, 37; **46**:2; **48**:4, 7, 19; **49**:8; **51**:30; **57**:1; **59**:1, 24;
    60:5, 10; **61**:1; **62**:1, 3; **64**:18; **66**:2; **76**:30

The Almighty—'Aziz/al-'Aziz

    a. **2**:129, 209, 220, 228, 240, 260; **3**:4, 6, 12, 62, 126; **4**:56, 158, 165; **5**: 38, 95, 118; **6**:96;
       8:10, 49, 63, 67; **9**:40, 71; **11**:66; **14**:1, 4, 47; **16**:60; **22**:40, 74; **27**:78; **29**:26, 42; **30**:27;
       31:9, 27; **33**:25; **34**:6, 27; **35**:2; **36**:38; **38**:9, 66; **39**:1, 5, 37; **40**: 2, 8, 42; **42**:3, 19; **44**:49;
       45:2, 37; **46**:2; **48**:7, 19; **57**: 1, 25; **58**:21; **59**:1, 23, 24; **60**:5; **61**:1; **62**:1,3; **64**:18; **67**: 2; **85**:8

    b. The Almighty, Ever-Merciful—al-'Aziz al-Rahim: **26**:9, 68, 104, 122, 159, 175, 191,
       217; **30**:5; **32**:6; **36**:5; **44**:42

The Always Returning/Relenting—al-Tawwab

    a. **4**:64; **24**:10; **110**:3

    b. Always Returning, Ever Merciful—al-Tawwab al-Rahim: **2**:37, 54, 128, 160; **4**:16,
       64; **9**:104; **49**:12

Appreciating/Appreciative—al-Shakir: **2**:158; **4**:147. Al-Shakur: **35**:30, 34; **42**:23; **64**:17.

The Best of Arbiters—Khair al-Fatihin: **7**:89. Khair al-Fasilin: **6**:57.

The Best of Forgivers—Khair al-Ghafirin: **7**:155

The Best of Helpers—Khair al-Nasirin: **3**:150

The Best of Judges—Khair al-Hakimin: **7**:87; **10**:109; **12**:80. The Most Excellent of Judges:
    10:109, **12**:80.

The Best of Protectors—Khair al-Muhafizin: **12**:64

The Best of Providers/the Best Provider—Khair al-Raziqin: **5**:114; **15**:20; **22**:58; **23**:72;
    34:39; **62**:11

The Best of Schemers—*Khair al-Makarin*: **8**:30

The Creator—*al-Khaliq*: **6**:102; **13**:16; **15**:28; **36**:81; **39**:62; **40**:62; **59**:24

The Debaser—*al-Khafid*: **56**:3 (also, *al-Mudhill* **3**:26)

Encompassing in Abundance—*Dhu al-Tawl*: **40**:3

The Ever Forbearing/Most Forbearing—*al-Halim*: **2**:225, 235, 263; **3**:155; **4**:12; **5**:101; **17**:44; **22**:59; **33**:51; **35**:41; **64**:17

The Ever Forgiving—*al-Ghaffar*: **20**:82; **38**:66; **39**:5; **40**:42; **71**:10

The Ever Giving/Bestower—*al-Wahhab*: **3**:8; **38**:9, 35

The Ever Gracious/Full of Grace/Full of Favor—*Dhu al-Fadl*: **2**:105, 243, 251; **3**:152; **8**:29; **10**:60; **27**:73; **40**:61. (See also The Most Gracious—*Dhu al-Fadl al-ʾAzim*.)

The Ever Living—*al-Hayy*

   a. **25**:58; **40**:65

   b. The [Ever] Living, the Self-Subsisting—*al-Hayy al-Qayyum*: **2**:255; **3**:2; **20**:111

The Ever Merciful—*al-Rahim*: **1**:1; **24**:20, 22. And many, many more, especially in doublets.

The Ever Near—*al-Qarib*: **2**:186, **11**:61; **34**:50

The [Ever/Most] Subtle/Most Gentle—*al-Latif*: **6**:103; **12**:100; **22**:63; **31**:16; **33**:34; **42**:19; **67**:14

The [Ever] Trustworthy—*al-Muʾmin*: **59**:23

The Ever Watchful—*al-Raqib*: **4**:1; **33**:52. (See also The All Seeing/All Watchful/Observant—*al-Basir*.)

The Exalter—*al-Rafiʿ*: **6**:83; **56**:3; **58**:11. *Al-Muʿizz*: **3**:26.

The Expander—*al-Basit*: **17**:30; **42**:27

The Expansive/All Embracing—*al-Wasiʿ*: **2**:115, 251, 247, 261, 268; **3**:73; **4**:130; **5**:54; **24**:32; **53**:32

The First—*al-Awwal*: **57**:3

Forbearing. See The All Kind/Forbearing—*al-Halim*.

Forever in Majesty and Munificence—*Dhu al-Jalali wa-l-Ikram*: **55**:27, 78

Forgiving of sin – *Ghafir al-dhanb*: **40**:3

Full of Favor. See The Ever Gracious/Full of Favor—*Dhu al-Fadl*.

Full of Forgiveness—*Dhu al-Maghfira*: **13**:6

Full of Mercy—*Dhu al-Rahma*: **6**:133; **18**:58

The Gatherer—*al-Jamiʿ*: **3**:9; **4**:140

Giver/Bringer of Death—*al-Mumit*: **2**:28, 258; **3**:156; **7**:158; **9**:116; **10**:56; **15**:23; **22**:66; **23**:80; **26**:81; **30**:40; **40**:68; **44**:8; **45**:26; **57**:2

Giver/Restorer of Life—*al-Muhyi*: **2**:28, 258; **3**:156; **7**:158; **9**:116; **10**:56; **15**:23; **22**:66; **23**:80; **26**:81; **30**:40, 50; **40**:68; **41**:39; **42**:9; **44**:8; **45**:26; **57**:2

The Glorious—*al-Majid*: **11**:73

The Grandeur—*al-Kibriyaʾ*: **45**:37

The Guardian—*al-Wakil*: **4**:81, 132, 171; **11**:12; **12**:66; **28**:28; **33**:3, 48; **39**:62; **73**:9

The Guide—*al-Hadi*: **22**:54

The Helper—*al-Nasir*: **4**:45; **8**:40; **22**:98; **25**:31

The Holy/the Sanctified—*al-Quddus*: **59**:23; **62**:1

The Heir(s)/Inheritor(s)—*al-Warithun*: **15**:23; **28**:58 (plural in both cases)

The Inner—*al-Batin*: **57**:3

The Irresistible—*al-Jabbar*: **59**:23

The Judge—*al-Hakam*

    a. **40**: 48

    b. The Judge, the All Knowing—*al-Fattah al-'Alim*: **34**:26

The Just—*al-'Adl*: **6**:115

The Last—*al-Akhir*: **57**:3

The Light—*al-Nur*: **24**:35 (5), **61**:8 (2)

Lord of Requital—*Dhu al-Intiqam*: **3**:4; **5**:95; **14**:47; **39**:37

Lord of the Stairs—*Dhu al-Ma'arij*: **70**:3

[Most] Able—*al-Qadir*: **6**:37, 65; **10**:24; **17**:99; **36**:81; **46**:33; **75**:40; **86**:8

The Most Bountiful—*Al-Akram*: **96**:3

The Most Exalted—*al-Muta'ali*: **13**:9

The Most Excellent of Judges—*Khair al-Hakimin*: **10**:109; **12**:80

The Most Gracious—*Dhu al-Fadl al-'Azim*: **3**:174; **57**:21, 29; **62**:4

The [Most] Great—*al-Kabir*: **4**:34; **13**:9; **22**:62; **31**:30; **34**:23 **40**:12

The Most Great/Supreme—*al-'Azim*: **2**:255; **42**:4; **56**:74, 96; **64**:33, 52

The Most High—*al-'Ali*

    a. **2**:255; **4**:34; **22**:62; **31**:30; **34**:23; **41**:12; **42**:4, 51; **43**:4

    b. The Most High—*al-A'la*: **16**:60; **79**:24; **87**:1 **92**:20

The Most Just—*al-Muqsit*: **33**:5

The Most Just of Judges—*Ahkam al-Hakimin*: **11**:45; **95**:8

The Most Kind—*al-Ra'uf*

    a. **2**:207; **3**:30; **9**:117; **33**:25; **57**:25; **58**:21

    b. The Most Kind, Ever Merciful—*al-Ra'uf al-Rahim*: **2**:143; **9**:117; **16**:7; **22**:65; **24**:20; **57**:9; **59**:10. Also *al-Barr al-Rahim*: **52**:28.

The Most Loving—*Wadud*: **11**:90; **85**:14

The Most Merciful of all—*Khair al-Rahimin*: **23**:109, 118

The Most Merciful of the merciful—*Arham al-Rahimin*: **7**:151; **12**:64, 92; **21**:83

The One—*al-Ahad*: **112**:1. Also *al-Wahid*: **12**:39; **13**:16; **14**:48.

The One Holding Sway/All Powerful—*al-Muqtadir*: **18**:45; **54**:42, 55

The One, Omnipotent/Supreme/Invincible—*al-Wahid al-Qahhar*: **12**:39; **13**:16; **14**:48; **38**:65; **39**:4; **40**:16

The Originator/Maker—*al-Bari'*: **39**:46; **59**:24. Also *al-Fatir*: **6**:14; **35**:1.

The Outer—*al-Zahir*: **57**:3

The Pardoner—*al-'Afuw*: **3**:155; **4**:9, 43, 99, 149; **5**:95, 101; **9**:43; **22**:60; **58**:2

Possessor of Power—*Dhu al-Quwwa*: **51**:58

The Powerful/the Strong/the Supremely Strong—*al-Qawi*: **8**:52; **11**:66; **22**:40, 74; **27**:39; **28**:26; **33**:25; **40**:22; **42**:19; **57**:25; **58**:21

The Praiseworthy—*al-Hamid*: **13**:1; **14**:8; **31**:12, 26; **41**:42. (See also Self-Sufficient—*al-Ghani*.)

The Preserver—*al-Hafiz*: **86**:4

The Prevailer—*al-Ghalib*: **12**:21

The Protector—*al-Mawla*: **2**:286; **3**:150; **6**:62; **8**:40 (2); **9**:51; **10**:30; **22**:78 (2); **47**:11; **66**:2, 4. Also *al-Wali*: **2**:257; **3**:68,150; **4**:45; **6**:127; **7**:155; **12**:101; **34**:41; **42**:9, 48; **45**:19.

The Reckoner—*al-Hasib*: **4**:6, 86; **33**:39

Relenting, Ever Relenting—*al-Tawwab*

    a. **4**:16, 64; **24**:10, **49**:12, **110**:3

    b. Relenting, Ever Merciful—*al-Tawwab al-Rahim*: **2**:37, 54, 128, 160; **4**:16, 64; **9**:104, 108

The Responsive—*al-Mujib*: **11**:61

The Restricter—*al-Qabid*: **25**:46

The Resurrector (the One Who Raises Up)—*al-Ba'ith*: **22**:7

The Self-Sufficient /Self-Sufficing—*al-Ghani*

    a. **2**:263; **3**:97; **6**:133; **10**:68; **14**:8; **27**:40; **29**:6; **39**:7; **47**:38

    b. The Self-Sufficient, Praiseworthy—*al-Ghani al-Hamid*: **2**:267; **4**:131; **22**:64; **31**:12, 26; **35**:15; **57**:24; **60**:6; **64**:6

The Severe/Stern in Requital—*Shadid al-'Iqab*: **2**:196, 211; **3**:11; **5**:2, 98; **6**:165; **7**:176; **8**:13, 25, 48, 52; **13**:6; **40**:3, 22; **59**:4, 7

The Shaper of Forms—*al-Musawwir*: **59**:24

The Source of Forgiveness—*Ahl al-Maghfira*: **74**:56

The Source of Mindfulness—*Ahl al-Taqwa*: **74**:56

The Source of Peace—*al-Salam*: **59**:23

The Sovereign/Ruler/King—*al-Malik*: **1**:4; **3**:26; **20**:114; **23**:116; **59**: 23; **62**:1; **114**:2

The Supreme—*al-Mutakabbir*: **59**:23. Also *al-'Azim*: **2**:255.

The Supreme in Strategy—*Shadid al-Mihal*: **13**:13

The Supreme in Strength—*al-Matin*: **51**:58

The Sustainer—*al-Razzaq*: **51**:58. Also *al-Muqit*: **4**:85.

The Swift in Reckoning—*Sari' al-Hisab*: **2**:202; **3**:19, 199; **5**:4; **13**:41; **14**:51; **24**:39; **40**:17. See also *Sari' al-'Iqab*: **6**:165; **7**:167.

The Truth/the True/the Reality/the True Reality—*al-Haqq*: **10**:32; **18**:44; **20**:114; **22**:6, 62; **23**:116; **24**:25; **31**:30

The Watchful—*al-Muhaymin*: **59**:23

The Witness—*Shahid/al-Shahid*: **3**:98; **4**:33, 79, 166; **5**:117; **6**:19; **10**:29, 46; **13**:43; **17**:96; **22**:17; **29**:52; **33**:55; **34**:47; **41**:53; **46**:8; **48**:28; **58**:6; **85**:3, 9

NOTES

Sura 1
The Opening (*Al-Fatiha*)

1:1   Although the *basmala*—"In the Name of God"—appears at the outset of every
sura in the 114 suras of the Qur'an except one (Sura 9, Repentance), it is only here
in the opening sura that it is treated as a verse. Its importance is underscored
by its two qualifiers, *al-rahman* and *al-rahim* in Arabic. Both are derived from
al-rahma (the mercy), which in turn derives from *al-raham* (the womb). Crucial
is the accent on God as encompassing mercy, just as the mother enfolds and
encompasses her child. Like the mother, God not only embodies mercy (*al-
rahman*) but also provides it again and again (*al-rahim*). Rendered here as "the
All Merciful" so as to mime certain semantic and poetic effects of the original,
God is also, always, the Ever Merciful. For those who think of Allah in gendered
terms, *al-rahman* and *al-rahim* are repeated as "His" defining traits. In the next
verses, *rabb* (Lord) and *malik* (Ruler) are solely masculine in their origin and
usage, but one can say, and should say, that Allah is neither male nor female.
Instead, the deity is depicted equally as feminine and masculine in traits, with
a stronger accent on the feminine due to the recurrent usage of Mercy, no less
than four times, in al-Fatiha. The vast expanse of Divine Mercy exceeds our
understanding but not our recognition: we recognize its performance daily in
our lives and also in the lives of others.

1:2   The definite article used in the Arabic is rendered as "All" in English to capture
the expanse of human gratitude to the Divine.

1:2   The Arabic for "universe" is '*alamin* (pl. of '*alam*), literally, "the worlds" or "all
worlds." It covers the spectrum of creations in the heavens and earth, land and
sea, at the same time that it also includes other creatures who are not human,
both jinn and angels (see multiple references in the Qur'an, especially Sura 55
on the jinn). The word "universe" is used here instead of "worlds" in order to
convey the fact that God's creation, while composed of many worlds and many
levels of being, is ultimately a unity. Also see Glossary, page 529.

1:4   *Al-din* can mean "religion" but here as *yawm al-din* it is clearly the final day or
the day of reckoning, reward, or punishment. See Glossary, page 530.

1:5   To "worship" God is also to be subservient to Him, and so the more graphic reference of worship is submission, servanthood, and slavery, connotations that are familiar in the Hebrew Bible and also in the Gospels.

1:7   It is crucial to stress that neither divine anger ("wrath") nor human deviance ("gone astray") is the final message of the opening sura. The two verbs used here are "to guide" (*hada*) and "to favor" (*an'ama*), and their respective nouns, *hidaya* (guidance) and *ni'ma* (favor), recur in the Qur'an as the insistent divine hope for all humankind and for all creatures in all worlds.

Sura 2
The Cow (*Al-Baqara*)

2:1   These letters are part of what is known as *muqatta'at*, or disconnected letters, different combinations of which are found at the beginning of several suras. See Glossary, page 531.

2:4   The Prophet Muhammad.

2:8   Arabic *wa-ma hum bimuminin*: literally, "But they are not among the believers."

2:14   In addition to the notion of a single Satan (Shaytan or Iblis), there are also multiple Satans or devils, like multiple jinn and angels, who can be, and are, seen to be part of Islamic cosmogony, acting in this world and the next.

2:22   Arabic *ja'alna lakum al-ard firash*: literally, "we made the earth a place spread out," an image found here and at 51:48. Similar to 40:64, God is projected here as a grand domestic architect, with earth as His habitat or couch, the sky His canopy.

2:29   "The seven heavens" is a metaphor for the entire cosmos, and like the number 7 in biblical literature it has a symbolic meaning, not a literal one.

2:30   The "regent" is Adam, who will appear by name in the next verse. Adam appears as regent or deputy for God on earth in several passages: see 7:69, 74; 10:14, 73; 27:62; and 35:39.

2:31   The word *ism* (name) implies use of reason and insight to distinguish between visible and invisible entities. The implication in the Arabic is that Adam is being given more profound knowledge than simply the "names" of things.

2:31   If the angels are right in their fear about the regent.

2:34   Iblis is another name for Satan, the enemy of humankind. Iblis's refusal to bow down to Adam is cited in several other passages: 7:11, 17:61, 18:50, 20:116, and 38:74–75.

2:36   God's speech is addressed to Adam, Eve, and Iblis. There are two other Qur'anic passages where the creation story features Satan/Iblis seducing Adam and Eve: 7:10–25 and 20:115–27.

2:41   Here is the first of several Qur'anic passages confirming the Qur'an as a completion of earlier scriptures. See *ahl al-kitab* in Glossary, page 529.

2:47   The word translated as "peoples" is the Arabic *'alamin*: literally, "all the worlds or the universe." See Glossary, page 529.

2:51   This is the "golden calf," depicted in Exodus 32:1–35; also cited in suras 7:148–53 and 20: 83–98.

2:53   On *furqan* (the criterion), see Glossary, page 530.

2:54   Arabic *fa-uqtulu anfusakum*: literally, "and kill yourselves," but here with a metaphorical meaning.

2:60   Arabic *kull unas*: literally, "all the people," but commentators agree that this refers to the tribes.

2:61   I.e., the children of Israel.

2:62   Since the Sabians, followers of the Queen of Sheba, were considered monotheists, and may be linked to the Mandaeans of southern Iraq, this passage echoes the Qur'anic message of inclusiveness: all who believe and do good will find salvation.

2:65   Arabic *kunu qirada khasiin*: literally, "be apes, despised." This figure of speech is also used elsewhere in the Qur'an, e.g., 31:19 and 62:5.

2:67   Arabic *a'udhu bi Allah an akun min al-jahilin*: literally, "I seek refuge with God from being among the ignorant."

2:70   This account can be compared to the biblical narrative in Numbers 19: 2–3, where the people of Israel are commanded to sacrifice a red heifer which is without defect or blemish and has never been placed under a yoke, as part of a purification ritual.

2:71   Arabic *ji'ta bil-haqq*: literally, "you have brought the truth."

2:87   Here and in v. 253 (as also in 4:171; 5:110; and 16:2, 102), the original uses the Arabic phrase *ruh al-quds*—literally, "the spirit of [God] the Holy." See Glossary, page 532.

2:95   Arabic *bima qaddamat aydihim*: literally, "on account of what their hands have sent forth."

2:98   Gabriel, often implied, is mentioned by name here and in one later sura (26:193), while Michael is mentioned only here. Both appear as quasi-angelic forces in Jewish literature, but since Gabriel was not only the holy or noble spirit but also the harbinger of death, some Jews saw him in a negative light.

2:101   Arabic *alladhina utu al-kitab kitab Allah waraa dhuhurihim*: literally, "Those given the Book put the Book behind their backs."

2:102   Solomon was not only king of Israel after David but, as a renowned source of wisdom, he also became the paragon of magicians and it is against this misuse of "Solomonic wisdom" that the current verse is warning.

2:102   Harut and Marut, two contrarian angels mentioned only here in the Qur'an, are said to be linked to the planet Venus; from there they allegedly derived special powers, at once magical and disruptive.

2:104 Some Jews in Medina opposed to the Prophet mispronounced *ra'ina* as *ra'ayna* (being a derogatory term in Hebrew, *ra'una* meaning "thoughtlessness") so that it became an abusive expression. The same derogatory verbal word game is cited elsewhere, at 4:46.

2:106 The technical word for "abrogation" is *naskh* (where a given verse is canceled or replaced by another); see Glossary, page 532.

2:110 A reference to the day of judgment echoed elsewhere; see especially 99:7–8.

2:112 Arabic *man aslama wajhahu li Allah*: literally, "whoever submits his face to God."

2:113 Arabic *laisat al-nasara 'ala shay*: literally, "Christians have nothing to stand upon."

2:125 The place near the Ka'ba where Abraham was said to have stood as he prepared to sacrifice his son Ishmael. See below, 37:100–111.

2:128 As elsewhere, the root verb, *s-l-m*, refers both to peace (*salam*) and submission (*islam*), and in the period when the Muslim movement had not yet coalesced into community aware of itself as such, the emphasis was on submitting to God and to God's will both as individuals and as a group.

2:129 Verses 124–29 are a kind of prayer consecrating the Ka'ba. Abraham's prayer here (v. 129) has been answered with the appearance of Muhammad. The religion of Abraham (*millat Ibrahim*) includes his covenant (through circumcision) with God, so that *millat Ibrahim* means "community of the covenant with Abraham." See also 2:135 and 16:123. Abraham becomes the prototype of the new community of believers, *al-muslimun*, those who submit (2:135–36). See Glossary, page 531.

2:132 The word *din*, here rendered as "religion," has multiple meanings. See Glossary, page 530.

2:133 Arabic *am kuntum shuhada'a idh hadara Ya'qub al-mawt*: literally, "did you witness when death approached Jacob?" This is directed to the Jews, who claimed Jacob as their forefather.

2:134 *Umma* is here rendered as "community" since the distinction of belief in One God is not limited to Jews or Christians, but applies to all who followed the example of Abraham. For other meanings, see Glossary, page 533.

2:138 The word for color (*sibgha*) distinguishes the creed of Abraham from others by its hue or color, for many signified as "green."

2:142 In Arabic, *qibla* signifies the direction of prayer, which was changed from Jerusalem to Mecca in the year 624 CE, and remains the direction of worship for Muslims today.

2:143 Arabic *umma wasat*: literally, "a community of the middle or the middle way," stressing that God is the God of East and West. To paraphrase 1:5, "the straight path" is also the middle path—at once moderate and broad, avoiding extremism or exclusion in all forms.

2:143   Arabic *lina'lama*: literally, "that We might know."

2:148   The Arabic pronoun *li-kull* is indefinite; it can refer to an individual or a collective, but the collective "community" seems best here.

2:156   Arabic *inna li-Allah wa-inna ilayhi raji'una* ("To God we belong, and to God we shall return") is one of the most important emblems of Muslim belief and practice in the Qur'an. It is often found on tombstones and is customarily recited on the news of anyone's death.

2:157   Arabic *ula'ika 'alayhim salawat min rabbihim wa-rahma*: literally, "on whom descend prayers from their Lord and mercy."

2:158   Safa and Marwa are two hills between which Abraham's wife Hagar ran in search of water for her son Ishmael. Her quest is commemorated by Hajj pilgrims, who walk or run between the two hills.

2:158   The Hajj is the major pilgrimage, to be performed during the pilgrimage season; the 'Umra, or minor pilgrimage, can be performed at any time of the year. The importance of the Hajj is accented by its placement in the obligations incumbent on each Muslim. 'Eid al-Adha is the feast of the near sacrifice of Ishmael by Abraham, celebrated every year, after the Hajj, as the major Islamic festival.

2:185   This is the signature event for Muslim observance of a monthlong fast, from sunrise to sunset. It lasts the entire month of Ramadan, ending in the Islamic calendar with a three-day festival, 'Eid al-Fitr. The actual revelation of the Qur'an took place over several years from 610 to 632 CE, with Sura 5:3 popularly thought to be the last revelation (though some have disputed that link). What is not disputed is the importance of *Lailat al-Qadr*. The high moment of Ramadan, it is marked in Sura 97 as "the Night of Decree" (see also 44:3), widely celebrated on the twenty-seventh night of Ramadan, when the entire Qur'an was said to be revealed to the Prophet, though articulated only in successive stages (17:106, 25:32).

2:187   Prior to Islam men used to lie secretly with their wives during the nights of fasting.

2:189   Before Islam, some Arabs, returning from the pilgrimage, entered their homes by the back door, imagining this to be a righteous act.

2:191   This is a critical instance—one among many—where the only correct sense of Qur'anic injunctions can be, and must be, gleaned from the whole context. There is not an unconditional directive "And kill them where you find them." The condition is: "Fight ... against those who fight you," *but within limits*. One must read the entire passage, vv. 190–94. See also 2:216–17. Cited here twice, the injunction to fight also recurs in 4:76, 84, 89, 91 and 9:5, 12, 14, 29, 36, 123. Although not as dramatic as the so-called verse of the sword (9:5), these verses nonetheless commend fighting, but solely in self-defense and within limits.

2:194   According to most commentators, there were four sacred months in the Islamic calendar in which fighting was prohibited: Rajab, Dhu al-Qaʾda, Dhu al-Hijja, and Muharram. However, if the polytheists attacked Muslims during a sacred month, the latter were permitted to defend themselves.

2:195 Arabic *la tulqu bi-aydikum ila al-tahluka*: literally, "do not cast yourself into ruin through your own hands." This verse is about charitable spending, and not, as some commentators have suggested, the prospect of suicide.

2:198 Trade is permitted during the pilgrimage.

2:198 The sacred site (*al-mashʿar al-haram*) is identified as Muzdalifa on the basis of Muhammad's practice. ʿArafat is about twenty-two kilometers (thirteen miles) from Mecca while Muzdalifa is about eight kilometers (five miles) beyond ʿArafat.

2:203 The appointed days are the days after the ʿEid al-Adha, celebrating the end of Ramadan. Pilgrims must spend at least two days in the valley of Mina, which is about five kilometers (three miles) east of Mecca.

2:222 This verse begins long section on marriage and divorce (through v. 242), with v. 228, like 4:34, seeming to elevate men above women. Yet in each case the "elevation" implies responsibility for taking fair action, and in the context of early-seventh-century Arabia, these verses curtailed rather than expanded both male dominance and the unbridled resort to patriarchal norms.

2:223 Arabic *anna shiʾtum*: literally, "as you wish."

2:226 Prior to the advent of Islam, husbands could swear abstinence from their wives indefinitely; Islam decreed that after four months, they would have to divorce them.

2:234 I.e., if they choose to remarry after the required waiting period.

2:235 A man may make known his interest in the woman during her ʿidda period but may not make a formal proposal.

2:237 Arabic *ʿuqdat al-nikah*: literally, "the knot of marriage."

2:240 Again, the reference here seems to be to a widow's decision to remarry after the required waiting period.

2:246 A reference to Samuel, as in 1 Samuel 8:19–20.

2:248 This is presumably the "ark of God" mentioned in 1 Samuel 3:3, the same ark that rescued Noah and assured the continuation of humankind. See 7:46.

2:255 This is the most beloved, and often quoted, section of the Qurʾan, after the initial sura, *al-Fatiha*. It embodies both invocation and petition to God, extolling His Beautiful Names at the beginning and the end. The Prophet Muhammad regarded this verse, which lays out the divine attributes of unity and eternal life, omnipotence and omniscience, transcendence and immanence, as the most exalted verse in the Qurʾan (Imam Abul Hussain bin al Hajja et al., eds., Nasiruddin al Khattab, trans., *Sahih Muslim* [Lahore: Darussalam, 2007], *hadith 810*, 1:556).

2:258 Despite the power of this narrative, its protagonist has never been identified, yet Abraham's debate with a king is often assumed to be Nimrod, with parallels in apocryphal literature, similar to speculations about the man and the town cited in 2:259. It can be linked to Sura 18:9–26, the story of the "companions of the Cave," which has parallels to the Christian legend of the Sleepers of Ephesus.

2:275   For other passages that address the Qur'anic prohibition of usury (or lending money for interest), see 3:130, 4:161, and 30:39.

2:282   This is the longest verse of the 6236 verses in the Qur'an. It offers a complex set of rules about the need to record loan agreements in writing. After announcing eight successive stages, it culminates in the directive "Be mindful of God," with the assurance "it is God Who will teach you—God Knows all things." The next verse (v. 283) provides limits to this command when traveling.

Sura 3
The Family of ʿImran (*Al ʿImran*)

3:1   On these disconnected letters, see *muqattaʿat* in Glossary, page 531.

3:7   Arabic *umm al-kitab*: literally, "the Mother of the Book"—that is, what gives it life and nurtures it, as does a mother. Here we have yet another instance of the gender-inclusive idioms that pervade the Qur'anic message. See Glossary, page 532.

3:7   This verse is the basis for abrogating verses; it is widely cited as a critique internal to the Qur'an of attributing one meaning to all its verses. See *naskh* in Glossary, page 532.

3:12   Arabic *mihad*: literally, "a place of rest." But the implication is that hell is the final destination of the disbelievers.

3:13   I.e., at the Battle of Badr, in March 624 CE.

3:14   Arabic *lil-nas*: literally, "to people or humankind," but clearly intending "men." See *nas* in Glossary, page 532.

3:19   Arabic *al-Islam*, here an inclusive term (as elsewhere in the Qur'an), not the religion of one group. See Glossary, page 531.

3:20   Arabic *aslamtu wajhiya li-Allah*: literally, "I have submitted my face to God," but clearly implying the entire person or whole self.

3:20   Arabic *ummiyyin*: literally, "unlettered," but here referring to those who have not yet received scripture. See also v. 75 and 2:78 ("Among them are unlettered people who don't know the Book").

3:28   Arabic *yuhadhdhirukum Allah nafsahu*: literally, "God warns you about Himself."

3:33   The phrases "the family of Abraham" and "the family of ʿImran" constitute the first, and only, such genealogical reference in the entire Qur'an. The family of Abraham is well-known, traceable to Isaac, Ishmael, and their descendants. The family of ʿImran refers to Miriam's lineage through her father, ʿImran, and his wife (cf. v. 35).

3:36   It seems to be implied that a girl, unlike a boy, could not serve in the Temple, but God chose to overlook this gender limitation.

3:38   Arabic *min ladunka*: literally, "from Yourself."

3:39   A reference to Jesus, since John later confirms Jesus as a Word from Him (v. 45).

3:52   The Arabic word *muslim* means one who submits to the will of God. See also 5:111, 112 and Glossary (page 531). It is significant that the disciples of Jesus assume this appellation for themselves.

3:61   Many authorities aver that several verses of this sura, but especially vv. 59–61, were revealed to Muhammad in 632 CE after a delegation of Christians visited the Prophet. Following an intense discussion, Muhammad challenged them to a prayer contest, and while the challenge was not accepted, a treaty was issued giving these Christians protection to practice their religion in territory controlled by the ascendant Muslims.

3:67   The word *hanif*, also used in 2:135, refers to a person who believed only in the one God even before Abraham. See Glossary, page 530.

3:70   Here the implication is that God's signs are also verses from the heavenly Book, itself the source for the Torah, the Psalms, the Gospels, as well as the Qur'an. See *ayat* in Glossary, page 530.

3:75   The dinar is a small unit of currency in some parts of the Arab world.

3:79   The addressees are Jews; see 5:44, where rabbis and the learned are invoked together.

3:93   Dietary laws laid down first by Noah (Genesis 9:3–4) and then by Jacob/Israel (Genesis 32:32).

3:96   The Arabic word *Bakka* is an old name for Mecca.

3:112   The two ropes, one from God, the other from humankind, are metaphors suggesting that only total reliance on God and full acceptance of other believers will elevate those among the people of the Book who are "true believers" (v. 110).

3:112   See 2:61 for identical words, referring there only to Jews; here, the disobedient who are "always transgressing" refers to all people of the Book.

3:113   In contrast with the preceding verse, *ayat* here has to be rendered as "verses" or "words," not "signs." See Glossary, page 530.

3:121   The historical incident to which this passage refers is the Battle of Uhud, which the Muslims thought they were winning, and then lost, in 625 CE. The Battle of Badr, which preceded it, marked the first victory of the nascent Muslim community in 624.

3:125   A similar divine insertion of angelic assistance occurred at the Battle of Badr; see 8:9–10, where the number of celestial mediaries is "a thousand angels, row upon row."

3:137   Arabic *sunan*: literally, "practices" or "customs."

3:140   Another reference to the Battle of Uhud (625 CE), where the Muslims, having flouted the commands of the Prophet, were defeated by the Quraysh.

3:140   Arabic *shuhada'*: literally, "witnesses [to Him]," and thus rendered as "martyrs."

3:147   Arabic *wa-israfana fi amrina*: literally, "and forgive us excess in our affairs."

3:152 I.e., victory over your enemies.

3:154 Arabic *jahiliyya.* "Ignorance" is the usual translation for this word, signifying the period preceding the advent of Islam; see also 5:50.

3:154 Arabic *wa-liyabtaliya Allah ma fi sudurikum wa-liyumahhisa ma fi qulubikum:* literally, "so that God could test your breasts and purify what was in your hearts."

3:174 Like *Dhu al-Fadl,* "Ever Gracious" in v. 152, *Dhu al-Fadl al-'Azim* here is not one of the canonical ninety-nine Beautiful Names of God, but "Most Gracious" clearly has the same power as other such names, and hence is here capitalized, as are numerous other noncanonical names, both affirming and critiquing humankind. See The Beautiful Names, page 536.

Sura 4
Women (*Al-Nisa*)

4:3   See v. 127, where it is clear that "orphan girls" are the subject of this directive.

4:3   The phrase "those you own" refers to concubines who, in addition to legal wives, were considered part of the household for seventh-century Arabs.

4:5   The property of the orphans.

4:6   Arabic *wabtalu:* literally, "and test."

4:15   This verse is often read in tandem with 22:2–3, where a different punishment is prescribed.

4:24   The intended meaning is to alter mutual agreements between husband and wife after the obligatory bride gifts, as indicated earlier in 4:4.

4:25   See v. 3.

4:29   Arabic *wa-la taqtulu anfusakum:* literally, "do not kill your selves," an expression that can be read as an injunction against both murder and suicide.

4:34   Arabic *min amwalihim:* literally, "from their wealth."

4:34   The most controversial directive about women in the Qur'an, it advises use of force but also, in context, with restraint; hence the qualifier "harmless force." The vast majority of exegetes agree that the force used should be very light, leaving no mark, and that its intent is merely to mark displeasure. Numerous sayings of the Prophet condemn the practice of beating women; Muhammad never even raised his voice to any of his wives.

4:46   The exchange here amplifies the reference above in 2:104—see the note there. In both instances, some Medinan Jews opposed to the Prophet would twist these words, using them against him.

4:49   There are also references to a date stone in vv. 53, 77, and 124.

4:75   Arabic *min ladunka:* literally, "from Yourself."

4:88   Arabic *wa-man yudlil Allah fa-lan tajida lahu sabil:* literally, "for those whom God allows to stray you can never find a way." But the repetition, on the heels of the question that precedes, sounds strained in English.

4:117 See a parallel reference in 53:19–20.

4:125 Arabic *hanif*. This refers to one who follows the primordial or natural religion of monotheism, considered to be the innate propensity of humankind. It is used of Abraham ten times, emphasizing his archetypal role as the founder of Judaism, Christianity, and Islam. The opposite of *hanif* in the Qur'an is the term *mushrik*, which means polytheist or idolater (literally, one who partners other entities with God). See Glossary, page 530.

4:128 In other words, the wife would agree to a decrease of her maintenance allowance.

4:129 Arabic *kal-mu'allaqa*: literally, "like one suspended."

4:153 The reference here is to recalcitrant Jews, who did not obey Moses (cf. Deuteronomy 1:26–36). See 2:55 for a similar exchange and word usage. Elsewhere it is Moses himself who implores, "Show yourself to me, so I may look upon you." To this comes the reply, "Never shall you see me," after which a mountain is crumbled (7:143).

4:154 "Gate" here is a metaphor for the land of Israel.

4:155 Arabic *ghulf*: literally, "wrapped, unable to be opened or penetrated." See also 2:88: "Our hearts are closed," with a similar lesson albeit using the stronger verb "curse": "No—God curses them for their disbelief; and little do they believe."

4:157 This is the sole Qur'anic dictum that a likeness of Jesus was crucified, not Jesus in the flesh. Elsewhere, the Trinity (4:171 and 5:73) and the divinity of Jesus (5:16, 72, 116; and 9:31) are denied.

4:158 The same action for raising Jesus is paralleled for Mount Sinai earlier in this sura (v. 154).

4:159 Arabic *qabla mawtihi*: literally, "before his death," reinforcing the notion that all Jews who reject Jesus' prophecy and all Christians who affirm his divinity will accept Jesus as a prophet before they die.

4:166 The parallelism is to Moses and to the revelation he received: both came directly from God, without mediation.

4:171 The Arabic word *ruh*, meaning "spirit," is also used to refer to the mediary of Mary's conception in 2:87 as *ruh al-quds*. Many translators (Yusuf Ali, Pickthall, Abdel Haleem, Alan Jones, Syed Qutb) render it as "Holy Spirit" but the reference to the spirit in the form of a man (i.e., Jabril or Gabriel) is specified in 19:17: "Then We sent Our spirit, appearing to her in the perfect form of a man." Here—as also in 2:87, 253; 5:110; and 16:2,102—the text translates the Arabic phrase *ruh al-quds*: literally, "the spirit of [God] the Holy."

4:173 Arabic *fa-yu'adhdhibuhum 'adhab alim*: literally, "He will punish them with a painful punishment."

4:175 Note the parallelism and contrast with vv. 168–69.

4:176 The discussion here harks back to vv. 11–12, when inheritance and the rules of its disbursement were first introduced. It grounds all the moral teachings of this sura in a final, concretized case.

Sura 5

The Table Spread (*Al-Ma'ida*)

5:2   Arabic *wa-la al-hadya wa-la al-qala'id*: literally, "nor of the offerings nor of the garlanded ones."

5:2   The Arabic *al-bait al-haram* clearly refers to the Ka'ba in Mecca, and the preceding elements relate to the rites of the Hajj, the annual pilgrimage.

5:2   Here as elsewhere, when a noncanonical Beautiful Name is invoked in the Qur'an, it will usually be capitalized to indicate its source, with appropriate stress, parallel to other Beautiful Names in the canonical list of ninety-nine. See the introduction for further explanation.

5:3   See v. 90, where divining arrows, as well as sacrifices at stone altars, are forbidden.

5:3   Arabic "*al-islam*": literally, "submission [to My will]." This is taken by most commentators to be the final revelation, revealed to the Prophet less than three months before his death in 632 CE. It is framed in a verse accenting obedience and forgiveness, each in tandem with the other.

5:5   Those "given the book" are Jews and Christians.

5:11   The Quraysh.

5:12   I.e., if you spend money legitimately earned in the way of God.

5:22   "They" here refers to the Canaanites, prior inhabitants of what became the Land of Israel.

5:30   Arabic *fa-qatalahu fa-asbaha min al-khasirin*: literally, "then he killed him and became one of the lost." But the repetition does not sit well in English.

5:32   Arabic *fasad fi al-ard*: literally, "spreading corruption on earth." This is a widely applicable moral imperative: to prevent broadscale physical violence or moral failure within the nascent Muslim community, concrete prohibitions and punishments are to be meted out. Their actual applicability has been, and continues to be, a matter of ongoing interpretation, with variant approaches and decrees.

5:41   In the opinion of most Qur'anic commentators, this refers to an incident in which a Jewish woman and man had committed adultery and were brought to the Prophet for his ruling. The Prophet asked about precedents from the Torah but was given false information. It was up to the Prophet to decide: if he opted for lashing, the accused were told to take it; but if stoning, they were warned to beware.

5:44   This is addressed to the rabbis and Jewish scholars.

5:50   Here again, as in numerous other passages, "ignorance" is the translation of *jahiliyya*, the period preceding the advent of Islam.

5:69   Since the Sabians were monotheists, the passage echoes a recurrent Qur'anic message of inclusiveness: all who believe and do good deeds will find salvation.

5:80   Arabic *labi'sa ma qaddamat lahum anfusuhum*: literally, "wicked is what their souls send forward for them" (to be added to their account on the day of judgment).

5:95   This rectangular building, which Muslims believe was built by Abraham, is at the center of the mosque in Mecca, around which pilgrims circumambulate.

5:103 There are Arabic terms for each of these domestic animals: *bahira, sa'iba, wasila,* and *ham.* All were deemed worthy of sacrifice, and efficacious, as part of Meccan idol worship prior to the coming of Islam.

5:104 Arabic *ma wajadna 'alayhi aba'ana*: literally, "what we found our forefathers doing."

Sura 6
Cattle (*Al-An'am*)

6:2   The two terms are presumed to be one's earthly span of life as fixed by God and the moment of final reckoning.

6:8   The "judgment" clearly refers to the day of judgment.

6:12   Arabic *kataba 'ala nafsihi al-rahma*: literally, "decreed for Himself the showing of mercy."

6:27   Arabic *wa-nakun min al-mu'minin*: literally, "and we would be among the believers."

6:35   Arabic *wa-in kana kabura 'alayka i'raduhum*: literally, "and if their turning away is hard on you," clearly a rhetorical question, implying that nothing could change the disbelievers.

6:38   The Arabic word *umam* (sing. *umma*) is usually "nation(s)" but here it's best rendered as "communities" see the next note, regarding v. 42. See also *umma* in Glossary, page 533.

6:42   Arabic *umam*: either "nations," as here, or "communities" (v. 38).

6:44   Arabic *fatahna 'alayhim abwab kull shay'*: literally, "we opened for them the gates of everything."

6:45   Arabic *fa-quti'a*: literally, "was cut off."

6:54   The expression in Arabic, *kataba 'ala nafsihi al-rahma* (literally, "decreed for Himself the showing of mercy"), is identical to v. 12 above.

6:61   The envoys clearly are angels.

6:73   Arabic *bi al-haqq*: literally, "in truth."

6:92   "The mother of cities" is another name for Mecca.

6:112 Arabic *zukhrufa al-qawl ghurur*: literally, "with adorned speech in deception."

6:113 Arabic *wa-liyaqtarifu ma hum muqtarifun*: literally, "and they commit the things they are committing."

6:114 Arabic *fa-la takunanna min al-mumtarin*: literally, "then do not be among those who doubt."

6:125 "Submission [to God's will]," here as elsewhere, is the literal meaning of the Arabic word *islam*. See Glossary, page 531.

6:135 Arabic *i'malu 'ala makanatikum*: literally, "act according to your place or station."

6:157 Arabic *su' al-'adhab bima kanu yasdifun*: literally, "We gave them a dread punishment for their turning away," but the repetition seems heavy in English.

6:158 Again, the repetition in Arabic—*ba'd ayat rabbika* (literally, "some signs of your Lord")—seems excessive in English.

Sura 7
The Heights (*Al-A'raf*)

7:1 On these disconnected letters, see *muqatta'at* in Glossary, page 531.

7:8 The "balance" refers to the divine scales of justice, which will weigh good deeds and bad deeds.

7:13 It is from Eden that Satan was banished.

7:16 Echoing Sura 1:7, "not astray," this verse confirms the agency of Satan as the one who leads humankind astray.

7:20 Both Satan and his son Khannas prefer "whispering" as a form of communication; see 114:4, where the "whisperer" is deemed to be Khannas.

7:29 Arabic *'aqimu wujuhakum 'inda kull masjid*: literally, "set your faces forward at each place of prayer."

7:34 The same Arabic word, *ajal*, is used for the fixed term of life for a community as for the fixed term of life for a single person; see 6:2 and Glossary, page 529.

7:40 A familiar image from the Gospels: see Matthew 19:24, Mark 10:5, and Luke 18:25. Here, it refers not just to a rich man, but to all sinners.

7:71 The "names" of idols are referred to elsewhere, in 12:40 and 53:23; they seem clearly to be the three stone idols or goddesses, al-Lat, al-Uzza, and Manat (53:19–20).

7:78 This same incident of prophecy, betrayal, and destruction—all linked to the she-camel of Thamud—becomes the backdrop for 91:11–14. It serves as the prototype for many punishment stories in the Qur'an.

7:79 Arabic *wa-lakin la tuhibbun al-nasihin*: literally, "but you dislike those who give advice."

7:84 Parallel to 11:82, which is also about Lot, "When Our command came to pass, We turned their town upside down, and rained upon it stones of baked clay, layer upon layer."

7:142 Most commentators suggest that the first thirty days were dedicated to fasting, and that the Torah was revealed only during the final ten days.

7:144 Arabic *kalimati*: literally, "My word"—i.e., God's direct word (without mediation)—and so the nickname for Moses is *kalimatu Allah*, "The word of God."

7:151 Arabic *arham al-rahimin*: literally, "the Most Merciful of the merciful."

7:155 Arabic *khair al-ghafirin*: literally, "the Best of Forgivers."

7:157 Muhammad is the "unlettered" prophet since he does not read or write yet understands and communicates to others what has been revealed to him and is then written down by others.

7:157   References to predictions about a coming prophet occur in Deuteronomy 18:15 and John 14:16.

7:165   Arabic *ba'is*: literally, "wretched."

7:166   For this phrase, see also, e.g., 2:65, 31:19, and 62: 5.

7:167   It is not clear who will be the agents inflicting punishment against the Jews, whether Assyrians or Babylonians, Greeks, Romans, Persians, or even Muslims.

7:169   Arabic *wa-darasu ma fihi*: literally, "they studied what was in it."

7:171   See parallel passage and imagery in 4:154.

7:172   This reference to the eternal covenant between the Divine and humankind is often evoked by the single question: *alastu bi-rabbikum?* (Am I not your Lord?) The day of resurrection is also known as *yawm alastu*.

7:180   Arabic *wa-li Allah al-asma' al-husna*: literally, "to God belong the Beautiful Names." The Beautiful Names of God recur throughout the Qur'an, as in this condensed expression here, and then again in 17:110, 20:8, and 59:24.

7:187   Arabic *thaqulat*: literally, "it weighs heavily."

7:202   Arabic *ikhwanuhum:* literally, "their brothers."

Sura 8
The Spoils of War (*Al-Anfal*)

8:11   Arabic *amana minhu*: literally, "a security from Him."

8:17   There is a tradition that the Prophet threw pebbles at the foe during the Battle of Badr.

8:34   The "sacred mosque" is the Ka'ba in Mecca.

8:38   Arabic *qad madat sunnat al-awwalin*: literally, "there preceded the practice or protocol of predecessors."

8:41   Arabic *yawm al-furqan*: literally, "[on] the day of the criterion [between right and wrong]." See Glossary, page 530.

8:42   That is, once the Meccans saw how large the Quraysh army was, they would have opted not to fight.

8:43   At first, the Quraysh army had appeared in a dream as few and weak, yet later they were many and fearsome. The divine strategy was to shift from the apparent small army to the actual huge enemy force.

8:48   Arabic *wa-inni jar lakum*: literally, "and indeed, I am a neighbor for you."

8:51   Arabic *dhalika bima qaddamat aydikum*: literally, "this is because of what your hands have sent forth."

8:68   Arabic *law la kitab min Allah*: literally, "had it not been a book from God."

8:68   The issue at stake here is what to do with prisoners taken at the Battle of Badr, since the divine decree has been clear: forgive them rather than kill them.

8:72   The emigrants have the right to inherit from the Medinans. The clear sense of this passage is that relatives (alone) are no longer kinsfolk but rather all who have become believers, at once emigrants (from Mecca to Medina) and those who strive "[with you] in the cause of God."

8:72   From Mecca to Medina.

8:72   They seek your help against those who would persecute them due to their religion.

8:75   This is likely synonymous with *umm al-kitab*, the ultimate source of all deeds, persons, and outcomes (3:7, 12:39, and 43:4; see Glossary, page 532). Most exegetes agree that this abrogates the implication regarding inheritance in v. 72, and it reaffirms that the sole rights of inheritance belong to blood relatives. Some commentators state that "allies" can inherit from someone only if the deceased does not have blood relatives.

Sura 9
Repentance (*Al-Tawba*)

9:4   The "term" indicated here are the months of Rajab, Dhu al-Qa'da, Dhu al-Hijja, and Muharram. They had been honored as a truce period by pre-Islamic Arabs, and this revelation confirms the continuation of that practice under Islam.

9:8   This refers to the first group of polytheists mentioned in the previous verse.

9:17   This and the next two verses appear to be directed at those who did not believe in Muhammad's prophecy but were still attached to the Ka'ba as a place of worship.

9:25   The Battle of Hunayn took place after the conquest of Mecca in 630 CE, in the neighboring town of Ta'if. Both vv. 25 and 26 depict the fortunes of this battle.

9:29   The *jizya* tax is levied on non-Muslims under Muslim rule, in return for protection of their homes, property, and persons by Muslim authorities. Though this is the single mention of it in the Qur'an, the *jizya* tax became an axial feature of Muslim law.

9:30   Ezra, esteemed by all Jews, is believed to be God's son only by some Jews from Arabia, while the affirmation that Jesus is the son of God is believed by all Christians—even though opinions vary wildly about what "sonship" means.

9:30   Sura 5:75 raises the same critique with the same wording: "how deluded they are!"

9:36   To wit, the months of Rajab, Dhu al-Qa'da, Dhu al-Hijja, and Muharram. See the note for 9:4.

9:36   The injunction here is similar to 2:194: "and for all violations, a fair requital. If anyone assaults you, you may respond in kind, equally against them."

9:37   This is a correction of the correction to calendrical time practiced by pre-Islamic Arabs, in order to synchronize the solar and lunar calendars. It is here explicitly rejected in order to maintain the Muslim difference, to wit, that a lunar calendar is rotated not just in ordinary time but in liturgical time, changing the dates for the Ramadan fast and the Hajj pilgrimage each year.

9:38   This and the next verse (v. 39), as well as several verses below, are related to the expedition that the Prophet organized to Tabuk, in order to oppose the Byzantines, in 630. The expected battle never occurred but the instigator of the Byzantine leader, Heraclius, was a Medinan notable opposed to the Prophet, Abu Amir. Some refused to fight and they are again rebuked in v. 81 below.

9:40   This moment, known as the *hijra* or "flight," marked Muhammad's escape from Mecca to Medina in 622 CE, which became 1 AH. His companion was Abu Bakr, later his successor, the first caliph of Islam.

9:42   Arabic *yuhlikun anfusahum*: literally, "they ruin themselves."

9:44   This and the next few verses seem to be calming Muhammad about the decision he made to accept halfhearted excuses from those who claimed to be Muslims but asked for exemption from the campaign at Tabuk. They were wrong not to assent to fight, though no fighting ever occurred, yet as the revelation explains, their faint participation would have created even greater problems for those who did agree to fight.

9:48   Arabic *laka al-umur*: literally, "your affairs."

9:52   A similar injunction, with nearly identical wording, occurs in 7:71.

9:60   *Sadaqat*, here translated as "alms," is not the same as *zakat*, also "alms." The latter is compulsory, the former voluntary, yet the aims for which both can and should be distributed are set by God as "an obligation" on all believers.

9:68   Arabic *hiya hasbuhum*: literally, "it suffices for them."

9:74   Arabic *wa-hammu bi ma lam yanalu*: literally, "and they planned what they could not attain." Most commentators take this to be a plot against the Prophet, inspired by those who wanted more than their share of booty.

9:81   See note for 9:38.

9:90   "Bedouin Arabs" are nomadic Arabs; they are discussed further in vv. 97–99 and are also mentioned later, in 48:11–16 and 49:14–17.

9:100 The forerunners (*sabiqun*) stand above all others, as also noted in 56:10; they are given special preference in the hereafter.

9:107 This verse seems to refer to a specific mosque, one built by opponents of the Prophet in Medina who claimed to be Muslims yet did not accept his authority. It was later destroyed.

9:118 Another reference to those who did not participate in the battle at Tabuk.

9:128 These final two verses (128–29) are thought to have been the last revealed to Muhammad; their hopeful tone lifts the mood of this entire sura to a realm of resolve that divine mercy will triumph in the end.

Sura 10
Jonah (*Yunus*)

10:1   On these disconnected letters, see *muqatta'at* in Glossary, page 531.

10:2   Arabic *awhayna ila rajul minhum*: literally, "We revealed to a man among them."

10:5   The lunar calendar in Islam is based on this and similar verses (6:96, 17:12).

10:12   Arabic *lijanbihi*: literally, "on his side." Elsewhere the same expression appears in the plural, "on their sides" (3:191, 4:104).

10:16   The Prophet Muhammad is here alluding to the fact that he was forty years old before receiving the initial revelation that subsequently became the Qur'an.

10:19   Arabic *law la kalima sabaqat min rabbika*: literally, "had it not been for a Word that preceded from your Lord."

10:19   The Word from God is that people will continue to disagree: "had God willed, they would not have fought—but God does as He intends" (2:253).

10:26   Arabic *ula'ika ashab al-janna hum fiha khalidun*: literally, "they shall be companions of the garden, where they shall live forever."

10:39   Arabic *kadhdhabu bima lam yuhitu bi 'ilmihi*: literally, "they deny that, the knowledge of which they cannot compass."

10:87   Arabic *qibla*: literally, "prayer direction." People could pray in their homes to avoid persecution.

10:103   Arabic *haqq 'alayna*: literally, "as is Our right or obligation," but since God cannot be obliged to do anything, it is His right to choose, or His choice.

10:105   Arabic *aqim wajhaka*: literally, "set your face."

10:108   Arabic *fa-man ihtada fa innama yahtadi linafsihi*: literally, "so whoever is guided, is guided for, or to, himself."

10:108   Arabic *yadillu 'alayha*: literally, "he strays against it."

Sura 11
Hud (*Hud*)

11:1   On these disconnected letters, see *muqatta'at* in Glossary, page 531.

11:1   Arabic *'uhkimat ayatuhu*: literally, "its verses made clear." This passage is parallel to 3:7 ("Some of its verses are clear in meaning"), where the original Arabic *ayat muhkamat* literally translates as "verses with clear meaning."

11:3   Arabic *yawm kabir*: literally, "a great day."

11:17   Arabic *wa-man yakfur bihi min al-ahzab fa-al-nar maw'iduhu*: literally, "and whoever among the groups denies it, the fire will be his appointed place."

11:21   Arabic *wa-dalla 'anhum ma kanu yaftarun*: literally, "and all that they invented strayed from them."

11:35   This verse is best understood as a parenthetic comment within the narrative about Noah. It is inserted to verify the truthfulness of the Prophet Muhammad, harking back to the reproof of vv. 13–14.

11:40   Arabic *wafara al-tannur*: literally, "and the oven boiled over."

11:44   Mount Judi is located near Lake Van, within the greater region known as Ararat.

11:49   Arabic *inna al-'aqiba lil-muttaqin*: literally, "the outcome belongs to those mindful of God."

11:50   I.e., their fellow countryman.

11:50   Arabic *in antum illa muftarun*: literally, "you are merely inventors [of gods]."

11:54   Arabic *anni bari' mimma tushrikun*: literally, "I am innocent of what you associate."

11:78   The implication seems clear: Lot wanted to commend his daughters as partners in preference to the guest messengers, males, whom his townsmen were intent on violating. But it is equally important to note that they were corrupt people "who before this had performed evil deeds." It is greed, selfishness, and inhospitality that marks these people, not their homosexuality.

11:83   Each stone had inscribed on it the person to be killed; parallel to 51:34.

11:88   Or "I only want to set things right."

11:101   Arabic *wa-ma zaduhum ghayra tatbib*: literally, "and increased them in nothing but ruin."

11:107   Arabic *fa''al lima yurid*: literally, "an Accomplisher of whatever He wishes."

11:108   The implication is that a higher reward exists for some of the most favored, to wit, those foremost in faith, noted in 56:10–11: "the foremost [in faith] shall be foremost [in place]; these will be nearest to God."

11:117   Some translators render *muslihun* as "reformers," but "righteous" seems to make better sense in this context.

Sura 12
Joseph (*Yusuf*)

12:1   On these disconnected letters, see *muqatta'at* in Glossary, page 531.

12:8   Arabic *wa-nahnu 'usba*: literally, "though we are a group."

12:9   Arabic *wajh abikum*: literally, "your father's face."

12:9   Arabic *wa-takunu min ba'dihi qawm salihin*: literally, "and after this, you can be a righteous people."

12:15   Arabic *wa-la yash'urun*: literally, "while they are not aware."

12:18   Arabic *bal sawwalat lakum anfusukum amr*: literally, "no, your souls have enticed you to a matter."

12:18   Arabic *fa-sabr jamil*: literally, "so patience is beautiful."

12:18   Arabic *tasifun*: literally, "you describe."

12:20   Arabic *darahim*: literally, "dirhams," a form of coinage.

12:26   Arabic *shahid min ahliha*: literally, "a witness from her family."

12:36   Arabic *min al-muhsinin*: literally, "one of those who do good."

12:41   Arabic *qudiya al-amr alladhi fihi tastaftiyan*: literally, "the matter has been decreed about which you both inquire."

12:52   Several translators attribute these words to the governor's wife but they do not make sense as such; Joseph specifically asked the king to question the women so that his name can be cleared.

12:54   Arabic *astakhlishu linafsi*: literally, "I may keep him for myself."

12:59   Benjamin.

12:61   Arabic *inna lafa'ilun*: literally, "we will certainly act."

12:102   This and the verses that follow are addressed to Muhammad.

Sura 13
Thunder (*Al-Ra'd*)

13:1   On these disconnected letters, see *muqatta'at* in Glossary, page 531.

13:14   Arabic *illa fi dalal*: literally, "nothing but in error or deviance."

13:38   Arabic *likull ajal kitab*: sometimes translated as "there is a decreed time for everything." See *ajal* in Glossary, page 529.

13:39   The phrase *umm al-kitab* means literally "the Mother of the Book," as also in 3:7. See Glossary, page 532.

Sura 14
Abraham (*Ibrahim*)

14:1   On these disconnected letters, see *muqatta'at* in Glossary, page 531.

14:2   Arabic *wa-wayl lil-kafirin min 'adhab shadid*: literally, "and woe to the unbelievers from a severe punishment."

14:9   'Ad and Thamud are the tribes to whom earlier prophets, Hud and Salih, had been sent, as recounted in 7:65–79.

14:9   Arabic *fa-raddu aydiyahum fi afwahihim*: literally, "then they placed their hands in their mouths."

14:12   Arabic *wa-'ala Allah falyatawakkal al-mutawakkilun*: literally, "and in God let all who trust, trust."

14:15   Arabic *wa-istaftahu wa khaba kull jabbar 'anid*: literally, "and they sought victory, and every obstinate tyrant was disappointed."

14:16   Arabic *ma' sadid*: literally, "purulent water," or pus mixed with blood.

14:19   Arabic *bi 'l-haqq*: literally, "with truth."

14:32   Arabic *wa-sakhkhara lakum al-fulk*: literally, "and He subjected the ships to you."

14:39   This is the sole verse where Isaac and Ishmael are mentioned together. 37:101–2 mention a son to be sacrificed, and commentators disagree about which of the two sons was to be sacrificed. Some give preference to Ishmael since there, like here, he is the first mentioned, though indirectly. The biblical story (Genesis 22:1–19) mentions only Isaac as a potential sacrifice.

14:43   Arabic *la yartaddu ilayhim tarfuhum*: literally, "their gaze not returning to them."

Sura 15
The Rocky Plain (*Al-Hijr*)

15:1   On these disconnected letters, see *muqatta'at* in Glossary, page 531.

15:4   Arabic *illa wa laha kitab ma'lum*: literally, "without its being decreed a fixed notice."

15:6   Arabic *innaka lamajnun*: literally, "you are possessed by jinn."

15:11   Arabic *ma ya'tihim min rasul illa kanu bihi yastahzi'un*: literally, "no messenger came to them that they did not mock."

15:13   Arabic *wa-qad khalat sunnat al-awwalin*: literally, "and the practice of the ancients had preceded [them]."

15:17   Arabic *shaitan rajim*: literally, "an accursed devil." This is the last part of an invocation, "I take refuge from the accursed devil," made before every recitation of the Qur'an.

15:18   A similar punishment, in parallel terms, is indicated for the "rebellious devil" in 37:7–10.

15:29   Similarly, it is the Archangel Gabriel who breathes God's spirit into Mary to form the child Jesus (see 66:12).

15:47   Arabic *ikhwan*: literally, "brothers."

15:54   Arabic *fa-bima tubashshirun*: literally, "about what do you give good news then?"

15:67   The angels who came to Lot were disguised as handsome boys, and the townspeople came with the intention of coercing them into being sexual partners.

15:70   Arabic *alam nanhaka 'an al-'alamin*: literally, "did we not forbid you from the worlds?" This phrase has been variously interpreted as Lot's people telling him not to interfere when they approached anyone with sexual motives or not to extend hospitality to any guests. Given the context, the former implication seems more plausible.

15:71   According to some commentators, as a last resort, Lot offers his own daughters in order to save the young men, whom he does not as yet apprehend to be angels. But "my daughters" could be interpreted more generically as referring to the women of the town, and as urging the townspeople to seek females in marriage.

15:78   The forest dwellers are thought to be the people of Midian, summoned by the prophet Shu'ayb (26:176–77).

15:80   An area north of Medina, linked to the tribe of Thamud, discussed in vv. 80–84.

15:87   The "seven much recited verses" are often thought to be the primary seven verses of the Qur'an, i.e., the seven verses of Sura 1, *al-Fatiha*, the Mother of the Book.

15:88   The same tender image of lowering one's wing is used in 17:24, with reference to protecting one's parents.

15:99   Arabic *hatta ya'tiyaka al-yaqin*: literally, "until the certainty (of death) comes to you."

Sura 16
The Bee (*Al-Nahl*)

16:2   Arabic *bi al-ruh min amrihi*: literally, "with the spirit by His command." See note for 16:102 and see also *ruh* in Glossary, page 532.

16:8   Arabic *wa zina*: literally, "as ornament."

16:10   Arabic *fihi tusimuna*: literally, "you graze in it."

16:25   Arabic *sa'a ma yazirun*: literally, "what they will bear is evil."

16:57   Arabic *wa-lahum ma yashtahun*: literally, "and to themselves what they desire"—i.e., sons. Ascribing daughters to God seems to refer to the goddesses of 53:19, prompting the alleged "Satanic verses" controversy.

16:59   A common practice among early-seventh-century Arabs, before the coming of Islam, was to bury unwanted female children in the sand, noted and critiqued in 81:8–9.

16:60   Most High (*A'la*) is one of the Beautiful Names, as well as the name of a Qur'anic sura, number 87.

16:62   That is, daughters rather than sons.

16:62   Sons are "the best things."

16:65   Arabic *ba'da mawtiha*: literally, "after its death."

16:74   Arabic *inna allaha ya'lamu wa-antum la ta'lamuna*: literally, "God knows and you do not know."

16:77   Arabic *wa-ma amru al-sa'ati*: literally, "and what is the command of the hour."

16:82   Arabic *al-balaghu al-mubinu*: literally, "the manifest message."

16:89   Arabic *shahidun 'alayhim min anfusihim*: literally, "a witness against them, from among themselves."

16:92   *Tafsir al-Jalalayn*, a classical Qur'anic commentary, speaks of a woman in Mecca who would weave her yarn all day and then undo it. Also, there is a famous precedent for this strategy in Homer's *Odyssey*, where Odysseus' wife, Penelope, wards off her suitors by telling them that she will make a decision concerning them when she has finished weaving a shroud for Odysseus' father, Laertes. She weaves it by day and unravels it by night.

16:98   This injunction has led to the practice of always renouncing Satan the accursed before reciting any sura or verse of the Qur'an.

16:101   The notion that God replaces one verse of the Qur'an with another, known technically as "abrogation," is a matter of great dispute. See *naskh* in Glossary, page 532. The burden of proof is on the interpreter, to understand each verse in context. See note for 2:106 and also 41:41–42, where it is declared that "it is a Book of great power that no falsehood might reach from any side."

16:102   The Archangel Gabriel, named as such here and also elsewhere (2:87, 253; 5:110; 16:2; 19:17; 40:15; 42:52; and 97:4), but not to be confused with the Holy Spirit linked to God the Father and God the Son in Christian belief. See *ruh al-quds* in Glossary, page 532.

16:103   The Arabic *a'ajami*, translated here as "a foreign tongue," literally means any language that is not Arabic, especially Persian. This may be a reference to scripture that the Prophet heard from Christians and Jews while he was still a merchant.

16:115   The command about forbidden food, combined with leniency for circumstances, is reiterated elsewhere in the Qur'an (2:173, 5:3, and 6:145–46).

16:118 See 6:146 for a parallel injunction.

16:126 Arabic *lahuwa khair lil-sabirin*: literally, "it will be better for those who are patient."

16:127 Arabic *wa-ma sabruka illa bi Allah*: literally, "and your patience is only in God."

Sura 17

The Night Journey (*Al-Isra'*)

17:1 In Arabic, "the farthest mosque" is Al-Masjid al-Aqsa. Revered by Muslims worldwide, it was constructed in the eighth century; nearby, a memorial to the Prophet's Ascent known as *Qubbat al-Sakhra*, or Dome of the Rock, was also built. Together they have become *al-Haram ash-Sharif*, the Holy Domain or the Temple Mount, marking Jerusalem as the third most sacred city in Islam, after Mecca and Medina.

17:2 The Book here is clearly the Torah, and what follows alludes to events depicted there.

17:4 It is unclear what events might be alluded to here, but certainly the destruction of the Temple in 70 CE seems likely, along with the catastrophes that followed it; see v. 7.

17:12 Compare with Sura 10:5, where the orderly succession of night and day is also invoked as a sign of God's care for humankind, and a means of calculating time.

17:13 The image of an invisible necklace measuring one's deeds calls to mind the frequent reference to a day of reckoning, when all actions are measured and sorted out as "good" or "evil"; see, e.g., 99:7–8.

17:24 See the same tender image in 15:88.

17:27 Arabic *al-shayatin*: literally, "the Satans or the devils." See *Shaytan* in Glossary, page 532.

17:30 Arabic *innahu kana bi-'ibadihi khabir basir*: literally, "He is All Aware and All Seeing of His servants."

17:33 On the day of reckoning.

17:40 On ascribing daughters to God, see note for 16:57.

17:51 Arabic *aw khalq mimma yakburu fi sudurikum*: literally, "or a creation of what is even greater in your breasts."

17:53 When speaking to people of religion.

17:59 See the extensive commentary on the people of Thamud elsewhere, e.g., 7:73–79 and 91:11.

17:60 The vision shown to the Prophet on the Night Journey; see v. 1.

17:60 See 37:62–65, where the tree of Zaqqum, created of fire, bears fronds like the heads of devils.

17:67 Arabic *man tad'una illa iyyahu*: literally, "whomever you invoke other than Him."

17:73 Other than a revelation.

17:76 Arabic *wa-in kadu layastafizzunaka min al-ard*: literally, "they were about to frighten you (to drive you) from the land."

17:77 The word *sunna*, here translated as "way," has come to represent the name for the majority Muslim community. Sunni Muslims are those who follow the *sunna*, or way of God, as also the *sunna* or way of the Prophet.

17:78 In Arabic the phrase *Qur'ana al-fajr* ("the Qur'an at dawn") is repeated here, just two lines after its previous usage.

17:79 This injunction connotes the special benefit of late night prayer (*tahajjud*). Even though it is supererogatory, it is said to have extraordinary power.

17:80 Arabic *adkhilni mudkhala sidq wa-akhrijni mukhraja sidq*: literally, "let me enter by a truthful entrance and leave by a truthful exit."

17:80 This language suggests a prayer by Muhammad before returning to Mecca on the Final Pilgrimage (630 CE), since it was then that the final Qur'anic sura was revealed to him: "When God's help comes and His victory . . ." (110:1).

17:84 Arabic *ahda sabil*: literally, "best guided to a path."

17:85 Arabic *al-ruh min amr rabbi*: literally, "the spirit is by the command of my Lord."

17:86 Arabic *la tajid laka bihi 'alayna wakil*: literally, "you would not find concerning it against Us an advocate."

17:92 Cf. Sura 34:9: "If We willed, We could make the earth swallow them, or fragments of the sky fall on them."

17:92 Cf. Sura 2:55: "And you said, 'Moses, we'll never believe in you until we see God, appearing.' Then the thunderbolt struck you, as you looked on."

17:101 These nine signs are never specified; they are also mentioned in 27:12.

17:104 Arabic *lafif*: literally, "motley crowd."

17:107 Arabic *lil-adhqan*: literally, "on their chins."

17:110 Arabic *al-asma' al-husna*: "the Beautiful Names" are laced throughout the Qur'an. See also 7:180, 20:8, and 59:24, as well as Glossary, page 530.

17:111 The Beautiful Name *Kabir*—(the Most) Great or Magnificent—provides the Qur'anic basis for the familiar phrase *Allahu Akbar*, God is the Greater, or Most Great. See also 4:34, 13:9, 22:62, 31:30, 34:23, and 40:12.

Sura 18
The Cave (*Al-Kahf*)

18:1 Arabic *'iwaj*: literally, "crookedness."

18:2 The Arabic *qayyim* is literally "straight," as translated here, but it can also mean "self-contained," with the same etymology as the Divine Name *Qayyum*: Self-Subsisting (2:255, 3:2, and 20:111).

18:2 Arabic *hasan*: literally, "good."

18:9 This is the first of three mysterious episodes that occur only here in the Qur'an:

the cave sleepers (vv. 9–26), Moses' encounter with a sly stranger (vv. 61–83), and the two-horned figure building a wall against Gog and Magog (vv. 84–99). The sweep of these stories evokes interstitial spaces: between death and rising from the dead, between two bodies of water (v. 61), between two mountain barriers (vv. 93–94). The interpretative possibilities stagger the imagination, leading mystics to see a spiritual depth that evokes what one observer, Norman O. Brown, calls the apocalypse of Islam. The cave dwellers here have been compared to the Seven Sleepers of Ephesus, but that narrative link only adds to the multitiered corridors of interpretative possibility for this verse and all that follows.

18:12 See v. 19 for an exchange between two parties concerning the length of time they had been sleeping the cave.

18:13 Arabic *naba'ahum bil-haqq*: literally, "their story in truth."

18:22 Arabic *rajm bil-ghaib*: literally, "casting stones at the unseen."

18:24 This is often taken to be the scriptural impetus for the everyday Muslim expression "if God wills."

18:25 This verse can be seen as a commentary on v. 22, which involves estimating the number of cave inhabitants. In other words, all such conjecture, whether about the cave dwellers or their length of stay, is guessing at what cannot be known.

18:26 This is one of many verses in the Qur'an that echo and register the Beautiful Names in multiple forms: as exclamatory phrases ("how clearly He Sees, how clearly He Hears"), as agentive noun ("no protector but Him"), and as object ("His judgment").

18:29 Arabic *wa-sa'at murtafaq*: literally, "and an evil resting place."

18:30 Arabic *man ahsana 'amal*: literally, "whoever does good."

18:33 The river metaphor in this parable anticipates, even as it parallels, the confluence of two waters in v. 61.

18:39 Arabic *ma sha'a Allah*: literally, "what God wills."

18:44 Arabic *al-haqq*: literally, "the truth."

18:45 Arabic *'ala kull shai' muqtadir*: literally, "the One Holding Sway over everything."

18:50 This is the only verse to identify Iblis as a jinn. Jinn recur in the Qur'an as both believers (46:29 and 72:14) and residents of hell (11:119). An entire sura (number 72) is dedicated to them, in which they attest to the truth of the Qur'an. See Glossary, page 531.

18:54 Some translate this as "more contentious than any other creature."

18:57 Arabic *ma qaddamat yadahu*: literally, "what his own hands have sent forth" (to be judged on the day of judgment).

18:61 Arabic *majma' al-bahrain*: literally, "the meeting of two waters," an echo of the river in v. 33, and also the point of separation as well as convergence between two persons. The mysterious stranger, not named here, has been identified through extensive commentary as al-Khidr, "the Green One," whose deep knowledge, or inner wisdom, contrasts with, even as it complements, the external wisdom conveyed to Moses through prophecy. The entire passage—vv. 60–82—has been the subject of extensive commentary, especially by Sufi masters who are also Qur'anic exegetes.

18:65 Arabic *wa-'allamnahu min ladunna 'ilm*: literally, "and We taught him a knowledge from within Us."

18:71 Arabic *hatta*: literally, "until."

18:71 Arabic *'akharaqtaha*: literally, "did you make the hole in it?"

18:78 Arabic *ta'wil*: literally, "interpretation." It signifies "deeper meaning" here as it often does elsewhere, especially in Joseph's dreams (see 12:6, 21, 36, 44, 45, 100 and 101).

18:81 Arabic *aqraba ruhm:* literally "nearer in affection."

18:83 Dhu al-Qarnain literally means "the two-horned." This figure serves as a symbol of power over disparate realms, East and West, and so many commentators have presumed it refers to Alexander the Great, also represented on his own coins with two horns. But the name's greatest significance may be the culmination of dyads, from the Cave Sleepers (between time) to the two travelers, Moses and al-Khidr (between water), and now the convergence of two mountains (v. 93) with only a pass between them.

18:91 This is the same expression used by al-Khidr to challenge Moses in v. 68, but here it becomes an affirmation, not a limitation: just as the knowledge of Moses did not encompass al-Khidr's actions, so Dhu al-Qarnayn is encompassed in all that he does by God's Knowledge.

18:94 Gog and Magog are also present in 21:96–97, and there as here they portend imminent destruction, so much so that many commentators have linked them to Mongols (Chinese warrior tribes) and to Tartars (Central Asian Turkic tribes).

18:109 Parallel to 31:27: "If all the trees on earth were pens, and the seas were ink, with seven more seas beyond, still the Word of God would not be exhausted."

Sura 19
Mary (*Maryam*)

19:1 On these disconnected letters, see *muqatta'at* in Glossary, page 531.

19:5 Arabic *wa-inni khiftu al-mawaliya min wara'i*: literally, "But I fear for my kin after me."

19:6 It is widely agreed that this "legacy" is not of wealth but prophethood. See also 3:38–39, which refers to God's granting Zachariah's prayer, and the angels giving him the good news that he would have a righteous son, a prophet.

19:7 The birth of John to his wife (Elizabeth, inferred but not named here) precedes the birth of Jesus in the Qur'an, as it does in the New Testament. See also 21:89–90.

19:8 The words "he said" are omitted here since the speaker is clearly Zachariah, and these words echo Abraham's words to the angel to the effect that Sarah is too old to conceive.

19:9   Arabic *min qabl*: literally, "from before (the time you were born)."

19:10   Arabic *sawiyya*: literally, "consecutively." Another common interpretation of *sawiya* is "[even though you are] sound or well," i.e. even though you are otherwise able to speak.

19:11   Cf. Sura 3:41 for a parallel passage: "Your sign is that you will not speak to people for three straight days, except by gestures." Here in Sura 19, the words "by gestures" are not explicitly stated in the original, only implied.

19:14   The word *al-jabbar*, translated here as "imperious," is also one of the ninety-nine Beautiful Names of God, usually translated as "The Compeller" (but we render as "The Irresistible" on page 536). See also v. 32, where the same attribute is imputed to Jesus; in both cases, it has a negative connotation.

19:18   The word "withdraw" is implied but not stated in the text.

19:27   Arabic *laqad ji'ti shai' fariy*: literally, "surely you've brought a terrible thing."

19:29   Arabic *ilayhi*: literally "to him."

19:34   Arabic *qawl al-haqq*: literally, "the true statement," as translated. This echoes 4:171: "Jesus, son of Mary, was but a messenger of God—His Word, conveyed to Mary, through His spirit."

19:37   Those who disbelieve or hide the truth will have their account reckoned or "witnessed" on the day of judgment.

19:43   Arabic *ma lam ya'tika*: literally, "which has not come to you."

19:50   Arabic *wa-ja'alna lahum lisan sidq 'aliy*: literally, "and We made for them a tongue of truth, exalted."

19:51   The distinction between "prophet" (*nabi*) and "messenger" (*rasul*) is based on function. While prophets were divinely inspired and taught what had already been revealed, messengers brought forth a new scripture from God. Therefore, every messenger was a prophet but not every prophet was a messenger. Hence, Moses was a messenger since he received the Torah, as was David since he received the Psalms, and Jesus also since he conveyed the Gospels. In contrast, Abraham, Solomon, and Idris were prophets but not messengers. Ishmael is the exception: while not bringing a book, he is lauded as both prophet and messenger (v. 54).

19:56   Idris is cited only here and in 21:85, where he is linked both to Ishmael and to Ezekiel.

19:84   Arabic *innama na'uddu lahum 'add*: literally, "We are only counting for them a (fixed) number." See *ajal* in Glossary, page 529.

Sura 20
Ta Ha (*Ta Ha*)

20:1   On these disconnected letters, see *al- muqatta'at* in Glossary, page 531. Unlike other such letters, these two, *ta* and *ha*, may indicate an abbreviated address: "O man," according to some early commentaries cited in Muhammad Asad, *The Message of the Qur'an* (Watsonville, Calif.: The Book Foundation, 2003), 525n1.

20:12 This valley, mentioned only here and in 79:16, is assumed to be near Mount Sinai.

20:25 Arabic *sadri*: literally, "my chest" or "my breast."

20:27 Arabic *wa-hlul 'uqda min lisani*: literally, "and untie the knot in my tongue."

20:40 The narrative of Moses in this verse is elaborated elsewhere (28:12–28), where characters, events, and places are explained.

20:70 Arabic *ulqiya*: literally, "were thrown down."

20:85 "Samiri" seems to refer to the Samaritans, but this group did not exist in Moses' time, so it may be a reference to strangers who joined the Jews fleeing Egypt.

20:87 Likely the spoils taken from the Egyptians; see Exodus 12:35–36.

20:99 Arabic *wa-qad atainaka min ladunna dhikr*: literally, "and We gave you a remembrance from within us." This passage is parallel to 18:65 ("and whom we had taught from Our Knowledge"), where the original Arabic *wa 'allamnahu min ladunna 'ilm* literally translates as "and We taught him a knowledge from within Us."

20:102 Arabic *zurq*: literally, "blue," but in this case with fear.

20:104 The play on perception of time is randomized: all life seems like ten days to the sinners, a single day to the wise.

20:107 Arabic *la tara fiha 'iwaj wa-la amt*: literally, "you will see in it neither crookedness nor curve."

20:110 An echo of 2:255, *Ayat al-Kursi*, the Verse of the Throne.

20:111 Again, the Beautiful Names are the same two as found in 2:255, *Ayat al-Kursi*: "God—there is no god but He, the Living, the Self-Subsisting."

20:129 Arabic *wa-lawla kalima sabaqat*: literally, "had it not been for a preceding word."

Sura 21
The Prophets (*Al-Anbiya'*)

21:4   Arabic *qala*: literally, "He said," yet both here and in v. 112, it seems preferable to translate as though it were a second-person-singular imperative: *qul*. The audience here, as elsewhere, is the Prophet Muhammad, though in a few instances of the more than three hundred in the Qur'an, *qul* can be used to address all believers (2:136, 3:84, 29:20, and 112:1).

21:19 Arabic *man 'indahu*: literally, "those with Him," which could refer to the angels or to those nearest him among the devout (56:11).

21:26 The reference here is to angels, whom the Meccans regarded as the daughters of God, elevated to a status comparable to that which Christians ascribe to Jesus.

21:28   The theme of omniscience and omnipotence, extending even to intercessory capability, echoes several Qur'anic verses, especially 2:255, *Ayat al-Kursi* (the Verse of the Throne).

21:33   Arabic *yasbahun*: literally, "they swim."

21:47   Arabic *wa-kafa bina hasibin*: literally, "We are sufficient as Reckoners," but carrying the sense of proficiency.

21:64   Another reading would be "They turned to reflect upon themselves."

21:65   Arabic *nukisu 'ala ru'usihim*: literally, "they were turned upside down on their heads." It is not clear whether they confirmed their disbelief or were convinced by Abraham's argument.

21:68   Arabic *in kuntum fa'ilin*: literally, "if you are doers (of what you deem to be correct)." One group of idolaters seems to be inciting another group.

21:91   Arabic *fiha*: literally, "in her," meaning Mary. For ease of expression, the order of the original is reversed; in Arabic the clause reads literally, "As for the one who preserved her chastity, We breathed into her of Our spirit."

21:95   Arabic Arabic *la yarji'un*: literally, "they will not return."

21:96   Gog and Magog are distant figures linked elsewhere to Dhu al-Qarnain, or Alexander, in 18:94. These legendary, "twin" giants are perhaps from Mongolia, though some commentators trace them to Turkic or Chinese ancestry.

21:105 This or similar phraseology is found four times in Psalm 37 (vv. 9, 11, 29, 34), as well as in Matthew 5:5.

21:112 Arabic *qala*: literally, "He said," but better "Say." See note to 21:4.

Sura 22
The Pilgrimage (*Al-Hajj*)

22:1   This word is famously used in John Donne's "A Valediction: Forbidding Mourning" to refer to the colossal movements of the planetary spheres, movements that are far larger than mere earthquakes; it seems especially apt in this context. Some Islamic commentators see this global convulsion, before the sun rises from the West (not the East), as one of the major signs of the end of the world.

22:6   The word *al-haqq* is usually translated as "the truth." But what appears to be indicated is that God is the ultimate reality, the ultimate ground of the reality of all things.

22:13   Arabic *darruhu aqrabu min naf'ihi*: literally, "one who is closer to harm than benefit."

22:15   There are several interpretations of this passage. Some commentators view "him" as the Prophet, referring to the fact that certain tribes allied with him were dubious as to whether he would receive God's help. Others think the verse refers to Muslims who were beginning to grow impatient for God's help.

22:17   Magians is the Arabic term for Zoroastrians.

22:25   The Arabic *al-badi*, translated here as "visitors," usually refers to pastoral nomads (e.g., see 33:20).

22:29   Here, as in v. 33, the "ancient house" refers to the Ka'ba.

22:30   Arabic *illa ma yutla 'alaykum*: literally, "except what has been recited to you."

22:32   The phrase "rituals of God" refers to not only the rites of the pilgrimage but also the places and actions linked to each of its successive stages.

22:39   This verse is the earliest pronouncement of what became the principle of self-defense in Islamic law, not invoked until after Muhammad had left Mecca for Medina in 622 CE (1 AH), the *hijra* or exodus. Sura 2:190–94, which also permits fighting in self-defense, was revealed about a year later.

22:45   Arabic *qasr mashid*: literally, "lofty palaces."

22:47   This bears comparison with Psalm 90:4: "A thousand years in your sight are like a day that has just gone by, or like a watch in the night" (New International Version).

22:58   To reinforce this notion, the next seven verses (59–65) have collocative Beautiful Names, each amplifying the message of how God is the Best Provider.

Sura 23
The Believers (*Al-Mu'minun*)

23:14   Arabic *khalq akhar*: literally, "another creature."

23:17   Arabic *sab'a tara'iq*: literally, "seven paths," but these paths refer to the orbits of the seven heavenly spheres or heavens (as elsewhere in the Qur'an: see 67:3 and 71:15).

23:20   Mount Sinai is the title and topic of Sura 52, but its full name is given only here and in Sura 95 where it is also linked to "the blessed olive tree," central to *ayat an-nur*, the Verse of Light (24:35).

23:21   There is a similar tribute to livestock in 16:5: "He created cattle for you, giving you warmth and other uses; you consume them for food."

23:53   Arabic *kull hizb bima ladayhim farihun*: literally, "each faction rejoicing in what they themselves have." This judgment applies to Muslims as well as to Jews and Christians, according to a well-known saying of the Prophet: "Jews have been divided into seventy-one sects, Christians into seventy-two, while my community will be divided into seventy-three."

23:60   This phrase echoes 8:2: "True believers are those whose hearts tremble in awe at the mention of God."

23:93   Arabic *imma turiyanni*: literally, "if you show me."

23:109   Arabic *khair al-rahimin*: literally, "the Best of those who show mercy"; also in v. 118.

Sura 24
Light (*Al-Nur*)

24:3   *Nikah* is contractual marriage within Islam, but here is an unusual instance where it clearly refers to those bonded in marriage outside Islam, with the adulterers being linked to polytheists—hence, both are outside Islam.

24:9   This is a private, nonjuridical procedure, designed to preserve marital harmony.

24:10   This conditional phrase is repeated four times in two sequences in this sura, with the echo for v. 10 coming in v. 14 and for v. 20 in v. 21.

24:11   This begins an extended Qur'anic revelation (vv. 11–20) that defends the Prophet's young wife, 'A'isha, against lies that were brought against her by some of the early Muslims, here defined as "liars in the eyes of God." The incident, known as "the affair of the lie," occurred in 627 CE when 'A'isha was left behind as a Muslim expeditionary force broke camp early, departing without her. Because a companion later found her and returned her to the Prophet, some rumors spread, occasioning this revelation to confirm her innocence as also the malevolence of those who brought the false charges.

24:15   Arabic *idh talaqqawnahu bialsinatikum*: literally, "when you received it with your tongues."

24:28   Arabic *azka*: literally, "purer."

24:31   Eunuchs or old men.

24:31   A reference to the anklets that women often wore.

24:33   Among pre-Islamic practices was the use of female slaves as prostitutes.

24:35   This verse has enjoyed a rich history of interpretation over the centuries. The "Light" has been variously interpreted as signifying divine guidance, knowledge, or power. Significantly, the verse stresses twice that God speaks in parables.

24:35   The word "soil" is introduced here for poetic effect. It does not alter the meaning.

24:37   See 14:42–43 for an expansion of this image: "till a day when their eyes will stare [in horror], racing forward, their heads craned back, their gaze fixed rigid, and their hearts void."

24:60   Arabic *la yarjuna nikah*: literally, "who have no desire for marriage."

24:61   Arabic *ma malaktum mafatihahu*: literally, "for which you own the keys."

Sura 25
The Criterion (*Al-Furqan*)

25:1   *Furqan* (criterion) is another name for revelation in general and the Qur'an in particular. See Glossary, page 530.

25:8   *Janna* (garden) is the same word as "paradise," hence this is a sarcastic comment.

25:15   Arabic *masir*: literally, "destiny."

25:20   That is, can you be patient when facing adversity or ridicule or rejection from unbelievers?

25:22	Another reading would be: "The angels will declare, 'None shall pass beyond this forbidden barrier.'"
25:28	A more literal translation would be "Woe unto me," but that seems too archaic.
25:30	Arabic *ittakhadhu hadha al-Qur'an mahjur*: literally, "have taken this Qur'an as a forsaken thing."
25:32	Both here and in 17:106, the process of revelation is depicted as piecemeal yet continuous. In 73:4, the same deliberate and measured process of recitation is enjoined on the Prophet.
25:38	These are pre-Islamic Arabian tribes who denied previous prophets, mentioned elsewhere in the Qur'an.
25:39	There is a clear contrast between God's lessons, here offered, and those offered above by the disbelievers (vv. 9 and 33).
25:40	Arabic *matar al-saw'i*: literally, "evil rain," referring to Sodom.
25:53	The word rendered as "barrier" is a Persian word, *barzakh*, in the original. See also 23:100 and Glossary, page 530.
25:56	Arabic *wa-nadhir*: literally, "and as a warner," but that expression is unidiomatic in English.

Sura 26
The Poets (*Al-Shu'ara*)

26:1	On these disconnected letters, see *muqatta'at* in Glossary, page 531.
26:9	This doublet of the Divine Names appears no less than eight more times in this sura—vv. 68, 104, 122, 140, 159, 175, 191, and 217—in similar sequence, an echo of the same protocol in Sura 55.
26:14	Moses had inadvertently killed an Egyptian. See below.
26:20	Moses is referring to an incident of false accusation, then further connivance to impugn him among the Egyptians. It is elaborated elsewhere, in 28:15–21.
26:30	Arabic *bishai' mubin*: literally, "something clear."
26:51	Arabic *awwal al-mu'minin*: literally, "the first believers."
26:58	The reference here seems to be the prosperity the Egyptians had enjoyed under Pharaoh, with the promise in the next verse (v. 59) that Israelites would be their eventual successors in kind once they completed their escape to a new home.
26:74	Arabic *wujudna aba'ana kadhalika yaf'alun*: literally, "we found our forefathers doing this."
26:88	Arabic *banun*: literally, "sons."
26:128	The word *aya* literally means "sign." Here it refers to a place of worship, so it's translated as "altar." See Glossary, page 530.
26:138	Arabic *wa-ma nahnu bimu'adhdhabin*: literally, "we are not the ones to be punished."

26:152   The reference here is to a bedrock element of Islamic ethics, *maslaha*, or the common, collective good.

26:158   The punishment predicted by Salih.

26:173   Arabic *fa-sa'a matar*: literally, "evil was the rain."

26:193   The Archangel Gabriel.

26:215   For a similar image, see 17:24: "lower over them both the wing of humility, with mercy."

26:224   This is the first, and sole, reference to poets in the sura named "The Poets." For deeper exegesis on the ambiguity of poetry in relation to Qur'anic discourse, see "About This Translation," pages xxxiii–xxxvii.

26:225   A metaphor to contrast the precision of Qur'anic rhetoric with the meanderings of poets.

Sura 27
The Ants (*Al-Naml*)

27:1   On these disconnected letters, see *muqatta'at* in Glossary, page 531.

27:5   Arabic *su' al-'adhab*: literally, "an evil torment."

27:8   The fire is here understood to be the Light of God.

27:10   The Arabic word for snake, *jann*, is a play on the word *jinn*. See 28:31 for the identical expression.

27:12   Arabic *fi jaybika*: literally, "in your pocket," referring to the opening in the cloak by his breast.

27:16   The phrase *mantiq at-tayr* has become a popular trope in Muslim spirituality, due to a Sufi poem of that title penned by the twelfth-century master Farid ud-din Attar, and known in English as "The Conference of the Birds."

27:18   The subtlety of this reference to ants must be underscored. Like bees and spiders, ants also are honored with a sura named after them because in their minute labor they mirror the marvel of divine creation. Solomon's appreciation for ants, and then birds, is deemed to be a measure of his own wisdom.

27:20   The hoopoe is the central figure, equivalent to a messenger from the unseen (Jabril/Gabriel), in Attar's "The Conference of the Birds."

27:22   Arabic *ahattu bima lam tuhit bihi*: literally, "I have encompassed what you have not encompassed."

27:22   *Saba'* is Sheba in English, and what follows is the encounter of Solomon with the Queen of Sheba. Solomon is clearly confronting her on account of the solar worship of her followers, the Sabians.

27:30   This is the sole passage in the Qur'an where the *basmala* is included in a verse not at the beginning of a sura.

27:31   Arabic *muslimin*: literally, "ones who have submitted"—i.e., "muslims," but here in a more general sense. See note to 27:91 and *muslim* in Glossary, page 531.

27:39   An *'ifrit* belongs to a class of jinn who are winged creatures, noted for their ruthlessness, power, and cunning, as well as their large size.

27:39   Before Solomon would rise at midday from his duties adjudicating.

27:40   Arabic *qabla an yartadd ilaika tarfuka*: literally, "before your own gaze returns to you."

27:45   See parallel reference in 11:61: "And to the people of Thamud We sent their brother Salih." The Thamud were said to be descendants of Noah. While not mentioned in the Bible, they appear repeatedly in the Qur'an: see also 7:73–79 and 26:141–58.

27:55   For the story of Lot and his recalcitrant people, see also 7:80–84, 11:77–83, and 15:61–79.

27:58   Arabic *sa'a matar*: literally, "evil was the rain."

27:61   Arabic *hajiz,* parallel to the Persian *barzakh* ("buffer" or "limit") as in 55:20. See *barzakh* in Glossary, page 530.

27:82   Arabic *dabba*: literally, "crawling or walking creature," often speculated to be a wild animal portending the end of the world and the day of judgment.

27:89   This phrase echoes the refrain of 55:60: "What is the reward for goodness beyond goodness?"

27:91   Arabic *min al-muslimin*: literally, "among the submitters." This group includes all those linked to the example of Abraham; see 4:125: "Who is better in religion than one who submits his entire self to God, does what is good, and follows the creed of Abraham, the pure in faith?" Here, as in vv. 31 and 38, Islam is implied but not stated since it did not exist as a formal religion at the time of Moses, Solomon, or Sheba—who are, along with Salih and Lot, the principal subjects of this sura. See *islam* in Glossary, page 531.

Sura 28
The Story (*Al-Qasas*)

28:1   On these disconnected letters, see *muqatta'at* in Glossary, page 531.

28:3   Arabic *bi al-haqq*: literally, "with the truth." This phrase is used both to refer to God and the Book below in three verses (vv. 48, 53, and 75). See Glossary, page 530.

28:4   Arabic *innahu kana min al-mufsidin*: literally, "he was among those who spread corruption."

28:6   Arabic *nuriya*: literally, "We might show."

28:6   Haman was the chief minister of Pharaoh.

28:11   Arabic *qussihi*: literally, "follow him."

28:13   The story of Moses the castaway child, recovered by an Egyptian, then returned to his mother and nurtured by her, is also recounted in 20:37–40, with parallels to Exodus 2:1–10.

28:15   This story is also noted in 20:40, with parallels to Exodus 2:11–15.

28:19   Arabic *min al-muslihin*: literally, "among those who promote the collective good."

28:20   Arabic *inni laka min al-nasihin*: literally, "I am among those who give you good advice."

28:22   The Arabs of Midian (also known as Madyan) were closely related to the Hebrews.

28:27   Arabic *fa-min 'indika*: literally, "that is from (within) you."

28:29   Arabic *inni anastu nar la'alli atikum minha bikhabar*: literally, "I saw a (distant) fire; perhaps I might bring you from it some news"—i.e., about which direction they might take on their journey.

28:32   Those who have fear raise their hand for protection.

28:35   This account of Moses' call, and God's direct speech to him, also occurs in 20:9–23, 26:10–68, and 27:7–14, with differing details and emphases in each narrative.

28:44   That is, Mount Sinai.

28:46   The repetition of the call to Moses on Mount Sinai underscores the intent of mercy which follows, and the recurrent emphasis on truth, harking back to v. 3.

28:47   The sentence seems to be deliberately incomplete: before they finish one line of argument, the disbelievers shift to another in the following verse (v. 48).

28:49   This is a challenge to the Quraysh similar to what is found elsewhere, e.g., 2:23 and 17:88.

28:53   The Word, the Book, the truth—all confirmed the right response for those listeners already inclined to submit (to God's will). Here again *muslimun* is better not translated as "Muslims." See note to 27:9 and *islam* in Glossary, page 531.

28:57   That is, a safe sanctuary in Mecca.

28:58   This is an invocation of the Beautiful Name *Warith* (Heir) in the plural. See also 15:23.

28:59   *Umm* here refers to Mecca, which is considered to be the "mother"—i.e., the center or capital—of towns around it.

28:70   Arabic *fi al-ula wa al-akhira*: literally, "in the first [world] and the last."

28:76   Korah (Qarun) is elsewhere linked to both Pharaoh and Haman; see 29:39 and 40:23–25.

28:77   Arabic *la tansa nasibaka min al-dunya*: literally, "do not forget your portion in this world," but also to share with others through charity and good works.

28:80   Arabic *illa al-sabirin*: literally "except those who are patient."

28:81   Arabic *fi'a*: literally, "party" or "group."

28:85   Arabic *ma'ad*: literally, "a place of return," which may refer to Mecca, since this verse, like most of the sura, was revealed on the *hijra*, or exodus, from Mecca to Medina. But it could also allude to the ultimate place of return, the next world.

Sura 29

The Spider (Al-'Ankabut)

29:1   On these disconnected letters, see *muqatta'at* in Glossary, page 531.

29:5   *Ajal* is the term used to refer to the time when each person is destined to die; no one can add to, or subtract from, the days allotted for their life. See Glossary, page 529.

29:6   Arabic *laghaniyy' an al-'alamin;* literally "without need of the worlds," where the "worlds" implies His creation or His created beings.

29:10   Arabic *al-'alamin:* literally, "worlds," as in v. 6, but here rendered as "creatures" to capture the idiom in English. See Glossary, page 529.

29:15   Arabic *li al-'alamin:* literally "for the worlds" but here connoting "for nations." See Glossary, page 529.

29:25   Arabic *yakfuru ba'dukum biba'd wa-yal'an ba'dukum ba'd:* literally, "some of you will deny others and some of you will curse others."

29:35   Arabic *minha:* literally, "of it."

29:41   The instance of the spider echoes the bee and the ant, other small creatures whose industry is heralded and recalled as the title of the sura in which they appear.

29:69   Arabic *fina:* literally, "in Us."

Sura 30
The Byzantines (*Al-Rum*)

30:1   On these disconnected letters, see *muqatta'at* in Glossary, page 531.

30:4   The earlier defeat of the Byzantines by the Persians had been hailed by the Meccans as a victory for pagans over the Christians, but it was not in God's plan that the Persians should prevail, save for a short time (a few years).

30:11   The creative and re-creative agency of God is accented throughout the Qur'an but repeatedly within different registers in this sura: see vv. 19, 40, 50, and 54.

30:13   Arabic *bishuraka'ihim:* literally "in their partners," but translated as "in these gods" to clarify the sense that the partners are associated with God.

30:18   These are the verses that established the hours and names for the daily ritual prayers incumbent upon all Muslims.

30:22   Coupled with 5:48, where differences in laws and revelations is a divine decree, we have here the strongest Qur'anic affirmation for linguistic and ethnic difference as a sign for those who can, and should, discern them.

30:28   Arabic *al-ayat:* literally, "the signs." Since they refer to God, they are marked as "Our signs." See Glossary, page 530.

30:30   Arabic *al-dinu al-qayyimu:* literally, "the steadfast faith." Here and in v. 43, it is equivalent to "the religion of truth" (9:33) and "the religion of God" (24:2). See *din* in Glossary, page 530.

30:30   Arabic *fitrat Allah:* literally, "the primordial nature of God," also echoed in the title of Sura 35, *al-Fatir* or "The Originator."

30:51   Arabic *min ba'dihi yakfurun:* literally, "they would continue to disbelieve after this."

30:53 *muslimun* is best translated as "those who submit [to the will of God]." See Glossary, page 531.

Sura 31
Luqman (*Luqman*)

31:1   On these disconnected letters, see *muqatta'at* in Glossary, page 531.

31:6   This may refer to al-Nadr ibn al-Harith, who diverted the attention of the Quraysh from the Qur'an using old Persian tales. The Arabic literally talks about someone who "buys" idle tales; some commentators say that the verse refers to a man who bought a maidservant to sing songs. Since the verb *yashtari* connotes business transactions, it is translated here as "who invests."

31:7   The Arabic word for "deafness," *waqr*, as pointed out by several commentators, means "heaviness." It's also used in 41:44.

31:16 Arabic *mithqal habba*: literally, "the weight of a mustard seed."

31:19 This line refers not to the pace at which one should walk but rather the demeanor of arrogance or modesty expressed in one's mode of walking.

31:19 Arabic *al-hamir*: literally, "of asses."

31:20 The "illuminating book," here as elsewhere, alludes to the Qur'an.

31:21 Arabic *ma wajadna 'alayhi aba'ana*: literally, "what we found our fathers on."

31:27 Arabic *kalimat*: literally "the words," but here emphasized as "the Word."

Sura 32
Prostration (*Al-Sajda*)

32:1   On these disconnected letters, see *muqatta'at* in Glossary, page 531.

32:3   Arabic *ma 'atahum min nadhir min qablika*: literally, "whom no one came to warn before you."

32:9   Arabic *al-af'ida*: literally, "hearts."

32:16 Arabic *junubuhum*: literally, "their sides."

Sura 33
The Allied Forces (*Al-Ahzab*)

33:4   Arabic *tudhahirun minhunna ummahatikum*: literally, "you made them appear like your mothers." This challenges a pre-Islamic practice of divorce that equated the wife with the mother's back—i.e., here wives are treated as "mothers." See 58:2, where the same practice is cited and eschewed.

33:4   The reference here is to a freed slave who became part of Muhammad's family.

33:5   Arabic *mawalikum*: literally "allies," "protectors," or "patrons."

33:6   Blood relatives alone should inherit; but one can still do one's friend a kindness by leaving them something in one's will.

33:9   This attack refers to the Battle of the Trench, which took place in 627 CE; it was the last major battle before the conquest of Mecca in 630.

33:13   Yathrib was the pre-Islamic name for Medina, where Muhammad settled after the *hijra* (exodus from Mecca) in 622 CE. The name was later changed to *al-Madina al-Munawwara*, i.e., City of Light.

33:20   The "allied forces" is the coalition arrayed against the Muslims at the Battle of the Trench in 627 CE (also known as the Battle of the Allied Forces, after which this sura is named). This coalition of Arab and Jewish tribes engaged in a twenty-seven-day siege of the town of Yathrib (later known as Medina), where the Muslims were enclosed.

33:20   It is implied that they would feel safe in the desert.

33:23   Their vow to fight until they win or die; the implication is that they died.

33:25   It is said that God repulsed the disbelievers (the Banu Qurayza) with a sandstorm.

33:37   The reference here is to Zayd, the adopted son of the Prophet. The Prophet married him to his own cousin Zaynab, but after Zayd divorced her, she became the Prophet's wife. This verse explains that the marriage is legitimate since adopted sons do not entail a blood relationship.

33:40   The "seal of the prophets" underscores Muhammad's status as the final messenger of God.

33:49   Arabic *'idda*: literally "reckoning"; in this case, the waiting period is the six months that is obligatory for a man who wants a divorce to ensure that the wife is not pregnant (see also 2:226–28).

33:55   The intent is to allow them to speak directly with close male relatives absent a protective screen, required otherwise (v. 53).

33:72   The notion of moral responsibility or trust as distinctive to humankind echoes the message of 59:21: "Had We sent down this Qur'an upon a mountain, you would have seen it humbled, cleave itself into a chasm, in fear of God." Yet, as the next verse goes on to say, not all humankind proved worthy of that trust, only believing men and women, those to whom "God is Forgiving, Ever Merciful."

Sura 34
Sheba (*Saba'*)

34:16   Likely the Ma'rib dam in Yemen.

34:19   They wished to flaunt their camels and possessions while traveling through the desert.

34:20   In 7:16–17, Iblis vowed to lie in wait for Adam's descendants, promising God: "You will find that most of them are not grateful to You."

34:26   Arabic *al-Fattah*: literally, "the Opener" or "the Decider." This is another Beautiful Name with multiple meanings, but here it is best rendered as "Judge."

34:33   Arabic *ta'murunana*: literally, "you were commanding us."

34:51   From the grave.

34:52   The "distant place" clearly refers to their life in this world.

34:54   A judgment repeated elsewhere: see 11:62, 110; and 14:9.

Sura 35
The Originator (*Fatir*)

35:10   Arabic *al-kalim al-tayyib*: literally, "good words."

35:18   Arabic *wa-la tazir wazira wizr ukhra*: literally, "no bearer of burdens can bear another's burden."

35:18   Arabic *bi al-ghaib*: literally, "in the unseen."

35:24   Arabic *illa khala fiha nadhir*: literally, "except there has been in it a warner."

35:37   Arabic *yatadhakkar fihi man tadhakkar*: literally, "for those who would be warned to be warned."

35:39   In 2:30 Adam is designated as God's regent.

35:39   This phrase is repeated in the Arabic, but its repetition would be too cumbersome in English.

Sura 36
Ya Sin (*Ya Sin*)

36:1   *Ya Sin*, according to many commentators, may be an abbreviated exclamation, with *sin* alluding to *insan* and meaning "O Human," or, in the rendition of Muhammad Asad: "O Thou Human Being" (Asad, *The Message of the Qur'an*: [Watsonville, Calif.: The Book Foundation, 2003], 758*n*1).

36:11   Regarding "unseen," see *al-ghaib* in Glossary, page 530.

36:14   These messengers are likely Moses and Jesus, each representing a scripture, first the Torah, then the Gospels.

36:18   Arabic *wa-layamassannakum minna 'adhab alim*: literally, "and a painful punishment from us will surely touch you."

36:26   Paradise, frequently evoked as a garden, contrasts with the Garden of Eden, fraught with peril as well as food. The garden of paradise anticipates the presence of God, where peace reigns.

36:42   Arabic *ma yarkabun*: literally, "which they ride."

36:46   Arabic *wa-ma ta'tihim min aya min ayat rabbihim illa kanu 'anha mu'ridin*: literally, "and no sign ever comes to them from the signs of their Lord except from it they turn away."

36:52   There is a mandatory pause here in the Arabic, indicating that the subsequent lines comprise a reply to the question just posed; but since this pause is not replicable in English, "A voice will answer" has been added.

36:63   The suffering of self-realization, experienced by sinners who deny God in this life, is a foretaste of the hell to come in the next world.

36:69   The Qur'an repeatedly denies its own status as poetry, though *saj'* or rhymed prose is commended. See "About This Translation," pages xxxiii–xxxvii.

36:75   Arabic *jund muhdarun*: literally, "an army present [to defend them]."

36:77   Again, the use of *insan* here seems to justify Muhammad Asad's decision to label

Ya Sin as an anticipation of the direct address in all that follows "O You Human." We have not followed his initiative due to the familiarity of the Arabic title for all Muslims.

Sura 37
Arrayed in Ranks (*Al-Saffat*)

37:1   Most commentators deem these first three verses as referring to angels; see v. 8.

37:5   Arabic *rabb al-mashariq*: literally, "Lord of the easts," but clearly evoking places where the sun rises.

37:19   See v. 2 and Sura 79.13 for the same image.

37:21   There is a mandatory pause here in the Arabic, indicating that the subsequent lines comprise a reply to the question just posed; but since this pause is not replicable in English, "A voice will say" has been added.

37:23   Arabic *sirat al-jahim*: literally, "path of hell," which rhymes with its opposite *al-sirat al-mustaqim,* "the straight path" (see 1:6).

37:26   The Arabic *mustaslimun* could be translated as "they seek to become Muslims," but that rendition would be anachronistic, as often noted above (e.g., note for 2:128), since the revelation is addressed to idolaters in a period before Islam had coalesced as a denominated movement.

37:28   Arabic *innakum kuntum ta'tunana 'an al-yamini*: literally, "it was you who would come to us from the right"—i.e., from a position claiming authority and influence.

37:49   Arabic *bayd maknun*: literally, "hidden eggs." Some translations render this as "hidden eggs [of ostriches]," often associated with beautiful women in Arabic poetry. See 56:23 for a parallel image in a similar eschatological setting.

37:62   A tree distinctive to hell, whose fronds cause great pain and disgust. See also 44.43 and 56.52.

37:75   Arabic *fa-lani 'ma al-mujibun*: literally, "how excellent are the responders."

37:79   Arabic *fi al-'alamin*: literally, "in all the worlds" or "in all the universe."

37:83   Arabic *min shi'atihi*: literally, "of his party."

37:97   Arabic *bunyan*: literally, "a structure."

37:102   Sources disagree about whether it was Isaac or Ishmael who was to be sacrificed, but the main point here is the son's willingness to be sacrificed. See also the notes to 14:39 and 37:101–2.

37:107   The sacrifice was the ram, said to be brought from God, the Unseen.

37:141   According to tradition, the ship's crew believed that the tempest that capsized the ship was due to divine wrath on account of misbehavior by one of its passengers. Jonah, who had disobeyed God when he fled Nineveh, was singled out; see also 21:87–88.

Sura 38
Sad (*Sad*)

38:1   On this and other disconnected letters, see *muqatta' at* in Glossary, page 531.

38:3   Arabic *wa-lata hin manas*: literally, "but there was no time to escape."

38:6   Arabic *inna hadha lashai' yurad*: literally, "this was certainly something to be desired."

38:7   Arabic *fi al-milla al-akhira*: literally, "in the last religion." Possibly, a reference to Christianity or a later form of pre-Islamic Arab paganism.

38:10   Arabic *asbab*: literally, "ropes'" or "bonds," as in 2:166, but also "paths" as in 40:36–37.

38:12   Sometimes translated as "tent posts," this is likely a reference to the remains of Pharaoh's monumental buildings, or to his practice of impaling his victims; see 7:137 and 89:10.

38:13   Probably a reference to the people of Midian who rejected the prophet Shu'ayb (26:176–89 as well as 15:78–79 and 50:14).

38:21   The "two litigants" are most likely angels sent to David after his contrivance to have Uriah, one of his soldiers, killed in battle so that he could marry Uriah's wife, Bathsheba. The full story, as related in 2 Samuel 11, does not appear in the Qur'an, but its sequel is clearly the topic here.

38:23   Arabic *wa-'azzani fi al-khitab*: literally, "and he dominated me in speech."

38:24   According to some commentators David realizes the similarity between this scenario and his own action in desiring another man's wife to add to the many wives he already had. Other commentators dispute this occurrence and state that David's "lapse" was his failing to account for both sides in the dispute before arbitrating.

38:25   Arabic *ma'ab*: literally, "place of return."

38:32   Arabic *hatta tawarat bil-hijab*: literally, "until they were hidden behind the veil" or "behind the barrier."

38:33   The sparse Qur'anic text suggests that both David and Solomon were tested in their obedience to God over their love of His creation.

38:38   See 21:82–83 for a similar depiction of devils obeying Solomon, while in 34:12–13 it is they who obey him.

38:44   According to commentators, this is a clear reference to God's willingness to forgive those who make oaths in haste (5:88); in this case, Job's pledge to beat his wife after she blasphemed is "fulfilled," without causing harm to her.

38:48   Arabic *Dhu al-Kifl*, also used in 21:85, and thought to be either Ezekiel or Elijah.

38:81   Arabic *ila yawm al-waqt al-ma'lum*: literally, "until the day of the known time."

Sura 39
The Crowds (*Al-Zumar*)

39:2   Arabic *mukhlis lahu al-din*: literally, "sincere to Him in religion."

39:6   Arabic *thamaniya*: literally, "eight."

39:6   On the three stages of darkness, see 22:5.

39:23   Arabic *mathaniya*: literally, "doubled." See 15:87.

39:36   Arabic *bi alladhina min dunihi*: literally, "with others besides Him."

39:39   Arabic *i'malu 'ala makanatikum*: literally, "act according to your standpoint."

39:42   The sense of this verse, that each night we die, and each morning are either restored or kept by God, is paralleled in 6:60: "It is He Who calls back your souls by night, knowing all you have done by day; then, He raises you up, to fulfill the appointed term. To Him you shall return—then He will inform you of all you have done."

39:45   Arabic *Allah wahdahu*: literally, "God alone."

39:74   Arabic *al-ard*: literally, "the land" or "the earth." But "realm" seems preferable here since it needs to be stressed that the location is paradise, not the earth or any earthly terrain.

Sura 40
The Forgiving (*Al-Ghafir*)

40:1   On these disconnected letters, see *muqatta'at* in Glossary, page 531.

40:3   Arabic, *dhi al-tawl*: literally, "Owner of Abundance." This unique occurrence of a Beautiful Name culminates a list of six from the long list of Divine Names, here accenting God's disposition to forgive again and again.

40:11   Arabic *amattana*: literally, "you caused us to die," but the term, according to most commentators, seems to refer to the state of non-being before and after life on earth.

40:24   Haman is said to have been Pharaoh's chief minister, while Korah (Qarun) was Moses' cousin.

40:36   Arabic *asbab*: literally, "ropes."

40:55   The "sin" here refers to the Prophet's impatience for God's help—through some miracle—when his followers were being persecuted.

40:69   Arabic *yusrafun*: literally, "they are turned away."

40:75   Some translators render this as "exulted in untruth."

Sura 41
Explained in Full (*Fussilat*)

41:1   On these disconnected letters, see *muqatta'at* in Glossary, page 531.

41:5   Arabic *fi akinna*: literally, "in coverings."

41:9   "Two days" is clearly an allegorical expression, as is "four days" in the next verse.

41:13   God's reprimand to the people of 'Ad and Thamud is detailed in 7:65–79.

41:14   Arabic *min bayni aydihim wa min khalfihim*: literally, "from between their hands and from behind them." The implication is that messengers tried to persuade them from various perspectives.

41:15   Arabic *bighayri al-haqqi*: literally, "without truth" or "without right."

41:25   Arabic *ma bayna aydihim wa ma khalfahum*: literally, "from in front and from behind them." Another rendering could be "this world and the hereafter."

41:25   Arabic *al-qawl*: literally, "the saying."

41:26   Arabic *taghlibun*: literally, "you will triumph."

41:33   Arabic *muslimun*, here rendered as "those who bow to God's will," is sometimes translated as "Muslims." However, the Muslims were not yet a self-conscious community, and not yet formed and named as Muslims. See Glossary, page 531.

41:34   Arabic *alladhi bainaka wa-bainahu 'adawa*: literally, "he between whom and you there was enmity."

41:35   Arabic *dhu hazz 'azim*: literally, "possessing a great portion." But clearly, what is indicated here is not material wealth but moral or spiritual substance. A parallel phrase occurs in 103:3: those who succeed are "those who believe, and do good deeds, urging one another toward truth, and urging one another toward patience."

41:42   Arabic *min bain yadaihi wa-la min khalfihi*: literally, "neither in front nor behind them." This is the third and final usage of a similar phrase in this sura.

41:44   The opponents are those with a veil between them and the Book (see v. 5). The reference to a non-Arab (*'ajam*) messenger echoes 26:198–99.

41:45   Arabic *law la kalima sabaqat min rabbika*: literally, "Had a word not gone forth from your Lord." That is to say, it was God who ordained dissension among humankind, as noted in 2:253 and expressed again, in similar words, in 10:19.

Sura 42
Consultation (*Al-Shura*)

42:2   On these disconnected letters, see *muqatta'at* in Glossary, page 531.

42:6   Arabic *awliya'*: "protectors" (sing. *wali*, "protector"). Others may be "protectors" but "Protector," one of God's Beautiful Names, alludes to the day of gathering when no one else can protect or intercede for the believer (see vv. 8, 31, 44, and 46). It is only God Who convenes, prevails, and protects on that day. He alone is "Ruler of the day of reckoning" (1:4), at once Protector and Restorer (v. 9).

42:7   A reference to Mecca.

42:15   "The Book" here clearly encompasses all scripture prior to the Qur'an, as is evident in 2:136: "Say, 'We believe in God, in what has been revealed to us, and what was revealed to Abraham, Ishmael, Isaac, Jacob, and the tribes, and in the Books given to Moses, Jesus, and the prophets, from their Lord; we make no distinction between any among them, and to God we submit our will.'"

42:16 Arabic *min ba'd ma ustujiba lahu*: literally, "after what had been responded to Him."

42:23 The promise of good in this life multiplying good in the next life recurs in 55:60: "What is the reward for goodness, beyond goodness?"

42:27 *Rizq* or "provision" (see also v. 12 above) echoes another of God's Beautiful Names, *al-Razzaq*, the Sustainer (51:58).

42:27 That is, man, by nature greedy and ungrateful (see v. 48), would have wanted even more than what God had provided.

42:43 These three verses (vv. 41–43) provide a case study in the importance of context for *all* declarations condoning violence in the Qur'an. Taken by themselves, vv. 41–42 seem to justify self-defense, but the clearly preferred response is given in v. 43: "whoever forbears and forgives, displays in this an ideal resolve." There is also the insistence on proportionality in response to wrong: the retribution cannot be greater than the initial offense.

Sura 43
Gold Adornments (*Al-Zukhruf*)

43:1 On these disconnected letters, see *muqatta'at* in Glossary, page 531.

43:4 Arabic *fi umm al-kitab*: literally, "in the Mother of the Book," a reference to the original tablet that is in God's keeping. The adjectives that follow refer both to the Book and to its keeper. See Glossary, page 532.

43:15 The pagan Arabs attributed daughters to God, as noted in 16:57.

43:17 This verse alludes to the fact that the pagan Arabs were often so dejected over the birth of a daughter—which they regarded as a liability—that they would bury her alive in the sand. A similar internal debate occurs in 16:56–59, where the practice of burying infant daughters is condemned. It concludes with this ominous query: "Should he keep her, to his ignominy, or bury her alive in the sand?" (16:59) The evil of this practice is underscored in 81:8–9.

43:18 This is how the pagan Arabs regarded girls.

43:28 Arabic *kalima baqiya*: literally, "an enduring word."

43:31 That is, Mecca and Ta'if.

43:35 The word order of the Arabic original of vv. 33–35 needs to be altered to make clear the divine motive for *not* making all humankind into one nation. This theme is raised elsewhere (16:93 and 42:8), yet without the disparities of wealth foregrounded here.

43:48 Arabic *min ukhtiha*: literally, "than its sister."

43:61 Arabic *wa-innahu la'ilm li al-sa'a*: literally, "and it gives knowledge of the hour." The sentence could, alternatively, be translated as "The Qur'an gives knowledge of the hour." But a well-attested *hadith* declares: "One of the signs of the hour will be the appearance of Jesus the son of Mary before the day of resurrection."

43:77   Malik is the angel who serves as the keeper of hell.

43:88   Arabic *wa-qilihi*: literally, "and his saying." What follows is an echo of the same
lament from 25:30: "The messenger said, 'My Lord, my people have forsaken
this Qur'an.'"

Sura 44
Smoke (*Al-Dukhan*)

44:1   On these disconnected letters, see *muqatta'at* in Glossary, page 531.

44:7   Arabic *in kuntum muqinin*: literally, "if only you were certain."

44:13   Arabic *rasul mubin*: literally, "a clarifying messenger."

44:20   Arabic *an tarjumuni*: literally, "if you seek to stone me," but here meant
allegorically.

44:24   Arabic *rahw*: literally, "at rest or calmed."

44:27   Arabic *na'ma*: literally, "a blessing."

44:32   Arabic *'ala al-'alamin*: literally, "over all the worlds." See Glossary, page 529.

44:33   Arabic *ma fihi bala' mubin*: literally, "in which there was a clear test." An example
of such testing through revelatory signs is God's command to Abraham that he
sacrifice his son (37:102–6), not mentioned by name but thought to be Ishmael.

44:37   A title for kings in South Arabia—that is, Yemen—since Tubba' is a town noted
also in 50:14 for rejecting the prophets.

44:43   A tree distinctive to hell, whose fronds cause great pain and disgust. See also
37:62 and 56:52.

44:59   That is, the unbelievers.

Sura 45
Kneeling (*Al-Jathiya*)

45:1   On these disconnected letters, see *muqatta'at* in Glossary, page 531.

45:14   References to "days of God" occur only here and in 14:5, addressed to Moses.
It is likely a reference to the day of final reckoning, also known as the day of
resurrection (v. 17 and elsewhere). The plural reference is yet another sign that
God's ways are not ours, nor His days like our days.

45:18   Here *shari'a* is rendered as "proper path [of religion]," to set Muhammad's mission
apart from those that preceded him. Subsequently *shari'a* became a technical
term for the expansive set of ethical and juridical norms in Islam.

45:20   Arabic *basa'ir*: literally, "visible proofs," echoing the Divine Name of God as
al-Basir, the All Observant, the All Seeing.

45:28   Arabic: *ila kitabiha*: literally, "to its book." It is also a reference to the ultimate
Book, *umm al-kitab*, "the Mother of the Book." See Glossary, page 532.

Sura 46
Sand Dunes (*Al-Ahqaf*)

46:1 On these disconnected letters, see *muqatta'at* in Glossary, page 531.

46:3 Arabic *bi al-haqq*: literally, "with truth" or "in truth." That is, God created the heavens and earth with just reasons and an appropriate purpose, since the word *haqq* can mean not only "truth" but also "right" or "just."

46:3 Arabic *'amma 'undhiru mu'ridun*: literally, "turning away from what they have been warned about."

46:15 Arabic *min al-muslimin*: literally, "among the submitters." See *muslim* in Glossary, page 531.

46:16 Arabic *wa'd al-sidq alladhi kanu yu'adun*: literally, "a true promise they had been promised."

46:35 Arabic *ulu al-'azm min al-rusul*: literally, "the resolute among the [prior] messengers," usually taken to refer to Noah, Abraham, Moses, and Jesus (all prior to Muhammad), due to the severe tests they underwent after being called to prophecy.

Sura 47
Muhammad

47:3 Arabic *yadrib Allah li al-nas amthalahum*: literally, "God coins their likeness for people," anticipating that God alone can judge their true likeness, as He does below in v. 38.

47:10 Arabic *afalam yasiru fi al-ard*: literally, "have they not traveled through the earth." Here, it's a metaphor of time as well as space, encompassing all preceding generations of humankind.

47:17 Arabic *atahum taqwahum*: literally, "He gives them their mindfulness."

47:19 Arabic *mutaqallabakum wa mathwakum*: literally, "your restlessness and your places of rest."

47:21 Arabic *qawl ma'ruf*: literally, "an honorable saying," but the qualifier *ma'ruf* means more than honor. It is part of the axial moral norm in Islam: *al-amr bil-ma'ruf wa al-nahy 'an al-munkar*—"Enjoining what is good and forbidding what is bad." Often used in the Qur'an (3:104, 110; 9:71, 112; 31:17), it highlights a collective duty to encourage righteous behavior and discourage immorality at all times, in peace and in war.

47:21 Arabic *fa-idha 'azama al-amr*: literally, "once the matter is determined."

47:23 Arabic *wa-a'ma absarahum*: literally, "and He blinds their sight."

47:31 Arabic *hatta na'lama*: literally, "so that We might know."

47:31 Arabic *akhbarakum*: literally, "your news."

Sura 48
Victory (*Al-Fath*)

48:9   Some commentators interpret "honoring" and "revering" as applying to the Prophet.

48:10   This verse equates loyalty to the Prophet with loyalty to God. It echoes a historical moment in 628 CE, when the Prophet was undertaking a return pilgrimage to Mecca. Encamped at Hudaybiyya, an area just outside Mecca, Muhammad requested a pledge of allegiance from his followers, and what later became known as the Treaty of Hudaybiyya was then secured with Muhammad's opponents, permitting Muslims to reenter Mecca peacefully as pilgrims—although only after a year's delay.

48:18   The actual pledge at Hudaybiyya was reported to have taken place under a tree, while the victory, with "many spoils of war yet to take" (v. 19), refers to the conquest of Khaybar, which took place in 629 CE, after the treaty but before the peaceful pilgrimage to Mecca in 630.

48:26   Arabic *kalimat al-taqwa*: literally, "the word of mindfulness of God." This refers, as in v. 18, to the promise that they had made to God under the tree at Hudaybiyya.

48:29   Arabic *simahum fi wujuhihim*: literally, "their mark is on their faces."

48:29   The reference in the Gospels is to the seed and mustard seed parables in Mark 4:26–32, while the Torah likely a reference to the command for bands of God's word to mark the forehead, as set forth in Deuteronomy 6:8 and 11:18.

Sura 49
The Private Apartments (*Al-Hujurat*)

49:1   Arabic *la tuqaddimu bain yadai Allah wa rasulihi*: literally, "do not advance [yourselves] before God and His messenger."

49:14   The priority of submission over faith is echoed in what is known as the *hadith* of Gabriel: conveyed to the Prophet Muhammad by the Archangel Gabriel, it explains *islam* ("submission") as the first step, followed by *iman* ("faith"), then *ihsan* ("virtue") the highest stage of human engagement with the Divine.

49:17   Arabic *sadiqin*: literally, "truthful."

49:18   Only the second of these accolades ("He Sees") echoes a Beautiful Name (Arabic *basir*: literally, Seer), but both it and "God Knows" are capitalized to underscore the consistency of God's presence in English.

Sura 50
Qaf (*Qaf*)

50:1   On this disconnected letter, see *muqatta'at* in Glossary, page 531.

50:4   Arabic *ma tanqus al-ard minhum*: literally, "what the earth diminishes of them."

50:4   A reference to *umm al-kitab*. See Glossary, page 532.

50:14   Nearly all these groups are identified elsewhere in the Qur'an as disbelievers and, in the case of Pharaoh, persecutors of believers. The people of Midian are *ashab al-aika* (literally, "people of the forest") since it is they who were sent, and rejected, the prophet Shuʿayb (26:176–89).

50:17 Arabic *yatalaqqa al-mutalaqqiyani:* literally, "Two receivers . . . receive." These are Nakir and Munkar, noted in 16:28–32.

Sura 51
Scattering Winds (*Al-Dhariyat*)

51:4 Like the first three verses of Sura 37, these four verses could refer to either winds or angels, but here winds seems more likely.

51:19 Arabic *wa-fi amwalihim haqq li al-saʾil wa-al-mahrum:* literally, "and both beggars and the needy have a right to their wealth."

51:36 Arabic *al-muslimin:* literally, "those who submit." See *muslim* in Glossary, page 531.

Sura 52
Mount Sinai (*Al-Tur*)

52:2 The Torah, delivered to Moses on Mount Sinai.

52:4 The Kaʿba, "maintained only by those who believe in God and the last day" (9:18).

52:5 The sky, as also in 21:32: "We raised the sky, a secure canopy."

52:21 Arabic *rahin:* literally, "a pledge."

Sura 53
The Star (*Al-Najm*)

53:5 The Archangel Gabriel.

53:16 Arabic *idh yaghsha al-sidra ma yaghsha:* literally, "when the lote-tree was cloaked with whatever cloaked it."

53:20 All three were pre-Islamic goddesses, whose stone idols the pagan Arabs worshipped.

53:21 This refers to the attribution of male offspring (considered desirable) to pagan Arabs, contrasting them with goddesses as God's daughters (daughters being deemed undesirable).

53:25 Arabic *fa li Allah al-akhira wa-al-ula:* literally, "to God belong the next life and the first."

53:31 The sense of goodness here is twofold, as it is elsewhere (e.g., 55:60): God is always "with those who are mindful of Him and those who do good" (16:128; see also 5:93), and then there is the reward of paradise: "that [paradise] is the reward of those who do good (5:85).

53:36 The Torah.

53:37 Upheld his belief in the One God.

53:47   Life after death.

53:49   A star worshipped by the polytheistic Arabs.

53:54   Arabic *fa-ghashshaha ma ghashsha*: literally, "So there covered them that which covered."

Sura 54
The Moon (*Al-Qamar*)

54:1   Some commentators have connected this verse to an alleged miracle of the Prophet Muhammad, while others have suggested that the split moon refers to a future event, auguring the end of the world and the day of resurrection. The message from v. 6ff. seems to favor the latter interpretation.

54:2   Another rendering would be "This is powerful sorcery."

54:29   Arabic Arabic *fa-ta'ata*: literally, "then he took hold."

54:29   A more extended account of this incident is furnished in 7:73–79, where the prophet Salih urges the people of Thamud to serve God alone and explains to them that God's she-camel, which was sent as a sign to them, should be left unharmed and allowed to pasture. But the leader of the most rebellious and proud faction in Thamud denounced the believers, and the disbelieving faction slaughtered the camel, thereby bringing divine retribution (Sura 91).

Sura 55
The All Merciful (*Al-Rahman*)

55:16   Although in the Arabic this refrain is repeated verbatim at v. 18 etc., it has here been varied across a range of word combinations and moods in a manner that is intended to retain its essential meaning. When the Arabic is recited, the refrain can be intoned in a variety of ways; if exactly the same refrain is repeated in English, it would not only come across as tedious and mechanical, but would fail to be faithful to the variation of tone that animates the Arabic.

55:17   Where the sun rises in winter and summer.

55:17   Where the sun sets in winter and summer.

55:29   Arabic *kull yawm huwa fi sha'n*: literally, "He is daily in a matter."

55:37   Arabic *ka al-dihan*: literally, "like dregs of olive oil" or "red leather."

55:54   Cf. 18:30–31: "those who believe and do good deeds ... will have eternal gardens, with rivers flowing beneath. There they will be adorned in bracelets of gold, and they will wear robes of green, of fine silk and rich brocade; they will recline there on raised couches—a blessèd reward, an excellent home."

55:60   The sense of goodness here is twofold, as it is elsewhere (e.g., 53:31): God is always "with those who are mindful of Him and those who do good" (16:128; see also 5.93), and then there is the reward of paradise: "that [paradise] is the reward for those who do good" (5:85).

55:72   Houri is the name for a large-eyed maiden of paradise.

Sura 56
The Inexorable Event (*Al-Waqi'a*)

56:8   Arabic *fa ashab al-maimana ma ashab al-maimana*: literally, "the companions of the right hand—who are the companions of the right hand?"

56:11   The ranking of divine judgment and reward is anticipated in the phrase "those on the right" (74:39) and then elaborated into three categories in another verse: "We gave the Book as a legacy to Our servants whom We favored. Some of them wrong their own souls, some are moderate, and others by God's leave are foremost in good deeds—the greatest grace" (35:32).

56:28   Arabic *fi sidr*: literally, "in lote-trees," said to be among the markers of paradise (53:14).

56:37   These women are the houris mentioned in v. 22.

56:52   On the tree of Zaqqum, a tree distinctive to hell whose fronds cause great pain and disgust, see also 37:62 and 44:43.

56:60   Arabic *qaddarna bainakum al-mawt*: literally, "We decreed death among you."

56:60   Arabic *wa-ma nahnu bimasbuqin*: literally, "and We are not to be overtaken."

56:62   God's power to create and re-create is echoed elsewhere, as in 29:20: "Say, 'Travel through the earth and see how He originated creation; then God will bring about a new creation, for God has Power over all things.'"

56:75   This may also refer to the staged revelation of the Qur'an that anticipates the following verses.

Sura 57
Iron (*Al-Hadid*)

57:7   To the war effort; see v. 10.

57:10   This refers to the capitulation of Meccan opponents to the ascendant Muslims in 630 CE.

57:25   The "balance" (*mizan*) indicates among other things the scales by which good and bad deeds are weighed or measured. It can refer to the body of religious law, which stipulates the criteria of such assessment, as well as the human faculties as harmonized in the notion of conscience.

57:27   The message here is that monasticism was not ordained by God, yet the chief fault of those (Christian monks and nuns) who followed it was their failure to observe fully its requirements.

57:28   The Light—recognition of the Prophet and obedience to God's commands—seems to be the same introduced earlier in v. 9, then developed in vv. 12–13 as a distinguishing mark between believers and hypocrites in the next life.

Sura 58
The Woman Who Pleads (*Al-Mujadila*)

58:2   Arabic *yuzahirun*: literally "made them appear [like their mothers' backs]"; this underscores the evil of *zihar*, the pre-Islamic practice of divorce—equating the wife to be divorced with the mother's back in order to nullify marriage—but it begs the question of why the marriage was initially deemed feasible. This practice is also cited and condemned in 33:4.

58:8   The passage is referring to certain Jews who would address the Prophet with the greeting *al-sam 'alaikum*, which means "death to you," instead of the conventional greeting "peace be to you."

58:11   The message here, as elsewhere, is the necessity of faith—but faith enhanced by knowledge is still better. This is often used to justify a class of religious specialists in Islam known as the *'ulama*, "those possessing knowledge."

58:22   Arabic *wa-ayyadahum biruh minhu*: literally, "and He strengthened them with a spirit from Him." This same accolade is found elsewhere only with reference to Jesus: 2:87 and 253; 5:110.

Sura 59
The Gathering (*Al-Hashr*)

59:2   The "gathering" is the gathering of a Jewish tribe that at first supported the new Muslim community in Medina, but then became their opponents, ca. 625 CE. It also provides the title for this sura.

59:11   The reference here, and throughout the sura, is to a group of Jews, the Banu Nadir, who were expelled from Mecca in 625 CE.

59:17   Arabic *fa-kana 'aqibatahuma annahuma fi al-nar*: literally, "the end of both will be in the fire."

59:24   *Al-asma' al-husna* is the key phrase in Arabic. Found here and in 17:110, it signals the recurrent importance of remembering God by His Beautiful Names. See Glossary, page 530.

Sura 61
In Ranks (*Al-Saff*)

61:8   Arabic *biafwahihim*: literally, "with their mouths."

61:14   Arabic *fa-asbahu zahirin*: literally, "they became dominant."

Sura 62
The Friday Prayer (*Al-Jumu'a*)

62:2   Cf. 2:78: "unlettered people who don't know the Book"—i.e., pagan Arabs.

62:6   Arabic *annakum awliya' li Allah*: literally, "that you are friends [or allies] of God."

62:6   The same critique is set forth in 2:94–95.

62:7   Arabic *bima qaddamat aydihim*: literally, "on account of what their hands have sent forth."

Sura 63
The Hypocrites (*Al-Munafiqun*)

63:8   Some translate this as "the more honorable."

Sura 64
Mutual Fraud (*Al-Taghabun*)

64:6   Arabic *dhalika biannahu*: literally, "that is because." The word "for" translates the expression more succinctly.

64:8   The Light is the Qur'an, as in 7:157: "those . . . guided by the light sent down with him [Muhammad]."

64:17   That is, if you spend money legitimately earned in the way of God; parallel to 5:12—see the note for that verse, page 547.

Sura 65
Divorce (*Al-Talaq*)

65:1   An interval in which a woman who is divorced cannot marry another man, equivalent to three full cycles of menstruation.

65:7   Arabic *ba'da 'usr yusr*: literally, "after a hardship comes ease." Cf. echo in 94:5–6: "with every hardship comes ease—yes, with every hardship comes ease."

65:12   The seven earths seem to complement each of the seven heavens. In both instances, the message is to reinforce the dictum that creation—of heaven(s) and of earth(s)—is a divinely ordained occurrence.

Sura 66
Prohibition (*Al-Tahrim*)

66:1   Tension among the Prophet's wives seems to have prompted this revelation, late in the Medinan period, ca. 629 CE. Abstention from marital privilege was the Prophet's response, here corrected by divine counsel.

66:4   Arabic *'alaihi*: literally, "against him," clearly here, the Prophet.

66:5   Arabic *sa'ihat*: literally, "traveling," but here "fasting" seems preferable.

Sura 67
Dominion (*Al-Mulk*)

67:9   Arabic *fi dalal kabir*: literally, "in a great straying."

67:16   Arabic *amintum*: literally, "do you have faith?"

Sura 68
The Pen (*Al-Qalam*)

68:1   On this disconnected letter, see *muqatta'at* in Glossary, page 531.

68:13   A reference to al-Walid ibn al-Mughira, a member of the Quraysh and a staunch critic of the Prophet.

68:17   The story that follows (vv. 17–32) seems to be cast in the form of a parable.

68:48   Arabic *sahib al-hut*: literally, "the companion of the whale."

68:51   Arabic *layuzliqunaka*: literally, "they would surely make you slip."

Sura 69
Reality (*Al-Haqqa*)

69:4   The fate of these unfortunate people has been described elsewhere (see 7:65–73)—a fate decreed by their denial of messengers sent to them.

Sura 70
The Paths of Ascent (*Al-Ma'arij*)

70:4   The rhetorical hyperbole accenting "fifty thousand years" stresses the difference between human and divine reckoning of time, as in 32:5, where the end occurs "on a day which spans a thousand years in your counting."

70:29   Arabic *lifurujihim hafizun*: literally, "guarding their private parts."

70:40   Arabic *birabb al-mashariq wa-al-magharib*: literally, "Lord of the Easts and the Wests" but clearly here as elsewhere (e.g., 37:5) evoking places where the sun rises and sets.

70:41   Arabic *wa-ma nahnu bimasbuqin*: literally, "and We will not be surpassed."

70:42   See also 43:83: "So leave them to gossip and frolic—until they encounter their promised day."

Sura 71
Noah (*Nuh*)

71:17   The earth equates with dust; cf. 40:67: "It is He Who created you from dust, then from sperm, then from a clot of blood."

71:23   These are Mesopotamian gods who were also worshipped in pre-Islamic Arabia, but mentioned in the Qur'an only here.

71:24   Arabic *la tazid al-zalimin illa dalal*: literally, "do not increase the wrongdoers except in error."

Sura 72
The Jinn (*Al-Jinn*)

72:1   The jinn are intermediate beings—neither humans nor angels. Jinn can transmit divine wisdom but are also expected to worship God and not be channels of misleading signs or outright magic. See Glossary, page 531.

72:9   A similar punishment is promised for any "rebellious devil" (37:7) with whom evil jinn are here linked, as in 37:10: "Any [devil] who eavesdrops, snatching an overheard fragment, shall be pursued by a luminous flame."

72:17   The message is subtle but strict: God's blessings are not just a boon but also a measure of human loyalty, requiring continuous awareness of the Giver as well as the gift.

72:19   That is, Muhammad. The implication is that the Arabs were worshipping him instead of God.

72:27   These are similar to the angels who monitor all humans; cf. 13:11: "Each person has a train of angels before them and behind them, guarding them by God's command."

Sura 73
The One Enwrapped (Al-Muzzammil)

73:2   Before five daily prayers became obligatory for Muslims, a night prayer was common practice. It remains a supererogatory prayer of high value, especially during Ramadan.

73:5   Arabic qawl thaqil: literally, "a weighty Word."

73:9   A description of God as Lord at sunrise and sunset, similar to those at 37:5, 55:17, and 70:40.

73:20   Since the injunction to jihad was sanctioned only after the hijra, this verse must date to the Prophet's stay in Medina. All the preceding verses belong to the early Meccan period.

73:20   That is, if you spend money legitimately earned in the way of God; parallel to 5:12—see corresponding note, page 547.

Sura 74
The One Enfolded (Al-Muddaththir)

74:1   Most commentators presume this to be an image of the Prophet covering himself as he prepared for the onset of revelation, but it can also refer to the fact that his prophetic mission is about to end his revelatory solitude as he is now instructed to "arise and warn."

74:11   Like an earlier passage (68:10–14), this directive (vv. 11–26) could refer to a specific opponent of the Prophet, al-Walid ibn al-Mughira, or it could apply generally to any disbeliever with wealth and children.

74:30   "Nineteen" may be the number of angels or the spectrum of human faculties.

74:47   Arabic hatta atana al-yaqin: literally, "until the certainty [of death] came to us." Cf. parallel passage at 15:99.

74:52   That is, they want the scripture to be self-evident, as noted in 2:118: "And those with no knowledge say, 'Why does God not speak to us?' or 'Why does no sign come to us?'"

74:56   Arabic huwa ahl al-taqwa wa-ahl al-maghfira: literally, "He is worthy of Mindfulness, and worthy to be Forgiving." The meaning of ahl here suggests the location rather than the state of the One, the Only God. Related to "people" or "family," the most common meanings of *ahl*, are notions of "home" or "origin," so "source" seems to capture both God as the focus (for *taqwa*) and as the force (for *maghfira*). These are Beautiful Names only found here in the Qur'an.

Sura 75
Resurrection (*Al-Qiyama*)

75:13   Arabic *bima qaddama wa-akhkhara*: literally, "what they advanced and what they delayed."

75:18   Through the Archangel Gabriel.

75:19   This directive is parallel to that given in 20:114: "And Prophet, don't be overhasty reciting the Qur'an before [each] revelation to you is completed. Rather, say, 'My Lord, increase my knowledge.'"

75:27   Arabic *man raqin*: literally, "who is a curer?"

75:35   Arabic *laka*: literally, "to you" but here personifying the end or death.

Sura 76
Humankind (*Al-Insan*)

76:18   A spring in paradise, mentioned only here.

76:23   Arabic *nazzalna alaikum al-Qur'an tanzil*: literally, "We sent down the Qur'an with a sending down," which seems to imply all at once, as in 97:1: "We revealed this Word on the night of decree," although others view it as having been sent down gradually or in stages.

Sura 77
Those Sent Out (*Al-Mursalat*)

77:4   The reference is clearly to angels as the mediators.

77:30   Arabic *shu'ab*: literally, "branches."

Sura 78
The Announcement (*Al-Naba'*)

78:19   Arabic *wa-futihat al-sama' fa-kanat abwab*: literally, "the sky was opened, and became doors."

78:20   Arabic *fa-kanat sarab*: literally, "and became a mirage."

78:30   Arabic *fa-lan nazidakum illa 'adhab*: literally, "We will not increase you except in torment."

78:38   A title of the Archangel Gabriel.

78:40   The ironic echo of dust at death comes elsewhere, e.g., in 56:47 where disbelievers protest: "When we die, when we are dust and bones, will we really be resurrected?" Instead of only being raised up, they also experience more torment (v. 30 above).

Sura 79
Those Who Force Out (*Al-Nazi'at*)

79:7   The first blowing of the trumpet brings about the last day when all perish, and the second blow resurrects them.

79:16   A valley near Mount Sinai.

79:20   Turning the staff into a serpent.

79:25   Arabic *al-akhira wa-al-ula*: literally, "in the last life and the first."

Sura 80
He Frowned (*'Abasa*)

80:1   The opening verse reflects the occasion for revealing this verse: the Prophet had ignored someone who was literally blind, while trying to convince others, pagan Meccan leaders, of the truth of his prophecy. The blind man, 'Abd Allah ibn Umm Maktum, became a devoted follower of Islam; he also served as one of the first muezzins, those who call other Muslims to prayer at the obligatory daily times.

80:4   Arabic *dhikra*: literally, "a reminder."

80:5   Arabic *man istaghna*: literally, "who considers himself free of need."

80:10   The theological lesson here is clear: God, not the Prophet, moves people to accept His revelation. Other verses confirm the same lesson (e.g., 28:56 and 18:28), but less directly.

Sura 81
The Folding Up (*Al-Takwir*)

81:3   Arabic *idha al-jibal suyyirat*: literally, "when the mountains are moved"; however, they actually vanish. See 20:105–7: "They ask you about the mountains. Say, 'My Lord shall blast them into fragments. He will leave them leveled as a plain. You shall see there neither peak nor vale.'"

81:7   The reference echoes a theme that recurs throughout the Qur'an: the cleaving of two groups on the right and the left, sorted into the good and the bad, some rewarded, others condemned, on the day of judgment.

81:19   The Archangel Gabriel, with Muhammad as his companion (v. 22).

81:23   A further reference to the vision of heaven, where Muhammad sees Gabriel; see 53:5–7: "one mighty in power has taught him, one imbued with great strength, who stood at the horizon's peak."

81:27   Arabic *'alamin*: literally, "all the worlds." See Glossary, page 529.

Sura 83
Those Who Defraud (*Al-Mutaffifin*)

83:7   Sijjin is a place in eternity equivalent to prison (*sijn*).

83:18   Arabic *'illiyyina*: literally, "lofty places," mirroring Sijjin (vv. 7, 8).

83:27   Another fountain in paradise.

Sura 84
The Splitting Asunder (*Al-Inshiqaq*)

84:7 Arabic *kitabahu* literally: "His book." It seems preferable to pluralize the two groups, since once again, this "record" refers to the ultimate record, the Mother of the Book, *umm al-kitab*. See Glossary, page 532.

Sura 85
The Constellations (*Al-Buruj*)

85:4 Those "who made the pit" could refer to the story of a Yemeni king, Dhu Nawas al-Yamani, who ordered a huge pit to be dug and filled with fire, into which were thrown those who had converted to Christianity before the advent of Islam (Tabari). It could also refer to disbelievers who make their own "hell," a related image of which appears in the Psalms (94:13, where "a pit is dug for the wicked").

85:18 The fate of Pharaoh is often described in the Qur'an (e.g., 7:103–17), while the people of Thamud are usually linked with the people of 'Ad (e.g., 7:65–73), their common fate decreed by their denial of the messengers sent to them.

85:20 Arabic *min wara'ihim*: literally, "from behind them."

85:22 "A preserved tablet" seems to be another name for "the repository of all scripture" (Arabic, *umm al-kitab*, literally "the Mother of the Book"), cited in 3:7, 13:39, and 43:4. See Glossary, page 532.

Sura 86
The Night Traveler (*Al-Tariq*)

86:11 Arabic *wa-al-sama' dhat al-raj'*: literally, "by the sky as it returns," implying the change of weather, the cycle of sun and rain.

Sura 87
The Most High (*Al-A'la*)

87:19 Abraham is not usually thought to have received a written revelation or scripture, but since there is the Testament of Abraham in Jewish-Christian apocrypha, scripture about Abraham may assumed to be scripture by him, all preserved in *umm al-kitab*, the Mother of the Book, the lodestone of all revelation (3:7).

Sura 89
The Breaking Dawn (*Al-Fajr*)

89:2 The number "ten" could refer to the first ten nights at the beginning of Muharram, the first month in the Muslim year, or it could refer to the first ten nights of Dhu al-Hijjah, the month of pilgrimage. See 2:196: "those without means should fast for three days during the major pilgrimage, and seven days upon your return, ten days in all."

89:3   If one accepts "ten nights" as a reference to the month of pilgrimage, it is marked both by "odd"—three plus seven—and "even"—ten. There are numerous other explanations of this elliptical reference.

89:9   The people of 'Ad and Thamud belonged to a pre-Islamic group that rejected the prophet Hud, cited in 7:65–72 (and repeated in 11:50–60 and 26:123–40).

89:10   Arabic *dhi al-awtad*: literally, "owner of the tent pegs."

89:24   Arabic *hayati*: literally, "my life [to come]," not the present life—i.e., good deeds accrued in this life will be of benefit in the life to come.

Sura 91
The Sun (*Al-Shams*)

91:11   A more extended account of this incident is provided in 7:73–79, where the prophet Salih urges the people of Thamud to serve God alone and explains to them that God's she-camel, which was sent as a sign to them, should be left unharmed and allowed to pasture. But the leader of the most rebellious and proud faction in Thamud denounces the believers and the disbelieving faction slaughters the camel, thereby bringing divine retribution.

Sura 92
Night (*Al-Layl*)

92:7   Arabic *fa-sanuyassiruhu li al-yusra*: literally, "We will ease for them the path to ease."

92:18   Arabic *yatazakki*: literally, "to promote purity."

Sura 93
Morning Light (*Al-Duha*)

93:1   The word *duha* refers to the period of time from after sunrise until before noon. In 91:1 and 79:29 it indicates the full brightness of the sun.

93:3   According to Ibn 'Abbas, as reported by Ibn Kathir, this verse was revealed after a lapse in the revelations given to the Prophet, which caused him great anxiety and which prompted the polytheists to taunt that "his Lord has abandoned him and hates him." The verse is intended to answer the taunt by reassuring the Prophet of his mission.

Sura 94
The Broadening (*Al-Sharh*)

94:2   Arabic *wizraka*: literally, "your burden."

94:4   Arabic *dhikraka*: literally, "your remembrance."

94:8   Arabic: *wa-ila rabbika fa-rghab*: literally, "and to your Lord be attentive" or "turn your attention."

Sura 95
The Fig (*Al-Tin*)

95:3   Mecca.

95:7   Arabic *din*: literally, "religion" as in 109:6 ("you have your religion and I have mine") but also connoting judgment as in 1:4 ("Ruler of the day of reckoning") and reward as in 24:25 ("their due recompense"). Here "reckoning" seems most apt. See Glossary, page 530.

Sura 96
Clot of Blood (*Al-ʿAlaq*)

96:9   From this verse to the end (vv. 9–19), the person recalled and rebuked is likely Abu Jahl, an early, fierce enemy of the Prophet. He and his companions will be ensnared by "the angels of hell" (v. 18).

Sura 97
The Night of Decree (*Al-Qadr*)

97:1   Arabic *inna anzalnahu*: literally, "We revealed it."

Sura 98
Clear Proof (*Al-Bayyina*)

98:5   The syntax is slightly inverted here.

98:7   Arabic *khair al-bariyat*: literally, "the best of creation."

Sura 99
The Earthquake (*Al-Zalzala*)

99:4   Arabic *akhbaraha*: literally, "her news."

Sura 100
Racing Steeds (*Al-ʿAdiyat*)

100:1   Arabic *wa-al-ʿadiyat*: literally, "by the racing steeds, panting." Since some commentators have taken the initial five lines to be an invocation not of Arabian horses but of wayward souls, charging after their own interests, it seems preferable to make that comparison explicit in the translation. "By those racing like steeds, panting" welds together the two parts of this sura (vv. 1–5 and 6–11), underscoring their stark ethical imperative: not to be ungrateful but mindful "that on that day, their Lord shall be fully Aware of them" (v. 11).

Sura 101
The Thundering Calamity (*Al-Qariʿa*)

101:1   Arabic *al-qariʿa*: literally, "the striking calamity," alluding to the day of judgment (v. 4).

Sura 102
Competing for Worldly Gain (*Al-Takathur*)

102:5   Arabic *'ilm al-yaqin*: literally, "knowledge of certainty."

102:7   Arabic *'ain al-yaqin*: literally, "eye of certainty."

Sura 104
The Backbiter (*Al-Humaza*)

104:9   Arabic *'amad mumadda*: literally, "extended pillars."

Sura 105
The Elephant (*Al-Fil*)

105:1   An Ethiopian army attempted to invade Mecca either in the 540s, two or three decades prior to Muhammad's birth, or in 570 CE, the year of his birth. The army had an elephant at its head. Birds are said to have pelted the soldiers with stones, providing the drama at the heart of this verse.

Sura 106
Quraysh (*Quraysh*)

106:1   This sura should be connected to the previous one, signaling that the Quraysh, the tribe of Muhammad, had survived the mid-sixth-century Yemeni assault due to God's grace, not their own military prowess.

Sura 108
Abundance (*Al-Kawthar*)

108:1   There are several *hadith* that relate *kawthar* ("abundance"), cited only here in the Qur'an, to a river in paradise. Its initial meaning, in reference to Muhammad and believers, is that in quality as well as measure, goodness will multiply for those God has favored.

108:3   They will have no progeny. Some of the Quraysh—specifically, As ibn Wa'il—had said that the Prophet was "cut off," that he would have no progeny since his three sons had died at an early age.

Sura 111
The Palm Fiber (*Al-Masad*)

111:1   Abu Lahab was an uncle of the Prophet who, together with his wife, fiercely opposed the Prophet, and so this sura is directed against them as a reminder to others that wealth and material gains will not prevail. The image of the cord around his wife's neck suggests that her "twisted" nature is evident to those who see her, while also reaffirming the Qur'anic dictum that "We have fastened every man's fate around his own neck" (17:13) also applies to women.

Sura 112
Unity/Sincerity (*Al-Ikhlas*)

112:2   Arabic *samad*: literally, "rock," but connoting someone or something stable and immovable, at once irreducible and unreproducible—i.e., the Absolute. It is among the Beautiful Names of God, found only here in the Qur'an.

Sura 113
The Dawn (*Al-Falaq*)

113:1   *Falaqa* means "to split," hence the image is that of the dawn which splits or breaks apart from night.

113:2   The evil here clearly refers to the evil practiced by God's creatures, those imbued with (moral) agency.

113:4   This refers to some hostile tribes in Medina whose members put a spell on the Prophet; this sura and the next were revealed in order to extricate him from their influence.

Sura 114
Humankind (*Al-Nas*)

114:5   As noted in 7:20, "whispering" is the preferred mode of communication for both Satan and his son, aka al-Khannas, "the whisperer."